COMMUNICATIONS LAW

Liberties, Restraints, and the Modern Media

Third Edition

John D. Zelezny

Attorney at Law

Wadsworth
Thomson Learning™

Australia • Canada • Mexico • Singapore • Spain
United Kingdom • United States

For Betty Zelezny

Mass Communication Editor: Karen Austin
Executive Editor: Deirdre Cavanaugh
Executive Marketing Manager: Stacey Purviance
Project Editor: Susan Walters
Print Buyer: Barbara Britton
Permissions Editor: Joohee Lee

Production Service: Johnstone Associates
Illustrator: Pat Rogondino
Cover Designer: Liz Harasymczuk
Cover Image: Globe, Bill Frymire/Masterfile
Compositor: G&S Typesetters, Inc.
Text and Cover Printer: R. R. Donnelley/Crawfordsville

Wadsworth/Thomson Learning
10 Davis Drive
Belmont, CA 94002-3098
USA

For more information about our products, contact us:
Thomson Learning Academic Resource Center
1-800-423-0563
http://www.wadsworth.com

International Headquarters
Thomson Learning
International Division
290 Harbor Drive, 2nd Floor
Stamford, CT 06902-7477
USA

UK/Europe/Middle East/South Africa
Thomson Learning
Berkshire House
168–173 High Holborn
London WC1V 7AA
United Kingdom

Printed in the United States of America
3 4 5 6 7 04 03 02 01

Asia
Thomson Learning
60 Albert Street, #15–01
Albert Complex
Singapore 189969

Library of Congress Cataloging-in-Publication Data

Zelezny, John D.
     Communications law : liberties, restraints, and the modern
media / John D. Zelezny.—3rd ed.
         p. cm.
     Includes bibliographical references and index.
     ISBN 0-534-51331-X
     1. Mass media—Law and legislation—United States.
2. Press law—United States. 3. Freedom of speech—United
States. 4. Libel and slander—United States. 5. Obscenity
(Law)—United States. I. Title.
KF2750.Z45 2000
343.7309′9—dc21   00-042872

Canada
Nelson Thomson Learning
1120 Birchmount Road
Toronto, Ontario M1K 5G4
Canada

Contents

CHAPTER THREE

Risks to Public Safety   71

CHAPTER FOUR

Damage to Reputation   99

CHAPTER FIVE

Privacy and Peace of Mind   153

CHAPTER SIX

Access to Places and Information   *197*

CHAPTER SEVEN

Media and the Justice System   *233*

CHAPTER EIGHT

Creative Property   279

CHAPTER NINE

Corporate and Government Speech   *329*

CHAPTER TEN

Commercial Speech   *359*

CHAPTER THIRTEEN

The Internet   485

Preface

Communications law is a fascinating, constantly evolving subject that permeates modern society. It is at the center of some of the most intriguing controversies of our time—from hidden news cameras to provocative music lyrics to television violence to porn on the Internet to advertising for cigarettes and liquor.

Communications law affects the day-to-day, nuts-and-bolts operating decisions of the mass media and related communications industries. At the same time, this subject cuts right to the heart of our nation's most lofty constitutional ideals—and our most basic philosophical conflicts.

Purpose and Approach

This book does not pretend to be an exhaustive treatise on communications law or on any one topic within that vast and complicated field. It does, however, aim to (1) instill a greater appreciation for freedom of expression and the First Amendment, (2) provide an overview of the diverse field of communications law, and (3) impart a functional understanding of the legal rules and principles that are generally most relevant to mass communications professionals in the United States. This book is concerned with the laws that directly shape communication, laws that determine the content and channels of expression. Rules concerning the routine business operation of the media, such as labor law and taxation, are left to courses in business law.

Communication professions today encompass increasingly varied yet overlapping methods of communication—from the traditional fare of newspapers, magazines, and broadcast stations to the blossoming use of company publications, specialized cable and satellite TV channels, consumer videos, and especially the Internet. Therefore, this book covers a broad area of the law. It includes some topics that have not traditionally been included in journalism law courses, such as trademark protection, music licensing, regulation of corporate political speech, and cable TV franchising.

To make room for this broader coverage while maintaining a readable text, treatment of a few traditional news-oriented topics, such as protection of journalistic sources, is more streamlined here than in some other books. Throughout the text, treatment is most extensive on topics that have the broadest professional relevance, such as libel and copyright law, and on topics that serve to illustrate First Amendment doctrine and conflict.

The text includes discussions of history, ethics, social custom, and legal philosophy. The overriding focus, however, is on practical application of current legal principles. This book is written primarily for students who anticipate working as professional communicators in such varied capacities as TV news anchors, sports editors, photojournalists, broadcast program directors, advertising account executives, magazine writers, government information officers, investigative reporters, video producers, website managers, and even gossip columnists. Therefore, in addition to providing a liberal arts perspective on the law, the book is designed as a kind of survival kit. I hope it will not only help students structure their thinking during a college course but also serve as a useful aid in avoiding legal pitfalls on the job—and in knowing when to consult a lawyer.

By the nature of the subject, any study of law is a formidable task. I have tried to stick to essentials and to fashion a user-friendly text. Footnotes and case names are used in moderation and the writing style is informal.

Special Features

To help promote learning, this third edition of *Communications Law* includes the following special features:

☐ An outline and a list of learning objectives on the first page of each chapter.

☐ An engaging hypothetical scenario near the beginning of each chapter that serves as a springboard into the discussions that follow.

☐ Key terms highlighted in the narrative by boldface type, followed promptly by their definitions.

☐ Diagrams, boxed features, sample documents, and other graphics to aid learning.

☐ Summary points, discussion questions, a list of key terms, web resources, and *InfoTrac* ® *College Edition* exercises at the end of each chapter.

☐ Dozens of Quick Check boxes scattered throughout the text to serve as reminders and as basic guides to analysis.

☐ An extensive glossary of nearly 200 legal terms that are particularly relevant to communications law.

This book also contains an entire chapter on Internet law (Chapter 13) that examines some of the unique problems of online services and Internet communication. Because it also reexamines the application of some legal topics discussed earlier, such as defamation, privacy, and copyright, Chapter 13 serves as an excellent way to conclude a course in communications law.

I hope this book will prove readable, useful, and stimulating, and that it will prompt a lifelong interest in the First Amendment and communications law.

For students and instructors who desire a more thorough, firsthand look at judicial reasoning in communications law, I have prepared a casebook that may be used as a companion. *Cases in Communications Law,* also published by Wadsworth, contains edited versions of about 60 actual court opinions, arranged in the same topical order as the chapters in this text.

Acknowledgments I am indebted to the following experts who, at various stages, reviewed this project and provided valuable suggestions: Richard Goedkoop, LaSalle University; Shannon Martin, Rutgers University; and Michael Ogden, University of Hawaii at Manoa. I also want to thank the reviewers of previous editions: Roy Alden Arwood, University of Idaho; Judith M. Buddenbaum, Colorado State University; Louis A. Day, Louisiana State University; William Hanks, Wright State University; W. Wat Hopkins, Virginia Polytechnical Institute; Robert Jensen, University of Texas; Allan D. Larson, Clarion University of Pennsylvania; Seong Lee, Appalachian State University; Val E. Limburg, Washington State University; Joan Lowenstein, University of Michigan, Ann Arbor; W. Robert Nowell III, California State University, Chico; David Protess, Northwestern University; Robert D. Richards, The Pennsylvania State University; Martin Sommerness, Northern Arizona University; Sara Capri Spears, Bowling Green State University; Elizabeth K. Viall, Lamar University–Beaumont; John Vivian, Winona State University; and Ruth Walden, University of North Carolina at Chapel Hill.

Professor Martin Sommerness of Northern Arizona University deserves special mention for helping to frame the first edition of this book more than a decade ago and for providing especially useful, written student evaluations of the text.

I am also grateful to my first-rate editorial team at Wadsworth Publishing company—in particular editor Karen Austin and former assistant editor Ryan Vesely—and to my production service, Johnstone Associates, managed by Judith Johnstone.

About the Author

John D. Zelezny is an attorney at law and senior vice president for communications at Community Medical Centers of Central California. He is a former professor who taught communications law for 15 years at universities in Arizona and California. He served as chairman of the mass communication and journalism department at California State University, Fresno, and subsequently as the university's chief public relations administrator.

Zelezny earned his bachelor's degree in journalism at Humboldt State University and his law degree at the University of the Pacific, McGeorge School of Law. He is an active member of The State Bar of California, a frequent speaker on communications law, and the author of First Amendment problems for major "moot court" competitions among law schools.

CHAPTER ONE

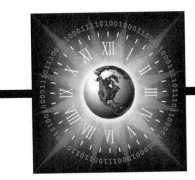

Chapter Outline

The U.S. Legal System

Upon completing this chapter you should

- [ ] **understand** why it is advantageous for communications students to study the law.
- [ ] **know** the principal categories of American law and how to distinguish them.
- [ ] **understand** the typical structure of court systems and the distinctions between trial and appellate courts.
- [ ] **possess** an overall understanding of how this nation's multiple-jurisdiction legal system functions and how individual disputes proceed through the courts.

■ Threat of a Lawsuit

Assume that you were hired recently as the program director for a commercial radio station, KBIG. The station format is primarily rock n' roll, but several news segments are broadcast each day. The problem is, very little money is budgeted for a news staff to cover local events. In fact, news staffing amounts to a single half-time position.

Under this staffing constraint, it has been particularly difficult to produce a good, original news show to fill the morning drive-time slot. Therefore, the KBIG news reporter has relied increasingly upon the local daily newspaper as the source for news material. On this particular morning, the news reporter filled the time simply by reading—word for word—the first few sentences from several stories that appeared in the morning paper.

A few hours later you receive a phone call from an angry editor at the newspaper. The editor delivers this threat: "You're stealing our work. You know that, don't you? You're reading our stuff without permission, and that's copyright infringement. You'd better knock it off right away, because we're mad enough to sue. Got it?"

You might soon contact a lawyer in order to get a detailed opinion about your rights. But in the meantime, you can answer some basic questions for yourself. Are the newspaper editor's threats based on language in the U.S. Constitution, in a legislative enactment, or in some other body of law? If the editor is right, is this a civil violation that could cost you money or a crime that could land you in jail? If you are sued, would the case be handled by a state court or by a federal court? Also, if the paper did decide to sue you, how would that lawsuit formally begin and what would be the sequence of procedural steps toward a resolution?

Studying the Law

In the United States today the law touches almost every aspect of everyone's life. This is particularly true for those who work in mass communication. What is communicated, how it is communicated, to whom it is communicated, when and where it is communicated, and the effects of that communication all may raise important legal concerns for those throughout the communications industries.

There are several reasons it is important that communications students study the law in college and maintain an interest in the law throughout their careers. One reason is daily survival. An understanding of the law helps communicators make prudent decisions in such day-to-day tasks as interviewing news sources, filming accident scenes, writing product advertisements, selecting the music to accompany TV productions, or wording corporate news releases. Even these routine assignments may be fraught with legal hazards that professionals must know how to avoid. Sometimes it is a matter of respecting others' legal rights; sometimes it is a matter of asserting your own. Daily survival also means knowing when to seek the advice of a seasoned professional in the office or when to consult a competent communications lawyer to avoid legal hassles.

It's also important for communicators to know the law so they can talk intelligently about it, defend it, critique it, and perhaps even help mold it. Like it or not, mass communicators have by necessity assumed the role of society's primary guardians of free speech. It is not always an easy role. The public expects the media to be vigilant of intrusions into freedom of expression and to protest them. On the other hand, when mass communicators are perceived as irresponsible, legislators and the public are quick to clamor for tighter legal controls. Communications professionals should be equipped to debate those issues. Furthermore, the mass media should be educating society on important points of law, on broader legal policy considerations, and on the ultimate virtues of free expression. Communicators are partly responsible for helping people to understand the relationship of media, government, and society. Much of that relationship involves law.

Yet another reason to study communications law is, simply, because it is fascinating. The law embodies America's unique history, its hottest philosophical debates, its most incendiary social issues, and its weirdest and least-expected turns of events. Study of the law opens our eyes to ethics, human nature, and public policy.

In addition to these direct benefits, a valuable byproduct of legal study is the cultivation of critical thinking skills. A field as complex as communications law requires effortful thinking; memorization alone is insufficient. The study of law is an ideal vehicle through which to better distinguish philosophical arguments, analyze factual scenarios, and apply settled principles in new contexts.

Before you can successfully study a particular field of law, however, some knowledge of the legal system is necessary, and that is the focus of this chapter. A few things are worth keeping in mind right from the start: One is that laws change, literally overnight in some cases. By the time a textbook is written, edited, printed, and distributed, new laws will be passed and new court decisions announced that might deserve your special attention.

Also, circumstances change. Slightly different factual scenarios may bring drastically different legal results, and the law is in a constant state of struggling to keep up with new controversies, often deciding them on a case-by-case basis. This means that the law is necessarily riddled with gray areas where hypothetical questions cannot be answered with certainty. Students need not be frustrated by this, but accept it as a part of the intellectual attraction of the law.

Another point to remember is that the law often differs from one place to another within the United States. This is because our nation's basic organizing principle is one of federalism—a union formed by separate, sovereign states. The states assigned certain specified powers to a central government, but they also reserved jurisdiction to handle a great portion of their internal affairs as they alone see fit. Therefore, on some subjects it is possible for the laws of neighboring states to be markedly different. The aim of this book is to convey the prevailing rules or to note the major variations on matters for which significant groups of states have adopted divergent policies.

Jurisdiction

The term **jurisdiction** is one of the most important concepts in the study of law. Jurisdiction is, in fact, at the heart of law itself, because it is the authority to make and administer the law. The concept of jurisdiction implies rights, powers, and limits. A government may be empowered to make and enforce its laws through its legislature, administrative agencies, and courts, but it can legally extend its power only to the limits of its jurisdiction.

In one sense, jurisdiction refers to the territory within which a governmental entity may exercise its legal authority. For example, one state may pass a law requiring that police officers' traffic accident reports be open for public inspection. But that law has effect only within the state's borders. The state would have no jurisdiction to enforce its law in a neighboring state, where the rule on accident reports might be different.

In another sense, jurisdiction refers to the subject or type of dispute over which legislatures and court systems have legal authority. In this respect, the most important distinction is between powers assigned to the federal government and powers reserved to the states collectively.

Federal Jurisdiction

When this nation was formed more than two hundred years ago, the states that joined to create it granted certain powers to a federal government in return for the benefits a centralized government would provide. But the federal government is one of limited, enumerated powers, as outlined in the U.S. Constitution. The enumerated powers include the authority to make treaties with foreign governments, to regulate interstate commerce, to coin money, to declare war, and so on. The federal government may exercise authority only to the extent granted in the Constitution, and the Tenth Amendment of that document declares that the powers not delegated to the federal government "are reserved to the States respectively, or to the people."

In terms of communications law, federal jurisdiction permits lawmaking in such areas as broadcasting, through Congress and the Federal Communications Commission; copyrights and trademarks, through Congress and the copyright and patent offices; and commercial advertising, through Congress and the Federal Trade Commission.

Exclusive versus Concurrent

When the federal government regulates within its granted powers, it may override or preempt any state regulation on the same topic. This federal right of preemption comes from the supremacy clause in Article VI of the Constitution. For example, as a legitimate exercise of its commerce power, Congress decided to regulate broadcasting. In doing so, it also specifically preempted that field; any state

EXHIBIT 1.1   *Jurisdiction over Subjects in Communications Law*

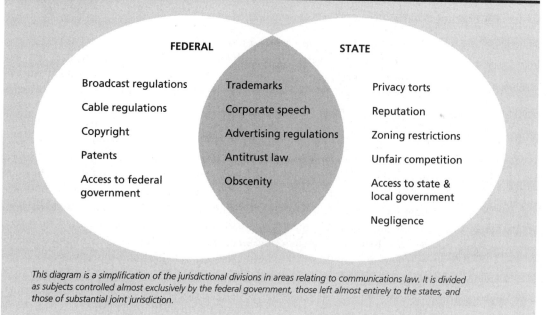

FEDERAL		STATE
Broadcast regulations	Trademarks	Privacy torts
Cable regulations	Corporate speech	Reputation
Copyright	Advertising regulations	Zoning restrictions
Patents	Antitrust law	Unfair competition
Access to federal government	Obscenity	Access to state & local government
		Negligence

This diagram is a simplification of the jurisdictional divisions in areas relating to communications law. It is divided as subjects controlled almost exclusively by the federal government, those left almost entirely to the states, and those of substantial joint jurisdiction.

laws attempting to regulate broadcasting, whether parallel to or in conflict with the federal laws, would be invalid. The same holds true for copyright regulation. In other words, not only does the federal government have jurisdiction in these fields but it has also chosen to exercise exclusive jurisdiction.

This isn't always the case, however. Sometimes Congress allows concurrent jurisdiction by the states. For example, Congress, again acting under its commerce power, has passed laws against deceptive advertising. But in this field the federal government has made no claim of exclusive jurisdiction. Therefore, as Chapter 10 relates, both the federal government and the individual states have laws against deceptive ads. The state laws are valid unless they conflict with federal law to the extent that both cannot stand. (See Exhibit 1.1 for a diagram of federal and state areas of jurisdiction.)

Federal Courts

In addition to its jurisdiction over legislation in certain subject areas, the federal government exercises jurisdiction, through its courts, over certain kinds of legal disputes. Federal courts are authorized to resolve legal disputes that arise under the laws passed by Congress and federal agencies, or under the U.S. Constitution. For example, the copyright dispute in the hypothetical scenario that opened this chapter would fall under the jurisdiction of the federal courts because the underlying copyright law is a creation of Congress. Also under federal court jurisdiction would be a dispute over whether police, by confiscating a news photographer's camera, violated the fundamental right of free speech guaranteed in the First Amendment of the federal Constitution.

Federal court jurisdiction, as with federal jurisdiction generally, does not necessarily mean exclusive jurisdiction. Only in areas the federal government has decided to preempt entirely—such as copyright law—do the federal courts represent the sole forum available. For example, many communications law cases involve claims that state laws improperly conflict with federal constitutional rights. These claims can be adjudicated in federal court or in a state court.

In addition to handling disputes arising from federal law, federal courts have jurisdiction to resolve controversies between citizens of different states. These are called **diversity-of-citizenship** cases, and they are very common in communications law. The theory behind this is that citizens of different states should have access to an impartial forum to resolve their legal disputes—even though no federal law is at issue. In diversity-of-citizenship cases, the federal courts apply state law to resolve the conflicts. Where the alleged legal violation occurred usually determines which state's law will be applied.

The federal system is composed of two kinds of courts: One is the **trial court,** where evidence is presented to determine the facts of a case and a decision is reached by applying the law to those facts. The second kind is the **appellate court,** where a panel of judges determines whether the trial court made any errors in its application of the law and whether those errors justify changing the trial decision. (This process will be explained in more detail later in this chapter.)

The main trial court in the federal system is called the **U.S. District Court.** At least one District Court is located in every state, and there are ninety-four in all.

The next level, an intermediate court for hearing appeals, is called the **U.S. Court of Appeals.** For appellate purposes the nation is divided into twelve geographic units, called *circuits,* each with its own Court of Appeals (Exhibit 1.2). A thirteenth circuit called the **Federal Circuit** has nationwide jurisdiction to hear appeals in certain specialized kinds of cases, including patent-law cases.

Finally, at the top of the federal judicial pyramid is the **Supreme Court of the United States,** with its nine justices in Washington, D.C. The Supreme Court has the authority to review decisions by any of the courts of appeals and, in some cases, decisions by the highest court in each of the states' own judicial systems. The Supreme Court is the final arbiter on all legal questions involving the U.S. Constitution and other federal laws.

State Jurisdiction

Those powers not specifically granted to the federal government are reserved by the individual, sovereign states. This means that the United States is a country, not of one legal system, but of fifty-one sovereign systems—one in each state, plus the federal system.

EXHIBIT 1.2   *The Thirteen Federal Judicial Circuits*

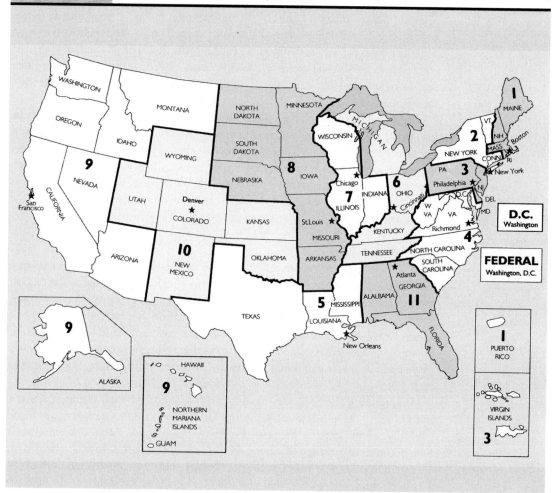

One effect is that each state government has jurisdiction within its borders over those fields of law not designated by the U.S. Constitution as the domain of the federal government. Therefore, many fields of law are primarily, if not entirely, matters of state concern. In the broad field of communications law, protection of individual reputations and protection of privacy, negligence laws, and zoning laws, for example, are matters traditionally within the domain of the states.

Also, because different states' legislatures and courts may decide similar issues differently, it is common for legal rules to vary significantly from state to state. For that reason, the states often are referred to as *laboratories for democracy,* where legal solutions to problems can be devised, tested, and ultimately adopted, modified, or rejected by other states and the federal government.

The concept of sovereign states with their own realms of legal jurisdiction is deeply rooted in the language and structure of the U.S. Constitution and even in American legal principles that predate the Constitution. The strength of state sovereignty was boldly reaffirmed by the U.S. Supreme Court in 1999 when it ruled that Congress generally lacks the authority to authorize private persons or corporations to sue the states.

For example, although the federal government has enacted an unfair-advertising law authorizing one individual to sue another or to sue a business, the law cannot be used to haul a state agency into court—that is, unless the state itself agrees to waive its **sovereign immunity** from such lawsuits.[1] An outgrowth of the notion of sovereign, politically autonomous states, the doctrine of sovereign immunity is that the state cannot be sued, even under authority of a federal statute, unless the state consents.

State Courts

Each of these sovereign, united states also has its own court system. As with the federal judicial system, state court systems consist of both trial and appellate courts. The trial courts go by many different names, including *justice court, municipal court, superior court, circuit court, county court,* and *court of common pleas.* Most states have intermediate courts of appeal, and each state has one court at the top of its hierarchy, usually referred to as that respective state's supreme court. (A diagram of the federal court system and a typical state system appears in Exhibit 1.3.)

Determining the proper court system for a particular legal dispute can be a tremendously complicated matter in the United States. One consideration is the allocation of jurisdiction between the state and federal courts, and another is the allocation of jurisdiction among the various states. Particularly in a field such as communications law, where disputes arise from communications dispersed across state lines, it may be that any one of several court systems would have jurisdiction. A state court system usually has jurisdiction if the alleged legal violation occurred in that state or if one of the people involved is a resident of that state. It is up to the aggrieved person to select a court of proper jurisdiction when initiating a lawsuit.

Categorizing Law by Source

In the United States it is sometimes difficult to decipher the law because it originates from a variety of sources. The main sources are constitutions, statutes, administrative regulations, and the common law of the courts. Which of these constitutes the law? Actually, each one is part of the whole cloth that makes up the law, and each has a place in an organized hierarchy. It is very important that stu-

EXHIBIT 1.3   *Court Systems*

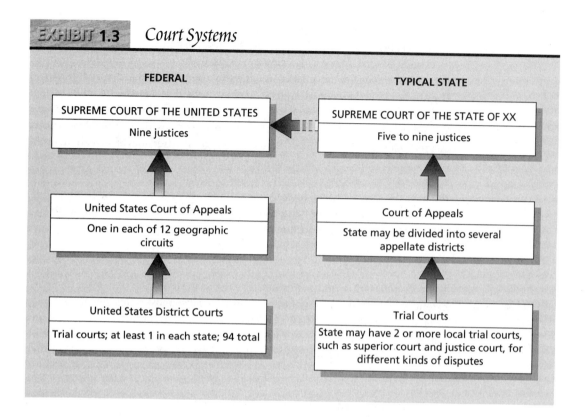

dents of communications law be able to categorize law according to its source, because the law from each source has different characteristics and a different degree of stature in the overall hierarchy. Therefore, we will consider each of these sources in some detail.

Constitutional Law

The most powerful laws are those that are constitutional in origin. A **constitution** is the most fundamental law of a particular jurisdiction. It serves as a charter for the government, specifying the government's form, functions, and operating procedures. Typically, constitutions also blueprint the relationship between the government and the governed, guaranteeing certain basic rights to the people. In most cases constitutions can only be enacted, altered, or amended with special involvement by the people, such as by a popular vote.

The U.S. Constitution

The highest law of this nation is the U.S. Constitution. It sets out the framework of the federal government, including its division into the executive, legislative, and judicial branches, and provides guidelines for the government's operation. As mentioned earlier, it also delegates to the federal government legal power over enumerated subjects and certain other kinds of legal disputes.

The U.S. Constitution also guarantees, in its first ten amendments, that certain rights and freedoms shall be retained by the people. Ratified as the **Bill of Rights** in 1791, these amendments long have served as a model for other nations and as a focal point of hope and inspiration for oppressed people in America and around the globe. This book is concerned at every turn with the First Amendment and its guarantee that Congress shall not abridge "the freedom of speech, or of the press." But this book also will examine rights under the Fourth Amendment (right against unreasonable searches and seizures) and the Sixth Amendment (right of the accused to a fair trial). In each amendment, the guaranteed rights are protections for the people against certain kinds of government action, but not against the actions of other private individuals.

State Constitutions

Each state has its own constitution. These constitutions are patterned to a great extent after the federal Constitution. This is because most states joined the Union after the adoption of the federal Constitution, and according to the U.S. Constitution's rules for admission of new states, the constitution of each applicant state must be approved by Congress. It seemed prudent, therefore, to include in a state constitution many of the same kinds of provisions that existed in the federal charter.

Most important for purposes of this course is that state constitutions also include free speech guarantees that are roughly equivalent to the First Amendment. Some are worded similarly to the First Amendment; others use very different language. For example, a provision in the Constitution of Arizona reads, "Every person may freely speak, write, and publish on all subjects, being responsible for the abuse of that right."

State constitutions may not restrict the minimum level of freedoms guaranteed for all U.S. residents in the federal Constitution. If it wishes, however, a state through its constitution may guarantee its citizens greater liberties than does the U.S. Constitution. For example, the California Supreme Court in 1979 held that the state constitution protects speech in privately owned shopping centers, contrary to the U.S. Supreme Court's interpretation of the First Amendment. The U.S. Supreme Court later acknowledged that the state is free to adopt civil liberties greater than those conferred by the federal Constitution.

Judicial Review

One problem with constitutions, and particularly the rather terse U.S. Constitution, is that their precise meaning isn't always clear. In the context of some new controversy it is often quite uncertain, from the document's language, whether a constitutional provision applies or is being violated. By necessity, then, some branch of government must have authority to *interpret* a constitution. In the United States that branch is the judiciary. Under the **doctrine of judicial review** it is the role of each court system to interpret that jurisdiction's constitution. The highest court in each jurisdiction is the final authority on the meaning of its constitution.

Therefore, the U.S. Supreme Court is the final authority on the meaning of the U.S. Constitution,[2] and that court's interpretations must be followed by all other federal and state courts when the federal Constitution is at issue. The Supreme Court of Arizona, however, is the final authority on the meaning of the Arizona Constitution; not even the U.S. Supreme Court may interpret that document differently.

Constitutional law, then, means not only the raw language of the documents but also the constitutions as interpreted by the courts. Constitutional provisions, as judicially interpreted, rank at the top of the legal hierarchy. If a court finds that the law from any other source within the jurisdiction conflicts with the interpretation of the constitution, that other law will be deemed unconstitutional and invalid.

Statutory Law   When most people think of the law, they think of **statutes.** These are the laws passed by legislative bodies—the acts of Congress and the fifty state legislatures. Statutes begin as bills that are introduced and then deliberated by the legislators. After passage the bills are formally signed into law or vetoed by the chief executives—state governors or the president.

In some fields, the law is almost entirely statutory. For example, all criminal laws in the United States are now in the form of statutes. The criminal statutes specify what sorts of conduct constitute crimes and what the penalties shall be. Another example is copyright law; all the basic rules may be found in the copyright statutes enacted by Congress.

As with constitutions, though, the courts also play a role in statutory law. Ultimately it is the courts that must interpret and apply the statutes in the context of specific disputes. **Statutory law,** then, refers to the actual language of the legislative enactments as well as any official interpretations rendered by the courts.

In most jurisdictions all statutes are systematically arranged by subject, numbered, indexed, and printed in bound volumes. These formal compilations, which must be updated continually, are usually called **codes.** Some legal publishers produce annotated codes that make legal research even easier. These codes list after each statute references to court rulings that have applied and interpreted that particular statute.

Statutes of the federal government—passed by Congress—are arranged by subject and published in the *United States Code,* abbreviated in citations as "U.S.C." Annotated versions of the official Code are available from private publishers. Newly enacted federal statutes, those passed since the last update of the Code, can be found first in the most recent volume of a government publication called *Statutes at Large.* This publication simply lists enacted statutes chronologically. To research the basic laws on copyright, for example, one of your resources might be the *United States Code.* You would look up "copyrights" in the general index and then turn to the appropriate volume. There you could read the actual language of statutory sections pertaining to such subjects as copyright, infringement, and exceptions to infringement. If you were to consult an annotated version of the Code, you also would be directed to specific court decisions interpreting those statutory sections.

The federal and state governments are not the only authorities that legislate. County commissions, city councils, and similar elected bodies also pass laws that relate to their local jurisdictions. At the city and county level, though, these legislative acts are called **ordinances.** Here again, ordinances are codified, printed, and typically made available in public libraries in bound or loose-leaf volumes with indexes.

Administrative Law

Though much more extensive than the provisions contained in constitutions, the enactments of elected legislative bodies still cannot possibly keep pace with all of today's fast-moving and often highly technical dilemmas. Therefore, legislative bodies over the years have delegated some of their lawmaking authority to administrative agencies. These agencies add to the body of law by passing **administrative regulations.**

For example, in the early 1900s the uncontrolled proliferation of radio stations in the United States caused havoc on the airwaves. Ultimately, the U.S. Congress, acting under its authority from the commerce clause of the federal Constitution, passed a licensing requirement to resolve the problem. But Congress itself could not possibly oversee the everyday details of the licensing process. So it created what today is the Federal Communications Commission (FCC) and authorized that agency to pass additional regulations pertaining to who may get a license and under what circumstances. And now it is the FCC, not Congress, that is the source of the greatest volume of law concerning broadcasting. The commission's regulations will be invalid, however, if they exceed the general scope of authority granted by Congress or if they conflict with a specific statute passed by Congress.

The federal government has a plethora of such administrative agencies. Some of the other important federal agencies are the Federal Trade Commission, the Securities and Exchange Commission, and the Interstate Commerce Commission. State governments have created an even greater number of administrative agencies, ranging from college governing boards to fish-and-game commissions, and covering almost every conceivable subject in between.

As with statutory law, administrative regulations currently in force are arranged systematically and then published in multi-volume sets. Official regulations of all federal agencies, such as those just mentioned, are published according to topic in a massive set called the *Code of Federal Regulations*—abbreviated "C.F.R." in citations. In most states, regulations of all agencies are published in

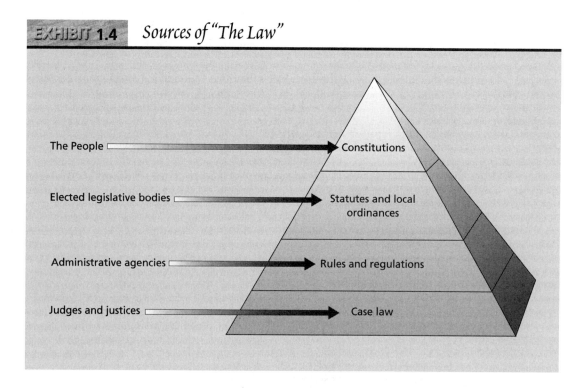

EXHIBIT 1.4   *Sources of "The Law"*

- The People → Constitutions
- Elected legislative bodies → Statutes and local ordinances
- Administrative agencies → Rules and regulations
- Judges and justices → Case law

comprehensive sets similar to the *Code of Federal Regulations.* In some other states, each agency is responsible for publishing its own regulations.

Case Law

Despite the escalated importance of statutory and administrative law during the twentieth century, case law remains the lifeblood of the U.S. legal system. Much of the law is not embodied in neat, codified provisions. Instead, our legal system has relied on the courts to create much of the law through their rulings in individual legal disputes. The term **case law** refers to the binding principles and rules that originate from these case-by-case judicial decisions. Case law may provide essential interpretation to the laws written by legislative and administrative bodies. Or, judges may create original legal rules as needed to resolve disputes; this kind of case law is called **common law.**

Historical Development

Our case law method has its roots in eleventh-century England and the king's courts. The system arose as an alternative to the local, ecclesiastical (church-controlled) courts that were prevalent at the time. The new system aimed to provide a uniform body of law for all of England, based on the common customs and standards of the land—thus the term *common law.* As cases were decided, principles of law were derived from them in order to guide the courts in future cases.

Eventually this common law system amassed a huge body of specific legal rules, each having evolved from court decisions made on a case-by-case basis.

By the fourteenth century, however, the common law rules had become rigid and technical, and aggrieved parties sometimes found that the common law courts simply did not offer an adequate legal remedy. Therefore, yet another supplemental system of courts arose. These courts were called the **courts of equity.** If an injured party could obtain no adequate remedy under the common law rules, he could then approach the court of equity and ask a judge to fashion a remedy based on simple fairness.

Thus another body of court-originated law—the **law of equity**—developed alongside the common law. One of the key differences between these two systems was that common law courts resolved disputes by ordering wrongdoers to compensate injured persons with money or property. The courts of equity, in contrast, would direct persons to alter their behavior in a particular manner so as to stop harming others.

When the American colonies won their independence, England's common law rules and its laws of equity were adopted together as a two-pillared foundation for American justice. By the mid-1800s, however, most states as well as the federal system had abolished the separate equity courts in an effort to merge the two forms of case law. In most jurisdictions today, the same courts administer both common law and equitable remedies, often through a single proceeding.

One confusing consequence of this evolution is that the term *common law* today is often used in a broader sense, synonymously with *case law*. Both terms may be used to mean all judge-made law, as opposed to law created by legislative enactment.

Some areas of communications law are almost entirely of case law development, such as the body of state law protecting individuals' reputations against attack. The legal rules were developed gradually by state judges, without the benefit of statutes, as they decided individual cases and attempted to reach fair conclusions.

The Role of Precedent

At the very core of case law development is the principle that courts are bound by their prior decisions or by the decisions of their superior courts. This is the **doctrine of precedent.** Without it, common law would be a worthless muddle of disjointed rulings. But with it, court decisions become reliable guides upon which future conduct may be based.

Under the doctrine of precedent, a prior judicial decision serves as a governing model—as precedent—for future cases arising under identical or similar facts. Generally speaking, a court *must* follow the precedent of an earlier case, unless the court considers the facts of the new case sufficiently different to warrant a different result.

The doctrine works as follows. First, an earlier judicial decision serves as a precedent only for courts in the same jurisdiction or judicial system. A Texas court decision is not a precedent for the courts of New York, and a New York decision is not a precedent that must be followed by the courts of Texas. At most, the Texas courts might look to the New York ruling as "persuasive authority." But it is not binding precedent.

Furthermore, even within the same jurisdiction, a decision is binding precedent only for the court that handed down the original decision and for other courts lower in the judicial hierarchy. A decision of the Supreme Court of Texas is binding on all lower Texas courts and generally binding as a precedent in later cases before the Supreme Court of Texas itself. But a decision of an intermediate appellate court in Texas is not a binding precedent in the Supreme Court of that state.

In the federal court system, a Supreme Court decision serves as precedent for later Supreme Court cases and for cases in all other federal courts. A decision by the Court of Appeals for the Ninth Circuit is precedent for that court and for all the federal trial courts within the boundaries of the Ninth Circuit, but not for courts in the other circuits. And a decision of a trial court, a U.S. District Court, is binding precedent only for that particular district court, since it is at the bottom of the federal judicial hierarchy.

You will find that in this book we sometimes refer to cases of the federal courts of appeals as being decided by the "U.S. Court of Appeals" or the "Court of Appeals"—without reference to the specific circuit that issued the ruling. The circuit may be found in the citation for that ruling listed in the notes at the end of the book, but the text may not differentiate among circuits unless there is a particular reason to do so. Keep in mind, however, that the various courts of appeals do have distinct personalities and may issue opinions that contradict one another. Unless and until the Supreme Court chooses to rule on the matter, the decisions of the respective circuits are binding precedent for the lower federal courts within their boundaries.

In the United States, the doctrine of precedent applies not only to traditional common law rules but also to court rulings that interpret constitutions, statutes, and regulations. This book is especially concerned with court interpretations of the First Amendment of the Constitution. When those interpretations come from the U.S. Supreme Court, they are binding precedent for all other courts, both state and federal.

As you can see from this system, decisions by the U.S. Supreme Court are of the greatest significance, not just in terms of the individual disputes in question but because they may set precedents for courts throughout the land. Appropriately, then, this book will focus on Supreme Court rulings. Some legal issues simply have never been ruled upon by the Supreme Court, however, or even by the highest courts of the various states. And, until they are, the rulings of lower courts serve as the best available authority.

Lawyers are trained to use case precedents to construct and support their arguments on behalf of clients. Because the facts of two different cases are never exactly the same, however, a judge can face a difficult decision as to which precedent actually controls the pending case. When the lawyers on each side cite different cases as precedent, the judge must decide which of the earlier cases is factually most similar to the case at hand.

A final word about precedent: Though the doctrine is taken very seriously by the courts, in rare instances a court will decide to overrule its own precedent and establish a new rule for the future. If this were done too often, it would jeopardize legal stability. Therefore, instead of overruling precedent, courts are more likely to sidestep an old rule by holding that the current case is factually distinguishable. But occasionally a precedent is directly overruled, or at least modified, when a court becomes convinced that its earlier decision is no longer proper. For example, in 1942 the U.S. Supreme Court ruled that commercial advertising did not qualify as protected expression under the Constitution. That precedent was followed by the Supreme Court and all other courts for more than three decades. Then, in 1976, in a case called *Virginia State Board of Pharmacy v. Virginia Citizens Consumer Council,* the Court repudiated its earlier rule and declared that commercial advertising is constitutionally protected. (In Chapter 10 we'll see why the Court changed its mind.)

Other Ways to Categorize Law

Not only may American law be categorized according to its various governmental sources but it may also be classified on the basis of its purpose, its subject matter, or its operational characteristics. Two of the most important distinctions are between civil law and criminal law and between contracts and torts.

Civil Law versus Criminal Law

The distinction between civil law and criminal law is based primarily on whether the wrongdoers are held accountable to the private, injured parties or to society as a whole. **Civil law** is essentially private law, the law under which harmed individuals or companies or even governments can sue other individuals, companies, or governments in order to extract some kind of legal remedy. The party claiming injury is using the court system and the civil law to obtain legal relief directly from the alleged wrongdoer. Usually the remedy sought is compensation in the form of money.

In most civil cases the applicable burden of proof is described as "a preponderance of the evidence." This means that the suing party, in order to win, must present evidence that outweighs by some degree that of the opposition. Under the preponderance-of-evidence standard, the evidence need not be overwhelmingly convincing, just more so than the other side's.

Under **criminal law,** the government prosecutes accused individuals on behalf of the public at large. The immediate purpose of the prosecution is to impose punishment, not to compensate an injured party. Usually the punishment is a fine or time behind bars.

The burden of proof in criminal cases is much tougher. In order to win a conviction, the government must prove that the accused person is guilty "beyond a reasonable doubt." In other words, the evidence of guilt must be totally convincing.

The laws protecting privacy and reputation, for example, are mainly civil. Under specified circumstances, injured people can collect monetary compensation from the parties that spread degrading or deeply private information (areas examined in Chapters 4 and 5). Also, the copyright problem presented in the chapter hypothetical would be a civil law matter because the threat was that a private company would sue you to protect its own rights. On the other hand, the law of obscenity is mainly criminal. Offended individuals don't sue adult-oriented magazines on a claim of obscenity; rather, it is a government prosecutor who seeks punishment under a state's criminal law on obscenity.

Contracts and Torts

Within the arena of civil law, another fundamental division is that between contract law and tort law. The categorization is based on the source of the rights and obligations involved.

Contract law is concerned with enforcing rights and obligations that arise when people enter voluntary agreements called **contracts.** Contracts are legally binding mutual promises to perform in a certain way under certain circumstances. They arise when one person makes a promise to another in exchange for a promise by the second person. The intent is to create certain expectations that did not exist prior to the agreement, and contract law enforces those expectations.

For example, a freelance reporter's promise to give a particular newspaper the exclusive story behind a tragedy the reporter witnessed, in exchange for the paper's promise to pay $2000, could form a valid contract. Courts are empowered to enforce the terms of the agreement. If one party to a contract believes the other has not performed as promised, that party may sue for monetary compensation. The formal basis for such a lawsuit is a legal claim for **breach of contract.** Contracts permeate the field of mass communication. Consider, for example, the agreement between an advertising agency and its client, the agreement between an author and a book publishing company, and the agreement between a commercial photographer and a model.

Communications law also involves a very broad classification of law called **torts.** A tort is any other wrong—other than breach of contract—for which the law gives the injured party some kind of remedy against the wrongdoer in civil court. The rights protected by tort law do not arise by agreement. Rather, they are rights—and corresponding duties—that a jurisdiction affixes universally to human relations. As the basic principle is stated in California, "Every person has, subject to the qualifications and restrictions provided by law, the right of protection from bodily restraint or harm, from personal insult, from defamation, and from injury to his personal relations."

The law actually recognizes many different torts, each with a separate name and definition. For example, it may be a tort to publish something derogatory about a person (libel) or to secretly bug someone's house with electronic devices (invasion of privacy), or to play a cruel practical joke over the radio (infliction of mental distress).

An important facet of any tort lawsuit is the applicable fault standard. That is, in addition to committing the harmful conduct itself, the alleged wrongdoer must be shown to have acted with a certain degree of dereliction. Depending on the tort, the fault requirement is usually stated as "negligence," "gross negligence," or "malice." The law does recognize a few "strict liability" torts, however. With these torts the alleged wrongdoer may be held accountable for his actions even if the resulting harm was in no way intended and could not reasonably have been foreseen. Historically, many states regarded libel as a strict liability tort, as Chapter 4 recounts.

In some cases the same act of wrongdoing may amount to both a tort, for which the injured party may file a civil lawsuit, and a crime, for which the government will prosecute. This is the case with some kinds of trespass, for example.

A substantial portion of communications law is simply the specialized application of general tort and contract principles that have evolved over many decades, and in some cases centuries. Communication law, then, is not a formal, separate branch of law that developed in a vacuum. Rather, it reflects many of the legal principles and social policies that underlie American civil law in general. For example, thinking back to the chapter hypothetical, suppose that you entered into a contract with the local newspaper by which you would be allowed to read some of its news material on the air. This contract would take the specialized form of a copyright license. But the basic principles for how that contract is formed and honored would be virtually the same as with any other kind of contract, such as a contract to provide gardening services. What makes communications law different from other fields of law is that the U.S. Constitution often intervenes and forces general legal rules to yield to a higher aim: freedom of speech. Elucidation of the influence of the Constitution begins in the next chapter.

The Judicial Process

Thus far this examination of the legal system has focused primarily on the origins and characteristics of substantive law—the actual rules of conduct people must live by. In any given legal dispute, however, the substantive rules of law may only begin to foretell the ultimate outcome. Equally important in the U.S. legal system are the procedural aspects of law. Procedural rules may determine when and how the substantive rules are applied or even if they will be applied.

Justiciable Controversy

The threshold principle of legal procedures is that courts can issue rulings only in conjunction with real controversies that are before them. No matter how much a judge may want to solve a problem in society, the judge cannot address that issue unless it is brought before the court, in the form of a lawsuit, by parties who have a true stake in the outcome. This is because the courts of this country operate in an adversary system. They are empowered only to resolve specific legal disputes between the people or entities whose legal rights are in jeopardy and who have formally asked the court, by filing a lawsuit, to intervene. In legal parlance, it is said that courts will consider only a **justiciable controversy,** as opposed to a question that is hypothetical or moot.

This principle explains why case law may take a long time to develop. Lawsuits are the necessary vehicle for case law, but a legal issue may arise in society long before an actual lawsuit on that issue works its way to the courts.

Pretrial Procedure

Many of the critical steps in a legal dispute occur prior to trial. And in this phase of the dispute vast differences exist between civil cases and criminal cases, so they are examined separately. What follows is a description of fairly typical procedure, but some steps and terminology do vary from state to state.

In Civil Cases

To continue the hypothetical problem that began this chapter, suppose your station was indeed sued for copyright infringement by the owner of the newspaper. That person would begin a civil case by filing at the trial court a legal document called a **complaint.** The complaint spells out the applicable law, identifies the wrongful conduct and those allegedly responsible for it, and asks for a certain amount of compensation for the harm done. The person complaining—in this case the newspaper owner—is called the **plaintiff.**

A copy of the complaint then is delivered to you, the **defendant.** A defendant is one against whom relief is being sought. There may be other defendants in this case, ranging from the individual news reporter to the corporation that owns the station. (Plaintiffs and defendants together are referred to as **litigants.**) You are required to file with the court an official response, known as an **answer.** In it your attorney will admit or deny each of the plaintiff's allegations and state, in general terms, why the plaintiff is not entitled to win against you.

After these initial documents, called the **pleadings,** are filed with the court, the lawsuit enters a phase called **discovery.** Unlike many of the dramatic depictions on film and television, in civil cases it is rare indeed for devastating testimony or a piece of evidence to be produced by surprise during trial. Instead, each lawyer knows ahead of time exactly what evidence the other side will present during trial.

This is learned during the discovery process, through which attorneys can compel plaintiffs or defendants or potential witnesses to answer detailed questions or hand over relevant documents. The discovery process can be time-consuming and expensive. The theory behind it, though, is to narrow the key issues prior to a full-blown trial.

As information becomes known, either side may make a variety of pretrial **motions,** which are simply formal requests that the judge make some kind of ruling in favor of the applicant. The most important is the motion for **summary judgment** because it seeks to end the case altogether. This motion is made when the applicant believes there is no contested issue of fact and that the applicant is entitled to an immediate legal judgment in his favor. Summary judgment motions have been used extensively by media defendants to cut frivolous lawsuits short.

If such motions are denied, a trial date will be set. Very few lawsuits make it that far, however. That is because more than 90 percent of all civil cases end with a **settlement** prior to trial. Often the trial judges encourage parties to settle. In a settlement, each side compromises and gives up something. Though the result is rarely ideal for either party, a settlement avoids the time, expense, and uncertainty of a full-blown jury trial. It is also common for the parties to agree that terms of their settlement shall not be made public.

In Criminal Cases

In criminal cases—those prosecuted by the government to obtain punishment—the pretrial procedure is significantly different from that in civil cases. It involves a greater number of formal steps along the way, due primarily to the need to safeguard the specific constitutional rights of an accused. Those rights include, for example, the right to notice of charges, the right to legal counsel, the right to a jury trial, the right not to testify against oneself, and the right to be presumed innocent until proven guilty beyond a reasonable doubt. The rights of a criminal defendant are more elaborate than those of civil defendants because in a criminal prosecution the defendant's liberty may be at stake.

Typically, the criminal case begins with an arrest by police, who then take their information about the suspect to the government prosecutor. A criminal complaint is promptly filed, and within a few days the defendant appears in court for an **arraignment.** Defendants are advised of the charges against them and then asked to plead either guilty or not guilty to each charge. (In federal cases this is called the **initial appearance.**)

Presuming the defendant pleads not guilty, the next formal step may be a **preliminary hearing.** The purpose of this hearing is to determine whether the government truly has enough evidence against the defendant to warrant a full-blown trial. During the hearing, the defendant is confronted with an abbreviated version of the prosecution's evidence. The defendant's lawyer may question the government's witnesses to discover the nature and credibility of their potential testimony at trial, but the defense does not present its own evidence at this stage. If the judge

EXHIBIT 1.5   *Major Steps in Legal Procedure*

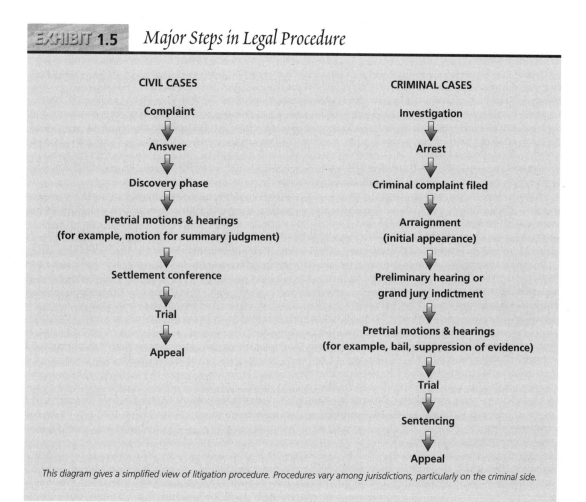

CIVIL CASES

Complaint
⬇
Answer
⬇
Discovery phase
⬇
Pretrial motions & hearings
(for example, motion for summary judgment)
⬇
Settlement conference
⬇
Trial
⬇
Appeal

CRIMINAL CASES

Investigation
⬇
Arrest
⬇
Criminal complaint filed
⬇
Arraignment
(initial appearance)
⬇
Preliminary hearing or
grand jury indictment
⬇
Pretrial motions & hearings
(for example, bail, suppression of evidence)
⬇
Trial
⬇
Sentencing
⬇
Appeal

This diagram gives a simplified view of litigation procedure. Procedures vary among jurisdictions, particularly on the criminal side.

is convinced that the evidence reasonably implicates the defendant, a trial will be ordered. (In some jurisdictions, including federal, this independent assessment of the evidence is more often made by a grand jury than by preliminary hearing. In such cases, the grand jury issues an **indictment**—the formal charge upon which the defendant will go to trial.)

As with civil cases, a number of motions may be filed with the court before a criminal trial begins. A common one, for example, is the **motion to suppress.** This request seeks to prohibit the introduction of any evidence that police may have obtained illegally. The merits of this request are debated at a pretrial suppression hearing. (An overview chart of the sequence of events discussed thus far is presented in Exhibit 1.5.)

Trial Procedure   Whether criminal or civil, cases that go all the way to trial are expensive. The costs escalate even more if a jury trial is requested because it takes additional time to select and instruct a jury.

In the ordinary trial, either criminal or civil, each side makes opening remarks. Then each side, starting with the plaintiff or prosecutor, presents its case by calling witnesses who are asked questions on the witness stand by the attorneys. Participants in a trial, including the plaintiff and defendant, may find themselves repeatedly and rigorously questioned about the events in controversy. Many have found it to be a grueling experience. Finally, each side makes closing arguments and the court comes to a decision.

In jury trials, it is the jury's responsibility to decide factual questions in controversy. For example, did your news broadcast actually harm the plaintiff? How badly? Was your version substantially similar to the copyrighted version? In jury trials it is the judge's role to rule on disputed questions of law. Should the testimony be declared irrelevant and therefore inadmissible to the jury? What degree of fault is the plaintiff legally required to prove? In proceedings where there is no jury, the judge decides both the legal and factual questions. In an effort to save time and costs, or perhaps for strategic reasons, it is fairly common for litigants to opt for a trial without a jury.

If the plaintiff wins in a civil trial, the defendant will be required to provide a legal remedy for the harm inflicted. In most cases, the remedy is a sum of money. These money awards to the plaintiff are called **damages.** Payment of damages is the traditional remedy employed in both contract and tort cases, even when the harm to the plaintiff was not actually monetary in nature. For example, in awarding damages a jury may be asked to place a monetary value on the wrongful loss of plaintiff's personal privacy.

For some kinds of harm, though, the payment of damages would be an entirely unsatisfactory remedy. Instead, a plaintiff may want the court to order the defendant to do something or refrain from doing something. For example, the plaintiff might desire an official order that a TV camera crew stop camping out in the plaintiff's front yard. This kind of court order is called an **injunction.** Injunctions are the most important of the so-called equitable remedies, developed by the courts of equity, that once operated as an alternative system. As a vestige of that once-distinct system, juries have no role in awarding equitable remedies; judges alone determine whether an injunction shall be issued.

Appellate Procedure   After the final judgment at trial, either the defendant or the plaintiff may wish to appeal. The losing party often wishes to do so. But sometimes the winning party may wish to appeal if, for example, he was not awarded the amount of damages requested. The appealing party is referred to as the **appellant** and the party against whom the appeal is filed is called the **respondent,** or sometimes the **appellee.**

Despite the common belief that appeals courts conduct the trial all over again, nothing is further from the truth. The factual questions in dispute were decided by the jury or judge in the trial court. And with very few exceptions, such as in prosecutions for obscenity, the appellate court will not reconsider the factual determinations. The appellate court will not view the witnesses giving testimony and will not reexamine the evidence firsthand. Instead, the job of the appellate court is to decide whether the trial court made an error in determining or applying the law. The appellate decision is based on a transcript of the trial, a written legal analysis, or a **legal brief** prepared by each attorney, and a short oral argument before the court by a lawyer from each side.

If the appellate court concludes that no significant errors were made by the trial court, its judgment will be **affirmed.** If it is deemed that the trial was not conducted in sufficient accord with the law, the trial judgment will be **reversed.** When the court reverses, a new trial may be necessary. But for this the case is **remanded,** or sent back down to the trial court.

In the first-level appellate courts, in both the federal and state systems, cases usually are decided by a panel of three judges. They usually are not the only judges for that appellate court; rather, they are the three assigned to the case. If parties are dissatisfied with the decision of a three-judge panel, they sometimes may obtain further review by the court's entire bank of judges. After a ruling by this first appellate court, most systems offer one more level of appeal. In most states it is termed the *supreme court* of that particular jurisdiction, and usually cases before the highest court are decided by the entire bench of five to nine justices. The highest court of a particular jurisdiction usually is the end of the line for the parties in a lawsuit. However, in some cases a decision of a state supreme court may be reviewed yet again by the U.S. Supreme Court. This final jump from a state high court to the federal high court is possible when the case involves a question of federal law, such as a claim that First Amendment rights have been violated.

Review by the highest appellate courts of a jurisdiction usually is discretionary. The U.S. Supreme Court, for example, actually decides about 100 cases a year, out of several thousand requests for review. So, in most kinds of cases there is no automatic right to appeal to the highest courts. Instead, these courts accept for review those cases that present the most important or most novel legal questions. When the U.S. Supreme Court decides to review a case, it usually does so through a formal order called a *writ of certiorari.* You will sometimes hear this referred to as a "granting cert."

When an appellate court judgment is announced, it is usually accompanied by a **majority opinion** that indicates why the court affirmed or reversed the lower court. A majority opinion is one that represents the views of a majority of the judges who considered the appeal. Judges sometimes write **concurring opinions** when they agree with the majority's final disposition of this case, but not with all of the majority's reasoning. Finally, appellate judges may issue **dissenting opinions** when they disagree altogether with the majority's ruling on a case. Although they do not represent the controlling view of the court, concurring and dissenting opinions may add valuable perspectives to the issues at hand. Also, the views

The U.S. Supreme Court justices, 2000.   *Back row (left to right): Justice Ruth Ginsburg, Justice David Souter, Justice Clarence Thomas, Justice Stephen Breyer. Front row: Justice Antonin Scalia, Justice John Paul Stevens, Chief Justice William Rehnquist, Justice Sandra Day O'Connor, Justice Anthony Kennedy.* (Collection, The Supreme Court of the United States, courtesy The Supreme Court Historical Society. Photographed by Richard Strauss.)

expressed in a concurring or dissenting opinion sometimes eventually gain the adherence of a majority of the court.

Appellate courts' majority opinions are the most important, or course, because of their strong value as precedent. But occasionally a court cannot muster a majority opinion, in which case a **plurality opinion** serves as a weaker substitute. A plurality opinion is an appellate opinion without enough judges' votes to constitute a majority but with more votes than any other opinion filed in the case. For example, suppose the U.S. Supreme Court voted 7–2 to uphold a federal restriction on liquor advertising. The seven justices would represent a clear majority supporting the Court's final judgment. However, if four of these justices reached their decision based on one rationale and three justices on another, the Court would be left without a majority agreeing to any one opinion. In this case, the Court's lead opinion would be a plurality opinion representing just four of nine justices.

Finding Court Decisions

When appellate opinions are issued, they are published chronologically, usually by jurisdiction, in extensive sets called **court reports.** More than 50,000 American case opinions are published each year. Thus, even when a dispute is concluded as far as the original litigants are concerned, the resulting court opinion may live on as precedent to guide the conduct of others.

In your study of communications law, you may want occasionally to look up the full text of important or interesting court opinions. This is a simple task when you have a case citation to go by.

Take, for instance, the case of *Hustler Magazine v. Falwell,* 108 S. Ct. 876 (1988). First in this citation is the name of the case. It reflects the names of two of the parties involved in the dispute, namely *Hustler* magazine and Jerry Falwell. (At the trial level, the suing party's name is always listed first. On appeal, however, some appellate courts will alter the original case name so that the party seeking the appeal is listed first, whether or not that was the suing party at trial.) The name is followed by a reference to a volume, a published set of court opinions, and a page. In the citation here, you find the abbreviation "S. Ct." This refers to the set of court reports called *Supreme Court Reporter,* so you would locate this set in your campus library or a local law library. Then you would refer to the first number in the citation and pull volume 108 from the shelf. Referring to the second number, you would turn to page 876. And there it is. The (*1988*) refers to the year the case was decided, and the material includes all opinions in the case to date.

It is common for the decisions of a particular court to be published by different publishers in different sets of court reports. Therefore, case names sometimes are followed by **parallel citations** to two or more sets of court reports in which the opinion may be found. Libraries often have lists to help you learn the citation abbreviations of the different sets of reports available.

For opinions of the federal courts, the following sets of court reports are the most important:

☐ The *United States Supreme Court Reports* (abbreviated "U.S.") and the *Supreme Court Reporter* ("S. Ct."), both for opinions of the U.S. Supreme Court.

☐ The *Federal Reporter* (abbreviated "F.," "F.2d," or "F.3d," depending on the series), for opinions of the U.S. Courts of Appeals.

☐ The *Federal Supplement* ("F. Supp."), for opinions of the United States District Courts. (Trial-level courts generally do not issue written opinions for publication. The federal District Courts are exceptions to this rule.)

The main libraries of colleges and universities commonly subscribe to these court reports, or at least to a couple of them. These libraries are less likely, however, to stock all the official sets of reports that carry the opinions of the various state courts individually. In some instances, though, libraries that don't carry the court reports of each state individually will stock all or a portion of the *National Reporter System*. Published by West Publishing Company, it is a collection of the case opinions from state courts, organized into seven regional sets of reports—the *Atlantic Reporter, North Eastern Reporter, Pacific Reporter,* and so on.

If you wish to look up a court opinion for which your regular library does not carry the necessary set of court reports, you should check with a law school library or your county law library, usually located at the courthouse. Another avenue—increasingly popular—is to find the case via computer. Some campus libraries offer access to commercial databases of legal materials, such as Westlaw and Lexis-Nexis, which can retrieve cases from any jurisdiction. More and more court systems also are making their decisions available for free via government Internet sites.

In this text the citations at the end of the book generally were selected on the basis of the case reports with the greatest availability. For state court decisions, the citations usually are to the appropriate regional sets in the *National Reporter System*. If a state court case does not appear in a regional reporter, the citation will be to a reporter for that individual state.

In a few instances you will find that a case has been given different citations in different places. This is because it may have been instructive to refer to judicial opinions from two different levels of courts, for which different sets of court reports were appropriate. For example, in one place you might find a reference to a federal district judge's opinion, and the note at the end of the chapter would cite the *Federal Supplement*. A later reference might be made to an opinion of the appellate court pertaining to the same case, but the citation would be to the *Federal Reporter*.

A final note about the citations of each chapter that appear at the back of the book: It is often necessary to cite the same case several times. Just as most journalists will use the *Associated Press Stylebook*, most lawyers use *A Uniform System of Citation*, which is quite specific about how to write various second references to a case. Because this book is for communications students, not lawyers, the format has been simplified somewhat. In the end-of-chapter notes, a second or third reference to *Hustler Magazine v. Falwell*, 108 S. Ct. 876 (1988), for example, will appear as Falwell, 878. That means that the material referred to in the text can be found on page 878 of volume 108 of *Supreme Court Reporter*.

Administrative Proceedings

In some specialized kinds of legal controversies between individuals and the government, legal proceedings may not actually begin in a trial court. Instead, the starting place may be an administrative hearing. Earlier, this chapter described the rule-making power possessed by many administrative agencies. In some cases, these same agencies are also authorized to issue rulings in specific controversies.

For example, suppose you are a broadcaster, and the FCC, after receiving numerous complaints about your using dirty words on the air, has decided to pull your license. You would receive notice of this decision. Your first forum in which to challenge the action would be an administrative hearing arranged by the FCC. You may be represented by an attorney, but there are no juries. Your arguments would be presented to an administrative law judge or perhaps to the full commission, and then a decision would be reached.

If you disagreed with the result of the administrative adjudication, you would have the right to take your legal argument to the regular court system. In the case of FCC rulings, your next step would be to bypass the trial court and appeal directly to the U.S. Court of Appeals. A similar process also applies in the states, where the quasi-judicial rulings of state administrative agencies are subject to review by a state appellate court.

Summary Points

As a result of the American concept of federalism, the United States is composed of fifty-one sovereign legal systems, each with its own legislature and court system.

Some fields of law are exclusively the domain of the federal government, some areas of law are reserved for the states, and in some cases the states and the federal government exercise concurrent jurisdiction.

The U.S. Constitution is the single highest ranking source of law in the United States. No other law may conflict with the Constitution as it is interpreted by the U.S. Supreme Court.

Within each legal system's hierarchy of law, constitutions are followed by statutes and then by administrative regulations. State law of any kind will be invalid, however, if it conflicts with any valid federal law.

Court decisions are an important source of communications law. Although court opinions are not neatly codified, they provide legal guidance by virtue of the doctrine of precedent.

Court opinions can be located easily by use of a citation, which includes the case name, the abbreviation for a particular set of court reports, the volume, the page number, and the year the decision was reached.

Court proceedings are either civil or criminal. Sometimes separate civil and criminal proceedings may result from the same incident of misconduct.

Some specialized kinds of legal disputes must be adjudicated first before a government agency rather than a court. Such is the case with broadcast licensing disputes, which are heard by the FCC.

In the chapter-opening hypothetical, several questions were presented about a threat to sue for copyright infringement. Copyright law will be discussed in

Chapter 8. But from the information presented in this chapter the following is apparent: If the newspaper sued you for infringement, it would be a civil case, not criminal. You would be in danger of losing money but not of going to jail. The lawsuit would begin formally when the newspaper, the plaintiff, filed a formal complaint in the court of proper jurisdiction. That court would be a federal District Court because the federal government has exclusive jurisdiction in the area of copyrights.

Key Terms

administrative regulations
affirm
answer
appellant
appellate court
appellee
arraignment
Bill of Rights
breach of contract
case law
certiorari
civil law
codes
common law
complaint
concurring opinion
constitution
constitutional law
contracts
court reports
courts of equity
criminal law
damages
defendant
discovery
dissenting opinion
diversity of citizenship
doctrine of judicial review
doctrine of precedent
Federal Circuit

indictment
initial appearance
injunction
jurisdiction
justiciable controversy
law of equity
legal brief
litigant
majority opinion
motions
motion to suppress
ordinances
parallel citations
plaintiff
pleadings
plurality opinion
preliminary hearing
remand
respondent
reverse
settlement
statutes
statutory law
summary judgment
torts
trial court
U.S. Court of Appeals
U.S. District Court
U.S. Supreme Court

Web Resources

http://www.law.cornell.edu/
Legal Information Institute (Cornell Law School)

http://www.uscourts.gov/
Federal judiciary home page

InfoTrac® College Edition

Using *Infotrac College Edition*, explore the way in which the concept of state sovereign immunity from federally authorized lawsuits was strengthened by a series of Supreme Court rulings in 1999. The rulings, based in part on language in the Eleventh Amendment, have been sharply criticized by some commentators who argue that they will permit state governments to violate federal laws, such as copyright and patent laws, with impunity. Find at least two articles that comment on the Court's recent sovereign-immunity rulings. Do you think the Supreme Court's rulings are good policy?

CHAPTER TWO

Chapter Outline

The First Amendment

Upon completing this chapter you should

- ☐ **appreciate** the philosophical underpinnings of the First Amendment to the U.S. Constitution.
- ☐ **know** what the First Amendment actually says and how the words have been interpreted by the Supreme Court.
- ☐ **understand** the general scope of First Amendment protection and the distinction between *expression* and *conduct*.
- ☐ **know** the standards and doctrines used by courts to decide First Amendment cases.
- ☐ **appreciate** some of the general circumstances in which freedom of speech may be limited by other, conflicting interests.

Hypothetical

■ A Bad Day at Flat Rock

Assume you are the editor of the *Flat Rock Folio,* a weekly newspaper that specializes in news analysis, entertainment, and commentary for your predominantly rural circulation area. On one particularly fateful day, a dozen angry Flat Rock residents enter your office. They are upset with your continuing editorials opposing a U.S. Air Force plan to base a detachment of its new warplane, the expensive F-39 Sleuth fighter, in your area. You have opposed the Sleuth, a super-secret jet that is virtually undetectable by current radar technology, on the grounds that it would cost too much, that its deployment would increase international arms buildups, and that training flights would shatter the serenity of the local environment.

The group of residents is concerned that your opposition might cause the air force, which is testing a prototype of the Sleuth at its high-security base nearby, to station the jets elsewhere, thus denying your region extra jobs and revenues. Your office visitors demand that you stop opposing the Sleuth. Your attempts to defend your views are unsuccessful. The confrontation quickly escalates to the point where several members of the group cripple your computers and printing press with hammers. The damage delays publication of your next edition by several days.

While you are cleaning up the mess in your office, the owner of your paper pays you a visit. She tells you that your coverage and commentary on the Sleuth issue have caused too much local resentment, and she orders you to lay off the story. You protest, but she says her decision is final.

Later that day a reporter tells you that the city council, which the week before had passed a resolution condemning your editorial stance, has just passed a newsrack ordinance. The law bans from town sidewalks the newsracks of all newspapers, which in its view create litter. Your newsracks, the council claims, are unsightly and the papers tend to create litter. The ban goes into effect immediately. Your newsracks already are being removed from the sidewalks, potentially causing you a large decrease in circulation.

In your next edition you respond to the city council by running some vulgar words in a front page headline. This causes a bit of a stir in the shopping malls where your few remaining newsracks are located. For this indiscretion the local prosecutor is charging you with disturbing the peace—a crime.

This scenario raises several questions about your rights to free expression. Which, if any, of the actions by the residents, your publisher, the city council, and the prosecutor are violations of the First Amendment? What would you do? What are your rights?

Background

Throughout human history, events have shown that freedom of expression stirs fear and anger, both within the citizenry and in government. Whether it is a rap music group recording provocative lyrics, a talk show host exploring unorthodox lifestyles, college students speaking frankly about race, an artist whose work expresses unpopular views of religion, or political protestors burning an American flag, many have faced—and many will continue to face—hostility for ideas freely expressed. This chapter examines the notion of freedom of expression as embodied in the First Amendment of the U.S. Constitution.

It is important that communications students understand First Amendment dynamics because the amendment has in some way influenced all of this nation's communications industries, and it will continue to permeate the communications issues of tomorrow. The First Amendment is the nation's ultimate protection for communicators. But its strength is not guaranteed forever; that depends upon vigorous application in the courts and the vigilance of professional communicators.

To appreciate the First Amendment, you must know something of its historical background in England and the American colonies. Even before the beginning of mass communication in Western civilization—the advent of the movable-type printing press in the mid-1400s—governments had attempted to control the free expression of ideas. Such freedom could lead to public criticism of those in power, and the powerful viewed criticism as a kind of disease that could topple them from command. So when the printing press arrived, with its ability to mass produce ideas at relatively little expense, it was greatly feared by those in control. In the seventeenth century the British government began to make steady attempts to control mass communication. Through a tight system of licensing, the government decided who would have the right to publish, both in England and in the colonies. Under this system the government also exercised prior restraint by prohibiting certain manuscripts or passages from being published at all, which is commonly called *censorship*. The crown justified this tight regulation of the media by citing the governmental responsibility to safeguard public welfare and civil stability.

One of the first arguments for freedom of the press was made by the poet John Milton in 1644 with the publication of *Areopagitica*. Milton's little book, which was subtitled *For the Liberty of Unlicensed Printing*, was written to support his efforts to publish unlicensed pamphlets about divorce—information that grew out of his own marital difficulties. Milton argued for what today would be considered a rather cramped notion of free expression: Only Protestant English men ought to have the right to free expression, argued Milton, who also served as a government book censor. Although *Areopagitica* had little effect when it was first published, Milton's eloquent call for freedom of expression has left its mark on the ages.

"Give me liberty to know, to utter, and to argue freely according to conscience, above all liberties,"[1] Milton wrote. Government does injury to truth by regulating communication, thus doubting the strength of truth, he said. Government should stay out of debates, Milton argued, and let truth and falsehood grapple, because in a free and open encounter truth would always come out on top.

Along with the ability to control publication in advance, of course, came the ability to punish after the fact those who did not follow the rules. And punish they did. Promoting ill opinions of the government and advocating change was regarded as a serious crime, often called **seditious libel.** In the seventeenth and eighteenth centuries, hundreds were convicted and commonly punished by fines, imprisonment, whipping, and the pillory.

In some cases publications critical of the king were even punished as treason. One such example is described by Pulitzer Prize–winning historian Leonard Levy:

> In 1663 William Twyn, for printing a book that endorsed the right of revolution, was held to have encompassed [imagined] the king's death; Twyn was sentenced to be hanged, cut down while still alive, and then emasculated, disemboweled, quartered, and beheaded—the standard punishment for treason.[2]

The power of the crown in Great Britain was curbed over time, as democratic tendencies increased. In the area of free speech, the first big step toward greater liberty came with the 1694 abolition of the licensing system in England. Governors of the colonies retained licensing a while longer. But public sentiment forced its demise there, too, in the early 1720s, after James Franklin, Ben's older brother, published his *New England Courant* in defiance of the license requirement and was jailed briefly.

Though the formal licensing scheme was beaten, other oppressive forms of control over expression remained in effect. Even after American independence, some of the controls, such as laws against seditious libel, were adopted in some form by the new nation.[3]

Reasons for Freedom of Speech

Since Milton's time many well-known writers, philosophers, legal scholars, and political figures have made forceful pleas for a policy of freedom of speech. But what does this concept actually mean? How much freedom? In what circumstances? Does freedom of speech simply mean the absence of any prior restraint on publication, as the great British judge and author William Blackstone argued in the 1760s?[4] Or should it mean something more?

Debate over the proper parameters of freedom of speech continues today. Some insight may be gained, however, by considering the main reasons, or justifications, that have been forwarded for protecting speech. These can be divided into social reasons and individualistic reasons.

Social Reasons

Social reasons for freedom of speech are those that presuppose some particular functional benefits to society. Among those most commonly cited are the following.

Discovery of Truth

The premise is that freedom of speech is essential if individuals, and ultimately society as a whole, are to select the best ideas and move toward truth. Such a process calls for many voices who are expounding all sides of an issue. Only when this process is continued can judgments truly be enlightened.

This theory argues that in a truly open marketplace of ideas the truth will ultimately prevail. Even widely accepted truths should be tested from time to time against seemingly absurd ideas, and the way to combat erroneous views is not to outlaw them but to inject superior views into the marketplace.

Participation in Democracy

Some of the founding fathers of this nation viewed free and continual expression of ideas as essential to the successful functioning of a democracy. Without freedom of speech voters would be more likely to remain ignorant or apathetic or be more easily deceived by the authorities in power. With freedom of speech, voters would be more likely to participate meaningfully in democracy. Thomas Jefferson wrote in 1787, "The basis of our government being the opinion of the people, the very first object should be to keep that right," and he urged that the people should have "full information of their affairs through the channel of the public papers."[5]

A more recent advocate of this self-governance justification was philosopher and educator Alexander Meiklejohn, who wrote in the 1940s that protection of free speech in America

> . . . is not, primarily, a device for the winning of new truth, though that is very important. It is a device for the sharing of whatever truth has been won. Its purpose is to give to every voting member of the body politic the fullest possible participation in the understanding of those problems with which the citizens of a self-governing society must deal.[6]

Meiklejohn believed this function was so important that any speech relating to public affairs should receive absolute protection under the First Amendment.

Check on Government

Another social justification for freedom of speech is that it serves to deter or bring to light abuses of power by public officials. One of the best examples of this check-on-government benefit was the uncovering of the Watergate scandal during President Richard Nixon's administration. The egregious abuses of authority—including campaign sabotage, wiretapping, laundering campaign money, and obstructing investigations—might never have been uncovered and punished had it not been for news media free to serve as aggressive watchdogs on government. History is replete, of course, with examples of government corruption. American media sometimes help to curb abuses by disclosing—at the local level, for example—squandered funds, payoffs, political favors, fraud, and conflicts of interest.

Social Stability

Another functional view is that freedom of speech actually helps assure social stability, contrary to the traditional assumption of some government officials that it disrupts society. This is because a free flow of information allows society to see its problems better and to respond with continual, incremental adjustments. It also allows displeased individuals to vent their anger before they reach the boiling point, a sort of therapeutic or safety-valve effect. On the other hand, government suppression of speech in a quest for "order" breeds fear, resentment, and hate, the perfect mix for social unrest and a violent eruption against authority.

Individualistic Reasons

Another approach to justifying freedom of speech is to argue that it is simply a natural or ethical right of individual human beings, that it is fundamentally good in itself, independent of any pragmatic benefits. The natural-right arguments have been stated in many different forms and over a prolonged period of time.

By the late 1700s, the founders of this nation and the framers of the U.S. Constitution, most notably Thomas Jefferson and James Madison, viewed government power as inherently limited. The limits are not determined by people, but by **natural law,** they argued. This term denotes rules of human conduct that conform to inherent, universal rights—rights emanating from nature or from God. In a natural-law system, government would be obliged to protect, not infringe upon, inherent individual liberties. As communications law scholar Frederick S. Siebert wrote in *Freedom of the Press in England, 1476–1776:*

> Under this theory of sovereignty, freedom of the press became one of the natural rights of man as derived from the law of God and incapable of infringement by any man-made power. According to this position, a government could not restrict the right to speak and to print, even to save itself from destruction.[7]

Another slant to this argument focuses on individual self-fulfillment. The theory is that free speech and free thought together are part of a person's essential nature and dignity and that, morally, people must be free to discover their true natures, to experience the unique characteristics of being human.

Rebuttal

The reasons cited for protecting speech, both social and individual, are of course open to some rebuttal. To the discovery-of-truth theory, for example, it may be argued that in a system of totally uncontrolled communication the theory's assumptions are not always correct. That is, in a marketplace of countless messages the truth may not always be sifted out; it may even be obscured. Furthermore, on the way to discovering truth, false messages may cause considerable harm over the short term. (In recognition of this, the courts have upheld laws against deceptive advertising, for example, as discussed in Chapter 10.) And it can be said that the promotion-of-democracy benefit will be realized only if the mass media cover public affairs thoroughly and responsibly and that some government prodding is necessary to assure such responsibility. Even the natural-law concept may be attacked as simply too vague to support specific legal policy and inadequately attentive to other inherent rights that may conflict with free speech.

For the most part American courts have upheld the notion that freedom of speech, as embodied in the First Amendment to the Constitution, is wise policy deserving of strict enforcement. Speech in the United States has never been totally free, however, and the protection of the First Amendment is not considered absolute.

Adoption of the First Amendment

Experience with suppressive policies of Great Britain during the American colonial period caused many Americans immediately following the Revolution to be fearful of any centralized government. Thus, in order to ensure popular support for adoption of the U.S. Constitution and the national government it would establish, the framers found it necessary to promise a bill of rights that would set limitations on the government. Those limitations were ratified in 1791 as the first ten amendments to the Constitution.

The First Amendment was written chiefly by James Madison, who had consulted the speech clauses in various state constitutions. Despite a commonly held belief to the contrary, no convincing evidence exists that the framers viewed the First Amendment as the most important in the Bill of Rights. Its position is merely an artifact of history. Two other amendments in the original Bill of Rights proposal actually preceded what is cherished today as the First Amendment. Because neither of those amendments was adopted, the free expression guarantee in effect defaulted into its number one position. The First Amendment reads in full:

> Congress shall make no law respecting an establishment of religion, or prohibiting the free exercise thereof; or abridging the freedom of speech, or of the press; or the right of the people peaceably to assemble, and to petition the Government for a redress of grievances.

This book is most concerned, of course, with the speech and press clauses. What did the framers of the Constitution actually mean by those clauses?

Despite the seemingly clear and absolute terms of the First Amendment, some form of interpretation has been necessary whenever free expression has come into conflict with other societal interests. For example, just as the First Amendment guarantee against restriction of speech appears uncompromising, so too does the Sixth Amendment dictate that those accused of crimes shall have the right to trial by an "impartial jury" seem absolute. What happens when two such rights collide? The answer is an interpretation by the courts. The raw language of the Constitution itself simply does not supply the answers.

The most obvious approach to interpretation is to look at the historical setting surrounding the adoption of the First Amendment to determine what its authors intended. This approach has proved of limited use, however. Constitutional history scholars generally conclude that the framers harbored broad disagreement over what "freedom of speech" meant in specific situations. Did the authors of the First Amendment intend to change the existing common law to abolish all central government restrictions on expression? Or did they presume that existing restrictions, such as criminal laws against seditious libel, were not within the scope of the amendment's prohibitions? Few of the framers bothered to write their views on such matters of specific application. Thus historical inquiries, as with references to the language itself, usually are inconclusive.

In the two hundred years since the First Amendment became the law, the courts have painstakingly weighed competing interests and considered public policy, in addition to pondering the language and history of the First Amendment, in order to flesh out the bare wording of the amendment. The remainder of this chapter looks at some of today's basic principles of First Amendment application, focusing on those of greatest relevance to the field of mass communication.

Nature of the Guarantee

What is the basic nature of the rights afforded under the First Amendment? In other words, in what kinds of situations is the amendment's guarantee even a relevant issue?

Liberty versus Government Power

Remember that the Bill of Rights was born specifically to counter fears of a strong central government. Thus, the First Amendment states only that "*Congress* [italics added] shall make no law. . . ." At the time the Bill of Rights was adopted, several state laws were on the books prohibiting blasphemy, obscenity, libel, slander, mockery of religion, and the like. The legality of these laws was never an issue when the Bill of Rights was being considered because the First Amendment was seen only as a safeguard against the tyranny of some future Congress. Over time, the First Amendment was interpreted to apply not only to congressional acts but to all federal government acts, by whatever branch or agency of the government. Still, it was understood that the Bill of Rights prohibited only *federal* encroachments on individual liberty, and this view was affirmed in a Supreme Court decision in 1833.[8]

The reach of the Constitution underwent a momentous extension beginning in 1925, however. In the landmark case of *Gitlow v. New York*,[9] the U.S. Supreme Court indicated for the first time that the First Amendment would be applied as a limit on *state* governments to the same extent as the federal government. This expanded application was linked to the Fourteenth Amendment, which states in part: "No State shall make or enforce any law which shall abridge the privileges or immunities of citizens of the United States; nor shall any State deprive any person of life, liberty, or property, without due process of law."

The Fourteenth Amendment, adopted in 1868 after the Civil War, was designed originally to prohibit individual states from limiting the rights that former slaves enjoyed as citizens of the United States. The Supreme Court in *Gitlow* interpreted the amendment's language more specifically to mean that the First Amendment's free speech guarantee had been incorporated as a standard for the states. For such an important development as this, the Court's pronouncement was made in a rather terse and incidental fashion:

> For present purposes we may and do assume that freedom of speech and of the press—which are protected by the 1st Amendment from abridgment by Congress—are among the fundamental personal rights and "liberties" protected by the due process clause of the 14th Amendment from impairment by the states.[10]

In later cases the Court similarly has applied most other provisions of the Bill of Rights to the states by way of the Fourteenth Amendment. This is referred to as the **doctrine of incorporation.**

The result of all this constitutional evolution is that today the First Amendment is read to prohibit all governmental bodies—local and state, as well as federal—from abridging free expression. The amendment remains a limit only on governmental action, however. As with the rest of the Bill of Rights, the issue is individual liberty versus governmental power. First Amendment liberty is not a matter of freedom from intrusions by other private citizens or private groups. Rather, the First Amendment serves as a restriction on government control over speech.

A privately owned and funded school, for example, may legally censor a student newspaper at will because this would not constitute governmental action. Similarly, an editor at a privately owned newspaper does not unconstitutionally censor a writer's article by editing it, and the MTV cable channel did not violate the First Amendment in 1990 when it deemed a Madonna music video too racy for its program. For the First Amendment protections to kick in, there must have been some **state action**—a term that's often used to apply to any governmental action that potentially infringes on expression. State action may come in the form of laws, court orders, or the judgments and actions of individual officials.

Consider again the hypothetical problem at the beginning of this chapter. From the basic structure of the First Amendment, it is clear that the destructive actions of the citizens' group would not amount to a violation of the Constitution, although civil and criminal actions for trespass, malicious destruction of property, and the like might well be appropriate. Nor is the First Amendment violated by the publisher's orders to lay off the story, though it may be spineless journalism. Neither of these incidents presents a confrontation between personal liberty and government intrusion.

Expression versus Conduct

One of the threshold problems in First Amendment law is to define what constitutes *speech* or *press*. Freedom of speech and of the press both are mentioned specifically in the First Amendment, but are the terms to be read in a narrow sense? What about expressive activity other than oral or printed words, such as pictures, dances, and gestures? What about actions that express ideas?

As culture and technology have evolved, the Supreme Court has interpreted the word *speech* to mean all forms of expression, verbal or otherwise, that are designed to communicate ideas. There would be little logic in reading the term so narrowly as to mean the relaying of information by word of mouth but not, for example, by means of modern videotape.

But implicit in the language of the First Amendment is that a distinction is to be made between expression and pure conduct, or action. Expression in its many forms is protected, but conduct is not. In most mass communications situations this distinction poses no difficulty. Communicators have a constitutional right to print that elected city officials should be recalled, for example, but no constitutional right to throw rocks through the windows at city hall.

Entertainment

Many forms of entertainment, including motion pictures, theatrical performances, and dancing, have been deemed protectable expression. Even nude dancing has been so classified, when performed specifically to entertain and communicate with others. The U.S. Supreme Court declared in a 1991 case involving nude barroom entertainment: "[N]ude dancing of the kind sought to be performed here is expressive conduct within the outer perimeters of the First Amendment, though we view it as only marginally so."[11]

On the other hand, activities undertaken predominantly for self-entertainment or recreation are labeled conduct, not expression, and are without First Amendment protection altogether. In a 1989 decision that recreational social dancing was not a form of expression, the Supreme Court explained: "It is possible to find some kernel of expression in almost every activity a person undertakes—for example, walking down the street, or meeting one's friends at a shopping mall—but such a kernel is not sufficient to bring the activity within the protection of the First Amendment."[12]

Symbolic Speech

Difficult cases sometimes result when speech seems closely intertwined with what normally would be pure conduct. Conduct—such as hoisting a flag, wearing a colored armband, or even burning a piece of paper—is referred to as **symbolic speech** or **expressive conduct** when performed in a manner intended to convey a particular message to others. The courts have deemed this hybrid form of speech to be within the guarantee of the First Amendment, though it is not always protected as broadly as other forms of expression.

One of the more hotly debated First Amendment issues in recent years involved a symbolic speech problem. Specifically, it was the emotional issue of flag burning. In 1984 Gregory Johnson, a member of the Revolutionary Communist Youth Brigade, torched an American flag outside the Republican Convention in Dallas. His conduct was part of a demonstration to protest foreign policies of the Reagan administration. Johnson was prosecuted under Texas law for "desecration of a venerated object" and was sentenced to a year in prison and fined $2000.

In a 5–4 decision, however, the U.S. Supreme Court held in 1989 that the flag burning in this case was expressive conduct protected by the First Amendment. The majority opinion in *Texas v. Johnson* was by Justice William Brennan, one of the high Court's most ardent First Amendment advocates from 1956 until his retirement in 1990. He wrote:

> The First Amendment literally forbids the abridgement only of "speech," but we have long recognized that its protection does not end at the spoken or written word. While we have rejected the view that an apparently limitless variety of conduct can be labeled "speech" whenever the person engaging in the conduct intends thereby to express an idea, . . . we have acknowledged that conduct may be "sufficiently imbued with elements of communication to fall within the scope of the [First Amendment]". . . .
>
> The expressive, overtly political nature of this conduct was both intentional and overwhelmingly apparent. . . .[13]

This case also serves to illustrate the broader political and emotional nature of some First Amendment debates. Following the Court's decision, President George Bush called for a constitutional amendment against flag burning. Congress instead decided to pass a statute, the Flag Protection Act. Along came another court test, this time involving four protestors who set a flag afire in front of the Seattle Post Office. The case found its way to the Supreme Court in 1990, and the federal statute, like the Texas law before it, was ruled unconstitutional.[14] At this writing, some members of Congress were pushing for a constitutional amendment that would authorize Congress and the states to prohibit physical desecration of the flag.

Gathering and Distributing

Another aspect of interpreting the words *speech* and *press* is whether they include the adjunct activities of gathering information in preparation for expressing oneself and then using distribution channels to deliver the expression to others.

On the first question, the answer generally has been no. The First Amendment usually is not interpreted to include a right to gather information, even if the gathering is closely linked to planned expression. Once information has been obtained, communicators have the general right to speak and publish. But the First Amendment only in limited circumstances guarantees that the doors to information be open in the first place (as discussed in Chapters 6 and 7). Except for a few narrowly defined circumstances, the amendment generally is not interpreted to guarantee a right to get or receive information. A major portion of this book deals with legal rights of access and information gathering, but those rights for the most part are not constitutional in origin. Of course, if someone wants to speak to you and the government interferes, this may be a violation of the speaker's First Amendment rights.

Speech generally has been interpreted to include distribution, however. Rights of free speech do not end when a pamphlet is printed or a TV show is videotaped. Speech rights include the right to disseminate to an audience. In the chapter hypothetical, for example, circulation of your newspapers, in this case through newsracks, is within the concept of speech. Still to be determined, however, is whether you are protected from the particular kind of state action in question.

Suspect Restrictions

The First Amendment is a shield that is available when free speech is being abridged (diminished) by government. The scope of protection does not extend to all situations in which speech is inadvertently affected or burdened in some way. For example, the taxation and labor laws that apply to businesses across the board also may be applied to media businesses. These laws may reduce the funds available for the business's news department and thus affect speech. But this is an unintended, secondary effect, not shielded by the First Amendment. On the other hand the amendment can provide freedom from very subtle interferences, indeed, if they are intended to suppress speech specifically because of its content. As we shall see, there need not be a complete ban on expression in order to raise First Amendment concerns.

Prior Restraints   The First Amendment guarantee protects most clearly against prior restraints upon the content of speech, typified by censorship schemes or court injunctions prohibiting publication. Even in cases where expression is not protected from after-the-fact lawsuits and prosecution, the First Amendment often is interpreted to bar any form of government censorship prior to publication.

Near v. Minnesota

Probably the single most important decision formalizing the doctrine against prior restraint was the 1931 case of *Near v. Minnesota*. As detailed in the aptly titled book about the case, *Minnesota Rag*, by Fred Friendly, *The Saturday Press* was at best a scurrilous publication. J. M. Near's newspaper attacked those who violated Prohibition, the constitutional amendment experiment that from 1919 to 1933 made it illegal to produce or sell alcoholic beverages. The newspaper, which also had a tendency to publish anti-Semitic barbs, was accused of extorting money from Prohibition lawbreakers. Those who got caught breaking the law and who did not want the publicity so generated could, if they bought enough advertising or simply made a large enough cash payment to the publication, keep their names out of the news. The newspaper also published articles charging that public officials were neglecting their duties to control bootlegging, gambling, and other crimes.

After nine issues of the paper were published, the local county attorney went to court without notifying Near and obtained an injunction prohibiting publication of future issues. The trial court upheld the injunction on the ground that *The Saturday Press* was a public nuisance. In a historic 5–4 decision by the U.S. Supreme Court, the state's prior restraint of future issues was held unconstitutional. Wrote Chief Justice Charles Hughes for the majority:

> [L]iberty of the press, historically considered and taken up by the Federal Constitution, has meant, principally although not exclusively, immunity from previous restraints or censorship. . . . The fact that for approximately one hundred and fifty years there has been almost an entire absence of attempts to impose previous restraints upon publications relating to the malfeasance of public officers is significant of the deep-seated conviction that such restraints would violate constitutional rights. The general principle that the constitutional guaranty of the liberty of the press gives immunity from previous restraints has been approved in many decisions under the provisions of state constitutions.[15]

The *Near* case, then, stands for the general principle that "Any system of prior restraints of expression comes to this Court bearing a heavy presumption against its constitutional validity."[16] Prior restraints are what the First Amendment most certainly was intended to protect against, the Court has concluded. The general theory behind this is that prior restraints create a great danger of government suppression and that societal interests are better served in the long run if abuses of free expression are dealt with after the fact—by civil lawsuits or criminal penalties.

This is not to say that prior restraints on speech are never allowed, however, as discussed in later chapters. In the *Near* opinion itself, the court noted a few exceptional instances when prior restraint might be permitted. Those instances were communications that would hinder a war effort, obscene publications, and incitements to acts of violence. But, as a general rule, prior restraint is considered the worst kind of abridgment, and it is permitted only in rare situations when harmful expression could not adequately be punished after the fact. One of the most famous First Amendment cases of all time, the 1971 case of the Pentagon Papers, was a high-stakes prior restraint duel that concerned national security. We will examine that case in the next chapter.

Licensing

One of the most blatant forms of prior restraint is a court injunction prohibiting publication, such as the one at issue in *Near v. Minnesota*. But prior restraints can take many other forms, including licensing schemes for communicators. Courts have frequently declared license requirements to speak or circulate to be forms of prior restraint on the content of expression and therefore presumptively unconstitutional. This can be true even for license requirements far less oppressive than the much-despised system enforced by England in the 1600s.

For example, a suburb of Cleveland passed an ordinance requiring annual licenses in order to place newsracks on public sidewalks. The mayor was given authority to grant or deny the license applications. The ordinance was challenged and held unconstitutional by the U.S. Supreme Court in 1988. Justice William Brennan, writing for the majority, said it was "time-tested knowledge that in the area of free expression a licensing statute placing unbridled discretion in the hands of a government official or agency constitutes a prior restraint and may result in censorship."[17] This is so, he said, because "unbridled" licensing schemes pose two major First Amendment risks: The first is self-censorship by communicators in order to avoid denial of a license. The second is the risk that officials will apply content-based censorship, in a manner difficult to detect, behind the mask of the licensing law.

This does not mean that all types of communication licensing are considered prior restraints on content; some may qualify as time/place/manner restrictions, discussed later in this chapter. Nor does it mean that a license requirement, even if a prior restraint, can never be constitutional. A federal licensing scheme for broadcasters has been upheld, for example, and is detailed in Chapter 11.

Informal Coercion

Prior restraint of expression also may arise through less formal actions by government officials, such as pressuring communicators to sign oaths or threatening to prosecute or to publicly chastise. Even government actions couched as friendly advice may actually amount to prior restraints of expression.

For example, in 1989 a controversial rap music recording titled "As Nasty as They Wanna Be" went on sale to the public. The recording by the group 2 Live Crew went on to sell more than a million copies in its first year. In Florida's Broward County, however, complaints about the record's sexually explicit lyrics prompted a sheriff's investigation. The sheriff's office purchased a "Nasty" tape from a record store, delivered it to a local judge, and obtained a court order stating there was "probable cause" to believe that the recording was obscene and illegal under Florida law.

Next the sheriff's office copied the court order and sent it to all retail stores countywide that might be selling the "Nasty" recording. This approach was taken to "warn the stores as a matter of courtesy,"[18] rather than making immediate arrests. Sheriff's deputies also paid personal visits to record stores and told the managers "in a friendly, conversational tone" that they should stop selling the recording. They were warned that further sales could lead to arrest. Within days all retail stores in Broward County stopped offering the recording for sale. This result was obtained even though there had yet been no formal criminal proceeding against the musical group or anyone else connected with the recording—and no formal ruling that the recording actually was obscene.

The musical group and its record company sued, and in *Skywalker Records v. Navarro* a federal judge declared the threatening actions of the sheriff's office an unconstitutional prior restraint of free speech:

When arguably protected work clothed in the presumption of constitutional free speech is removed from public distribution, the state has imposed a prior restraint. . . . Although the music store operators were the immediate parties who stopped distributing the recording, they so acted only after the police visits and the delivery of the court's probable cause order.[19]

The ruling would be different, the court said, if police had simply informed stores how generally to comply with the law—without stating or implying threats over specific material.

Another classic example of informal restraint was addressed by the Court in the 1963 case of *Bantam Books v. Sullivan*. Rhode Island had created a commission to combat juvenile delinquency, and one of its powers was to inform the public of literature that contained obscenity or that otherwise tended to corrupt youth. The commission's practice was to notify distributors of certain books or magazines that had been declared objectionable by a majority of the commission. The list of objectionable publications also was supplied to police departments. The effect of the notices was to intimidate wholesale distributors and retailers and cause them to cease selling or even ordering the materials.

Four publishers of paperback books sued, claiming that sales of some of their books, which were not actually obscene, had been suppressed by this process and that their First Amendment rights had been violated. The Supreme Court agreed, holding that the activities of the commission were unconstitutional. Wrote Justice Brennan for the majority:

It is true that [the publishers'] books have not been seized or banned by the State, and that no one has been prosecuted for their possession or sale. But though the Commission is limited to informal sanctions—the threat of invoking legal sanctions and other means of coercion, persuasion, and intimidation—the record amply demonstrates that the Commission deliberately set about to achieve the suppression of publications deemed "objectional" and succeeded in its aim.[20]

Punishment After the Fact

Considerable agreement exists among legal historians that the First Amendment was intended primarily as a protection against prior restraints on expression. Punishment after publication was, and is, generally considered a more acceptable way to deter irresponsible speech because it allows the communicator to make a reasoned decision about whether something can and should be expressed—and only thereafter pay the penalty if the decision was improper. In theory subsequent punishment is less oppressive than prior restraint because, to be punishable, the alleged abuses must be specifically and individually proved in court.

However, the Supreme Court has recognized that there often is little practical difference between prior restraint and subsequent punishment of expression. Particularly when the laws are vague, or the sanctions overly harsh, the prospect of after-the-fact punishment may serve to chill expression every bit as much as a prior order not to publish. Sometimes the distinction itself seems illusory. For example, a portion of the court order at issue in *Near v. Minnesota* perpetually enjoined Near from producing any defamatory publication in the future. Is that injunction (a typical form of prior restraint) truly any different from a criminal statute prohibiting defamation and specifying penalties?

Given the functional haziness of the distinction, it is well established today that subsequent sanctions, too, may abridge free expression in violation of the First Amendment. Punishment is allowed for many kinds of errant speech, as you will see throughout this book, but only within carefully tailored lines set by the courts. Sanctions based on the content of expression do indeed raise a First Amendment issue.

Subsequent sanctions against speech usually come in the following three basic forms: (1) contempt citations issued by courts, under which communicators may face fines or jail time; (2) enforcement of criminal statutes and regulations, which may lead to fines, loss of privileges, or even prison; and (3) private lawsuits for torts or breach of contract. (These lawsuits qualify as state action against communicators because government's laws and enforcement mechanisms are what make the lawsuits possible.)

Even the punishment of speech that appears highly irresponsible, derogatory, and hateful can raise serious First Amendment concerns. For example, the late 1980s saw an alarming increase in racial intolerance on some college campuses. In response, several public colleges and universities adopted stricter policies prohibiting "racist" or "sexist" speech on campus. The University of Michigan instituted a broad policy that prohibited students, under penalty of sanctions, from "stigmatizing or victimizing" individuals or groups on the basis of race, ethnicity, religion, sex, sexual orientation, creed, national origin, ancestry, age, marital status, handicap, or Vietnam-era veteran status. Many other campuses enacted similar policies.

Does such a policy violate rights of free speech under the First Amendment? In 1989 a federal District Court said yes, to the extent that such policies are applied to pure speech. The court ruled in favor of a University of Michigan psychology student who feared that discussion of certain theories about biological race and gender differences might be perceived as racist and sexist and therefore sanctionable under the campus policy. The court began its opinion by noting: "It is an unfortunate fact of our constitutional system that the ideals of freedom and equality are often in conflict."[21] But no matter how well intentioned the university's policy, the court said, rules that punish speech solely on the grounds that it is unseemly or offensive are consistently held to be unconstitutional.

In 1992 the U.S. Supreme Court reached a similar result in a highly publicized hate-speech case. The case, *R.A.V. v. City of St. Paul*, arose when a teenager burned a crudely made cross inside the fenced yard of a black family. The conduct could have been punished under a variety of laws, such as laws against arson, damage to property, or trespass. Instead the prosecutor decided to charge the juvenile with a violation of the city's bias-motivated crime ordinance, which made it a misdemeanor to place on public or private property any symbol that one knows would arouse anger or resentment in others on the basis of race, color, creed, religion, or gender. The Court held the ordinance unconstitutional because it prohibited speech solely on the ground of the nature of the speaker's views. The First Amendment does not permit a city to impose special prohibitions on those speakers who express disfavored or offensive views on particular subjects, Justice Antonin Scalia said in his majority opinion.[22]

This principle that offensive speech is generally protected also would apply to the hypothetical at the beginning of this chapter. Recall that some vulgar words in a front page headline had prompted the local authorities to initiate a prosecution for "disturbing the peace." In reality, it appears the effort is directed solely at punishing language that was too raw for the tastes of many people. Though the choice of words may not have been journalistically wise, the First Amendment generally prohibits punishing someone for a failure to live up to the majority's standards for good taste or proper judgment in expression.

Financial Burdens

General business taxes, as noted earlier, do not raise First Amendment concerns when applied uniformly to media and nonmedia businesses. However, when taxes, fees, or other financial burdens discriminate against communicators, or among them, those financial burdens do indeed raise serious First Amendment concerns.

Government's power to tax and levy fees may not be employed to punish or subdue expression. Furthermore, even when no such censorial motive is present, discriminatory financial burdens are adverse to the First Amendment because of their chilling potential for abuse. Courts sometimes categorize financial burdens as prior restraints. But whether or not they are so classified, it is clear that financial burdens may run afoul of the First Amendment.

A leading case on this point is *Simon & Schuster v. Crime Victims Board,* a 1991 ruling by the U.S. Supreme Court. At issue was a New York statute that aimed to prevent persons who had committed crimes from unjustly profiting from their stories. The statute required that a convicted person's income from works describing his crime be deposited in an escrow account to benefit the crime victims. If any medium contracted with the convicted person to produce the work, it was the medium's responsibility to turn over the author's income to the Crime Victims Board. Thus, the statute imposed a financial burden that could discourage people who had committed crimes from publishing their stories or contracting with the media to do so.

Book publisher Simon & Schuster had contracted with an organized-crime figure turned government witness, Henry Hill, to produce a book about Hill's life.

The book, *Wiseguy*, was favorably reviewed as an insightful look into crime in America. However, the Crime Victims Board sought to invoke the escrow statute, and Simon & Schuster sued to have the law declared unconstitutional.

The Supreme Court began its analysis by noting a basic principle from earlier cases: "A statute is presumptively inconsistent with the First Amendment if it imposes a financial burden on speakers because of the content of their speech."[23] The Court found that New York's statute was indeed content-based, singling out income from works that recount crimes and thereby serving as a "financial disincentive" that could inhibit Simon & Schuster's ability to produce books about crime. Though the state clearly had an interest in aiding crime victims and preventing criminals from profiting on their crimes, New York's statute was too broadly drafted to overcome the presumption against constitutionality, the Court said.

Taxes

General business taxes, as noted earlier, don't violate the zone of First Amendment protection when applied uniformly to media and nonmedia businesses alike. However, when tax laws discriminate against media businesses, or among them, the laws become a form of prior restraint. Government's power to tax may not be employed to punish or subdue expression. Furthermore, even when no such intent is actually present, discriminatory taxation schemes qualify as prior restraints because of their chilling potential for abuse.

For example, in 1987 a Supreme Court case involved a challenge to Arkansas's general sales tax. Certain kinds of media products were exempt from the tax, including "religious, professional, trade and sports journals." General interest magazines, however, were subject to the tax. The Court held the selective taxation invalid.

"Our cases clearly establish that a discriminatory tax on the press burdens rights protected by the First Amendment," Justice Thurgood Marshall wrote for the majority. Even when there is no evidence of an improper censorial motive, he said,

> [S]elective taxation of the press—either singling out the press as a whole or targeting individual members of the press—poses a particular danger of abuse by the State. . . . [T]he basis on which Arkansas differentiates between magazines is particularly repugnant to First Amendment principles [because] a magazine's tax status depends entirely on its *content*.[24]

Compelled Speech

The First Amendment is offended not only by government efforts to prohibit or punish speech but also by laws that compel speech. A corollary of the right to speak one's mind is the right not to be a government-coerced messenger for other's views.

This principle is basic and long-established, but it can become complex and controversial when applied in mass media situations. The typical scenario is this: Government passes a law mandating some degree of individual access to the mass media in order to increase the plurality of voices—an effort clearly in the spirit of free speech and an open marketplace of ideas. But the media take exception because, from their perspective, they are being made unwilling conduits for others' expression.

Media Access Laws

The theory of forced access gained wide acceptance after the Commission on Freedom of the Press, the so-called Hutchins Commission (named after its chairman, University of Chicago President Robert Hutchins), released its famous and somewhat controversial 1947 report, *A Free and Responsible Press.* In that publication, the commission argued that although the media should be free, marketplace forces were constricting ownership, which in turn lessened the number of voices in the free marketplace of ideas. This the commission argued, was just as deadly as governmental censorship. Therefore, the government should play a residual role in assuring responsible press performance.[25]

The commission's recommendation, though seemingly well thought-out, was fraught with logical fallacies. For example, a thorough critique of the recommendations of the commission is John Merrill's *The Imperative of Freedom,*[26] in which the author notes that a decrease in media owners does not necessarily mean a decrease in message plurality. In addition, once a free press is forced to be responsible it is certainly not free and arguably not necessarily responsible—only chained. Nevertheless, some media law scholars, such as lawyer and professor Jerome Barron, have argued that individuals should have a right of access to the American mass media.[27] The issue came to the U.S. Supreme Court in the 1974 case of *Miami Herald Co. v. Tornillo.*

Pat Tornillo, a 1972 candidate for the Florida House of Representatives, had been taken to task in an editorial in the *Miami Herald.* The newspaper had criticized him for his role a few years earlier as a teachers' union leader who had led an illegal strike. Tornillo demanded an opportunity to respond. His demand was based on a state statute that required a newspaper to publish free replies by political candidates who had been criticized by the newspaper. It was a crime for the paper to refuse to publish verbatim the candidate's reply in the same type size and in as conspicuous a location as the original editorial. The newspaper did refuse, however.

The Florida trial court found the statute unconstitutional, but the state supreme court reversed the decision, holding that free speech was enhanced, not abridged, by the right-of-reply statute. The case went next to the U.S. Supreme Court. In a unanimous ruling, the Court struck down the access law as an unconstitutional violation of the newspaper's First Amendment rights. Wrote Chief Justice Warren Burger for the Court:

> A responsible press is an undoubtedly desirable goal, but press responsibility
> is not mandated by the Constitution and like many other virtues it cannot be

legislated. . . . A newspaper is more than a passive receptacle or conduit for news, comment, and advertising. The choice of material to go into a newspaper, and the decisions made as to limitations on the size of the paper, and content, and treatment of public issues and public officials—whether fair or unfair—constitutes the exercise of editorial control and judgment. It has yet to be demonstrated how governmental regulation of this crucial process can be exercised consistent with First Amendment guarantees of a free press.[28]

Chapter 11 will detail how forced access to radio and television to reply to certain kinds of attacks *is* considered constitutional. This distinction, said the Supreme Court in *Red Lion Broadcasting Co. v. FCC*,[29] is due to the limited nature of the broadcast spectrum and the need for the government to regulate that limited resource in the public interest.

Compelled Financial Support

Another interesting application of the principle against compelled speech arises when people are required to *finance* others' expression. Financing expression is itself a form of expression, and the Supreme Court has held that people cannot be compelled by government to fund political speech with which they disagree.

For example, the Court held in the 1990 case of *Keller v. State Bar of California*[30] that the State Bar could not use lawyers' mandatory dues to fund political and ideological activities, including lobbying. The Court said mandatory dues could fund activities germane to the Bar's central purpose of regulating the legal profession, but not ideological activities outside that central purpose.

Another interesting angle to this First Amendment principle can arise on college campuses. Several students at the University of Wisconsin–Madison, for example, sued the university on the ground that a portion of their mandatory, $165-per-semester activity fee was being used to subsidize private student groups whose political and ideological speech they found objectionable. The student plaintiffs objected to funding eighteen campus organizations, including the Student Labor Action Coalition, the Militant Student Union, and the International Socialist Organization. A federal Court of Appeals in 1998 held that forcing the objecting students to fund such organizations violated the First Amendment.[31]

In 2000, however, a unanimous U.S. Supreme Court reversed the Court of Appeals. In *Board of Regents of the University of Wisconsin v. Southworth,* the Court concluded that, unlike the situation in *Keller,* it would be virtually impossible to determine which of the extracurricular campus speech was "germane" to the broad educational mission of the university and which was not. Therefore, Justice Kennedy wrote, the First Amendment permits a public university to charge an activity fee to fund speech by student groups—so long as the method for allocating the funds is entirely viewpoint neutral.[32]

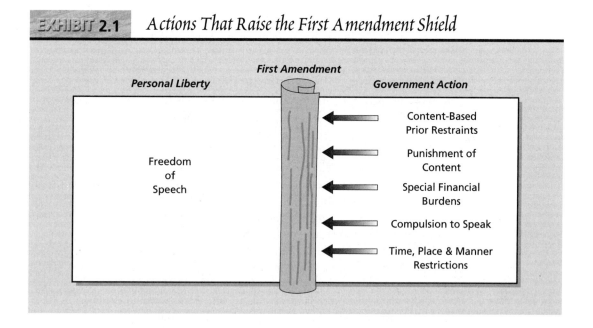

EXHIBIT 2.1 *Actions That Raise the First Amendment Shield*

First Amendment

Personal Liberty   **Government Action**

Freedom
of
Speech

Content-Based
Prior Restraints

Punishment of
Content

Special Financial
Burdens

Compulsion to Speak

Time, Place & Manner
Restrictions

Time, Place, and Manner Restrictions

The scope of protection discussed thus far has concerned freedom from government efforts to influence the content of expression. What if government attempts to control an avenue of expression, but for reasons allegedly unrelated to its content? Examples would be a city ordinance requiring all billboards to be at least ten yards from streets for traffic safety reasons or an ordinance limiting the hours and volume for sound trucks in residential neighborhoods.

These kinds of controls are known as **time, place, and manner (TPM) restrictions.** They may result in significant inconvenience or added expense for communicators, but the restrictions are not intended to limit or control any particular sort of content. TPM restrictions do indeed raise First Amendment concerns. The protection against TPM restrictions is weaker, however, than the protection against most content-based interferences. Therefore, it is important to distinguish between a TPM restriction and a content restriction.

Many court cases have focused on whether government action actually qualified as a TPM restriction. To do so, the restriction must be honestly **content neutral.** That is, the real purpose of the restriction may not be to curb certain messages on the basis of their content: If the action is actually a content restriction in disguise, the scope of First Amendment protection against the restriction is much greater and the government action is more likely to be unconstitutional.

To pass the content-neutral test, the government action must leave no room for administrative discretion. In other words, a government official must not hold authority to prevent the communication of some messages, while allowing others to proceed, on the basis of personal bias. TPM restrictions must use consistent, across-the-board guidelines. For example, laws that require door-to-door leaflet distributors to first obtain the approval of some government official—usually based upon a showing of "proper purpose" or "good moral character"—are not constitutionally valid. Such restrictions invest too much administrative discretion in the government officials, so they do not pass the content-neutral test.

On the other hand, the U.S. Supreme Court in 1981 upheld a rule that restricted literature distribution and fund solicitation to an area of fixed booths at the Minnesota State Fair. The rule was challenged by the International Society for Krishna Consciousness because members could not wander the grounds freely to sell religious literature. But the Court found that the rule was content neutral. All literature distributors were automatically under the same restrictions, with no unbridled discretion vested in state fair officials.[33]

In the last two decades, attempts of cities to regulate the placement of news-racks on their streets has been an often-litigated First Amendment issue. Those cases provide additional illustrations of attempted TPM restrictions.

Ordinances that prohibited newsracks where they would unreasonably interfere with traffic on streets or sidewalks, where they would interfere with sidewalk cleaning machinery, and where they would obstruct access to mailboxes and emergency facilities such as fire hydrants have been upheld as constitutional. Ordinances specifically drafted to prevent interference with traffic, to protect people from defective racks, and to advance significant aesthetic interests also have been upheld.[34]

On the other hand, laws that authorized the revocation of newsrack permits by an administrator for no given reason, that failed to set standards for controlling the discretion of a mayor or city council in issuing newsrack permits, that vested review boards with standardless discretion to review newsrack designs, that required a newspaper to obtain a permit from the chief of police—who was vested with vague and virtually limitless decision power—and that discriminated against newsracks containing free or adult-oriented tabloids, were deemed to violate the First Amendment.[35]

Would the blanket newsrack prohibition and seizure mentioned in the hypothetical at the beginning of this chapter qualify as a TPM restriction? Most certainly the answer is no. It allowed too much administrative discretion for it to bypass the First Amendment shield. The ordinance could too easily be a veil behind which the city council might punish a particular newspaper for its content. For that ordinance to be a valid TPM restriction, it would need to state specific criteria for the acceptability of newsracks and leave no room for discriminatory application.

Resolving Conflicts

So far we have looked at the general structure of the First Amendment and examined the sorts of government interference that are deemed to raise First Amendment concerns. But even if speech is clearly involved and government action clearly interferes with it, the questions remains: Is this interference acceptable under the First Amendment, or is it a violation of the law? Most of the major interpretation battles involve this question. Is some speech simply too worthless to command protection? Or, even if the speech is worthwhile, are the government's reasons for interfering so significant that they override protection?

Rights Not Absolute

The First Amendment guarantee is absolute on its face. Yet majorities of the Supreme Court have long believed that guarantees in the Bill of Rights must bow to some limitations.

Over the years some distinguished scholars and jurists have pleaded for an absolute approach to applying the First Amendment. The **absolutists** argue that speech should be subject to *no* government restrictions or penalties, just as the actual language of the amendment states, though typically these thinkers have taken a narrow view of what constitutes *speech.*

For example, scholar Alexander Meiklejohn argued that speech that contributes to self-governance should be afforded an absolute protection, regardless of its motive or nature. "No one who reads with care the text of the First Amendment can fail to be startled by its absoluteness," Meiklejohn wrote in his 1948 book, *Free Speech and Its Relation to Self-Government.* "The phrase 'Congress shall make no law . . . abridging freedom of speech,' is unqualified. It admits no exceptions."[36] Others who have argued for some form of absolutist approach to interpretation of the First Amendment include former Supreme Court Associate Justices Hugo Black and William O. Douglas. Black interpreted his absolutism narrowly, arguing that because speech and press freedoms were mentioned explicitly, only those strict forms of expression were protected. Douglas took a broader view. He considered even symbolic speech—wearing armbands, burning draft cards, and the like—within the scope of complete First Amendment protection. In 1951 Justice Douglas wrote:

> The First Amendment provides that "Congress shall make no law . . . abridging the freedom of speech." The Constitution provides no exception. This does not mean that the Nation need hold its hand until it is in such weakened condition that there is no time to protect itself from incitement to revolution. Seditious *conduct* can always be punished. But the command of the First Amendment is so clear that we should not allow Congress to call a halt to free speech. . . . The

First Amendment makes confidence in the common sense of our people and in their maturity of judgment the great postulate of our democracy. . . . Unless and until extreme and necessitous circumstances are shown our aim should be to keep speech unfettered and to allow the processes of law to be evoked only when the provocateurs among us move from speech to action.[37]

Ten years later Justice Douglas admonished his Supreme Court colleagues for their tendency to weigh the value of particular speech to determine whether it deserved protection:

In recent years we have been departing, I think, from the theory of government expressed in the First Amendment. We have too often been "balancing" the right of free speech and association against other values in society to see if we, the judges, feel that a particular need is more important than those guaranteed by the Bill of Rights. . . . This approach, which treats the commands of the First Amendment as "no more than admonitions of moderation," . . . runs counter to [James] Madison's views of the First Amendment.[38]

Absolutist approaches to First Amendment interpretation—though often expressed in eloquent terms—have never commanded a majority of the Supreme Court, however. Through the years the Court has carved out dozens of limitations and exceptions to First Amendment protection. This book will examine many of them, including libel, invasion of privacy, incitement to violence, interference with justice, and deceptive advertising. The Court has used a variety of methods to arrive at its limitations to First Amendment freedoms. Thus a key question to ask in any clash over First Amendment rights is what standard the court will use to resolve the conflict. (A streamlined graphic depiction of First Amendment application is found in Exhibit 2.2.)

Unprotected Speech

One way the Supreme Court has limited First Amendment freedoms is to place certain categories of expression outside the amendment's protection. One of the best examples of an unprotected category is obscenity, covered in Chapter 12. ("This much has been categorically settled by the Court, that obscene material is unprotected by the First Amendment,"[39] wrote Chief Justice Burger in 1973.) Some other unprotected categories include false or misleading commercial advertising, perjury, so-called fighting words, and libel that is published with a requisite degree of fault. Another classic category of unprotected speech is incitement to violent or dangerous conduct—a topic that will be examined in the next chapter.

For each of these categories the Supreme Court has established a particular test, or definition. In a given case, the key task may be to determine whether the speech actually fits the Court's definition of an unprotected category. Theoretically, setting aside several clearly defined categories of unprotected speech—and

EXHIBIT 2.2   *Application of the First Amendment*

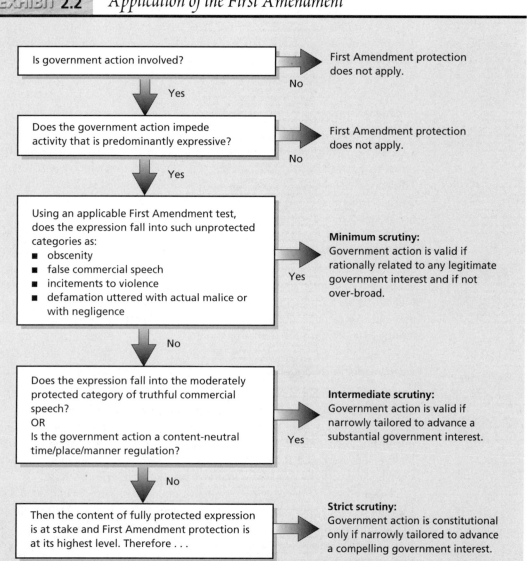

Is government action involved? → **No** → First Amendment protection does not apply.

↓ **Yes**

Does the government action impede activity that is predominantly expressive? → **No** → First Amendment protection does not apply.

↓ **Yes**

Using an applicable First Amendment test, does the expression fall into such unprotected categories as:
- obscenity
- false commercial speech
- incitements to violence
- defamation uttered with actual malice or with negligence

→ **Yes** → **Minimum scrutiny:** Government action is valid if rationally related to any legitimate government interest and if not over-broad.

↓ **No**

Does the expression fall into the moderately protected category of truthful commercial speech?
OR
Is the government action a content-neutral time/place/manner regulation?

→ **Yes** → **Intermediate scrutiny:** Government action is valid if narrowly tailored to advance a substantial government interest.

↓ **No**

Then the content of fully protected expression is at stake and First Amendment protection is at its highest level. Therefore . . .

→ **Strict scrutiny:** Government action is constitutional only if narrowly tailored to advance a compelling government interest.

This diagram is a simplified depiction of how the First Amendment is applied by the courts. Some doctrines add further complication. For example, if the expression at issue is categorized as "symbolic speech," either strict or intermediate scrutiny may apply, depending on whether the government action is aimed at the conduct portion or the speech portion. Also, the doctrine against prior restraint may cause actions against even unprotected expression to undergo tougher scrutiny.

declaring all other speech to be protected—provides greater guidance and certainty than a system in which virtually all speech may be subjected to a case-by-case, circumstantial review. In practice, however, the application of category definitions often is accompanied by its own degrees of uncertainty. For example, Chapter 12 relates how lower courts have been inconsistent in their attempts to apply the Supreme Court's three-part test for obscenity.

Minimum Scrutiny

Once it is determined that some particular expression falls within an unprotected category—meaning no First Amendment freedom is at stake—the government action that interferes with that speech typically will be upheld as constitutional. This is because the government has no special First Amendment hurdle to clear. The government action is scrutinized in court only to the extent that it must be rationally related to a legitimate government interest.

The **rational basis standard** represents the minimum level of justification that all government restrictions on freedom must meet in order to comply with the due process clauses of the Fifth and Fourteenth amendments. In cases involving restrictions on unprotected speech, this standard is easily met unless government is achieving its purpose in some patently arbitrary fashion. For example, a ban on obscenity would generally be valid, but not if it arbitrarily targeted only materials costing $100,000 to $200,000 to produce.

Overbreadth and Vagueness

For a statute or other government action to be upheld, however, it is further required that its impact be limited to the targeted speech. Legislation that punishes protected speech as well as the targeted, unprotected expression typically is held unconstitutional under the **doctrine of overbreadth.** Restrictions on speech will be deemed overbroad if they encompass any significant amount of protected speech along with the expression that may be regulated legitimately.

The overbreadth doctrine is commonly employed in First Amendment cases. Even though the speech involved in a particular controversy may be unprotected, the government restriction may be attacked as unconstitutional on the ground that it would, in other situations, penalize protected speech. For example, suppose that, in an effort to ban obscenity, a state passed a law making it illegal to distribute any materials that "depict sexual conduct or nudity." A person who is prosecuted under this statute for selling materials that were indeed obscene, and therefore unprotected, could nevertheless challenge the validity of the statute because its wording is so broad as to also outlaw materials that are protected under the First Amendment. Laws may be challenged as either overbroad *on their face,* meaning as written, or overbroad *as applied* by government officials.

Valid Content Restrictions

☐ Does the government restraint apply to a narrow, non-protected category of expression?

☐ Or is the restraint limited to commercial speech or symbolic speech and supported by a substantial justification?

☐ Or is the restraint supported by a compelling justification?

☐ And, in any case, is the restraint no broader than necessary to serve the government's purpose?

Closely related to the overbreadth doctrine is the **void-for-vagueness doctrine.** Statutes and regulations that restrict speech, if they do so in terms too vague to provide clear guidance, may be struck down as unconstitutionally vague. The rationale is much the same as that behind the overbreadth doctrine. That is, if a law fails to paint clear distinctions between the speech that is prohibited and that which is not, a danger of inconsistent and unpredictable enforcement exists, and the law may effectively stifle speech well beyond its intended range.

The Balancing Approach

Limitations to First Amendment protection also are arrived at by weighing in a given situation the considerations favoring freedom against the considerations favoring government intervention. Former Harvard Law School Dean Zechariah Chafee has been one of the proponents of the basic balancing approach that has commanded a majority of the Supreme Court in recent years. Chafee contends that all parts of the Constitution must be examined together in relation to one another so as to define the extent and limits of each in harmony with the others. However, when balancing First Amendment rights against other constitutional rights or obligations, freedom of expression should begin with extra weight. As he argued in his 1941 book, *Free Speech in the United States:*

> One of the most important purposes of society and government is the discovery and spread of truth on subjects of general concern. This is possible only through absolutely unlimited discussion. . . . Nevertheless, there are other purposes of government, such as order, the training of the young, protection against external aggression. Unlimited discussion sometimes interferes with these purposes which must then be balanced against freedom of speech, but freedom of speech ought to weigh very heavily in the scale.[40]

In other words, no category of speech is absolutely protected in Chafee's view. Instead, speech is always subject to balancing against other governmental/ societal interests to determine whether interference is legally acceptable. In the balancing process, however, the scales are not set evenly. Speech weighs heavily from the beginning, so that competing government interests must always be important in order to justify restraints on expression. This general approach to interpreting the scope of First Amendment protections is sometimes called **preferred position balancing.** The inquiry begins with speech occupying a preferred position, and the government must overcome that position by demonstrating sufficient reasons why the speech in a given situation should not be constitutionally protected.

The specific balancing standard—sometimes referred to as the **standard of judicial review**—is determined by the nature of the speech or the circumstances in which the speech appeared. Presuming the speech in question does not fall into one of the narrow categories of unprotected expression discussed earlier, the government must show at least a "substantial" interest, and usually a "compelling" interest, in order to override the First Amendment. Another way to state this is that, in comparison with the minimum level of scrutiny given to restraints on unprotected speech, government restrictions on protected speech must undergo either **intermediate scrutiny** or **strict scrutiny.**

Strict Scrutiny

In most cases, restrictions on protected expression can be upheld only if they directly further a compelling government interest and are no broader than necessary to advance that interest. This means that government interference is allowed only if the government proves the gravest of justifications. A **compelling interest** is a justification of great magnitude, for example, directly protecting the nation's very existence, safeguarding life or limb, or shielding children from lasting emotional harm. It is the strictest of standards—one that the government rarely can meet when attempting to justify a restriction on speech. (See the sample case excerpt from *Cohen v. California* that follows, in which the Supreme Court ruled that even a profane phrase was protected speech in the absence of a compelling reason to prevent it.)

Not only must restrictions on fully protected speech be justified by a compelling interest but the restrictions themselves must also be "narrowly tailored." This means they must indeed accomplish the government's purpose, and their scope must be no broader than necessary.

The best general example of speech that receives this highest level of protection is that which is intended primarily to convey political or social ideas or facts. Restrictions aimed at the content of such speech must typically undergo this strict level of judicial scrutiny. As Chief Justice William Rehnquist wrote in 1988, "*At the heart* [italics added] of the First Amendment is the recognition of the fundamental importance of the free flow of ideas and opinions on matters of public interest and concern."[41]

Cohen v. California

403 U.S. 15 (1971)

CASE

EXCERPT

From the majority opinion by Justice John Harlan:

This case may seem at first blush too inconsequential to find its way into our books, but the issue it presents is of no small constitutional significance.

Appellant Paul Robert Cohen was convicted in the Los Angeles Municipal Court of violating that part of California Penal code §415 which prohibits "maliciously and willfully disturb[ing] the peace or quiet of any neighborhood or person . . . by offensive conduct. . . ." He was given 30 days' imprisonment. . . .

the facts

[The conviction was based on the following facts: In 1968 Cohen was observed in the corridor of the Los Angeles County Courthouse wearing, in the presence of other people, a jacket bearing the plainly visible words, "Fuck the Draft." Cohen testified that he wore the jacket as a means of informing the public of the depth of his feelings against the Vietnam War and the draft. Neither he nor anyone else threatened to commit any act of violence.]

I

In order to lay hands on the precise issue which this case involves, it is useful first to canvass various matters which this record does *not* present.

speech, not conduct

The conviction quite clearly rests upon the asserted offensiveness of the *words* Cohen used to convey his message to the public. The only "conduct" which the State sought to punish is the fact of communication. Thus, we deal here with a conviction resting solely upon "speech," . . . not upon any separately identifiable conduct. . . .

unprotected category?

. . . [T]his case cannot be said to fall within those relatively few categories of instances where prior decisions have established the power of government to deal more comprehensively with certain forms of individual expression simply upon a showing that such a form was employed. This is not, for example, an obscenity case. . . .

not obscenity

not "fighting words"

This Court has also held that the States are free to ban the simple use, without a demonstration of additional justifying circumstances, of so-called fighting words, those personally abusive epithets which, when addressed to the ordinary citizen, are, as a matter of common knowledge, inherently likely to provoke violent reaction. *Chaplinsky v. New Hampshire*, 315 U.S. 568 (1942). While the four-letter word displayed by Cohen in relation to the draft is not uncommonly employed in a personally provocative fashion, in this instance it was clearly not "directed to the person of the hearer." No individual actually or likely to be present could reasonably have regarded the words on appellate's jacket as a direct personal insult. . . .

no exception for "unwilling audience"

Finally, in arguments before this Court much has been made of the claim that Cohen's distasteful mode of expression was thrust upon unwilling or unsuspecting viewers, and that the State might therefore legitimately act as it did in order to protect the sensitive from otherwise unavoidable exposure to appellant's crude form of protest. Of course, the mere presumed presence of unwitting listeners or viewers does not serve automatically to justify curtailing all speech capable of giving offense. . . . [I]f Cohen's "speech" was otherwise entitled to constitutional protection, we do not think the fact that some unwilling "listeners" in a public building may have been briefly exposed to it can serve to justify this breach-of-the-peace conviction. . . .

II

Against this background, the issue flushed by this case stands out in bold relief. It is whether California can excise, as "offensive conduct," one particular scurrilous epithet from the public discourse, either upon the theory of the court below that its use is inherently likely to cause violent reaction or upon a more general assertion that the States, acting as guardians of public morality, may properly remove this offensive word from the public vocabulary.

overriding rationale present?

The rationale of the California court is plainly untenable. At most it reflects an "undifferentiated fear of apprehension of disturbance [which] is not enough to overcome the right to freedom of expression." *Tinker v. Des Moines Indep. Community School Dist.*, 393 U.S. 503, 508 (1969). . . .

Admittedly, it is not so obvious that the First and Fourteenth Amendments must be taken to disable the States from punishing public utterance of this unseemly expletive in order to maintain what they regard as a suitable level of discourse within the body politic. We think, however, that examination and reflection will reveal the shortcomings of a contrary viewpoint.

At the outset, we cannot overemphasize that, in our judgment, most situations where the State has a justifiable interest in regulating speech will fall within one or more of the various established exceptions, discussed above but not applicable here, to the usual rule that governmental bodies may not prescribe the form or content of individual expression. Equally important to our conclusion is the constitutional backdrop against which our decision must be made. The constitutional right of free expression is powerful medicine in a society as diverse and populous as ours. It is designed and intended to remove governmental restraints from the arena of public discussion, putting the decision as to what views shall be voiced largely into the hands of each of us, in the hope that use of such freedom will ultimately produce a more capable citizenry and more perfect polity and in the belief that no other approach would comport with the premise of individual dignity and choice upon which our political system rests. . . .

To many, the immediate consequence of this freedom may often appear to be only verbal tumult, discord, and even offensive utterance. These are, however, within established limits, in truth necessary side effects of the broader enduring values which the process of open debate permits us to achieve. That the air may at times seem filled with verbal cacophony is, in this sense not a sign of weakness but of strength. . . .

no compelling reason

It is, in sum, our judgment that, absent a more particularized and compelling reason for its actions, the State may not consistently with the First and Fourteenth Amendments, make the simple public display here involved of this single four-letter expletive a criminal offense. . . .

conviction unconstitutional

Reversed.

Intermediate Scrutiny

In a few kinds of free speech cases, the government can override the First Amendment guarantee by showing that a restraint on speech furthers a substantial government interest and is no broader than necessary to advance that interest. A **substantial interest** is an important or significant one, though not necessarily one of the utmost gravity. In other words, when this level of scrutiny applies, the speech has a markedly lower degree of protection than in strict scrutiny situations. Court cases have identified as substantial such justifications as promoting smooth operation of a government program, protecting community order and tranquility, safeguarding private economic interests, indirectly promoting public health, and upholding basic notions of morality.

Truthful commercial advertising is one of the best examples of speech that is afforded only a moderate degree of First Amendment protection. The Supreme Court has said that because commercial speech is intended mainly to generate a self-serving transaction, rather than to contribute to social discourse or understanding, it is not the kind of speech that warrants the fullest extent of protection. Thus, when the state of New York banned all promotional advertising by electrical utilities on the ground that such ads were contrary to state energy-conservation goals, the Supreme Court applied the substantial interest standard. The state's interest in conserving energy was indeed substantial, the Court said in 1980. (However, the complete advertising ban ultimately was ruled unconstitutional on the ground of overbreadth.) [42]

Time, place, and manner restrictions pertaining to any kind of protected speech also are reviewed at the intermediate scrutiny level. Remember, TPM restrictions must, first of all, be content neutral. If this is the case, a restriction will be upheld if in addition it (1) furthers a substantial government interest, and (2) leaves open ample alternative channels for communication of the message.

For example, in a case mentioned earlier, the U.S. Supreme Court upheld a rule that restricted literature distribution to an area of fixed booths at the Minnesota State Fair. The rule was challenged by the International Society for Krishna Consciousness, which wanted to distribute literature throughout the grounds. Once the Court concluded that the rule was truly content neutral, it proceeded to apply the intermediate standard of scrutiny. The Court identified a substantial

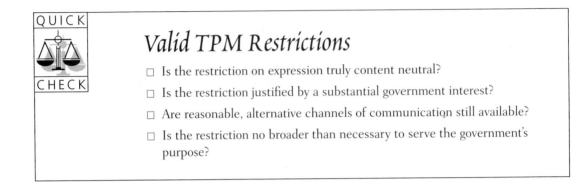

QUICK
CHECK

Valid TPM Restrictions

☐ Is the restriction on expression truly content neutral?

☐ Is the restriction justified by a substantial government interest?

☐ Are reasonable, alternative channels of communication still available?

☐ Is the restriction no broader than necessary to serve the government's purpose?

government interest (assuring orderly crowd movement), and the rule left ample opportunity to distribute literature effectively from a booth. Therefore, it was a constitutionally valid time, place, and manner restriction.[43]

Cases involving expressive conduct (symbolic speech) also may be decided at the intermediate scrutiny level. Recall that these cases involve the application of some restriction to conduct that has been injected with a particular message.

The constitutional inquiry in these cases begins by determining whether the government restriction was aimed at the conduct element or at the expression. If the government regulation was aimed strictly at the conduct, the regulation will be upheld in most cases, under essentially the same inquiry used in TPM cases. But if the aim was really to suppress the underlying expression, the regulation is judged at the strict scrutiny level and nearly always will be held unconstitutional.

In the case of *United States v. O'Brien*, for example, a man had burned his military draft registration certificate on the steps of a Boston courthouse in the presence of a large crowd. His action was intended as a demonstration against the war in Vietnam. O'Brien was convicted under a federal statute that made it a crime to knowingly destroy draft cards, and he appealed on First Amendment grounds.

The Supreme Court in 1968 ruled that the punishment against O'Brien's expressive conduct could be upheld as long as the federal restriction (1) was not aimed at suppressing expression, (2) was in furtherance of a substantial government interest, and (3) was no greater than necessary to achieve that interest. These requirements were met, the Court held, because the legislation was adopted not to suppress political expression but to protect the government's substantial interest in maintaining a smooth and efficient Selective Service System. Availability of the draft cards allowed officials to quickly verify a man's Selective Service status. Therefore, the Court concluded that O'Brien was convicted not for his message of protest, but purely because of the noncommunicative conduct—the burning itself—that frustrated the government's organizational efforts.[44]

In contrast, recall the flag-burning case of *Texas v. Johnson*, discussed earlier. Justice Brennan concluded that the Texas law against burning a flag actually was aimed at the expressive component of the symbolic act—at the message behind burning the flag, not purely at the conduct. This conclusion had the effect of bumping the level of judicial scrutiny up to the highest level. For the law to be constitutional, the state needed a compelling justification, and Brennan found none: "If there is a bedrock principle underlying the First Amendment, it is that the Government may not prohibit the expression of an idea simply because society finds the idea itself offensive or disagreeable,"[45] he wrote.

Special Problem: Government Media

A special perplexity arises when government attempts to control speech within its own media or facilities, such as county parks, city-owned auditoriums, public-school newspapers, or government employee newsletters. Should controls in these places be classified as a prior restraints, just as they would be in other instances? Or is government merely exercising a right to control its own medium, much as the publisher of a commercial newspaper may dictate that paper's content?

The Forum Theory

The legal answer depends on whether the facility or medium is maintained by the government as a **public forum,** a place either specifically designed or traditionally used for the exercise of free speech by the public. As a general rule, government has the power to exercise control over the use of its own property. However, if a public forum has been created, government attempts to control the content of speech in that forum are presumptively invalid prior restraints. In essence, once government installs a soapbox for the public, it cannot restrict the ideas expressed thereon.

If a city traditionally allowed speeches, plays, and dance performances at its civic auditorium, for example, a public forum would exist. Denial of access to a particular speaker or organization, on the basis of its message, would amount to a prior restraint on expression.[46] In a public forum, such restraint virtually always will be unconstitutional, unless government can prove the restriction is necessary to serve a compelling interest.

On the other hand, courts are unlikely to declare such places as government office lobbies or military bases to be public forums.[47] To qualify as a forum, the facility must be one where free exchange of ideas is traditionally a principal purpose—such as public parks—or where free speech is a specifically designated purpose. All other government facilities for communication are nonpublic forums, where government generally may control speech on any reasonable ground, without risk of a First Amendment violation.

A U.S. Supreme Court decision in 1998 dealt with this distinction. The Arkansas Educational Television Commission is a state agency that operates a network of noncommercial TV stations. Its staff planned a one-hour, televised debate among the leading contenders for one of the state's congressional districts. An independent candidate asked to participate, but the AETC's executive director denied the request, saying viewers would be better served in the short time available by limiting the debate to the major-party candidates. The independent candidate sued, claiming that he had a First Amendment right to participate because the government-owned broadcast operation had set up a public forum.

Howerever, the Supreme Court ruled in *Arkansas Educational TV Commission v. Forbes*[48] that the debate was a nonpublic forum because it was designed from the start with very selective participation in mind, not with the intent to open the doors of AETC facilities to all candidates. The debate was never designed as an open-microphone format. Furthermore, the majority held, the decision to exclude the independent candidate was a reasonable, journalistic judgment. The Court noted that the candidate was excluded not because of his specific views, but because he had not generated significant public interest. Therefore, the selective debate was not a violation of any candidate's First Amendment rights.

Student Media and the Hazelwood Case

The forum theory has played a particularly important role in free speech disputes involving student media at public high schools and colleges. A long line of federal and state court cases has declared that school administrators possess no legal authority to censor student publications just because the publications are owned by the school. Rather, the critical question is whether the school was operating a forum for student expression. Furthermore, courts typically have ruled or assumed that student publications indeed constitute forums. Even when publications were part of the curriculum and were closely supervised by school employees, courts traditionally held an open forum existed if the publication aired student viewpoints on a variety of subjects.[49] And once a student forum exists, censorship is unlawful except when necessary to protect other students' legal rights or to prevent substantial disruption of the school environment.[50]

Although many lower courts adjudicated student press cases in the 1970s and 1980s, the U.S. Supreme Court did not rule on the student press until 1988. That year, in *Hazelwood School District v. Kuhlmeier*,[51] the Court significantly narrowed application of the forum theory on campus. In *Hazelwood* the Court upheld censorship by a high school principal in Missouri.

The *Hazelwood* dispute arose over two scheduled stories in the high school's newspaper. One described three high school students' experiences with pregnancy; the other discussed the impact of divorce on students at the school. During his customary prepublication review, the principal concluded that the stories were written unfairly and were inappropriate for younger students at the school. He ordered that the two pages containing those stories be withheld from publication. Three of the student staff members sued.

The majority of the Supreme Court characterized the school newspaper as a laboratory paper—not as a public forum. School facilities become public forums, wrote Justice Byron White, only if school officials open the facilities for "indiscriminate use" by the students. And that had not occurred at Hazelwood East High, even though the paper traditionally covered a wide range of subjects and even published letters to the editor. Weighing against forum status, the Court said, were the facts that the newspaper was solely the product of a regular journalism class, taught by a faculty member who selected the editors and assigned and edited the stories. Without forum status, the newspaper's content could be regulated by the school "in any reasonable manner" without having to overcome a strict First Amendment test.

Some student press experts were concerned that the *Hazelwood* decision would swell the incidence of censorship on campuses. A nationwide survey conducted the following year concluded that high school publications had been experiencing a high level of censorship prior to the case and that the *Hazelwood* decision increased that level slightly. The survey also found that 8 percent of the surveyed principals and 17 percent of the newspaper advisers believed the Court's opinion had changed the legal status of their campus papers.[52] The Supreme Court in *Hazelwood* declined to state whether the same analysis would apply to publications produced on college and university campuses, where a more liberal tradition of free speech exists, or whether a broader standard for forum status would apply.

A federal appeals court addressed this issue in the 1999 case of *Kincaid v. Gibson*.[53] Two student writers at Kentucky State University sued campus officials on grounds that they prevented distribution of the 1992–94 student yearbook and interfered with content of the student newspaper. Campus officials were displeased with the yearbook because of its vague theme ("Destination Unknown"), because many of the photographs were unrelated to campus, and because many of the campus photos lacked captions. Plaintiffs contended that the vice president for student affairs attempted to stifle content in the campus newspaper, as well, by directing the publications coordinator not to publish a particular letter and to publish more positive news in the paper, and by transferring the publications coordinator to another post when she refused to cooperate.

A federal district court granted summary judgment for the defendants on the First Amendment claims, and the Court of Appeals for the Sixth Circuit agreed. It applied the Supreme Court's *Hazelwood* framework to the yearbook and held that the publication was not a public forum. Though the yearbook was not a product of the classroom and was not subject to the same degree of daily control as the high school paper in *Hazelwood*, the court nevertheless found no evidence that the university had intended to set up a public forum. The court noted a Kentucky State policy that the yearbook "shall be under the management of the Student Publications Board." Because the yearbook was a nonpublic forum, officials were entitled to regulate it in any reasonable manner. Confiscation of the yearbook was reasonable, the court said, because the book failed to accomplish its intended purpose of chronicling and promoting the campus. The decision not to circulate was based on poor quality, not political viewpoint discrimination, which would have been improper, the court said. Thus, *Kincaid* became the first case to apply the *Hazelwood* approach to a college student publication.

As to the Kentucky State newspaper, the appellate court said the student plaintiffs lacked standing to pursue their First Amendment claims because there was no showing that speech was actually restricted by the university. An *attempt* to influence speech was not enough, the court said. With the claims dismissed for lack of standing, the court had no occasion to rule on whether the student newspaper, unlike the yearbook, might qualify as a public forum.

Most litigation involving the student press has concerned efforts by public school officials to control news-editorial content. But what about the question of access to the school-owned media by advertisers or others? Would it make a difference whether the medium is a public forum? Should the law allow student editors of forum publications to be free from content controls by officials while also allowing the editors to deny access requests by outsiders? Should school officials have the power to bar access by outsiders, based on content?

In 1989 the U.S. Court of Appeals answered some of these access questions. Planned Parenthood had sought to place an ad in high school newspapers, yearbooks, and athletic event programs in Las Vegas. The family planning group's ad simply stated its address and announced the availability of routine gynecological exams, birth control methods, pregnancy testing, and pregnancy counseling. However, the ads were rejected at some of the high schools under guidelines that prohibited publishing ads for birth control products or information.

Planned Parenthood sued, claiming a First Amendment right of access to the taxpayer-supported publications. The Court of Appeals ruled in favor of the schools. Citing *Hazelwood,* the court said the publications were not set up or operated as public forums. Therefore, school officials were free to regulate their content in any reasonable or rational manner. School principals rejected the ads because they believed it was best for their schools to appear completely neutral on such controversial subjects as birth control methods. The court deemed this reasoning sufficient to support the restriction.[54]

Waiver of Rights

Under certain circumstances individuals may effectively waive, or relinquish, their constitutional protections—including the protections of the First Amendment. Fundamental constitutional rights, such as the right to freedom of speech, are never relinquished involuntarily, however. For a waiver to occur there must be some voluntary action or agreement by the individual. And if the facts are unclear, the judicial presumption is that a waiver of rights has not taken place.

In some cases, a waiver of First Amendment freedom may occur when an individual accepts government benefits, knowing in advance that they come with strings attached. Government may not condition its benefits upon a complete relinquishment of a constitutional right in all facets of a person's life. However, it may stipulate restrictions on how the benefit will be put to use. Once individuals proceed to accept such benefits, they have agreed implicitly to the terms and cannot at the same time challenge the restrictions.

In 1991, for example, family planning clinics and physicians who received government funds under the Public Health Service Act challenged government regulations that prohibited the funds from being used to support abortion counseling or advocacy. In a 5–4 decision, the Supreme Court in *Rust v. Sullivan* held that the restriction did not violate the First Amendment. Doctors and clinic staff members were not generally prohibited from engaging in abortion counseling or advocacy, the Court majority said. Rather, the rule simply prohibited the public funds from being spent for those purposes. The clinic staffers and doctors could continue speaking freely on abortion—as long as it was done through avenues or programs separate from those that voluntarily use the government funds.[55]

In contrast, the Supreme Court in *FCC v. League of Women Voters of California* invalidated a federal law that provided that noncommercial television and radio stations that receive federal grants may not "engage in editorializing." Here, too, the justices split 5–4, though the decision went the other direction. Under the federal regulation, a recipient of funds was barred absolutely from all editorializing as a condition for receiving funds. In effect, the law meant that an educational station that received just 1 percent of its overall income from federal grants was nevertheless completely prohibited from airing editorials. The Court ruled in the 1984 case that the government's ability to condition its funding did not extend that broadly.[56]

Another way in which First Amendment rights may be voluntarily relinquished is by agreeing to restrictive provisions in a government employment contract. In a couple of cases, the federal government has successfully used employment agreements to prevent former CIA employees from revealing agency information in books. The courts deemed these restrictive agreements reasonable and upheld them, even without a showing that the former CIA employees' writings would contain secret or dangerous information. The agents had signed the agreements when they were first hired.[57]

Summary Points

The First Amendment to the U.S. constitution is a single sentence that must be interpreted by the courts in order to have any meaning in real conflicts.

It is not clear exactly what the founders intended when the First Amendment was drafted, but at the very least they intended to prevent a central government from imposing prior restraints such as licensing and censorship schemes, as the Crown had done in earlier decades.

The leading advocates of free speech in the new nation saw it as a natural, fundamental right of individuals and also as a functional social policy, necessary to the operation of a democracy.

Since 1925 the First Amendment guarantees have served as restrictions on all government—local, state, and federal.

In recent decades the U.S. Supreme Court has interpreted the words *speech* and *press* broadly to cover all methods of expression, but protection does not apply to pure conduct.

Although direct prior restraint on content is the least tolerable form of interference in speech, after-the-fact penalties, well-meaning access rules, and even restrictions not based on content may be abridgments of speech.

Though the First Amendment's guarantees are stated in absolute terms, courts have always allowed some government interference in expression. Speech rights may be outweighed by competing interests in a given situation, and they are limited by some categorical exceptions to constitutional protection.

No regulation can withstand First Amendment scrutiny if it restricts more communication than necessary to achieve its purpose; if a less restrictive alternative is available, the law is overbroad.

In the chapter hypothetical, the pressroom destruction by the citizens' group and the order to lay off the story by the newspaper owner would not amount to First Amendment violations; neither represents government action against you. The city council's newsrack ordinance would be highly suspect, however. Circumstances suggest the ordinance was directed at punishing your views, and the council apparently had unfettered discretion to decide which newsracks promote litter. The ordinance would not qualify as a valid TPM restriction for either reason. Finally, the attempted prosecution based on your vulgar headline would be unconstitutional under the standard applied in *Cohen v. California.*

Discussion Questions

1. If the U.S. Supreme Court did adopt an absolutist approach to the First Amendment, what are the worst consequences that might realistically result from that decision? How, realistically, might society benefit from an absolutist approach to free speech?

2. In today's mega-media society, are there any serious flaws in the marketplace-of-ideas, discovery-of-truth justification for freedom of speech?

3. What, exactly, should be the dividing line between speech and conduct? Is topless barroom dancing speech or conduct? How about simply posing topless in the bar? If posing topless or naked is not considered speech, would a videotape of the posing be considered speech? Would it matter how the tape was made? What if the tape were recorded by a stationary camera with no creative human control? Should playing the tape still qualify as an inherent form of expression?

4. The courts have long distinguished between prior restraints on speech and subsequent punishments, the latter being more likely to be upheld. Might this distinction be entirely illusory? What is the practical difference between a statute prohibiting false advertising and a court injunction ordering a magazine not to publish a particular ad because of its false content? In *Near v. Minnesota* the injunction against the paper was considered a classic form of prior restraint and a particularly bad form of speech abridgment. But in this

hypothetical example is there any practical difference between the injunction and the general statute? In both cases, violation will result in some form of punishment. Would the injunction have any more chilling an effect on advertising than the statute?

5. The mass media are sometimes criticized for hiding behind the First Amendment when they behave in an ethically questionable fashion. Some media consumers indeed harbor doubts as to whether the amendment is a particularly beneficial device in modern society. How, specifically, might the mass media better educate and convince the public of the merits of the First Amendment?

Key Terms

absolutist
compelled speech
compelling interest
content neutral
doctrine of incorporation
doctrine of overbreadth
expressive conduct
intermediate scrutiny
natural law
preferred position balancing
prior restraint

public forum
rational basis standard
seditious libel
standard of judicial review
state action
strict scrutiny
substantial interest
symbolic speech
time, place, and manner restriction
void-for-vagueness doctrine

Web Resources

http://www.FreedomForum.org/first/welcome.asp
The Freedom Forum, First Amendment page

http://www.splc.org
Student Press Law Center

InfoTrac® College Edition

Rating schemes for the content of TV programs have been hotly debated in recent years. Even if the ratings are assigned by the TV industry itself or by a citizens group it appoints, and even if they are intended to warn parents of potentially objectionable material, some argue that any such government-urged scheme violates at least the spirit of the First Amendment. Find an opinion piece that speaks to this issue. Do you find it persuasive?

CHAPTER THREE

Chapter Outline

Risks to Public Safety

Upon completing this chapter you should

- [ ] **know** how the Supreme Court's clear-and-present-danger test evolved and how the modern version of that test is applied.
- [ ] **appreciate** the legal issues involved when national security is jeopardized by mass communication.
- [ ] **understand** how communicators may become civilly liable when individuals suffer physical harm as a result of media content.
- [ ] **be able** to analyze a given set of facts for legal danger signs of criminal or civil liability.

■ Worse Days at Flat Rock

Assume once again that you are editor of the weekly *Flat Rock Folio*. Driving home along a rural road, you notice smoke rising from behind a nearby hill. Grabbing your camera, you quickly hike to the top of the hill. Crashed in a field below is what you suspect to be a Sleuth fighter jet—although the Air Force has never released photographs of it. Military personnel and equipment are beginning to arrive from the local air base. You are apparently the only nonmilitary observer of this news event. As a crane loads the aircraft onto a large truck, you take as many photographs as you can and hurry home to develop the film. A few hours later, there is a knock at your door. Several federal marshals have brought a court order forbidding you to publish anything about the aircraft.

You abide by the order. But in your next issue you again publish an editorial urging local citizens to oppose deployment of the Sleuth fighters in your area. This time you urge specific action:

> The *Folio* urges citizens to show where they stand. It's time to draw the country's attention to this problem—time to force some changes in government thinking. We should not sit by quietly while the Air Force shoves deafening, dangerous warplanes down our throats.
>
> We must send a strong message by taking to the streets. Let us gather, all of us, at the gates of Flat Rock Air Force Base. All Air Force vehicles, entering or leaving, should be swarmed by the people and tipped on their sides. As a further sign of the public's resolve, starting today all citizens of this town should begin fasting in protest. Let us consume nothing but water until the Air Force agrees to hold public hearings. Fasting is a way that every person, young or old, can protest. Begin now! It's time to act.

That afternoon you are arrested and charged with violating a state statute that makes it a crime to "knowingly and willfully advocate the necessity of sabotage, violence, or destruction of property as a means to achieve political reform." The following day brings even more bad news. A teenage girl who fasted for twenty-four hours suddenly lapsed into unconsciousness and died. The girl, a diabetic, was captivated by your editorial but did not realize that, for her, fasting could be very dangerous. Her distraught mother calls and vows to sue you for everything you've got.

Have you risked public safety sufficiently to warrant the legal actions against you? Is the court order against publication a valid prior restraint? Are the criminal prosecution and the civil lawsuit likely to be successful against you?

Introduction

If speech is ever to be justifiably curtailed or punished despite the First Amendment, perhaps the most likely time would be when speech directly causes physical harm—or creates a high risk of such harm. That could occur, for example, if speech caused fighting or widespread civil disobedience, if it compromised military secrets such that troops or entire cities were put in danger, or in a wide array of circumstances in which individuals might injure themselves or others while imitating actions reported in the media. This chapter begins with historical attempts by government to prevent insurrection and ends with recent cases in which private people have sued the media for harm sustained. What many of these cases have in common is judicial application of the so-called clear-and-present-danger standard to determine when the expression has created too great a risk.

Law and Order

Freedom of speech became a point of controversy quite early in this nation's history, when Congress passed the **Sedition Act** of 1798. The law made it a crime, punishable by up to two years' imprisonment, to publish "any false, scandalous and malicious writing" with intent to stir up contempt for the federal government, government officials, or their official acts. Many political leaders, including James Madison, believed the law violated the First Amendment, either because it punished free discussion of government and politics or simply because it infringed on the states' rights to regulate expression.

The Sedition Act was vigorously enforced to punish opponents of the Federalist-controlled government. About two dozen editors and a number of private citizens were prosecuted. The Sedition Act expired by its own terms in 1801, however, and the new president, Thomas Jefferson, pardoned all people convicted under the act.

By today's standards, the Sedition Act would appear to have been a patent violation of the First Amendment. The constitutionality of the act, however, was never tested in the U.S. Supreme Court, and the zealous prosecutions show that First Amendment protection can be illusory in the absence of strong backing by the courts.

The Supreme Court did not begin to interpret the scope of First Amendment protections for more than one hundred years—until the time of World War I. This is not to say that freedom of speech was unhindered by government. Most government suppression of speech, though, was at the state level, where the First Amendment did not apply. (Remember, the First Amendment guarantees were not made applicable to the states until 1925.)

The period leading up to the Civil War was particularly troublesome. For example, many Southern states feared that antislavery speech could bring down the institution of slavery, so they placed harsh restraints on abolitionist expression. These official restraints were exacerbated by unofficial acts of intimidation, violence, and censorship.

Clear and Present Danger

Finally, in 1919 the Supreme Court began giving form and life—and, eventually, strength—to the First Amendment. The first case was *Schenck v. United States.* Congress had enacted the **Espionage Act** of 1917 after declaring war against Germany. The act said in part that

> . . . whoever, when the United States is at war, shall willfully cause or attempt to cause insubordination, disloyalty, mutiny, or refusal of duty, in the military or naval forces of the United States, or shall willfully obstruct the recruiting or enlistment Service of the United States . . . shall be punished by a fine of not more than $10,000 or imprisonment for not more than twenty years, or both.

Schenck was convicted under the act for sending to drafted men pamphlets that urged insubordination in the armed services and obstruction of the draft. The Supreme Court unanimously upheld the conviction and legally established a First Amendment exception for such dissident expression. The opinion, by Justice Oliver Wendell Holmes, explained the court's reasoning and constitutional standard:

> The character of every act depends upon the circumstances in which it is done. . . . The most stringent protection of free speech would not protect a man in falsely shouting fire in a theatre and causing a panic. . . . The question in every case is whether the words used are used in such circumstances and are of such nature as to create a clear and present danger that they will bring about the substantive evils that Congress has a right to prevent. It is a question of proximity and degree. When a nation is at war many things that might be said in time of peace are such a hindrance to its effort that their utterance will not be endured so long as men fight and that no Court could regard them as protected by any constitutional right.[1]

Thus the **clear-and-present-danger** test—an attempt to define the point at which speech comes close enough to triggering serious harm that it loses First Amendment protection—was born. The legal debate had just begun, however. The Espionage Act was amended in 1918 to include many other kinds of speech that could be punished, including "any disloyal, profane, scurrilous, or abusive language about the form of government of the United States, or the Constitution of the United States, or the military or naval forces of the United States, or the flag of the United States." Criticizing the unpopular war or government institutions became extremely hazardous. More than 2000 prosecutions took place under the Espionage Acts of 1917 and 1918, and almost 900 people were convicted. This, in turn, led to many more appellate challenges, several of which reached the U.S. Supreme Court.

The clear-and-present-danger test was not always followed at first, but later cases further refined it and clearly established it as the constitutional standard for government restraints of this kind. A 1927 case, *Whitney v. California,* is noted in particular for the articulate concurring opinion of Justice Louis Brandeis, which was joined by Justice Holmes. Brandeis argued in spirited detail for a clear-and-present-danger standard that would assure greater latitude for free expression:

> Fear of serious injury cannot alone justify suppression of free speech and assembly. Men feared witches and burnt women. It is the function of speech to free men from the bondage of irrational fears. To justify suppression of free speech there must be reasonable ground to fear that serious evil will result if free speech is practiced. There must be reasonable ground to believe that the danger apprehended is imminent. There must be reasonable ground to believe that the evil to be prevented is a serious one. . . . Even advocacy of violation [of the law], however reprehensible morally, is not a justification for denying free speech where the advocacy falls short of incitement and there is nothing to indicate that the advocacy would be immediately acted upon. . . . In order to support a finding of clear and present danger it must be shown either that immediate serious violence was to be expected or was advocated, or that the past conduct furnished reason to believe that such advocacy was then contemplated. . . . Only an emergency can justify repression. Such must be the rule if authority is to be reconciled with freedom. Such, in my opinion, is the command of the Constitution.[2]

So, in the increasingly sophisticated views of Justices Holmes and Brandeis at least, the standard should require a *reasonable fear of serious and imminent danger caused by incitement* before speech could be suppressed. Despite this more liberal view of two of the justices, however, the Court voted unanimously to uphold the conviction of Charlotte Whitney, under the California Criminal Syndicalism Act, for her active membership in the pro-violence Communist Labor Party.

As a whole, the Supreme Court was not yet ready to adopt the more liberal standard articulated by Brandeis. Nevertheless, top legal authority was clearly turning toward expanded freedom for political dissent. The Supreme Court in the mid-1900s entered an era during which sedition convictions were overturned as often as they were upheld.

The World War II years and the Cold War era that immediately followed brought another wave of anti-sedition legislation in the states and at the federal level. The main federal statute was the **Smith Act** of 1939, which outlawed speech that advocated either forceful overthrow of the government or disloyalty among members of the military. As it turned out, Smith Act prosecutions were very rare during the war. This is due largely to the fact that Americans, having suffered the devastating surprise attack at Pearl Harbor, were much more united in support of the war effort than they had been in World War I.

After World War II, however, the Cold War tension between Western democracy and Soviet communism brought years of suspicion, fear, and suppression of socialist views in this country. Suddenly the Smith Act rose to prominence as a vehicle for prosecuting Communist party members in America. By the late 1950s more than 140 people had been indicted under the act. A number of the convictions were reviewed by the Supreme Court, with some upheld and some reversed.

Smith Act prosecutions came to a virtual halt in 1957, however, following the Supreme Court's opinion in *Yates v. United States*.[3] In that case fourteen members of the Communist party in California had been convicted under the Smith Act for conspiring to advocate violent overthrow of the government. The Supreme Court reversed the convictions, ruling that the prosecution had failed to distinguish between the mere advocacy of abstract doctrine, which is protected speech, and the advocacy of specific, illegal action. The government concluded that it could rarely meet that tougher standard of evidence, and most of the pending Smith Act prosecutions were dismissed. A majority of the Supreme Court never deemed the Smith Act itself to be unconstitutional, however; it simply narrowed the statute's application. The Smith Act remains on the books.[4]

The Incitement Standard

The foregoing discussion compressed drastically a great deal of legal history and philosophical struggle. The important lesson is to appreciate how the Supreme Court, through years of case opinions, carved out an exception to freedom of speech and then refined it by slowly adjusting and clarifying the line between protected expression and that which could be punished. It is also important, of course, to know the Supreme Court's current standard in these kinds of cases, which is stated in the 1969 case of *Brandenburg v. Ohio*.

In *Brandenburg*, a Ku Klux Klan leader had made a speech at a rally, and the episode was filmed by a TV news crew. The Klan leader made highly derogatory remarks about African Americans and Jews and then in his speech said: "If our President, or Congress, or Supreme Court, continues to suppress the white, Caucasian race, it's possible that there might have to be some revengeance [sic] taken." In all, the film showed twelve hooded figures at the rally, some of whom carried firearms. The Klan leader was convicted under the Ohio Criminal Syndicalism statute for advocating "crime, sabotage, violence, or unlawful methods of terrorism as a means of accomplishing industrial or political reform."

Was the conviction constitutional? The Supreme Court said no, and in so doing further extended the scope of First Amendment protection. After analyzing its own precedent, the Court ruled that a new standard had evolved and stated it succinctly as follows:

> The constitutional guarantees of free speech and free press do not permit a State to forbid or proscribe advocacy of the use of force or of law violation except where such advocacy is directed to inciting or producing imminent lawless action and is likely to incite or produce such action.[5]

Does this sound familiar? More than forty years earlier, Justice Brandeis had argued that the clear-and-present-danger test should mean incitement of likely and imminent danger. Now in *Brandenburg* the full Court had distinctly recognized that view as the constitutional standard. Even presuming that the Klan leader had

QUICK
CHECK

The Brandenburg Incitement Test

☐ Does the expression advocate the use of illegal force or violence?

☐ Is it directed toward actually inciting such illegal conduct?

☐ Would the advised conduct be imminent, or immediate?

☐ Is the expression actually likely to produce that illegal conduct?

called for specific action rather than mere adoption of abstract doctrine, that would no longer be sufficient to convict. The speech remains protected until the point when it is actually *likely* to incite unlawful action. Not only did the Supreme Court reverse the Brandenburg criminal conviction but it also invalidated the underlying Ohio statute.

This modern interpretation of the clear-and-present-danger test, sometimes referred to as the **incitement standard,** was reinforced by the Supreme Court in 1973. In May 1970 about 150 antiwar demonstrators had moved from the campus of Indiana University into a public street and blocked traffic. A group of law enforcement officers dispersed the demonstrators by walking up the street. As the sheriff passed, one of the demonstrators standing at the curb said to other demonstrators and onlookers nearby: "We'll take the fucking street again." The demonstrator was arrested and convicted under the state's disorderly conduct statute.

The Supreme Court held that the statute had been applied in this case only to punish spoken words, not conduct, so constitutional guarantees were at issue. The court then recited its *Brandenburg* test and concluded that the demonstrator's words did not fall within the narrowly limited class of speech that could be punished: "At worst, [the words] amounted to nothing more than advocacy of illegal action at some indefinite future time."[6]

Expression that threatens to seriously disrupt the safe functioning of government, then, is one of the classic, long-presumed exceptions to First Amendment protection. The standard developed to determine the boundaries of this excepted class of speech was the clear-and-present-danger standard, which has evolved over several decades into the stricter incitement test, thus narrowing the exception and putting a greater burden of proof upon the government when it seeks to punish speech. Over the decades the Supreme Court also strengthened the role of judicial inquiry, giving less deference to the judgments of legislative and executive branches of government when First Amendment rights are at stake.

The incitement test of *Brandenburg v. Ohio* is not the standard used to settle all First Amendment conflicts. The standard was designed for those situations in which dangerous, illegal conduct was being advocated generally, for political purposes, and in which government wanted to prevent or punish such expression. As we will see later in this chapter, lower courts in recent decades have employed the incitement test in some other kinds of cases, such as personal tort cases where plaintiffs allegedly suffered physical injury as a result of faulty instructions or some other kind of speech. But the incitement test has been applied inconsistently and sometimes awkwardly in those civil cases for which the test was not designed.

National Security

Even in a democracy the government must be allowed to maintain certain secrets in order to be effective. Most people would concede, for example, that the identities of undercover narcotics agents or the location of troops during wartime are legitimate secrets. On the other hand, government often has a tendency to be too secretive, sometimes just to avoid embarrassment or opposition.

As mentioned earlier in this chapter, the First Amendment as interpreted does not generally empower communicators to open the doors of government. But what if, through inside sources or your own observation, you discover secrets that you think should be made public? May the government intervene? Think back to the chapter hypothetical, for example. News that a very expensive new warplane had crash-landed might be important for taxpayers to know. Which should win, your free-speech rights or the court order against publication?

National defense would seem to be a logical justification for government restrictions on publication. Especially in today's tense world of increasingly sophisticated and lethal weapons technology, most legal experts presume there must be some First Amendment exception to allow punishment or censorship of mass communications that would threaten national security. Little agreement or legal authority exists, however, regarding the boundaries of that exception. This is a developing area of First Amendment law, one that may unfold in the decades ahead. Instructive decisional law is virtually nonexistent where the issue is sanctions or restraints directly against the mass media, as opposed to restrictions on government employees who might be tempted to write books or leak information to the press. Just two modern cases have raised this issue, and only one of them reached the Supreme Court. Even in that case the fractured court published nine separate opinions that failed to establish one guiding standard. Though the boundaries of the national security exception remain problematic, it is instructive to examine these two cases.

The Pentagon Papers Case

The first is the **Pentagon Papers** case of 1971, formally titled *New York Times Company v. United States*. It all started when a consultant who had worked for the Pentagon on an extensive, classified history of the Vietnam War leaked copies of the secret manuscript to both *The New York Times* and the *Washington Post*. The study was titled *History of U.S. Decision-Making Process on Viet Nam Policy,* and it dealt with a war in which the nation was still engaged. As soon as the two newspapers began to publish their planned series of excerpts from the document, the Justice Department sought restraining orders against further publication, claiming that **national security** was at stake.

The opinion in *Near v. Minnesota* decades earlier had acknowledged that threats to national security were not protected by the First Amendment and might even be subject to prior restraint. But this was the first time the government had ever sought a federal court order to prevent publication. At the lower court levels, the government effort to enjoin publication met success in New York, but in Washington, D.C. its requests for a restraint against the *Post* were denied.

The issue posed a historic First Amendment clash of utmost significance — and of some urgency. If the Nixon administration's argument was correct, the *Post* was about to publish information that would endanger national security. If the restraining order was not justified, however, the *Times* was being subjected to flagrant political censorship each day that passed. Recognizing the gravity of the situation, the U.S. Supreme Court granted immediate review of the cases and reached its decision just two weeks after the controversy first arose.

The official opinion added little guidance to this area of First Amendment law, however. In a brief, unsigned opinion, the Court simply said that the government "carries a heavy burden of showing justification" for prior restraints and that it did not meet the burden in this case. So the papers were free to publish. The vote was 6–3. This brief opinion was followed by nine separate concurring or dissenting opinions, with the justices exhibiting a wide variety of reasoning. Here is a sampling.

Justice Douglas took the absolutist approach to the First Amendment:

It should be noted at the outset that the First Amendment provides that "Congress shall make no law . . . abridging the freedom of speech or of the press." That leaves, in my view, no room for governmental restraint on the press.[7]

Justice Brennan favored a balancing approach, but concluded that in this case the government had not met the necessary standard of proof:

The entire thrust of the Government's claim throughout these cases has been that publication of the material sought to be enjoined "could," or "might," or "may," prejudice the national interest in various ways. But the First Amendment tolerates absolutely no prior judicial restraints of the press predicated upon surmise or conjecture. . . . Only governmental allegation and proof that publication must inevitably, directly and immediately cause the occurrence of an event kindred to imperiling the safety of a transport already at sea can support even the issuance of an interim restraining order.[8]

Justice Marshall focused on the lack of federal legislation authorizing prior restraints for national security reasons:

It would . . . be utterly inconsistent with the concept of separation of power for this Court, to use its power of contempt to prevent behavior that Congress has specifically declined to prohibit.[9]

Justice Potter Stewart, in a concurring opinion joined by Justice White, was the only member of the Court to suggest at a specific test for deciding such cases. He wrote:

I cannot say that disclosure of any of [the documents] will surely result in direct, immediate, and irreparable damage to our Nation or its people. That being so, there can under the First Amendment be but one judicial resolution of the issues before us.[10]

In dissent, Justice Harlan favored a policy of greater deference to judgments of the executive branch on matters of foreign affairs:

It is plain to me that the scope of the judicial function in passing upon the activities of the Executive Branch of the Government in the field of foreign affairs is very narrowly restricted. This view is, I think, dictated by the concept of separation of powers upon which our constitutional system rests.[11]

The government never attempted to prosecute the newspapers after the series had run, though under some federal statutes a case might theoretically have been fashioned. Also, several justices hinted in the Pentagon Papers case that subsequent punishment under appropriate criminal statutes might be constitutionally permissible.

Ultimately, it appeared that the government in this case had been more concerned about preventing embarrassment than about protecting national security, strictly speaking. The document, after all, detailed past decision making in the war—events that had occurred some 3 to 20 years previously—much of which was of questionable quality.

The H-Bomb Case

Probably the closest this nation has come to stopping publication on the basis of national security was the 1979 case of *United States v. Progressive, Inc.,* though outside developments essentially dissolved the conflict before it could reach the appellate courts. The case arose when a freelance writer for the *Progressive* magazine, a political journal, completed an article describing in detail the design and operation of a hydrogen bomb. Prior to publication, a copy of the article was sent to the U.S. Department of Energy with a request that the department verify the accuracy of the technical information. But the government decided instead that portions of the article should not be published.

The author and his editors claimed that all information in the article came from unclassified, public sources and would convey no secrets. The government nevertheless argued that the article was dangerous because it connected and explained various H-bomb concepts in a manner not available in the public realm. It claimed that portions of the article must be classified as "restricted data" under the Atomic Energy Act, and the government went to federal court to stop publication.

The District Court, after wading through stacks of affidavits containing complex, scientific information, decided to issue the preliminary injunction. The court, groping for some specific test, concluded that the government had "met the test enunciated by two Justices in the *New York Times* case, namely, grave, direct, immediate and irreparable harm to the United States."[12] The judge's opinion stated in part:

> Does the article provide a "do-it-yourself" guide for the hydrogen bomb? Probably not. . . . One does not build a hydrogen bomb in the basement. However, the article could possibly provide sufficient information to allow a medium size nation to move faster in developing a hydrogen weapon. It could provide a ticket to bypass blind alleys. . . . What is involved here is information dealing with the most destructive weapon in the history of mankind, information of sufficient destructive potential to nullify the right to free speech and to endanger the right to life itself.[13]

The *Progressive* promptly announced it would appeal, and the nation's news media began bracing for an ultimate, landmark ruling that many feared would restrict freedom of the press. Unlike the Pentagon Papers case, which was based upon a general claim of a threat to national security, this case was based upon a specific federal statute. And unlike the Pentagon Papers case, this one involved a technology still sought by many countries, not a purely historical document.

The higher level of legal precedent never materialized, however. In the months before an appeal could be heard, two other writers compiled H-bomb articles similar to the one that had been enjoined. These articles began appearing in newspapers, and soon the government's preliminary injunction against the *Progressive* became pointless. The government dropped its case before any further legal proceedings could be held. And here again, no attempt was made to prosecute the media following publication.

The national security decisions thus far provide rather indefinite guidelines for solving the question raised by the chapter hypothetical—the validity of a court order preventing publication of news about the warplane. Whatever the specific test might be, however, the Pentagon Papers ruling conveyed the message that the courts are not obliged to defer entirely to the judgment of the executive branch. Instead, it is the government's burden to convince a court that real danger exists. In the warplane scenario, it is hard to imagine how the information that might be published would pose anything but a very speculative loss of competitive advantage in the future.

Wartime Access Restrictions

Restrictions that *have* been imposed in the name of national security, to date without a successful court challenge, are controls on media access to actual military operations. As later chapters will show, this is in keeping with the general rule that the First Amendment does not guarantee a right of access to newsworthy information, only the right to communicate it after it is learned. Nevertheless, news media have complained bitterly in recent years that the military's controls on war reporting have become increasingly heavy handed and that reporters are being deprived of a traditional freedom to assume the risk of injury and cover the front lines in battle.

News access was prohibited altogether, for example, when U.S. Marines invaded the Caribbean island of Grenada in 1983 to oust a Marxist regime. Numerous media organizations approached the island in private boats but were intercepted by a virtual military blockade and ordered to turn back. One First Amendment lawsuit was filed against the U.S. Department of Defense, but because the Grenada press ban had been lifted a few days after the invasion, the federal Court of Appeals declared the case moot and ordered it dismissed.[14]

The debate over battlefront access was renewed in 1991 when the United States military and allied forces launched Operation Desert Storm against Iraq in the Persian Gulf. Shortly before the Gulf War began, the Department of Defense adopted a set of rules governing media coverage. One rule was that combat reporting would be allowed only through selected media "pools," each headed by a military escort. Pool members had to agree to share their products, such as videotapes. Further, pool products were subject to security review checks prior to dissemination to determine whether they contained any "sensitive information" about the military or its plans.

The Department of Defense declared the rules were necessary to protect reporters' physical safety, to prevent the release of information that might jeopardize soldiers, and to avoid having more than a thousand free-roaming reporters physically hamper operations. Media people complained that the Gulf War restrictions were not for legitimate security reasons and were instead used to limit the character of the information reported to the American public. *The Nation* magazine and several other media filed a lawsuit challenging the restrictions. A federal court ruled the plaintiff's claims of harm were too conjectural and dismissed the case.

The U.S. Supreme Court has never addressed directly the question of whether news media may be denied access to military operations. It is widely assumed that the Court would uphold such restrictions, however, especially if they are related to protecting life or limb. The Court has upheld access restrictions pertaining to many other government-controlled settings, including prisons and military bases. Historically the judicial branch has been inclined to defer to the judgment of military experts on matters pertaining to actual conduct of an ongoing war.

Personal Injury

In the fifty years between 1919 and 1969, the Supreme Court fashioned and refined the clear-and-present-danger check on prosecutions of speech thought to evoke mass lawlessness. In the 1970s the nation witnessed two high-profile cases in which information allegedly would threaten national security. But the 1980s were primarily responsible for yet another kind of legal duel involving expression and safety—personal injury claims against the media.

In the area of civil litigation, a substantial portion of the nation's lawsuits are for "personal injury." Typically they are lawsuits by physically injured people against drivers, machinery operators, manufacturers, medical professionals, and others who allegedly caused the harm. In the 1980s, however, the number of personal injury lawsuits against mass communicators—lawsuits claiming that injury or death was traceable to the content of a publication, broadcast, or sound recording—increased.

Negligence versus Incitement

In most kinds of personal injury cases the legal basis for a lawsuit is a very broad tort called **negligence.** In general usage *negligence* is simply another word for carelessness. In law it means a failure to exercise the degree of care that a reasonable person would have exercised under the circumstances—often referred to as a failure to exercise **reasonable care** or **due care.**

In order to be legally actionable as a tort, two elements are required in addition to the careless conduct itself. Thus, the tort of negligence is committed when:

1. the defendant owed a legal duty to use due care (this duty exists whenever there is a reasonably foreseeable risk of direct harm to others);

2. the legal duty was breached (this is the negligent conduct itself);

3. and the breach was the proximate cause of the resulting injury.

Stated another way, a negligence lawsuit generally has grounds when there is careless conduct in the face of reasonably foreseeable harm, and the conduct indeed causes that harm.

For example, suppose you were driving along a four-lane highway when the vehicle next to you suddenly swerved into your lane, causing you to run into an embankment and to be injured. In your lawsuit for negligence against the other driver, the key is whether the defendant failed to use due care. You need not prove that the other driver intended to harm you, nor that the other driver thought he probably would harm you. Rather, the test is whether a reasonable driver would have been more careful than this defendant. Negligence might be proved simply by showing that the defendant failed to look in your direction before changing lanes.

When a personal injury lawsuit is based not on conduct but on expression, however, the defendant's First Amendment freedoms enter the equation. A constitutional dimension is added. In such cases should a showing of mere negligence be enough to win? Or should a First Amendment screen be applied, thus making the plaintiff's burden tougher? For example, should the clear-and-present-danger standard be the applicable test?

In most cases the courts have indeed held that the traditional tort law standard of negligence is insufficient and that the constitutional standard of clear and present danger, or specifically incitement, is what must be proved. As justification for the tougher rule, courts often speculate that, if mere negligence were the standard, it would (1) create a chilling effect on potentially valuable speech, and (2) give rise to a spate of lawsuits based on media content. This area of law is not entirely settled, however, and media liability may depend on the nature of the allegedly negligent message.

Harm Through Imitation

In some of the lawsuits alleging media responsibility for death or injury, the harm occurred when something described or shown in the media was imitated by a member of the audience. Sometimes it is the imitator who is harmed; sometimes the imitator causes harm to someone else. These so-called Pied Piper cases are particularly troublesome for mass communicators because the imitation typically was not an intended result.

For example, the 1981 case of *Olivia N. v. National Broadcasting Co.* arose from a TV broadcast of a film drama titled *Born Innocent,* about the effects of a state-run home on an adolescent girl. As described in the court records:

> In one scene of the film, the young girl enters the community bathroom of the facility to take a shower. She is then shown taking off her clothes and stepping into the shower, where she bathes for a few moments. Suddenly, the water stops and a look of fear comes across her face. Four adolescent girls are standing across from her in the shower room. One of the girls is carrying a "plumber's helper," waving it suggestively by her side. The four girls violently attack the younger girl, wrestling her to the floor. The young girl is shown naked from the waist up, struggling as the older ones force her legs apart. Then, the television film shows the girl with the plumber's helper making intense thrusting motions with the handle of the plunger until one of the four says, "That's enough."[15]

The lawsuit against NBC was brought by a 9-year-old girl who, four days after the broadcast, was attacked and artificially raped with a bottle by adolescents at a beach. The assailants had viewed and discussed the scene in *Born Innocent.* The lawsuit alleged that NBC should have known, based on studies of child violence, that susceptible people might imitate the crime depicted in the broadcast and that NBC was therefore negligent in broadcasting the scene. Even if that were true, however, the California Court of Appeal ruled that mere negligence was not the proper standard:

> [The plaintiff] does not seek to impose a prior restraint on speech; rather, she asserts civil liability premised on traditional negligence concepts. But the chilling effect of permitting negligence actions for a television broadcast is obvious. . . . The deterrent effect of subjecting the television networks to negligence liability because of their programming choices would lead to self-censorship which would dampen the vigor and limit the variety of public debate. . . . If a negligence theory is recognized, a television network or local station could be liable when a child imitates activities portrayed in a news program or documentary.[16]

To win, the court said, the plaintiff would have to show that the program was directed at inciting imminent lawless action and was likely to produce such action—the incitement requirement of *Brandenburg*. Because that could not be shown in this case, the broadcast remained constitutionally protected, and the girl could not win her case against NBC. Of course, the victim could sue the boys who actually assaulted her at the beach, and the government also could prosecute those youths.

In another case from the early 1980s, the programming in question was a stunt performed on *The Tonight Show with Johnny Carson*. A guest on the show, a professional stuntman, announced that he would attempt a stunt that involved dropping through a trapdoor with a noose around his neck. He made it clear, however, that the stunt was dangerous and should never be attempted by members of the audience. Following a commercial break, the stunt was performed successfully, using comic Carson as the subject.

Several hours after the broadcast, a 13-year-old boy was found dead, hanging from a noose in front of his TV set. The set was still on and was tuned to the channel upon which *The Tonight Show* had appeared. The boy's parents sued NBC but lost, for failure to demonstrate incitement.[17]

In a 1987 case it was an adolescent's reading of a magazine article that apparently prompted him to commit an act that proved fatal. *Hustler* magazine had published an article titled "Orgasm of Death," which discussed "autoerotic asphyxia"—the unorthodox practice of masturbation while hanging oneself in order to temporarily limit blood supply to the brain at the moment of orgasm. A prominent editor's note stated: "*Hustler* emphasizes the often-fatal dangers of the practice of 'autoerotic asphyxia,' and recommends that readers seeking unique forms of sexual release DO NOT ATTEMPT this method." The two-page article began by noting cases in which the practice had resulted in death. However it went on to include details of how the act is performed.

A 14-year-old boy attempted the practice. The next morning his body was found hanging by the neck in a closet, with a copy of the "Orgasm of Death" article near the feet. The boy's mother and his closest friend, who discovered the body, sued *Hustler* and claimed the article had implicitly incited the boy to perform the act. A jury agreed and awarded the plaintiffs almost $200,000 in damages.

The federal Court of Appeals reversed, however. Wrote the court:

> Even if the article paints in glowing terms the pleasures supposedly achieved by the practice it describes, as the plaintiffs contend, no fair reading of it can make its content advocacy, let alone incitement to engage in the practice. [The plaintiffs] complain that the article provides unnecessary detail about how autoerotic asphyxiation is accomplished. . . . Although it is conceivable that, in some instances, the amount of detail contained in challenged speech may be relevant in determining whether incitement exists, the detail in "Orgasm of Death" is not enough to permit breach of the first amendment.[18]

A different twist on this line of cases is presented by *Zamora v. Columbia Broadcasting System,* a 1979 case in which the plaintiffs argued that it was the cumulative effects of television violence that caused the harm. When he was 14, Ronny Zamora shot and killed his 80-year-old neighbor in Miami Beach. Ronny was convicted of charges stemming from the killing and was imprisoned. Ronny and his parents then sued the TV networks, claiming that the teenager's problems were caused by negligent, excessive broadcasts of violence to which the boy became addicted and "subliminally intoxicated."

The federal court dismissed the claim, in part on First Amendment grounds. The plaintiffs sought to impose a duty upon broadcasters that was simply undefinable and therefore incompatible with free speech, the court said. "[T]he liability sought for by plaintiffs would place broadcasters in jeopardy for televising Hamlet, Julius Caesar, Grimm's Fairy Tales, more contemporary offerings such as All Quiet On The Western Front, and even The Holocaust, and indeed would render John Wayne a risk not acceptable to any but the boldest of broadcasters."[19]

Is there any situation in which excessive detail in entertainment programming, even without incitement, should be the basis for tort liability? For example, in 1990 a 10-year-old boy was arrested in Southern California on suspicion of planting a homemade time bomb in his school restroom. The bomb, which was safely detonated a few minutes before it was set to go off, was made from model rocket engines, batteries, and a digital timer. The boy told sheriff's deputies that he learned how to make the explosive device entirely by watching an ABC television show, *MacGyver,* though network officials said that was impossible. Suppose the bomb had seriously injured other children, and suppose the TV show actually had provided all the detail necessary for home construction of the device? Should the network be liable? Should the legal standards for a tort claim in this case be significantly different from the standard for obtaining a prior restraint in the *Progressive* case? Cases of this nature are on the horizon, and a few courts have already indicated that the incitement test does not seem entirely appropriate for these kinds of situations.[20]

In 1995 the issue of excessive media detail rose to the level of national debate, this time in the context of news. In one instance the issue grew out of coverage of the Oklahoma City federal-building bombing that killed 169 people and injured hundreds more. Some news accounts gave details about how the 4800-pound homemade bomb was constructed from fuel oil and a chemical fertilizer. Another case, six months after the Oklahoma bombing, involving the fatal derailment of an Amtrak train in Arizona. Some news accounts detailed how the saboteurs loosened 19 feet of rail, removed a 3-foot steel connecting plate, and bridged the gap with wire in order to disable an electronic warning system. Both cases raised the question whether the detailed media accounts would serve to instruct would-be terrorists. Under any circumstances, could persons injured in a later, copycat attack hold the media legally responsible? From the case law discussed in this segment of the chapter, it appears the answer is no.

Harm from Advice or Instructions

In the cases mentioned so far it was not the desire of communicators that members of the audience imitate the depicted conduct. In fact, imitation was expressly discouraged in two of the cases. Sometimes, however, communicators do urge or invite the audience to act in a certain way. It may be anything from a medical advice column to a product instruction booklet to a political editorial. Recall that in the chapter hypothetical, for example, the newspaper editor specifically urged citizens to fast in protest. If the advice leads to harm, are communicators and the media in a dangerous legal position?

Radio and TV

A classic case in this area, and one often relied upon by plaintiffs, is *Weirum v. RKO General, Inc.* A Los Angeles radio station with a large teenage audience conducted a contest that rewarded the first driver to locate a disc jockey, "The Real Don Steele," as he moved from one location to another in his red car. In typical radio style, the contest was promoted directly over the air, with audience members specifically urged to be the first to catch up with the DJ. Two teenage drivers, jockeying for position, raced to the next location at speeds of up to 80 miles per hour. In the process, they forced another car off the road, killing its driver. The driver's widow sued the radio station, as well as the young drivers, for the wrongful death.

In 1975 the California Supreme Court upheld a jury finding that the rock station was indeed liable for the accident. The language of the court's opinion was broad and highly critical of the station's manner of expression. The court declined to apply a heightened First Amendment standard, but even if it had it might have reached the same conclusion. In *Weirum,* the court noted, there was a specific attempt to generate a competitive scramble on the public streets, "accelerated by repeated importuning by radio" to be the first one to arrive at a destination.[21]

In a later case involving instructions for action, however, the Supreme Court of Georgia ruled in favor of the media. *Walt Disney Productions, Inc. v. Shannon* arose from an episode of the *Mickey Mouse Club,* a television show aimed at children. A special feature on the show as "all about the magic you can create with sound effects." One demonstration was how to produce the sound of a wheel coming off a car by putting a BB pellet inside a round balloon, filling the balloon with air, and then rotating the BB inside. An 11-year-old boy tried to repeat what he had seen on TV, using a piece of lead twice the size of a BB, and a "large, skinny balloon." The balloon burst, shooting the lead into the boy's eye and partially blinding him. He sued the producer, the syndicator, and the local broadcaster of the TV show.

The Georgia court upheld summary judgment in favor of the defendants after determining that the show was protected under the First Amendment by virtue of the clear-and-present-danger doctrine. Wrote the court: "Although it can be said that what the defendants allegedly invited the child to do in this case posed a foreseeable risk of injury, it cannot be said that it posed a clear and present danger of injury."[22] As evidence of this, the court noted that, of an estimated 16 million children watching the program, this was the only reported injury relating to the techniques shown.

Recordings

Turning to a different medium, a lawsuit in the late 1980s involved a 19-year-old who killed himself in his bedroom while listening to the recorded rock music of Ozzy Osbourne. The victim, who reportedly had emotional and alcohol abuse problems, had listened to certain Osbourne recordings repeatedly on the night of the suicide. The victim's parents sued Osbourne and others connected with the recordings, claiming that the lyrics conveyed the message that "suicide is not only acceptable, but desirable"[23] as a way to avoid despair and alleging that Osbourne should have known his music would influence emotionally unstable listeners.

However, in its 1988 ruling the California Court of Appeal applied the *Brandenburg* test and concluded that Osbourne's music was neither directed toward bringing about imminent suicide nor likely to produce such a result. Therefore, the legal claim was barred by the First Amendment. This court also concluded that even under the traditional tort law of negligence the plaintiffs would not win. Suicide was not a reasonably foreseeable consequence of the music, the court said.

In a similar case heard before a federal court in Georgia,[24] two parents sued Ozzy Osbourne and CBS Records, claiming that lyrics in the song "Suicide Solution" incited the plaintiffs' son to kill himself by firing a pistol at his head. Unlike the California case, though, these plaintiffs charged that the suicide directive was contained in subliminal lyrics aimed at the subconscious mind. The message, they alleged, is intelligible to the conscious mind only when the music is electronically adjusted.

The federal court said that if the Osbourne recording contained surreptitious, subliminal messages it would be relegated to a class of speech worthy of little, if any, First Amendment protection. In this instance, however, the court held that plaintiffs' expert witnesses had failed to produce any credible evidence that subliminal messages actually existed in the recording. Therefore, the recording was fully protected by the First Amendment, and, the court held, the parents could not possibly demonstrate that the lyrics incited imminent suicide. Accordingly, summary judgment was granted in favor of the defendants.

Books

With its tremendous volume of detailed how-to titles, book publishing is another area in which the courts have been careful not to open the floodgates to litigation concerning authors' particular choices of words. In one recent case a woman died, allegedly of sudden complications caused by a liquid protein diet she was following, as described in a book titled *When Everything Else Fails . . . The Last Chance Diet*. (The woman had lost over 100 pounds in about six months but then died of heart failure.) The administrator of the woman's estate sued the pub-

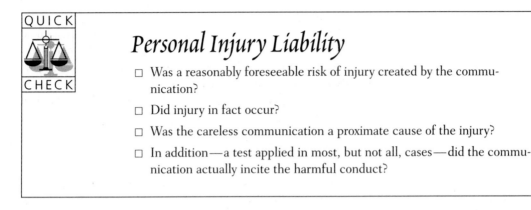

Personal Injury Liability

☐ Was a reasonably foreseeable risk of injury created by the communication?

☐ Did injury in fact occur?

☐ Was the careless communication a proximate cause of the injury?

☐ In addition—a test applied in most, but not all, cases—did the communication actually incite the harmful conduct?

lisher and several other parties connected with the book, claiming it was published negligently.

A Pennsylvania appellate court upheld summary judgment in favor of the defendants. Here again, the incitement standard was applied, and the court disagreed that the diet book was "an incitement to immediate unreflecting action such as the action arising from shouting 'Fire!' in a crowded theater."[25]

In a 1991 case the U.S. Court of Appeals faced a similar claim. But the federal court did not directly discuss the incitement standard; it said that even under basic negligence law a publisher was not liable for harm to readers. The case arose when two mushroom enthusiasts, relying on information in *The Encyclopedia of Mushrooms,* became severely ill from picking and eating wild mushrooms. Descriptions in the book led the readers to believe the mushrooms they harvested were safe. But in fact, the plaintiffs had eaten one of the most deadly species of mushrooms; both plaintiffs required liver transplants as a result.

The readers sued the book publisher for negligence, alleging that the descriptions in the book were erroneous and led to their illnesses. But the District Court granted summary judgment for the publisher, ruling that publishers do not have a legal duty to assure the accuracy of the books they publish. The Court of Appeals agreed:

> We conclude that the defendant has no duty to investigate the accuracy of the contents of the books it publishes. A publisher may of course assume such a burden, but there is nothing inherent in the role of publisher or the surrounding legal doctrines to suggest that such a duty should be imposed on publishers. . . .
> Were we tempted to create this duty, the gentle tug of the First Amendment and the values embodied therein would remind us of the social costs.[26]

What if the advice is entirely accurate but pertains to an illegal and intentionally harmful activity? Should communication of this kind be given the First Amendment shield of the *Brandenburg* incitement test? Or should this kind of speech be deemed undeserving of any First Amendment protection? Should the answer depend on the degree of detail in the advice? These were the issues in what has come to be known as the "Hit Man" case. A flight attendant was found dead in her Maryland home, shot through the eyes. Nearby were the bodies of her disabled 8-year-old son and a housekeeper, also brutally killed. Police soon traced the killings to the flight attendant's ex-husband and a contract killer he had hired, and the two men were convicted of the murders.

An interesting civil lawsuit arose from the slaying because when police searched the contract killer's home they found a copy of a book titled *Hit Man: A Technical Manual for Independent Contractors*. Published by Paladin Press of Colorado, it was a self-described "instruction book on murder" and contained step-by-step tips and diagrams on how to sneak into homes, kill with cruel certainty using a variety of weapons, and then avoid the law. It appeared that advice in the book had indeed been followed by the trigger man, so the family of the victims sued Paladin Press for aiding and abetting wrongful death.

Paladin argued that the book was mere entertainment or abstract advocacy that should be protected by the First Amendment under *Brandenburg v. Ohio*. But in 1997 a federal court of appeals disagreed, holding that the book's content was so detailed and coldly calculating that it became an integral part of the crime, undeserving of any First Amendment shield:

> Paladin's astonishing stipulations, coupled with the extraordinary comprehensiveness, detail, and clarity of Hit Man's instructions for criminal activity and murder in particular, the boldness of its palpable exhortation to murder, the alarming power and effectiveness of its peculiar form of instruction, the notable absence from its text of the kind of ideas for the protection of which the First Amendment exists, and the book's evident lack of any even arguably legitimate purpose beyond the promotion and teaching of murder, render this case unique in the law. In at least these circumstances, we are confident that the First Amendment does not erect the absolute bar to the imposition of civil liability.[27]

Absent First Amendment protection, Paladin agreed to pay a multimillion-dollar settlement in 1999, just days before a jury trial in the case was set to begin.

The Internet

Free-speech issues similar to those in the Hit Man case are arising with greater frequency on the Internet. Commonly referred to as "hate speech" and "extreme speech," the fundamental legal question is whether the online communication amounts to a "true threat" that should be regarded as a form of illegal conduct rather than protected expression.

The World Wide Web is home to thousands of sites dedicated to discrimination, violence, violent pornography, weapons, murder, suicide, and hate. Some of these sites actually urge violent acts or provide detailed instructions on how to commit violence, or both. Such sites have come under increasing public scrutiny, especially after the 1999 massacre at Colorado's Columbine High School, in which two students scattered bullets and bombs about the school, killing or wounding nearly 40 people before the two students committed suicide. One of the killers reportedly maintained a hate-filled website and accessed other sites that provided instructions on how to make pipe bombs.

A high-profile case involving extreme speech arose in Oregon when Planned Parenthood and several physicians sued a number of anti-abortion activists and groups that contributed information to a website called the "Nuremberg Files." The site labeled abortion providers as "baby butchers" and listed hundreds of abortion doctors and clinic staff members with such details as their home addresses, license-plate numbers, and the names of their spouses and children. Doctors who had been killed by anti-abortion activists were listed with lines through their names, and the names of wounded abortion providers were shown in gray type. Though the website did not expressly threaten anyone or urge specific, violent acts, the plaintiffs argued that a true threat was implicit. The plaintiffs sought, under a variety of state and federal statutes, damages and an injunction.

In 1999 a federal jury and judge sided with the plaintiffs. The jury awarded more than $107 million in damages to Planned Parenthood and the physicians, and the judge issued an injunction forbidding the defendant anti-abortion activists from providing any additional information about the plaintiffs or their families to the Nuremberg Files or any similar website. The federal district court judge held that, in light of the surrounding factual context of violent debate over abortion, the website did amount to a "true threat" to do bodily harm and that the threat was released into a known atmosphere of violence against abortion providers. Such personal threats are not protected by the First Amendment, the court held.[28] Defendants in the case vowed to appeal.

The Hypothetical

So, how about the call for a protest fast in the *Flat Rock* hypothetical? Could the newspaper and its editor be held liable for wrongful death? Presuming the court were to employ the modern version of the clear-and-present-danger standard, liability would be highly unlikely. First of all, implicit in the *Brandenburg* concept of incitement is the notion of immediacy. Though the editorial called for prompt action ("starting today," "begin now"), the nature of the medium lends itself to calm reflection on the reader's part, rather than an atmosphere of frenzy or impulsiveness. (In the *Hustler* magazine case, the federal court even raised the question of whether written material could ever be found to create culpable incitement.) Furthermore, it would be highly questionable whether the kind of harm that transpired was likely to occur as a result of the editorial.

Consider another hypothetical: How about manuals or videotapes containing highly specific information about physical behavior—information that is presented as fact and that both speaker and listener know is fully intended as guidance to be immediately followed. Examples might be manuals on safe sex, contraception, or first aid for snakebites. Suppose such a manual, through carelessness, contained a *should* where it was supposed to read *should not,* thereby causing harm to the reader? Should the writer be insulated from a tort case to any extent greater than if the advice had been given in person? Should it matter how the materials are distributed? What if the faulty advice were on a subscription website? [29]

Harm Through Advertising

Sometimes personal injury lawsuits are prompted by advertising content. Should the standard for liability be any different in such cases? Is advertising any less deserving of First Amendment protection than other kinds of speech? In lawsuits against the medium, as opposed to the advertiser, would it be fair to hold the medium accountable for the content of ads written by others?

Soldier of Fortune I

The 1989 case of *Eimann v. Soldier of Fortune Magazine, Inc.* raised these issues. The magazine, which focused on mercenary activities and military affairs, ran a classified ad that read as follows:

> EX-MARINES: 67–69 'Nam Vets, Ex-DI, weapons specialist—jungle warfare, pilot, M.E., high risk assignments, U.S. or overseas. [phone number]

A man named Hearn later testified that he placed the ad to recruit veterans for work as bodyguards and that "Ex-DI" meant ex-drill instructor, "M.E." meant multi-engine planes, and "high risk assignments" referred to security work. However, Hearn also stated that about 90 percent of those responding to the ad sought his help in illegal activities such as beatings, kidnappings, bombings, and murders. And that was the problem.

One caller proposed to pay Hearn $10,000 if he would kill the caller's wife. Hearn said he would consider it, and a few weeks later he did commit the slaying. Hearn was convicted and received a life sentence. But the incident also spawned a civil lawsuit against *Soldier of Fortune* by the son and the mother of the victim. Their claim: that the magazine negligently published the ad.

The plaintiffs presented evidence that as many as nine other classified ads in *Soldier of Fortune* had previously been tied to crimes or criminal plots around the country. This suggested that the magazine had reason to know that such ads, including those with ambiguous code words and abbreviations such as Hearn's, posed a threat to public safety. The jury agreed, and it awarded the plaintiffs $9 million in damages, based purely on a negligence standard.

A federal Court of Appeals reversed the judgment, however. Without deciding whether it was proper for the trial court to apply general negligence principles rather than a more protective First Amendment standard, the court ruled that even under negligence rules the magazine could not be held liable. By publishing this particular ad, the magazine did not fail to exercise reasonable care, the court held.

> SOF owed no duty to refrain from publishing a facially innocuous classified advertisement when the ad's context—at most—made its message ambiguous. [The ad's] bare terms reveal no identifiable offer to commit crimes, just as a locksmith's ad in the telephone director reveals nothing about that particular advertiser's willingness to commit burglaries or steal cars. . . . Without a more specific indication of illegal intent than Hearn's ad or its context provided, we conclude that SOF did not violate the required standard of conduct by publishing an ad that later played a role in criminal activity.[30]

Soldier of Fortune II

Soon *Soldier of Fortune* found itself in court again. And in 1993 a different federal Court of Appeals reached a different conclusion. This time the magazine was held accountable for publishing a classified ad that read as follows:

> GUN FOR HIRE: 37-year-old professional mercenary desires jobs. Vietnam veteran. Discreet and very private. Bodyguard, courier and other special skills. All jobs considered. [phone and P.O. box]

The sons of a slain businessman sued the magazine for negligence, claiming that their father's associate used the ad to arrange their father's brutal assassination and that the magazine should have foreseen this consequence. Again the magazine's defense was that it had no legal duty to investigate every advertiser and that the ad contained no identifiable risk that it was an offer to commit crimes. In this case, however, *Braun v. Soldier of Fortune Magazine, Inc.*, the court upheld a nearly $4.5 million jury verdict against the magazine.

The Court of Appeals upheld the judgment for the following reasons:

1. Unlike *Eimann,* the trial judge in *Braun* instructed the jury that it could hold the magazine liable only if the ad on its face contained a *clearly identifiable* unreasonable risk of harm to the public; this was the proper negligence standard.

2. The sinister language in the ad made it apparent there was a substantial danger of harm to the public; the magazine should have recognized this as a solicitation for illegal jobs involving a gun, "as readily as its readers obviously did."

3. Because the First Amendment does not protect commercial speech related to criminal activity, there was clearly no need to employ a heightened constitutional standard for liability (such as "incitement").

4. By instructing the jury that the magazine could be liable only if the ad *on its face* would have alerted a reasonable publisher to the danger, the magazine

would not suffer an impermissible "chilling effect" on speech. The court referred to this as a "modified" negligence standard that provided all the First Amendment protection necessary.[31]

As a general rule publishers and broadcasters are not considered liable for harm caused to individuals by advertised products and services (though the advertiser is within the chain of potential liability). This is because the media usually would have no reason to suspect that a particular product is defective. Only when the medium actually should have known of the danger can it be held accountable, and there is no legal duty to investigate all products and ad claims in advance. Courts have often noted that a rule to the contrary would open the doors to lawsuits that could not reasonably be anticipated and that such an economic burden on the media would adversely affect editorial content.[32]

When it should be clear from the face of an ad itself that it presents a public safety risk, the media that run the ad anyway may indeed be deemed negligent and potentially within the chain of liability. The *Soldier of Fortune* cases demonstrate that in such instances not all courts feel obliged to provide special First Amendment protection by requiring plaintiffs to meet the tougher incitement test.

Undoubtedly, the courts will continue to see many variations and twists on this basic personal injury theme in the years ahead. For example, one case concerned *Boy's Life* magazine and its publication of a special advertising supplement titled "The Shooting Sports: Aiming for Fun." Immediately after reading the supplement, a 12-year-old boy and several of his friends located a .22-caliber cartridge and an old rifle that belonged to one of their fathers. The rifle accidentally discharged, and the boy was killed. His mother sued the Boy Scouts, which publishes the magazine; Remington Arms Company, which advertised in the supplement; and the Shooting Sports Foundation, which sponsored the supplement. She alleged that her son was motivated to experiment with the rifle and cartridge as a direct result of negligent publication of the supplement in a magazine for young, impressionable readers.

In 1993 a Texas appellate court upheld summary judgment in favor of the defendants. The court held that the boy's "experimentation" with the rifle was not a reasonably foreseeable consequence of the publication. It noted that photos and features in the supplement emphasized adult supervision and the use of firearms in a structured, safety-conscious environment. Because the accident was not a foreseeable result, the defendants did not have a legal duty under negligence law to avoid such publications. The court barely mentioned the First Amendment, but it did note that truthful commercial advertising had been accorded some degree of constitutional protection by the U.S. Supreme Court.[33]

The standards for personal-injury cases against the media are not entirely settled. As we have seen, courts usually excuse the media from liability, either under basic negligence law principles or by applying a First Amendment buffer such as the *Brandenburg* incitement test. Media liability appears most likely in cases involving commercial advertising or promotions for hazardous and illegal products or services, where the danger is foreseeable to the media. Another area to watch—though rarely an issue for mainstream media—is hateful or depraved expression sufficiently detailed or targeted that it may constitute a threat of bodily harm. It remains unclear exactly when such speech will fall entirely outside the First Amendment, becoming subject to civil lawsuits and criminal statutes, and when it will qualify for some degree of First Amendment shield, such as the *Brandenburg* test.

Summary Points

The initial line of First Amendment cases considered by the Supreme Court dealt with speech that was aimed at arousing others to commit harmful acts. The Court used the standard of clear and present danger to determine when the speech posed a serious enough threat to be punishable by government.

Over time the constitutional standard for the government became tougher and thus the realm of protected speech greater. To be punishable, the court looked for incitement to imminent harmful conduct that was likely to occur.

In cases in which information dissemination might threaten national security, the courts have not employed the incitement standard. But neither has another specific test emerged. In the Supreme Courts' only national security case, that of the Pentagon Papers, the message was generally that the government would need to convince the Court of grave danger before a prior restraint could be valid.

The last fifteen years have seen an increase in tort cases against the media for personal harm relating to content. Though the U.S. Supreme Court has yet to enter this area, lower courts have often, though not always, employed the incitement test rather than allow liability on negligence alone.

The hypothetical at the beginning of this chapter presented three separate problems: a court order against publication of warplane information, a criminal prosecution for advocating violence, and a civil lawsuit by a distraught parent. The principles discussed in this chapter suggest that you should be safe from all three legal assaults. The court order is a classic prior restraint and, following the lead of the Pentagon Papers case, it would need to be supported by a clear and overriding national security threat that does not seem apparent from the facts in the hypothetical. The criminal prosecution could be successful only if the government could meet the constitutional test of showing incitement, and the wording of the newspaper editorial makes this highly unlikely. Finally, the negligence lawsuit would probably fail because of the plaintiff's inability to show that the editorial incited the girl's fasting.

Discussion Questions

1. Is it likely that the incitement test as stated in *Brandenburg v. Ohio* could ever be met by a mass media communication, as opposed to in-person, live expression? Or should the courts adopt a solid rule that impersonal expression through the mass media can never be deemed directly to incite hazardous behavior? Suppose, in the chapter hypothetical, that the editorial urging violence at the military base had aired live on TV and had urged citizens to act "now." Could that broadcast qualify as incitement?

2. The courts have on many occasions found manufacturers liable to consumers who were injured after relying on erroneous or misleading product instructions. Lawsuits based on faulty instructions are called *product liability* lawsuits. How are such cases distinguishable from the lawsuit against the publisher of *The Encyclopedia of Mushrooms*? Should the authors of product instructions have less constitutional or common law protection than the authors and publishers of books, where the "product" is the expression itself?

3. A few of the cases described in this chapter (the "Hit Man" and "Nuremberg Files") concerning highly detailed or personal information about how or whom to harm raise serious questions about the applicability of the *Brandenburg* test or any other First Amendment inquiry. Are there times when media content should amount to a criminal or civil violation of law without regard to the First Amendment?

Key Terms

clear and present danger
due care
Espionage Act
incitement standard
national security

negligence
reasonable care
Sedition Act
Smith Act

Web Resource

http://www-cse.stanford.edu/class/cs201/Projects/nuremberg-files
The Nuremberg Files (a case analysis by Stanford University students)

InfoTrac® College Edition

Many people are dismayed by what they believe is an increased tendency for motion pictures to portray violence and depravity in a manner that inspires, if not incites, copycat crimes. Yet few critics are able to suggest a workable legal mechanism to deal with the problem. Find two pieces of commentary regarding media content and harmful copycat behavior. Do either of them suggest ways the law might be changed to hold media accountable, or do they advise other, social rather than legal, tactics?

Chapter Outline

Damage to Reputation

Upon completing this chapter you should

- ☐ **appreciate** the justifications behind laws that aim to protect people's reputations.
- ☐ **know** the elements that libel or slander plaintiffs must prove to win a lawsuit against mass communicators.
- ☐ **know** the defenses and procedural rules that may protect mass communicators from libel and slander claims.
- ☐ **be able** to analyze a factual situation to determine whether a risk of libel or slander liability is present.
- ☐ **understand** why much sentiment exists for major reforms in this area of the law.

Hypothetical

■ The Disparaged Sheriff

You are the local advertising manager for a small daily newspaper. One afternoon during the political campaign season, you are visited by three members of a citizens' group called People Opposed to Scandal and Soft Enforcement (POSSE). The group, composed of business leaders, educators, political activists, and others concerned about crime, is opposing the reelection of local sheriff Angelo "Jake" DiPunto. The POSSE leaders ask you to run a half-page display ad that reads as follows:

> Enough already! Our community is one of history, pride, and decent people. But crime is taking that away from us. Violence, theft, drugs—crime has become an insidious cancer in our neighborhoods, and it's time to fight back!
>
> You can begin on election day by saying NO to another term for one of America's most vile and backward sheriffs, Jake DiPunto. At a time when we need leadership in law enforcement, we instead have a lazy, pathetic slob for a sheriff. He's had eight years to prove himself, but all he has proved is that he's more like a spineless politician than a leader for justice. How long will he keep looking the other way? The evidence makes us wonder, is he taking bribes? Join with the citizens of POSSE in voting out this sleazy man who himself may soon be indicted for crimes.

POSSE is an aggressive and outspoken organization, but also a reputable one, and you would run the political ad with a disclaimer reading "Political ad paid for by People Opposed to Scandal and Soft Enforcement." On the other hand, your own newspaper's reporters say they don't think the sheriff has ever been investigated for criminal activity, and you don't think the sheriff is a slob.

Under these circumstances, would publication of the ad present legal dangers for you? If so, what specific changes would you require before accepting the ad?

Evolution of Defamation Law

For many centuries, in cultures around the globe, humanity has recognized the importance of an individual's reputation. Reputation is what a person is seen to be in the eyes of others—the individual's projection of self within a society. Resting upon this projection are personal dignity and honor and, oftentimes, extensive tangible benefits such as patronage in the marketplace. A good reputation may be the fruit of prolonged dedication and hard work, whether in a trade or in the building of personal relationships.

Yet, however well it may have been nurtured, a reputation can be poisoned by rumors or, in modern times, shattered literally overnight by accusations in the mass media. This is why most countries have long had laws against what is now called **defamation**—an attack upon the reputation of another person.

Historically, many of these laws were harsh indeed. United States defamation law can be traced to England's infamous Court of the Star Chamber, established in the late 1400s to take a tough stand on law and order. The Star Chamber, sitting without a jury, punished defamation by ordering money payments to the defamed party and by maiming and imprisoning the guilty. That the defamatory statements might be true was no defense. This harsh system of "justice" was replaced by a practice hardly more civilized—the medieval tradition of dueling to vindicate honor.

Through the centuries the laws protecting reputation have been refined, and in most cultures the penalties are imposed with greater restraint than the Star Chamber exhibited. Yet the underlying sentiment for defamation laws remains strong. Wrote Justice Potter Stewart of the United States Supreme Court: "The rights of a man to the protection of his own reputation from unjustified invasion and wrongful hurt reflects no more than our basic concept of the essential dignity and worth of every human being—a concept at the root of any decent system of ordered liberty."[1] Furthermore, the penalties today may still be harsh—financially. In 1990 a lawyer who sued the *Philadelphia Inquirer,* claiming he had been defamed by a series of articles, won a whopping $34 million in damages from a Pennsylvania jury. As the decade and the century drew to a close, jury awards for defamation were commonly exceeding a million dollars.

Some legal scholars have predicted that the emerging laws of privacy or mental distress (discussed in the next chapter) eventually will eclipse defamation law, but today the relatively ancient laws of defamation still pose the most pervasive legal threat to American media. And even though media defendants ultimately win most defamation lawsuits, the costs of defending in court may run into the hundreds of thousands, even millions, of dollars.

Development by the States

From the beginning of this nation, defamation law fell almost exclusively under the domain of the various states, not the federal government. And in most respects the states adopted their rules from the English common law. For more than 150 years the various states compiled, unfettered, an enormous body of law pertaining to civil and criminal defamation. Primarily through court decisions, and occasionally through legislation, there evolved a complicated web of defamation rules involving careful distinctions and a list of legal terminology all its own. Some of the time-honored rules were of questionable value by mid–twentieth century, however. Wrote law professor William Prosser in his authoritative treatise on torts: "It must be confessed at the beginning that there is a great deal of the law of defamation which makes no sense."[2]

Libel versus Slander

By mid–seventeenth century in England two separate branches of defamation law had evolved: **libel,** which was written defamation, and **slander,** which was spoken defamation. The various states carried the distinction forward in this country. Since people seemed all too eager to run to the courts and sue one another for spoken insults, and since the spoken words were fleeting in nature, the courts set stricter rules of proof for people complaining of slander. Also, only specified kinds of defamatory remarks could be grounds for a lawsuit.

In contrast, written defamation tended to be longer lasting and more broadly distributed (and was therefore considered more harmful); it involved more premeditation on the defendant's part and it was of course easier to prove. Therefore, in libel cases the balance of fairness was seen to weigh more heavily on the plaintiff's side. Thus libel lawsuits were permitted in a broader range of accusations, and injury to the plaintiff often was presumed, without proof.

Eventually, however, the rules of libel and slander began to converge. In the United States today the libel/slander distinction has all but disappeared. The only significant remnant found in some states is a requirement that slander plaintiffs prove some financial injury in order to recover any damages—a burden usually not required of plaintiffs in libel cases.

Further blurring the distinction today is that defamation in the electronic media is not easy to categorize as either libel or slander. Statements made on a radio program are more fleeting than those in print—a characteristic of slander. But they are capable of very broad dissemination and usually involve premeditation—characteristics of libel. In most states today, the rule is that defamation by way of any mass medium is considered libel, though some states, including California, do classify broadcast defamation as slander. This book will use the term *libel* to refer generally to libel and slander.

Crimes and Torts

In the eighteenth and nineteenth centuries most defamation law, in the colonies and then the states, was criminal. The government prosecuted instances of defamation, and punishment could be particularly harsh for seditious libel—disparaging remarks about government officials—as noted in Chapter 2. Over time, however, most of the action shifted to the civil arena where, treating libel and slander as torts, individuals could sue to collect money for the harm suffered. By the mid-1900s, defamation had evolved almost entirely into a matter of civil law.

The Constitution Intervenes

Amazingly, it was not until 1964 that a direct confrontation with the First Amendment altered the course of common law defamation. The alteration came through a U.S. Supreme Court case called *New York Times v. Sullivan,* and it began the era of defamation law that continues today. It is an era marked by the injection of constitutional free expression safeguards into defamation law across the land. It is an era of careful balancing between reputation rights and First Amendment principles of free expression, an era of increasing constitutionalization of defamation law.

During the colonial era it was juries, interestingly, that came to the rescue of the media and began to insulate them from authoritarian courts. In the celebrated 1735 trial of printer John Peter Zenger, for example, a New York jury refused to convict for seditious libel, despite the letter of the law. Today, however, it is often the courts, injecting constitutional safeguards, that give the media some protection *from* juries.

Application of the First Amendment also has furthered the decline of criminal prosecutions for defamation. The U.S. Supreme Court has never ruled that criminal defamation statutes are, per se, unconstitutional, and in almost half the states criminal statutes remain on the books. But, just eight months after it entered the defamation field with *New York Times v. Sullivan,* the Court reversed a criminal defamation conviction and significantly limited the reach of criminal defamation statutes.[3] Criminal defamation prosecutions, already rare and unpopular by the 1960s, now are constitutionally suspect as well.[4]

Though civil libel lawsuits are a pervasive threat to mass communicators, very few libel cases today actually go to trial. Rather, they are frequently dismissed on summary judgment in favor of the media, often on constitutional grounds. However, when libel cases do go before a jury, the media stand a good chance of losing large judgments. For example, the Libel Defense Resource Center reported that in 1998 there were just sixteen libel trials nationwide against mass media defendants. But the media lost half of those cases, and the average jury verdict against the media was $1.3 million.

Ingredients for a Lawsuit

Not all disparaging remarks about a person amount to a tort of libel. For our purposes, libel may be more fully defined as a false statement of fact that is disseminated about a person and that tends to injure that person's reputation.[5] This working definition adds insights to the tort, but it is just a beginning. To truly understand the likelihood and validity of libel claims, it is important to view libel as a tort composed of six main elements. A libel plaintiff usually must prove all six elements in order to win a case against a mass medium or individual communicator. (It is said that the plaintiff has the "burden of proof" in these elements.) The elements are

1. defamatory content,
2. falsity,
3. publication,
4. identification,
5. fault, and
6. harm.

Defamatory Content

To win a lawsuit, a libel plaintiff must pinpoint the specific defamatory content that is the source of complaint. Regardless of the form of the communication, this content often is referred to as the *defamatory statement.*

The Meaning of "Defamatory"

Defamatory content is that which would tend to injure the plaintiff's reputation among some respectable segments of society. Typically it is statements that call into question an individual's honesty, integrity, professional competence, sanity, solvency, morality, or social refinement. The *Second Restatement of the Law of Torts,* a definitive treatise that serves as a model for the states, says: "A communication is defamatory if it tends so to harm the reputation of another as to lower him in the estimation of the community or to deter third persons from associating or dealing with him."[6]

Threat to Reputation

Note that a statement is not considered defamatory simply because the affected person doesn't agree with it, doesn't like it, is embarrassed by it, or believes that it is less than accurate. The statement must tend to injure reputation. When analyzing a potential libel situation, the first thing communicators should do is determine whether there is indeed some defamatory content.

In most cases a defamatory statement is recognizable as defamatory "on its face." This means that no additional information is needed in order to convey defamatory meaning. Such language is also referred to as *libel per se.* Examples: accusations that a banker "has ties to organized crime," that a physician "is an alcoholic," that a public official "takes bribes" (as in the chapter hypothetical), that a college student "has AIDS," or that a married person is "out having affairs" (Exhibit 4.1, pages 106–107).

Such factors as geographical location, historical period, and the nature of the audience may have some bearing in determining whether words are considered defamatory on their face. For example, a charge that a minister has "lost his faith" might cause his congregation to dismiss him, whereas he might suffer little or no reputational damage in society at large. Similarly, in many communities falsely asserting that someone is a homosexual might be defamatory, but it might not be deemed defamatory within a community with a large gay population.

Sometimes, however, a defamatory statement is present even though the defamatory meaning is not apparent on its face. The defamatory meaning comes into focus only when considered in light of additional facts. Such language is sometimes called *libel per quod.* For example, a false and unauthorized newspaper report that a college student has given birth to twins would not, on its face, be considered defamatory. The student might be bothered and inconvenienced by the report, but reputational harm would not be a natural result. Acquaintances would tend to send congratulation cards. However, the report would become defamatory if readers know that the plaintiff's husband is in the Navy, that he has been stationed overseas for the past thirteen months, and that she has not seen him during that time.

Though libel claims usually are based on verbal accusations, this is not a requirement. The notion of a defamatory statement must be considered more broadly. Photographs and cartoons (either alone or in combination with captions or narration) and gestures (of a TV news anchor, for example) also could qualify as defamatory statements. Particularly in this era of computer-generated images, defamation through modified pictures is a danger. Such would be the case if two photographs, one of a local banker and one of an organized crime figure, were blended to make it look as though the two people were conversing on a secluded park bench.

Living Persons and Businesses

Any living individual can be defamed and can sue for libel. However, lawsuits cannot be maintained on behalf of people who were deceased at the time of publication. The rationale for this, of course, is that a dead person probably will not suffer from a tarnished reputation in society. Libel is considered a personal tort, and it is often said that the ability to sue dies along with the potential plaintiff.

Communicators must be careful, however, because derogatory comments about deceased people sometimes may also defame the living. An example of this might be an erroneous report that a fraternity member's deceased roommate had had AIDS. The living fraternity member might sue on his own behalf.

In addition to individuals, many kinds of formal business, charitable, and labor entities can be defamed and have been allowed to sue for libel in their own names. These include profit-making and nonprofit corporations, partnerships, and labor unions. Therefore, statements that a corporation's pricing policies are fraudulent could injure the corporate reputation and could lead to a libel lawsuit by the corporation. These entities, as such, are not defamed by statements about individual employees or officers, however, unless the accusations also cast aspersions upon the entity's conduct.

Are business entities or individuals within them defamed by negative statements about the company's products? As a general rule, no. To defame the manufacturer, comments about the product would have to be so negative as to imply deceit by company officials, for example. Saying that a product is poorly made or unequal to the competition is not enough to defame the manufacturer. However, a specialized tort called **trade libel** or **product disparagement** may apply in these circumstances. This tort allows companies to recover for false statements about the nature of their products. Although the elements of this tort are the same as those for personal libel in most respects, trade libel is a less attractive claim for plaintiffs because damage awards are usually limited strictly to direct, monetary loss.[7]

In the 1990s more than a dozen states passed special product disparagement statutes giving farmers and food companies a right to sue when their food products are publicly and falsely criticized. The impetus for the laws was a CBS News *60 Minutes* segment in 1989 that linked cancer with the chemical Alar, which some apple farmers sprayed on their trees. The demand for apples plummeted following

EXHIBIT 4.1   *Words of Warning*

The following list of selected words and phrases can spark libel lawsuits and/or demands for retraction. These "warning" words or phrases should be scrutinized carefully before publishing or broadcasting.

abortion	brothel	delinquent	herpes
abuse	bulimic	derelict	hit man
abuser	bum	devil worship	Hitlerian
accomplice	buys votes	disbarred	HIV positive
addict		disorderly house	homosexual
adopted	call girl	double-crosser	hooker
adulteration of products	charged	drug addict	hypocrite
adultery	cheats	drug dealer	
AIDS	collusion	drunkard	idiot
alcoholic	communist (or red)	DUI	illegal
altered records	compulsive liar		illegitimate
Alzheimer's	con		illicit relations
ambulance chaser	con artist	evil	immoral
anorexic	confidence man	ex-convict	incompetent
arrested	conspirator		indicted
ass	convicted	fag	industrial espionage
atheist	correspondent	fairy	infidelity
attempted suicide	corrupt	fascist	informer
	corruption	felon	insane
bad moral character	cosa nostra	fired	insider trading
bagman	coward	fix	insolvent
bankrupt	crazy	fixed	intimate
bigamist	crime family	flim flam	intolerance
bilk	criminal	flit	
bimbo	cronyism	fraud	jerk
bisexual	crook		junkie
blackmail	crooks	gambling house	
bootlegger	cult	gangster	kept woman
brainwash		gay	kinky
bribery	deadbeat	graft	Ku Klux Klan
	defaulter	guilty	

the broadcast, and some apple growers went bankrupt.[8] The new "veggie libel" laws, as they are sometimes called, give the producers of disparaged food products a right to sue even if no particular producer or food company is criticized. Television talk-show host Oprah Winfrey was sued by Texas cattlemen under such a statute following a 1996 broadcast suggesting that it was dangerous to eat U.S. beef because of Mad Cow Disease.

liar	Peeping Tom	scam	suicide
lies	perjurer	scandalmonger	swindle
live-in friend	pervert	scoundrel	swindler
	pimp	seducer	
Mafia	pirate	sexual harassment	thief
malfeasance	plagiarist	sharp dealing	thug
malpractice	pockets public funds	short in accounts	traitor
mental disease	profiteering	shyster	
misappropriated funds	prostitute	sleazebag	unethical
mobster	pusher	slumlord	unmarried mother
moral delinquency	pyramid scheme	slush fund	unprofessional
		slut	unscrupulous
Nazi	quack	sneak	unsound mind
necrophiliac	queer	sodomist	unworthy of credit
		sold influence	
overdose	racist	sold out	V.D.
	racketeer	spy	vice den
paramour	rapist	stool pigeon	
paranoid	rip off	street person	whore
patronage		stuffed the ballot	widow robber
payoff	satanism	box	witch
	scab	stupid	

Any other words or expressions imputing:

- a loathsome disease;
- a crime or words falsely charging arrest, indictment for, or confession or conviction of a crime;
- anti-Semitism or other imputation of religious, racial, or ethnic intolerance;
- connivance or association with criminals;
- lying;
- involvement in a racket or complicity in a swindle;
- membership in an organization which may be in ill repute at a given period of time;
- financial embarrassment or any implication of insolvency or want of credit;
- unwillingness or refusal to pay or evading payment of a debt;
- poverty or squalor.

Copyright © 1990 by the law firm of King & Ballow. Reprinted with permission. King & Ballow, with offices in Tennessee and California, concentrates its practice in communications law.

Unlike corporations, government entities are not permitted to sue for libel. Individual government officials, however, are capable of being defamed and often do sue for libel.

Interpreting the Statements   Often the meaning of language is unclear, and a statement may be susceptible to two or more interpretations, only one of which is defamatory. In such cases a jury ultimately determines the precise sense in which a statement was likely to be understood. When interpreting potentially defamatory statements, the courts will look to overall context and the natural effect of language as guidelines.

Overall Context

First, statements should be considered in light of their overall context. This means that courts will not simply scrutinize the literal meaning of words in isolation or out of context. Rather, the language will be examined in light of the entire article or story, sometimes even in light of the overall nature of a publication or broadcast program. For example, a Texas sheriff sued for libel over a book passage about a shooting that described him as "the police executioner."[9] But this was held not to be defamatory because the overall context clearly described the shooting as an act of justifiable self-defense.

While overall context can help erase a defamatory impression in some cases, context in other instances can have the opposite effect of inflaming what otherwise might be a passage of insignificant defamatory effect. This may be especially true in television and other dramatic, high-tech media. As one federal court explained:

> Television broadcasts add new and potentially significant variables to the defamation analysis. Courts must scrutinize the juxtaposition of the audio and video portions of a television program. In subtle ways, a television director can alter the tone of an otherwise innocuous broadcast. With the emerging popularity of self-styled "magazine" news programs, courts should be sensitive to the possibility that a transcript which appears relatively mild on its face may actually be, when the total mix of creative ingredients are considered, highly toxic. Indeed, a clever amalgamation of half-truths and opinion-like statements, adorned with orchestrated images and dramatic video accompaniment, can be devastating when packaged in the powerful television medium.[10]

Special Problem: Headlines   Though context is typically considered when determining defamatory content, courts have been inconsistent in their approach to headlines. Bold and sketchy by their very nature, headlines are frequently the source of anger for the subjects of articles and thus the impetus for lawsuits as well. Some courts have employed the general rule of considering the overall article to determine whether the headline was a defamatory communication.[11] Others have scrutinized a headline as it stands alone, on the rationale that newspaper readers often have only the time or interest to read the headline and not the story.[12] So, while overall context usually is considered when determining the existence of defamation, you should presume that headlines and titles alone may be deemed defamatory, even if the body of the accompanying article is accurate and inoffensive. A recent federal appeals case makes this clear.

One week after the famous O.J. Simpson murder trial ended in his acquittal in 1995, the front page of the *National Examiner* proclaimed in a headline "Cops Think Kato Did It!" The headline referred to Brian "Kato" Kaelin, who became publicly known during the trial as the long-term guest at Simpson's estate. Actually, police did not think Kaelin committed the murders, and neither did the *Examiner,* apparently. The text of the story made it clear that "it" in the headline referred not to the murders, but rather to lying on another point. Kaelin sued the tabloid for libel, seeking $15 million. The *Examiner* sought summary judgment, claiming that the full published story protected the paper.

In an important decision, however, the U.S. 9th Circuit Court of Appeals ruled that headlines alone can be libelous. The court said a reader could reasonably interpret the *Examiner's* headline to mean that police suspect Kaelin committed the slayings of Nicole Brown Simpson and Ronald Goldman. It was for a jury to decide whether the headline alone was indeed libelous and malicious, the court said.[13] In 1999 the parties agreed to a settlement.

Natural Effect

As a second and related guideline to context, statements should be analyzed for their natural effect on the average reader or listener. Potential libel plaintiffs often attach hypersensitive, even neurotic, meanings to statements about them in the mass media. When determining whether a defamatory statement has been made, however, it is not the plausible meaning advanced by the plaintiff that is determinative. Rather, it is the statement's natural and probable effect upon the mind of the average reader or listener. During prepublication review, communicators should ask "How would most people understand this?"

For example, language that an average person would understand purely as a joke, satire, or **rhetorical hyperbole** (emotional, exaggerated name-calling) is regarded as nondefamatory. This is because the listener or reader knows the statements don't amount to anything, that they are not to be taken literally. Therefore statements that a police officer was a "clown and a big, fat ape,"[14] and references to a TV talk-show guest as a "fat bitch" and a "pair of tits with legs"[15] were held nondefamatory. Jokes, put-downs, and unflattering nicknames may generate amusement within an audience, but such expression typically does not damage the subject's reputation.

However, if statements of ridicule also imply sincere and specific allegations, the communicator cannot escape liability by claiming they were intended in jest. It is the natural understanding of the proverbial reasonable person that is controlling.

Defaming by Implication

The principle of natural effect is also illustrated by a developing area of the law referred to as **libel by implication.** This occurs when the individual statements communicated are literally true or nondefamatory, but taken together they leave the ordinary audience member with a false and defamatory conclusion.

In *Newton v. National Broadcasting Company* a federal court concluded that just such an implication arose from an NBC *Nightly News* story aired in 1980. The script read in part as follows:

[Guido] Penosi is a New York hoodlum from the Gambino Mafia family, a man with a long criminal record, now believed to be the Gambino family's man on the West Coast, in the narcotics business, and also in show business. Penosi is also a key figure in a federal grand jury investigation . . . that involves one of the big casinos here [Las Vegas], the Aladdin; and one of Las Vegas' top performers, singer Wayne Newton. . . . [L]ast week, Newton and a partner were given state approval to buy the Aladdin Hotel in Las Vegas for $85 million. A federal grand jury is now investigating the role of Guido Penosi and the mob in Newton's deal for the Aladdin. Despite his big income, authorities say Newton has had financial problems. Investigators say that last year, just before Newton announced he would buy the Aladdin, Newton called Guido Penosi for help with a problem. Investigators say whatever the problem was, it was important enough for Penosi to take it up with leaders of the Gambino family in New York. Police in New York say that this mob boss, Frank Piccolo, told associates that he had taken care of Newton's problem and had become a hidden partner in the Aladdin Hotel deal.[16]

Literally speaking, almost all the individual facts reported by NBC were true. However, the problem for which Newton contacted Penosi, as it turned out, was that members of an organized crime syndicate had directed threats at Newton and his daughter. Newton asked Penosi if he could stop the threats. Penosi in turn contacted Piccolo, who arranged with another family, which was threatening Newton, to stop the threats.

The District Court ruled that quite a different implication arose from the story, however:

> The clear and inescapable impression made by the broadcast was that the plaintiff did not have enough money to buy the Aladdin Hotel so he called a friend, Guido Penosi, who had ties to organized crime; and that Mr. Penosi helped him raise the money and thus obtained a hidden interest in the Aladdin Hotel.[17]

This impression was defamatory, the court ruled, because arranging for someone to obtain a hidden interest in a casino is a crime. (Newton ultimately lost in the Court of Appeals on other grounds.)

Thoughts, Not Mere Words

Many libel experts have compiled lists of words and expressions that have generated lawsuits or that have indeed been held defamatory in some court. The purpose of such lists is to help communicators see the kinds of language that should raise red flags. One such list, Exhibit 4.1, appeared in this chapter. It is important to remember, however, that the element of defamatory content actually concerns the particular thoughts delivered to an audience. Words are but one tool for conveying thoughts, and words themselves are subject to differing meanings. To quote Justice Oliver Wendell Holmes: "A word is not a crystal, transparent and unchanged; it is the skin of a living thought and may vary greatly in color and content according to the circumstances and the time in which it is used."[18]

Therefore, an exhaustive list of defamatory words and "safe" words would be impossible to compile. And communicators should not screen for defamatory content based on a rigid list of memorized language. Defamatory meaning is determined by the particular circumstances of the communication, including the environment in which the statements were made and who the target of the offending language happens to be. Language deemed nondefamatory in one setting might indeed be defamatory in another. And even where the circumstances are nearly identical, different jurisdictions occasionally may reach different conclusions.

You need to keep sight of the underlying rationale for libel law and recognize important distinctions in differing factual settings. For example, in one case an article/illustration left readers with the impression that a particular trucking company was going out of business. This was held to be defamatory.[19] On the other hand, a premature report that an individual had died was held not to be defamatory *per se*.[20] How might these differing results be explained? Why is an erroneous report of a business's demise more likely to be defamatory than a false announcement of an individual's demise?

What about the hypothetical problem at the beginning of this chapter? Would the disparaged sheriff have any difficulty identifying defamatory content in the newspaper ad? No. Virtually all of the accusations would be understood as sincere allegations and would tend to lower the reputation of a sheriff. Most damning are suggestions that the sheriff is probably taking bribes and may soon be indicted. The terms *spineless, vile, sleazy, lazy,* and *slob* might be deemed mere rhetorical hyperbole in other contexts, but given the grave tenor of this ad, they may be taken as serious allegations here. *Spineless* would not be taken literally, of course, but could reasonably be understood to convey the idea that the sheriff lacks courage and is manipulated by criminals. Similarly, the term *sleazy* in this context might suggest someone with shoddy morals and imply criminal wrongdoing. Many of the accusations would be defamatory, then, suggesting criminal activity and incompetence, and the sheriff would have the first ingredient for a successful libel claim. This does not mean, however, that we can pronounce him the winner of a libel lawsuit.

Falsity

In addition to being defamatory in nature, statements also must be false in order to support a libel lawsuit. This has long been the prevailing view in the United States. Often in libel lawsuits, however, the truth or falsity of the derogatory accusations is murky. Evidence is provided on both sides. Therefore, a key question is who has the burden of proof. Must the plaintiff convince, by a majority of the evidence, that the statements are false? Or must the defendant muster the majority of evidence and thus prove truth?

**Burden
of Proof**

Technically speaking, the traditional common law rule in America was that truth was a defense to libel. This meant it was the libel defendant's burden to raise the question of truth and to prove it by a majority of the evidence. If this could be done, in most states truth was a complete defense to libel, even if the offensive statements were born from malicious intent. But in the modern era of constitutionalization, U.S. Supreme Court rulings have shifted the burden in most cases to the plaintiff to prove falsity.

The Court addressed this issue directly in the 1986 case of *Philadelphia Newspapers, Inc. v. Hepps.* Hepps was the primary owner of a corporation that franchised a chain of snack stores. The *Philadelphia Inquirer* published a series of articles suggesting that Hepps and the company were linked to organized crime. Hepps and the corporation sued for libel, but the Pennsylvania courts disagreed over which side had the burden of proof on the question of truth or falsity.

In a 5–4 decision, the U.S. Supreme Court held that libel plaintiffs must shoulder the burden of proving falsity, at least when the speech in question relates to a matter of public concern—as almost all mass media content does. This made falsity one of the libel elements that a plaintiff must prove. This burden can be the deciding factor whenever the factual evidence in a case is ambiguous. Justice Sandra Day O'Connor recognized this and wrote for the majority: ". . . [W]here the scales [of evidence on truth or falsity] are in such an uncertain balance, we believe that the Constitution requires us to tip them in favor of protecting true speech."[21] This is necessary, she wrote, to ensure that true speech on matters of public concern is not deterred simply because the speaker might have difficulty proving truth in court.

In the dissenting opinion, Justice John Paul Stevens called the majority ruling a "blueprint for character assassination" and a "wholly unwarranted protection for malicious gossip."[22] Stevens thought that the Court's existing fault standards, discussed later in this chapter, already were enough of a burden on libel plaintiffs and that unscrupulous communicators might now be tempted to tell deliberate lies, knowing that some lies are very difficult to prove false. For the majority, however, the burden of proving falsity was simply a logical extension of the existing requirement that the defendant be proved at fault.

This is an interesting and important philosophical argument, as well as a procedural one. In practice, however, communicators should not feel overly secure in the fact that falsity has been added as a plaintiff's burden at trial. The fact is that clear, provable truth is the best deterrent to a libel lawsuit and one of the best ways to win one. And should a controversy actually reach the courtroom, communicators will need to answer the plaintiff's claim of falsity with their own evidence of truth.

**How False
Must It Be?**

How false must a communication be in order for the plaintiff to win on this point? It is not necessary that material be precisely accurate in every detail in order to be protected from libel. The question is whether the material is substantially false or substantially true. A communication remains substantially true if it is accurate as to those assertions that go to the heart of the defamation alleged—even though relatively minor, accompanying facts may turn out to be false.

For example, suppose you write that a particular chemical company illegally dumped toxic wastes into Trout River on April 24. You'd better be correct about the allegations that toxins were dumped into that river, by that chemical company, and that the action was illegal. However, if you were wrong about the date—the chemicals were dumped on April 26, not 24—your story still would be considered substantially true in the eyes of the law. The portions of your account that are truly reputation-threatening are true.

Special Problem: Fact versus Opinion

Implicit in the constitutional requirement that statements considered libelous must be proven false is also the requirement that the statements indeed lend themselves to a truth-or-falsehood determination. In other words, as a logical outgrowth of the requirement that libel claims be based on falsehoods, it is also required that the complained-of statements be allegations of fact, not mere judgment or opinion that cannot be proven true or false.

For decades a **fair comment privilege** has been recognized under common law. The privilege allows the media to make "good-faith" critiques of speeches, plays, books, and other matters of general public interest. This important but relatively narrow common law privilege has in most cases been eclipsed, however, by the broader, constitutionally based standards for libel articulated by the U.S. Supreme Court. Today, good faith or not, expressions of pure judgment are not subject to libel lawsuits. (Other common law privileges will be discussed in a later section.)

In recent years media defendants increasingly have won early summary judgments in libel cases because judges have declared the offending statements to be protected opinion rather than assertions of fact. This fact/opinion distinction has become so important in the disposition of libel cases that it was made an explicit part of this book's working libel definition (a false statement *of fact* disseminated about a person that tends to injure that person's reputation). The problem, however, is that this is a distinction far more difficult than it first appears.

Scope of Protected Opinion

The constitutional protection for opinion is substantial, but it is not so broad as to automatically protect all statements that happen to be labeled "opinion" or are preceded by the words *I think*. According to the Supreme Court, the issue is whether the statement in question has some specific, factual content, so that a plaintiff could prove it false as required under *Hepps*. This was made clear by the Supreme Court in the 1990 case of *Milkovich v. Lorain Journal Co.,* where the court admonished the lower courts for interpreting too broadly the scope of constitutionally protected opinion.

The case was filed by a high school wrestling coach, Milkovich, whose team had been involved in a brawl and then placed on probation by a state athletic association. In a legal proceeding successfully challenging the probation, Milkovich testified about his role in the altercation. In the following day's newspaper, sports columnist Ted Diadiun, who had witnessed the brawl and the testimony, wrote that Milkovich had "lied at the hearing"[23] in order to avoid the probation. The column appeared under the standing title *TD Says.* . . .

Milkovich sued for libel, but the Ohio appellate court ruled that the accusation of lying, in light of its context in a piece of commentary, was constitutionally protected opinion. The U.S. Supreme Court reversed, and in the majority opinion Chief Justice William Rehnquist wrote:

> Expressions of "opinion" may often imply an assertion of objective fact.
>
> If a speaker says, "In my opinion John Jones is a liar," he implies a knowledge of facts which lead to the conclusion that Jones told an untruth. . . . Simply couching such statements in terms of opinion does not dispel these implications; and the statement, "In my opinion Jones is a liar," can cause as much damage to reputation as the statement, "Jones is a liar." . . .
>
> . . . *Hepps* ensures that a statement of opinion relating to matters of public concern which does not contain a provably false factual connotation will receive full constitutional protection. . . .
>
> We are not persuaded that . . . an additional separate constitutional privilege for "opinion" is required to ensure freedom of expression. . . .[24]

The chief justice then wrote that the key questions were simply (1) whether the column reasonably implied that Milkovich actually lied in court (as opposed to the column's making that allegation in pure jest), and (2) whether the charge is sufficiently factual to be proved true or false. Rehnquist concluded it was.

Application of the Principle

Under the constitutional rule, then, it is important to isolate the defamatory statement and ask whether it states or implies a provably false assertion of fact. Suppose someone writes that a professional football coach is part of an illegal gambling operation and bets thousands of dollars on his games. These are verifiable assertions of fact, and they could be the basis for a libel lawsuit. On the other hand, suppose someone writes that the coach is one of the ugliest men in professional sports. This most likely becomes a protected expression of opinion—a loose, judgmental statement that cannot be proven one way or the other by reference to some accepted standard.

Between these examples, though, lies a vast, murky area where context may indeed be important because of the need to determine the sense in which words were used. Is it a provably false assertion of fact to label someone an idiot? witch? fascist? racist? traitor? The answer is, it depends.

While *Milkovich* made it clear that the context of an opinion column does not automatically protect the otherwise factual allegations therein, context may nevertheless be critical to determining the sense in which words were used. Just as we considered context to determine if words were used in a reputation-reducing sense, we must now consider context to see if words were used in a factual sense. Specifically, in murky cases the courts are likely to consider such factors as the common usage of the challenged language; the type of column, book, or program in which the statement appears; and the broader social circumstances in which the statement was made.[25] Some examples of recent opinion rulings:

In a high school newspaper, a math teacher was described as a "babbler" and "the worst teacher" at the school. The teacher sued the school district, the principal, the newspaper adviser, and the students who made and reported the statements. In 1990 a California court held the statements to be incapable of being proved true or false, and thus protected opinion under the First Amendment.[26]

The former principal of an elementary school sued parents over statements that were made during a campaign to remove her. One parent told reporters that the principal was "insensitive" to the needs of the community and that she was a "racist." A federal court held these assertions to be constitutionally protected opinion in this context, merely forms of name-calling that were not objectively verifiable. On the other hand, assertions that the principal was "sick" and "under a doctor's care" and that she was "using an illegal testing system" were deemed statements of fact. They were of precise meaning and were objectively verifiable, the court said, and thus could be grounds for a libel lawsuit.[27]

A Texas television station prepared an investigative report on the work habits of Dallas County's criminal district court judges by obtaining courthouse parking records. The aired report stated that "records suggest" a particular judge leaves the courthouse early 67 percent of the time, works only a half day 50 percent of the time, and appears to work an average work week of about 27 hours. The caveat "records suggest" does not insulate appellants' statements as protected opinion, a Texas appellate court ruled, because the statements in the investigative report nevertheless implied verifiable assertions of fact.[28]

Now reconsider the hypothetical at the beginning of this chapter, keeping the Supreme Court's *Milkovich* approach in mind. Which statements about the sheriff are protected opinion and which are factual assertions that may lead to liability?

A good case could be made that some of the terms used in the ad are too judgmental to be provable as false—terms such as *lazy, slob,* and *spineless politician.* Normally, these are words with no objective standards for meaning. However, some danger exists that, in the context of this ad, the term *spineless* might reasonably be understood to imply specific, underlying facts, such as collaboration with criminals. This potential problem can be avoided in many cases if writers simply make known the underlying bases for their conclusions (for example, "He's a spineless politician because his stands on the issues are not tough enough"). In the hypothetical, two of the remaining allegations—that the sheriff appears to take bribes and may soon be indicted—are almost certainly factual assertions that would support a lawsuit under the *Milkovich* test.

Determining that certain statements are protected as opinion under the law does not necessarily mean that the language is acceptable under standards of professional ethics, of course. Profane or emotional mudslinging is generally avoided by mainstream media unless it appears in a highly newsworthy quotation. Furthermore, audiences are ethically entitled to know the grounds for opinions expressed by mass communicators—a major problem with the ad in the chapter hypothetical.

State Protection of Opinion

Although in *Milkovich* the Supreme Court said there is no blanket First Amendment protection for otherwise factual-sounding statements that appear in opinion contexts, the states are free to add such protection if they wish — or at least some degree of contextual protection beyond the constitutional minimum articulated in *Milkovich*.

In 1991 New York state's highest court became the first specifically to disagree with the *Milkovich* approach and to add contextual protection for opinion under state law. The New York case arose when a medical company sued over a letter published in a scientific journal that criticized the company's treatment of research animals. The court ruled that letters to the editor and other forms of commentary automatically deserve greater protection from libel lawsuits because the context in which they appear makes it clear that they tend to convey opinion more than fact. Wrote the court: "We believe that an analysis that begins by looking at the context of the whole communication, its tone and apparent purpose, better balances the values at stake than an analysis that first examines the challenged statements for expressed and implied factual assertions."[29]

Publication

Because libel law is intended to protect reputation, it is a logical requirement of the tort that the defamatory statement be disseminated to people other than the plaintiff. To win a libel suit, the plaintiff must show that the defendant intentionally communicated the defamatory statements to at least one other person, the so-called third person.

This dissemination element, called **publication** in libel law terminology, is relatively straightforward, and in mass communication cases it is rarely an issue. In most libel lawsuits against mass communicators the statements in question were clearly disseminated to thousands, even millions, of third parties.

One point about publication that is often misunderstood, however, is that each person who repeats a libelous statement has separately met the requirements of dissemination and commits a separate tort. It is no defense that you, as a disseminator, were not the originator of the statement. As one court put it in 1896: "Tale-bearers are as bad as talemakers."[30] Again, this is logical. Particularly in instances of republication by today's mass media, the medium may cause far more reputation damage than the original source of the defamatory remarks.

In practice, this means that attributing the libelous statements to someone else is of no help to the mass communicator. It is not enough that professional communicators accurately quote someone else and clearly attribute the quote. When the media republish, they take legal responsibility for the content of the quote. Some states are carving out a narrow exception to this rule, often referred to as the *neutral reportage privilege,* which will be discussed later in this chapter. But it is very important to understand the general rule on republication, for it is a major constraint on mass communicators.

Perhaps the best illustration of the principle of liability for republication is the publication of letters to the editor in newspapers and magazines. Cases from many jurisdictions have established that these media may be liable for the content of published letters, even though it is clear that the media defendant is not the original source of the libelous statements. Similarly, the media may be responsible for libel contained in advertising, if they were aware of the defamatory content.

In the chapter hypothetical, therefore, clearly labeling the submission about the sheriff as a "political ad" would not automatically protect the newspaper or its advertising manager against tort liability for the content. The key question will instead occur later, under the element of fault, when it is asked whether the newspaper had reason to know the content was false and defamatory.

In terms of the chain of liability, each person and entity that takes part in the publication and republication of defamation may be named as a defendant in the lawsuit. This includes the original source, the corporate entities of media that disseminate the libel (but not the stockholders), individual publishers and station owners, editors, and writers.

Identification

In addition to showing that a defamatory and false statement of fact has been disseminated, a plaintiff also must prove that the libelous statements were reasonably understood to apply to him. Or, as this element is stated in many of the libel cases and statutes, the defamatory content must specifically be "of and concerning the plaintiff."

The plaintiff need not be identified by name, so long as other information led some of those who heard or read the defamatory statements to believe, reasonably,

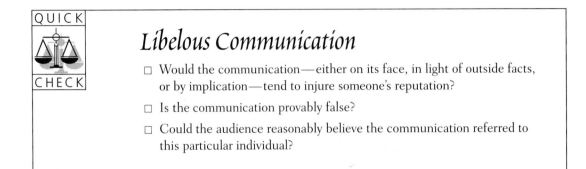

QUICK

CHECK

Libelous Communication

☐ Would the communication—either on its face, in light of outside facts, or by implication—tend to injure someone's reputation?

☐ Is the communication provably false?

☐ Could the audience reasonably believe the communication referred to this particular individual?

that this particular plaintiff was the person portrayed. Physical descriptions, job titles, nicknames, or circumstantial information may be enough to establish identification.

Note that here again the critical question is the reasonable interpretation by members of the audience, not the intent of the defendant communicator. The fact that a libel defendant might have intended the defamatory statements to refer to another person, not to this plaintiff, is irrelevant. Therefore, media writers have a legal reason to get in the habit of identifying people completely—by name, age, city, and occupation, for example. Even when writers disseminate information that is entirely accurate about the people to whom they intended to refer, sloppy or negligent identification could lead to a libel lawsuit from a plaintiff unanticipated by the writer.

Special Problem: Group Defamation   The identification element often becomes an issue when the defamatory content is directed against a group. The question then is whether individual members of the group can claim that the defamatory statements specifically referred to them.

As a general rule, when defamatory statements refer to a large group or class of people, individuals from the group cannot sue for libel unless they were specifically singled out. Statements about ethnic groups, political parties, religions, professions, or geographic regions fall under this rule. The theory is that these kinds of statements are understood by reasonable people as gross generalizations and that even when references are to all members, this cannot be taken literally.

For example, an organization of game hunters and four of its members sued CBS News over a 1975 documentary "The Guns of Autumn," which was critical of sport hunting. The plaintiffs alleged that CBS defamed American hunters, and especially those in Michigan, when it emphasized the slaughter rather than the spirit of the hunt. The individual hunters' claims were tossed out of court, however, because "Vague, general references to a comparatively large group [in this case, more than a million Michigan hunters] do not constitute actionable defamation."[31] Similarly, the hunting organization itself was not specifically implicated as a proponent of the questionable hunting practices depicted, so its defamation claim, too, was deemed without merit.

At the other end of the scale, defamation directed at all members of a small group does give rise to libel claims by each of the individual members. In this case readers or listeners could reasonably assume that the statements truly concerned all individuals. When is a group considered small? According to the *Second Restatement of Torts,* "It is not possible to set definite limits as to the size of the group or class, but the cases in which recovery has been allowed usually have involved numbers of twenty-five or fewer."[32] In a few reported cases, libel claims have been allowed for groups as large as fifty or more, however.

The final group libel scenario involves defamation aimed at just some or a few members of a small group. Should all members of the group be allowed to recover for libel? The courts are divided on this question, but it would be wise to assume that this is still a dangerous practice. In a classic group defamation case from 1952, three classes of Neiman-Marcus department store employees sued over the contents of a book. The authors wrote that "most" of the twenty-five salesmen in the Dallas store were "fairies," that "some" of the nine models were "call girls," and that an undisclosed portion of the 380 saleswomen were also "call girls." The federal court dismissed the libel claims of the individual saleswomen, but it allowed the lawsuits by the models and salesmen.[33]

Fault

It is well established today that when mass communicators are sued for libel the plaintiff must prove some degree of fault on the defendant's part. This wasn't always the case, however. Traditionally, libel was a **strict liability** tort. This meant that if the defendant intentionally disseminated information that turned out to be defamatory and false, the plaintiff could win a lawsuit even if the defendant had taken all customary precautions to assure that the information was true.

By way of analogy, suppose that while you were driving you collided with another car at an intersection. Strict liability would mean that you could be held legally responsible for the other driver's injuries without a court even asking whether you were at fault. You might have taken all the precautions of a defensive driver, but you would still be held liable—simply because you were driving, an accident occurred, and someone was injured. Of course, the law doesn't work this way with regard to traffic accidents, and today it doesn't work this way with libel, either.

It was with this element—fault—that the U.S. Supreme Court first infused constitutional standards into state libel law. And the significance of this infusion could hardly be overstated. By requiring that some fault be shown, the balance shifted from a tort in which plaintiffs generally held the upper hand to one in which mass media defendants have the breathing space—in some cases, great breathing space—to make "honest mistakes." Why did the Court see fit to mandate this additional element, which is sometimes referred to as the media's *constitutional privilege?* The reasons are well illustrated in *New York Times Co. v. Sullivan,*[34] the landmark 1964 case that was the Supreme Court's initial foray into libel law.

New York Times Co. v. Sullivan

The New York Times had carried a full-page political advertisement titled "Heed Their Rising Voices," in which a committee of civil rights activists in the South charged that peaceful student demonstrations were being met with a "wave of terror." The ad described several alleged events to illustrate government suppression. Among them were claims that after a student demonstration police armed with tear gas and shotguns in Montgomery, Alabama ringed the college campus and later padlocked the student dining hall. It also charged that authorities bombed the home of Martin Luther King, Jr., and harassed him with seven arrests for minor offenses.

The problem was that these accounts of events were not accurate. Though police were deployed near the campus in large numbers, they never did ring the campus or padlock the dining hall. King's home was indeed bombed, but police were not implicated, and King had been arrested just four times, not seven.

L.B. Sullivan, the Montgomery commissioner responsible for the police department, sued the *Times* under Alabama's common law of libel. Though he was not mentioned by name in the ad, he claimed that the charges against police would be read as referring to him. A jury awarded Sullivan $500,000 in damages, the full amount claimed, and the Supreme Court of Alabama affirmed. This brought the case to the U.S. Supreme Court, where for the first time the Court was faced with the issue of whether the First Amendment limits the states' power to award libel damages, in this case under a rule of strict liability.

In a unanimous ruling the Court reversed the judgment. Justice William Brennan wrote the opinion for the Court, in which he focused on the basic First Amendment principle that speech concerning public issues and officials should be free and uninhibited. Libel awards based on inadvertent errors could have a

Justice William Brennan during his early years at the Supreme Court. Collection of the Supreme Court of the United States.

marked chilling effect on such speech. Therefore, he said, public officials could recover libel damages only when the defamatory statement was made with "actual malice." (See the case excerpt that follows.)

New York Times Co. v. Sullivan

376 U.S. 254 (1964)

CASE
EXCERPT

From the opinion of the Court by Justice Brennan:

We are required in this case to determine for the first time the extent to which the constitutional protections for speech and press limit a State's power to award damages in a libel action brought by a public official against critics of his official conduct. . . .

We consider this case against the background of a profound national commitment to the principle that debate on public issues should be uninhibited, robust, and wideopen, and that it may well include vehement, caustic, and sometimes unpleasantly sharp attacks on government and public officials. . . . The present advertisement, as an expression of grievance and protest on one of the major public issues of our time, would seem clearly to qualify for the constitutional protection. The question is whether it forfeits that protection by the falsity of some of its actual statements and by its alleged defamation of respondent. . . .

A rule compelling the critic of official conduct to guarantee the truth of all his factual assertions—and to do so on pain of libel judgments virtually unlimited in amount—leads to . . . "self-censorship." Allowance of the defense of truth, with the burden of proving it on the defendant, does not mean that only false speech will be deterred. . . . Under such a rule, would-be critics of official conduct may be deterred from voicing their criticism, even though it is believed to be true and even though it is in fact true, because of doubt whether it can be proved in court or fear of the expense of having to do so. . . . The rule thus dampens the vigor and limits the variety of public debate. It is inconsistent with the First and Fourteenth Amendments.

The constitutional guarantees require, we think, a federal rule that prohibits a public official from recovering damages for a defamatory falsehood relating to his official conduct unless he proves that the statement was made with "actual malice"—that is, with knowledge that it was false or with reckless disregard of whether it was false or not. . . ."

There is evidence that the Times published the advertisement without checking its accuracy against the news stories in the Times' own files. The mere presence of the stories in the files does not, of course, establish that the Times "knew" the advertisement was false, since the state of mind required for actual malice would have to be brought home to the persons in the Times' organization having responsibility for the publication of the advertisement. With respect to the failure of those persons to make the check, the record shows that they relied upon their knowledge of the good reputation of many of those whose names were listed as sponsors of the advertisement, and upon the letter from A. Philip Randolph, known to them as a responsible individual, certifying that the use of the names was authorized. There was testimony that the persons handling the advertisement saw nothing in it that would render it unacceptable under the Times' policy of rejecting advertisements containing "attacks of a personal character"; their failure to reject it on this ground was not unreasonable. We think the evidence against the Times supports at most a finding of negligence in failing to discover the misstatements, and is constitutionally insufficient to show the recklessness that is required for a finding of actual malice. . . .

The judgment of the Supreme Court of Alabama is reversed. . . .[35]

Thus a new standard was added to the law of defamation in all jurisdictions. And in Sullivan's case the Court also ruled the evidence insufficient to find "actual malice" in the *Times'* failure to discover and remove the ad's misstatements. It is important to understand the justification behind the Court's new fault requirement. It is not necessarily that defamatory falsehoods, in themselves, deserve to be protected. Rather, it is that some latitude for inaccuracies is necessary in order to safeguard truthful expression. The truth defense by itself is not enough, Justice Brennan wrote. As long as strict liability is the rule, it is more than just falsehoods that will be deterred. The media would tend to steer wide of the unlawful zone, and thus the law would have a chilling effect on truthful speech as well.

For example, if newspapers were to lose cases such as this, where at the time of publication they had no reason to doubt the veracity of the statements, they would feel pressured to play it safe by rejecting similar political advertising altogether. Even a line-by-line fact check would not insulate the paper because heretofore reputable sources could turn out to be wrong. By injecting the fault standard into libel law, the Court gave the media a better chance to control their own fate.

Until Justice Brennan's opinion in the *Sullivan* case, the Supreme Court had never acknowledged that defamatory speech deserved any constitutional protection against civil lawsuits. This was true for the vast majority of state courts as well. One reason the judiciary had not accepted a First Amendment defense is that the amendment had historically been viewed only as protection against direct government action. But in *Sullivan* the Court noted that government support of civil laws that place unreasonable burdens on the press can be just as offensive to constitutional liberties as a state criminal law that punishes the media.

Requiring some showing of fault is a reasonable enough proposition. Unfortunately, however, what has followed the *Sullivan* case has been a tortured, confusing, piecemeal approach to determining precisely how the fault element should work. Today a thorough assessment of communicators' potential liability means deciding exactly what degree of fault the plaintiff must prove, and this, in turn, depends upon who the plaintiff is.

The Meaning of Actual Malice

In *Sullivan* the plaintiff was a government official, and he was therefore required to prove a degree of fault called **actual malice.** This is a high degree of fault that has nothing to do with *malice* as that word is commonly used, to mean spite, ill will, or hatred. Actual malice—sometimes referred to as **constitutional malice**—means that when the defamatory statements were published the communicator either (1) knew they were false, or (2) published with reckless disregard of truth or falsity, that is, with serious doubts that the statements were true.

Today the actual malice standard applies in cases where the libel plaintiff is a public official or a public figure. Later, this chapter will look more closely at how these categorizations are made. But first, it is necessary to take a closer look at the actual malice standard.

State of Mind

The question in actual malice inquiries is what the defendant actually believed at the time of publication, not simply whether a prudent person would have published or whether most professionals would have done more checking. This is a difficult task for plaintiffs. Furthermore, not only must certain plaintiffs demonstrate that the defendant acted with actual malice, but this fact must be proved by "clear and convincing evidence." This heightened degree of proof makes the actual malice standard even tougher for plaintiffs to overcome. Yet case results show that the actual malice requirement is not insurmountable. Remember that the civil discovery process includes powerful methods for uncovering evidence.

A 1979 Supreme Court ruling established that plaintiffs faced with proving actual malice may inspect a writer's notes and compel answers to detailed questions in order to piece together circumstantial evidence of the defendant's actual state of mind during the editorial process. The case *Herbert v. Lando* involved a *60 Minutes* broadcast in which a retired army colonel, Anthony Herbert, claimed he was wrongly depicted as a liar. The broadcast concerned Herbert's public accusations that the military had covered up atrocities committed by U.S. troops in Vietnam.

In his effort to prove actual malice against the producer of the *60 Minutes* segment, Herbert's lawyers pressed for thousands of pages of detailed testimony. The defendant protested, arguing that such inquiries into an editor's state of mind would produce an unconstitutional, chilling effect on speech. But the Supreme Court disagreed, holding that such an inquiry is valid as long as it is directed to producing evidence relevant to the proof of actual malice.[36]

Knowing Falsehood

Actual malice can be proved most easily when a defendant simply fabricates defamatory "facts" out of thin air. Making up a story and presenting it as fact would, of course, amount to publication of a known falsehood—one of the two ways to establish actual malice. Equally egregious would be publication of facts fabricated by someone else while knowing that the material was indeed fiction. Fortunately, very few lawsuits against professional communicators actually involve such gross abuse of journalistic license.

What if a writer concocts quotations and attributes them to a source, perhaps believing that the fabricated quotes are a reasonable interpretation of what the speaker said, but knowing full well that the passages aren't really direct quotes? In the 1991 case of *Masson v. New Yorker Magazine, Inc.* the Supreme Court addressed this more problematic angle to "knowing falsehood." The case concerned an article about Jeffrey Masson, a controversial psychoanalyst who had been interviewed by a writer for the *New Yorker.* Masson claimed that several passages in quotation marks, which were attributed to Masson and amounted to boastful self-description, were deliberately fabricated and injurious to his own reputation. Furthermore, he argued that falsification of quotations should automatically constitute publication with knowing falsity—and thus actual malice.

The Supreme Court did not entirely agree. It held that deliberate alteration of the words uttered by a plaintiff, even if more substantial than the correction of grammar or syntax, does not equate with knowledge of falsity for actual malice purposes unless the alteration changes the meaning conveyed by the statement. Placing quotation marks around substantially accurate paraphrases, though a poor journalistic practice, is not evidence of actual malice for purposes of a libel lawsuit.

On the other hand, wrote Justice Anthony Kennedy for the Court, readers assume that a passage in quotation marks reproduces the speaker's words verbatim, and hence, erroneous quotations may be a particularly "devastating instrument" for convening false meaning. The Court said that false quotations can defame the person to whom they are attributed in at least two ways: The first way is by the falsity of the factual assertion in the quote. The second way is by the false attribution of the remark to this particular speaker, regardless of the truth or falsity of the statement within quotation marks. A false attribution alone may injure reputation because the manner of expression or even the mere fact that the statement was made could indicate a negative personal trait that the speaker does not actually possess. Therefore, the deliberate alteration or fabrication of a quotation, if it substantially changes the substance of a person's remarks, *is* a statement made with knowledge of falsity for purposes of proving actual malice. This may be true, said the Court, even if the writer at the time thought, mistakenly, that the made-up quotes were a reasonable interpretation of what the speaker said.

In the *New Yorker* article Masson is quoted as referring to himself as an "intellectual gigolo" and the "greatest analyst who ever lived." The Supreme Court sent the case back down to the lower court to determine whether the quotes attributed to Masson were indeed significantly different from Masson's actual statements.[37] In 1994 a jury found the article nonlibelous.

Reckless Disregard

"Reckless disregard" might be established if a news story were based wholly on un-verified information from an anonymous telephone call or from a caller with a history of unreliability. And in some cases the facts of a story may be so inherently improbable that to disseminate them without verification would smack of reckless disregard for the truth. The key is whether the communicator had ample reason to be highly suspicious of the information at the time and chose to run it anyway.

Still, sloppy or even unethical journalistic practices do not, by themselves, equate to reckless disregard for the truth. Nor is a communicator's motive a deciding factor in this inquiry. Rather, these facts are just part of the overall relevant circumstances that may be considered by a jury when determining whether a libel defendant was reckless with the truth.

In *Harte-Hanks Communications, Inc. v. Connaughton* the U.S. Supreme Court in 1989 agreed unanimously that an Ohio newspaper had published information about a judicial candidate with actual malice. The plaintiff in the case, Daniel Connaughton, lost a local judgeship election after the newspaper reported a woman's allegations that he had promised jobs, fancy dinners, and a Florida vacation to her and her sister "in appreciation" for her help in providing information about corruption in the incumbent judge's office.

The Supreme Court found clear and convincing evidence of actual malice in the facts that

(1) the woman's allegations had been denied by Connaughton and five other witnesses before the story was published;

(2) Connaughton had made tapes of conversations with the woman's sister available to the newspaper, but no one there had bothered to listen to them;

(3) no attempt had been made to interview the source's sister, though she was closely connected to the allegations; and

(4) a tape of the interview between the newspaper and the source evidenced inconsistencies and other reasons to question the veracity of the charges.

Wrote Justice Stevens for the Court:

> It is likely that the newspaper's inaction was a product of a deliberate decision not to acquire knowledge of facts that might confirm the probable falsity of [the woman's] charges. Although failure to investigate will not alone support a finding of actual malice, the purposeful avoidance of the truth is in a different category.[38]

Simple failure to investigate, even when coupled with feelings of ill will by the defendant toward the plaintiff, is not enough to establish that the defendant published a known falsehood or with reckless disregard. This is illustrated by another 1989 case in which the World Boxing Council sued sportscaster Howard Cosell over comments contained in his book *I Never Played the Game*. The book referred to the organization as "a conspirator in rigging ratings" and an "instrument of extortion." Wrote the federal District Court:

> [T]he WBC argues that Cosell harbors ill-will towards the WBC, and that Cosell failed adequately to investigate the charges he lodged at the WBC in his book. Even conceding the truth of these factual assertions, it does not follow that Cosell knew or should have known that the allegations in his passage were false.[39]

But obvious signs of ill will, particularly evidence of an intention to harm someone's reputation, may be considered relevant support for charges that the defendant invented the defamatory information. In a 1983 Mississippi case, for example, statements by the defendant writer that "I've got him now" and "I tore him up," coupled with testimony that the defamatory statements "were made up through anger," were considered sufficient to prove actual malice.[40]

An issue in many cases is the hectic pace of decision making that typifies media professionals working on deadline. The deadline environment may breed careless decisions, but haste alone does not equate to actual malice. This point is illustrated by a 1994 case in which a newspaper carried a story based on an Associated Press dispatch labeled URGENT. The dispatch had also been marked MORE, indicating that additional information about the story would soon arrive. However, the journalist did not wait for the additional information and prepared a story based on the initial dispatch alone. Though the second dispatch did arrive before deadline, the journalist never saw it. The plaintiff claimed that the story would not have been libelous had the journalist incorporated the second dispatch, and the failure to do so was offered as evidence of actual malice. The federal Court of Appeals disagreed. Even though the journalist was alerted to expect additional information and went ahead without it, the court held this did not prove the journalist had serious doubts about the accuracy of the story crafted on the first dispatch.[41]

Consider once again the chapter hypothetical. If you were to publish the line about a pending criminal indictment of the sheriff, would you have done so without actual malice? From the information provided in the hypothetical, you did not know that to be a falsehood. But would you be publishing with serious doubts about its accuracy (reckless disregard)? The group sponsoring the ad was reputable. But reporters at your paper gave you actual reason to doubt the truth of that charge. This would not look good before a jury and might well qualify as reckless disregard for the truth.

Gertz and the Negligence Standard

For nearly a decade following the *Sullivan* case, the Supreme Court consistently expanded application of the actual malice standard to a wide range of "public" plaintiffs. In 1971 a fractured Supreme Court, led again by Justice Brennan, decided to take an even bolder approach and extend the standard to any case in which the content of the offending communication was of general public concern. In *Rosenbloom v. Metromedia, Inc.* the Court plurality decided that the constitutional buffer against libel laws should depend not on the status of the plaintiff, but on the subject matter of the communication.

Thus the Court in that case required the libel plaintiff, a distributor of nudist magazines, to prove actual malice in his lawsuit against a Philadelphia radio station. The defamatory statements were made in the context of news reports on the distributor's arrests for allegedly selling obscenity—clearly a matter of legitimate public concern. Wrote Justice Brennan:

> We honor the commitment to robust debate on public issues, which is embodied in the First Amendment, by extending constitutional protection to all discussion and communication involving matters of public or general concern, without regard to whether the persons involved are famous or anonymous.[42]

The *Rosenbloom* approach seemed both logical and less complicated. It was short-lived, however.

The Gertz Ruling

In 1974 a majority of the Supreme Court decided that the *Rosenbloom* approach granted too much latitude to mass communicators and tread too heavily upon state libel laws protecting the reputation of private individuals. So in *Gertz v. Robert Welch, Inc.* the Court retrenched. It reverted to the approach in which the constitutional malice standard is triggered by the public status of the libel plaintiff—the approach still followed today.

The *Gertz* case involved a libel lawsuit by a respected Chicago attorney, Elmer Gertz, against *American Opinion*, a magazine disseminating the views of the far-right-wing John Birch Society. Gertz had earlier filed a civil lawsuit on behalf of the family of a young man shot by a police officer. On that basis *American Opinion* reported, falsely, that Gertz was part of a giant communist conspiracy to destroy local police departments. Gertz lost his libel case in the lower courts because it was held that the article concerned was a matter of public interest and there was no evidence of actual malice by the magazine.

But the Supreme Court reversed, 5–4. It held that Gertz was a private figure and that private figures are in greater need of protection from defamation than public figures, who enjoy greater media access with which to counteract false accusations. Wrote Justice Lewis Powell for the majority: "We hold that, so long as they do not impose liability without fault, the States may define for themselves the appropriate standard of liability for a publisher or broadcaster of defamatory falsehood injurious to a private individual."[43]

So, any libel plaintiff not deemed a public official or public figure is automatically characterized as a private person. And in libel cases filed by private people, the *Gertz* ruling allows each state to determine the precise degree of fault the plaintiff must prove. There is no constitutionally mandated fault standard in private person cases, except that some degree of fault must be shown. The states are not free to impose strict liability on mass communicators.

Reasonable Care

A few states have decided to require a showing of actual malice in all libel cases against mass communicators, regardless of *Gertz.* But among the states that have specifically addressed the issue, a majority has decided to allow private person plaintiffs to recover upon evidence of mere **negligence,** a far lesser degree of fault. Remember from Chapter 3 that people are considered negligent when they fail to exercise ordinary or reasonable care. In libel cases it means that the defendant failed to take the precautions that a reasonable communicator would have taken under similar circumstances to assure that libelous communications were not disseminated.

In most cases, the negligence inquiry focuses on the adequacy of a communicator's efforts to verify information. It is not necessary that all possible avenues of verification be exhausted in every case, of course. But the question is whether all reasonable efforts were taken, as indicated by the overall circumstances and by custom within the applicable communications profession.

For example, a federal court in 1989 held that the newspaper editors at *USA Today* could be deemed negligent for condensing a twenty-minute interview into a single paragraph of quotes and then failing to verify their accuracy—either with the original source or with the part-time correspondent who had relayed the entire interview to the editors by telephone. The court wrote:

> This is especially so in a case like this one, where (1) time was not a critical problem (there were four full working days between deadline and publication), and (2) the means of checking were readily at hand (a telephone call to the plaintiff would have prevented the blunder). In light of these facts, we cannot gainsay the jury's determination that reasonable editors under the totality of the circumstances would have made some further attempt at confirmation.[44]

The reason the negligence standard is much less favored by professional communicators, and what makes it different from the actual malice standard, is that it essentially invites a jury to impose liability by second-guessing communicators' methods and judgments. In his *Gertz* dissent, Justice Brennan wrote about negligence: "The reasonable-care standard is 'elusive' . . . ; it saddles the press with 'the intolerable burden of guessing how a jury might assess the reasonableness of steps taken by it to verify the accuracy of every reference to a name, picture or portrait.'"[45] In sharp contrast, the known falsehood or reckless disregard standard provides greater certainty for communicators because the focus isn't on what a reasonable person would have done, but on what the communicator actually knew at the time of dissemination.

Still, communicators can be fairly certain of avoiding negligence by observing the basic professional principles that are taught in college journalism courses. Some of the more important principles, from both a legal and ethical standpoint, are: Don't rely on information from anonymous phone calls; seek out both sides of a story; and provide the targets of defamatory allegations with an opportunity to respond.

It is also important that journalists and other communicators behave like true professionals when interviewing others. The legal reason for this is that techniques and offhand comments might later be used against the interviewer—perhaps as evidence of a tendency to be biased or sensationalistic. Juries will not look favorably upon the use of scare tactics or derogatory and exaggerated comments about others during efforts to gain information from a source.

Categorizing the Plaintiff

Analyzing the facts of a particular libel case under one of the fault standards can be a laborious and inexact process. Equally as difficult, however, may be the threshold determination of which standard shall apply. Whether the plaintiff must show actual malice on the defendant's part, or just negligence, is a determination that often will ordain the ultimate outcome of a libel lawsuit. This critical determination is in turn based on whether the plaintiff is a public or a private person. In practice, though, this categorization can be difficult, and courts in the various jurisdictions sometimes reach different conclusions.

In *Sullivan* the Court required a public official to prove actual malice, and a few years later the requirement was extended to litigation in which the plaintiff is a public figure. For private person plaintiffs, however, it is constitutionally permissible to win a libel lawsuit by showing a lesser degree of fault.

The rationale behind this double standard is based on assumptions about the relative importance of the speech and the reasonable expectations and influence of defamed people. Speech concerning the conduct of public officials is considered, socially speaking, to be among the most important classifications of speech—speech that goes right to the heart of the First Amendment and the ideals of an open democracy. Similarly, criticism of public figures is of particular public importance because famous people serve as role models and influence policies and events of concern to society at large.

Also, the Supreme Court has noted that both public officials and public figures in most cases have voluntarily exposed themselves to the risks of closer public scrutiny. And in both cases they enjoy greater access to the mass media, where they can counteract defamatory charges. Private people don't have the same opportunity, however, and thus need greater help from libel laws.

For all these reasons the Supreme Court has chosen to distinguish between public and private libel plaintiffs. When the plaintiffs are public people—public officials or public figures—mass communicators receive greater constitutional protection through application of the actual malice standard. The next question is, who is a public official or public figure.

Public Officials

The Supreme Court has loosely defined the term **public official** as applying to "government employees who have, or appear to the public to have, substantial responsibility for or control over the conduct of government affairs."[46] Thus the designation of "public official" does not apply to everyone who receives a government paycheck, but neither is it reserved exclusively for the very highest levels of government.

In practice the question is whether the government job carries with it the authority to influence public policy or otherwise to affect directly the health, liberty, or property of the public. In most cases the individual's title and the general nature of the office will provide the answer.

Likely examples of public officials include elected representatives, high-ranking officers in the armed forces, judges, prosecutors, public defenders, county clerks, building inspectors, and, yes, the sheriff in the chapter hypothetical. In the vast majority of cases the courts have also deemed police patrol officers to be public officials, with reference to their authority to affect personal liberty. Various school and college authorities, including school board members, principals, and college deans, also have been deemed public officials. More difficult, however, has been the classification of public school teachers, and courts have reached different conclusions.[47]

Even when it is determined that the plaintiff in a libel lawsuit is a public official, the actual malice standard is said to apply only if the defamatory statement pertains to the plaintiff's official conduct. This limitation on the reach of the actual malice rule was stated in the *Sullivan* opinion. However, the limitation is of scant practical significance because later decisions have clarified that the actual malice rule applies whenever statements might touch on the suing official's general fitness for office. Even statements about very personal attributes, such as dishonesty or improper motivation, may be germane to fitness for office.[48]

Public Figures

The extension of the actual malice standard to public figures was first announced by the Supreme Court in the 1967 case of *Curtis Publishing Co. v. Butts* and a companion case, *Associated Press v. Walker*. The first case involved a report by *The Saturday Evening Post* that University of Georgia athletic directory Wally Butts had conspired with coach Bear Bryant of the University of Alabama to fix a football game between their respective schools. The *Walker* case involved an erroneous Associated Press report that retired Brigadier General Edwin Walker had helped instigate a University of Mississippi campus riot. Because Butts was paid by a private alumni association and Walker had retired from the army, neither of these libel plaintiffs could be classified as public officials. However, both men had acted in such a fashion as to invite public attention and comment, one as a major sports figure and one as a political activist. The Supreme Court declared both plaintiffs public figures to whom the actual malice standard should logically apply.[49] (See Exhibit 4.2, page 132, for a chronological summary of important Supreme Court cases pertaining to libel.)

The **public figure** classification, then, applies to plaintiffs who have assumed special prominence in the resolution of public issues or the character of public events. This determination is generally tougher to make than the determination of who is a public official. As a federal judge once described it, defining public figures is "much like trying to nail a jellyfish to the wall."[50]

In an effort to better structure the analytic task, courts often further categorize public figures as **all-purpose** or **limited purpose.** All-purpose public figures are those who have achieved pervasive fame. They are household names, either across the nation or at least in the region where the defamatory content was published, and they must prove actual malice in regard to virtually any defamatory statement. Film stars, TV celebrities, sports heroes, and big-name social critics may fall into this category. Courts have ruled that entertainer Johnny Carson and author-commentator William F. Buckley, Jr. are all-purpose public figures, for example.

At the other end of the public-figure spectrum are limited-purpose public figures—those who have entered the public spotlight, but only within a narrow context. As libel plaintiffs they are considered public figures only if the defamation was related to that public context. These are people who voluntarily have thrust themselves into the forefront of specific public controversies in an effort to influence the outcome; they are sometimes referred to as "vortex public figures."

Typical examples of people who would tend to be limited-purpose public figures are local candidates for public office and their campaign managers, lobbyists, union leaders, top-level corporate executives, and people who lead the charge on one side of a public controversy—vocal abortion rights advocates, leaders of a grassroots campaign to stop construction of a dam, and so on. Criminal defendants may be limited public figures, but only if they injected themselves into a preexisting public controversy. Criminal prosecution by itself does not automatically convert the defendant into a public figure under libel law.[51] In deciding whether limited public-figure status shall apply, the plaintiff's position or title alone is rarely determinative. Rather, courts look to the individual's actual, voluntary involvement in a public debate.

When the plaintiff in a libel lawsuit is a corporation, the determination of public-figure status is made in the same way as with individuals. The corporate entity will be deemed a public figure if it had injected itself into the struggle or debate over public issues, such as pollution controls, foreign policy, minority hiring practices, or federal fiscal policy. Generally speaking, large corporations will tend to be public figures, but the determination does not rest on size alone.

EXHIBIT 4.2   *Highlights in the Constitutional Evolution of Libel Law*

1964   The First Amendment bars a "public official" from collecting damages for defamatory falsehoods relating to his official conduct unless it is shown with convincing clarity that the falsehood was published with "actual malice." *(New York Times Co. v. Sullivan.)*

1967   The actual malice standard of *Sullivan* extends to libel lawsuits filed by "public figures" as well as lawsuits by public officials. (Associate Press v. Walker and Curtis Publishing Co. v. Butts.)

1971   The *Sullivan* actual malice standard is applicable to all libel lawsuits in which the defamatory communication relates to matters of public or general concern (plurality opinion). *(Rosenbloom v. Metromedia, Inc.)*

1974   *Rosenbloom* repudiated; the actual malice standard is not constitutionally required in libel lawsuits brought by "private" persons, though liability may not be imposed without some degree of fault. Plaintiff limited to damages for "actual injury," however, unless actual malice is shown. *(Gertz v. Robert Welch, Inc.)*

1979   During the discovery process a libel plaintiff, who must prove actual malice, may inquire into the details of a defendant's "mental process" of preparing the communication. *(Herbert v. Lando.)*

1985   The *Gertz* limitation on damages does not apply in cases where defamatory statements do not involve matters of public concern; in such cases presumed and punitive damages may be awarded without proof of actual malice (pluarity opinion). *(Dun & Bradstreet, Inc. v. Greenmoss Builders, Inc.)*

1986   Trial courts must dispose of libel cases at the summary judgment stage when it is apparent that public-person plaintiffs cannot meet the heavy burden of proving actual malice by clear and convincing evidence, as required by the First Amendment and *Sullivan*. (Anderson *v. Liberty Lobby, Inc.)*

1986   A libel plaintiff bears the burden of proving falsity, at least in cases in which the plaintiff seeks damages against a media defendant for speech involving matters of public concern. *(Philadelphia Newspapers, Inc. v. Hepps.)*

1989   A newspaper's purposeful avoidance of information that might refute defamatory allegations about a plaintiff is sufficiently reckless to qualify as actual malice. *(Harte-Hanks Communications, Inc. v. Connaughton.)*

1990   The fact that defamatory statements might be labeled "opinion" is not enough to warrant a constitutional privilege against libel claims if the statements imply an assertion of objective fact. *(Milkovich v. Lorain Journal Co.)*

1991   Fabrication of direct quotations does not necessarily equate to actual malice, though it may amount to actual malice if the altered words change the meaning of the plaintiff's actual remarks. *(Masson v. New Yorker Magazine, Inc.)*

This list shows the chronological order of some of the U.S. Supreme Court's most important libel decisions. By no means is it a complete list of the Court's rulings pertaining to libel.

In some cases a corporation's public discussion about the merits of its own product may be a sufficient basis for public-figure status. For example, a federal court ruled that a manufacturer of loudspeakers was a public figure for purposes of a lawsuit against *Consumer Reports* magazine, which had published an allegedly defamatory product review. The public figure determination was based on the manufacturer's extensive advertising and publicity efforts, designed to encourage tests and reviews of its product.[52]

Can a person involuntarily become a public figure? For example, how about the bystander who jumps into a freezing river to save a child, who now finds herself the subject of media and community attention she never wanted? Or an Air Force pilot, shot down in enemy territory, who escapes to safety only to find his picture now appearing in media across the country? The usual answer is no. Especially where the attention-getting conduct is a single event, and the individual was not actually seeking the attention, courts are not likely to deem the plaintiff a public figure.

However, involuntary public-figure status is more likely if the plaintiff had engaged in some notorious conduct over a significant period, knowing full well that it could lead to widespread publicity, and had already attracted some media attention. A leading case for this point is *Rosanova v. Playboy Enterprises,* in which *Playboy* magazine had referred to the plaintiff as a "mobster." The federal Court of Appeals declared Rosanova a public figure—even though he had not sought public attention—because he engaged in conduct that was of significant public interest and had been the subject of prior media reports.[53]

Change of Plaintiffs' Status

Does a public figure always remain a public figure in the eyes of the law? Or does the passage of time convert a person to private person status, thus easing the obstacles to winning as a libel plaintiff? This remains an unsettled point in defamation law. The U.S. Supreme Court has not ruled directly on this question, and other courts have disagreed.

A person who has been out of the public eye for many years may no longer command easy access to the media and may no longer be said voluntarily to accept the closer scrutiny that comes with the public spotlight—two of the justifications for the public-figure distinction in the first place.

Using the standpoint of the greater public interest, however, most courts have reached a different conclusion—at least when the communication related to events while the plaintiff was in the public eye. In a case involving a plaintiff who had been a limited-purpose public figure forty years earlier, the Court of Appeals reasoned:

> Once a person becomes a public figure in connection with a particular controversy, that person remains a public figure thereafter for purposes of later

EXHIBIT 4.3   *Classifying the Plaintiff: A Rough Guide*

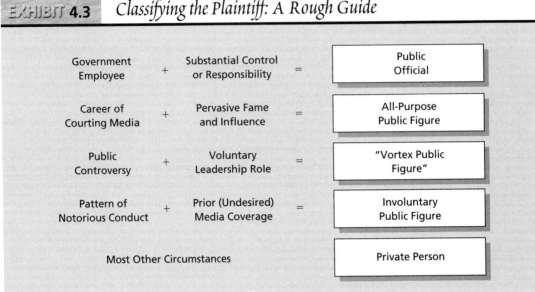

commentary or treatment of *that controversy*. . . . The mere passage of time does not automatically diminish the significance of events or the public's need for information. A nation that prizes its heritage need have no illusions about its past. It is no more fitting for the Court to constrain the analysis of past events than to stem the tide of current events.[54]

A Practical Warning

Since 1964 this nation's courts have generated thousands of pages of judicial opinions concerning the proper categorization of libel plaintiffs. Not surprisingly, the critical legal distinction between public and private plaintiffs also tends to be a much-discussed topic in books and courses such as this. Despite the intellectual attention, however, categorizing libel plaintiffs will never become an exact science. Also, not all public figures neatly fit the all-purpose and limited-purpose molds as they have been defined.

For example, would a *Playboy* magazine centerfold "playmate" qualify as a public figure? A federal court said yes, at least for purposes of an allegedly defamatory satire of *Playboy* that appeared in *National Lampoon*. Though the plaintiff had not actually sought to influence any specific controversy, the court noted that she had voluntarily posed for nude photos and consented to their publication, thereby inviting public attention and comment regarding her role as a model. But another federal court ruled that a "Miss Wyoming," who had competed in the Miss America pageant and had won several other beauty contests and hundreds of regional and national baton-twirling championships, did not merit the public figure designation in her lawsuit against *Penthouse* magazine.[55]

In terms of practical, day-to-day advice, law firms urge their media clients: Do not assume that individuals portrayed in the media are public figures. The wise practice is generally to assume that potential libel plaintiffs are private figures and may be able to win a libel case on the basis of ordinary negligence. Only when the potential plaintiff is a high-ranking federal government official or a media celebrity of the grandest stature might an assumption of public-person status be safe.

Harm to Plaintiff

As the final element of libel the plaintiff must provide evidence that he or she actually suffered an injured reputation as a direct result of the defamation. Normally the compensable injuries are not limited to a plaintiff's tangible, out-of-pocket losses. In most cases the bulk of the claimed injuries is intangible—a loss of esteem in social circles, being shunned by neighbors, personal humiliation, and so on.

Realistically, some people are much more susceptible to reputation damage than others. For example, a heart surgeon with a terrific regional reputation would tend to be highly susceptible to such injury. An erroneous report that the doctor is a drug addict could easily cause reputation damage worth hundreds of thousands or even millions of dollars. But suppose that a drug-addict charge is made about a convicted felon—a man who has recently served prison time for burglary, firearms violations, and animal abuse, and who last year was caught by an FBI sting operation because he applied for a job as a hit man with people he thought were members of the mob. In reality, the facts of this person's life may have already led to such a sorry reputation that a false drug claim could hardly damage it further. In recognition of this reality, courts have occasionally declared plaintiffs with highly unsavory pasts and despicable reputations to be "libel-proof" as a matter of law and therefore incapable of winning a libel lawsuit.[56]

Under the common law as it existed for decades in this country, a libel plaintiff was not actually required to prove the extent of injury. The jury was allowed to presume the extent of harm, taking into account the plaintiff's prior reputation, the harshness of the defamation, and the scope of dissemination. This procedure has been greatly restricted by the Supreme Court, however.

Awarding Damages

The only legal remedy available to a libel plaintiff is to recover money because courts will not enjoin publication of potential libel. Whether or not the injury to a defamed person is financial in nature, the jury will decide upon a monetary award for the plaintiff in order to compensate for the harm. This award is called **compensatory damages.** Compensatory damages may further be subdivided into three categories, and these terms are worth noting because they often appear in cases and statutes dealing with libel. The three kinds of compensatory damages are **presumed damages** (the broadest category possible, based on a jury's presumption of what the harm is likely to be), **actual damages** (an award based strictly on evidenced harm, of any kind), and **special damages** (an award limited to evidenced harm of a direct, monetary nature).

In addition to compensatory damages, most states have traditionally allowed juries to tack on an award of **punitive damages** in cases in which the defendant's behavior was shown to result from spite or other detestable motives. These additional damages are for the sake of example, as a way of punishing the defendant in the context of a civil lawsuit.

There are no solid standards for ascertaining the dollar value of a plaintiff's injured reputation, so juries have great latitude in awarding compensatory damages. Trial and appellate judges have the authority to reduce jury awards that are grossly excessive, but only rarely are judges willing to upset juries' determinations. Similarly, few guidelines exist for setting the amounts of punitive damages. In some cases they have amounted to several times the amount of compensatory damages. For example, in 1989 a Pennsylvania court upheld a $2.2 million libel verdict against the *Pittsburgh Post-Gazette* that was just $200,000 in compensatory damages but $2 million in punitive damages.[57]

With the 1980s came the advent of so-called mega-verdicts in libel law. In that decade juries in more than two dozen cases awarded damages in excess of $1 million. And while the vast majority of these awards were overturned or reduced on appeal, media professionals and their lawyers began warning that such awards, particularly in the punitive category, could have a stifling effect on freedom of speech.

Limits on Damages

The U.S. Supreme Court has injected just two constitutional limitations on damage awards, and those were announced in the *Gertz* case back in 1974. First, the states' common law doctrine of presumed injury was greatly restricted. Wrote the Court:

> The largely uncontrolled discretion of juries to award damages where there is no loss unnecessarily compounds the potential of any system of liability for defamatory falsehood to inhibit the vigorous exercise of First Amendment freedoms. Additionally, the doctrine of presumed damages invites juries to punish unpopular opinion rather than to compensate individuals for injury sustained by the publication of a false fact. . . . It is necessary to restrict defamation plaintiffs who do not prove knowledge of falsity or reckless disregard for the truth to compensation for actual injury.[58]

So, private figure plaintiffs at trial must offer solid evidence of their injuries, both tangible and intangible, unless they can prove the higher standard of fault, actual malice. States may no longer allow awards of presumed damages, at least in libel cases involving matters of public concern, unless actual malice is proved.

The second restriction laid down in *Gertz* is that punitive damages may not be awarded unless, again, the libel plaintiff proves actual malice on the defendant's part. While the *Gertz* ruling eased the constitutional fault requirement in libel cases brought by private people, it also withheld from plaintiffs the potential wind-falls—punitive damages and damages based on presumed injury—unless the plaintiff proves additionally that the defendant is guilty of actual malice.

Remember that these restrictions are constitutional minimums, limitations deemed necessary under the First Amendment so that adequate breathing space would exist for freedom of speech. And, while the Supreme Court has declined in recent years to require further restrictions on awards of libel damages, the in-dividual states are free to do so and have done so. A few states prohibit punitive damages for libel altogether, for example.[59] And many other states require a show-ing of "common law malice" (ill motives) as well as constitutional actual malice be-fore punitive damages may be obtained. Furthermore, both state and federal courts are free to reduce awards of punitive damages that they deem to be "grossly excessive."

Matters of Private Concern

Most of the Supreme Court's libel decisions, and most of this chapter, deal with cases in which the defendants were mass media—newspapers, TV networks, and so on—and the offending communication naturally related to news or commen-tary on a matter of broad public interest. Communicators may receive lesser First Amendment protection against libel lawsuits, however, when the communication in question was of a purely self-serving or private nature.

In *Dun & Bradstreet, Inc. v. Greenmoss Builders, Inc.* a plurality of the Supreme Court limited application of the *Gertz* standards to public-oriented communica-tions. In *Greenmoss* a credit reporting agency had issued a confidential report to several subscribers stating that a contractor, Greenmoss Builders, had filed for bankruptcy. The report was in error, however, and the contractor sued for libel. In state court the contractor was awarded both presumed and punitive damages, even though actual malice was never shown. But the U.S. Supreme Court affirmed, holding that the rule of *Gertz,* which prohibits awards of presumed and punitive damages without a showing of malice, does not apply when the defamatory state-ments do not involve matters of public concern. The plurality opinion states:

> We have long recognized that not all speech is of equal First Amendment impor-tance. It is speech on "matters of public concern" that is "at the heart of the First Amendment's protection." . . . In contrast, speech on matters of purely private concern is of less First Amendment concern. . . . While such speech is not totally unprotected by the First Amendment . . . its protections are less stringent.[60]

Greenmoss leaves many important questions for the future. For example: Could the contents of mass communications ever be deemed not of public concern? What if this same, mistaken bankruptcy report had appeared as a news item in a newspaper? What about the self-serving, commercial pitches of advertisers?

This public concern distinction raised in the *Greenmoss* case is one that professional communicators will need to watch carefully. Recall that when a public concern classification was proposed in *Rosenbloom*, it was later rejected by the Supreme Court in *Gertz*. Yet in two later cases, *Greenmoss* and *Hepps*, the Court again used the qualifying language "matter of public concern," thereby indicating that some degree of subject-matter classification is still alive and that it may determine precisely which libel safeguards apply. (Recall that in *Hepps* the Court said private-person plaintiffs had the burden of proving falsity in cases involving matters of public concern.) The Supreme Court has not announced criteria for distinguishing subjects of public concern from subjects of private concern. For now, though, *Greenmoss* at least serves as a warning that the law of libel still is evolving.

Privileges, Defenses, and Other Protections

This chapter so far has focused on the elements that plaintiffs must prove in order to win a libel lawsuit against mass communicators. You should recognize that, under the common law of the states, and particularly under the additional constitutional limitations laid down by the Supreme Court, considerable protections for communicators are built into these elements.

Even if libel plaintiffs can prove the basic elements of the tort they are not guaranteed victory. This is because the law recognizes more than a dozen additional defenses, privileges, and procedural protections that may shield defendants from liability for defamation. This section considers just a few of those protections—the ones that are most important to professional communicators. (Two of the most important common law privileges, truth and fair comment, were incorporated in the discussion of the falsity element earlier in this chapter.) This section also looks at other means by which mass communicators can at least diminish or discourage libel claims.

Reports of Official Proceedings

For newspeople, particularly, one of the most useful protections is the privilege to report fairly and accurately what is said in official government proceedings. Known as the **fair report** or **public record privilege,** it is premised on the public's overriding right in a democratic society to be informed about the functioning of government and the behavior of government officials. Therefore, media may republish or broadcast allegations made in official proceedings even, in most states, when the media know the allegations are defamatory or false. Obviously, this is a major exception to the rule that anyone who repeats defamation is independently liable for it.

For example, suppose that during a city council meeting the chief of police testifies that the student-body president of the local college is running a prostitution ring out of a campus dorm. The testimony is defamatory, and you might even suspect it is false. But under the fair report privilege the public's right to know how its police chief is performing takes priority over the student's ability to sue for defamation, so you would be free to report the chief's remarks. (By the way, those participating in the official proceeding are also covered by a privilege.)

A Qualified Privilege

In most jurisdictions this is a conditional, or qualified, privilege, not an absolute one. That's because the privilege applies only so long as communicators live up to their end of the bargain. Specifically, they must meet two related conditions. First, the republication or broadcast must be fair. This means that the account must not employ selective omission and inclusion in such a way as to lose all reasonable balance or otherwise evidence a malicious, vengeful motive. As a second condition, the selected quotes and paraphrases must be accurate. If the defamatory report is a distortion of what was said in the proceedings, the privilege may be destroyed. As an Illinois court phrased it, the republication may not carry a greater sting than what was actually said in the official proceeding or documents.[61] If the republication meets these qualifications, the privilege applies—regardless of whether the plaintiff is a public figure or private figure.

Types of Proceedings Covered

The precise scope of the fair report privilege varies significantly from state to state. Generally, though, the privilege applies both to the content of live proceedings and to documentary information, so long as the proceedings or documents are open to the public and only if they indeed represent official public business. For example, the privilege typically will apply to accounts of the following: lawyers' and witnesses' statements in open court, legislators' comments during floor sessions or open committee hearings, official reports and studies by executive branch agencies, and information in police agencies' official arrest records.

On the other hand, pieced-together accounts of what transpired in a closed court proceeding, or a report on the contents of a nonpublic, police investigative record, may not be privileged. (Chapters 6 and 7 will include more about the kinds of proceedings and records that the states deem public.) Also, reports on the unofficial statements or materials volunteered to you on the side by lawyers, police officers, and witnesses may not be privileged.

This point is illustrated by a 1998 federal district court ruling. A Minnesota man was killed by a shotgun blast to the head while sleeping in his home. A sheriff's department investigation focused on the victim's wife as the prime suspect, but after five months investigators still had insufficient evidence to arrest the wife. During the end of this period a CBS television station approached the lead sheriff's investigator, seeking an update on the investigation. After consulting with his superiors, the investigator described to the station a calculated killing and indicated the wife was the likely culprit. These statements were broadcast, and the victim's wife then sued CBS for defamation. Would the fair report privilege protect CBS? The TV station "did much more than reiterate or summarize official documents or proceedings," the court said, by broadcasting statements "nowhere to be found in any public record." Consequently, the fair report privilege did not apply.[62]

Would the result be different if the sheriff investigator's statements had been distributed to media via a news release? Not necessarily. Though the release is a more formal statement, it may still depend on whether the release was based on official government documents or proceedings. In one case, a federal district court in Pennsylvania extended the state's fair report privilege to protect a newspaper's story based on a *foreign* government news release. One person identified in the release and the story as "associated with planning illegal activities in Israel" sued the newspaper for libel. But the court found that the release summarized official Israeli government action of public concern and that the paper was therefore privileged to report fairly on the contents of the release. The court cautioned that not all statements issued by a foreign government agency would, if repeated, give rise to the fair report privilege.[63]

Some states have extended the media privilege even to accounts of non-governmental public proceedings on matters of public concern, such as speeches made during political campaigns. And the *Second Restatement of Torts* suggests that the privilege should apply to reports of "any meeting, assembly, or gathering that is open to the general public and is held for the purpose of discussing or otherwise dealing with matters of public concern."[64] You should check the statues and case law to see how liberally your state applies this very important privilege.

Neutral Reporting	The fair report privilege, with origins both in case law and state statutes, is well established throughout the country. By contrast, a constitutionally based privilege known as **neutral reportage** has been floundering at the doorstep, waiting to gain full-scale acceptance by the courts. It is of potentially great importance. The neutral reporting privilege essentially picks up where the fair reporting privilege leaves off. It would shield the media from libel judgments when reporting in a fair, neutral, and accurate fashion the newsworthy allegations made by others about public officials or public figures—without the requirement of an official or public setting.

The neutral reporting privilege was born in 1977 in the federal appellate court case of *Edwards v. National Audubon Society, Inc.* The case arose when Audubon Society officials labeled as paid liars certain scientists who denied links between pesticide use and harm to wildlife. *The New York Times* reported the charges and was sued for libel, but the U.S. Court of Appeals ruled that under these circumstances the *Times* could not be punished. Wrote the court:

> When a responsible, prominent organization like the National Audubon Society makes serious charges against a public figure, the First Amendment protects the accurate and disinterested reporting of those charges, regardless of the reporter's private views regarding their validity. . . . What is newsworthy about such accusations is that they were made. We do not believe that the press may be required

under the First Amendment to suppress newsworthy statements merely because it has serious doubts regarding their truth.[65]

Other courts and legal scholars expressed grave concerns, however, that such a privilege would be too broad an exception to the rule in libel law against repeating unverified accusations. In the 1980s and 1990s the privilege languished, with some courts declining to recognize the privilege and others adopting it, but with ill-defined and differing contours. For example, the Eighth Circuit adopted the privilege, while the Third Circuit expressly declined to follow it. And in 1989 the U.S. District Court for the District of Columbia applied an expansive version of the privilege, one that covers "all republications of serious charges by one partici-pant in an existing public controversy against another participant in that contro-versy, regardless of the trust-worthiness of the original defamer."[66] The case in-volved comments made by a Hawaiian environmental activist, who vanished soon thereafter, that a member of the state land board was "the Godfather of Hawaii's underworld." The charge was carried by the United Press International wire ser-vice. The U.S. Supreme Court has not yet spoken on the neutral reporting privilege.

The Wire Service Defense

A number of courts have recognized a so-called wire service defense. It is available when a media organization republishes material from a reputable news service without substantial change and without suspecting the content to be false.

For example, in one case a newspaper in Alaska published an Associated Press wire service story in its entirety, exactly as transmitted by AP. All the paper added was its own headline: "Alaska Bush Pilot Accused in Arizona Drug Trafficking." The paper made no attempt to verify or investigate independently. But neither did anyone at the paper have reason to doubt the accuracy of the report. A federal court promptly dismissed a resulting libel claim against the newspaper.[67]

In essence, this defense is little more than a formalized application of the ba-sic fault standards covered earlier. Unless something on the face of the wire serv-ice release would put the local media organization on notice that the release may be inaccurate, or unless the local medium knows the story to be inaccurate, it is not an act of negligence to run the story from a reputable news agency without fur-ther verification. A similar rule generally applies to advertisements submitted to a medium by a reputable advertiser or agency. Note, however, that this defense might not apply when the local medium fails even to read the submitted material prior to publication.

Retractions

About thirty states have enacted **retraction statutes** that provide the media with varying degrees of protection from libel lawsuits. In all cases these laws are an ef-fort to encourage the resolution of libel disputes outside of court. Typically, this is done by limiting a potential plaintiff's recoverable damages if the media publish a timely correction or retraction. Unlike the privileges mentioned earlier, retraction statutes are only a partial shield against libel claims. A lawsuit may still be filed after a retraction is published, but the amount of the plaintiff's potential recovery is restricted to some degree.

California's retraction statute will serve to illustrate. It reads that in any defamation lawsuit against a newspaper or broadcast station the plaintiff may recover no more than special damages unless a formal retraction had been demanded and had not been published or broadcast.[68] Special damages are only those provable losses of a monetary nature, such as loss of income in a business or profession. These business losses are generally much smaller and harder to prove than the actual damages normally recoverable under the *Gertz* decision, and a valid retraction eliminates the threat of punitive damages. In other words, the statute encourages potential plaintiffs to first give the media a chance to set the record straight and encourages the media to run a correction if there was indeed an error. Under the statute a libel lawsuit becomes much less attractive to the plaintiff if the media were not notified of the error promptly or if the media disseminated a legally sufficient correction.

Some states' retraction statutes are of less benefit to the media. For example, they may preclude punitive damages if the plaintiff failed to make a retraction demand or if an appropriate retraction is published, but the full scope of actual damages is still recoverable. Or a statute might not include the requirement that plaintiffs first make formal retraction demands before filing their lawsuits. But in a half-dozen states the requirement on the plaintiff is even greater than in the California example. Under these statutes a potential libel *must* first make a timely retraction demand as a condition of the right to sue for defamation. Another important variable among the retraction statutes is the range of defendants covered. For example, some statutes apply only to alleged libel by the print media; the California statute cited earlier applies to newspapers and broadcast stations, but not to magazines.

Whether or not a statute applies, demands for a retraction should always be taken seriously by mass communicators. You should not be bullied or frightened into backing down when you are convinced you were accurate, for this would sacrifice professional integrity. On the other hand, responding to complaints with sincerity and tact is an important way to ward off libel lawsuits. Responding with rudeness and disdain is a good way to provoke legal trouble. And if you have indeed been inaccurate on a matter of any significance, it is of course a matter of professional ethics that you set the record straight. (See Exhibit 4.4 for additional insights on provoking libel lawsuits.)

Summary Judgment

Media defendants have been able to end many libel lawsuits prior to trial by obtaining summary judgment, a procedure described in Chapter 1. It is essentially a determination by a judge that the lawsuit could have only one outcome and therefore there is no need to proceed with trial. The judge simply applies the law to the known facts and makes a ruling.

| EXHIBIT 4.4 | *Five Sure Ways to Tempt Fate* |

1. Write memos to your editor or news producer about the "holes" in a story. Make plenty of copies and pass them out to everyone. Keep the original memo; it will give the libel plaintiff's lawyer a road map to your company's bank vault.

2. Disregard pleas that it would be premature to publish or broadcast a sensitive story. Railroad the story through.

3. Don't waste a lot of time verifying routine police blotter or court stories. Even though they account for the single greatest percentage of libel claims, these humdrum stories are tiresome to check.

4. Hype a lead or headline, or if you're in broadcasting inflate a "promo," "teaser," "toss," "bumper," or other device used to promote or maintain audience interest during commercial breaks. Jurors always understand economic incentive and they quickly grasp why reporters have to publish or air interest-grabbing stories.

5. Harbor some personal animus toward your news subject. Better yet, tell someone how you can't wait to get that "sleazebag." Even better, put it in writing, in scatalogical detail.

From "Some Lessons in Libel," by media defense attorney Bruce Sanford. Washington Journalism Review, March 1986, p. 29. Reprinted by permission.

Summary judgment has been obtained by media defendants most often in cases filed by public figures and public officials when the plaintiffs could collect no evidence to support a finding of actual malice. Jurisdictions differ in their attitudes toward summary judgment, however. Some court systems encourage it as a way to avoid the chilling effect that prolonged and costly litigation may have on First Amendment rights. Other jurisdictions are less inclined to grant requests for summary judgment, believing that plaintiffs have a right to their day in court unless the lawsuit is clearly a groundless attempt to harass the media.

According to the U.S. Supreme Court, however, summary judgment must be granted in public person cases unless the plaintiff has "clear and convincing" evidence that raises a "genuine issue" of whether actual malice exists. The Court addressed summary judgment at length in *Anderson v. Liberty Lobby, Inc.* in 1986.[69]

Counter-Attacks by the Media

In the mid-1980s, during a time of increased libel lawsuits against the media, communicators in several instances began fighting back, not only by seeking early summary judgment but also by suing the libel plaintiffs in turn. The countersuits are most frequently based on claims of **malicious prosecution** and **abuse of process.**

The tort of malicious prosecution is the initiation of an unsuccessful lawsuit that the plaintiff never reasonably believed could be successful and that caused

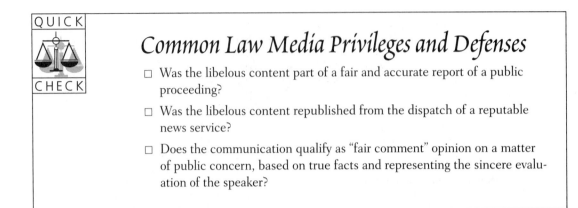

Common Law Media Privileges and Defenses

☐ Was the libelous content part of a fair and accurate report of a public proceeding?

☐ Was the libelous content republished from the dispatch of a reputable news service?

☐ Does the communication qualify as "fair comment" opinion on a matter of public concern, based on true facts and representing the sincere evaluation of the speaker?

the defendant significant expense or damage to reputation. For example, if an individual filed a groundless libel claim against a TV station, perhaps in a quest to force a settlement, the station might countersue for malicious prosecution. Abuse of process, a related tort, is the improper use of any legal procedure—that is, the use of legal power for some ulterior purpose. A libel plaintiff could commit this tort by, for example, filing a civil complaint to intimidate a newspaper and delay publication of information about the plaintiff.

Anti-SLAPP Statutes

In 1988 the acronym SLAPP (strategic lawsuits against public participation) was coined by two University of Denver professors to describe lawsuits without merit that are filed to dissuade or punish the exercise of First Amendment rights by others. In the typical kind of case studied by law professor George W. Pring and sociology professor Penelope Canan, a libel lawsuit is filed by a business entity against an ordinary citizen who, on public interest grounds, has opposed the entity in a government proceeding. For example, a shopping-center developer sues a local resident who publicly opposes zoning approval for the developer's construction project in an effort to intimidate and silence the citizen.

Operating under the perception that these so-called SLAPP cases were on the rise, several states in the 1990s enacted **anti-SLAPP statutes** that create a streamlined procedural avenue for defendants to get such lawsuits tossed out of court. Under the typical anti-SLAPP law, courts must promptly dismiss libel cases concerning statements on public issues unless the plaintiff can demonstrate a probability that the lawsuit has legal merit and is not merely an effort to intimidate. The scope of these statutes varies considerably from state to state. As of 1999, there were fifteen states with anti-SLAPP laws: California, Delaware, Georgia, Indiana, Louisiana, Maine, Massachusetts, Minnesota, Nebraska, Nevada, New York, Oklahoma, Rhode Island, Tennessee and Washington.

In some states these statutes may be drawn broadly enough to also protect the mass media when they are sued for libel concerning statements about a public issue. In California, which possesses one of the most sweeping anti-SLAPP laws, an appellate court ruled that the *San Francisco Chronicle,* a large, corporate media defendant rather than the typical private-citizen SLAPP target, could nevertheless seek to have a libel case dismissed under the anti-SLAPP law. The *Chronicle* had been sued by a private, alternative university following a series of published stories about a zoning dispute between the school and the county. The stories included some unflattering characterizations of the school and its leaders. The university sued for libel, and the *Chronicle* filed a special motion to dismiss the lawsuit, under the anti-SLAPP law, saying the university could not demonstrate a probability that it would prevail because the stories were true.[70]

Libel Insurance   An adverse verdict in one libel lawsuit could force some media organizations out of business. Therefore, many mass-communication businesses carry libel insurance. However, libel insurance does not eliminate all risk. For one thing, only a handful of companies write libel insurance in the United States, and communication businesses deemed as high-risk sometimes find they cannot obtain the insurance. Also, even where insurance can be obtained, some smaller businesses have decided that it is just too costly.

Another limitation on libel insurance is that most insurers' policies do not cover punitive damages. In fact, most states do not allow insurance companies within their borders to protect against punitive damages, the theory being that the public interest is not served by covering malicious behavior.

In the case of broadcasters and newspapers, leading trade organizations have arranged to provide libel insurance coverage for their members through private insurance carriers. The cost of the insurance depends mainly on the amount of coverage desired, the circulation or viewership of the paper or station, and the business's history as a libel risk.

Statutes of Limitations   Regardless of the merit of a defamation claim, a plaintiff must file the lawsuit within a time period specified by law—or the claim is forever barred. The specified time period for filing lawsuits is called the **statute of limitations,** and for defamation claims it ranges from six months to three years, depending on the state. In some states the period is shorter for slander claims than for libel. In the overwhelming majority of states, however, the applicable statute of limitations for all defamation claims is one or two years.

In most states the time period for filing a defamation claim begins running from the day of publication or broadcast, not the date when the plaintiff actually learned of the defamation, which could be much later. For publications that distribute nationally, the statute of limitations does not serve as a solid protection

against a lawsuit until it has expired in the states with the longest filing periods—
three years.

Libel Reform Efforts

The libel rules presented in this chapter are the result of extensive evolution and
balancing by the courts over numerous decades. Still, many of the nation's top
authorities on libel law have in recent years been highly critical of the way the
system works in practice. In the past twenty-five years some high-profile cases
have come to symbolize the tortuous curves and hurdles of modern defamation
lawsuits.

Reasons for Change

For example, in 1976 actress Carol Burnett sued the *National Enquirer* for $10
million. The supermarket tabloid had erroneously reported that Burnett had become boisterous, argued with the secretary of state, and otherwise made a spectacle of herself at a Washington, D.C. restaurant. The *Enquirer* ran a retraction,
but it was ruled of no legal value under the California retraction statute because
the *Enquirer* was not a "newspaper." In 1981 a jury awarded Burnett $1.6 million,
most of it in punitive damages. The trial judge reduced the award to $800,000, and
in 1983 an appellate court further reduced the award to $200,000. The court gave
Burnett the option of a new trial on the issue of damages, however, and she chose
that option.[71] The lawsuit finally ended in 1984 with a settlement of undisclosed
terms, after eight years and the accumulation of millions in attorney's fees.

Burnett's attorney, Barry Langberg, has since handled many other libel cases.
In a telephone conversation in July 1990 he told the author of this book that Burnett "had the time, the money, and the inclination" to pursue her case to the end.
But when injured plaintiffs are without substantial resources, he said, "then it's
very hard to see the justice in the system."

The case of *Newton v. NBC*, mentioned earlier in this chapter, was first initiated by Wayne Newton in 1981. A trial took place five years later, and in 1986 a
federal jury awarded Newton more than $19 million in compensatory and puni-
tive damages. The trial judge then sliced the total award to $5 million. Both par-
ties appealed. Finally in late 1990—almost ten years later—the Court of Appeals
threw out the libel award altogether, ruling there was insufficient evidence of actual malice.

Indeed, many other libel cases have had similar, tortured procedural histories.
From all parties' viewpoint the flaws in the system are apparent: First, even though
media defendants ultimately win most libel lawsuits, the legal costs of the defense
can be enormous. Perhaps the specific libel rules have reached a reasonable balance between freedom of speech and the need to safeguard reputations. But now
it may be the prospect of a lengthy and expensive lawsuit that works a chilling effect on speech, encouraging the media to steer clear of controversial stories.

Second, the process can be prohibitively expensive and wearisome for plaintiffs, too. This means that people who were truly harmed by erroneous information in the media may conclude they have no practical, legal avenue to obtain vindication. And even if a substantial sum is awarded at trial, by the time appeals are completed the award might do little more than cover the legal expenses.

Finally, from the public's standpoint the process of a libel lawsuit, with its complicated turns and lengthy delays, rarely supplies satisfactory answers on the question of truth or falsity or on the virtue of the communicator's performance. Depending on the case, these matters of public concern may not even be the focus of the lawyers' efforts. These criticisms may be overstated to some extent, but a movement has indeed been building—in Congress, state legislatures, and legal and media policy organizations—for some kind of reform.

The Annenberg Project

One of the more ambitious reform efforts was undertaken in 1987 by the Annenberg Washington Program, a communications policy forum sponsored by Northwestern University. Eleven experts, including libel plaintiff attorneys, defense attorneys, and members of the media, were brought together in Washington, D.C. Their goal was to hammer out a model for a better system, operating from the philosophy that "the law of defamation and the First Amendment should not work at cross-purposes, but should function in harmony to serve the compelling public interest in the pursuit of truth."[72]

The project resulted in publication of a model libel reform act, which the team hoped would serve as a precursor to passage of reform laws in the state legislatures or in Congress. The major features of the Annenberg proposal were as follows:

☐ The potential plaintiff would first be required to ask for a retraction or opportunity to reply. If the request is honored, *no* lawsuit would be allowed.

☐ If a lawsuit did result, either side could dictate that it simply be for a "declaratory judgment" by the court, rather than for an award of damages. In this streamlined proceeding, the sole issue would be the truth or falsity of the statements. The court would make a public announcement of its findings, but the only money paid by the loser would be the winner's attorney fees.

☐ The parties could decide to tangle in a full-fledged lawsuit where money damages would be at stake and where the constitutional fault standard would have to be proved. But in all cases presumed and punitive damages would be eliminated.

The real crux of this bold proposal was to encourage both sides in a defamation conflict to patch up their differences outside of court or to settle on the declaratory judgment route. Plaintiffs would give up the possibility of collecting big damages, but would gain a relatively quick and affordable way to clear their name. Defendants would be without the protection of the constitutional fault standards, but would avoid the risk of having to pay huge damage awards.

Despite the ultimate unity achieved by the diverse members of the reform project, the proposal did not prompt changes in the law. Many in the media opposed the declaratory judgment aspect, fearing that it would open the gate to a flood of "truth suits" that taken together could cost plenty in defense attorneys' fees.

The Uniform Correction Act

An even more weighty libel reform effort was undertaken by the National Conference of Commissioners on Uniform State Laws, a prestigious organization of legal experts that drafts model legislation for possible adoption by the states. The commissioners address legal matters where consistency among the states would be particularly advantageous. In 1993, after several years of work, the commissioners approved the Uniform Correction or Clarification of Defamation Act (UCCDA).

In early drafts, the commissioners attempted a thorough overhaul of defamation law. But these drafts met considerable resistance from the media. In its final form, the UCCDA is a narrower proposal that appeared to have good prospects of adoption by the states. Similar to the retraction statutes already existing in some jurisdictions, the UCCDA seeks to encourage timely corrections of defamation and to provide a means of settling disputes without going to court. But the act is substantially broader and more detailed than most preexisting state retraction statutes.

The UCCDA applies in all defamation situations, regardless of whether the potential plaintiff is a public or private person, or whether the would-be defendant is a mass medium or an individual. The act requires that, in all such cases, the aggrieved party formally request a correction within ninety days from first learning of the defamatory communication. If a ninety-day request is not made, the aggrieved party may still sue but is limited to recovery of provable economic loss; punitive damages and damages for general injury to reputation would be precluded. Furthermore, even if a plaintiff makes a timely correction request, the defendant can still limit the plaintiff to recovery of economic loss by publishing a "timely and sufficient" correction.

The American Bar Association endorsed the UCCDA in 1994, and shortly thereafter state legislatures began considering the model bill. In 1995 North Dakota enacted the proposal into law, and, it appeared that many other states would follow. The American Society of Newspaper Editors backed the UCCDA, and many legal experts believe it is a realistic, rational proposal for resolving disputes and reducing the "chilling effect" posed by lengthy lawsuits and huge damage awards. In addition, it would give national media, for the first time, a uniform set of legal rules governing corrections. However, as of 1999 North Dakota still was the only state to have adopted the model legislation.

Summary Points

The law of defamation can be traced back hundreds of years; it is based on the common law right of people to protect their good reputations against attack.

Defamation law encompasses the twin torts of libel (written defamation) and slander (spoken defamation), but in terms of the legal rules, these torts are nearly identical today. Some states also have criminal laws against defamation, but criminal prosecutions are rare and constitutionally suspect.

Beginning with the 1964 landmark case of *New York Times v. Sullivan,* the Supreme Court has forced remodeling of the states' defamation rules so that mass communicators would have adequate breathing space to pursue First Amendment ideals.

To win a libel lawsuit against a mass medium, a plaintiff today must prove in court all of the following:

defamatory statement (one tending to injure reputation),

falsity of the statement,

publication to third persons,

identification of the plaintiff,

fault on the part of the communicator (actual malice or at least negligence), and

injury to the plaintiff as a result of the defamation.

To establish actual malice, public person plaintiffs must prove through direct or circumstantial evidence that the defendant published with knowledge of falsity or with serious doubts about the accuracy of the material.

In addition to the libel elements, communicators have several privileges and other protections. Perhaps most important, communicators cannot be liable for simply relaying, accurately, the contents of public proceedings and documents.

Also, broadcasting or publishing a retraction has, in many states, the statutory effect of limiting the extent of potential liability.

In the chapter hypothetical about the sheriff, some of the comments made in the newspaper ad would be protected as pure opinion. Others, such as the charges that the sheriff is "looking the other way," may be "taking bribes," and may "soon be indicted," suggest facts that could be proved true or false and therefore could support a libel claim. If so, an important question becomes whether the newspaper and you, as advertising manager, were at fault in allowing the ad to run. The sheriff as a public official would have to prove actual malice, but some evidence of actual malice exists in the fact that reporters specifically told you, in advance, that they thought one of the serious allegations was false.

Discussion Questions

1. In recent decades the courts have gone to considerable effort to achieve the proper balance between the right of free speech and the right of defamed people to seek compensation for their injured reputations. In your opinion, considering the many legal rules discussed in this chapter, has the proper balance been reached? If so, has the legal framework become too cumbersome to do justice, as some charge? Do any reasonable alternatives exist, other than the kind of declaratory judgment lawsuit described at the end of this chapter?

2. Suppose, in the chapter hypothetical, that the charges of bribery against the sheriff had been typed in a flyer and distributed all over town by the citizens' group. The flyers are causing quite a stir, and you, as a news reporter, would like to repeat in a news story exactly what the group is alleging. Could you legally do so, even if you suspected the allegations were false? In a jurisdiction that recognizes the neutral reportage privilege, what conditions would have to be satisfied before the privilege would protect you?

3. Suppose you were a speech writer for the disparaged sheriff in the chapter hypothetical, and the sheriff is giving a speech tomorrow in which he wants to go on the offensive against Sam Smith, a member of the opposition citizens' group. Would any of the following comments be privileged or otherwise safe from a libel claim? "I think Smith must be a cocaine dealer." "I think Smith is the kind of man who would be a cocaine dealer." "Half the people in this town think Smith is the kind of man who would be a cocaine dealer." "Smith has the kind of weak moral values I often observe in cocaine dealers."

Key Terms

abuse of process	libel
actual damages	libel by implication
actual malice	limited purpose public figure
all-purpose public figure	malicious prosecution
anti-SLAPP statutes	negligence
compensatory damages	neutral reportage
constitutional malice	presumed damages
defamation	product disparagement
fair comment privilege	publication
fair report privilege	public figure

public official   slander
public record privilege   special damages
punitive damages   statute of limitations
retraction statutes   strict liability
rhetorical hyperbole   trade libel

Web Resource

http://www.ldrc.com
Libel Defense Resource Center, Inc.

InfoTrac® College Edition

Hundreds of U.S. newspapers are now accessible via the Internet, and defamation issues have followed the traditional media into the online arena. The law must evolve to catch up to this seemingly overnight development. One interesting question is: To what extent will existing retraction statutes be interpreted to cover online corrections? Find a journal article that analyzes this question.

Chapter Outline

Privacy and Peace of Mind

Upon completing this chapter you should

- ☐ **appreciate** the rationales behind laws that aim to protect privacy and peace of mind.
- ☐ **learn** the distinguishing elements of the four main privacy torts.
- ☐ **understand** the role of related torts that may arise along with claims of privacy invasion.
- ☐ **know** some of the typical criminal laws that aim to protect privacy and restrict media content.
- ☐ **be able** to analyze a given set of facts to determine which media practices would violate privacy laws, which would be safe, and which would fall into the risky gray area, which can be quite substantial in privacy law.

Hypothetical

■ The Spicy Private Life

Assume you are a producer for a TV news show, and you are preparing a special segment titled "Who's Teaching Our Kids?" about the private lives of educators. You hear seamy rumors from two students at the local college about one of their psychology instructors, Vera Grundy, and you decide to check it out. After hours of searching through old police logs at the city records office, you discover that Grundy was arrested once, eight years ago, for drunk driving. Also, a former friend of Grundy's tells you that when they were freshmen in college the two women hid behind the dormitory one night and smoked marijuana. They had kept this a closely guarded secret ever since. The ex-friend also tells you that Grundy recently made several visits to a psychiatrist's office for treatment of acute depression. Finally, you stake out Grundy's secluded home on the outskirts of town. Her property is surrounded by a wooden fence and thick vegetation, but you and a camera operator climb high into a tree across the road. From your perch you can see a portion of Grundy's backyard. Using a video camera equipped with a powerful lens, you get footage of Grundy naked in her hot tub with a man who is not her husband.

Your station decides this segment is worth promotion. Between a couple of late-afternoon soap operas, one of the news anchors comes on the air and announces: "Vera Grundy, the hot-tub teacher. Get the full story on tonight's eleven o'clock news, right here on Channel Seven." The scenario raises serious ethical concerns for you, of course, and perhaps some legal ones. From a strictly legal standpoint, would you be safe in broadcasting all of that information? Some of it? Have you or your station already crossed the legal barrier, even if you never broadcast the details of what you learned? Would you answer differently if Grundy were running for a seat on the city council?

Origins of Privacy Law

Privacy law is among the most complicated and potentially far-reaching legal concerns facing mass communicators today. It is also a rather young and unsettled area of law. When this nation was formed there was no privacy law to inherit from the common law of England. Nor did the U.S. Constitution specifically recognize the right of individual privacy, and the early legislatures did not feel a need to address it.

But by 1900 times had changed radically. Perhaps most important was the advent of commercial mass media that were highly competitive and pervasive. Extremely private matters could be made public overnight—and the media seemed increasingly inclined to do just that. Today, with assaults on privacy coming not only from the mass media but also from computer databases, telemarketing, and sophisticated electronic taping and surveillance devices, the public seems increasingly concerned about protecting what's often called a "right to be left alone."

Legal scholars often trace the privacy laws of today to an influential 1890 article by law partners Louis Brandeis and Samuel Warren, published in the Harvard *Law Review*. The authors were reacting to the personal affronts of gossip-oriented newspapers in that era of yellow journalism when they proposed that the law recognize a right of privacy. They wrote:

> The press is overstepping in every direction the obvious bounds of propriety and of decency. Gossip is no longer the resource of the idle and of the vicious, but has become a trade, which is pursued with industry as well as effrontery. . . .
> To occupy the indolent, column upon column is filled with idle gossip, which can only be procured by intrusion upon the domestic circle. The intensity and complexity of life, attending upon advancing civilization, have rendered necessary some retreat from the world, and man, under the refining influence of culture, has become more sensitive to publicity, so that solitude and privacy have become more essential to the individual; but modern enterprise and invention have, through invasions upon his privacy, subjected him to mental pain and distress, far greater than could be inflicted by mere bodily injury.[1]

States in the early 1900s began to recognize a civil-law right of privacy. Some states passed statutes, and in others the courts developed the right through common law. These early laws prohibited using without consent a person's name or picture for advertising purposes. From this beginning the courts slowly expanded privacy law to cover the publication of truthful but embarrassing private facts— the kind of protection that Brandeis and Warren had proposed. Lawmakers have added criminal statutes to protect privacy in some narrow circumstances.

As the century drew to a close, privacy-related lawsuits against the media were escalating. As in prior decades, the media successfully defended against most of these 1990s lawsuits. Yet there were enough plaintiff's victories to rouse more plaintiffs, and enough instances of offensive media conduct to spark new legislation against hidden cameras and intrusive paparazzi-style tactics.

Four Distinct Torts

This chapter actually encompasses several distinct torts, as well as a few misdemeanor crimes. Most notable are the four separate privacy torts that have evolved in most of the states, each tort with different rules and purposes. They are:

1. Commercial appropriation of name or likeness

2. Public disclosure of embarrassing private facts

3. Placing an individual in a false light

4. Intrusion upon physical seclusion

A slight majority of the states now recognizes all four branches of invasion of privacy, either by statute or common law. However, a significant number of states have not clearly adopted all of them. In many instances states simply have not had reported appellate cases directly on point, making those states' positions uncertain. In a few instances, courts have specifically declined to recognize one or more of these privacy torts.

Privacy-invading circumstances often give rise to a combination of tort claims, including not only the above privacy torts but also such claims as fraud and intentional infliction of emotional distress. Although multiple tort claims are often made by plaintiffs, it important to avoid mentally commingling them. As you improve your ability to analyze potentially dangerous situations, you must know the separate purposes and elements of these torts. We will begin by looking at the four privacy torts.

Appropriation

The first form of privacy invasion, **appropriation,** may be defined as the commercial use of a person's name or likeness without consent.

Here's the typical scenario: You take a photograph of an accomplished marathon runner as she crosses the finish line and provide the photo to a newspaper. The picture finds its way to the advertising department. The photo then is used prominently in an ad for a brand of running shoes without the athlete's consent. The woman feels exploited by the profit actions of others—by the advertiser, the paper, and you—and she has potentially a good legal claim.

Appropriation is the best established form of invasion of privacy, and it is of particular concern to photographers and advertising and public-relations practitioners. This civil wrong is also referred to as **misappropriation** or infringement of an individual's **right of publicity.** The theory behind this law is that individuals should have the sole right to control the marketing or exploitation of their own persona.

Some legal scholars view this as more of a business or property right than a privacy right. Indeed, lawsuits are often brought by people who are upset, not about their appearance in an advertisement, but about the lack of payment. Yet this law, like the other privacy torts, is intended to compensate individuals for the infliction of embarrassment or shame—highly personal forms of injury—that can accompany unwanted publicity. Commercial appropriation lawsuits are often initiated by celebrities seeking to protect or control their commercially valuable images, but exploited private people may sue as well.

As with libel, it is best to separate and examine the key elements of this privacy tort.

Commercial Use

First of all, **commercial use** generally means exploitation directly for trade or self-enrichment purposes. Modern courts have consistently made the critical distinction between commercial and noncommercial uses, though it is not always easy to make.

Advertisements or promotions, for products or services, are typical examples of messages with a commercial purpose, so the use of a person's image in those messages is usually deemed commercial. The clearest form of commercial use is the product endorsement ad, such as the running shoe example. But product manuals, promotional contests, corporate recruiting films, and picture posters are other examples of productions that courts are likely to deem commercial.

At the other end of the scale, use of a name, photo, or sketch in the context of news is not deemed a commercial use. And an otherwise news-oriented context is not classified as commercial simply because the medium is operated for profit, as most newspapers and broadcast stations are. To be deemed a commercial use there must be some direct, self-serving link between the individual's identity and the promotion of a product, service, or organization. When the individual appears in news reports, the commercial element is insufficient, even if the individuals' appearance might, secondarily, help sell newspapers. These are well-settled points, addressed by the *Restatement (Second) of the Law of Torts:*

> The value of the plaintiff's name is not appropriated by mere mention of it, or by reference to it in connection with legitimate mention of his public activities. . . . The fact that the defendant is engaged in the business of publication, for example of a newspaper, out of which he makes a profit, is not enough to make the incidental publication a commercial use of the name or likeness.[2]

Unfortunately, the rule that news content cannot spark appropriate lawsuits has been clouded to a small degree by the U.S. Supreme Court's only decision in an appropriation case. It was an odd case, decided 5–4 by the Court: In 1972 Hugo Zacchini performed as the "human cannonball" at a county fair in Ohio. In each fifteen-second performance he was shot from a cannon into a net 200 feet away. One day a television news reporter videotaped the act and it was shown on the eleven o'clock news. The human cannonball sued for damages, claiming that the TV station unlawfully appropriated his professional property and threatened the future economic value of his act. What was the result?

Despite the usually solid rule that appropriation claims cannot arise from news content, the Supreme Court in this case held that no First Amendment privilege applies when a professional performer's entire act is broadcast without consent under the context of news. The state of Ohio was therefore free to allow tort liability if it wished. This opinion is much criticized and should be viewed as a narrow and rare exception to the usual principles of appropriation law.[3]

The general rule is that appearances in product advertising and promotions are usually commercial uses; appearances in news contexts are not. But this still leaves plenty of communications that are hard to categorize, such as corporate public relations publications that include legitimate news or educational information. Retail magazines and books can also be problematic.

Magazines and Books

In one case, *Playgirl* magazine contained an illustration, unrelated to any particular news or commentary, of a nude black man seated in the corner of a boxing ring. The man was recognizable as former heavyweight champion Muhammad Ali. He sued the magazine under New York's broad privacy statute, which stated that "any person whose name, portrait or picture is used within this state for . . . the purposes of trade" without the written consent of that person may sue for damages and an injunction. The court, ruling in favor of Ali, said:

> It is clear that the picture has been used for the "purpose of trade" under [the statute]. It is the established law of New York that the unauthorized use of an individual's picture is not for a "trade purpose" . . . if it is "in connection with an item of news or one that is newsworthy" . . . In the instant case there is no such informational or newsworthy dimension to defendants' unauthorized use of Ali's likeness. Instead, the picture is a dramatization, an illustration falling somewhere between representational art and cartoon, and is accompanied by a plainly fictional . . . bit of doggerel.[4]

So inclusions in a magazine of works that are purely fictional—solely for entertainment—may be deemed commercial uses in some states, even if the use is not directly connected with an advertising pitch. On the other hand, a news or educational article in a magazine is likely to fall outside the scope of appropriation law.

Frequently it is the covers of magazines or books that cause trouble. The general rule is that a cover picture is safe if it is derived from the newsworthy or educational content within. If the person depicted on the cover is not a subject of the content, however, the picture is deemed to be for a purely commercial, promotional purpose.

For example, when a magazine cover photo showed a man dressed in green at a St. Patrick's Day parade to illustrate an article about Irish immigrants, a court said the photo was related to the story and could not be the basis for an appropriation claim.[5] But in New York a black teenager won an appropriation lawsuit against the publisher of a book about getting into college. The teen was not a subject of the book, but her picture, obtained from a freelance photographer, was used on the cover to help boost sales to members of minority groups.[6]

These distinctions draw some fine lines; remember that courts from different jurisdictions may not be entirely consistent. Therefore, publications dealing with non-news content often play it safe by obtaining written consent. In the book-cover case the publisher was unaware that the freelancer had never obtained a written photo release.

Incidental Uses

Categorizing the overall context of a message as commercial, as opposed to news or educational, helps determine whether individuals' appearances in those messages will be deemed commercial uses. But often the analysis must go deeper. Frequently there is some degree of commercial purpose behind a media message or production, and the ultimate question then is whether the individual's identity is incidental to the commercial purpose or directly in support of it.

Even in a product advertisement, for example, it is possible that an individual's appearance would not be considered a commercial use. This is because it is not the purely technical, or incidental, inclusion of someone's name or likeness that gives rise to this tort. Rather, it is the exploitation of some individual attributes—capitalization upon some values associated with the name or likeness.

For example, suppose you took a long-range picture for that running shoe ad—a photo of 150 runners crowded near the starting line. Technically speaking, each runner is identifiable. Yet these people cannot each bring an appropriation claim because their identities are immaterial to the message. They are not appearing in the ad for any individual value, such as reputation, good looks, or even a particular pose. Nor would the circumstance imply a product endorsement by all these runners.

So it is the value of a person's name or likeness—some identifiable qualities—that must be appropriated for this tort, not the merely incidental appearance of the likeness. Communicators must be careful, though; rarely is a person's appearance in a commercial message purely incidental. When in doubt, it is wise to get consent or refrain from using the name or likeness in a commercial context. (The rules of consent are discussed later in this section of the chapter.)

Special Problem: Self-Promotion

A tricky area of dispute has been that of "house ads," "teasers," or other media self-promotions. A 1986 case from Oregon will illustrate. A television news cameraman filmed an auto accident scene, including footage of a victim who was bleeding and receiving emergency medical treatment. The video did not appear on that night's news program, but it was used later—in a promotional spot for an upcoming special report on emergency care. The accident victim sued for appropriation, claiming his likeness was used without consent for the TV station's own commercial advantage. But the Supreme Court of Oregon ruled in favor of the station. While the footage was used for a commercial purpose, the victim's appearance was merely incidental to that purpose, the court said. The promotion did not imply that the victim endorsed the forthcoming program about emergency care, and "the identity of the accident victim was immaterial," the court said.[7]

Suppose newspaper editors use a photo of a movie star on page 20 of the newspaper and also reproduce it in a little box at the top of page 1. Along with the photo, the box reads: "A Film Star's Career Examined—See Page 20." Now the individual's identity is an integral part of the promotional message. But even here, the media are generally immune from appropriation claims because the name or likeness is being used to illustrate the legitimate contents of the paper, courts have said. This is essentially the sort of promotion that was described in the hypothetical problem for this chapter. The result will be different, though, if the promo implies an endorsement or any other commercial connection between the individual and the medium.

For example, in *Cher v. Forum International, Ltd.,* the U.S. Court of Appeals held a magazine liable for exploiting an interview with the entertainer Cher. She had given an interview to *US* magazine under the condition that she could bar publication if she did not like the results. Cher decided not to allow publication. However, the interviewer then sold the interview to *Forum,* a magazine of which Cher did not approve. In addition to publishing excerpts from the interview, the magazine used Cher's name on a pullout subscription card. The card claimed that Cher told *Forum* things she would not tell *US* magazine, and it read, "So join Cher and *Forum*'s hundreds of thousands of other adventurous readers today." This was held to be a highly misleading and commercial use of the public figure's likeness.[8]

Name or Likeness

Individuals must be readily identifiable in order to sue successfully for appropriation. This element is easy to recognize when it is a plaintiff's name or photograph that appears in the message. But the concept of **name or likeness** is broader than this. It could also be the plaintiff's nickname, voice, or other mark of personal identity.

A 1983 case illustrates that name or likeness can really mean personal identity by whatever method of reference. A company had begun doing business under the name Here's Johnny Portable Toilets, Inc., and it referred to its product as "the world's foremost commodian." As you might guess, the company was sued by TV comedian Johnny Carson, who had hosted *The Tonight Show* since 1962. On the show each night he was introduced with the phrase "Here's Johnny," and the phrase came to be associated with Carson by a substantial segment of TV viewers.

Carson believed his identity had been wrongfully capitalized upon, and the appellate court agreed. Wrote the court: "The right of publicity . . . is that a celebrity has a protected pecuniary interest in the commercial exploitation of his identity. . . . Carson's identity may be exploited even if his name, John W. Carson, or his picture is not used."[9]

A particularly troublesome area of the law in recent years has involved the use of celebrity look-alikes and sound-alikes. Under the traditional rule it is not considered commercial appropriation to feature in advertising someone who looks or sounds like a particular celebrity, without the celebrity's consent. This is simply because it is not the celebrity plaintiff's actual picture or voice that is being used. However, when the look-alike or sound-alike is used in a manner likely to confuse the public, some courts recently have allowed the celebrity to recover damages, either on a right-of-publicity theory or on some other ground.

For example, a 1988 federal appellate court decision involved the following facts: The advertising agency of Young & Rubicam had approached Bette Midler to perform her 1970s hit "Do You Want to Dance?" in a series of commercials for Ford Motor Company. Midler refused, so the agency, without Midler's consent, hired one of her former backup singers to imitate Midler's voice as closely as possible. The imitation was convincing, and Midler sued for appropriation. The U.S. Court of Appeals acknowledged the usual rule that imitation does not amount to appropriation, but the court nevertheless held that in the narrow circumstance "when a distinctive voice of a professional singer is widely known and is deliberately imitated in order to sell a product, the sellers have appropriated what is not theirs and have committed a tort in California."[10] A jury eventually awarded Midler $400,000.

Another 1988 case involved the well-known entertainer and filmmaker Woody Allen. Allen sued a clothing store and an advertising agency for unauthorized exploitation of his likeness through the use of a look-alike. A magazine ad for the store had featured Allen look-alike Phil Boroff, posed with a clarinet. The Federal District Court in New York reiterated the usual rule in that state that invasion-of-privacy law extended protection only to likenesses of the plaintiff, not to photographs of someone else. However, the court awarded summary judgment to Allen on another theory—unfair competition under the federal Lanham Act. All that was required for Allen to have a valid claim under this federal statute was a false representation that the store's products were associated with Allen in some way. Such a likelihood of confusion existed, the court held, despite a small disclaimer that appeared under the photo.[11]

Taking the element of likeness a step further was the 1992 case of *White v. Samsung Electronics*. The electronics company ran a magazine advertising campaign in which its products were depicted in humorous futuristic settings. The basic theme was that its products were of such quality that they would remain in operation well into the new millenium. One of the ads, for Samsung video recorders, depicted a robot dressed in a wig, gown, and jewelry. The robot was posed next to a game-show board resembling that of the hit show *Wheel of Fortune*. This, of course, conjured up the image of game-show host Vanna White. White sued for appropriation.

The federal district court granted summary judgment against White on grounds that the ad did not actually use White's name or likeness, nor would readers confuse the robot for an actual picture of White. But the Court of Appeals reversed.

Applying California law, the court said appropriations of identity in that state could be accomplished through many means other than name, picture, look-alike, or sound-alike. If a celebrity's identity is commercially exploited, the court noted, then the celebrity's rights have been invaded no matter how that identity was conveyed. And in this case, the court concluded, the total circumstances of the ad clearly evoked the identity of Vanna White.[12]

Following these cases a number of other celebrities have filed their own lawsuits claiming that unauthorized imitations have infringed upon their rights. A few of these plaintiffs have won in court, others have lost, and still others have obtained settlements for undisclosed amounts. Suffice it to say that, as of this writing, the law concerning imitations in advertising remains unsettled in many jurisdictions. National advertising campaigns must conform to the law in states known to be the strictest.

Consent

There is a tendency to think that people won't sue for appropriation unless their images are used in some offensive fashion, or that if they do sue it won't be a case worth much money. But these can be dangerous assumptions, especially when using names and images of celebrities.

A case in point: *Los Angeles Magazine* without consent published a photo of actor Dustin Hoffman as he appeared in the successful 1982 film *Tootsie,* dressed in a gown and high heels. Through computer manipulation, however, the photo had been altered so that the gown and shoes looked like those of particular fashion designers. The text read: "Dustin Hoffman isn't a drag in a butter-colored silk gown by Richard Tyler and Ralph Lauren heels." The photo ran in a section with similar computer-altered images of celebrities wearing fashions by designers who were also advertisers in the magazine. Hoffman, who during thirty years of celebrity status had refused to permit commercial uses of his identity, sued for violation of his right of publicity. In 1999 a federal court approved an award of $1.5 million in compensatory damages to Hoffman, representing the fair market value of his name and likeness used for endorsement purposes.[13] Another $1.5 million was awarded in punitive damages.

So, unless it is clear that the use of a person's name or likeness is not for a commercial purpose, communicators should protect themselves by obtaining consent. Even if the initial intent is not to use the material in a commercial context, that opportunity may present itself later on. This is especially true for freelance photographers and the publications that use their work. A photo may have first been taken and published simply because it seemed newsworthy; later an advertiser may offer to buy the picture for use in a campaign. At that point, having the prior consent of the individual in the photo serves a dual purpose: It protects against appropriation lawsuits and it makes the photo more marketable.

In some states the appropriation laws say consent for commercial uses is valid only if it is in writing. And that's the prudent way to document consent, whether it is required in writing or not. For photographs, consent is normally obtained on

EXHIBIT 5.1   *Sample Model Release*

In exchange for valuable consideration, I hereby irrevocably consent to the use and reproduction by you, [photographer's name], or anyone authorized by you, of any and all photographs that you have this day taken of me, for any purpose whatsoever and through any or all media, without restriction as to alterations, and without further compensation to me. All negatives, positives, and prints shall constitute your property, solely.

Date: _____

Model signature: _____

Address: _____

the spot by photographers who carry forms known as **model releases** or **photo consent forms.** Aware that the law is not always clear about what constitutes a commercial use, many magazines and book publishers require a signed model release in all cases. A typical release form might read something like the one in Exhibit 5.1.

Of course, some release agreements are much more complicated than this, at the desire of one or all parties concerned. For example, the release might be very specific, either about the degree to which photos or video may be altered or about the purposes for which they may be used. It is generally in the best interest of the media to have releases worded in broad terms to cover future, unforeseen uses. On the other hand, the individuals being used—especially if they are highly marketable models or celebrities—will sometimes consent only to clearly specified, restrictive uses.

In any case, there are a few important points to remember about consent. First, people under 18 years of age, **minors,** are deemed incapable of giving valid consent. Therefore, a parent or guardian must also sign the release form on the minor's behalf.

Second, when consent is given gratuitously—that is, not in exchange for money or something else of value—the consent may legally be withdrawn at any reasonable time prior to publication. Gratuitous consent is not a binding contract, so the individuals giving consent retain the right to change their minds. If communicators want to lock in consent for the long term, the release must be worded in the form of a contract, and something must be paid in exchange for the consent obtained. The sample release language in Exhibit 5.1 is in contract form because it begins: "In exchange for valuable consideration. . . ." The "consideration" may be as little as one dollar, but something of value must be exchanged in order to solidify a contractual form of consent.

Appropriation

☐ Is the context commercial, such as a product advertisement or promotion?

☐ Is someone identified by name, photo, voice, or otherwise?

☐ Is the person being exploited for commercial gain rather than appearing incidentally?

☐ Was proper consent obtained (e.g., a written photo release)?

Finally, even though a release may be worded in broad, open-ended terms, courts have often held that reasonable limitations are implied. For example, the consent might be deemed invalid after the passage of many years unless the terms are specific on this point. Similarly, courts might not interpret blanket consent language to cover either drastic alterations to a photo or degrading uses of it. It is also highly unlikely that courts would uphold an individual's consent to be libeled, even if the consent language specifically attempts to absolve you of such liability, unless the defamatory portrayal has been clearly specified. Under the law only a **knowing consent** is a valid consent.

Special Problem: Deceased Celebrities

In appropriation law, one of the ongoing debates is whether a legal right over publicity should survive death. In other words, if you publish in an advertisement the picture of a famous football player who died last year, should the athlete's widow be allowed to sue you for appropriation, just as the football player could if he were alive? In many states this question has not been settled. And, among those jurisdictions where it has been settled, the states are split.

Generally speaking, in states that distinguish a separate right-of-publicity offshoot of appropriation, that right is viewed as essentially a property interest. As such, a celebrity may assign the right to others, and enforceability of the right survives the celebrity's death. In states where a separate right of publicity is not recognized apart from the personal privacy protections of appropriation law, the typical rule is that the claim must be filed and pursued, if at all, by the individual whose name or likeness was used.[14]

At least eight states have passed statutes that allow appropriation claims to be filed after death by the appropriated individual's heirs or the heirs' assignees. An important example is the California statute that establishes a transferable property right in an individual's "name, voice, signature, photograph or likeness" if it had commercial value at the time of death.[15] The right expires fifty years after death. Certain unauthorized uses, such as for news reporting, are privileged. The significance of such statutes is that advertisers sometimes have to pay substantial licensing fees to the heirs of deceased celebrities before using their identities in advertising campaigns. The statutes generally apply only in cases in which people, such as film and music stars, commercially exploited their persona during their lifetime.

First Amendment Issues

Historically, most appropriation cases concerned relatively easy distinctions between permissible news uses of people's identities and impermissible exploitation of their identities for advertising purposes. However, many of the recent appropriation cases raise significant First Amendment concerns and beg for further court clarification of the line between free speech and invasion of personal right of privacy or publicity.

For example, an artist specializing in charcoal sketches of celebrities produced and sold prints and T-shirts bearing a sketch of the famous deceased comedy personalities, the Three Stooges. Under California's deceased-celebrity statute, the owner of the Stooges' publicity rights sued to collect the profits and attorney fees. The defendant raised the First Amendment, arguing that his selling of the sketches should be fully protected as art, as expression of a message, and as expression about people who remain newsworthy. But a state appeals court said no, that the First Amendment offered no protection because the artist was not seeking to convey any message, political or social. Rather, he was just selling the celebrities' images. Nor was there automatic protection against an appropriation lawsuit just because the work might be deemed art.[16]

Cases such as this raise many interesting questions: Would the result be different if the T-shirts depicting the Three Stooges also contained the words "In Memory" or "We Miss You, Stooges" or some other message?[17] What if the images had been altered somewhat so that they became parody, a form of commentary on current social or political affairs?

Disclosure of Private Facts

Mention invasion of privacy by the mass media and it is this second kind—unwarranted publicity about private life—that often comes to people's minds. For a working definition, this tort is the public disclosure of embarrassing private facts that are not newsworthy and when such disclosure would be highly offensive to a reasonable person.

Note that this law runs contrary to traditional American precepts about freedom of expression by allowing mass communicators to be sued for the dissemination of truthful information. Strong sentiment exists for legally protecting an individuals' personal secrets and private moments because the mass media have the power to obliterate privacy in short order. The perceived threat of mortifying exposure by the mass media is probably as great today as it was in 1890, when Warren and Brandeis published their influential law review article.

To a large extent this privacy issue must be relegated to society's ethical discourse and standards, not to legal rules, and the courts have recognized this. If applied broadly, this tort could work a tremendous chilling effect on legitimate media activity. So the tort has been confined to narrow boundaries, and successful lawsuits against the media have been infrequent.

Here again, it is necessary to break down the definition of this tort to examine its important elements.

Private Facts

First of all, this tort concerns the dissemination of accurate information—facts. In that respect it is easily distinguishable from defamation. Truth is no defense; rather, it is part of the problem. But these disclosed facts must also have been truly *private* facts. No liability exists under this tort for giving further publicity to information that was already generally available to the public. It is not enough that an individual now wants to keep certain information private. The plaintiff must prove that the information *was* private until the media came along and let the cat out of the bag. The disclosed information must indeed have been treated confidentially by the plaintiff, not spread across town to anyone who would listen.

But prior disclosures by an individual plaintiff, if limited and selective, will not necessarily diminish the private nature of those facts in the eyes of the law. Information relayed in confidence to family, close friends, or an employer, for example, may still be private in character. Following are some additional guidelines for determining whether information is private.

Public Places

Events that occur in public view are almost always considered public, not private, information. A 1976 case against *Sports Illustrated* is often cited as an example of this principle. A photographer for the magazine took pictures of some Pittsburgh Steelers fans who were hamming it up atop a dugout before a football game. From thirty photos of the fans, the magazine published one to illustrate an article titled "A Strange Kind of Love," about the Steelers' rowdy fans. The picture, however, was a close-up of one of the fans with his trousers left unzipped; that fan sued, claiming his slovenly behavior was a private matter.

Though the photo was not anatomically revealing, a federal court agreed that the magazine had deliberately exhibited the fan in an embarrassing manner. Yet this wasn't enough. The court denied the plaintiff's claim because the photo simply did not reveal anything that was private. The fan's embarrassing behavior had been observable by the general public, and he had even dared the photographer to take pictures. The court wrote: "A photograph taken at a public event which everyone present could see, with the knowledge and implied consent of the subject, is not a matter concerning a private fact."[18]

This principle—that events in public places are fair game—is often observed by the courts. Rare exceptions can be found, however. For example, contrast the Pittsburgh case with a 1964 case against an Alabama newspaper. A woman and her two sons had decided to wander through the fun house at a county fair, unaware of what to expect. As she exited, the woman's dress was blown up by air jets beneath the fun house platform. As fate would have it, a newspaper photographer captured this instant on film. A few days later the photo ran on the front page, showing the woman exposed from the waist down except for her panties.

The Alabama Supreme Court upheld an invasion-of-privacy judgment in favor of the woman, even though it acknowledged the scene had occurred in public. Unlike the case of the Steelers fan, this woman's embarrassing predicament was instantaneous and involuntary. The court wrote: "To hold that one who is involuntarily and instantaneously enmeshed in an embarrassing pose forfeits her right of privacy merely because she happened at the moment to be part of a public scene would be illogical, wrong, and unjust."[19]

Public Records

Another principle is that information cannot be deemed private in nature when it is obtained from the public record. This is the rule from an important 1975 U.S. Supreme Court case, *Cox Broadcasting Corp. v. Cohn.*

A teenage girl in Georgia had been raped, and she died. Six youths were soon indicted in the death and rape. These facts were reported prominently in the media, but a state law prohibited public disclosure of the victim's identity. During court proceedings several months later, a TV reporter was allowed to examine the indictments and from them learned the name of the victim. He broadcast the name later that day. The girl's father sued the reporter and station owner Cox Broadcasting, arguing that his own right to privacy had been invaded by the broadcast of his deceased daughter's name.

The Court ruled in favor of the defendants, based on First Amendment rights. The Court first noted the well-established privilege under defamation law, that those who see and hear what transpires at trials and other public proceeds can in turn report it with impunity. Then the Court turned to the privacy arena and concluded that "even the prevailing law of invasion of privacy generally recognizes that the interests in privacy fade when the information involved already appears on the public record."[20]

Finally, the Court put its own, constitutional stamp of approval on that developing principle in privacy law. Wrote Justice White:

> We are reluctant to embark on a course that would make public records generally available to the media but forbid their publication if offensive to the sensibilities of the supposed reasonable man. Such a rule would make it very difficult for the press to inform their readers about the public business and yet stay within the law. . . . Once true information is disclosed in public court documents open to public inspection, the press cannot be sanctioned for publishing it. In this instance as in others, reliance must rest on the judgment of those who decide what to publish or broadcast.[21]

This **public record privilege** is applied to all branches of government; it is not limited to court records. Nor is the privilege actually limited to information in documents; it encompasses generally the words and events of public proceedings. Communicators must be careful, however, because the privilege is limited to *public* records and proceedings. And not all government records are legally classified as public. (Detailed discussions of this problem appear in Chapters 6 and 7.) Therefore, if through clandestine or persuasive means you gain access to such material, you might end up disclosing facts that are deemed private. In such cases you might need to fall back on the newsworthiness defense, to be discussed shortly.

Note also that the *Cox* case stands only for the rule that neither criminal nor civil law may prohibit the disclosure of information that already has been learned from the public record. The *Cox* ruling does not prohibit a privacy-conscious government from trying to prevent the media from learning the information in the first place, by sealing certain court documents, for example, or by concealing names. In court documents, the identities of parties to a legal proceeding are sometimes kept confidential by using the fictitious names Roe or Doe.

Other Lawfully Obtained Facts

The Supreme Court in 1989 added further constitutional standards to this tort in the case of *Florida Star v. BJF.* The *Star,* a small weekly in Jacksonville, Florida, had published a one-paragraph story about a sexual assault, including the victim's name. The name was obtained from a report available in the police department pressroom. Signs in the pressroom warned that rape victims' names were not considered part of the public record, however, and publication of the name was contrary to the paper's own internal policy. Also, a state statute specifically made it unlawful to publish the names of rape victims.

Under authority of the statute, the assault victim sued the *Star* for invasion of privacy and was awarded $97,000 by a jury. In a 6–3 decision, the Supreme Court reversed. "If a newspaper lawfully obtains truthful information about a matter of public significance," wrote Justice Thurgood Marshall for the majority, "punishment may lawfully be imposed, if at all, only when narrowly tailored to a state interest of the highest order."[22] Punishing the *Star* would not serve an interest of that magnitude, he wrote, as evidenced by the fact that, in this case, the government itself was making the information public.

Some commentators believe the *BJF* ruling has taken a huge bite out of the private facts tort. However, the Court emphasized the narrowness of its ruling, and it expressly declined to hold that dissemination of the truth is always protected by the First Amendment against civil sanctions. Also, the Court found the news item to concern "a matter of public significance." In that respect, the constitutional standard of *BJF* simply coincides with the usual common law rule limiting this tort to non-newsworthy disclosures.

Privacy in a Name?

Under what circumstances, if any, might a person's name, telephone number, or address be considered a private fact for purposes of a lawsuit? Consider this actual case. About midnight a woman (Jane Doe) returned to her apartment and found the dead body of her roommate on the floor. She had been beaten, raped, and strangled. Doe then looked up and found herself face to face with a man. She fled the apartment, found a police officer, and provided a description of the suspect. A summer intern for the *Los Angeles Times* was assigned to cover the story. She learned Doe's real name and in an article published the next day identified Doe by name as the discoverer of the body. The article also reported that "one witness" gave police a description of the suspect, who was still at large. Doe, who then lived in fear that the killer would track her down, sued the *Times* and the reporter for invasion of privacy.

Would it matter in this case how the news reporter obtained Doe's name? Would it matter if the reporter did not know that the person who discovered the body and the person who described the suspect were one and the same? This case was eventually settled out of court for an undisclosed sum.[23]

Highly Offensive

Even if truly private information is disclosed, no privacy claim exists unless the disclosure is one that would be highly offensive and objectionable to a reasonable person of ordinary sensibilities. The question is not merely whether a plaintiff was agitated and embarrassed by the disclosure of facts; rather, the plaintiff must convince the court that it is reasonable to react in that manner. In other words, the disclosure must have clearly overstepped prevailing notions of decency.

While they may have been guarded secrets, some kinds of information simply don't meet this offensiveness test. For example, publication of a secret family meat loaf recipe would not tend to shock the reasonable person's sensibilities. But you should approach very cautiously disclosures of sexual confidences, unusual or stigma-laden physical disorders, mental disorders, or extremely bizarre personal habits.

Newsworthiness Defense

Despite the presence of the elements discussed so far, private facts claims cannot succeed unless the court is also convinced that the disclosures were not newsworthy. One might publish facts that are both private and highly objectionable, but the disseminator is safe from liability if the facts are reasonably related to a newsworthy event or issue. This **newsworthiness defense** is legal acknowledgment that the public has a **right to know** in some cases, even at the expense of an individual's privacy.

The big difficulty, of course, is drawing a legal line between what is newsworthy and what is not. This has been a tough definition for the courts, and the articulated newsworthiness tests vary from state to state. One general approach has been to avoid the quagmire of strict definitions altogether by simply asking juries to consider whether the disclosures were in line with customary news content. Other courts, such as those in California, profess to use a more structured balancing test that weighs (1) the social value of the facts disclosed against (2) the depth of the intrusion into private affairs.

Courts may weigh a third factor: the extent to which the plaintiff voluntarily sought a position of notoriety. Private facts about public figures are more likely to be considered within the scope of legitimate public concern. Courts have often ruled, however, that even public figures are entitled to keep private some facts of their domestic activities and sexual relations.

As a further guideline, courts have often stated what will not be considered newsworthy: information that represents a morbid or sensational prying into private lives for its own sake. In the fun house case, for example, the photo of indecent exposure was characterized by the court as a mere curiosity piece, published precisely because of its embarrassing quality and not because it added insights to the write-up on the state fair.

Legitimate Public Interest

Most contemporary courts would likely reach a different conclusion about the fun house photograph and give greater latitude to editors. Here's an example from *Sports Illustrated*, in which a court gave broader meaning to the notion of newsworthiness. The magazine had prepared an article about a dangerous body-surfing beach in California that was known as the Wedge. The story included information about a man, Mike Virgil, who was considered the most daring surfer at the beach. When the magazine telephoned the surfer to verify some facts, he learned that the article would deal not only with his surfing prowess but also with some bizarre behavior in his personal life. This behavior included diving head first down flights of stairs, eating live spiders and other insects, and extinguishing a cigarette in his mouth.

Virgil asked that he not be mentioned in the article, but the magazine published the story as planned. In a lawsuit for invasion of privacy the court sided with the magazine. The facts did not represent sensational prying for its own sake, said the judge, but instead were related to a legitimate story. He wrote:

> "Body surfing at the Wedge is a matter of legitimate public interest, and it cannot be doubted that Mike Virgil's unique prowess at the same is also of legitimate interest. Any reasonable person . . . would have to conclude that the personal facts concerning Mike Virgil were included as a legitimate journalistic attempt to explain Virgil's extremely daring and dangerous style of body surfing at the Wedge."[24]

In a 1991 case a Texas appellate court discussed the newsworthiness defense specifically in terms of a constitutional privilege. A newspaper had published a photo, taken during a high school soccer game, in conjunction with an article about the game. The plaintiff was shown in the photo running full-stride after the soccer ball, but in the picture his genitalia also happened to be exposed. The exposure was caused by the student athlete's failure to wear the customary athletic supporter, the court noted.

The newspaper responded to the student's lawsuit for invasion of privacy by claiming that the suit was barred by the First Amendment and the free speech provision in the Texas Constitution because, it claimed, those provisions do not allow civil damages against a newspaper for the publication of a photo taken at a newsworthy public event. The Texas court concluded there was indeed a constitutional privilege to report private facts when connected with a newsworthy event such as a soccer game, even though offensive to ordinary sensibilities. The newspaper does not lose constitutional protection simply because it embarrasses the people it refers to; the privilege ceases to operate only when editors abuse their broad discretion to publish matters that are of legitimate public interest, the court said. The Texas court noted the contrary result in the fun house case discussed earlier in this chapter, but it said that case was not persuasive because the Alabama Supreme Court had not analyzed the applicability of First Amendment protection. Summary judgment was affirmed for the newspaper.[25]

Humiliation for Its Own Sake

Contrast the above cases with the 1983 case of *Diaz v. Oakland Tribune*. *Tribune* columnist Sidney Jones wrote this paragraph in a multiple-topic column: "The students at the College of Alameda will be surprised to learn that their student-body president, Toni Diaz, is no lady, but is in fact a man whose real name is Antonio. Now, I realize that, in these times, such a matter is no big deal, but I suspect his classmates in P.E. 97 may wish to make other showering arrangements." That was the entire reference to Diaz, who had undergone sex-change surgery some years earlier and went to great trouble to conceal this from the public and start a new life. Diaz sued for the publication of highly embarrassing private facts and was awarded $775,000 in compensatory and punitive damages at trial. Wrote a state appeals court:

> Contrary to defendants' claim, we find little if any connection between the information disclosed and Diaz's fitness for office. The fact that she is a transsexual does not adversely reflect on her honesty or judgment. . . . Nor is there merit to defendants' claim that the changing roles of women in society make this story newsworthy. This assertion rings hollow. The tenor of the article was by no means an attempt to enlighten the public on a contemporary social issue. . . . Jones' attempt at humor at Diaz's expense removes all pretense that the article was meant to educate the reading public. Here Jones knew that Diaz would certainly suffer severe emotional distress from the publicity alone. Nevertheless, he added to the indignity by making Diaz the brunt of a joke. . . . The jury could reasonably have inferred from these facts that Jones acted with the intent to outrage or humiliate Diaz . . . .[26]

As this case shows, plaintiffs can prevail when the private information is used, not to illustrate or prove a point of legitimate interest, but rather for its own sake to shock or embarrass.

You may be irked by the less-than-precise boundaries of this tort. However, that is reality. Boundaries are taking shape through court opinions, but they are inexact. This imprecision can—and should—cause occasional ambivalence on the part of students and professional communicators. In all the main elements addressed here—whether facts are private, whether their disclosure would be highly offensive, and whether they are of legitimate public concern—the legal standards ultimately take into account the prevailing mores of society. These mores, of course, are subject to some change and a lot of interpretation.

Your task as a communications expert is to learn the basic rules and the factual situations that typically signal danger. But you also must realize there will always be new situations that fall into a zone of uncertainty. To some extent this is true of most areas of the law. But this tort, publication of private facts, is an especially good example of hazy boundaries that can have a chilling effect on the media.

Furthermore, there is some argument about whether prior restraints should be available in these kinds of privacy cases. Recall that, in defamation cases, plaintiffs must sue for money damages after publication; no prior restraint (injunction) is available. This is generally accepted as the principle of privacy lawsuits as well. But the decisions in private facts cases are dotted with exceptions, and the U.S. Supreme Court has not ruled directly on the First Amendment question. Judges occasionally may be responsive to requests for injunctions in private facts cases because, unlike libel situations, the plaintiff cannot use counterspeech to set the record straight and prop up a damaged reputation. Since complaints over private facts don't rest on the inaccuracy of statements—but upon unwanted publicity—no sort of retraction, correction, or counterattack could ease the plaintiff's suffering.[27]

Special Problem: Lapse of Time

What about media disclosures of information that, though once public, had been buried in a person's distant past and publicly forgotten? This has been an occasional problem, typically involving past criminal activity or prosecutions.

The classic example is an old case from California, *Melvin v. Reid,* popularly known as the *Red Kimono* case. In 1918 Gabrielle Darley, a prostitute, was tried for murder. It was a notorious case, but she was acquitted and then changed her life dramatically. She married, left the state, became a housewife, and "thereafter at all times lived an exemplary, virtuous, honorable and righteous life." But seven years later a filmmaker produced *The Red Kimono,* a movie based on the deeds of the housewife's prior life. The film used her real maiden name—Gabrielle Darley—as the name of the principal character, and the movie was advertised as a true account of her escapades. The former prostitute sued the filmmaker and won, in one of the earliest private facts cases.[28]

The case would be decided differently in most states today, however. First of all, much of the information in the film probably came from the public record, from the trial. Second, the initial media coverage of her prosecution surely included additional information about her life, and that information probably would

Disclosure of Private Facts

☐ Has publicity been given to heretofore private facts of another's life?

☐ Would the publicity be highly offensive or embarrassing to a reasonable person?

☐ Is the disclosed information of no legitimate public interest?

no longer be considered private. And finally, she had forever become a newsworthy personality, whether she liked it or not.

As a general rule, that which was public does not later become private, and people or events once newsworthy remain newsworthy topics of legitimate recall. Furthermore, the Supreme Court in its *Cox* ruling never suggested that a lapse of time could make the contents of public records somehow private.

Communicators should be wary, however, of the "Guess Where He Was Twenty Years Ago" exposé that does not rely on information from a public record. An example of this would be a news story revealing that a local man, now a dentist, had many years ago tried to kill himself with a revolver. If the suicide attempt had been released as news at the time, legal authorities agree that the media are safe in reporting it again. This comes under the general rule that recall of past news events is a legitimate public endeavor.

But if the suicide attempt had been a guarded secret all these years, it should not be assumed that the passage of time now makes disclosure less objectionable. Long-past private matters should not be published unless they would be legitimate news today. Consider the basic guidelines for newsworthiness as they would apply today. For example, if the dentist is now running for high public office, many private aspects of his past may come within the scope of legitimate public interest.

A final, important note of advice: The best way to avoid this tort is to get the affected individuals themselves to talk with you, on the record, about their private lives. Be as persuasive as you can if you think the information is important. That way you have the consent of the individual, and he cannot turn around and sue you when the information is printed or broadcast.

Ethical Concerns

Of course, the law is just one of the concerns when media are about to broadcast or publish private facts. Another one is professional ethics, and its sweep is much broader than that of the law. In most cases, the private information does not rank particularly high on the ladder of newsworthiness, and the dissemination may cause severe trauma for the individual. You may want to conduct your own public benefit/private trauma balancing test. When a significant public benefit may result, don't be timid—run it. But when the potential public benefit is next to nil and the privacy factor high, don't appear indifferent—hold off.

The media have sustained some of their worst black eyes when they seemed to be cold-heartedly preying on people's private moments, particularly with pictures. The daily *Bakersfield Californian* learned this in 1985 when it ran a front-page photograph showing the grieving family of a boy who had just drowned in a river, with the boy's body in the foreground. The scene was at a public park, so the photo presented no legal problem. But many readers thought the paper crossed the lines of decency and invaded the family's privacy. Readers were so offended, in fact, that the paper received more than five hundred phone calls of protest—and a bomb threat.

The codes of ethics for the Society of Professional Journalists and the Radio-Television News Directors Association both specify that practitioners shall respect the dignity and privacy of people encountered in the course of reporting the news.

Private Facts in the Hypothetical

Consider again the chapter hypothetical concerning Vera Grundy. Would broadcast of any of the information learned, or scenes you filmed, constitute the private facts tort? Grundy's drunk driving arrest, though several years old, was on the public record and thus would be fair game legally. The marijuana incident had been kept private, but its release probably would not be sufficiently offensive to support a legal claim. Reporting her psychiatric treatments, however, could be trouble. If you were the reporter and wanted to air this, it would be wise to see if Grundy would talk about it first.

And finally, what about the hot-tub video? If the tape shows intimate frolicking in the hot tub and lots of skin, broadcasting it would normally cross the legal line. If the tape shows the two people simply sitting in the water chatting, the question is whether the core information itself—that these people not married to each other sit together naked in her hot tub—is still too private a matter to be broadcast without being highly offensive.

In any event, it is difficult from an ethical perspective to see the justification for broadcasting any of this material. What public purpose is served by broadcasting private and embarrassing information of this kind for a simple feature series on the lives of educators? Note how the legal and ethical balance may shift, however, if Grundy is embroiled in a public controversy to which this information relates. Suppose she is running for a city council seat and her campaign pledge is to serve as a model citizen for today's youth. Courts now would likely deem all this information newsworthy under law, except perhaps for video of intimate conduct. From an ethical perspective, would you reach the same conclusion?

The hypothetical presents legal and ethical problems beyond the private facts issue. For example, if Grundy is married, video of her and the man sitting in a hot tub probably would imply to viewers that she is having an affair. What if this were not true? Perhaps Grundy's husband and the other man's wife are also there, but just happened to be inside getting sodas while you were in the tree. The false impression you created could lead to a lawsuit for another privacy tort, false light.

False Light

The third branch of privacy invasion, **false light,** is a tort similar to defamation. False light is the representation of an individual in a false and highly offensive manner before the public.

It is common for a claim of false light invasion of privacy to accompany a defamation claim, because both torts concern false information published in either a news or commercial context. And the major elements of the false light claim are similar to those of defamation. The plaintiff must prove that the information was made public, was about the plaintiff, and was substantially false.

One thing that distinguishes a false light claim is that its aim is to compensate the individual for personal embarrassment and anguish, not for damage to reputation. Therefore, false light alone may be the appropriate claim when an erroneous public portrayal has caused personal trauma, but when there is no evidence of injury to reputation.

For example, in one of the classic early cases, a ten-year-old girl was nearly run over by a car, and a newspaper photographer took a dramatic picture of the child being lifted to her feet by a bystander. The picture was published in the paper the following day, and that newsworthy publication was privileged. But two years later the photo was published again—this time to illustrate a magazine article about pedestrian carelessness, titled "They Ask To Be Killed." Said the federal appeals court:

> This use of her picture had nothing at all to do with her accident. It related to the general subject of traffic accidents and pedestrian carelessness. Yet the facts . . . show that the little girl, herself, was at the time of her accident not careless and the motorist was. The picture is used in connection with several headings tending to say that this plaintiff narrowly escaped death because she was careless of her own safety. That is not libelous. . . . But we are not talking now about liability for defamation. We are talking about the privilege to invade her interest in being left alone.[29]

The court concluded that the publication exceeded legal bounds, and it upheld a $5000 judgment for the girl. This 1951 case never referred to the false light tort by name, but the court clearly recognized the emergence of this separate branch of privacy invasion. Had the context of the publication been accurate, no other privacy theory could have allowed the girl to recover. The difference between false light and defamation also was apparent. Labeling the girl as a careless pedestrian would not tend to injure her reputation. She would not be likely to lose friends or job opportunities or be ostracized at school. Yet it is the kind of erroneous characterization that would tend to be deeply aggravating in a personal sense.

Though the false light tort aims to protect a fundamentally different interest than does defamation, there is of course much overlap in the applicability of these torts. Some jurisdictions regard claims for false light and libel as duplicative. After all, any false publication that harms reputation is also likely to injure the individual's peace of mind. As long as three decades ago some legal scholars began wondering if the false light tort would eventually engulf the whole law of defamation. But this has not happened. One explanation, perhaps, is that even though false light is a broader tort in some respects it is in some ways narrower than defamation. For example, while corporations are free to sue for defamation, only individuals can sue for false light or other kinds of privacy invasion.

False Light Situations

False light cases generally fall under three categories: distortion, embellishment, and fictionalization. The distortion category is illustrated by the case of the young pedestrian described earlier. Typically it is a matter of photographs or video being used out of context. To avoid this, communicators must be extremely careful about using file pictures to illustrate stories. For example, suppose a news photographer takes a picture of a young man shopping at a convenience store. The picture is not used at the time and is filed. But six months later the newspaper is running a piece about shoplifting, so editors dig into the file and publish that photo along with the article, simply for purposes of graphic illustration. By doing this the newspaper is begging for legal trouble. This is a common danger in TV news also, mismatching the audio and video.

The embellishment category includes cases in which false information was added to journalistic accounts. In other words, writers should not take liberty with the news. The U.S. Supreme Court case of *Cantrell v. Forest City Publishing Co.* was a prime example of this. A bridge collapsed in 1967 and forty-four people were killed, one of them Cantrell. Several months later a reporter for the *Cleveland Plain Dealer* wrote a follow-up story on the impact of the disaster. The story stressed the poverty of the remaining Cantrell family members and the deteriorating condition of their home, but many of the facts clearly were embellished. For example, the reporter wrote:

> Mrs. Cantrell will talk neither about what happened nor how they are doing. She wears the same mask of non-expression she wore at the funeral. She is a proud woman. She says that, after it happened, the people in town offered to help them out with money and they refused to take it.[30]

In reality, though, only the children were home when the reporter visited; he never saw nor talked with their mother, contrary to the clear implication. Other significant misrepresentations were contained in the detailed descriptions of the Cantrells' poverty. The Court affirmed a $60,000 judgment for the Cantrells.

QUICK
CHECK

False Light

☐ Has a person been placed before the public in a false light?

☐ Would the false portrayal be highly offensive to a reasonable person?

☐ Did the communicator act with negligence or, if the subject is a public person, with reckless disregard for the truth?

The fictionalization category is typified by the use of real, identifiable characters in tales that are born of imagination. The article, book, or whatever it may be, is neither pure fiction nor pure documentary, but a dangerous combination of the two. For example, suppose you wrote a story—labeled "fiction"—for a regional literary magazine. Your story is about a mild-mannered dermatologist who on weekends leads a ring of eco-guerrillas, sabotaging construction projects, blowing up oil-drilling rigs, and threatening the lives of loggers. Although your story is primarily fiction, the main character you describe is similar to a real physician in your town who is indeed known as a controversial environmental crusader. Your fictional character is described with the same kind of beard, the same medical specialty, and a similar first name.

The test is this: Could a reasonable person reading your story believe the fictional character is in fact this particular real person? If so, you may have to deal with a lawsuit for false light (or perhaps for libel). The lesson from these fictionalization cases is that audiences must not be misled. If the work is one of fiction, don't send a contrary message to readers or viewers by injecting real people. And if the piece does begin with real people and events but shifts into fiction, this must be made clear to the audience. Also, disclaimers—stating, for example, that "any similarities to real people are purely coincidental"—will not necessarily protect against liability.

The Elements and Privileges

Once the basic nature of the wrong—a highly offensive characterization, by the standards of a reasonable person—is distinguished, the remaining elements of the false light tort are much the same as those for libel. Plaintiffs must show that they were identified and that the damaging messages were substantially false. And those messages must be made public, though this publication requirement is applied differently in privacy cases. Courts have consistently held that, in the privacy torts discussed so far, there must be dissemination to a segment of the general public. This is contrary to the rule in defamation where communication to one other person is enough to satisfy the publication requirement.

Some of the constitutional privileges and procedural safeguards that apply in defamation cases also have been applied to false light claims. Most notably, the U.S. Supreme Court has decided that the actual malice standard fashioned in the libel case of *New York Times v. Sullivan* should also apply in false light cases. This decision was reached in the 1967 case of *Time, Inc. v. Hill,*[31] the first false light case to reach the Supreme Court. The Court held that in false light privacy cases involving matters of public interest, the plaintiffs must prove that defendants disclosed the information with knowledge of its falsity or in reckless disregard of the truth. This is easily proved in deliberate falsification or embellishment cases, such as *Cantrell,* but in other kinds of cases it can represent a tough roadblock for plaintiffs, as discussed in Chapter 4.

Since the *Hill* ruling, the Supreme Court has narrowed application of the actual malice standard in libel law; it is no longer a public interest test that determines application but whether the plaintiff is a public figure. It is widely speculated, therefore, that this would also be the controlling factor in false light cases, though the Supreme Court has yet to make such a ruling.

Other substantive and procedural standards from the law of defamation also have been applied in false light cases. For example, courts have held that statements of opinion cannot give rise to a false light claim and that the retraction statutes designed for defamation situations also apply when the claim is false light. Remember, too, that some states have yet officially to recognize the false light tort or have specifically declined to do so.[32]

Intrusion

The invasion of privacy branch known as **intrusion** may be defined as the intentional invasion of a person's physical seclusion or private affairs in a manner that would be highly offensive to a reasonable person.

Note first of all that this privacy tort is different because it occurs in the information-gathering process, not by publication or broadcast. The aim of this law is to compensate people for the shock and embarrassment of learning that peering eyes, focused camera lenses, or live microphones were present at a time when there should have been safety from unwanted observation. When and if publication occurs in an intrusion case, it can serve to increase damages and might give rise to a related privacy tort, such as private facts.

Sometimes intrusion claims go hand in hand with claims for trespass. (Trespass is discussed in detail in Chapter 6.) But intrusion may occur even when there is no trespass—when snooping occurs with the aid of powerful camera lenses or telescopes, for example. Intrusion is a privacy tort that fills the gaps left by other laws, including trespass, nuisance, infliction of mental distress, criminal eavesdropping laws, and civil rights laws.

Expectation of Privacy

You might think that intrusion claims would be frequent against the mass media. But they are not particularly common, and the plaintiffs rarely win. An important reason for this is the threshold question that the law will ask: Was the individual in a place where she could reasonably expect privacy?

In most instances the answer to this question is no, in which case there can be no valid claim for intrusion. Generally speaking, a reasonable expectation of privacy can't exist on public sidewalks, at parks, on public beaches, in the aisles of department stores, or in the open dining rooms of restaurants. Individuals in these places cannot reasonably think they are entitled to go unobserved or even unphotographed.

A reasonable expectation of privacy *is* likely to exist in a private residence. The right to be free from unwanted observation also has been acknowledged for a few other closely controlled places, including hospital rooms, ambulances, hotel rooms, private offices, dressing rooms, and public toilet stalls. To be deemed legally secluded for purposes of this tort, it is not required that the individual be hidden from all others. As a federal court in Illinois explained in 1986: "[A plaintiff's] visibility to some people does not strip him of the right to remain secluded from others. Persons are exposed to family members and invited guests at their homes, but that does not mean they have opened the door to television cameras."[33]

A couple of actual cases will help illustrate these points. In one case, a television camera crew was working on a mini-documentary about paramedics. A Los Angeles paramedic unit had been called to a private residence, and the camera crew followed, right into the bedroom, where a heart attack victim lay on the floor. The crew filmed the resuscitation efforts without obtaining the consent of the victim's wife, who waited in another room. Could a lawsuit for intrusion conceivably succeed? The California Court of Appeal said yes.[34]

Compare this case from the state of Washington. A television station was pursuing a story about a pharmacist who was facing criminal charges. A cameraman walked up to the exterior window of the closed pharmacy and filmed the pharmacist talking on the phone inside. The court held there could be no claim for intrusion and explained: "It is not contended that the film recorded anything other than that which any passerby would have seen."[35]

One of the most closely watched intrusion cases of the late 1990s was *Shulman v. Group W Productions*,[36] which reached the California Supreme Court. Ruth Shulman was injured when her car veered off the highway and tumbled down an embankment into a ditch, coming to rest upside down. She was pinned under the vehicle and had to be freed with a device called the "jaws of life." A television cameraman arrived to record the rescue effort for later broadcast on a show titled "On Scene: Emergency Response." The cameraman captured the dialog between Shulman and an emergency nurse as Shulman was being removed from the car. Then, when Shulman was placed in a rescue helicopter, the cameraman also accompanied the patient and continued to tape Shulman's strained dialog with the flight nurse, who agreed to wear a microphone. Though the taping was done with the consent of the air ambulance personnel, Shulman was unaware that she was being videotaped. Shulman, left a paraplegic by the accident, sued the program producers for disclosure of private facts and for intrusion.

The California high court held that the broadcast material was newsworthy and therefore could not support a claim for disclosure of private facts. On this claim, summary judgment in favor of the media was appropriate. But the court reached a different conclusion on the intrusion claim. While the cameraman's mere presence at the accident scene and filming of the events there could not be deemed an intrusion into Shulman's seclusion, two particular aspects of the cameraman's conduct could amount to intrusion, the court said. First, Shulman might have a reasonable expectation of privacy in the interior of the rescue helicopter. The court drew an analogy to media entering a hospital room during treatment without a patient's consent. Second, the court said Shulman was entitled to some degree of privacy in her conversations with the emergency nurse at the accident scene. The cameraman didn't intrude into that zone of privacy merely by recording conversations that others at the public scene could hear with unaided ears. But by placing a microphone on the nurse and amplifying and recording everything she said and heard, the cameraman may have listened in on conversations that Shulman could reasonably have expected to be private. Therefore the court declined summary judgment on the intrusion claim. It was for a jury to decide whether Shulman had a reasonable expectation of privacy in those instances, the court said.

In the chapter hypothetical, you'll recall, you climbed a tree to peer into a secluded, private yard. You might have committed the tort of intrusion already, even if the videotape is never broadcast. One key question would be whether the couple in the hot tub had a legitimate expectation of privacy. In answering this question a court might consider whether neighborhood children frequently played in that tree, whether neighboring hillside homes overlooked the yard, and exactly where in the yard the hot tub was located. The fact that you had to climb a tree to get the video suggests that you may have crossed the legal line, but not necessarily.

Though most intrusion cases deal with surveillance of the plaintiffs themselves, examining private papers and records also may constitute intrusion. Again, the threshold question is whether the papers were placed where the plaintiff could reasonably expect others would not have access. What if the private records had been discarded? Does an individual retain a reasonable expectation of privacy once the private papers have been placed in a trash container near the street? Not likely. In a case involving the legality of a police search, the Supreme Court held that criminal defendants had no reasonable expectation of privacy with respect to trash placed by the side of a public street for collection. It was common knowledge, the Court said, that such trash was readily accessible to scavengers, snoops, and other members of the public.[37]

Intrusion

☐ Does this person have a reasonable expectation of solitude or seclusion, such as would be found in a private residence?

☐ Is the seclusion intentionally intruded upon, either physically or otherwise?

☐ Would the intrusive conduct be highly offensive to a reasonable person (e.g., by subterfuge or deception)?

Offensiveness   When considering intrusion situations, remember that the standard of "highly offensive" is a part of this tort, just as it is with false light and private facts claims. (See Exhibit 5.2 for a comparison of the four privacy torts.) Intrusion law aims to protect people from the kind of disregard for privacy that shocks the public consciousness; it is not intended as a technicality to trap media people who are simply being assertive or thorough in seeking the news.

Courts will also look to other laws and the intruder's purpose to help determine offensiveness. Intrusive behavior will typically be held offensive for purposes of an intrusion lawsuit if the conduct also violated criminal laws, such as Peeping Tom statutes, or laws against wiretapping or breaking and entering. Intrusive behavior will be held not offensive when a public benefit clearly outweighs the individual's privacy. This might be the case, for example, when an apartment building owner enters to investigate an unsafe condition. However, the courts have yet to recognize an overriding public benefit for newsgathering. In the 1998 *Shulman* case, California's high court explained the offensiveness standard as follows:

> In deciding whether a reporter's alleged intrusion into private matters (i.e., physical space, conversation or data) is "offensive" and hence actionable as an invasion of privacy, courts must consider the extent to which the intrusion was, under the circumstances, justified by the legitimate motive of gathering the news. Information-collecting techniques that may be highly offensive when done for socially unprotected reasons—for purposes of harassment, blackmail or prurient curiosity, for example—may not be offensive to a reasonable person when employed by journalists in pursuit of a socially or politically important story. . . .
>
> The mere fact the intruder was in pursuit of a "story" does not, however, generally justify an otherwise offensive intrusion; offensiveness depends as well on the particular method of investigation used. At one extreme, routine reporting techniques, such as asking questions of people with information could rarely, if ever, be deemed an actionable intrusion. At the other extreme, violation of well-established legal areas of physical or sensory privacy—trespass into a home or

tapping a personal telephone line, for example—could rarely, if ever, be justified by a reporter's need to get the story. Such acts would be deemed highly offensive even if the information sought was of weighty public concern; they would also be outside any protection the Constitution provides to newsgathering.

Between these extremes lie difficult cases, many involving the use of photographic and electronic recording equipment. Equipment such as hidden cameras and miniature cordless and directional microphones are powerful investigative tools for newsgathering, but may also be used in ways that severely threaten personal privacy. California tort law provides no bright line on this question; each case must be taken on its facts.[38]

Use of Subterfuge

What, then, about the use of disguises, false pretenses, hidden cameras, and the like? To what extent do these time-tried investigative reporting techniques risk lawsuits for intrusion? Consider the facts of a classic 1971 federal court case, *Dietemann v. Time, Inc.*

Two reporters for *Life* magazine visited the plaintiff's private home to investigate claims that he was a medical quack who professed healing with clay, minerals, and herbs. The reporters rang a bell and when the plaintiff answered they said that they needed medical help and had been sent by a friend, a Mr. Johnson. This was a trick to gain entrance, and it worked. All three went into the plaintiff's den, where one of the reporters complained of a lump in her breast. She was examined by the plaintiff, who at one point employed some unusual gadgets and what appeared to be a wand. He concluded that the reporter had eaten some rancid butter eleven years, nine months, and seven days before.

While all this was going on, the conversation was being sent by a radio transmitter hidden in the "patient's" purse to a tape recorder in a parked car. The car was occupied by another magazine employee and two law enforcement officials. Also, the second reporter was using a hidden camera to photograph the plaintiff.

A few weeks later the plaintiff was arrested for practicing medicine without a license. Nevertheless, he sued the magazine publisher for invasion of privacy—and won. Where did the reporters go wrong?

One key was that the plaintiff's den was a place where he could reasonably expect privacy from news people; he did not advertise his home as a place of business. In this case, the reporters' presence admittedly was gained by consent, and the court concluded that the consent was valid, even though it was gained by subterfuge. The problem occurred later, however, with the use of the audio and visual eavesdropping devices in the private den. Wrote the court:

> One who invites another to his home or office takes a risk that the visitor may not be what he seems, and that the visitor may repeat all he hears and observes when he leaves. But he does not and should not be required to take the risk that what is heard and seen will be transmitted by photograph or recording . . . to the public at large or to any segment of it that the visitor may select. A different rule

could have a most pernicious effect upon the dignity of man and it would surely lead to guarded conversations and conduct where candor is most valued, e.g., in the case of doctors and lawyers.[39]

Tort liability, then, does not necessarily attach to uses of subterfuge or "white lies" in order to gain access or get a source to talk. (*Note*: There are criminal laws against impersonating law-enforcement officers and other government authorities.) The intrusion tort will come into play if electronic or mechanical devices are used to record or intercept the conversations and events that occur in private spheres.

The *Dietemann* case also illustrates that there is no blanket newsworthiness privilege, no First Amendment immunity, in intrusion cases. Recall that newsworthiness is a complete defense to claims of publication of private facts. But in the gathering of information there is no similar defense, even if the information clearly turns out to be newsworthy, as in the *Dietemann* case. Said the court:

> We agree that newsgathering is an integral part of news dissemination. We strongly disagree, however, that the hidden mechanical contrivances are "indispensable tools" of newsgathering. . . . The First Amendment has never been construed to accord newsmen immunity from torts or crimes committed during the course of newsgathering. The First Amendment is not a license to trespass, to steal, or to intrude by electronic means into the precincts of another's home or office. It does not become such a license simply because the person subjected to the intrusion is reasonably suspected of committing a crime.[40]

The Dietemann cases serves as a warning to journalists considering the use of modern photographic, taping, and surveillance equipment. The secret use of such equipment does not always amount to a tort, however. Courts in the 1990s considered many hidden-camera cases arising out of television journalism. When the equipment is used in the commercial workplace, and the journalist gains valid entry by posing as a routine customer, the courts generally do not find intrusion.

Illustrative is the 1995 case of *Desnick v. American Broadcasting Companies, Inc.* The ABC program *PrimeTime Live* had decided to produce a segment on cataract surgery and focused on Desnick Eye Center offices, which were performing more than 10,000 cataract operations a year. ABC dispatched persons equipped with concealed cameras to several of the Eye Center offices, where they requested eye exams. The physicians were secretly videotaped while examining these "patients" and while making their recommendations concerning surgery. Some of this video footage was aired on *PrimeTime Live.* Two of the physicians sued ABC for various torts, among them intrusion. But the federal Court of Appeals concluded there was no intrusion because the taping did not invade truly private affairs or conversations. The *Desnick* court had this to say about *Dietemann*: "The parallel to this case is plain enough, but there is a difference. Dietemann was not in business and did not advertise his services or charge for them. His quackery was private."[41]

EXHIBIT 5.2	*Overview of Privacy Torts*			
	Type of interest invaded	**Nature of defendant's invasion**	**Public dissemination required?**	**Main defense**
Private facts	Right to keep private information private	Highly offensive	Yes	Newsworthiness
Intrusion	Right to private, secluded moment	Highly offensive	No	Privacy expectation unreasonable
False light	Right to be represented accurately before public	Highly offensive	Yes	Truth*
Appropriation	Right to control commercial use of persona	Simply without consent	Yes	Written consent

This diagram is a simplified comparison of some key features of the four privacy torts.

*Absence of actual malice is another important bar to a false light lawsuit when the false representation deals with a matter of public interest.

Still, this does not mean that infiltrating a commercial workplace with hidden cameras will never amount to intrusion. In another case involving ABC, a reporter obtained employment as a "telepsychic" in the Los Angeles office of the Psychic Marketing Group. She wore a small video camera hidden in her hat to covertly tape her conversations with coworkers, one of whom later sued for intrusion. The California Supreme Court in 1999 held that in a workplace such as this where the public generally does not have access, employees may enjoy a legitimate expectation that their conversations with co-workers will not be secretly videotaped—even if those conversations are not completely private from all others in the workplace.[42] Thus, the tort of intrusion does not allow a bright-line rule that journalists are always free to tape their conversations in an office or other workplace. (In some cases, clandestine taping can lead to other legal claims, such as fraud, trespass, and criminal violations of wiretap statutes. These will be discussed later in this chapter and in Chapter 6.)

In order to be liable for intrusion, one must have actually ordered or participated in the intrusive acts. This point was illustrated in *Pearson v. Dodd,* a 1969 Court of Appeals case. Former employees of a U.S. senator entered the senator's office without authorization, removed documents from files, and copied them. The copies were turned over to columnist Jack Anderson, who was aware the copies had been obtained by stealth. Dodd sued Anderson for intrusion, but the court ruled in favor of the columnist. Anderson had not requested the documents, so he did not become liable for intrusion simply by accepting them. The court explained:

A person approached by an eavesdropper with an offer to share in the information gathered through the eavesdropping would perhaps play the nobler part should he spurn the offer and shut his ears. However, it seems to us that at this point it would place too great a strain on human weakness to hold one liable in damages who merely succumbs to temptation and listens.[43]

Public Places

As mentioned earlier, it is a nearly steadfast rule that the media are safe to observe, follow, or photograph people in public places. This is certainly true as long as the observer is not using electronic eavesdropping or taping devices that significantly expand what other observers could see and hear. Even in public, however, the law recognizes a small zone of privacy. The most notable case is *Galella v. Onassis,*[44] a protracted legal battle involving a freelance photographer who habitually hounded former First Lady Jacqueline Kennedy Onassis and her children. The photographer jumped into the path of young John Kennedy while he was riding his bicycle; he invaded the children's private schools; and at one time he came uncomfortably close in a power boat to where Onassis was swimming. Galella often jumped and postured while taking pictures of Onassis and the Kennedy children at extremely close range whenever they ventured out in public.

Onassis sought an injunction against Galella, claiming that he invaded her privacy, assaulted her, harassed her, and intentionally inflicted mental distress. The court granted the injunction. It did not prohibit Galella from taking photos, but it did forbid him to approach within twenty-five feet of Onassis and thirty feet of her children. On what legal basis could such an injunction be granted?

The photographer's conduct fell within the definition of criminal **harassment** under New York law. The violation occurs "when with intent to harass, a person follows another in a public place, inflicts physical contact or engages in any annoying conduct without legitimate cause." Conduct sufficient for criminal harassment could also amount to the tort of intrusion, the court wrote:

> [Galella's] endless snooping constitutes tortious invasion of privacy. . . . He has intruded into her children's schools, hidden in bushes and behind coat racks in restaurants, sneaked into beauty salons, bribed doormen, hatcheck girls, chauffeurs, fishermen in Greece, hairdressers and schoolboys, and romanced employees. In short, Galella has insinuated himself into the very fabric of Mrs. Onassis' life and the challenge to this court is to fashion the tool to get him out. . . . As we see it, Galella's conduct falls within the formulation of the right of privacy. . . .
> The surveillance, close-shadowing and monitoring were clearly "overzealous" and therefore actionable.[45]

This was a very unusual case, of course. Surveillance of people in public places generally poses no legal problem. But if the surveillance is clearly overzealous, habitual, and obnoxious, in rare cases the courts may declare an illegal intrusion upon privacy or find some other legal theory by which to protect the plaintiff.

Fraud

The tort of fraud, misrepresentation, or deceit is not a traditional component of courses in communications law. However, in recent years numerous plaintiffs have alleged fraud in cases where the media, armed with hidden cameras and microphones, have implied or expressly stated falsehoods to gain access to private meetings, workplaces, and sources' homes.[46] Therefore, a brief discussion of this tort is warranted.

Fraud is committed when a defendant (1) makes a false representation of significant fact, (2) knowing the representation is false, (3) intending to induce reliance upon the misrepresentation, and (4) where the plaintiff did justifiably rely, resulting in damage. The tort is commonly alleged in connection with the sale of vehicles, real estate, and other investment properties, where buyers often must rely upon the inside information provided by sellers and trusted experts. But mass communication professionals can run some risk of this tort, too, when they misrepresent themselves or their intentions.

The most publicized of the media fraud cases has been *Food Lion v. ABC*.[47] In 1992 producers of ABC's *PrimeTime Live* received tips alleging that Food Lion stores were engaging in unsanitary meat-handling practices, such as grinding out-of-date beef with new beef and re-dating meat not sold by its expiration date. ABC decided to investigate under cover by having two reporters obtain deli-department jobs with the grocery chain. They submitted applications with false identities and references and misrepresented their work experience. Based on these false applications the reporters were given jobs at Food Lion stores in South and North Carolina. One reporter worked for a week, the other two weeks, and during that time they used tiny concealed cameras to record several apparent unsanitary actions by employees. Some of the footage was used in a *PrimeTime Live* broadcast.

Food Lion sued ABC and its reporters, challenging not the accuracy of the broadcast but the methods by which the video was obtained. A federal jury found ABC liable for fraud and awarded $1400 in compensatory damages and $5.5 million in punitive damages. The district court judge ruled the punitive award excessive and reduced it to $315,000.

But in 1999 the court of appeals altogether eliminated the damage award for fraud. The court said that under North and South Carolina law the plaintiff could collect only for damage resulting directly from reliance on the misrepresentations, and the court found no such damage. Food Lion suffered reputational harm from the broadcast, but to recover for such harm the store would have to sue for defamation, the court held. Furthermore, the court said the loss of consumer good will in this case was not the result of the ABC reporters' misrepresentations, but rather from Food Lion's own actions. Food Lion sought to recover at least its administrative costs of making the short-term hires. But the court said the reporters made no representation about how long they would work and that they did work suitably for the short time they were on the job. Therefore, there was no proved harm from the false applications.

One of the three judges wrote a dissenting opinion, however, indicating he would have upheld the jury's finding of fraud because the reporters "never intended to work as loyal employees for Food Lion and to promote the business of Food Lion," as the employer had a right to expect.

Emotional Distress

Another tort, **intentional infliction of emotional distress,** has crept into communications litigation in recent years. Though the law is not aimed specifically at privacy invasions or at mass communications, it is a tort theory that is advanced occasionally in the kind of privacy situations discussed in this chapter. The tort may be defined as outrageous conduct that is calculated to cause, and does cause, severe mental or emotional distress. In some states the tort goes by the simpler name of **outrage.**

Typically, this legal claim has been used to recover for such indiscretions as practical jokes that far exceed the bounds of ordinary behavior and cause extreme humiliation. But emotional distress lawsuits have also been brought, sometimes successfully, against mass communicators in situations involving disclosure of private facts, false light, and intrusive surveillance.

The elements of this tort are relatively simple. First, there must be outrageous or highly offensive conduct, as judged by the reasonable person of average sensibilities. Note that this element is similar to elements in three of the privacy torts (false light, private facts, and intrusion). Second, the defendant must have acted with the intent to cause mental distress or with reckless disregard of the probability that such distress would occur. Finally, the plaintiff must prove that severe emotional distress did result. By no means has there been a rash of emotional distress cases against the media, but by 1980 some legal scholars were speculating whether the tort would evolve to supplant claims for defamation and invasion of privacy.

Harsh Satire and the *Hustler* Case

The U.S. Supreme Court in 1988 curtailed the advancement of this tort to some extent with its opinion in *Hustler Magazine v. Falwell.*[48] The inside front cover of the November 1983 issue of *Hustler* magazine featured a parody of an advertisement for Campari liqueur. It was titled, "Jerry Falwell Talks About His First Time." Copying the general form of the real Campari ads, *Hustler's* editors drafted a mock interview with the nationally known minister and described his "first time" as a drunken sexual encounter with his mother in an outhouse (Exhibit 5.3).

Falwell sued for libel, invasion of privacy, and intentional infliction of emotional distress. He lost on the first two claims, but a jury awarded him roughly

EXHIBIT 5.3

Jerry Falwell talks about his first time.*

FALWELL: My first time was in an outhouse outside Lynchburg, Virginia.

INTERVIEWER: Wasn't it a little cramped?

FALWELL: Not after I kicked the goat out.

INTERVIEWER: I see. You must tell me all about it.

FALWELL: I never really expected to make it with Mom, but then after she showed all the other guys in town such a good time, I figured, "What the hell!"

INTERVIEWER: But your mom? Isn't that a bit odd?

FALWELL: I don't think so. Looks don't mean that much to me in a woman.

INTERVIEWER: Go on.

FALWELL: Well, we were drunk off our God-fearing asses on Campari, ginger ale and soda—that's called a Fire and Brimstone—at the time. And Mom looked better than a Baptist whore with a $100 donation.

INTERVIEWER: Campari in the crapper with Mom . . . how interesting. Well, how was it?

FALWELL: The Campari was great, but Mom passed out before I could come.

INTERVIEWER: Did you ever try it again?

FALWELL: Sure . . .

lots of times. But not in the outhouse. Between Mom and the shit, the flies were too much to bear.

INTERVIEWER: We meant the Campari.

FALWELL: Oh, yeah. I always get sloshed before I go out to the pulpit. You don't think I could lay down all that bullshit sober, do you?

© 1983—Imported by Campari U S A New York, NY 48°proof Spirit Aperitif (Liqueur)

Campari, like all liquor, was made to mix you up. It's a light, 48-proof, refreshing spirit, just mild enough to make you drink too much before you know you're schnockered. For your first time, mix it with orange juice. Or maybe some white wine. Then you won't remember anything the next morning. Campari. The mixable that smarts.

CAMPARI You'll never forget your first time.

*AD PARODY—NOT TO BE TAKEN SERIOUSLY

$200,000 in compensatory and punitive damages on the emotional distress claim. The U.S. Supreme Court reversed, however, ruling that the standard of *New York Times v. Sullivan* must also apply to this tort. Chief Justice William Rehnquist, writing for a unanimous Court, said that to uphold Falwell's claim would be to also subject political cartoonists and satirists to liability even though no one had been falsely defamed, and this would be a result abhorrent to the First Amendment.

Wrote the chief justice:

> [Falwell] would have us find that a State's interest in protecting public figures from emotional distress is sufficient to deny First Amendment protection to speech that is patently offensive and is intended to inflict emotional injury, even when that speech could not reasonably have been interpreted as stating actual facts about the public figure involved. This we decline to do.[49]

The upshot of the *Falwell* case is that a public person may not recover for emotional distress inflicted by critical expression without showing in addition that the defendant published with actual malice false statements that were represented as truth. When the expression is clearly satire no such representation exists. It remains to be seen whether this *Falwell* standard, which significantly limits the ability to sue for emotional distress caused by publication, also will be applied to private plaintiffs.

In addition to the *Falwell* case's direct impact on intentional infliction cases, the unanimous ruling also serves as a strong reaffirmation of the Court's support for the actual malice standard when public figures sue the media. In the twenty-some years after he introduced actual malice as a First Amendment standard (in *New York Times v. Sullivan*), Justice William Brennan remained concerned that the Court might renounce or soften the rule. However, in October 1988, in a brief conversation with the author of this text, Justice Brennan expressed his view that the *Falwell* ruling had anchored actual malice as a solid doctrine for the foreseeable future.

Shocking News Content and Tactics

The *Falwell* decision is not the answer to all emotional distress situations, however. Consider this 1991 case from Florida. A six-year-old girl had been abducted in Orlando. About two years later a construction worker in nearby Oviedo discovered a sun dress and a child's skull, which were taken into possession by the Oviedo police. When it was determined that the remains were those of the abducted girl, her family was notified and a memorial service planned. On the day of the service a local TV news reporter drove to the Oviedo Police Department and asked to see the girl's skull. The police chief complied, and the reporter made a close-up videotape of the skull as it was removed from a box. The video was aired throughout central Florida on the 6 o'clock news in conjunction with coverage of the memorial service. Among the audience was the unsuspecting family of the girl, and the emotional impact of the tape was devastating. The abducted girl's twelve-year-old sister reportedly fled from the room screaming "That's not my sister."

Family members sued the station for the tort of outrage. The Florida Court of Appeal refused to dismiss the claim. The court wrote: "We have no difficulty in concluding that reasonable persons in the community could find that the alleged conduct of Channel 2 was outrageous in character and exceeded the bounds of decency so as to be intolerable in a civilized community. . . . Indeed, if the facts as alleged herein do not constitute the tort of outrage, then there is no such tort."[50] The court did not employ the *Falwell* standard or any other special First Amendment protection. In fact, this case demonstrates the narrow applicability of *Falwell*.

Infliction of emotional distress might also occur during news *gathering*, without publication or broadcast, as a 1995 California case illustrates. A mother had murdered her two young children at home and then committed suicide. Meanwhile, three young playmates of the murdered children, girls aged five, seven, and eleven, were at home next door, unaware of the violent tragedy. A TV reporter and cameraman covering the story came to the front door and the three girls answered. With the camera rolling in the doorway, the reporter questioned the girls and established that no adults were home, that the girls knew the children next door, thought they were nice, and played with them "all the time," and that the girls had no idea what had happened. At that point the reporter stated "Well, the mom has killed the two little kids and herself." One of the girls exclaimed "Oh, my God!" The reporter asked a few more questions and then terminated the interview; no portion of the interview was broadcast.

The girls sued for intentional infliction of emotional distress, and California Court of Appeal refused to order summary judgment for the TV station. The station argued that the interview, as revealed in the resulting videotape, was not conducted in an offensive or threatening manner. The reporter did not provide details about the deaths, and he apparently spoke in a tone of voice appropriate to young children. But the court said a jury could nevertheless conclude that the elements of intentional infliction were present: "A jury could find that a television reporter who attempts deliberately to manipulate the emotions of young children for some perceived journalistic advantage has engaged in conduct 'so outrageous in character, and so extreme in degree, as to go beyond all possible bounds of decency.'"[51]

Criminal Statutes

In addition to the four privacy torts and some other civil laws, such as fraud and infliction of mental distress, some state and federal criminal statutes also work to protect privacy from invasion by the mass media. These criminal laws may be categorized generally either as restrictions on disclosure of information or as restrictions on methods of information gathering.

Restrictions on Disclosure

The most direct way to legislate confidentiality in the public arena is to prohibit the media and others from disclosing certain kinds of information, under threat of criminal penalty. The problem with this approach, of course, is that it conflicts with basic First Amendment principles. As noted in Chapter 2, once the media or other third parties have obtained information, it is a rare instance when the government may step in to prohibit publication categorically. This point is illustrated by a U.S. Supreme Court case from 1979, *Smith v. Daily Mail Publishing Co.*[52] At issue was the constitutionality of a West Virginia law that made it a crime for newspapers to publish the names of juveniles who were the subject of juvenile court proceedings. In this instance there had been a killing at a junior high school, and reporters at the scene learned the suspect's name by asking witnesses and police. The newspapers published the name and were indicted.

The Supreme Court ruled in favor of the newspapers, holding that the state's method of protecting confidentiality in juvenile proceedings was unconstitutional. The state's interest in protecting juveniles and fostering their rehabilitation was important, the Court agreed, but not important enough to prevail over the newspapers' First Amendment rights. Several Supreme Court opinions have fallen into this same mold, striking down laws and lower court orders that attempted to protect confidentiality by prohibiting third-party disclosure. (Note the similarities with *Cox Broadcasting Corp. v. Cohn* and *Florida Star v. BJF,* the civil cases discussed earlier.) At the end of its *Smith* opinion, however, the Court included a warning of sorts. Describing its holding as a narrow one, the Court specifically reserved judgment on how the balance might be struck in cases where the media obtain information illegally or where the privacy issues are more compelling. Despite this caveat, any law that categorically prohibits the media from publishing truthful information is presumptively unconstitutional if the law's sole purpose is to protect individual privacy.

It is quite a different matter when statutes prohibit government employees or the actual participants in government proceedings from relaying information to the media and other outsiders. Although government rarely may stop the media from disclosing what they know, it usually *is* constitutional for lawmakers to prevent media and the public from obtaining information in the first place. Therefore, many statutes take this tack, some of them purely in the interest of protecting personal privacy. They deem a particular kind of information confidential and then set penalties for government employees who release that information to the public or media.

Florida, for example, is among the more restrictive states. It classifies more than fifty kinds of information as confidential, including abortion records, motor-vehicle accident reports filed by the people involved, birth records, and the cause-of-death sections of all death records.

Restrictions on Information Gathering	In the civil law, the tort of intrusion is responsible for protecting people against shockingly intrusive forms of information gathering. Criminal laws, however, also play a major role in this regard by contributing more specific restrictions.

Wiretap Laws

At the federal level, the Electronic Communications Privacy Act of 1986 is a particularly extensive package of legislation that added numerous sections to the federal code. Among other things, the act makes it a crime for any person willfully to intercept or record another's oral or wire communications through the use of an electronic, mechanical, or other device.[53] Violators are subject to fines and imprisonment and also are liable for civil damages. However, interception or recording is privileged under this anti-wiretap statute when it is done by a party to the conversation or when one of the parties to the conversation has given prior consent, as long as the communication is not recorded for a criminal or tortious purpose.

In a 1990 case a New York physician with a national reputation for his controversial diet program sued the producer of a nationally syndicated news show, *Inside Edition*, claiming that the defendant violated the federal statute banning nonconsensual recording of communications. One of the producers had infiltrated the doctor's office by posing as a patient and had surreptitiously videotaped the doctor during alleged medical malpractice. The physician managed to obtain a temporary restraining order prohibiting the producer from broadcasting the videotape. The Court of Appeals promptly reversed, however. Although the electronic privacy law prohibits certain conduct, the court held, it in no way provides for a prior restraint of the press in its exercise of First Amendment rights, even if the media's conduct clearly violates the statute.[54]

Similar laws prohibiting wiretapping, bugging, or other forms of electronic and mechanical surveillance exist at the state level. Of particular importance to communicators, because it concerns a relatively common practice, is how state laws treat the audio taping of telephone conversations. Some states, led by Florida[55] and California,[56] are more restrictive than the federal law. In these states even participants in a phone conversation may not tape-record the conversation without the consent of *all other parties* involved. In other states, taping is allowed as long as at least one participant agrees. In other words, participant taping would always be permissible in these more lenient states, but secret taping by a nonparty to the conversation would not.

The Federal Communications Commission has a specific rule on recording telephone conversations for purposes of broadcast, and the rule requires the consent of all parties to the conversation. Violation of the rule can result in a penalty being levied against the broadcast license holder. The FCC rule reads as follows:

> Before recording a telephone conversation for broadcast, or broadcasting such a conversation simultaneously with its occurrence, a licensee shall inform any party to the call of the licensee's intention to broadcast the conversation, except where such party is aware, or may be presumed to be aware from the circumstances of the conversation, that it is being or likely will be broadcast. Such awareness is presumed to exist only when the other party to the call is associated with the station (such as an employee or parttime reporter), or where the other party originates the call and it is obvious that it is in connection with a program in which the station customarily broadcasts telephone conversations.[57]

It is also a violation of criminal laws to remove official government documents, to knowingly receive stolen property, to impersonate a law enforcement officer, or to bribe government employees.

Anti-Paparazzi Legislation

Public sentiment against **paparazzi**—photographers who aggressively stalk and photograph celebrities for profit—erupted following the 1997 death of Diana, Princess of Wales. The princess died tragically in a Paris car crash, some said because her driver was attempting to elude paparazzi who were chasing the car on motorcycles.

Though a variety of state laws are already on the books to combat the dangerous pursuit of others—laws against intrusion, harassment, stalking, battery, reckless driving—federal lawmakers in 1997, 1998, and 1999 introduced bills intended specifically to restrict photographers. The bills would have made it a federal crime to pursue someone in a way that risks bodily harm in an effort to photograph or tape the person for commercial purposes.[58] As of January 2000, none of these proposed criminal laws against paparazzi had actually been enacted. However, California did pass a civil statute declaring it an invasion of privacy to attempt to capture "in a manner that is offensive to a reasonable person, any type of visual image, sound recording, or other physical impression of the plaintiff engaged in a personal or familial activity under circumstances in which the plaintiff had a reasonable expectation of privacy. . . ."[59] It remains to be seen whether such a statute will be upheld as constitutional.

Summary Points

Privacy protection, unlike defamation, is a relatively young area of law that reflects modern society's changes in attitudes, lifestyles, and technology.

A majority of states has recognized four separate torts that come under the rubric invasion of privacy: appropriation, disclosure of private facts, false light, and intrusion. In addition, the overlapping tort of intentional infliction of mental distress has been claimed against the mass media with increasing frequency in recent years.

Thus far these torts have been kept under control by a few rulings from the U.S. Supreme Court and by narrow application in the lower courts. But some legal scholars believe that eventually a single privacy or emotional distress tort will evolve to supersede the law of defamation.

Some criminal statutes are also on the books to protect privacy. In most cases, they are concerned with the secret use of electronic eavesdropping devices.

As some general legal guidelines, it should be remembered that:

☐ Scenes open to public view can be photographed, and information in public records may be reported, without consent.

☐ Private information about an individual, once you have it, may always be published or broadcast if a legitimate news purpose exists.

☐ In areas specifically intended for privacy, such as private homes and motel rooms, you may not secretly snoop, tape-record, or photograph, even if a newsworthy motive exists.

☐ Written consent must be obtained before using a person's name or picture in a commercial message.

☐ People should not be represented in a misleading and highly objectionable context without consent.

In recent years plaintiffs have increasingly alleged intentional infliction of emotional distress against media defendants. Although the claim is probably viable in some circumstances, the Supreme Court has limited this tort by ruling that public figures, at least, must show that the highly offensive communication alleged facts and was disseminated with actual malice.

The hypothetical at the beginning of this chapter presented numerous potential privacy problems. From a legal perspective some things would clearly be safe to report, such as Grundy's drunk driving arrest, discovered in public police logs. On the other hand, reporting much of the additional material, such as videotape from the hot tub, could pose a realistic danger of a lawsuit for disclosure of private facts. The outcome of such a lawsuit would depend on an examination of many detailed facts relating to the degree of privacy at issue and the connection to legitimate news. Disclosing the psychiatric treatment, for example, could lead to liability if not related to a matter of legitimate public concern. Another privacy tort, intrusion, might also have been committed when you climbed into the tree and used a powerful camera lens. Again, an examination of more detailed facts would be needed to determine whether Grundy had a reasonable expectation of privacy in her backyard.

Discussion Questions

1. Should wrongful intent or news-gathering methods by defendants have any bearing on the outcome of privacy lawsuits? For example, suppose a trespassing news reporter slipped unnoticed into a physician's office, stole an individual's medical file, and then published information from the file—including the fact that the individual was infected with the AIDS virus. If the medical information was legitimately newsworthy, would the reporter's wrongful methods be the slightest bit relevant in a lawsuit brought by the individual subject of the story? Has the Supreme Court answered this question, or has it left the door open to such a lawsuit?

2. For purposes of the appropriation tort, the trick sometimes is determining whether the individual's name or likeness was used for a commercial purpose. How would you categorize the following unauthorized uses:

   (a) Putting an employee's picture on the front of the company's monthly employee newsletter?

(b) Using a business customer's picture on the cover of the company's share-holder magazine?

(c) Using a campaign contributor's name in a political ad urging support for the senatorial candidate?

(d) Using an individual doctor's picture on a flyer for a cancer society fund-raising event?

(e) Using a college professor's picture in a calendar being sold on campus to raise funds for a fraternity?

3. It has been extremely rare for plaintiffs actually to win lawsuits against mass communicators for invasion of privacy or infliction of emotional distress. Yet it appears these kinds of lawsuits are being filed with increasing frequency. How would you explain this? Have these lawsuits become more frequent because of changing tactics by the media? A changing mood among media consumers? An increasingly litigious society?

Key Terms

appropriation	model release
commercial use	name or likeness
false light	newsworthiness defense
fraud	outrage
harassment	paparazzi
intentional infliction of emotional distress	photo consent form
	private facts
intrusion	public record privilege
knowing consent	right to know
minors	right of publicity
misappropriation	

Web Resource

http://www.epic.org/privacy
Electronic Privacy Information Center

InfoTrac® College Edition

Privacy is a hot issue with the American public. But the various types of privacy law discussed in this chapter can raise serious conflicts with First Amendment ideals. Find an article that describes a current, unresolved issue pitting privacy interests against free speech ideals.

Chapter Outline

Access to Places and Information

Upon completing this chapter you should

- ☐ **recognize** the limited role of the U.S. Constitution in media access problems.
- ☐ **understand** the basic rules of trespass law.
- ☐ **understand** the typical framework of statutes that grant rights of access to government meetings and records.
- ☐ **know** the most common exceptions to state and federal access laws.

Hypothetical

■ Get Lost and Keep Out

Now assume that you are working as a staff writer for a consumer affairs magazine, and the editor has assigned you to cover a story about contaminated drinking water in a Midwestern town. Some physicians suspect that a recent marked increase in leukemia cases is linked to the water. One of the first things you do after arriving in town is visit city hall and ask to see a copy of a special water quality report completed just a few days ago by the city's department of health. The clerk at the front desk asks "Why do you want to see it?" You tell her you're working on a magazine story about the city's bad water and the corruption that may be behind it. The clerk says "Sorry, that report is being kept confidential because it's highly technical. It would be too confusing to media people and the public."

Later that evening you show up at the weekly city council meeting, during which local residents are expected to speak out against the city's water policies. However, a guard stops you at the door to the council chambers. "You with the media?" he asks. You nod, and the guard says "No media allowed."

You're getting frustrated now and you decide to do some investigating firsthand. The next morning you drive to the edge of town and begin hiking across a field in the direction of the city's water wells. After about half a mile you encounter a red sign reading "Warning—Private Property. No Trespassing." About fifty yards ahead you can see ponds of brackish water on the private industrial property. An odor fouls the air, and lots of rusty metal barrels are scattered around. You figure what lies ahead is a dump site for toxic wastes. You disregard the sign, approach the ponds, and take dozens of photographs of the sickening mess. Just then, two men wearing gas masks emerge from behind a pile of canisters. One of them says to you "This is private property and you're trespassing. Hand over all your film, or you'll get in trouble with the police." Instead, you turn and run as fast as you can. As you're racing back through the field, you wonder about the legalities of your actions.

Would the law help you gain access to the city's water report and to the council meeting? Who holds the upper hand, legally, in the confrontation at the dump site?

Access to Places

Sometimes the threshold question for media professionals is whether they may gain access to the newsworthy places—the house where a homicide occurred, the scene of a traffic accident, a military testing site, or the private industrial yard where toxins are being dumped illegally. Chapter 5 discussed the narrow tort of intrusion, which in the interest of personal privacy prohibits the media from snooping in certain places or by certain methods. This chapter considers the much broader, more commonplace situations in which laws affect access. The discussion includes laws that limit access as well as laws that help open the doors.

The first thing to realize is that the First Amendment is usually impotent in confrontations over access. With limited exceptions the First Amendment is not interpreted to guarantee public or media access, either to places or to information. As Chief Justice Burger wrote in 1978: "There is an undoubted right to gather news 'from any source by means within the law,' . . . but that affords no basis for the claim that the First Amendment compels others—private persons or governments—to supply information."[1] In other words, the First Amendment works defensively as a shield against government suppression, but not offensively as a battering ram to open doors to the newsgathering process. It does not, for example, make communicators immune to the law of trespass.

Trespass on Private Property

Trespass may be defined as the intentional, unauthorized entry upon property that is rightfully possessed by others. As the definition suggests, the elements of this common tort are relatively simple. All that is required is that a person physically invade land or structures without the consent of those who lawfully control the property. Typically the tort occurs when newspaper photographers, TV camera crews, or news reporters wander onto private property in hot pursuit of a story.

Consent: Express or Implied

Consent is a complete defense to trespass. It may be **express consent,** if you are invited or granted specific authorization to enter property. But that is not the only kind of consent recognized by law. People enter private property routinely—to shop, eat at a restaurant, or knock on a front door, for example—without specific authorization and without becoming liable for trespass. That's because most of those entries follow general custom or a pattern of usage, and under the law there is **implied consent** to follow the custom.

Trespass may occur at the moment of entry, such as when a reporter hops a fence. Or, if a visitor originally had either express or implied consent, the trespass could occur later—when the visitor exceeds the scope of consent or when consent is revoked and the visitor fails to leave. For example, suppose you entered a restaurant during its regular business hours. No trespass has occurred because under the legal doctrine of **custom and usage** there is implied consent for the public to enter. But the implied consent would not extend to all activities, such as roaming through the restaurant to photograph patrons. Furthermore, the restaurant manager could end any claim of implied consent by simply asking you to leave. If you linger, trespass will occur. In other words, the initially lawful entry has lapsed.

A 1978 New York case involved a CBS camera crew that had been directed to visit restaurants cited for health code violations and to enter unannounced, "with cameras rolling." The crew entered the plaintiff's restaurant and, it was claimed, immediately began filming the patrons in a noisy and obtrusive fashion. Patrons waiting to be seated instead decided to leave the restaurant, and the manager had to push the crew from the premises. A jury found CBS liable for trespass, and an appellate court upheld the verdict. The trespass occurred when the crew first entered the restaurant, the court noted, because the crew had no intention of entering the establishment for any of its customary purposes.[2]

What if the entry is for a customary or approved purpose, but there is another, undisclosed and unapproved purpose as well? Is the consent still valid? This thorny legal question often arises in cases where videotaping was done secretly by undercover reporters whose presence was otherwise welcome. Unfortunately, courts across the country have not been consistent in dealing with these cases. Some have stood by the general rule that consent to enter property can be legally valid even if obtained by misrepresentation or concealed intentions.[3] But other courts have sided with plaintiffs who allege that covert taping by guests can turn them into trespassers.

For example, a Minnesota television reporter applied for a volunteer position with a local religious organization that operated care facilities for the mentally retarded. She did not disclose that she was actually a reporter, and during 120 hours as a volunteer at various facilities she secretly videotaped what she observed. The TV station broadcast a report using portions of the video that allegedly showed improper care by the staff. The Court of Appeals of Minnesota in 1998 ruled that although the reporter's volunteer work was welcomed initially, "if she exceeded the scope of her consent by secretly videotaping their activities, her continued presence became unpermitted and unlawful."[4]

Tagging Along with Police

News photographers and reporters have run into legal trouble by assuming that the right of police or other emergency personnel to enter property also implies consent for the news media to follow. Courts usually reject this contention. In fact, even the express consent of police or fire officials may be insufficient.

The often-cited 1986 ruling in *Miller v. National Broadcasting Co.* serves to illustrate: As you may recall from Chapter 5, a television crew working on a mini-documentary about paramedics obtained consent to accompany a unit of Los Angeles Fire Department paramedics and film all aspects of their work. The unit was called to a private residence, and the camera crew followed—right into the bedroom where a man lay on the floor dying of a heart attack. The TV crew stayed to film the resuscitation efforts, but never sought consent to enter from the one person who, under the circumstances, could give it. That person was the victim's wife, who anxiously waited in another room of the apartment and realized only later that a television crew had been present. The California Court of Appeal held that she could pursue a trespass claim, as well as the claim for invasion of privacy, against the TV station.[5]

The Florida Supreme Court reached a different verdict ten years earlier, holding that no trespass occurred when a newspaper photographer accompanied fire officials into a burned-out house without the owner's consent.[6] But the case may be factually distinguishable because the owners of the house were out of town at the time, and the authorities in this situation could be viewed as the temporary custodians of the property, legally able to authorize others' presence. Whether other courts would follow this reasoning is uncertain, however.

What is certain is that tagging along with authorities, which has become increasingly popular in television, is legally risky. Various torts can grow out of this practice, and from the plaintiff's standpoint the easiest claim is usually trespass. Sometimes for the media it is a calculated risk. The subject of a police narcotics raid is likely to have other, more pressing concerns than to pursue a trespass claim against the media. Furthermore, trespass damages often are minor, a point discussed in the next section. Still, media people should approach the tag-along scenario with caution.

A pair of U.S. Supreme Court cases decided on the same day in 1999 is likely to reduce the tag-along opportunities for media. In *Wilson v. Layne*[7] and *Hanlon v. Berger*[8] the Court held that, in addition to the media violating trespass law, police may violate the Fourth Amendment of the Constitution by allowing the media to accompany them into private residences. The Fourth Amendment prohibits unreasonable government searches and generally confines searches to what is stipulated in judge-approved warrants.

In *Wilson,* a team of U.S. and Maryland law enforcement officers invited a *Washington Post* reporter and photographer to tag along in the early morning as the team executed a search warrant at a private home. The team expected to find a dangerous fugitive inside, but instead found only his parents, Charles and Geraldine Wilson, dressed in their night clothes. Mr. Wilson angrily confronted the officers and was then subdued on the floor, all while the *Post* photographer took numerous pictures.

In *Hanlon,* agents of the U.S. Fish and Wildlife Service searched the Montana ranch house of Paul and Emma Berger, where the agents sought evidence that Mr. Berger had killed protected eagles. But, when the USFWS agents arrived with a search warrant, they also brought along a crew of photographers and reporters from Cable News Network (CNN). In accordance with a special access agreement between CNN and the USFWS, the cable channel collected eight hours of audio and video tape at the ranch, unbeknownst to the Bergers. One USFWS agent even wore a hidden microphone that continuously transmitted audio to the CNN technical crew.

The residents in each case sued the law enforcement officers, contending that they violated the plaintiffs' Fourth Amendment rights by expanding a government search into a media production. The Supreme Court agreed. "We hold that it is a violation of the Fourth Amendment for police to bring members of the media or other third parties into a home during the execution of a warrant when the presence of the third parties in the home was not in aid of the execution of the warrant," the Court said in *Wilson*. The "possibility of good public relations for the

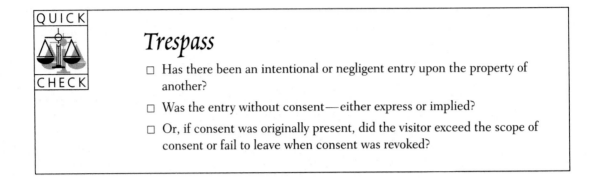

Trespass

□ Has there been an intentional or negligent entry upon the property of another?

□ Was the entry without consent—either express or implied?

□ Or, if consent was originally present, did the visitor exceed the scope of consent or fail to leave when consent was revoked?

police is simply not enough, standing alone, to justify the ride-along intrusion into a private home."

In the *Hanlon* case the ranch owners also sued CNN for trespass. The federal Court of Appeals held that the government agents' temporary control of the Berger ranch during the search did not authorize the agents to invite media onto the property. Therefore, CNN could indeed be liable for the tort.[9]

Thus, court decisions in the Wilson and Berger cases have dealt a multi-pronged blow to the decades-old practice of media ride-alongs with police—a practice increasingly popular in recent years as the public appetite has grown for televised scenes of dramatic, in-the-trenches engagement between police and crime suspects. When those scenes are on suspects' private property, and especially in the home, both law enforcement and the media must consider the risks of continued media presence.

Damages

Often in trespass situations there is no damage—no fences broken, no merchandise taken, no flowers trampled. In such cases a lawsuit for trespass rarely looms as an ominous threat. When plaintiffs in trespass cases are unable to show they were actually harmed, courts traditionally have awarded **nominal damages** to the plaintiff—usually one dollar. These nominal awards are supposed to vindicate the plaintiff in theory, while at the same time declining to enrich the uninjured property owner.

On the other hand, whenever some damages can be proved, trespass is a particularly threatening kind of tort for the mass media. This is because *all* harm traceable to the trespass is subject to compensation—injury to the land, to personal property, even to peace of mind.

Criminal Trespass

Plaintiffs need not show that defendants entered their property with any mischievous or malicious intent in order to win a civil trespass case against the defendants. If a trespass is "willful," though, it can sometimes constitute a crime as well as a tort. State statutes specify a variety of **criminal trespass** situations, such as refusing to leave clearly posted or fenced lands after being asked to do so. In general, trespass rises to the level of a crime when the trespasser acts in defiance of the landowner's clear wishes. In the hypothetical scenario that began this chapter, for example, you defied the landowner's clear wishes by hiking past the No Trespassing sign. In many states that would amount to a misdemeanor.

The criminal trespass statutes vary widely from state to state, though in all cases the crimes pertain to a narrower class of activity than do the laws of civil trespass. To be punishable as a criminal offense, the statutes typically specify a particular intent that must have been present, such as willfulness or malice. And trespasses are especially likely to become criminal if they involve the use of force or some other breach of the peace. As an example, the criminal trespass statute of California reads in part as follows:

> Every person who willfully commits a trespass by any of the following acts is guilty of a misdemeanor:
>
> . . . (m) Driving any vehicle . . . upon real property belonging to or lawfully occupied by another and known not to be open to the general public, without the consent of the owner, his agent, or the person in lawful possession.
>
> (n) Refusing or failing to leave land, real property, or structures belonging to or lawfully occupied by another and not open to the general public, upon being requested to leave by . . . the owner, his agent, or the person in lawful possession. . . .[10]

Can you envision situations in which the media might violate criminal trespass provisions such as these? In Oklahoma, news reporters were convicted of criminal trespass after they followed demonstrators into the fenced construction site for a nuclear power plant. The utility had warned reporters in advance that they would be arrested along with the demonstrators.[11]

Special Problem: Confiscation

In the chapter hypothetical, what are your rights when the landowners or their employees attempt to confiscate your film? Admittedly, you are trespassing. The landowner could sue you for damages, and you might even be guilty of a misdemeanor.

Are you legally bound to comply when they say "Hand over your film"? Does the act of trespass somehow give others an instant right to your possessions? No. The mere act of trespass does not give the property occupant authority to seize your film, notes, or equipment, though this is often presumed. The legal remedy for trespass is through the courts. Confiscation of your film by force or threat would in turn be a violation of your property rights.

One warning about this, however. The rule can be different if your actions could amount to a crime and it is police who are seizing your film or other property as evidence. The next chapter will say more about that.

Special Problem: Contractual Limitations

Remember that even when communicators are welcomed upon privately controlled property the consent does not necessarily extend to the full range of newsgathering activities. In fact, the consent to enter may specifically be contingent on the entrant's refraining from certain activities—typically photography and taping.

The problem arises most frequently when the media cover privately sponsored entertainment and sporting events. For example, you might find on the back of your ticket to an ice skating exhibition the printed stipulation "No photographing of this performance is allowed." It might be that the sponsor wants to prevent distractions to other patrons. Or perhaps the intent is to maximize marketing opportunities; the promoters might wish to offer exclusive photography rights to a particular magazine. In any event, the sponsors of such events are essentially selling a product, and they may package and sell it in almost any way they wish. The fact that the event may also be newsworthy does not change the rules of proprietary control. When you accept admission to such an event, you have agreed implicitly to the stated restrictions; they become part of a binding contract between you and the proprietor. Generally speaking, you can assume that advance permission is required before you may commercially photograph stage productions or sporting events to which attendance is controlled.

Accident, Crime, and Disaster Scenes

Even in the most public of places there are times when police or other authorities may close areas in the interest of public safety or an investigation. Typical examples are traffic collisions, chemical spills, scenes of violent crime, or areas damaged by earthquake, storm, or fire. Unauthorized people who enter these enclosed sites may be arrested and prosecuted for misdemeanors.

Of course, it is just such newsworthy areas to which journalists and photographers often want access. Fortunately, newspeople are granted access rather routinely. Some law-enforcement agencies issue standing **press passes** to employed newspeople—something reporters and photographers should inquire about before a newsworthy calamity strikes. These passes serve as a handy form of identification for the agency, and letting credentialed newspeople past the barricades is common policy. But in most cases this practice, which newspeople may come to take for granted, is not required by law. So even with a pass there are times when the media might be held behind the lines with the general public.

In California a unique statute specifically allows newspeople to cross police lines, thus formalizing the common practice legally.[12] But even that statute is interpreted narrowly. A court in 1986 said the statute was meant to allow newspeople to assume the risk of injury and enter sites that were closed solely for public safety. But if authorities believe media access will impede emergency operations, or if the closure is related to investigation of a crime, no media privilege exists. For example, the California court upheld the conviction of a TV news cameraman who disobeyed police orders and entered an airline crash site where officers were investigating a cause that could have been criminal.[13]

If authorities at a calamity scene do order you to stay away, don't expect an on-the-spot argument to prove fruitful. In fact, if you force a confrontation you could be arrested and prosecuted for interfering with a police officer, even if your presence was consistent with prevailing policy. Courts are likely to defer to the judgment of police officers in emergency situations.[14] If you believe an officer is unreasonably or even illegally standing in the way of your doing your job, ask to speak to a superior officer, or avoid the impeding individual and find another vantage point. File a complaint later. For the benefit of your long-term working relationship, editors at your organization may want to set up a media/law-enforcement meeting at which both sides can discuss problems and agree to some guidelines in areas where state law does not specify your rights.

Polling Places

Suppose your state passed a statute that prohibits the conduct of any public opinion poll within 300 feet of a polling place on election day. One purpose of the law is to protect the integrity of polling places. Another is to eliminate the early broadcasting of projections based on exit polls, in the belief that early projections discourage voter turnout. Indeed, the 300-foot buffer would make it virtually impossible for the media to conduct valid exit polls. Would this law be constitutional?

Just such a law was passed by the state of Washington in 1983. Several news organizations challenged the restriction on First Amendment grounds, claiming that it effectively eliminated a legal form of expression—accurate exit-polling information. The federal Court of Appeals agreed. The court held the law was a restriction on speech, not merely on access to polling places or sources, because it drastically limited communication opportunities between voters and pollsters and prevented the dissemination of polling information. Furthermore, it was a content-based restriction, not a time/place/manner restriction, because it aimed to restrict discussion about voters' choices.

As a content restriction on speech, the law could be upheld only if it were narrowly tailored to serve a compelling government interest. But to the extent that the law attempted to prevent disruption at the polling place, the restriction was far broader than necessary; it banned nondisruptive polling as well. And, to the extent that the law attempted to protect the integrity of elections and voter participation rates, the court held that the general interest of protecting voters from outside influences was simply not sufficient to justify a restriction on speech.[15] The U.S. Supreme Court has not decided a case relating to exit polling. Presumably, though, restrictions could be drawn narrowly enough to avoid being categorized as content-based limitations on speech.

Government Property

Government property—military bases, prisons, power plants, schools, airports and so on—exist for a public purpose, but that does not mean they must be open to the public or to the media. Entry can be limited to that which serves the property's purpose, and the laws of civil and criminal trespass apply.

However, an important difference exists between government-controlled property and purely private property. For the most part, owners of private property may invite or exclude whomever they wish. But government, once it does open property or proceedings to the general public, usually may not single out the media or certain members of the media for exclusion. Discriminatory access practices by government typically are struck down on constitutional grounds. Selective access is discussed more fully near the end of this chapter.

Jails and Prisons

In terms of media access to government facilities, one of the more common points of contention has been access to jails and prisons. The Supreme Court decided such a case, *Houchins v. KQED, Inc.,*[16] in 1978. Following a suicide in a county jail, a San Francisco television station sought access to the jail in order to get the full story and to photograph the facilities. But the sheriff refused to admit the news crew. Soon thereafter the sheriff announced that monthly jail tours would be available, and a KQED reporter went on the first group tour. Important sections of the jail were not included on the tour, however, and tour members were not allowed to bring cameras or tape recorders or to see or talk to inmates. KQED filed a lawsuit, claiming that the denial of more effective access was a violation of its First Amendment rights.

The Supreme Court held that no First Amendment right was applicable. In his majority opinion Chief Justice Burger acknowledged that conditions in jails and prisons are matters of great public importance and that the media serve an important function as the "eyes and ears of the public." Nevertheless, he wrote, many other avenues were available for learning about jail conditions, and the First Amendment simply did not provide a right for the public or the media to enter these institutions, with or without cameras, to hunt for information.

Though media access is not a constitutional right, state laws or prison regulations may allow the media to interview inmates. The policies typically are quite limited, however. For example, they may limit the number of interviews an inmate may grant per month, limit interviews only to certain categories of inmates, require prior approval of interview requests, or prohibit cameras and tape recorders.

Executions

In the early days of this nation, executions customarily were public events. Today, however, they often present access frustrations for journalists. The federal government and about three-quarters of the states permit imposition of the death penalty, but typically under very tightly controlled conditions, with a limited number of witnesses.

For example, New York's statute dictates that the state corrections commissioner shall select and invite "six adult citizens" to witness executions. There is no mention of who those citizens should be or whether a media representative should be among them.[17] In some other states the law specifically provides for media attendance at executions, but not with cameras or recorders.

Efforts to claim First Amendment access rights have been unsuccessful. In 1990 television station KQED again raised the question, this time when it sought to videotape an execution in a California prison. The prison traditionally had allowed reporters to witness executions with notebooks and pencils, but it had a strict rule against cameras. KQED argued that decisions about the method of news coverage should rest with the media, not with the state. Furthermore, executions in the 1700s and 1800s typically were public events. There now should be a First Amendment right for the public to at least observe the execution through television, KQED argued. The federal District Court ruled against a constitutional right to camera access, however, and said it was reasonable for the prison to conclude that cameras and video coverage would pose an additional threat to prison security.[18]

In some states where lethal injection is used, execution witnesses are permitted to see the condemned prisoner only after he or she has been strapped to a gurney and the intravenous tubes have been inserted—a process that may take twenty minutes. The Society of Professional Journalists and the California First Amendment Coalition challenged such a policy in that state, arguing that they had a constitutional right to view the entire execution procedure at the prison. But in 1998 the federal Court of Appeals held there was no such First Amendment right of access.[19]

Access to Government Proceedings

When the media seek access to government meetings, hearings, and similar proceedings, the law swings more forcefully to the media's aid. The federal government and all fifty states have enacted **open meeting laws** that require government deliberations to be open to the public. Here again, the First Amendment is not interpreted to provide a general right of access, but it is widely agreed that government decision making in a democracy should take place in the open. Thus Congress and the state legislatures have created these access rights by statute. The rights belong to the general public, not just to the media.

If you ever work in the news business, it will be particularly important for you to understand the provisions of your own state's open meeting law. Generally speaking, legal hotlines for the news media receive more inquiries regarding access to meetings than any other area of communications law.

State Open Meeting Laws

State open meeting laws vary greatly and can be quite complicated, covering an array of governmental units in the executive and legislative branches at both local and state levels. The statutes make two general requirements: first, the agencies must provide advance public notice of their meetings; second, the agencies must conduct these meetings openly. The laws do allow closed meetings for specified topics of deliberation.

To Whom Do the Laws Apply?

When examining a state's open meeting law, the first thing to ascertain is which government bodies are subject to the law. Typically the laws apply to the multi-member, deliberative bodies of local government, such as city councils, county planning commissions, and school boards. The laws also tend to cover multi-member agencies of state government, though it is less common for open meeting laws to cover proceedings of the legislatures.

Often it is presumed that the question of which government bodies are covered by an open meeting law is simple and straightforward. In some cases it is. The county planning commission is covered. The state fish and game commission is covered. Nevertheless, the statutes don't always provide definitive answers on this question. How about a volunteer advisory board appointed by the planning commission? How about the student government at a state college or university? Sometimes the courts must be called upon to answer these questions by interpreting the statute.

What Is a Meeting?

For those government entities covered by an open meeting law, the meetings must be open to the public. Naturally, this raises the critical question of what a meeting is. A *meeting* is generally defined under these laws as a gathering of a quorum of the governmental body, no matter how informal, whenever official business is discussed or voted upon.

Thus a meeting is determined by the number of agency members present (enough to make binding decisions) and the nature of the discussion, not by the place where discussions occur. If all members of a city council gathered at one member's house for a hot-tub party, it would qualify as a meeting, subject to requirements of the open meeting law, if the members discussed matters pending before the council. The theory is that the media and public have a right to witness the government's decision-making process, whatever it may be. Agencies cannot sidestep the open meeting requirements simply by meeting in an unusual place and calling the gathering a "social" or "fact-finding" session. This is not to say that government bodies don't engage in such practices. All too often they do, and all too often these informal arrangements go unchallenged, by the public and by the media.

The Notice Requirement

In most cases, advance public notice must be given for the times and places of meetings. Otherwise, of course, the guarantee of public meetings could be circumvented easily by officials who prefer to meet without an audience. Furthermore, open meeting laws often require that an agenda for each meeting be available in advance. The law may even prohibit the agency from discussing or acting on topics absent from the posted agenda. The specifics of the notice-and-agenda requirements may take many forms. In California, for example, one of the leading states in open meeting legislation, local government agencies must set, by ordinance or bylaw, the time for their regular meetings. In addition to this standing notice, the local agency must conspicuously post the agenda for each regular meeting at least seventy-two hours in advance. For state agencies, however, the form of notice is different. A written notice of the time, date, and place of a meeting, along with an agenda, must be mailed at least ten days in advance to all who request the information.

The state open meeting laws contain several exceptions to the notice-and-agenda requirements. For example, in emergency situations such as work stoppages or crippling disasters, agencies may be allowed to meet under a reduced notice requirement, or in some cases with no advance public notice.

Permissible Closed Sessions

While recognizing the general right of the public to witness government proceedings, state legislatures also have recognized a need for candor and uninhibited debate among public officials. In some situations this candor would tend to be suppressed if the public and media were present. Also, some kinds of information, if discussed in public, could greatly hinder government effectiveness or disrupt individual privacy.

Therefore, the open meeting laws authorize closed sessions, sometimes called **executive sessions,** where certain topics are discussed. During closed sessions only the members of the agency and perhaps the support staff are present. The states vary significantly in the extent to which their courts will recognize implied justifications for closed sessions. In some states exceptions to the open meeting requirement are broadly construed or freely implied; in others exceptions are very narrowly construed and are limited to express statutory authorization. In any event, state open meeting laws typically identify dozens of exceptions to the public meeting requirement. Some of the most common exceptions are made for the following reasons:

1. To promote candid discussion and avoid embarrassment for public employees, a *personnel exception* typically allows workers to be employed, dismissed, or evaluated in closed sessions.

2. To avoid compromising an agency's legal positions, a *pending litigation exception* may allow agencies to confer with their legal counsel regarding lawsuits by or against the agencies.

3. To discuss threats to public facilities or services, a *public security exception* may permit agencies to meet in closed session with law enforcement officials.

4. To negotiate salaries and benefits for public employee organizations, a *labor negotiations exception* allows agencies to meet in private with bargaining representatives.

5. To discuss purchase, sale, or lease of property by an agency, a *real estate negotiation exception* permits agencies to meet in confidence with their negotiators.

Though a governmental body may be authorized to conduct a closed session, it still may be subject to the notice requirement for that meeting. Also, laws may require that agencies prepare written justification for meetings or portions of meetings that are closed to the public. Many times a meeting will begin in public and shift to executive session when a certain topic is raised. If this happens, it may be smart to stick around; just because officials have gone into executive session doesn't mean they won't come out of it ten minutes later.

What To Do If You Are Shut Out

If you find yourself shut out of a government meeting or learn that you will be, don't just presume the agency has legal authority to do so. First contact the agency or its attorney and ask for justification. If you then believe the meeting is being closed unlawfully, follow the complaint procedure recommended by your organization, if one exists, and promptly contact your editor or supervisor. Your organization may want to consult its lawyer. Open meetings violations occur frequently, especially with small, local government bodies that may be ill-informed of the open meeting requirements. Often one call from a lawyer is enough to prompt the proper open door policy.

If the agency still insists on meeting in private, legal action may be necessary. Here again, the state laws differ in the penalties and remedies available for violations of the open meeting requirements. Civil remedies are by far the most common. As one civil remedy, the laws typically provide that you may go to court to obtain an injunction—a court order preventing further or future violations. Furthermore, some of the laws specify that government actions taken in violation of the open meeting requirements be declared void. If you win your case, the law also may require the errant agency to pay your legal fees.

In addition to these civil lines of recourse, some statutes provide that misdemeanor criminal penalties may be imposed upon public officials who meet in knowing violation of the law. Proving a knowing violation is difficult, though, so even in states where criminal sanctions are on the books, prosecutions are rare.

The Federal Statute

The federal law, called the **Sunshine Act** of 1976,[20] is structured similar to the states' open meeting statutes. The Sunshine Act, aptly named because it opens government to the light of scrutiny, pertains to about fifty federal agencies and commissions. Of these governmental bodies the law makes two general require-

The Federal Sunshine Act

☐ Is the meeting one of a federal, executive-branch agency headed by two or more presidentially appointed members?

☐ Has the agency provided one week's advance public notice of its meeting?

☐ Is the meeting open to the public and media, except for deliberations that fall within 10 specified exception categories?

ments: first, the agencies must provide advance public notice of their meetings; second, the agencies must conduct these meetings openly.

Unlike some of the state laws, the federal Sunshine Act applies only to the executive branch of the government and only to agencies "headed by a collegial body composed of two or more individual members, a majority of whom are appointed to such position by the President with the advice and consent of the Senate." This leaves out much of the federal government, of course, but virtually all the important regulatory agencies are covered, including the Federal Trade Commission, the Securities and Exchange Commission, the Federal Communications Commission, and the Nuclear Regulatory Commission.

Congress did not include itself under the act, and it may decide on a case-by-case basis whether its own proceedings will be open to the public. (Traditionally, sessions of the full House and Senate have been open, and in the past twenty years a greater number of committee meetings and investigative hearings also have been conducted in public. The push toward openness even has led to gavel-to-gavel cable TV coverage of congressional sessions.)

For the covered agencies, meetings are defined broadly as "the deliberations of at least the number of individual agency members required to take action on behalf of the agency where such deliberations determine or result in the joint conduct or disposition of official business." Public notice must be made of all meetings, even those that might legally be closed, at least one week in advance of the meeting. The notice, which must appear in the *Federal Register* and some other public place, must specify the time, place, and general subject of the meeting.

The federal Sunshine Act lists ten exceptions to the requirement that meetings be open to the public—fewer exceptions than most state statutes provide. The act says that agencies may vote to hold closed meetings when it is determined that the meeting would concern:

1. National defense or foreign policy secrets

2. Internal personnel practices of the agency

3. Information specifically exempted from disclosure by a separate federal statute

4. Trade secrets of private business

5. Accusations of crime

6. Personal information that if disclosed would constitute an unwarranted invasion of privacy

7. Investigative information compiled for law enforcement purposes

8. Reports on government oversight of financial institutions

9. Information that would significantly frustrate implementation of agency actions or would threaten the stability of a financial institution or the economy

10. The agency's participation in a lawsuit or its own quasijudicial functions, such as conducting hearings or issuing subpoenas

The law presumes openness. Closed sessions must be justified under one of the statutory exceptions. Even in those cases where the act does not require an open meeting, however, the agency is usually free to hold an open meeting if it wishes.

Remedies for Violation

To enforce the provisions of the Sunshine Act against a federal agency, a lawsuit must be filed in federal District Court. The court can issue an order requiring further deliberations to be open, and if the plaintiff is victorious, it can award the plaintiff court costs and lawyers' fees. The court cannot, however, void the actions taken at improperly closed meetings or punish individual officials.

Access to Government Records

Just as with government proceedings, all state legislatures and the Congress have concluded that government records should generally be open for public inspection. Here again, the First Amendment is not interpreted to force government records into the open, but the legislatures have passed statutes that pick up this slack. In passing **open record laws,** Congress and the states have agreed that the availability of documents relating to the public's business should not be left to the whims of government officials or clerks.

The Freedom of Information Act Congress passed the Freedom of Information Act (FOIA)[21] in 1966 and thereby opened a huge—even mind-staggering—storehouse of government documents. As with the Sunshine Act passed ten years later, the FOIA created a system of presumptive availability. The public and the media have a right to inspect government documents unless the information they seek is properly classified under one of nine statutory exemptions. It is important to note that the FOIA was created for the benefit of the public at large, not just the news media. The goal was to help assure that people who want to learn more about the workings of their government can do so.

The FOIA applies to a much broader range of government than does the Sunshine Act, however, since the FOIA isn't limited to multi-member, presidentially appointed bodies. The FOIA covers virtually every unit in the executive branch of the federal government except for the president and the president's immediate staff. In addition to independent regulatory agencies such as the Federal Trade Commission, the FOIA covers the executive-branch departments (such as the Defense Department and the Justice Department—including the FBI) and government-controlled corporations (such as the Postal Service). The act does not cover the legislative or judicial branches of the federal government, however.

Communicators from every type of medium—from giant television networks to small weekly newspapers to trade journals—have relied on documents obtained through the FOIA. FOIA documents have been used by the media to uncover developing news stories, to double-check theories and facts, or to elaborate on historical events. In all, federal agencies receive hundreds of thousands of FOIA requests a year, not only from journalists but also from private individuals, attorneys, and businesses. For example, in 1998 NASA received about two thousand FOIA requests; the Securities and Exchange Commission received 3000; the CIA received 6000; the Environmental Protection Agency received 21,000; and the Department of Justice received 181,000 FOIA requests.

Which Records Are Covered?

The FOIA broadly covers agency-generated documents that are in the agency's possession. This means that the act covers only documents that the agency wrote, commissioned, or ordered. It does not cover documents such as presidential transition-team recommendations, which might end up in agency file cabinets but which were not compiled at the behest of the agency in the course of its official business. Nor does the act require agencies to generate or retrieve records not in their physical possession at the time of the request.

What about items created solely for personal convenience, such as phone message slips or notations on a calendar? These are not considered agency records under the act unless they also are used for some official agency purpose. On the other hand, the term *records* is interpreted broadly to include any reproducible form of documentary information, such as papers, electronic databases, films, sound recordings, and photographs.

Exemptions from Disclosure

The FOIA specifies nine disclosure exemptions that agencies may use to keep documents secret. The exemptions cover records relating to:

1. National defense and foreign policy secrets
2. Internal agency personnel rules and practices

3. Information specifically exempted by other federal statutes (a catchall exemption)

4. Trade secrets and commercial or financial information obtained from businesses in confidence

5. Internal agency memos and policy discussions

6. Personal information, such as medical reports, that if disclosed would invade privacy

7. Law enforcement investigative information

8. Federally regulated financial institutions

9. Oil- and gas-well data of private companies

Other than Exemptions 5 and 9, the FOIA exemptions are similar to those of the federal Sunshine Act pertaining to open meetings. And, other than some of the laws incorporated under Exemption 3, the exemptions are not mandatory. This means that the government is permitted, but usually not required, to withhold information that properly falls within these categories.

Critics of the FOIA over the years have said that it is riddled with too many broad exceptions and that it is still too easy for the government to keep records secret. In 1974 Congress enacted, over President Gerald Ford's veto, several amendments that significantly strengthened the FOIA. In 1996 another package of strengthening amendments was enacted that is known as the Electronic Freedom of Information Act Amendments.

The FOIA is an important tool for journalists—one that is used each year to uncover many important stories. The act is also used by businesspeople and special interest groups to gain information about markets, competitors, and government decision making. But many variables come into play in determining how well the act will work for you in practice — variables such as the attitude toward openness by a presidential administration or the rules put into place by a particular agency chief or the backlog of FOIA requests facing an agency.

Exemption 1

Some of the FOIA exemptions have proved particularly bothersome for journalists. One of these is Exemption 1, dealing with national security. Under this exemption the White House is given broad discretion to establish through executive order the specific criteria by which documents related to national defense or foreign affairs will be classified as confidential. While certainly necessary up to some point, this discretion also opens the door to abuse.

In 1974 Congress tightened the exception slightly. In an amendment to the FOIA it gave federal courts the power to inspect classified documents in private to determine whether they were properly classified under the president's criteria.

QUICK CHECK

The Freedom of Information Act

☐ Were the sought-after records generated by, and are they now housed by, an executive-branch agency of the federal government?

☐ Did the agency respond within ten working days of a formal, written FOIA request?

☐ If the records were not disclosed, did the agency specify which of the nine exemptions it deems to permit confidentiality?

(This is called an *in camera* review). Nevertheless, the courts may not second-guess the classification criteria; they may determine only whether the criteria could reasonably apply to the documents in question.

Exemption 3

Exemption 3, a sort of catchall exemption, is another one often cited by federal agencies. This exemption incorporates federal statutes—other than the FOIA—that specifically prohibit the release of certain information. For example, federal laws require confidentiality for Census Bureau records,[22] individuals' tax returns,[23] and patent applications.[24] Remember that these separate statutes are different from the usual structure of the FOIA in that they *require* confidentiality rather than merely allowing it.

Exemption 5

Another widely used exemption is the fifth, pertaining to "interagency or intra-agency memorandums or letters." According to the U.S. Supreme Court, this exemption is intended to shield from FOIA requests the same kinds of documents that would normally be privileged in the civil discovery phase of a lawsuit.[25] Therefore, Exemption 5 incorporates the attorney-client privilege, which protects communications between an agency and its lawyer, and the so-called **executive privilege,** which protects the working papers, draft reports, or preliminary opinion memos that are used in the advisory and deliberative processes within government. The purpose of this privilege is to sustain the sort of frankness that is necessary for sound decision making.

In 1974 President Nixon claimed executive privilege when several of the infamous White House tapes were subpoenaed by the special prosecutor for use in the Watergate cover-up trial of Nixon's aides. Nixon argued that release of the tapes would damage the constitutional integrity of presidential decision making. In

United States v. Nixon[26] the Supreme Court recognized the need for executive-level candor and thus for the privilege. But it is also said that, absent a need to protect military, diplomatic, or national security secrets, the executive privilege is not absolute. The Court conducted an in-camera review of the tapes and then weighed the need for presidential confidentiality against the need for fair administration of criminal justice. In the end the Court ordered Nixon to honor the subpoena. The *Nixon* decision was based on constitutional doctrine, not the FOIA. But apparently the courts are similarly free to examine the requested material and weigh the competing public interests in FOIA Exemption 5 cases.

Exemption 6

The personal privacy exemption, 6, generally applies to intimate personal or family-life details deemed not to be of important public interest. The exemption essentially requires a balancing of the individual's privacy rights and the public's right to government information. Therefore, application of this exemption requires a context-specific analysis by the agency. Not all information labeled "medical" would necessarily be exempt, for example. And information requests in this area can be made more persuasive by stating the reasons behind them.

A case involving NASA serves to illustrate the balancing nature of this exemption. In January 1986 the space shuttle *Challenger* exploded shortly after take-off, killing the entire crew. An audio tape had been made in the cockpit during the brief flight, and that tape was recovered from the ocean floor by NASA. *The New York Times* made an FOIA request for the tape, which contained brief conversations of the *Challenger* astronauts. NASA responded by providing a written transcript of the tape, but it refused to duplicate the actual tape.

In 1990 a sharply divided U.S. Court of Appeals held that the actual audio might indeed intrude on privacy, that it was similar in nature to personnel and medical files, and that it could fall under Exemption 6. The case was sent back to the lower court to determine whether public dissemination of the tape would indeed invade the privacy of the astronauts' families by exacerbating their grief and to determine whether the public interest in access outweighs those privacy interests.[27] The lower court ultimately ruled that the tape need not be disclosed.

Exemption 7

Finally, Exemption 7, which pertains to information compiled for law-enforcement purposes, is another exemption often confronted by the media. This exemption was significantly revised in 1986. The revision, in the words of *The New York Times*, "gives federal law-enforcement agencies new authority to withhold documents they believe might compromise current investigations."[28]

Generally, the exemption allows law enforcement records to be kept confidential if their release could (a) reasonably be expected to interfere with enforcement proceedings, (b) deprive a person of a fair trial, (c) unnecessarily invade personal privacy, (d) disclose the identity of confidential sources, (e) reveal investigative techniques, or (f) endanger the life of any individual. In some cases, the agency may refuse to confirm or deny that certain records even exist.

Among the law enforcement records that might be most useful to the news media are the computerized criminal histories kept by the FBI. These complete histories, often called "rap sheets," list the arrests, criminal charges, convictions, and sentences of more than 24 million people. But in 1989 the Supreme Court ruled against public access to these records. In *U.S. Department of Justice v. Reporter's Committee for Freedom of the Press,* a CBS journalist had requested from the FBI the rap sheet for an individual whose business was dominated by organized-crime figures. The FBI declined to release the document, citing FOIA Exemption 7(C), an unwarranted invasion of personal privacy. The Supreme Court agreed, even though the individual events summarized in rap sheets are typically a matter of public record at the applicable court houses and police stations around the country.

In Justice Stevens' opinion for the unanimous Court, he drew a practical distinction between the privacy-invading potential of scattered bits of information and a comprehensive, computerized file: "Plainly there is a vast difference between the public records that might be found after a diligent search of courthouse files, county archives, and local police stations throughout the country and a computerized summary located in a single clearinghouse of information."[29] Having concluded that privacy was indeed at stake, the Court then considered whether the invasion of privacy in this case would be unwarranted. Exemption 7(C) applies only to *unwarranted* invasions of privacy. In order to answer this question, the Court referred to the basic purpose of the FOIA: to open agency action to the light of public scrutiny. If the requested document relates to that statutory purpose, then the sacrifice of privacy would be warranted. But in this case, the Court concluded, disclosure of historical information about a private individual would reveal little or nothing about the FBI's own conduct. The Court noted that "in none of our cases construing the FOIA have we found it appropriate to order a Government agency to honor a FOIA request for information about a particular private citizen."[30]

A 1999 court decision involving exemption 7(C) concerned an issue similar to the one addressed in the NASA case under exemption 6: Can records be withheld to protect the privacy of people other than the subjects of the records? The case began in 1993, when National Park Service employees were alerted to a dead body found in Ft. Marcy Park in Virginia. Found dead was Deputy White House Counsel Vincent Foster, Jr., with a revolver in one hand and a fatal gunshot wound to his head. Various government inquiries concluded that Foster committed suicide. But Accuracy in Media, Inc. (AIM) requested photos of the body, seeking to shed light on rumors of an illegal government plot. The Park Service resisted disclosure under exemption 7(C), claiming that release would constitute an unwarranted invasion of close relatives' personal privacy.

The federal Court of Appeals held that nondisclosure was warranted. First, it concluded that disclosure of the photos would indeed invade privacy:

> AIM cannot deny the powerful sense of invasion bound to be aroused in close survivors by wanton publication of gruesome details of death by violence. One has only to think of Lindbergh's rage at the photographer who pried open the coffin of his kidnapped son to photograph the remains and peddle the resulting photos. While law enforcement sometimes necessitates the display of such ghoulish materials, there seems nothing unnatural in saying that the interest asserted against it by spouse, parents and children of the deceased is one of privacy—even though the holders of the interest are distinct from the individual portrayed.[31]

Second, the court said in order for AIM to demonstrate that disclosure was nevertheless warranted, it must show "compelling evidence" of illegal activity by the agency and that access to the photos would help confirm or refute that evidence. Accuracy in Media pointed to differing preliminary descriptions of the gunshot wound by some authorities. But the court said this was far from compelling evidence of agency wrongdoing.

Obtaining Information Under the FOIA

The FOI Service Center in Washington, D.C., a journalists' organization, recommends that anyone seeking information from government documents should first try to obtain the documents through informal means. Simply contact the public information or FOIA officer at the appropriate agency, identify yourself, and then specify the records you want to see. If you are turned down, the next step is to send the appropriate agency, by registered mail, a formal FOIA request. (A sample FOIA request letter is shown in Exhibit 6.1 on pages 220–21.) Advice on how to prepare a request is contained in a popular booklet, "How To Use the Federal FOI Act," available from the FOI Service Center.[32] An automated FOIA letter generator is also available online at the center's website listed at the end of this chapter.

Generally, the more precise a request, the quicker the response. This means identifying documents by name, number, and date, if possible. But if you lack this information, just provide a description reasonable enough to allow the agency employee to locate the records you seek. Learning what documents are on file can be an investigative task in itself. Many federal agencies maintain document indexes that may be of assistance. You may even be uncertain which agency has the kinds of records you want. In this case, check the *United States Government Manual* at your library. It describes the responsibilities and offices of all government agencies.

Once a formal request is made under the FOIA, certain legal obligations apply to the agency. The agency has twenty working days to respond to the FOIA request, although in practice delays are common. If your request is denied, or the agency fails to respond, you should follow with an appeal letter to the head of the agency. The agency has twenty working days to respond to the appeal. (A sample FOIA appeal letter is shown in Exhibit 6.2 on pages 222–23.)

If an appeal letter still does not bring results, and you believe the agency has not adequately justified its refusal to release documents, your next step is to go to the federal District Court nearest you. If the agency fails to convince the court that the requested documents fall within one of the act's nine exemptions, the court will order the documents released.

It is important to realize, too, that the FOIA does not authorize an agency to withhold an entire document when only isolated portions of that document contain information that is exempt from disclosure. In such cases, the agency may excise the exempted portions—by blacking them out, for example—but it must release the remainder of the document.

Most federal agencies will permit you to visit their offices and inspect the released FOIA documents in person. Or you may ask that the agency send copies of the requested documents, either by mail or electronically. In any case the agencies sometimes collect fees for responding to requests. The act allows agencies to charge commercial users reasonable fees for searching and duplicating documents. However, news organizations and noncommercial scientific or educational organizations can be charged only for the costs of duplication and not for the agency's costs in conducting the search. This is significant because the fees for complicated records searches can run into thousands of dollars.

Regardless of these requester categories, however, you may be entitled to a waiver or reduction of fees if, under the words of the act, "disclosure of the information is in the public interest because it is likely to contribute significantly to public understanding of the operations or activities of the government and is not primarily in the interest of the requester." Therefore, even though you are not required to say why you want certain documents in order to make an enforceable FOIA request, you will need to volunteer that information if you also request a fee waiver.

The Electronic FOIA Amendments of 1996

By the early 1990s many federal agencies were suffering from backlogs of FOIA requests and were routinely failing to meet their required time limits for responding. The Clinton administration in 1993 made an effort to reduce the response time by requiring agencies to apply a presumption in favor of disclosure. But the number of FOIA requests continued to grow. A growing number of information seekers were requesting documents in various electronic forms and formats. Many agencies were slow to respond to the computer age of public document requests,

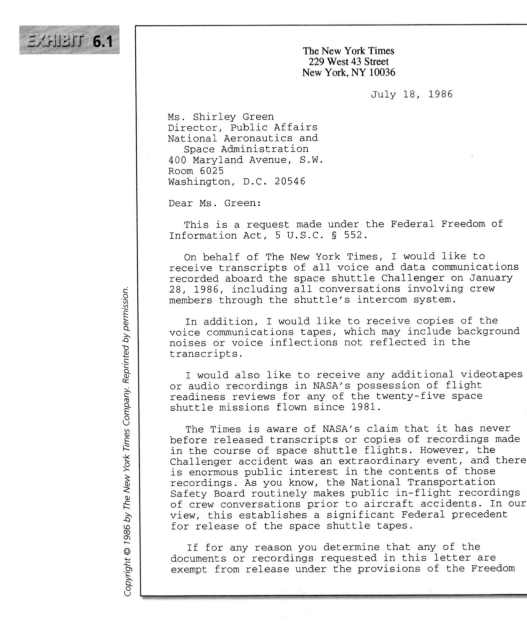

EXHIBIT **6.1**

The New York Times
229 West 43 Street
New York, NY 10036

July 18, 1986

Ms. Shirley Green
Director, Public Affairs
National Aeronautics and
    Space Administration
400 Maryland Avenue, S.W.
Room 6025
Washington, D.C. 20546

Dear Ms. Green:

This is a request made under the Federal Freedom of Information Act, 5 U.S.C. § 552.

On behalf of The New York Times, I would like to receive transcripts of all voice and data communications recorded aboard the space shuttle Challenger on January 28, 1986, including all conversations involving crew members through the shuttle's intercom system.

In addition, I would like to receive copies of the voice communications tapes, which may include background noises or voice inflections not reflected in the transcripts.

I would also like to receive any additional videotapes or audio recordings in NASA's possession of flight readiness reviews for any of the twenty-five space shuttle missions flown since 1981.

The Times is aware of NASA's claim that it has never before released transcripts or copies of recordings made in the course of space shuttle flights. However, the Challenger accident was an extraordinary event, and there is enormous public interest in the contents of those recordings. As you know, the National Transportation Safety Board routinely makes public in-flight recordings of crew conversations prior to aircraft accidents. In our view, this establishes a significant Federal precedent for release of the space shuttle tapes.

If for any reason you determine that any of the documents or recordings requested in this letter are exempt from release under the provisions of the Freedom

and there was even some ambiguity under the FOIA whether some kinds of electronic information were covered by the act.

All this prompted Congress to enact the Electronic Freedom of Information Act Amendments (EFOIAA) of 1996.[33] The amendments are of two main types: (1) administrative reforms intended to ease the backlogs and delays, and (2) tech-

EXHIBIT 6.1

—2—

of Information Act, I would appreciate a written
explanation describing the basis for such a decision.

Since I am making this request on behalf of a daily
newspaper, and because the information is needed on a
timely basis, I would appreciate your communicating with
me by phone concerning the status of this request. I can
be reached either through the Washington Bureau of The
Times at 202-862-0300, or in New York at 212-556-5818. In
any event, I look forward to receiving a reply within 10
business days, as required by law.

Sincerely,

David E. Sanger

/sf

nological reforms intended to update the FOIA for the computer age of communicating with citizens. Among other things, the EFOIAA accomplished the following:

- ☐ clarified that electronic agency records are equally subject to the disclosure requirement as paper records,

- ☐ obliged agencies to provide records in the electronic format requested, where technically feasible,

- ☐ extended the time period allowed for responses to FOIA requests (to 20 days), but also requires agencies to adopt procedures for meeting "expedited requests" by persons "primarily engaged in disseminating information" who demonstrate urgency to inform the public,

- ☐ increased the scope of each agency's required annual FOIA report to Congress,

- ☐ required that public records created after Nov. 1, 1996 be made available within one year of their creation by "computer telecommunications," and required agencies to create indexes of records available by computer,

- ☐ narrowed the "exceptional circumstances" provision of the FOIA that allows a court to extend the time limit for an agency to respond to requests,

- ☐ required that agencies affirmatively publish certain kinds of information online, including final agency opinions and policies and any requested, non-exempt material that is likely to be requested again.

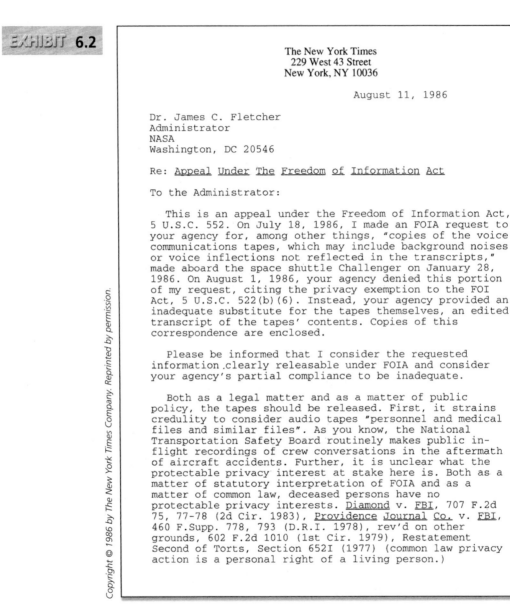

EXHIBIT **6.2**

The New York Times
229 West 43 Street
New York, NY 10036

August 11, 1986

Dr. James C. Fletcher
Administrator
NASA
Washington, DC 20546

Re: Appeal Under The Freedom of Information Act

To the Administrator:

This is an appeal under the Freedom of Information Act, 5 U.S.C. 552. On July 18, 1986, I made an FOIA request to your agency for, among other things, "copies of the voice communications tapes, which may include background noises or voice inflections not reflected in the transcripts," made aboard the space shuttle Challenger on January 28, 1986. On August 1, 1986, your agency denied this portion of my request, citing the privacy exemption to the FOI Act, 5 U.S.C. 522(b)(6). Instead, your agency provided an inadequate substitute for the tapes themselves, an edited transcript of the tapes' contents. Copies of this correspondence are enclosed.

Please be informed that I consider the requested information clearly releasable under FOIA and consider your agency's partial compliance to be inadequate.

Both as a legal matter and as a matter of public policy, the tapes should be released. First, it strains credulity to consider audio tapes "personnel and medical files and similar files". As you know, the National Transportation Safety Board routinely makes public in-flight recordings of crew conversations in the aftermath of aircraft accidents. Further, it is unclear what the protectable privacy interest at stake here is. Both as a matter of statutory interpretation of FOIA and as a matter of common law, deceased persons have no protectable privacy interests. Diamond v. FBI, 707 F.2d 75, 77-78 (2d Cir. 1983), Providence Journal Co. v. FBI, 460 F.Supp. 778, 793 (D.R.I. 1978), rev'd on other grounds, 602 F.2d 1010 (1st Cir. 1979), Restatement Second of Torts, Section 652I (1977) (common law privacy action is a personal right of a living person.)

Critics in the late 1990s complained that many agencies were slow to comply with their obligations under the EFOIAA. But while the amendments created new obligations for agencies to store, search, and disseminate information electronically, the legislation did not supply additional funding for the costs of compliance.

EXHIBIT 6.2

continued

−2−

Even legitimate privacy concerns, however, according to the U.S. Supreme Court, must be balanced with "the preservation of the basic purpose of the Freedom of Information Act <u>to open agency action to the light of public scrutiny.</u>" <u>Department of the Air Force</u> v. <u>Rose</u>, 425 U.S. 352, 372 (1976) (emphasis supplied). According to the August 1 letter, NASA has considered only the public's interest in the astronauts' awareness of the developing problems of Challenger in balancing the issues. Such public interest is a very significant reason for release. But NASA has neglected the crucial element emphasized above, namely the interest in opening agency action to the light of public scrutiny. NASA's actions as an agency have recently been the subject of intense scrutiny and considerable controversy, and the agency has been less than candid in a similar situation (following the 1967 Apollo disaster). Only the release of a copy of the actual tape can satisfy the balancing requirement.

It also appears that NASA has waived the privacy exemption because, by releasing the transcripts, the contents of the tapes have become part of the public record. <u>See Simpson</u> v. <u>Vance</u>, 648 F.2d 10 (D.C.Cir. 1980).

I trust that on reconsideration you will reverse the decision denying me access to this material and grant my original request.

As I have made this request in the capacity of a reporter for a daily newspaper and this information is of timely value, I will appreciate your expediting the consideration of my appeal in every way possible. I would appreciate your communicating with me by phone concerning the status of this request. I can be reached in New York at (212) 556-5818. In any event, I will expect to receive your decision within 20 business days, as required by law.

Thank you for your assistance.

Sincerely,

David E. Sanger

Enclosures
cc: Bill Kovach,
         Washington Bureau Editor
     George Freeman, Esq.

State Open Records Laws

The states have adopted open records statutes that cover most statewide governmental agencies as well as the records of local government units—cities, counties, school districts, and so on. Generally speaking, these statutes are in the general mold of the federal FOIA, and they typically do not cover documents of the judicial branch of government or the records of state legislatures (though many court and legislative records are made available to the public in keeping with tradition or internal rules).

As with the federal law, most states provide that all records are presumptively open and then list certain exceptions. Some states take the opposite approach, however, specifically listing the kinds of records that are open to inspection. Also, in line with the federal law, the reasons for your access request are normally considered irrelevant to the legal duty to release documents. Recall the hypothetical at the beginning of this chapter. A clerk in a city health department responded to your document request by asking "Why do you want to see it?" Normally you are not obliged to answer this question, though it is often asked. If you do answer, the usual rule is that neither your intended use nor your identity may properly be the basis for an agency decision to keep records secret.

Numerous Exceptions

In comparison to the federal law, however, most state open records laws are far more complicated. This is particularly evident in the lists of exceptions to required disclosure—the kinds of information that agencies may or must keep confidential. While the federal law lists nine exemptions, state statutes often list twenty or more. To some extent, at least, this can be traced to the fact that state and local agencies encompass a much broader range of public services and records than does the federal government. In addition to the kinds of exemptions listed in the federal FOIA, for example, the state statutes may exempt disclosure of such materials as adoption records, welfare records, test questions for professional licensing exams or academic exams, library borrower records, and student files kept by public schools.

It is important to note that many of the exemptions to these access laws are born not out of a need to ensure effectiveness and efficiency in government but out of a perceived need to protect the personal privacy of residents. In other words, the open records laws are another arena where government and the courts must balance the public's right to know about government against the individual's right to privacy. This, of course, was the problem discussed earlier, when the U.S. Supreme Court allowed criminal rap sheets to be kept confidential under the federal FOIA. At the state level the privacy question may arise in an even broader range of circumstances.

For example, in 1989 the California Legislature limited access to driver's license records that indicate home addresses. The restriction was prompted by the slaying of a television actress, Rebecca Schaeffer. The man accused in her death had used a private detective to obtain her address through the state Department of Motor Vehicles. Though media organizations generally opposed the access restriction, one of the state's leading newspapers supported it, saying that agency records "ought not be a research library for the depraved and the demented."[34]

State open records laws differ considerably in their lists of exemptions and also in such specifics as methods of enforcement and the maximum agency response times. For example, Arkansas, Colorado, Georgia, Kansas, Kentucky, Louisiana, and Missouri have adopted a stringent requirement that agencies respond to records requests within three business days. Maryland allows a more lenient thirty-day response time. Texas simply requires that responses be made "with reasonable speed," and in almost twenty states no specific response time is legislated.

It is important that print and electronic journalists be familiar with the open records laws of their state because government records at the state and local level are an important and expanding source of information. Sometimes such records are the only reliable or quotable source of information. Furthermore, agency employees are not always well informed about the open record laws. You may need to educate them.

Special Problem: Police Records

Among the records most frequently sought by the news media are those kept by law-enforcement agencies. The laws pertaining to these records are often complicated and vague, however, with different rules pertaining to different kinds of records. Most often the media desire for information would fall under one of these three categories: (1) routine police-blotter information about incidents and arrests, (2) information about the progress of an ongoing investigation, and (3) rap sheets —the detailed criminal histories of individuals, including arrests, charges, and convictions.

The first category of information, basic data on incidents and arrests, is typically the most readily available for public inspection. Most state laws require that public access be allowed to such information as the nature, time, and location of reported crimes; the names, ages, and addresses of people arrested; the dates, times, and places of the arrests; the charges for which the arrests were made; and the circumstances surrounding arrests. Such information is listed chronologically at police stations. In most cases, 911 tape recordings are considered open records too.

The second category of law-enforcement records, information about ongoing investigations, is usually more difficult to obtain. This is because investigative records are specifically exempted under the typical state public records statute and under exemption 7 of the federal FOIA. As with the federal law, though, most of the state exemptions simply mean that the police agency may keep the records confidential; in most cases they don't require that such records be kept secret.

All in all, it is the third category, individuals' criminal histories, that is the most difficult kind of police record to obtain. As you read earlier in this chapter, the Supreme Court has ruled that the FBI is allowed to keep such compilations confidential on privacy grounds. But many of the state laws go further, *requiring* that rap sheets be kept secret from the public and the media. The history file might contain nothing more than items that appeared at one time on a police blotter. Yet the theory is that the release of such a convenient compilation, perhaps dating back many years, could be a highly unwarranted and devastating invasion of privacy. Also, rap sheets are notoriously incomplete. They might indicate an arrest, for example, without also noting that criminal charges were dropped.

Of course, the individual states may differ significantly from the general summary here. In Florida, for example, criminal histories are generally considered open public records that may be sealed only under an appropriate court order. When you research your own state's access statutes and the court opinions interpreting them, determine too whether tighter rules apply to police records that identify juvenile offenders.

Media Hotlines

To learn more about your state's access laws, both for records and for meetings, you might begin by locating and reading the statutes. Statewide press associations, the offices of state attorneys general, and the individual record-keeping agencies sometimes publish helpful guides to the access laws.

Access problems frequently arise that cannot be solved simply by reading the applicable statute or a pamphlet. The statutory language may be vague, or the situation may be an unusual one not addressed by the statute. Sometimes the government blocks access even when the plain language of a statute does mandate openness. Where can you turn for prompt legal help, particularly if you work for a small media organization without a standby lawyer for such matters?

The answer in many areas of the country is a media law hotline. About twenty hotlines are in operation, some of them logging five hundred or more calls a year. The hotlines are organized and funded in a variety of ways. Most commonly, the hotlines are linked to law firms and are funded by contributions from a coalition of news media and media associations. In some cases individual press associations operate their own hotlines, funded by dues or subscription fees from their member organizations. The hotline lawyers can provide an informed judgment about your legal rights and also may be able to generate quick results for you with a phone call or letter to the offending government officer.

Selective Access by Government

This chapter has described how access statutes can force government officials to open meetings and records to the public. But these statutes do not apply to all branches or offices of government or to all kinds of information. In those cases where statutes don't dictate the disclosure rules, officials are generally free under the U.S. Constitution to restrict access and keep information and proceedings confidential.

There are some exceptions to this—some narrow circumstances, despite the general principle stated early in this chapter, when provisions in the U.S. Constitution *do* work to guarantee access to newsworthy places and information. One of these circumstances—court trials—is discussed in the next chapter. Another such circumstance is when government officials voluntarily grant access or information to segments of the public but then seek to deny access to the media or certain members of the media.

Even though government officials may not be required to grant access, once they voluntarily do so, constitutional principles of free speech and equal treatment do come into play. The **equal protection clause** in the Fourteenth Amendment to the U.S. Constitution requires that similarly situated people not be treated differently with respect to personal rights. Discrimination must be justified by strong government interests. The **due process clause** of the Fifth Amendment also may provide some protection. It requires that government clearly identify the factual bases for denying benefits to a person when those benefits are routinely granted to others. Courts have used the First Amendment, in tandem with the equal protection clause or the due process clause, to prohibit some instances of **selective access** by government. But there are other instances when selective access will pass these constitutional tests, or when it is not even deemed to raise constitutional concerns.

One of the classic cases is *Borreca v. Fasi,* which in 1974 pitted the mayor of Honolulu, Hawaii against a reporter for the *Honolulu Star-Bulletin.* The mayor thought the paper's regular city hall reporter had been biased, irresponsible, and malicious in his reporting on the mayor and his administration. So the mayor instructed his staff to keep the reporter out of future news conferences, though all media representatives were generally free to attend. The reporter and his newspaper sought a court injunction to gain entry to the conferences, and won. The federal District Court said First Amendment freedom of the press includes a limited right of reasonable access to news in "the public galleries, the press rooms and the press conferences dealing with government."[35] To overcome that right, the mayor would have to show a compelling government interest, the court said, and stifling a critical or even reckless reporter is not reason enough.

The *Borreca* case left many questions, however. Does the equal-access right mean the mayor would have to answer all journalists' questions? Does it prohibit the mayor from selecting only certain reporters to meet with individually? These questions were answered by another federal court in the 1999 case of *Snyder v. Ringgold.* Journalist Terrie Snyder specialized in coverage of the Baltimore City Police Department. In the mid-1990s her relationship with the police department's public information officer soured. The PIO, Samuel Ringgold, told other officers not to trust Ms. Snyder and never to go off the record with her. When Snyder's TV station arranged for an exclusive interview with officers in the homicide division, Ringgold contacted the station and said that if the TV crew included Snyder access for the interview would not be granted. Ringgold contacted another of Snyder's employers, a newspaper, and announced that he would no longer talk with her individually about any story. And when Snyder requested an interview with the police commissioner, her interview was limited to just five minutes.

Snyder sued, claiming a violation of her First and Fourth Amendment rights to equal access. But the court distinguished this case from Borreca, which concerned general news conferences open to all media. In contrast, Snyder was not denied information generally available to all media. Rather, Ringgold was merely exercising his right not to speak with particular representatives of the media whom he may regard as untrustworthy, the court said. It wrote:

> No reporter has a right to access to a particular interview, exclusive story, or off the record statement. Snyder, therefore, is not seeking equal access to public information, but the kind of preferential treatment that public officials can provide to certain journalists, and that, in Ringgold's opinion, she does not merit. While a constitutional right to equal access for members of the press may well exist, extending the right to encompass preferential treatment would completely change the longstanding relationship and understandings between journalists and public officials.[36]

Another question is where the government may constitutionally draw the line when space for the media is limited. In a 1970 case the Los Angeles Police Department denied press passes to reporters at the *Los Angeles Free Press,* a weekly newspaper. The department had been issuing thousands of press passes each year but decided to restrict this practice in order to protect against chaos at disaster scenes. Under the new policy the departments would issue passes only to reporters who needed them in connection with their regular newsgathering duties. *Free Press* employees were denied passes on the ground that their weekly paper was not regularly engaged in spot coverage of police activities. Rather, the paper was primarily for features and analysis. The *Free Press* sued, but the California Court of Appeal sided with the government.

The court ruled that the denial of press passes did not arbitrarily discriminate against the newspaper in violation of its right to equal protection of the law:

> There is no constitutional requirement that [the department] show uniform treatment to all publications or news media in issuing press passes, the only requirement being that there be a reasonable basis for the classification imposed. . . . Regular coverage of police and fire news provides a reasonable basis for classification of persons who seek the privilege of crossing police lines.[37]

The law concerning selective media access to government needs further development. As a general summary, however, government may not broadly allow access but then exclude certain individuals unless the individuals clearly belong to a different classification of people, the exclusion of which is reasonable, or unless some compelling interest justifies the exclusion of a particular individual. For example, the White House could decide to conduct presidential news conferences but, in light of limited seating, restrict access to professional, Washington-based journalists. A different class of people—high-school journalism students—might reasonably be excluded. Furthermore, even a professional, Washington-based journalist might be excluded legally if a compelling reason is shown—for example, a security risk if the journalist has made death threats against the president. But personal dislikes for certain reporters or media, differences of political philosophy, or even prior instances of misleading reporting, would not be constitutionally sufficient to support exclusion.

Selective access problems are fairly common. Another example was the hypothetical at the beginning of this chapter. A guard barred you from the city council meeting because, he said, "no media allowed." Even if this particular council session were not required to be open under the state's open meetings law, the decision apparently had been made to allow entry to members of the general public. If so, it would now be a constitutional violation to single out members of the media for exclusion. A persuasive call to the city attorney, preferably from your lawyer, might have been enough to gain your entry to the meeting.

In some states the access statutes specifically command that access among media be equal, thus giving shut-out reporters a statutory argument as well as a constitutional one. This extra statutory language can be important when one particular reporter is given access to records or meetings that would not otherwise have to be open. Under these statutory provisions other reporters then acquire the right to see the information. For example, the Colorado Open Records Act states that if a right to inspect exempt materials is given any employee of a newspaper, radio station, TV station, or other newsgathering agency, "it shall be allowed to all such media."[38]

Summary Points

In most situations the First Amendment is not interpreted to convey special privileges for gathering information. Courts do speak of a "limited First Amendment right of access," but this right arises only in limited situations involving government information.

Without constitutional access rights, members of the media are subject to the same laws of trespass as members of the general public. Civil trespass laws may be enforced by the occupiers of both private and government property, and some willful trespasses may amount to a crime.

Recognizing the strong public policy in favor of openness in government, however, all states and the federal government have passed freedom-of-information statutes that assure public access to government documents and meetings. These are important laws for the newsgatherer, but they also contain numerous exceptions permitting information to be withheld, and they do not cover all branches and offices of government.

At the federal level the primary open meeting law is the Sunshine Act, and the law granting rights of access to records is the Freedom of Information Act, after which many of the state laws are modeled.

In some instances, specific statutes also prohibit officials from allowing access to certain kinds of information, usually in the interest of personal privacy rights.

When government does grant general access to information, it may not discriminate against particular media or individuals with whom it happens to disagree. Unwarranted exclusion may violate the First Amendment and the equal protection clause of the Fourteenth Amendment.

In this chapter's hypothetical you would find that open records and open meeting statutes would help you gain access to the city council meeting and the health department report. You would not have to give an acceptable reason to authorities as a condition of access. As to your trespassing in the field, this conduct on your part would not be privileged under the First Amendment or any other legal authority. However, an act of trespass does not give property owners or their employees a right to seize your journalistic property.

Discussion Questions

1. In TV journalism it has become rather common to create dramatic video by having a camera crew follow police right into a private residence or business to film an arrest or drug raid. Considering the trespass principles discussed in this chapter, can such newsgathering methods be legal without the consent of the rightful occupier of the property? What kinds of factors would, or should, a TV station consider before deciding whether to send camera crews onto private property without consent?

2. For a plaintiff whose privacy has been invaded in her own home by a TV news crew that burst through the door, why exactly would trespass be a more appealing lawsuit than the intrusion tort discussed in the preceding chapter?

3. Suppose a city council decided to cover press relations expenses by charging a fee to attend the mayor's press conferences. The fee—$15—is the same for all media representatives for all press conferences. Do you think this practice would violate the constitutional requirement of equal access? Could the mayor grant exclusive interviews to some reporters and grant no interviews to others? If so, how is this legally distinguishable from holding a press conference exclusively for the mayor's five favorite reporters?

Key Terms

criminal trespass	implied consent
custom and usage	nominal damages
due process clause	open meeting laws
equal protection clause	open records law
executive privilege	press pass
executive session	selective access
express consent	Sunshine Act
Freedom of Information Act (FOIA)	trespass

Web Resources

http://www.rcfp.org/foi.html
The Reporters Committee for Freedom of the Press, FOI Service Center

http://www.usdoj.gov/04foia/04_6.html
FOIA Annual Reports of Federal Agencies, compiled by U.S. Dept. of Justice

http://www.spj.org
The Electronic Journalist, Society of Professional Journalists (includes FOIA Resource Center)

InfoTrac® College Edition

Public document seekers in recent years have expressed considerable frustration about their ability to obtain government records kept in electronic form, and open records laws are being updated to more clearly outline rights and obligations with respect to electronic data. Find an article that addresses this computer-age issue.

CHAPTER SEVEN

Chapter Outline

Media and the Justice System

Upon completing this chapter you should

- □ **understand** the potential conflict between the First and Sixth Amendments to the Constitution.
- □ **know** the customary means by which courts may assure fair trials and the limited circumstances in which courtrooms may be closed or the media silenced.
- □ **understand** the courts' traditional aversion to cameras and the current status of camera access rules.
- □ **know** when the law may accord you a special privilege of not revealing sources or information to the government.

■ The Mystery Homicide

A pregnant woman is found battered and stabbed to death in the upstairs bedroom of her expensive, lakefront home. The victim's husband, a well-known physician, notifies police. He tells detectives that he was napping on the couch downstairs when he was awakened by his wife's screams. As he reached the top of the stairs he was knocked unconscious, he says, by a large, masked figure. The next day the doctor is arrested and charged with killing his wife.

Naturally, this quickly becomes a sensational mystery story for the media. You are a resourceful reporter on the cop-and-courts beat of the local daily newspaper. Over the next few weeks you talk with dozens of neighbors, friends, and acquaintances of the doctor and his deceased wife. You learn that the socialite couple had lately been exhibiting a rocky marriage and that just two days before the slaying the doctor had learned his wife was having a romance with another man.

A few days before the doctor's trial you begin publishing what you learned—details of the couple's domestic arguments and adulterous flings. But after your story hits the newsstands the judge issues a restrictive order. It prohibits your newspaper from publishing anything further about the case until after the trial. The judge is concerned that stories like yours would make it nearly impossible to impanel an unbiased jury. Your paper decides to appeal the judge's order.

On the first day of trial you and dozens of other reporters arrive to find the courtroom closed to spectators and the media. The judge had decided to close her courtroom to head off what she thought would surely be a distracting, circus-like atmosphere created by a pack of anxious reporters and their equipment.

Meanwhile, you pursue your own investigation. You find someone who has information tending to implicate others as the killers. Your source, a local bookie, says he will talk to you only on condition of complete anonymity. You agree, and he tells you that the doctors' wife was deeply involved in illicit gambling and owed hundreds of thousands of dollars to organized crime figures who have reputations for tough collection tactics. Observing the court's restrictive order, you don't publish this immediately. But you do mention your interview to editors, and word somehow reaches the doctor's defense attorney. Next thing you know, you are subpoenaed to appear in court. The doctor's attorney wants to put you on the witness stand and have you answer detailed questions about what you heard and from whom you heard it.

May you refuse to answer these questions in court, without going to jail? Would it be a breach of ethics if you did answer? Should you expect to win your appeal of the judge's restrictive order? Was it proper for the judge to close the courtroom?

Media and Courts: A Unique Relationship

The relationship between this nation's justice system and the media, especially the news media, has long involved tension, distrust, and misunderstanding—and unique legal problems. This becomes most evident in high-profile trials. It was painfully evident in the 1994–95 double-murder trial of sports celebrity O. J. Simpson, a case that presented many of the legal issues discussed in this chapter.

The relationship between media and the courts is vitally important. Coverage of crime and justice is among the most useful and expected services that a local news organization can provide the public. Even the justice system benefits, over the long term, when the public understands the system's procedures, rulings, and limitations. Research suggests that public understanding of the justice system is lagging and that the media should seek ways to improve judicial coverage.[1]

Recognizing the need for media and the justice system to associate closely, and the unique opportunities for friction and legal clashes, some communities have formed **bench/bar/media committees.** These are groups of judges, lawyers, police officers, and newspeople that meet periodically to discuss problems and, ideally, build cooperation. Most problems that bench/bar/media committees debate fall within two broad scenarios, which this chapter will examine.

In the first, the media want to publish or broadcast information related to a court proceeding. But judges or litigants see the media as a threat to a fair trial and seek to limit media access or publication. Chapter 2 examined the basic doctrine against prior restraint of speech, and Chapter 6 looked at rules of access. This chapter revisits those subjects—this time in the unique context of covering the justice system.

The second scenario is nearly a reverse of the first: The media have information, and the justice system wants it. The media may resist disclosure for a variety of reasons, such as the protection of a confidential source. But the justice system, with its substantial power to compel desired behavior, may be equally determined to uncover the information.

Media and a Fair Trial

One of the oldest continuing legal debates in this country arises from a perceived conflict between the media's right to free expression and an accused's right to a fair jury trial. To understand this conflict, you must appreciate how the model jury system was envisioned.

The concept of a trial by jury was brought to England nearly a thousand years ago with the Norman Conquest of 1066. Trial by jury gradually took the place of tyrannical methods of justice, as typified by the secretive Court of the Star Chamber, which continued to impose ruthless penalties until 1641. The initial practice was that neighbors of the accused would serve as jurors. These people presumably were in the best position to pass judgment, based not only on the evidence revealed in court but also on what they otherwise knew or heard from the community. Over time the rules of courtroom evidence became more refined and so did the role of the jury. It was seen that out-of-court gossip and innuendo were terribly unreliable, yet potentially devastating to the accused. In the 1600s it became settled that juries would reach their verdicts based solely on the evidence presented in court. This also meant, of course, that jurors must not come to the courthouse with their minds already decided.

Thus the ideal concept of the jury system had changed by the time this nation was formed. The jury's role no longer was to bring community-born perceptions into the decision-making process. Rather, it was to apply unclouded judgment to legally admissible, court-presented evidence alone. The ideal jury had become a safeguard against two separate dangers: On the one hand it was to rise above the shallow prejudices and rumors that may influence a general population; on the other, the jury continued as an alternative to a totally government-controlled justice system that, history shows, can become politicized and oppressive.

The Sixth Amendment Guarantee

The modern conception of the jury system was incorporated in the Sixth Amendment of the Constitution along with other guaranteed protections for criminal defendants. The amendment reads in part: "In all criminal prosecutions, the accused shall enjoy the right to a speedy and public trial, by an impartial jury of the State and district wherein the crime shall have been committed. . . ."

Courts have held that the **impartial jury** guarantee refers to a jury that is in an open, unprejudiced frame of mind at the beginning of trial and is influenced only by the evidence legally presented during the trial. It is not required, however, that the jury have no prior knowledge of the case. Indeed, the requirement of a jury from the locale "wherein the crime shall have been committed" is an indication that the jury should have some knowledge of the circumstances. In short, the requirement is that the jury be fair.

Though the Sixth Amendment applies only to criminal prosecutions, state constitutions or statutes typically set similar fair-jury standards for civil trials. The main focus in this chapter, however, will be on criminal proceedings, where the bulk of free press/fair trial conflicts arise.

The Sixth Amendment's standards apply to state prosecutions as well as federal ones because the provisions are applied to the states through the Fourteenth Amendment's due process clause. Chapter 2 detailed how most of the Bill of Rights, including the First Amendment, became applicable to the states.

The First Amendment Conflict

A constitutional dilemma often occurs in the coverage of notorious crimes, when the media's First Amendment rights of free expression seem to conflict with the defendant's right to an impartial jury. The concern is that pervasive media coverage, replete with damning information of all sorts, may make it impossible to find or maintain an impartial jury. Chief Justice Warren Burger described the First Amendment/Sixth Amendment dilemma in his 1976 majority opinion in *Nebraska Press Association v. Stuart*:

> The problems presented by this case are almost as old as the Republic. Neither in the Constitution nor in contemporaneous writings do we find that the conflict between these two important rights was anticipated, yet it is inconceivable that the authors of the Constitution were unaware of the potential conflicts between the right to an unbiased jury and the guarantee of freedom of the press. . . .
>
> The authors of the Bill of Rights did not undertake to assign priorities as between First Amendment and Sixth Amendment rights, ranking one as superior to the other. . . . It is unnecessary, after nearly two centuries, to establish a priority applicable in all circumstances. Yet it is nonetheless clear that the barriers to prior restraint remain high unless we are to abandon what the Court has said for nearly a quarter of our national existence and implied throughout all of it.[2]

Thus the challenge is one of ad hoc constitutional balancing, of devising the right tests to be applied on a case-by-case basis so that both of these important constitutional guarantees can be accommodated. The Sixth Amendment conflicts presented by media coverage can arise through both pretrial publicity and trial publicity—and they often raise different problems. With *pretrial* publicity the concern is whether impartial jurors can be found by the time trial is scheduled to begin. This is what the judge was worried about in the chapter hypothetical when she ordered the newspaper to cease publishing stories about the case. With *trial* publicity the concern is whether jurors, presuming they were impartial when impaneled, will be improperly influenced by media accounts of the proceedings or perhaps even by the mere presence of the media. This was the concern that led the judge to close the courtroom in the hypothetical.

Warnings from the Supreme Court

Conflicts between the justice system and media reporting can be traced at least as far back as the 1830s, when newspapers began to achieve mass circulation. The U.S. Supreme Court reviewed its first trial publicity case in 1851—a case in which two jurors in a murder trial had read newspaper accounts of the evidence. The Court was unconvinced that the defendant deserved a new trial, however.

By the early 1900s, press coverage of crime and justice had reached a notably aggressive level with frequent use of sketches and photographs. In 1935 it became evident that print and radio journalists could dominate criminal proceedings of national interest. In that year Bruno Hauptmann was tried for the kidnapping and death of Charles Lindbergh's infant son. Lindbergh was the nation's leading aviation hero at the time, and it is estimated that nearly one thousand reporters and photographers converged to cover the trial in a tiny New Jersey town. It was more than twenty years, however, before the U.S. Supreme Court began to reverse convictions on the ground of excessive media publicity.

In a series of cases between the late 1950s and mid-1960s, the U.S. Supreme Court clearly indicated to the nation's justice systems that the mass media could indeed jeopardize the constitutional standards of a fair trial. Five times during that period the Supreme Court reversed criminal convictions—three of them in murders—because of prominent media coverage of the cases.

Mad Dog Irvin

In the 1961 case of *Irvin v. Dowd,* Irvin was indicted by a grand jury in Vanderburgh County, Indiana in the slaying of one person. The media then generated a flood of maligning stories about the suspect and, to avoid local prejudice, he was granted a change of trial location to neighboring Gibson County. (Movement of a trial to another location is called a **change of venue.**) After being denied a second change of venue, Irvin was convicted and sentenced to death.

The U.S. Supreme Court eventually nullified the conviction, however. The High Court found a "pattern of prejudice" created by extensive newspaper and broadcast coverage beginning at the time of Irvin's arrest. For example, the media reported that "Mad Dog Irvin" had confessed to six murders and that he was "remorseless and without conscience." The media also blanketed the rural area with reports about his juvenile criminal convictions, parole violations, and a military court martial for going AWOL. The Supreme Court reviewed the trial court's efforts to select a jury in the case. It found that 430 prospective jurors were examined and 268 of them were excused for having fixed opinions as to guilt. All twelve of the jurors finally seated told the judge they would be fair and impartial. Yet eight of the twelve also said they assumed Irvin was guilty.

In the Court's unanimous opinion, Justice Tom Clark wrote:

> With such an opinion permeating [the jurors'] minds, it would be difficult to say that each could exclude this preconception of guilt from his deliberations. The influence that lurks in an opinion once formed is so persistent that it unconsciously fights detachment from the mental processes of the average man. When one's life is at stake—and accounting for the frailties of human nature—we can only say that in light of the circumstances here the finding of impartiality does not meet constitutional standards. Two-thirds of the jurors had an opinion that petitioner was guilty and were familiar with the material facts and circumstances involved. . . .[3]

Following the Supreme Court's reversal and remand, Irvin was convicted in a second trial and sentenced to life imprisonment.

Rideau's Confession Film

A 1963 case, *Rideau v. State of Louisiana,* involved a man who was suspected of robbing a bank, kidnapping several bank employees, and killing one of them. During a jailhouse interrogation by the local sheriff the suspect, Wilbert Rideau, admitted that he had perpetrated the crimes. The interrogation was filmed, and later the same day a community TV station broadcast the confession film. The film was again broadcast on the following two days, thereby reaching a substantial portion of the citizens in the Louisiana parish. After Rideau was arraigned on robbery, kidnapping, and homicide charges, his lawyers requested a change of venue on the ground that the TV broadcasts prevented the defendant from receiving a fair trial in the parish. The request was denied, and Rideau was convicted and sentenced to death. At least three members of the jury had seen the televised confessions.

The U.S. Supreme Court reversed the conviction without requiring proof that the jurors' minds were swayed by the film. Wrote Justice Potter Stewart:

> We hold that it was a denial of the due process of law to refuse the request for a change of venue, after the people of Calcasieu Parish had been exposed repeatedly and in depth to the spectacle of Rideau personally confessing in detail to the crimes with which he was later to be charged. For anyone who has ever watched television the conclusion cannot be avoided that this spectacle, to the tens of thousands of people who saw and heard it, in a very real sense *was* Rideau's trial—at which he pleaded guilty to murder. Any subsequent court proceedings in a community so pervasively exposed to such a spectacle could be but a hollow formality.[4]

Dr. Sam Sheppard

In 1966 the Supreme Court decided *Sheppard v. Maxwell*, which involved facts similar to those that began the chapter hypothetical. Sheppard's pregnant wife was bludgeoned to death in the couple's home in Bay Village, Ohio, and the doctor was charged with homicide. Before and during the nine-week trial Sheppard was the subject of relentless, damning media coverage. The public read that Sheppard had refused to cooperate with the homicide investigation, that he surely was guilty because he had hired a famous criminal lawyer, and that Sheppard allegedly had had sexual relations with many women. One newspaper story announced "The prosecution has a 'bombshell witness' on tap who will testify to Dr. Sam's display of fiery temper. . . ."[5] No such evidence was presented in court. Furthermore, at trial the media maintained a dominating presence in the courtroom, even occupying a press table near the front of the courtroom, adjacent to the jury box.

Sheppard was convicted, and after he had spent about ten years in prison the U.S. Supreme Court took his case for review. The Court ruled that Sheppard had not had a fair trial, and it ordered him released from prison unless a new trial were provided. The Court's opinion, again by Justice Clark, chastised the trial judge for allowing a "carnival atmosphere" in the courtroom and for failing to control the media publicity:

> The fact is that bedlam reigned at the courthouse during the trial and newsmen took over practically the entire courtroom, hounding most of the participants in

the trial, especially Sheppard. . . . Having assigned almost all of the available seats in the courtroom to the news media the judge lost his ability to supervise the environment. The movement of the reporters in and out of the courtroom caused frequent confusion and disruption of the trial. . . .

As the trial progressed, the newspapers summarized and interpreted the evidence, devoting particular attention to the material that incriminated Sheppard, and often drew unwarranted inferences from testimony. At one point, a front-page picture of Mrs. Sheppard's blood-stained pillow was published after being "doctored" to show more clearly an alleged imprint of a surgical instrument. . . .

The court should have made some effort to control the release of leads, information, and gossip to the press by police officers, witnesses, and the counsel for both sides. Much of the information thus disclosed was inaccurate, leading to groundless rumors and confusion. . . .

From the cases coming here we note that unfair and prejudicial news comment on pending trials has become increasingly prevalent. Due process requires that the accused receive a trial by an impartial jury free from outside influences. Given the pervasiveness of modern communications and the difficulty of effacing prejudicial publicity from the minds of jurors, the trial courts must take strong measures to ensure that the balance is never weighed against the accused. . . .[6]

The state decided to retry Sheppard on the homicide charge. Following a sixteen-day trial, this time with tight media restrictions, Sheppard was acquitted and released from prison.

Thus the Supreme Court in a series of opinions verified for trial judges a constitutional reason to be leery of the media. More than that, the Sheppard opinion in particular seemed to command judges to take virtually any steps necessary to assure that cases were tried in the courtroom and not in the media.

Justice Warren's Commission

Further drawing attention to the threat of publicity to the judicial process was the 1964 *Report of the President's Commission on the Assassination of President John F. Kennedy,* often referred to as the *Warren Commission Report.* The commission criticized the clamorous media coverage of accused assassin Lee Harvey Oswald and questioned whether he could have received a fair trial, had he not been killed just days after his arrest:

The Commission recognizes that the people of the United States, and indeed the world, had a deep-felt interest in learning of the events surrounding the death of President Kennedy, including the development of the investigation in Dallas. An informed public provided the ultimate guarantee that adequate steps would be taken to apprehend those responsible for the assassination. . . .

However, neither the press nor the public had a right to be contemporaneously informed by the police or prosecuting authorities of the details of the evidence being accumulated against Oswald. Undoubtedly the public was interested in these disclosures, but its curiosity should not have been satisfied at the expense of the accused's right to a trial by an impartial jury. The courtroom, not the newspaper or television screen, is the appropriate forum in our system for the trial of a man accused of a crime.[7]

Thus by the mid-1960s, with impetus from the Supreme Court and the prominent Warren Commission, sentiment was building within the legal community to better insulate the judicial process from media influence. Was this sentiment among lawyers and judges really justified?

The True Effect of Publicity

Most media historians will readily concede that journalists have on occasion been reckless, disruptive, and sensationalistic in their coverage of legal proceedings. Coverage of Sheppard's prosecution may have been the lowest point—a case in which a physician was found not guilty by a second jury but nevertheless had lost his license and his livelihood and spent ten years in prison.

You should take a few minutes to think in terms of a broader perspective, however, before concluding that the media are an incessant threat to the justice system—as some judges and lawyers have grown to believe. First of all, consider some of the positive effects of trial and pretrial publicity upon the general public.

Accurate news coverage of serious crimes and their prosecutions can actually work to limit rumors and to reduce the terror of an uninformed public. Say a serial killer is at large in your town; thus far he has brutally maimed fourteen college students who strolled near campus at night. Wouldn't you breathe more easily knowing that an arrest has been made, that substantial evidence has been collected, and that a prosecution is proceeding?

Also, it is through detailed and timely coverage of legal proceedings that the public is most readily able to learn about the quality of the justice system itself—clearly a substantial public interest.

Take care not be hasty in assuming that media coverage will prejudice jurors' deliberations at trial. In fact it is extremely rare that new trials are granted on the basis of prejudicial media influence, and such influence may be more theory than reality. Empirical studies have shown that, where publicity existed prior to trial, potential jurors often have difficulty recalling it by the time trial rolls around. And, where jurors do recall news reports, they may nevertheless be quite capable of purging preconceptions about a case and focusing on the trial evidence objectively.

Admittedly, empirical studies concerning jury performance have many weaknesses. Most involve experimental simulations, for example, rather than the study of real jurors. But taken as a whole these studies by social scientists can provide useful insights into the likely influence of media publicity. One researcher, Rita J. Simon, summarized the empirical studies in an article for the *Stanford Law Review*:

Experiments to date indicate that for the most part juries are able and willing to put aside extraneous information and base their decisions on the evidence. The results show that when ordinary citizens become jurors, they assume a special role in which they apply different standards of proofs, more vigorous reasoning and greater detachment.[8]

Among the legal profession, too, many experts believe prejudicial media influence is mostly a myth. Experienced trial lawyer and law professor John Kaplan is another whose observations on this subject have appeared in the *Stanford Law Review*:

> The short of my conclusions is that newspaper publicity, or any other assertions of facts of a case made outside of court, have virtually no impact upon the jury trying the case. . . . In deciding the case before them, the jurors almost invariably assumed as a matter important to their status that they knew more about the facts of the case than any newspaper reporter and that their superior understanding was due to their close observation of the trial itself.[9]

Also, when the media report little more than what jurors hear at trial, prejudicial influence is improbable. It is only with the publication of highly inflammatory commentary or facts that also are deemed inadmissible as evidence at trial that a real problem of media influence may exist. Such could be the case with publicity about a coerced confession or about a criminal defendant's unsavory past, but cases involving such volatile information are relatively rare.

Therefore, the news media understandably protested when the justice system, following the *Sheppard* decision, began to effect sweeping restrictions on reporting.

The Aftermath of *Sheppard*

One of the most notable developments in the years immediately following *Sheppard* was the 1968 adoption by the American Bar Association of detailed standards for the courts. The highly restrictive standards, which were based on a two-year study called the *Reardon Report,* were not legally binding. But they served as a model for the states and became working standards for many courts and lawyers.

Under the ABA standards, the flow of information to the media from law enforcement officers, lawyers, witnesses, and other participants in the judicial process was greatly restricted from the time of arrest until the end of trial. Many kinds of information, such as prior criminal records of defendants, were not to be released to the media under any circumstances by participants in judicial proceedings. Beyond these prohibited kinds of statements, most other statements to the media were forbidden if there were "a reasonable likelihood that such dissemination will interfere with a fair trial or otherwise prejudice the due administration of justice."[10] (These fair trial standards have since been revised by the ABA in recognition of greater First Amendment rights of witnesses and others to speak publicly.) The original standards also urged judges to use their contempt powers broadly to enforce the rules of silence upon the justice system participants.

The ABA standards never attempted to impose prior restraints directly on the media, as they did upon the media's sources. But the standards did authorize judges under certain circumstances to choke off media access by closing preliminary and pretrial hearings and by sealing court records. Soon judges were treading even beyond the ABA recommendations, however. It became fashionable to close hearings and even trials, and judges began issuing restraining orders directly upon the media.

Two positive results came out of all this. One was increased incentive on the part of the media to form the bench/bar/media committees mentioned earlier in this chapter and to seek some middle ground. More than half of the states have such committees at the state level that meet with widely varying degrees of formality and frequency. Most statewide committees have even established voluntary, written bar/press guidelines of their own.

The second positive result of the court's clampdown on publicity was that the U.S. Supreme Court entered the free press/fair trial controversy again, this time to come to the rescue of First Amendment rights.

Preventing Publication

In the years following *Sheppard,* trial judges produced a wave of restrictive orders to guard against prejudicial publicity. Most orders, sometimes called **gag orders,** barred lawyers and other trial participants from commenting publicly about a case. These were only indirect restrictions on the media, by way of potential sources. If the media did obtain information, they were not legally prohibited from publishing it. But a worrisome number of orders did take the form of direct restrictions on media publication.

Gag Orders on the Media   Various studies have indicated that about forty restrictive orders directly prohibited publication or broadcast by the media during the period 1967–75.

For example, in 1975 Lynette "Squeaky" Fromme went on trial in the attempted shooting of President Gerald Ford. Fromme was a member of the notorious Charles Manson "family." Fearing prejudicial influence upon the jury, the judge banned the telecast of a documentary about the Manson group. The restrictive order extended to twenty-six counties around Sacramento, California, the trial site, and it was lifted only after the jury was confined in a place where such programming could be screened out.

Prior restraints were discussed earlier in this book. In the Pentagon Papers case, for example, the Supreme Court indicated that the government held the heavy burden of showing a legitimate national-security threat before freedom of speech could be restrained on that ground. But how about instances in which the argument for prior restraint is linked to another provision in the Bill of Rights—the guarantee of an impartial jury? Must the doctrine against prior restraint yield?

The Nebraska Press Case

That was the question that came before the Supreme Court in *Nebraska Press Association v. Stuart.* Six members of a family had been slain in a Nebraska town of about 850 people. Charged with the crimes was an unemployed handyman who confessed to law-enforcement officers. The case attracted widespread media coverage, both locally and nationally.

The defendant's lawyer and the prosecutor jointly requested a court order restricting the public disclosure of evidence prior to trial. In its final form the order barred media publication or broadcast of information about confessions or any other facts "strongly implicative" of the defendant.

A unanimous U.S. Supreme Court ruled that the gag order was unconstitutional. In the majority opinion, Chief Justice Burger summarized the Supreme Court's earlier efforts to protect a defendant's right to a fair trial from widespread publicity. But he also referred to the Court's earlier rulings on prior restraint, writing: "The thread running through all the cases is that prior restraints on speech and publication are the most serious and the least tolerable infringement on First Amendment rights."[11] And those restraints are particularly harmful, said the Court, when they fall upon the dissemination of news and commentary about current events, including reports of criminal proceedings.

With this in mind, the Court constructed a classic balancing test. Gag orders aimed at media coverage of legal proceedings could be constitutionally valid only in extremely rare circumstances, when the trial judge specifically finds that:

1. Pretrial publicity about the case would be intense and pervasive

2. No alternative measures would work to offset the effects of the publicity

3. A gag order on the media would indeed operate to prevent the danger of prejudicial influence

Furthermore, the opinion stated as an absolute rule that there may be no prior restraints on reporting what transpires during open court proceedings.

According to the Supreme Court, the trial judge in the *Nebraska Press* case was justified in concluding there would be pervasive pretrial publicity. But the judge failed to determine whether alternative measures, such as a change of venue, might have protected the accused's right to a fair trial. Furthermore, whether the gag order would really work to guarantee an impartial jury was far from clear, the Court held.

In his concurring opinion, Justice White expressed doubt that a similar gag order on the media would ever be justifiable. And in fact, a line of later cases confirms that *Nebraska Press* left very little room for gag orders on media publicity related to judicial proceedings. The majority opinion concluded: "We reaffirm that the guarantees of freedom of expression are not an absolute prohibition under all circumstances, but the barriers to prior restraint remain high and the presumption against its use continues intact."[12]

Alternative Measures

For gag orders on the media, *Nebraska Press* all but sounded the death knell. In the years since the decision, trial judges usually have refused to issue gag orders, and, when they have, the orders typically have been reversed on appeal. Instead, trial judges must look to one or more alternative means of assuring a fair trial—means that do not conflict with the First Amendment. Some of these traditional alternatives are:

1. **Continuance**—delaying trial until prejudicial publicity has died down

2. **Change of venue**

3. Intensive **voir dire**—questioning potential jurors to determine whether they have been prejudiced by news coverage

4. **Jury admonitions**—instructing jurors, for example, not to read or listen to media accounts of the case

5. **Sequestration** of the jury—providing a monitored place for jurors to stay for the duration of the trial, so they will not be exposed to news reports.

Of these, the first three are most appropriate for diminishing the effects of pretrial publicity. Jury admonishment and sequestration are available only after a jury is selected, and they are most likely to work against any effects of publicity concurrent with the trial.

Sample Cases

The approach of appellate courts following *Nebraska Press* is illustrated in the 1984 case of *C.B.S. v. U.S. District Court.* Auto-industry executive John DeLorean was being prosecuted on drug charges, and before the trial CBS obtained copies of videotapes the government had made while DeLorean was under surveillance. On a Saturday the trial judge issued an order restraining CBS from disseminating any portion of the tapes. But on Sunday a Court of Appeals panel invalidated the order.

Following the *Nebraska Press* test, the court said the trial judge improperly concluded that the publicity would be pervasive enough to warrant a gag order. "If it is to be restrained," the appeals court ruled, "the publicity must threaten to prejudice the entire community so that twelve unbiased jurors cannot be found."[13] It was unlikely that broadcasting portions of the tapes would produce such a community-wide, inflammatory effect, said the court, especially in such a large,

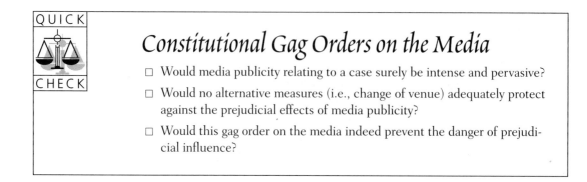

Constitutional Gag Orders on the Media

☐ Would media publicity relating to a case surely be intense and pervasive?

☐ Would no alternative measures (i.e., change of venue) adequately protect against the prejudicial effects of media publicity?

☐ Would this gag order on the media indeed prevent the danger of prejudicial influence?

heterogeneous area as Los Angeles, the trial site. The trial judge also failed to give sufficient consideration to the second part of the test, the alternatives. Extensive use of voir dire and emphatic instructions to the jury were reasonable alternatives in this case, the appeals court ruled.

Similar scrutiny is given to gag orders in civil cases, where it is often litigant privacy, rather than Sixth Amendment rights, that is at stake. For example, in 1994 Procter & Gamble Co. sued the Bankers Trust Co., alleging a $100 million loss due to fraud. The case attracted widespread coverage in the business press. Therefore, during the discovery phase of the lawsuit the parties drafted a judge-approved stipulation that many of the documents collected would be labeled as confidential trade secrets and placed under seal. Months later, the parties alerted the judge that *Business Week* magazine had somehow obtained litigation documents that the parties wanted to remain secret. At the urgent request of the parties, the trial judge transmitted a gag order to *Business Week*, prohibiting it from publishing the documents.

But in 1996 the federal Court of Appeals held the gag order unconstitutional. The documents in question were standard litigation filings, and the court said: "The private litigants' interest in protecting their vanity or their commercial self-interest simply does not qualify as grounds for imposing a prior restraint."[14]

Students should not conclude from this discussion, however, that gag orders on the media are now merely a curious point of history. A majority of the Supreme Court did leave the door ajar for gag orders under extremely rare circumstances, so not only do trial judges still issue them occasionally but they also are sometimes upheld on appeal.

For example, in 1998 the Supreme Court of South Carolina upheld a gag order on the following facts: A man who had been indicted for several violent crimes was awaiting a trial where the state sought the death penalty. While he was in prison, a confidential conversation between the criminal defendant and his lawyer was secretly videotaped and then provided to WIS-TV in South Carolina. Upon learning this, the defendant sought a restraining order to prevent broadcast of the tape. The trial court issued the restraining order, prohibiting the station and other local media from disseminating the substance of the tape until after a jury was empanelled and sequestered in the defendant's case.

The state's high court applied the *Nebraska Press* balancing test and concluded the prior restraint was justified. First, the court found there would be a level of pretrial publicity, particularly with the tape, pervasive and damaging enough to impair the defendant's right to a fair trial. Second, while other measures might have been used to lessen the prejudice to the defendant, they would not be enough to ensure him a fair trial in the face of disseminated details about an attorney-client conversation. And third, the restraint on speech was narrowly tailored in time and scope and was effective in preventing potential jurors from learning the contents of the private prison conversation.[15]

In 1990 the U.S. Supreme Court revisited the gag order issue in an unusual case that also involved tapes of jailhouse conversations. It concerned Cable News Network (CNN) and the criminal prosecution of deposed Panamanian dictator Manuel Noriega. CNN had obtained by legal means tape recordings of Noriega's telephone conversations with several people, including his defense attorneys. Noriega at the time was in jail awaiting trial on drug charges, and the jail routinely recorded inmates' phone calls.

Upon learning that CNN planned to broadcast excerpts from the tapes, Noriega's lawyers filed for a court order prohibiting CNN from airing any attorney–client conversations. A federal district judge issued a temporary restraining order and also ordered CNN to turn the tapes over to the judge so that he could determine whether their broadcast would violate the attorney–client privilege. CNN immediately appealed, but in the meantime it also aired excerpts from one tape. In its appeal to the Supreme Court, CNN argued that the District Court's gag order was improperly based on mere speculation of harm and that the gag order contradicted Supreme Court precedent.

The Supreme Court, however, in a brief order joined by seven justices, refused to lift the district judge's order. This essentially forced CNN to turn the tapes over to the district judge for review, which it did. The judge then determined that broadcast of the remaining unaired conversations would not threaten the attorney–client privilege, and the restraint on playing the tapes was lifted.[16] Though the broadcast ban was ultimately dissolved, this case serves as evidence that the Supreme Court does not view such gag orders as unconstitutional per se. Rather, the justifications alleged for prior restraint must be considered.

As for the gag order in the hypothetical at the beginning of this chapter, it appears to be unconstitutional. A court would need more facts to show why alternative measures would not suffice to assure selection of an impartial jury. Can you envision circumstances in which the gag order on the newspaper and other media would be the only practical way to obtain an impartial jury?

Gag Orders on Participants

Although direct gag orders on the media now have only a narrow window of constitutional support, the Supreme Court has more readily supported restrictive orders on out-of-court statements by *participants* in legal proceedings. These participants include plaintiffs and defendants, lawyers, witnesses, jurors, and court officials. The Supreme Court's endorsement of gag orders on participants came more than twenty-five years ago in the *Sheppard* case, and many state and federal appellate courts have upheld such orders when they are aimed at preventing prejudicial statements that are not already part of the public record.

However, some limits also apply to participant gag orders because modern courts have recognized that the participants, too, have free speech rights that must be weighed. To avoid constitutionally overbroad gag orders, some appellate courts have required a showing by the trial judge that the prohibited statements would pose a clear and present danger to a fair trial and that reasonable alternatives to the gag order do not exist. Others have adopted the standard of a reasonable likelihood of a serious threat to a defendant's right to a fair trial. The bottom line here is that gag orders on participants are upheld fairly often, but only if the orders are narrowly tailored and accompanied by some specific justification.

For example, such a restrictive order was upheld during the 1997 trial of Timothy McVeigh, a suspect in the bombing of the Oklahoma City federal building two years earlier. The bombing killed 168 people and injured hundreds more. Media coverage was so intense that it compelled the unusual step of a change of venue from Oklahoma to Colorado. But, before the jury was selected, the trial court took the additional step of restraining all out-of-court statements about the case by the lawyers and other support personnel in the trial. The step was necessary, the court said, to keep jurors from being exposed to misleading, out-of-court pronouncements by lawyers in the highly complex and emotionally charged case.[17]

Lawyers' Rules of Conduct

In some states enforceable disciplinary rules work as a partial gag on attorneys in all cases, even without an individual tailored order from a judge. These rules, many of them modeled after Rule 3.6 of the American Bar Association's *Model Rules of Professional Conduct,* may discourage lawyers from cooperating with the media.

ABA Rule 3.6 forbids a lawyer to make a statement to the media if the lawyer "reasonably should know that it will have a substantial likelihood of materially prejudicing an adjudicative proceeding."[18] The rule goes on to list several kinds of statements that would ordinarily be deemed prejudicial, including comments relating to the reputation of a party or witness or their expected testimony, the existence or substance of a confession, the results of any examination or test, and even the fact that a person has been charged with a crime. About half the states have adopted some version of Rule 3.6. Lawyers who violate the rule are subject to disciplinary action.

In 1991 the U.S. Supreme Court gave its general approval to disciplinary rules that limit lawyers' out-of-court comments, but the Court invalidated Nevada's rule on the ground that it was too vague. Following the arraignment of his client on felony theft charges, a Nevada lawyer held a press conference in which he declared his client innocent and questioned the integrity of people who had testified before the grand jury. The Nevada Bar later disciplined the attorney for violating Nevada Supreme Court Rule 177—a provision nearly identical to ABA Rule 3.6. The rule prohibited lawyers from making out-of-court statements that the lawyer should know "will have a substantial likelihood of materially prejudicing an adjudicative proceeding." The U.S. Supreme Court agreed that lawyers may be subject to speech restrictions more stringent than possible restraints on the media or the public. In this case, though, the wording of the rule was not specific enough to give lawyers clear notice of the kinds of remarks that would be considered a violation. Therefore, the Court held, the rule was unconstitutionally vague.[19]

Media as Participants

When a mass medium itself is a party to a lawsuit, it may encounter a major exception to the tough standard against gag orders on the media. The exception was set down by the Supreme Court in *Seattle Times Co. v. Rhinehart,* a 1984 case, and it pertains to media dissemination of information obtained in the civil discovery process.

The *Times* and other newspapers were defendants in a libel and privacy lawsuit filed by members of a small religious group that the papers had been investigating. The papers' lawyers then made extensive use of the civil discovery process to obtain information about the group. But a Washington state court issued a protective order prohibiting the papers from publishing anything they learned solely through the court-supervised discovery process. The U.S. Supreme Court unanimously affirmed. The Court noted that discovery is a powerful tool for litigants—essentially a court-compelled intrusion into normally confidential matters. The protective order was justified, the Court ruled, to prevent media abuse of this process for journalistic purposes.[20]

Access to Proceedings

The case of *Sheppard v. Maxwell,* you'll recall, involved not only problems of trial and pretrial publicity but also of disruptive media conduct at the trial. To prevent this threat to proper decorum, as well as some of the perceived publicity problems, it was logical that trial judges in the late 1960s began using another remedy with increasing frequency: the closed courtroom.

Constitutionally speaking, it was also the general rule then and now, that government is free to deny access to the media and public so long as the denial is nondiscriminatory. (This general rule was discussed in Chapter 6.) Therefore, closing court proceedings, though contrary to the courtroom tradition in this country, was not regarded as a violation of the media's First Amendment rights.

This changed beginning in 1980, however, with a series of Supreme Court opinions that dealt directly with the problem of closed criminal proceedings. The public and the media now have a recognized First Amendment right, albeit qualified, to attend proceedings in a courtroom.

Access to Trials   The landmark case for courtroom access rights was *Richmond Newspapers, Inc. v. Virginia*. The story began in 1976 when John Paul Stevenson was prosecuted in the stabbing death of a hotel manager in Virginia. Stevenson was tried and convicted of second-degree murder. But the Virginia Supreme Court reversed the conviction on grounds that a bloodstained shirt had been improperly admitted as evidence. A second trial began, but it was declared a mistrial when one of the jurors suddenly had to be excused. A third attempt also ended in a mistrial when it was learned that one of the prospective jurors had read newspaper accounts of Stevenson's prior trials and had told other prospective jurors about the case.

As the fourth trial was set to begin, Stevenson's lawyer requested that the trial be closed to the public. (The Sixth Amendment guarantees criminal defendants a right to a public trial, but defendants may waive this right.) The defense attorney said he was concerned that courtroom spectators might relay accounts of testimony to prospective witnesses. The prosecutor did not object to the motion for closure, and the judge ordered the courtroom closed to all spectators. The order was not immediately contested by the two reporters present, representing the *Richmond Times-Dispatch* and the *Richmond News-Leader*. Later that day, however, Richmond Newspapers obtained a hearing to attack the closure order. Lawyers for the reporters argued that the judge failed to consider less drastic measures before ordering the closure. But the judge left his order in place, stating that "having people in the courtroom is distracting to the jury."[21] The trial continued the next morning with the public and press excluded.

The trial ended swiftly, this time with the verdict that Stevenson was not guilty. Though the homicide case now was over, Richmond Newspapers continued to seek a legal determination that the closure had been unlawful. Eventually the matter reached the U.S. Supreme Court, and the Court ruled 7–1 in favor of the newspapers. For the first time, the Court had found a specific right of access under the First Amendment. For its efforts in championing access to the legal system, Richmond Newspapers was awarded the Society of Professional Journalists' prestigious Freedom of Information Award in 1982.

The Richmond Newspapers Rationale

Why should a constitutional right of access apply to criminal trials when such a right has not been declared for other government places or forums? In the Court's plurality opinion, Chief Justice Burger stressed two things. One was historical context: Trials traditionally have been open to the public for hundreds of years. Second, Burger noted an important function of openness: The openness of trials had long served a vital purpose by providing an outlet for community concern, hostility, and other emotions triggered by crime. In modern society, he said, it is the mass media, operating as "surrogates for the public," that relay the important trial information to the people. And this information is essential to public confidence in the judicial system. Having made these historical and functional arguments, the chief justice concluded that "a presumption of openness inheres in the very nature of a criminal trial under our system of justice."[22] Then he gave that presumption constitutional stature:

> Free speech carries with it some freedom to listen. . . . What this means in the context of trials is that the First Amendment guarantees of speech and press, standing alone, prohibit government from summarily closing courtroom doors which had long been open to the public at the time that amendment was adopted. . . .
> We hold that the rights to attend criminal trials is implicit in the guarantees of the First Amendment; without the freedom to attend such trials, which people have exercised for centuries, important aspects of freedom of speech and of the press could be eviscerated.[23]

Justice Burger concluded his opinion by observing that in this case the trial judge had made no specific findings of a threat to a fair trial, nor did he investigate whether alternative solutions could have ensured fairness. Therefore, the closure was improper: "Absent an overriding interest articulated in findings, the trial of a criminal case must be open to the public."[24]

The chief justice declined, however, to specify the kinds of circumstances that could override the public's newfound right of access. This imprecision in the plurality opinion was exacerbated by the seven separate opinions the justices produced in the case—opinions that evidenced significant differences of thinking about the breadth of this First Amendment right and the constitutional standard for overriding it.

Nevertheless, the case was remarkable in that it added a whole new arm to the First Amendment. The significance was underscored by Justice Stevens in his own opinion: "Until today the Court has accorded virtually absolute protection to the dissemination of information or ideas, but never before has it squarely held that the acquisition of newsworthy matter is entitled to any constitutional protection whatsoever."[25]

Protecting Victims and Witnesses

The Supreme Court further solidified this First Amendment right of access to criminal trials in the 1982 case of *Globe Newspaper Co. v. Superior Court*.[26] The Court in that case struck down a Massachusetts statute that required closure of trials during testimony by juvenile victims of sexual offenses. Justice Brennan, writing for the majority, reiterated the principle and rationale of *Richmond Newspapers* and then went a step further by ruling that a strict scrutiny standard of review would apply to courtroom closures. To be constitutional a trial closure must be supported by a compelling government interest, and the closure must be narrowly tailored to serve that interest, the Court ruled in *Globe*.

The Massachusetts statute aimed to protect juvenile victims from further trauma, embarrassment, and intimidation, and the Court ruled that this was indeed a compelling interest. But the statute was not narrowly tailored. It categorically closed all such testimony, whether or not the victim actually needed such protection. But a less sweeping discretionary closure rule, rather than a mandatory one, could satisfy the state's goals.

Justice Brennan emphasized that the *Globe* ruling was a narrow one. It did not mandate open trials at all times. In fact, one of the commonly accepted justifications for closed trials is the protection of juvenile crime victims and witnesses from further trauma and embarrassment, especially in sex offense cases. But *Globe* suggests that such trial closures must be justified on a case-by-case basis, with the trial judge considering such factors as the victim's age and maturity, the nature of the crime, and the victim's desires regarding closure. (In the *Globe* case, for example, the victims were 16 and 17 and indicated no qualms about testifying in public.) Many lower court decisions have since employed the constitutional test articulated in *Globe* and have upheld partial closures of trials to protect the psychological well-being of juvenile crime victims or witnesses.

Jury Selection

Later opinions by the Supreme Court added further detail to the test for determining when courtroom closures are constitutional, and they also expanded the test's application. In 1984 the Supreme Court held unanimously that the public access rights apply even to the jury selection phase of a criminal trial. The case was *Press-Enterprise Co. v. Superior Court* (often called *Press-Enterprise I*).[27] A man was charged in the rape and killing of a teenage girl. The trial judge in the homicide case had excluded the public from the lawyers' questioning of prospective jurors, one of the earliest phases of a trial. The stated purpose of the closure was to encourage candor in the prospective jurors' responses by protecting against public disclosure of sensitive answers. But the Supreme Court held that jury selection was a critical part of the trial process and was subject to the same presumption of openness as the main portion of the trial. In this instance the trial judge had failed to articulate specific dangers and had not considered whether less drastic measures might have worked to protect jurors' privacy. Therefore, the closure order was vacated.

What has evolved from *Press-Enterprise I* and later cases is essentially a four-pronged test. Criminal trial closures will be constitutional only if:

1. A substantial probability exists that overriding interests (such as the accused's right to an impartial jury) will be damaged by conducting the proceeding in public

2. No reasonable alternatives to closure would protect against the danger

3. The reasons behind these conclusions are fully articulated as findings in the trial record

4. The closure is no broader than necessary to protect the overriding interest

The final prong of this test means that, even when some form of closure appears warranted, judges must take care to fashion the closure as narrowly as possible in order to avoid undue harm to the First Amendment access rights of the public and media. Therefore, closure orders usually are limited to isolated segments of the proceedings—during testimony of a particular witness, for example.

How about the closed courtroom you encountered in the chapter hypothetical? All you were told was that the judge anticipated substantial distractions if the courtroom were open to journalists. First, you should wonder whether specific findings were articulated to support this closure. If not, the closure could be vacated by a higher court on that basis alone. What is the likelihood that the judge could articulate a specific finding of likely danger to a fair trial? Pretty slim, it seems, because the judge would not yet have known how many reporters would attend the trial or how respectful they would be of the trial process. And even if the judge did have sufficient evidence to find a likelihood of danger, could the danger reasonably be diffused by alternative measures or by a more selective closure? This was a closure that a good journalist would not fail to protest.

The upshot of all this is that U.S. Supreme Court rulings during the 1980s greatly curtailed closures of criminal trials, just as gag orders on the media were reined in during the 1970s. Again, it is not that closures are banned altogether, but rather that a strict constitutional standard—one that mandates a look toward alternatives—makes valid closures extremely rare.

Pretrial Proceedings

Criminal trials actually are but a small part of the overall criminal justice process. Another significant aspect of the system involves pretrial proceedings of many types, such as arraignments, bail hearings, and hearings to suppress the release of certain kinds of evidence. Therefore, as the Supreme Court was molding a First Amendment right of access to criminal trials, the question naturally arose whether the right would apply to these other proceedings as well.

In 1986 the Supreme Court began to answer this question when it extended the qualified right of courtroom access to preliminary hearings, at least as they are conducted in California. In a preliminary hearing the criminal defendant is confronted with a streamlined version of the prosecution's evidence, and the defense is allowed to cross-examine the prosecution's proposed witnesses. The purpose of the hearing is for the judge to determine whether evidence sufficient to warrant a

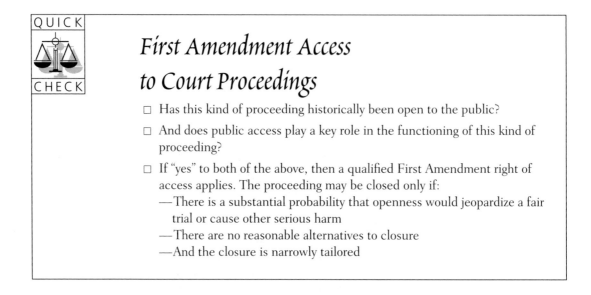

QUICK

CHECK

First Amendment Access to Court Proceedings

☐ Has this kind of proceeding historically been open to the public?

☐ And does public access play a key role in the functioning of this kind of proceeding?

☐ If "yes" to both of the above, then a qualified First Amendment right of access applies. The proceeding may be closed only if:
—There is a substantial probability that openness would jeopardize a fair trial or cause other serious harm
—There are no reasonable alternatives to closure
—And the closure is narrowly tailored

full-fledged trial exists against the accused. The preliminary hearing is thus an important stage that may last many days.

In a case again titled *Press-Enterprise Co. v. Superior Court,* often referred to as *Press-Enterprise II,* the U.S. Supreme Court ruled against closure of a particularly lengthy preliminary hearing in California. A nurse named Robert Diaz was accused of killing twelve patients by administering massive doses of a cardiac drug, and the prosecution was seeking the death penalty. Naturally the case attracted national publicity, and the defense requested that the preliminary hearing be closed. The judge agreed, citing a danger that "only one side may get reported in the media."[28]

But the Supreme Court found that there had been a long tradition of accessibility to preliminary hearings as conducted in California. It also found that public access served a significant, positive function in these hearings, which resemble trials in many ways. Access serves as a safeguard against corruption and also as a bridge to public confidence in the system. Essentially the same considerations that led to a First Amendment right of access to criminal trials in *Richmond Newspapers* were present in this case, and the Court appropriately extended the right.

After concluding that the right of access extended to California preliminary hearings, the Supreme Court in *Press-Enterprise II* applied the four-part test from *Press-Enterprise I.* The Court ruled that the test had not been met and struck down the closure.

Press-Enterprise II is an encouraging decision for journalists, though along with it has come much uncertainty. Just how far will the qualified right of access evolve? It is not yet clear whether the constitutional right of access extends to most other kinds of pretrial proceedings in criminal cases. As a practical matter, other kinds of hearings are rarely closed or considered newsworthy, so the issue doesn't come up often. Much speculation also exists about whether the Court's tradition/function analysis might eventually be used to extend the access right to entirely different scenarios, such as congressional hearings or executions.

Civil Proceedings

Thus far, we have looked at courtroom closures only in the context of criminal cases. The issues and litigants in civil proceedings may also be of great news value, however. Although the Sixth Amendment right to an impartial jury does not apply to civil cases, a fair jury in civil cases is guaranteed under common law and state constitutions. Also, other important interests—such as privacy rights and trade secrets—sometimes work against openness.

The U.S. Supreme Court has not decided directly whether the right of access recognized in criminal proceedings also extends to civil cases. However, the plurality opinion in *Richmond* noted that both criminal and civil trials historically have been open in this country from the time of the ratification of the Constitution. And a few of the justices in their *Richmond* concurrences suggested that the rationale behind the right of access would apply to civil trials as well.

Therefore, lower courts directly confronting the issue in recent years have tended to hold that a constitutional right of access applies to civil trials.[29] And in some instances in which the courts have declined to find a First Amendment access right, they nevertheless have ruled in favor of access based on a common law presumption of openness.[30]

Privacy Interests

On the other hand, some courts have balked at extending access rights to certain classes of civil proceedings in which privacy interests typically are high. This is true primarily with family relations cases, involving such matters as divorce and child custody, and with mental health proceedings. In upholding closures, courts often note that family law proceedings do not have the same tradition of openness as most other kinds of court proceedings. In fact, many kinds of family law proceedings historically have been closed to the public by state statutes. Still, the Supreme Court's ruling in *Globe Newspaper* would seem to preclude blanket closures and require judges to assess the need for closure in each case.

Civil Discovery

The presumption of openness that now applies to most civil trials and hearings does not extend, however, to the pretrial discovery phase of civil lawsuits. During discovery the litigants attempt to collect all pertinent information about the case—from potential witnesses and from each other—by asking many detailed questions and requesting documents. The responses are mandated by law and made under oath. It is a phase that may last many months or even years, and its

EXHIBIT 7.1   *Access to Courts: Key Supreme Court Cases*

1966	Criminal convictions will be overturned if trial judges fail to "take strong measures" to ensure an impartial jury free from outside influences (*Sheppard v. Maxwell*).
1976	Judicial gag orders on the media are valid only in rare circumstances where no other measure exists to control pervasive and prejudicial publicity (*Nebraska Press Association v. Stuart*).
1980	The public and the media have a First Amendment right of access to criminal trials, absent an overriding justification for closure (*Richmond Newspapers v. Virginia*).
1981	Media cameras in the courtroom, if properly controlled, do not violate a criminal defendant's right to a fair trial (*Chandler v. Florida*).
1986	The First Amendment right of access extends beyond criminal trials to other proceedings with a tradition of openness and where public access serves an important function—in this case criminal preliminary hearings (*Press-Enterprise v. Superior Court* [*Press-Enterprise II*]).

goal is to clarify the issues for trial. The discovery phase may produce reams of information that are never actually presented as evidence at trial.

Because of the expansive and unfiltered nature of the civil discovery process, courts typically have declined to grant media access rights to oral depositions or the lawyers' extensive discovery files. Note, however, that if litigants voluntarily provide the fruits of discovery to you, you have a First Amendment right to disseminate that information (though subject to the usual tort restraints, such as invasion of privacy). Some kinds of discovery documents are routinely made part of the public file, open for inspection at the courthouse.

Special Problem: Cameras in the Courtroom

As discussed, courtrooms traditionally have been open to the public and the media, with the exception of a few kinds of proceedings. And in the last twenty years the Supreme Court has declared a First Amendment right of access that enforces the traditions and goes even further. On the other hand, although the courts generally have accepted and even required a right of access for those with notepads and pens, access with cameras has been an entirely different matter.

Judges long have abhorred both television and still photography in their courtrooms. Unlike the presence of reporters with mere notepads, the use of cameras, it was thought, presented a serious danger of (1) distracting juries, (2) intimidating witnesses, (3) encouraging "showboating" by lawyers and witnesses, and (4) generally disrupting proper decorum. These effects could jeopardize a fair trial. Furthermore, cameras were not equated with access. Cameras were not necessary for keeping the public informed about justice; they were viewed rather as devices for the "showbiz" side of journalism. So, for decades, most court systems across the nation maintained strict bans on the use of cameras.

Supreme Court Cases

The U.S. Supreme Court first confronted the issue in 1965. A man linked to then-President Lyndon Johnson had been convicted of big-time fraud in Texas, and despite the defendant's objections the trial judge permitted the proceedings to be televised. Texas was one of just two states that allowed televised trials at the time. The Supreme Court later overturned the man's conviction, ruling that the use of TV cameras had contaminated the constitutional ideals of a fair trial and due process.[31]

But in the years that followed, the media lobbied vigorously for the use of cameras, and technology aided the cause by providing equipment that was less conspicuous and easier to use. By the mid-1970s the courts had begun to experiment. By 1980 a majority of the states had either lifted their bans on photography or were studying the issue.

In 1981 the U.S. Supreme Court faced the issue again in the case of *Chandler v. Florida.* The context was a criminal trial in which two Miami police officers were convicted of conspiracy to commit burglary. TV cameras had been present in the courtroom over the defendants' objections, though only a few minutes of the trial were broadcast.

This time the Supreme Court allowed the convictions to stand, ruling that the presence of cameras does not inherently render a trial unfair. Wrote Chief Justice Burger for the majority:

> An absolute Constitutional ban on broadcast coverage of trials cannot be justified simply because there is a danger that, in some cases, prejudicial broadcast accounts of pretrial and trial events may impair the ability of jurors to decide the issue of guilt or innocence uninfluenced by extraneous matter. . . . The risk of juror prejudice is present in any publication of a trial, but the appropriate safeguard against such prejudice is the defendant's right to demonstrate that the media's coverage of his case—be it printed or broadcast—compromised the ability of the particular jury that heard the case to adjudicate fairly.[32]

In *Chandler* the Supreme Court made it clear that cameras in the courtroom were generally constitutionally permissible. The ruling further opened the door for experimentation with cameras. Still, the Supreme Court has never ruled that access with cameras is constitutionally required under the First Amendment. Therefore, the various court jurisdictions—via statutes or formal court rules—have been free to set their own guidelines.

State Rules

Today the majority of states do allow cameras in their courtrooms. By the mid-1990s, filming of criminal trials was permitted in 35 states, and in most of those states cameras were also allowed in appellate proceedings.

Camera access comes with some strings attached, however. Modern court rules seek a balance between journalists' legitimate photo and video needs and the parties' rights to dignified legal proceedings. For example, most modern rules reserve for judges the broad discretion to determine whether camera coverage will be allowed in a particular case, and how. States often require written, judicial approval in advance. Some states also require permission of the parties. And, in proceedings with extraordinary media interest, the court may require a pool arrangement for all media—one or two camera people are admitted to the courtroom and then share the photos and video with the others. Some states' rules also contain specific prohibitions on close-up shots of jurors or the use of motorized drives or special lighting. Photographers are often limited to a certain area of the courtroom.

As a practical matter you might increase your chances of camera access by introducing yourself to the judge in chambers in advance of the trial or hearing. Show the judge how your camera works, and convey your appreciation for the need to be unobtrusive.

Federal Rule

Generally speaking, camera access rules have worked smoothly in the states, and many judges today allow camera access routinely. A major exception, however, has been the federal court system. Rule 53 of the *Federal Rules of Criminal Procedure* prohibits the use of media cameras during federal court proceedings. Therefore, media covering federal cases have had to rely on photos of people entering or leaving the courtroom or on artists' sketches of the courtroom drama.

In 1991 the federal court system began a three-year pilot program that permitted camera coverage of civil proceedings in selected trial and appellate courts, at the discretion of a presiding judge. Federal courts in six states were chosen to participate. The pilot program generated positive feedback from the participating judges and lawyers, who generally found the cameras to be unobtrusive. However, in 1994 the U.S. Judicial Conference voted to discontinue the program and return to a system-wide ban on cameras in federal court. In 1996 the Judicial Conference again changed its mind and voted to allow each circuit temporarily to set its own camera rules, but only in civil cases. In 1998 the U.S. House of Representatives approved a Judicial Reform Act that contained provisions to allow cameras in the federal trial courts and the circuit appeals courts. The bill then died in the Senate, but it was reintroduced in 1999. The U.S. Supreme Court has yet to allow cameras in any of its proceedings.

The Simpson Aftermath

The O. J. Simpson trial—or "spectacle," as some called it—refocused national attention on the cameras-in-court debate. Prior to the Simpson criminal proceedings, camera access had evolved to the point of routine in many states. But the lengthy, often-theatrical Simpson case rekindled the controversy over cameras.

Fallout from the Simpson case remains difficult to assess. Even before the criminal verdict was announced in 1995, the case helped convince judges in other cases to deny cameras access. And on the same day Simpson was acquitted of murder charges, California's governor asked the state's judicial council to consider banning cameras in criminal proceedings. In various state legislatures, too, the topic was cropping up in debates over justice-system reform.

Yet as the nation entered the year 2000, there was very little evidence of actually turning back the clock on cameras. New York had allowed its camera-access law to lapse, but other states' laws remained on the books. Most judicial experts seemed to recognize that the theatrical O.J. case was an aberration, with or without cameras, and that cameras were presenting no problem in most courtrooms. In a 1999 speech before the National Press Club in Washington, D.C., the president of the American Bar Association urged the Supreme Court to open its doors to cameras so that the public could witness the "majesty" of the American justice system.

Special Problem: Juvenile Court

In contrast to most other kinds of court proceedings, the proceedings in juvenile court—where persons under age 18 are prosecuted—have traditionally been closed to the public in order to protect the anonymity of the defendant. Behind this tradition is the notion that the juvenile justice system is not intended primarily to punish but rather to rehabilitate immature offenders. Publicity can hamper rehabilitation, the theory goes, because juveniles are stigmatized when their names and crimes are made known to the community at large.

Because juvenile court has traditionally been closed, it is uncertain whether any First Amendment right of access might apply to these proceedings. The U.S. Supreme Court has not directly addressed the issue. And, meanwhile, other courts have upheld continued closure. For example, the Supreme Court of Vermont in 1981 held that the First Amendment right of trial access announced in *Richmond Newspapers* did not apply to juvenile court proceedings.[33]

However, recent years have seen a troublesome rise in juvenile crime rates and high-profile violent crimes by juveniles that have sparked a change in public attitude. The public is demanding closer scrutiny of the juvenile justice system, and many would say the public's right to know about violent juvenile crimes should override the young offender's right to rehabilitate in privacy.

Therefore, many states are revising their statutes to open juvenile court proceedings and records in certain instances—such as when the offender is 13 or older and the offense would constitute a violent felony. Furthermore, in many jurisdictions judges have the discretion to open juvenile court proceedings under certain conditions—such as when the media agree in advance not to reveal the minor's identity. Examine your own state's statutes and case law, and keep in mind that the law of access to juvenile court is in a state of significant change.

Also, remember that even in states that strictly limit access to juvenile court proceedings and records, the media cannot be punished for revealing juvenile information they lawfully obtain in another manner. This was the U.S. Supreme

Court's holding in *Smith v. Daily Mail Publishing Co.*,[34] discussed in Chapter 5. This principle was also illustrated in a 1998 decision by the Supreme Court of Mississippi. A reporter for the *Delta Democrat Times* attended an open-court manslaughter sentencing hearing. The prosecutor discussed portions of the adult defendant's prior juvenile record in order to persuade the judge to impose a harsh sentence. Following that discussion, the judge asked the reporter to approach the bench and told the reporter that the juvenile record information was "not to be recorded in the paper." But the reporter's story nevertheless contained this line about the defendant: "As a juvenile, Hollingsworth was charged with such crimes as manufacturing of marijuana, grand larceny, auto burglary, possession of alcohol and others." The reporter was sentenced by the judge to seventy-two hours in jail for contempt. But the state's high court reversed because the reporter was not obliged to obey the judge's order not to publish. Once the confidential record was made public in open court, anyone in attendance had a further right to disseminate the information.[35]

Ethics and Etiquette of Court Coverage

As a practical matter, and over the long term, media interests in access and publication will not be assured wholesale by the Supreme Court. Instead, the media must continually earn the confidence of judges and lawyers. This is accomplished in part by appreciating the constitutional and moral rights of those directly involved in legal proceedings. Often the media are wise (and perhaps ethically bound) to exercise a little self-restraint so that principles of justice are not trampled while guarding the public's right to know. Even when media behavior does not give rise to a question of ethics, it may nevertheless concern a point of courtroom etiquette—something that judges take seriously.

The law does not dictate most aspects of the media–justice system relationship, and it is for this reason that the dialogue encouraged by bench/bar/media committees remains so important. At the very least these committees can foster a greater understanding by the legal profession of journalists' professional principles, and vice versa. Some committees have agreed upon statements of ethical and professional principles and even on specific, voluntary policies (Exhibit 7.2).

Access to Court Evidence and Records

With access to courtroom proceedings now guaranteed by law in most cases, the next question involves access to the court documents in those proceedings. This is an evolving area of law, complicated by the fact that there are several different kinds of records that may be accumulated during a legal case. Remember, too, that state and federal open records statutes, discussed in the previous chapter, don't cover the courts.

Earlier, this chapter noted the general rule that the media have no access rights to information gathered by lawyers through the pretrial discovery process in civil cases. But some access rights do apply to actual court records. Unfortunately the U.S. Supreme Court has provided little guidance in this area, and courts in the various states and federal circuits have conflicting views. With this in mind the general trend of the opinions concerning access to judicial records is as follows.

A First Amendment right of access to judicial records has not been widely recognized. However, in both *Press-Enterprise I* and *II* the newspaper sought access to transcripts of the judicial proceedings as well as access to the actual proceedings. When the Supreme Court ruled in those cases that there existed a First Amendment right to attend the proceedings, it implicitly held that the transcripts of such proceedings must be open to public and media inspection. As Chief Justice Burger wrote in *Press-Enterprise II:* "Denying the transcripts of a 41-day preliminary hearing would frustrate what we have characterized as the 'community therapeutic value' of openness."[36] Thus a First Amendment right of access to court records is evolving, and some lower courts have extended the right to documents other than the transcripts of open court proceedings.

More widely recognized, though, is a common law right to inspect and copy judicial records pertaining to open proceedings. These presumptively open records include not only transcripts of proceedings but also pleadings and motions, court orders, and any materials formally admitted into evidence. This common law right of access is not absolute, however; it is subject to the reasonable discretion of the trial judge. For the most part, access is allowed unless a judge specifically finds that public dissemination would threaten rights to a fair trial or would invade personal privacy.

Many cases in recent years have dealt with requests by broadcasters to copy video or audio tapes used as evidence in criminal trials. The majority of appellate court decisions has favored these requests, provided that the tapes had already been formally submitted as evidence and had been played in open court.[37]

Some kinds of court records typically are kept secret and are not subject to a common law presumption of openness. For example, transcripts of grand jury proceedings are very rarely made public. Also, journalists usually may not gain access to the settlement agreements in civil cases. As part of a settlement agreement the parties typically promise to keep the terms of the agreement confidential, and judges often seal the written agreements at the parties' request.

Extracting Evidence from the Media

Another point of friction between the media and the justice system often arises when legal authorities want the news media to provide information they've obtained in the course of their business. In a sense, the authorities want to take advantage of the same sort of aggressive reporting work that often irritates them.

The problem typically begins when a news reporter or editor is served with a legal document called a **subpoena.** The subpoena orders a person who has evidence relevant to a legal proceeding either to testify in person or to produce specified documents or other physical evidence. Subpoenas are issued by lawyers

EXHIBIT 7.2   *Joint Declaration Regarding News Coverage of Criminal Proceedings in California*

STATEMENT OF PRINCIPLES

The bench, bar, and news media of California recognize that freedom of the press and the right to fair trial, as guaranteed by the First and Sixth Amendments to the Constitution of the United States, sometimes appear to be in conflict. They believe, however, that if the principles of fair trial and free press are applied responsibly in accord with high professional ethics, our society can have fair trials without limiting freedom of the press.

Accordingly, the following principles are recommended to all members of the bar and the press in California.

1. The news media have the right and responsibility to gather and disseminate the news, so that the public will be informed. Free and responsible news media enhance the administration of justice. Members of the bench, the bar, and the news media should cooperate, consistent with their respective ethical principles, in accomplishing the foregoing.

2. All parties to litigation, including the state, have the right to have their causes tried fairly by impartial tribunals. Defendants in criminal cases are guaranteed this right by the constitutions of the United States and the State of California.

3. Lawyers and journalists share with the court responsibility for maintaining an atmosphere conducive to fair trial.

4. The news media and the bar recognize the responsibility of the judge to preserve order in court and to conduct proceedings in such a manner as will serve the ends of justice.

5. Editors in deciding what news to publish should remember that:

(a) An accused person is presumed innocent until proved guilty.

(b) Readers, listeners, and viewers are potential jurors or witnesses.

(c) No person's reputation should be injured needlessly.

6. No lawyer should use publicity to promote his version of a pending case. The public prosecutor should not take unfair advantage of his position as an important source of news. These cautions shall not be construed to limit a lawyer's making available information to which the public is entitled. Editors should be cautious about publishing information received from lawyers who seek to try their cases in the press.

7. The public is entitled to know how justice is being administered, and it is the responsibility of the press to give the public the necessary information. A properly conducted trial maintains the confidence of the community as to the honesty of its institutions, the competence of its public officers, the impartiality of its judges, and the capacity of its criminal law to do justice.

8. Journalistic and legal training should include instruction in the meaning of constitutional rights to a fair trial, freedom of the press, and the role of both journalist and lawyer in guarding these rights.

9. A committee of representatives of the bar, the bench, and the news media, aided when appropriate by representatives of law enforcement agencies and other interested parties, should meet from time to time to review problems and to promote under-standing of the principles of fair trial and free press. Its purpose may include giving advisory opinions concerning the interpretations and applications of these principles.

These principles have been endorsed, as of February 15, 1970, by the following: The State Bar of California, California Freedom of Information Committee, California Newspaper Publishers Association, California Broadcasters Association, Radio and TV News Directors, and the Executive Board of the Conference of California Judges.

STATEMENT OF POLICY

To give concrete expression to these principles in newsmen's language the following statement of policy is recommended for voluntary adoption by California newspapers and news broadcasters.

Our objective is to report the news and at the same time cooperate with the courts to assure the accused a fair trial.

Protection of the rights of an accused person or a suspect does not require restraint in publication or broadcast of the following information:

—His or her name, address, age, residence, employment, marital status, and similar background information.

—The substance or text of the charge, such as complaint, indictment, information, and, where appropriate, the identity of the complainant.

—The identity of the investigating and arresting agency, and the length of investigation where appropriate.

—The circumstances surrounding an arrest, including the time and place, resistance, pursuit, possession and use of weapons, and a description of items seized.

Accuracy, good conscience, and an informed approach can provide nonprejudicial reporting of crime news. We commend to our fellow newsmen the following:

Avoid deliberate editorialization, even when a crime seems solved beyond reasonable doubt. Save the characterizations of the accused until the trial ends and guilt or innocence is determined.

Avoid editorialization by observing these rules:

—Don't call a person brought in for questioning a suspect.

—Don't call a slaying a murder until there's a formal charge.

—Don't say solution when it's just a police accusation or theory.

—Don't let prosecutors, police, or defense attorneys use us as a sounding board for public opinion or personal publicity.

Exercise care in regard to publication or broadcast of purported confessions. An accused person may repudiate and thereby invalidate a confession, claiming undue pressure, lack of counsel, or some other interference with his rights. The confession then may not be presented as evidence and yet has been read by the jurors, raising the question whether they can separate the confession from evidence presented in court. If you do use a "confession" call it a statement and let the jury decide whether the accused really confessed.

In some circumstances, as when a previous offense is not linked in a pattern with the case in question, the press should not publish or broadcast the previous criminal record of a person accused of a felony. Terms like "a long record" should generally be avoided. There are, however, other circumstances—as when parole is violated—in which reference to a previous conviction is in the public interest.

Records of convictions and prior criminal charges which are matters of public record are available to the news media through police agencies or court clerks. Law enforcement agencies should make such information available to the news media upon appropriate inquiry. The public disclosure of this information by the news media could be prejudicial without any significant contribution toward meeting the public need to be informed. The publication or broadcast of such information should be carefully considered.

In summary:

This Statement of Policy is not all-inclusive; it does not purport to cover every subject on which a question may arise with respect to whether particular information should be published or broadcast. Our objective is to report the news and at the same time cooperate with the courts to help assure the accused a fair trial. Caution should therefore be exercised in publishing or broadcasting information which might result in denial of a fair trial.

in both civil and criminal cases, and they also are issued by grand juries investigating crime. The recipient of a subpoena may not ignore it. One who fails to comply without showing legal justification can be jailed or fined for contempt of court.

A strong societal interest lies behind the enforcement of subpoenas because they are a powerful—even essential—tool for arriving at the truth. Without the authority to subpoena witnesses and documentation, prosecutors and civil litigants often would find it impossible to compile sufficient evidence in their favor. Potential witnesses who simply do not want to be bothered would be free to ignore the pleas for information. For criminal defendants, furthermore, the federal Constitution recognizes that the subpoena power is vital to the basic notion of due process. It is another of the Sixth Amendment's guarantees that an accused person "shall enjoy the right . . . to have compulsory process for obtaining witnesses in his favor. . . ."

But a strong public interest also exists in allowing journalists, particularly, to decline to serve as sources of legal evidence. This is because tapping journalists for testimony, notes, negatives, and videotape is likely to hinder the free flow of information to reporters and thus to the public. Often sources will talk with news reporters only in confidence, as did the bookie in the chapter hypothetical. But if prosecuting authorities or civil litigation opponents could obtain that information via subpoena, such sources would tend to dry up.

Also, the routine use of journalists as auxiliary investigators for the legal system could be highly disruptive for the media. Few news operations could count on meeting their deadlines if reporters and editors were frequently compelled to appear in grand jury investigations, depositions, preliminary hearings, and trials. Therefore, the fear is that the news media under such circumstances would simply choose to shy away from aggressive reporting on crime and impropriety. This would indeed be society's loss, for such watchdog reporting is what often brings crimes to light in the first place.

Furthermore, media organizations prefer to avoid answering subpoenas because of the appearance that may be created—that media are essentially an arm of law enforcement. This perception could be damaging to the media's credibility because the media usually must be perceived as autonomous in order to be credible.

Historically, journalists in this country have taken great pride in their aggressive reporting of crime and corruption, and they have resisted—even to the point of going to jail—attempts to force disclosure of journalistic confidences. Journalists claimed that First Amendment rights were at stake, though that legal issue remained unsettled for decades. In the late 1960s, however—an era of civil unrest and increasingly sophisticated TV news operations—there came a sharp rise in the frequency of disclosure orders served upon the media. In the two-year period of 1969–70, the three major TV networks alone were the targets of more than 150 subpoenas. The time had come to determine whether a "reporter's privilege" truly protected journalists against having to respond.

Forced Disclosure and the First Amendment

The U.S. Supreme Court directly considered the forced disclosure issue in 1972, in four separate cases collectively known as *Branzburg v. Hayes*. Each of the cases arose when a news reporter was subpoenaed to testify before a grand jury.

In the first case, a reporter named Paul Branzburg had written a story for the *Louisville Courier-Journal* that described how two Kentucky youths made money by converting marijuana into hashish. Branzburg observed firsthand the illegal synthesizing of hashish, but only after promising anonymity to the young chemists. When Branzburg was ordered before the grand jury he refused to disclose his sources' identities.

The second case involved the same reporter. This time Branzburg ran a story about the use and sale of illicit drugs, based on dozens of first-hand interviews with drug users. Again the grand jury subpoenaed Branzburg to testify as to the crimes and individuals he observed.

In the third case, a Massachusetts TV reporter covering civil unrest had gained entrance to a headquarters of the Black Panther party, a militant black organization. He was allowed to observe the events inside upon condition that he report none of what he saw or heard, except in the case of a police raid. No raid occurred, but two months later the reporter was ordered before a grand jury. He discussed what he had seen outside Panther headquarters but refused to answer questions about events inside.

The fourth case involved a reporter for *The New York Times* who had written stories about the Black Panthers in the San Francisco area. A federal grand jury investigating possibly criminal conduct by the Panthers ordered the reporter to answer questions and to turn over notes and tapes of interviews. He refused.

The Branzburg *Plurality*

The Supreme Court considered the cases together, and it came away deeply divided. In the Court's plurality opinion, written by Justice White, it declined to recognize a special First Amendment privilege for the journalists. The Court reiterated the basic principle that the media have no constitutional immunity from laws affecting the general public. It also noted that the cases did not involve direct controls on what the media must or must not publish: "The sole issue before us is the obligation of reporters to respond to grand jury subpoenas as other citizens do and to answer questions relevant to an investigation into the commission of crime."[38]

Under the specific facts of these cases, in which crimes were perhaps being concealed, the Court ruled that reporters were not constitutionally excepted from the duty to comply with grand jury subpoenas. It did note, though, that the subpoenas must be issued in good faith, not in an effort to harass the media.

The Court's ruling and the plurality opinion are but a small part of the *Branzburg* story, however. Only four members of the Court plurality believed that newsgatherers possessed absolutely no First Amendment privilege. Four other justices dissented, and the critical swing voter, Justice Powell, wrote his own concurring opinion, which took the middle ground.

Branzburg *Concurrence and Dissents*

The dissenting justices argued for recognition of either an absolute or qualified First Amendment privilege for journalists. And Justice Powell, though voting against the reporters in these grand jury cases, wrote that he saw the Court's holding as a narrow one and that a constitutional privilege might indeed apply in other situations. Powell wrote that the proper approach should be a case-by-case balancing between freedom of the press and the legitimate needs of the justice system.

The vote in *Branzburg* was 5–4 against the reporters. But when the lower courts looked to the Supreme Court for guidance in other cases, they saw that five justices apparently believed that at least a qualified reporter's privilege should exist. Ironically, the *Branzburg* decision has led to a substantial body of case law recognizing a reporter's limited privilege, under the First Amendment, to resist subpoenas. Most of the federal courts of appeals have recognized the privilege, as have many state courts, and this body of case law prevails—at least until such time as the U.S. Supreme Court again examines the question.

To summarize, the *Branzburg* decision is significant for the following reasons:

1. It established that journalists do not have an absolute, constitutional right to resist subpoenas.

2. It means that journalists must comply with relevant grand jury subpoenas in situations similar to the *Branzburg* cases.

3. It led to the specific recognition in many lower courts that journalists do have a qualified constitutional right to withhold unpublished information and sources' identities in other situations.

First Amendment Privilege Applied

In dealing with the qualified reporter's privilege, many state and federal appellate courts have articulated specific tests for the trial courts to follow. The tests vary from one jurisdiction to another, but the courts commonly consider the following factors:

1. The relevance and importance of the requested information. The trial judge must determine whether the information elicited from the reporter will bear directly on the issues in the case and whether a claim or defense could hinge on the information.

2. Availability through alternative means. In order to override the journalist's qualified privilege, courts often require a showing that the information could not be obtained from other, nonjournalistic sources.

3. The type of controversy. The public interest in resolving criminal charges is considered weightier than the interest in resolving purely private disputes. Therefore, the journalist's right to safeguard confidential information is more

likely to be upheld in a civil proceeding and more likely to be overridden in a criminal prosecution.

4. How the information was gathered. Courts tend to recognize a greater need for privilege when the media gain information through confidential relationships and a lesser need when the information is gained from first-hand observation without a confidential source.

The required consideration of these factors is an important First Amendment safeguard against fishing expeditions at the expense of the media. The constitutional privilege is far from absolute, however. Under this minimum level of protection it is still common, particularly in criminal cases, for courts to order journalists to testify or produce materials. Also, the privilege applies only to unpublished information. Once the media decide to publish information, there is no privilege against reiterating those facts in a judicial proceeding.

The 1995 case of *Shoen v. Shoen* illustrates how some courts consider various balancing factors. The case involved an underlying civil lawsuit for defamation. Leonard Shoen, founder of the U-Haul Corporation, had made public statements implicating two of his sons in the death of another family member. The sons sued their father for libel. Meanwhile, investigative author Ronald Watkins, who was working on a book about the Shoen family feud for control of U-Haul, conducted extensive interviews with Leonard Shoen. The Shoen brothers were not alleging that their father made libelous comments to Watkins; nevertheless the brothers, seeking evidence of actual malice by their father, served Watkins with a subpoena ordering him to appear for a deposition and produce all interview notes and recordings. Watkins refused. The trial court found Watkins in contempt and ordered him to jail until he agreed to comply. But the contempt citation was reversed by the U.S. Court of Appeals for the Ninth Circuit.

The Court of Appeals held that, in a civil lawsuit where the journalist is not a party and the information sought is not from a confidential source, the journalist's First Amendment privilege may be overcome by showing three things: that the information is unavailable elsewhere, is noncumulative, and is clearly relevant to the case. The information sought from Watkins was not relevant to the issue of actual malice, the court said, because there was no evidence that Shoen actually discussed his motivation for making the particular defamatory statements. Furthermore, to the extent the information was sought to demonstrate Shoen generally harbored ill will toward his sons, the information was merely cumulative. In other words, rather than providing a new element to the case, the information would simply add to existing evidence of ill will—in this case statements made by Shoen in a deposition. Therefore, in *Shoen* the journalist's privilege was upheld.[39]

In contrast to *Shoen,* however, the U.S. Court of Appeals for the Fifth Circuit in 1998 interpreted *Branzburg* as creating First Amendment protection only when subpoenas are being used to harass the media. In *United States v. Smith,* a television reporter taped an exclusive interview with Frank Smith, who was under suspicion for setting fire to a large distribution center in New Orleans. Some days later Smith was arrested, and the TV station broadcast a small portion of the interview in which Smith said he heard the manager of the center plotting to set the fire. The federal government subpoenaed the station for the unaired portion of the interview. But the station sought to avoid answering the subpoena based on First Amendment privilege.

The Court of Appeals held that no privilege applies in this situation:

> WDSU-TV seeks to protect only nonconfidential information obtained from a person who wanted it aired when he gave it. . . . WDSU-TV's fears that non-confidential sources will shy away from the media because of its unholy alliance with the government are speculative at best. . . .
>
> Banzburg will protect the press if the government attempts to harass it. Short of such harassment, the media must bear the same burden of producing evidence of criminal wrongdoing as any other citizen.[40]

Keep in mind that these cases are just examples. Courts continue to wrestle with the legal ramifications of *Branzburg,* and application of the First Amendment reporter's privilege is inconsistent from jurisdiction to jurisdiction.

State Shield Laws

The various states are at liberty, of course, to provide journalists with greater protection than the limited privilege derived through First Amendment interpretation. In a few states this has been done judicially, through interpretation of a state constitution or common law. More important, about half the states have done so legislatively, by passing specific statutes or state constitutional provisions known as **shield laws.** These state laws vary tremendously. In some the language is narrow and conditional; in others the stated privilege is in absolute terms. In any event, state shield laws are not controlling in federal court proceedings.

As of this writing, shield laws were on the books in thirty states and the District of Columbia. The states were Alabama, Alaska, Arizona, Arkansas, California, Colorado, Delaware, Florida, Georgia, Illinois, Indiana, Kentucky, Louisiana, Maryland, Michigan, Minnesota, Montana, Nebraska, Nevada, New Jersey, New Mexico, New York, North Dakota, Ohio, Oklahoma, Oregon, Pennsylvania, Rhode Island, South Carolina, and Tennessee.

Though the scope of state shield laws varies widely, they tend to provide a more dependable form of protection than the privilege derived thus far from the federal Constitution. This is because the shield laws establish more formal categorical guidelines and rely less on case-by-case balancing tests. Some of the most important ways in which the shield laws of the various states differ are as follows:

1. Some provide protection only in narrow arenas, such as before grand juries; others apply to virtually any government demands for information.

2. Some shield only the confidential sources of information; others protect the information itself.

QUICK
CHECK

Protection Against Subpoenas

☐ Does the state have a shield law? Does it protect confidential sources? Journalistic work product? Testimony about events witnessed firsthand?

☐ If a shield law does not apply, would a First Amendment balancing test provide protection?
—Does the newsperson have evidence clearly relevant to the proceeding?
—Is there no other source for the information?
—Does the requestor have a legitimate need for the information?

☐ Is it a criminal defendant seeking the information, thus raising a Sixth Amendment right to compel evidence in defendant's behalf?

3. Some protect only the information obtained through confidential sources; others apply to evidence journalists witness firsthand.

4. Some grant protection only to regular employees of traditional news media; others extend to both employees and freelancers in a broader range of the mass media.

Often shield laws do not make these distinctions clearly: In such cases it is left to the courts to interpret the statutes in light of public policy concerns and legislative intent. To understand your state's shield law fully you must read not only the language of the statute but also the leading court opinions interpreting the statute.

Despite the existence of shield laws in many states, media subpoenas are fairly common. In a nationwide survey by the Reporters Committee for Freedom of the Press, 600 news organizations reported receiving 2725 subpoenas in 1997. The committee's report, *Agents of Discovery: A Report on the Incidence of Subpoenas Served on the News Media in 1997,* also revealed that media in shield-law states were just as likely to receive subpoenas as media in states without formal shield laws. The average number of subpoenas per television station (10) was far higher than the average for newspapers (2).

Shield Laws and the Sixth Amendment

State shield laws may indeed provide journalism with a broader privilege against forced disclosure than does the First Amendment. But shield laws may not work so broadly as to push aside a criminal defendant's fair trial rights under the U.S. Constitution. Recall that criminal defendants are guaranteed certain due-process rights, including the Sixth Amendment right to compel testimony and other evidence on the defendant's behalf. Therefore, when it is a criminal defendant seeking evidence from a journalist, even the strongest shield laws might have to yield to the defendant's request.

This point is illustrated by a 1990 decision out of California, a state with one of the broadest shield laws in the country. A *Los Angeles Times* reporter and a photographer had accompanied police on patrol, and they watched as officers searched a man for illegal drugs. The search turned up a set of brass knuckles, and the man was prosecuted. In his defense, the man questioned the legality of the police search, and the *Times* employees were summoned to tell what they had observed.

The California Supreme Court held that the state shield was indeed very broad and that it protected reporters' firsthand observations in public—usually. But the court said the state shield law cannot restrict a criminal defendant's federal constitutional right to a fair trial. Therefore, the state privilege must give way if a criminal defendant demonstrates a reasonable possibility that the information will assist his defense.[41]

Media Defendants

Another limitation on shield laws may arise when a medium is a party to a lawsuit. The courts will tend to order disclosure of any information legitimately sought through the legal process by the opposing party. The dilemma for a news medium is most acute when it is sued for defamation and the plaintiff seeks the identities of confidential sources who provided the defamatory information.

On the one hand, forced disclosure of confidential sources clearly could have a chilling effect on important news-gathering efforts, and the discovery process could be abused by those wishing to retaliate against such sources. On the other hand, defamation plaintiffs have a difficult task under modern libel rules, and they should be able to compel disclosure of the evidence that might establish actual malice. In these situations the courts usually have used some version of a First Amendment balancing test to determine whether the plaintiff truly needs the requested information from the defendant and whether a shield law therefore should be overridden.[42]

Ethical Concerns

In deciding whether to provide evidence to grand juries, the courts, or other government agencies, journalists often face serious ethical concerns as well as legal ones. Reporters sometimes conclude they have a societal duty to comply with evidentiary requests, even if the law does not require them to do so. Few news organizations believe that journalists must categorically shun all requests for evidence, no matter the circumstances. Circumstances could arise when a sobering matter of justice rests on the requested information and when the reporter's cooperation would be unlikely to compromise journalistic effectiveness and the greater public good.

But history is full of examples of journalists convinced that good ethics precluded disclosure—even when the law compelled it. This dilemma often arises when a reporter promises confidentiality to a source. It is a dilemma raised in the chapter hypothetical. Recall that you promised complete anonymity to a source who then told you of the dead woman's gambling debts. The source might now be essential to the defense of the man accused in her death so you might legally be ordered to disclose the source's identification, even in a shield law state. But what is your ethical obligation? Under what circumstances would you go back on your word, if ever? Would it depend on the extent of your punishment for disobeying the law? Would it depend on whether you thought the defendant was innocent, and the nature of the punishment? Or should ethics simply follow the law?

Legal Obligation to the Source

Several courts in recent years have addressed a different side to this topic of journalists and confidential sources. Suppose a journalist promises confidentiality to a source and receives information in exchange for that promise. But later the journalist (or the journalist's editor or news director) decides unilaterally to reveal the source. Has there been a breach of any legal duty owed to the betrayed source?

The Supreme Court considered such a claim in *Cohen v. Cowles Media Co.* In the closing days of a Minnesota gubernatorial race one of the candidate's campaign consultants, Dan Cohen, approached reporters from two newspapers and offered to provide newsworthy documents concerning the opposing party's candidate for lieutenant governor. Cohen made it clear that he would provide the information only if he was promised confidentiality. The reporters promised to keep Cohen anonymous, and he in turn provided copies of court records showing that the candidate, Marlene Johnson, had been convicted twelve years earlier for shoplifting six dollars' worth of sewing materials. The editors at both newspapers decided independently that it was important to publish Cohen's name as part of their stories concerning Johnson. Cohen was identified as the source of the records, and on the same day the stories appeared Cohen was fired from his job at a public relations agency.

Cohen sued the newspapers, alleging breach of contract, and a jury awarded him $200,000 in damages. The Minnesota Supreme Court reversed, however, concluding that enforcement of the confidentiality promise would violate the papers' First Amendment rights to make editorial decisions. The U.S. Supreme Court, in a 5–4 decision in 1991, reversed the Minnesota high court and ruled that enforcing the promises of confidentiality would not violate the newspapers' constitutional rights. Writing for the majority, Justice White said the case was controlled by the "well-established line of decisions holding that generally applicable laws do not offend the First Amendment simply because their enforcement against the press has incidental effects on its ability to gather and report the news."[43]

In his dissenting opinion, Justice Harry Blackmun said the application of contract law to this scenario would amount to more than an incidental burden on speech. Furthermore, he said laws may not be enforced in such a way as to restrict the expression of truthful information or opinion unless the restriction is justified by a compelling government interest. In this case, the publications at issue were factually correct, and the state's interest in enforcing the reporters' promises was far from compelling, Blackmun argued.

The Supreme Court returned the *Cowles Media* case to the Minnesota Supreme Court to determine whether a contract had indeed been formed and whether enforcement of such an agreement would violate the Minnesota Constitution. The Minnesota high court in 1992 declined to construe the state constitution as providing broader protection to the media than the U.S. Constitution. It concluded that the promises made to Cohen were enforceable based on a variation of contract law called "promissory estoppel." This contract theory applies when a promise is reasonably relied upon, to the substantial detriment of the relying party. The Minnesota court therefore awarded Cohen the $200,000.[44]

As a consequence of *Cowles Media,* journalists need to be doubly careful about entering agreements in which they create specific expectations of confidentiality. Some media lawyers are advising their clients to adopt clear policies regarding vows of confidentiality so that reporters in the field are less likely to make promises that editors will overrule back in the newsroom.

Police Searches   With shield laws and the First Amendment providing journalists with avenues to resist answering subpoenas, law enforcement officials may be tempted to obtain evidentiary materials from the media with a more direct tool—the search warrant. In the classic 1971 case, police were called to remove demonstrators who had seized the administrative offices at Stanford University Hospital. When police forcibly entered a hallway they were attacked and beaten by some demonstrators armed with clubs. The *Stanford Daily* published photos of the demonstration, and the police believed this student newspaper had additional photos that would help identify the perpetrators of the criminal assault upon police. The police decided to obtain the additional photos in the most direct manner possible: They showed up at the *Daily* office with a search warrant and proceeded to search the photo labs, file cabinets, desks, and wastepaper baskets. They found nothing that had not already been published. The *Daily,* however, sued the police chief and other officials, claiming that the search violated the paper's First Amendment rights.

The search process, argued the *Daily,* is physically disruptive, intimidating to the news staff, and a threat to the cultivation of confidential sources. The case eventually reached the U.S. Supreme Court where the paper lost. The Court held in *Zurcher v. Stanford Daily*[45] that as long as a search warrant is supported by probable cause to believe that evidence of a crime will be found, a search is acceptable. Nothing in the Constitution gives the press a special privilege to avoid this process, the Court said in the 1978 decision.

Some states and Congress, however, accepted the notion that the press should be protected against the intrusiveness of police searches and that news organizations' materials should be requested by subpoena instead — an avenue that at least gives the media time to consult legal counsel and plan a response. In the Privacy Protection Act of 1980,[46] Congress provided the protection that the Supreme Court would not. The federal statute prohibits newsroom searches and seizures except when (1) the person possessing the materials is the criminal suspect, (2) immediate seizure of materials is deemed necessary to prevent death or serious injury, (3) serving a subpoena would likely result in destruction or concealment of the materials, or (4) a subpoena and court order to comply have already been unsuccessful. In the absence of one of these exceptions, law enforcement personnel must use a subpoena rather than a search warrant to obtain evidence from news organizations.

Contempt of Court

Journalists who refuse to reveal a source or to provide other evidence in defiance of a judge's order risk being slapped with stiff sanctions for **contempt of court.** Actually, almost any activity that directly interferes with a court's administration of justice may be considered contempt of court. A photographer's refusal to abide by a court's rules of decorum, for example, could bring a citation for contempt.

The Penalties for Contempt

Contempt of court is punishable by fines, jail time, or both. For example, in the late 1970s a *New York Times* reporter, Myron Farber, published a series of stories about mysterious deaths that had occurred at a New Jersey hospital. The stories led to a lengthy homicide trial, and the defendant's attorney subpoenaed Farber's notes. A court upheld the subpoena. Farber and the *Times* refused to comply, however, and were cited for contempt. The newspaper was fined $100,000, plus $5000 per day, until it complied. Farber was sentenced to an indeterminate amount of jail time until he complied, plus a six-month jail term to begin after he surrendered the notes.[47]

Citations for contempt of court are often categorized as either criminal or civil, both of which were present in the Farber case. A finding of criminal contempt typically results from conduct that defies the dignity and power of the court, such as repeated disruptive behavior during court proceedings. The sanction, intended as punishment, comes in the form of a fixed fine or term of imprisonment.

A finding of civil contempt typically results when a reporter refuses to answer questions or provide journalistic materials that would benefit one of the parties. The sanction in this case is not punitive but coercive: The fine or imprisonment accumulates day by day, and it will end whenever the journalist decides to comply with the court order—or until the order becomes a moot point.

Perhaps the most important thing to remember about contempt in most jurisdictions is that, if you violate a court order, you may not ward off a contempt citation by claiming that the underlying court order was invalid. For example, suppose a trial court judge orders you to comply with a subpoena and turn over your negatives of a traffic-accident scene to the plaintiff in a civil lawsuit. Instead, you disregard the order and destroy the negatives. You are cited for criminal contempt. You cannot defend against your contempt citation by claiming that the underlying order to produce the negatives was improper. Your only appropriate legal avenue, according to the general rule, is to challenge the initial order—through the courts. Until such time as a court order is actually ruled improper by a higher court, it must be obeyed.

The problem with this general rule, often called the *Dickinson rule*,[48] is that an obviously improper court order could nevertheless delay publication, hamper reporting efforts, and otherwise tie up the media in expensive legal procedures for quite some time. Such a result can be particularly disruptive for the mass media, where daily deadlines are so important. A few courts, therefore, have broken with the *Dickinson* rule in situations in which court orders amounted to clearly invalid prior restraints on speech. In such cases, these few courts have ruled, media that disobey the order are not liable for contempt.[49] However, you should *never* disobey a court order without first consulting a lawyer.

Recall the CNN case discussed earlier in this chapter. CNN had aired portions of the Noriega jailhouse tapes despite a federal judge's temporary restraining order. Though the allegedly unconstitutional restraining order was ultimately dissolved, CNN in 1994 was found in criminal contempt for willfully violating the order while it had been in effect.[50] The court imposed an $85,000 fine, and CNN agreed to broadcast, in lieu of additional fines, an admission of error. In December 1994, CNN aired a statement that read in part: "CNN realizes that it was in error in defying the order of the court. . . . We do now and always have recognized that our justice system cannot long survive if litigants take it upon themselves to determine which judgments or orders of the court they will or will not follow."

Though the contempt power of courts is broad, it is not without legal limitations. For example, the U.S. Supreme Court has clearly established that public criticism of judges, levied by the media or members of the public, is protected speech that only in the rarest of circumstances could be punished as contempt. The general standard is that public criticism of a judicial officer cannot be punished absent evidence of "a clear, present and imminent danger to the investigation . . . and to the proper administration of justice."[51]

Summary Points

For the mass media there is hardly a more traditional and important activity than covering the justice system. Sometimes coverage may compromise other important interests, however, such as the right to a fair trial.

Judges in the lower courts are responsible for assuring the fairness of proceedings, and they have many tools for mitigating the potential effects of media publicity. Most of these tools, such as the change of venue or admonishment of the jury, do not infringe on the First Amendment rights of the media.

Prior restraints on the media (gag orders) and closure of traditionally open proceedings are two judicial actions that are considered interferences with free expression. Therefore, these actions are constitutional only under very rare circumstances, when the courts have specific evidence to show they are necessary. Gag orders on trial participants are more likely to be valid, however, and a few kinds of court proceedings are closed by tradition.

Sometimes the tables are turned, and it is the justice system that wants the media to provide testimony, notes, negatives, or other work-product materials as evidence in a proceeding. A practice of answering subpoenas may be deleterious to news-gathering efforts, however. Many courts have recognized a limited First Amendment privilege for the media to keep their unpublished information confidential.

Many states have gone even further by enacting shield laws for the media, though the scope and strength of these laws vary considerably from state to state. Under the Privacy Protection Act of 1980, law-enforcement agencies generally cannot resort to newsroom searches in an effort to obtain information directly. Rather, they must use the subpoena process.

When journalists or other people disrupt court proceedings or disobey court orders, judges may have the authority to punish that behavior by issuing citations for contempt. Criminal contempt is punishment for past misconduct and results in a fixed fine or jail term. Civil contempt is an effort to coerce compliance with a court order and thus the fine or jail time is indeterminate.

The chapter hypothetical raised three separate legal issues: whether you had a privilege to refuse to testify in court, whether you could overturn the judge's gag order, and whether the courtroom closure was valid. Most likely you would be required to testify in court, even if the state had a strong shield law. This is because it is a criminal defendant seeking the testimony—a Sixth Amendment right—and the testimony is relevant and probably not available from others. The judge's gag order, on the other hand, would be unconstitutional because it was issued without the accompanying findings required by the *Nebraska Press* case. As for the courtroom closure, it, too, was ordered without the requisite judicial findings and would likely fail the other three prongs of the closure test that evolved from the *Press-Enterprise* cases.

Discussion Questions

1. Many of the access questions discussed in Chapter 6 could be much simplified, it seems, if the Supreme Court would extend the rule of *Richmond Newspaper v. Virginia,* discussed in this chapter, to government proceedings

and information in the executive and legislative branches. Is the argument equally compelling, for example, that city council meetings have traditionally been open and that their continued openness therefore should be guaranteed by the First Amendment? If such a First Amendment right of access were extended to all traditionally public government meetings and records beyond the judicial realm, would this be an improvement over the current jurisdiction-by-jurisdiction system of access statutes?

2. With camera access to courtrooms now the rule rather than the exception, broadcast and cable television channels, such as Court TV, sometimes offer live, gavel-to-gavel coverage of both criminal and civil trials. Occasionally these trials include graphic testimony that many would consider unfit for children. In the long run, do you think such television coverage is in the public's best interest? Or is there an overriding public interest in letting some kinds of judicial proceedings be decided behind closed doors?

3. In the *Stanford Daily* case, the newspaper essentially argued that it is less troublesome for journalists to be served with subpoenas than with search warrants. Why? Why, exactly, would news organizations prefer to deal with subpoenas for materials than with search warrants?

Key Terms

bench/bar/media committees
change of venue
contempt of court
continuance
gag order
impartial jury

jury admonitions
sequestration
shield laws
subpoena
voir dire

Web Resources

http://www.rcfp.org/csi/
Confidential Sources and Information, by the Reporters' Committee for Freedom of the Press (a practical online guide to the status of the reporter's privilege in all 50 states)

InfoTrac® College Edition

All but a few states allow at least some kind of camera access in their courtrooms, at a judge's discretion. Yet there remains considerable debate about the appropriateness of cameras in various kinds of courts and proceedings. Find an article that details a recent debate over cameras in judicial proceedings.

Chapter Outline

Creative Property

Upon completing this chapter you should

- [ ] **understand** the separate purposes of copyright and trademark laws and the general scope of those laws.
- [ ] **know** the legal requirements for attaining copyright or trademark protection and the benefits of government registration schemes.
- [ ] **know** some common ways in which creative property rights are licensed to others in the major media industries.
- [ ] **know** how infringement lawsuits can arise and applicable remedies and penalties for infringement.
- [ ] **understand** the extent to which the creative property of others may be used without violating the law.
- [ ] **know** how unfair competition law can be applied to fill in the gaps between copyright and trademark laws.

Hypothetical

■ The Tangled Documentary

Suppose that you are producing a two-hour TV documentary about horse racing in America—its history, present, and future. You hope to market the program to dozens of independent, commercial stations across the country. This is a complicated project, of course, and the final version will blend information derived from hundreds of sources.

You and your production team generate much of the content from scratch, including taped interviews with leading trainers and jockeys and video of the horses going through their daily training regimens. You are particularly proud of these interviews and behind-the-scenes video segments because they were accomplished with a lot of effort and artistic flair.

But you also draw from materials that were created by others. For instance, in the historical portion of the documentary you rely heavily on newspaper and magazine commentary describing such highlights as War Admiral's Kentucky Derby victory in 1937 and the record-shattering performance by Secretariat in the 1973 Belmont Stakes. Paragraphs from the previously published columns of well-known sportswriters are reproduced visually on your videotape and the narrator quotes large portions of the commentaries. You also reproduce photographs, as they originally appeared in newspapers and magazines, without asking anyone for permission.

You need lots of music for this dramatic documentary, so you decide the best solution is to purchase records and tapes of popular hits from the last few years and to integrate that music into your action video segments.

You title the documentary *Hooves,* and a distinctive logo is designed to assist in marketing. It combines the program's title with a sketch of a pounding horse hoof. As the project nears completion, you become worried that others may attempt to capitalize on your title and logo by using similar names and artwork. You are also concerned about protecting your entire documentary against other producers who would love to tape your program off the air and use portions of it in their own programming.

Does your liberal quoting from the sportswriters' columns and the reproduction of photographs present potential copyright infringement problems for you? How about the way you obtained music for your program—do you need special permission to use those tunes and, if so, how is it obtained? What steps, if any, can you take to protect your documentary and its logo against unauthorized use by others?

Introduction

Property laws are concerned with the rights of ownership in things. With ownership of a personal computer, for example, comes exclusive legal rights—such as the right to determine whether the machine will ever be lent or rented to others. Less obviously, perhaps, disputes involving copyrights and trademarks also involve the principles of property law. The property concept is not limited to physical things like computers, cars, and office buildings; it includes intangible creations, such as arrangements of musical notes, pictures, and words.

These creative forms of property are sometimes called **intellectual property** because they are products of the mind and have legal status apart from any physical product upon which they may be fixed. For example, suppose a business owner dreams up an advertising script and writes it on a piece of paper. A visiting competitor happens to glimpse the paper, copies the script into his electronic notepad, and then uses the material in his own business. The competitor never took anything tangible. Yet he may well have violated the intellectual property rights of the scriptwriter.

This chapter discusses two main forms of intangible property: copyrights and trademarks. It also looks briefly at how the law of unfair competition has evolved to fill the gaps between copyright and trademark protection.

Copyright

Copyright may be defined as a proprietary right of control over literary or artistic creations. It is the lifeblood of television and film production companies, magazines, book publishers, record companies, and freelance writers and artists in all fields. Copyright is also an important asset of news organizations. But copyright law also drastically restricts these same companies' and individuals' freedom to borrow material from others.

Under the sanction of copyright, owners are afforded virtual monopolies over their protected works of expression. The primary purpose of copyright protection is not to make writers and artists rich, but to encourage creative production for the ultimate benefit of society at large. This is accomplished by giving individual writers, artists, and media organizations control over how and when their works will be exploited commercially. Without this legal protection creators would be discouraged from producing because anyone else could copy and market the original creators' works and usurp their rightful profits. Also, publishing and production companies would hesitate to invest in major projects, knowing that the creations could be pirated without restraint by their competitors. The theory of copyright law, then, is to give creators economic incentive so that society will benefit from creative production.

The power of Congress to enact copyright laws is derived directly from Article I, Section 8 of the U.S. Constitution, which states in part: "The Congress shall have power . . . to promote the progress of science and useful arts, by securing for limited times to authors and inventors the exclusive right to their respective writings and discoveries. . . ." Under authority of this clause Congress has enacted patent legislation to create ownership rights in inventions as well as copyright laws to protect expression.

The first copyright statute in the United States was adopted by Congress in 1790 and the law has been substantially revised many times since. The last comprehensive revision came with the Copyright Act of 1976, which took effect on January 1, 1978.[1] This chapter focuses on the 1976 act, although some sections of the act it replaced, the 1909 Copyright Act, are still relevant to copyrights in existence before the new act took effect.

Congress has since updated the 1976 law in an effort to keep pace with advancing technology and international agreements. For example, the Berne Convention Implementation Act of 1988, which took effect on March 1, 1989, sought to bring U.S. law into accord with an international copyright agreement, the Berne Convention for the Protection of Literary and Artistic Works. In 1998 Congress passed the Copyright Term Extension Act, adding years to the duration of copyright protection, as some other nations had done. That same year Congress also enacted the Digital Millennium Copyright Act to address issues relating to copyright in cyberspace. That act will be discussed in more detail in Chapter 13, "The Internet."

In the United States today copyright law is a matter of federal jurisdiction. The Copyright Act of 1976 specifically preempts state common law protections that existed along with federal law until that time. Copyright disputes arising under the 1976 act are heard only in the federal courts. The day-to-day administration of copyright formalities is delegated to the U.S. Copyright Office, which is part of the Library of Congress. The office registers copyright claims, accepts copies of works, and records documents relating to copyright ownership and transfers.

Protected Works

Copyright protection applies to "original works of authorship, fixed in any tangible medium of expression."[2] To understand the copyright law, it is essential to understand the components of this description of copyrightable works.

Expression

The term *work of authorship* refers to any creation that is primarily expressive in nature. Copyright protects the creator's particular manner of expression, as distinguished from ideas or underlying facts. No particular degree of literary or artistic merit is required in order to attain protection. But the work must have involved some expressive effort.

For purposes of illustration, the 1976 Copyright Act lists the following seven categories of works of authorship:

1. literary works;
2. musical works, including accompanying words;
3. dramatic works, including accompanying music;
4. pantomimes and choreographic works;
5. pictorial, graphic, and sculptural works;

6. motion pictures and other audiovisual works; and

7. sound recordings.[3]

Computer programs are considered literary works and thus are copyrightable under the first category. Likewise, test questions—and essay answers—may qualify for copyright protection as literary material. Photographs, maps, charts, technical drawings, and diagrams are all copyrightable forms of expression under the fifth category, pictorial and graphic works. Cartoon characters such as Mickey Mouse or Charlie Brown are protected as pictorial works.

Remember that it is not the information contained in, say, a news story or a map that is protected by copyright. Such a rule would have the repressive effect of preventing others from writing about the same event or publishing a map of the same region. Rather, it is the particular manner of expression that is covered by copyright—the phrasing of the news story, the graphic method of depicting mountains and highways on the map. As a general rule, if there is only one way to state something, it is not copyrightable. For example, the scientific equation $E = mc^2$ could not have been copyrighted by Albert Einstein.

Similarly, raw ideas—including ideas that underlie an expressive work—cannot be protected. For example, the general idea or plot for a screenplay cannot be protected. Nor can the basic idea for a literary character. But the actual dialogue, the detailed traits of the characters, and the specific scene descriptions all are forms of expression that can be protected by copyright.[4] Fictional literary characters such as James Bond can be protected by copyright, independent of a particular story, to the extent that an author has delineated sufficiently distinctive characteristics to transcend the setting of an individual screenplay or novel (Exhibit 8.1).

An important limitation is that names, titles, and other short phrases, even though expressive, do not qualify as works of authorship for purposes of copyright protection. Depending on how they are used, names and short phrases—including the names of literary characters or periodicals—may be protected under the more limited scope of trademark or unfair competition laws. For copyright protection, however, a more extended work of expression—something beyond a label or identification—is required. If this weren't the rule, simple newspaper headlines and mere terms, such as *star wars,* could be preempted from the marketplace.

Originality

In addition to the requirement of being a work of expression, copyright law specifies that the work be original. Originality simply means that the author created the work—that it is not simply a reproduction of existing material. There is no requirement that the work be unique, however. Two or more photographers might take pictures of the Grand Canyon from the same vantage point, at the same time of day and year, such that the photos are barely distinguishable. But as long

EXHIBIT 8.1

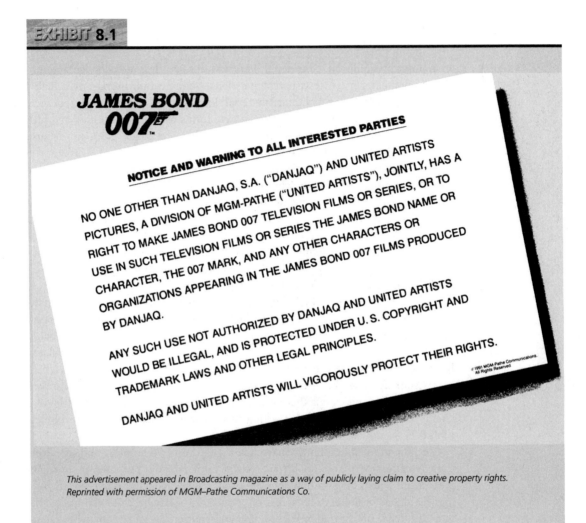

This advertisement appeared in Broadcasting magazine as a way of publicly laying claim to creative property rights. Reprinted with permission of MGM–Pathe Communications Co.

as each performed the camera work independently, rather than copying someone else's photo, the photographers will have created copyrightable works. The photos need not be novel or distinctive, just original. In this respect copyright law is much different from patent law, which applies only to novel inventions, and from trademark law, as discussed later in this chapter.

Works may be copyrightable even though they include some unoriginal components, however. The Copyright Act specifically affords protection to **compilations** and to **derivative works**.[5] In both cases original, creative effort is added to preexisting material in such a way that a new, copyrightable work of authorship is created.

A compilation is a work formed by the collection and assembly of preexisting information. Examples may include business directories, databases, and stock price lists. The individual bits of information contained in such works are not original creations of the compilation author, and taken individually they may not even be copyrightable. Yet the compilation as a whole is an original, copyrightable work if the information is selected, arranged, and presented through independent effort and with "a modicum of creativity," to use the judicial phrase.

For example, a federal District Court concluded in 1991 that *O'Dwyer's Directory of Public Relations Firms,* an annual listing of over one thousand PR agencies, was a copyrightable compilation. Each individual listing, which included a firm name, address, and list of employees, was purely rote information that lacked the requisite originality to support a copyright, the court said. But O'Dwyer's creative effort in soliciting the listings and determining which firms qualified for inclusion was significantly creative to render the directory as a whole a copyrightable compilation.[6]

In contrast, the U.S. Supreme Court held in 1991 that the white-page listings in a telephone directory did not amount to a copyrightable compilation. Although the telephone company did hold a valid copyright on other portions of the directory, said Justice O'Connor for the unanimous Court in *Feist Publications, Inc. v. Rural Telephone Service Co.,* the white-page listings lacked the originality necessary to qualify as a protected compilation. Not only were the raw data—telephone subscribers' names, towns, and phone numbers—uncopyrightable facts, but the way in which the company selected and arranged that data was not original in any way, the Court concluded. Wrote Justice O'Connor:

> The originality requirement is not particularly stringent. A compiler may settle upon a selection or arrangement that others have used; novelty is not required. Originality requires only that the author make the selection or arrangement independently (i.e., without copying that selection or arrangement from another work), and that it display some minimal level of creativity. Presumably, the vast majority of compilations will pass this test, but not all will. There remains a narrow category of works in which the creative spark is utterly lacking or so trivial as to be virtually nonexistent.[7]

Compilations may be made up of contributions that are themselves expressive works. These compilations are called **collective works.** Examples would include a magazine containing freelancers' articles or an anthology of short stories by various writers. Though the creator of the collection did not write the contributions, the added elements of selection, editing, and arrangement amount to an original, copyrightable work of authorship. This does not mean that the collection author

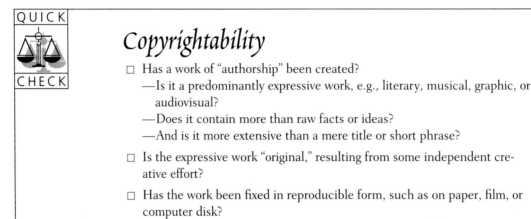

Copyrightability

- ☐ Has a work of "authorship" been created?
  - —Is it a predominantly expressive work, e.g., literary, musical, graphic, or audiovisual?
  - —Does it contain more than raw facts or ideas?
  - —And is it more extensive than a mere title or short phrase?
- ☐ Is the expressive work "original," resulting from some independent creative effort?
- ☐ Has the work been fixed in reproducible form, such as on paper, film, or computer disk?

gains copyright control over the individual contributions to the collection, however. It may even be that the individual contributions are protected by separate copyrights and that the collection author was able to reprint them only with permission. But there now exists a copyrightable work apart from those individual components.

A derivative work is defined as a work based upon one or more preexisting works, such as a translation, dramatization, fictionalization, condensation, or any other form in which the preexisting work is recast or adapted in some way. Here again, the creator of the derivative work is adding sufficient amounts of original, creative effort to the preexisting material so that a new, copyrightable work is created. (But this doesn't mean one is always free to make a derivative work. If the underlying work is protected by copyright, making a derivative work from it without consent can amount to copyright infringement, as discussed later.)

Fixation

Finally, in order for copyright protection to apply, the original work of authorship must be fixed in a tangible medium. In other words, the work must be embodied on paper, film, tape, computer disk, or other medium such that the work can be reproduced. Copyright law does not protect sounds or images of purely transitory duration, such as a live broadcast of an impromptu news report. The report would be fixed, however, if it had been written on paper, videotaped in advance, or taped, at the author's direction, simultaneously with the broadcast transmission. Live sports broadcasts typically are protected by copyright because the broadcasts are simultaneously fixed in tangible form, on videotape or audio tape.

To use another example, a college professor's spontaneous lecture, though certainly an original work of authorship, would not qualify for copyright protection because of the lack of fixation. But a lecture could indeed meet this basic copyright requirement if the speaker were operating from a set of notes or if the lecturer were taping the performance. Also, although a lack of fixation would preclude copyright, the speaker is not left totally unprotected by law. For example, the law of appropriation, discussed in Chapter 5, could prevent unauthorized people from commercially marketing the comments under the speaker's name.[8]

Ownership

Ownership of copyright can be an extremely valuable property asset. Sometimes this value is a function of time, such as when the early recordings of a musical group become more marketable as the group gains stature over the years. Or the work could be of significant value immediately, even when the creator is not well known. An example of this is the bystander's film of President John Kennedy's assassination, the Zapruder film, which was purchased by Time, Inc. In some cases, copyrights are marketed for significant value even before they are finished. In 1988, for example, Warner Books bid nearly $5 million for the right to publish the authorized sequel to *Gone with the Wind,* even though the book would not be completed until 1991. Copyright ownership, then, is something to be taken seriously.

Contrary to popular belief, ownership rights in copyright are not acquired through any formal procedure, such as registration or public notice. Rather, copyright ownership begins at the moment a work that can be protected is created. Public notice and government registration are significant for other reasons, as explained shortly, but ownership accrues without these formalities.

Another basic principle to remember about copyright ownership is that it is entirely distinct from ownership of the physical object that embodies a copyrighted work. Therefore, ownership of the tangible object does not necessarily include ownership of the copyright. For example, courts have held that when the writer of a letter sends the letter to another person, the recipient becomes the owner of the physical object—the actual piece of paper. But absent an agreement to the contrary, the writer typically retains copyright ownership over the contents. Thus the recipient would not have the right to publish the letter, absent an understanding to the contrary.[9]

Work Made For Hire

Generally speaking, when an individual writer or artist creates a work, she immediately becomes the original owner of the copyright. When the work is created at the behest of someone else, however, initial ownership may belong to the buyer rather than to the individual creator of the work. The key legal question is whether the creator was acting as an employee of the buyer. If so, the copyrightable material is called **work made for hire,** and ownership vests automatically with the employer, absent an agreement to the contrary.[10]

Typical work-for-hire materials include the stories written by staff reporters at a newspaper, the video shot by camera operators at a TV station, and the diagrams created for a magazine by its full-time graphic artist. In these cases the creators are formal, salaried employees, and the copyright to the works they produce within the scope of their employment belongs to their employers. But in many cases, such as with freelance artists working on assignment, determining whether works are made for hire has been a cloudy legal question.

In the 1989 case of *Community for Creative Non-Violence v. Reid*[11] the U.S. Supreme Court helped clarify the meaning of *employment* under the work-for-hire doctrine. The Community for Creative Non-Violence (CCNV), a nonprofit organization concerned with homelessness in America, hired artist James Reid to produce a sculpture for a display that would dramatize the plight of the homeless. Reid and CCNV reached a general understanding about how the sculpture would look and how much it would cost. But the parties had no agreement about who would own the copyright; that topic was never mentioned.

Reid worked on the sculpture for two months, and during that time CCNV members occasionally visited the studio to check on his progress and make suggestions. Reid delivered the completed statue of three human figures to CCNV for use in a Christmastime display. Reid was paid $15,000 for his work. After the display CCNV returned the statue to Reid for minor repairs and began making plans to take the work on a nationwide fundraising tour. But when CCNV asked Reid to return the sculpture, he refused, claiming he owned the copyright. CCNV sought a court order requiring Reid to return the sculpture.

The copyright question hinged on whether Reid was an employee of CCNV, in which case CCNV would own the copyright, or whether he was an independent contractor, in which case Reid would retain the copyright. It is essentially a distinction based on which party maintained the greatest degree of control over creation of the work. The Supreme Court held that whether a person is an employee for copyright purposes is to be determined by examining several factors, such as which party supplies the instrumentalities and tools, the location of the work site, the length of the working relationship between the parties, the hiring party's right to control how the work is accomplished, and the extent of the artist's discretion over when and how long to work.

By applying the factors the Court concluded that Reid was not an employee but an independent contractor. Reid worked in his own studio in another city and supplied his own tools; he was retained for only two months; he had absolute freedom to control his work schedule; and CCNV was not in a position to supervise the work closely. Therefore, without a formal agreement that the work would be considered made-for-hire or that the copyright would be assigned to CCNV, Reid retained the copyright to his work.

Despite the Supreme Court's list of factors, though, the work-made-for-hire doctrine still carries an area of uncertainty. Furthermore, as a practical matter many communications professionals are entirely unfamiliar with the doctrine and do not even think about copyright ownership until a dispute arises. A common point of contention, for example, is whether the copyright in an advertising design belongs to the client advertiser or to the ad agency that created it. Controversies also have arisen over whether the materials created by student newspaper staffs are owned entirely by the schools or whether the individual students retain the copyright to their works. Such disputes and uncertainty over copyright ownership can almost always be avoided if the parties simply enter a written agreement in advance, designating who the owner will be.

For one common scenario, though, the Copyright Act does provide greater certainty. When a freelancer is commissioned to contribute to a collective work, such as a magazine or newspaper, the contribution is a work made for hire only if the parties expressly agree in writing to that designation.[12]

Joint Authorship

Sometimes works entitled to copyright protection have more than one author. The Copyright Act calls these **joint works,** defined as material "prepared by two or more authors with the intention that their contributions be merged into inseparable or interdependent parts of a unitary whole."[13] In such cases the authors are co-owners of the copyright and share in its profits. A common example of this is the musical composition for which one person writes the lyrics while another creates the melody. Another example would be a textbook on which two or more authors collaborated, each writing a portion of the chapters.

Note that the intent of the authors is critical to the definition. To qualify as a joint work, two or more authors must have intended to merge their efforts into a cohesive product at the time the work was created. If a composer created a tune as an instrumental solo, for example, a lyricist's addition of words sometime later would not convert the song into a joint work. The later version would be a derivative work.

Though Congress provided a definition for joint works, it did not attempt to specify all the rights and duties of the co-owners. That task was left for the courts, and it has been filled with difficult questions. For example, does each joint author own an equal interest in the joint work, regardless of the author's level of contribution? (Generally, yes.) May one joint owner, without the consent of the other joint owners, authorize outsiders to copy the work? (In most cases, yes.) May one joint owner transfer his entire share to another party, without the other joint owners' consent? (Yes, absent an agreement to the contrary.)

The joint ownership picture can be further complicated in the eight community property states (Arizona, California, Idaho, Louisiana, Nevada, New Mexico, Texas, and Washington). *Community property* is a form of marital ownership. Its basic tenet is that any property earned by one spouse during marriage is automatically co-owned by the other spouse. This rule would apply to copyrights created or otherwise acquired during marriage, unless husband and wife entered a written agreement to the contrary. Therefore, the spouses of joint authors also may acquire joint ownership privileges in their own right.

In determining the rights of ownership of joint works, the courts generally have adopted the rules that apply to other kinds of property, such as real estate. It is a highly complicated area, and the details are well beyond the scope of this book. However, two general points are worth remembering: The first is that joint copyright ownership, profitable though it might be, is also a formula for legal complications down the road. These complications typically arise when the creative team breaks up, perhaps after the death of one member, and the joint owners, including the heirs of the deceased member, disagree over how the copyright should be marketed.

The second point is that, here again, the legal problems can be avoided to some extent if the joint authors enter a written agreement spelling out the terms of their relationship in advance. These are called **collaboration agreements,** and they are enforceable contracts. Vital to any well-drafted agreement is a section concerning how the copyright will be owned and managed. For example, an agreement might stipulate that no one author may grant outsiders permission to use the copyrighted work without the consent of all joint owners. Collaboration agreements also are useful for clarifying such non-copyright matters as how the joint authors will divide the expenses and share the income, how the team's production and decision-making process will work, and how the credits will appear on the work.

Government Works

Works of the U.S. government, such as reports, consumer publications, films, regulations, and judicial opinions, are specifically precluded from copyright ownership.[14] Such taxpayer-funded works may be copied and used by anyone, barring some other legal restriction. However, this rule applies only to works created by federal government employees as part of their official duties. Materials prepared for the government by private consultants are protected. Also, the federal government is not precluded from owning copyrights that are transferred to it—for example, by bequest.

Nothing in the Copyright Act prevents state or local governments from owning copyrights to the works created by their employees. However, as a practical matter, governments rarely seek to enforce the prerogatives of copyright ownership against residents. Also, as to official government enactments, such as statutes, courts have ruled consistently that these are not copyrightable.[15]

Duration of Ownership

The U.S. Constitution gives Congress the power to protect copyrights only for limited periods. The 1976 act specifies the periods of protection for works created after January 1, 1978. When the applicable period expires, the work falls into the

| EXHIBIT **8.2** | *Copyright Duration* |

Category of Work	Term of Protection
Published prior to 1923	Copyright has expired
Published 1923 to 1963	95 years, if renewed in 28th year
Published 1964 to 1977	95 years
Created, but not published, before 1978	Author's life plus 70 years
Created 1978 or later, by sole author	Author's life plus 70 years
Created 1978 or later, by joint authors	Life of longest-living co-author plus 70 years
Created 1978 or later, as work for hire	95 years from year of first publication or 120 years from creation, whichever comes first

Note: This exhibit does not list all possible copyright terms.

public domain forever. This means that the copyright can never again be owned; the work is available to be freely copied or published by anyone without fear of infringing on copyright. The general period of protection is the lifetime of the author, plus seventy years. For works made for hire, it is ninety-five years from the year of first publication or 120 years from the year of creation, whichever occurs first.

Works created prior to 1978 may have different terms of protection, however, because they initially were governed by the federal Copyright Act of 1909 or by state common law, both of which specified ownership durations different from the modern act. Under the 1909 act, federal copyright protection began when the work was published or registered, and it ran for an initial period of twenty-eight years. The author then could renew for one more 28-year term. The 1976 act contains special duration provisions for works that were under a subsisting copyright term as of January 1, 1978, in an attempt to bring the terms of protection into greater conformity with the new law. Under these special provisions the term of protection differs according to whether the work was published or unpublished as of 1978 and whether a renewal application had been filed in accordance with the 1909 act.[16]

In 1998 Congress passed the Sonny Bono Copyright Term Extension Act which amended the 1976 act by adding 20 years of protection for most works. See Exhibit 8.2 for a summary of copyright durations.

Sometimes it's easy to determine whether the copyright protection for another's work has expired. But other times it's hard to determine. Copies may have been published with missing or incorrect copyright notices, for example. Such irregularities could easily lead a person to miscalculate the duration of protection. Therefore, it is highly advisable to consult a qualified attorney before copying works on the assumption they are in the public domain. A search of Copyright Office records may be necessary, and a lawyer may need to analyze documents pertaining to the ownership and transfer of a copyright.

Copyright protection in a work may be cut short if the copyright owner voluntarily places it into the public domain. Under the modern copyright statute, however, you cannot assume that a work belongs to the public domain absent a specific direction from the owner, such as "I hereby grant this work to the public domain." Even for works governed by the prior statute, extensive distribution and news media coverage does not signal a lack of copyright protection. For example, a federal appeals court held in 1999 that Dr. Martin Luther King, Jr. did not place his famous "I Have a Dream" speech into the public domain when he delivered it in front of the Lincoln Memorial in 1963—even if 200,000 people were present and millions more were listening via live radio and television.[17]

Moral Rights

Historically in the United States the owner of a copyrighted work enjoyed virtually complete freedom to treat it as she or he wished—to edit it, change its color, alter its title, even to destroy it. However, this prerogative of ownership raises serious ethical questions when the owner is not the original creator of the work and the work is a piece of significant art. Painters, sculptors, photographers, and filmmakers do not always own the copyrights to their works, having transferred the ownership to others or created the material as work for hire. But these artists often feel emotional attachment to their work, their reputations are connected to the work, and they—rather than owners whose main concern may be a financial investment—are considered the best arbiters of artistic form. Therefore, artists in the United States have lobbied with increasing intensity in recent years for the recognition of some perpetual **moral rights** to their works, distinct from the rights of copyright ownership. Institutional owners of copyrights have opposed any changes in the law that would diminish their traditional rights to alter and market their property as they see fit.

Moral rights of artists long have been recognized by law in some other countries, particularly in Europe. The concept, first developed by French courts in the early 1800s, typically involves two components: (1) a right to attribution, meaning the right of an artist to control the use of his name in association with the work; and (2) a right to integrity, meaning an artist's right to control alterations and prevent distortion or destruction of the work.

Since 1928 protection of moral rights has been a tenet of the international Berne Convention copyright agreement. When the United States joined the convention in 1989, it became necessary for this country to recognize moral rights or risk falling into noncompliance. Initially, Congress declined to add specific moral rights provisions to the Copyright Act, concluding that adequate protection could be achieved through an existing patchwork of rights arising under contract law, privacy law, defamation law, unfair competition law, and a handful of state statutes protecting moral rights.[18]

But in 1990 Congress enacted the Visual Artists Rights Act, amending portions of the Copyright Act to provide some limited federal protection for moral rights.[19] The law protects both a right to attribution and a right to integrity. Artists have a right always to be known as the creators of their works, as well as a right to prevent use of their names on modified versions of their work if the modifications could harm their reputations. Artists also have the right to prevent any intentional distortion or mutilation of their works.

The Visual Artists Rights Act is narrow in its scope, however—narrower than the protections called for in the Berne Convention. The act applies only to paintings, drawings, prints, sculptures, and exhibition photographs and only if they exist in a single copy or in limited editions of no more than 200 copies. Furthermore, the moral rights provisions do not apply if the works were made for hire, and the term of any moral rights protection is limited to the life of the artist. It remains to be seen how vigorously the courts will employ this act, as well as other legal theories, to secure moral rights for creators of artistic works.

Formalities

For an asset that can be worth huge sums of money, copyright ownership is remarkably simple to originate; it is basically self-executing. Ownership begins automatically as soon as work is fixed in a tangible form. There is no need for prior investigation or approval by a government agency. However, two optional formalities—registration and notice—do offer significant advantages for the copyright owner.

Registration

The owner of a copyright may register it with the federal government at any time within the life of the copyright, either before or after publication. Registration is obtained by sending to the Copyright Office the following items:

1. *Completed registration form.* The appropriate form is determined by the class of material. For example, works of the visual arts are registered using Form VA; Form TX is for textual material; and Form SR is for sound recordings.

2. *Filing fee of $30.* Works in unpublished form sometimes may be registered as a collection, under one application fee. This would be particularly advantageous, for example, for a series of fifty photographs.

3. *Nonreturnable deposit of the work being registered.* The general requirement is one complete copy of unpublished works, two complete copies of works already published.[20]

The Copyright Office receives more than 500,000 registration applications per year. The office briefly examines each application to determine that all requested information has been provided and that the material is of a copyrightable nature. A certificate of registration is issued, effective the date application materials were received.

Though not a requirement for ownership, registration establishes a public record of the copyright claim and serves as court evidence (though not necessarily conclusive evidence) of the validity of ownership. Furthermore, registration is necessary before the copyright owner may file an infringement suit in court. If the registration is made promptly—within three months after publication of the work or prior to an infringement—the owner may collect attorney's fees and certain statutory damage amounts from infringers. (Otherwise, only an award of actual damages and profits is available to the copyright owner. These remedies are discussed in more detail shortly.)

Copyright Notice

A proper copyright notice should be affixed to all publicly distributed copies of protected works, and it should appear in a position where the public would reasonably look for it. Notice consists of the following elements:

1. The word *copyright,* or the international symbol © (or in the case of sound recordings, the letter *P* in a circle)

2. The year of first publication

3. The name of the copyright owner

Traditionally, failure by the owner to affix a notice on all publicly distributed copies of a work meant automatic loss of copyright protection. Legally speaking, lack of notice was taken as a signal that the owner was allowing the work to pass immediately into the public domain. The 1976 act was less harsh than the earlier law; it allowed copyright ownership to continue if the notice was omitted only from a small portion of the distributed copies or if the owner made an effort to add the notice as soon as the omission was discovered.

However, in accord with the Berne Convention, notice became entirely optional for works publicly distributed after March 1, 1989. The Copyright Act now reads that a copyright notice "may" be placed on a publicly distributed copies.[21] The main legal advantage of including a notice is that it warns potential infringers and prevents a copyright infringer from receiving leniency on grounds of innocent infringement.

Infringement

Earlier in this chapter it was stated that a copyright owner possessed a virtual monopoly over the protected work. More specifically, the owner of copyright is accorded by law a bundle of exclusive, overlapping rights. The owner may do, or authorize others to do, any of the following with respect to the copyrighted work:

☐ Display publicly

☐ Distribute publicly

☐ Reproduce

☐ Adapt (prepare derivative works)

☐ Perform publicly[22]

Copyright infringement occurs when one or more of these exclusive rights of ownership is violated. For example, professional photographer Art Rogers of California produced a photo of a married couple posed on a bench with their eight German shepherd puppies. The memorable picture, titled *Puppies,* was exhibited in art museums and then licensed by Rogers to be reproduced on notecards. A few years later Jeff Koons, a well-known New York sculptor who had purchased some of the notecards, produced a sculpture modeled directly after the photograph, without the photographer's consent. Three of the 62-inch-long sculptures were sold for a total of $367,000. When Rogers learned of this, he sued Koons for infringement.

In his defense, Koons argued that no infringement occurred because copyright protection was limited to use of the work as a photograph. But the District Court disagreed. The manner in which Rogers arranged his subjects and carried out his photographer's art constituted a protected, original act of expression, the court held, and reproduction in sculpture form violated Rogers' exclusive right to make derivative works. A change in medium did not avoid infringement.[23]

To prove infringement plaintiffs must first show that they indeed own a valid copyright interest. The next step is simply to establish that the defendant engaged in substantial, unauthorized copying from the protected work. This is easily accomplished when exact reproduction is involved, as would be the case if a radio news director conducted his show by reading stories word for word from the local newspaper. (This was the problem in the hypothetical scenario that began Chapter 1.)

More commonly, though, lawsuits involve some altered use of the protected material. In such cases infringement typically is proved by two-pronged evidence: access to the copyrighted work coupled with substantial similarity.

Substantial Similarity and Access

Substantial similarity is a matter of degree, to be decided by the jury. Suppose, for example, that the radio news director obtained his material from the local newspaper but altered the wording somewhat. In an infringement case brought by the newspaper the jurors would be asked to compare the newspaper stories with transcripts of the radio reports and decide whether the allegedly infringing work bears a remarkable resemblance to the plaintiff's stories.

The jury also must distinguish between similarity in the underlying facts or ideas and similarity in manner of expression. Only in the latter case is the similarity evidence of copyright infringement. It would be entirely permissible, for example, for the radio announcer to take facts from the newspaper stories and rework the manner of expressing them. Facts, remember, are not copyrighted and therefore cannot be infringed.

To complete a case for infringement, it also must be established that the defendant had access to the copyrighted work prior to creating the alleged infringement. It is possible, after all, that the defendant, working entirely independently, created a substantially similar work. Such a creation would not infringe copyright. But if the defendant had previously seen or heard the copyrighted work, the jury may legally conclude that the similarity was indeed the result of copying and that infringement has occurred.

Access may be established by circumstantial evidence, such as a defendant's subscription to the newspaper in which an allegedly infringed story appeared. Furthermore, it is not necessary to show that defendant copied directly or intentionally from the protected work. In one high-profile case it was even found that illegal copying had occurred subconsciously. In 1976 a federal court held that musician George Harrison, formerly of the famous rock group the Beatles, had infringed a tune recorded previously by the Chiffons. Harrison's song, "My Sweet Lord," contained a melody almost identical to portions of the earlier work, "He's So Fine." No evidence suggested that Harrison deliberately copied from the Chiffons or that he was even specifically aware of their tune. Yet the court concluded that Harrison had indeed heard the song at some point, and that "his subconscious knew . . . a song his conscious mind did not remember."[24]

Enforcement

When a copyright is being infringed, the first step for the owner in most instances is to send a cease-and-desist letter to the culprits, informing them of the owner's rights and demanding a stop to the unauthorized use. Most infringements are resolved out of court through an initial letter, some telephone negotiations, and perhaps a settlement agreement.

Should these efforts fail, a copyright owner whose works are being infringed also has several remedies available through the courts. The first is an injunction ordering the defendant to stop using the owner's work. The injunction, issued by a federal district judge, is a relatively quick remedy intended to prevent further harm to the owner's copyright interest.

A copyright owner also may sue an alleged infringer to obtain actual damages and profits. *Actual damages* is a sum of money equal to what the owner lost as a result of the infringement. For example, if a college professor without permission photocopied a textbook and provided free copies to his students, the publishing company would not make the money it otherwise would have from sales. This lost amount would equal actual damages. Sometimes the plaintiff's actual loss is not nearly as much as the infringer's wrongful gain, however. In this case, the plaintiff also may be awarded an amount representing the defendant's additional profits from use of the copyrighted work. For example, suppose the professor had sold photocopies of the pilfered manuscript to students at a price nearly double the retail price of the book. The publisher could sue to collect the infringer's extra profits.

Instead of collecting actual damages and profits, a copyright owner may elect to recover **statutory damages** from the infringer. This is particularly likely when the amount of the owner's actual loss, or the defendant's profits, is negligible or hard to determine. In such cases the Copyright Act nevertheless specifies amounts the owner may be awarded. For non-willful infringement, the amount ordinarily is between $500 and $20,000, at the judge's discretion, for each work infringed. If the copyright owner can prove the infringement was committed willfully—with full awareness of its illegality—the statutory award may go as high as $100,000.[25]

For example, in a 1984 case several record companies together sued for willful infringement of thirty-five copyrighted sound recordings. Defendants were found to have produced counterfeit copies of the recordings—exact copies made and marketed without permission. The plaintiffs were able to prove actual damages and infringer profits of less than $100,000. But the judge granted statutory damages at near the maximum allowable, for a total of $1.5 million.[26]

If done willfully and for purposes of financial gain, copyright infringement can also amount to a criminal offense. Willful infringers may be indicted and prosecuted under federal criminal statutes, in addition to the civil proceedings described previously. If convicted, first offenders generally face fines of as much as $25,000 and/or imprisonment for as long as a year.[27] Criminal prosecution is most likely in piracy cases, where counterfeit copies of tapes, films, or other materials are produced and marketed in blatant disregard of their copyright protection.

Clearly, copyright infringement can become an expensive and embarrassing legal problem for the infringer. Thinking back to the chapter hypothetical, it is clear that such legal hassles are looming. Recall that in the hypothetical a video documentary included musical recordings, previously published magazine photos, and paragraphs from published sports columns. These materials were most likely protected by copyright. And, under the principles discussed thus far, their unauthorized use in the commercial documentary—a form of reproduction—would probably amount to infringement. The best way to avoid infringing someone else's copyright, while still getting to use the work, is to get written permission from the owner.

Licensing Agreements

The rights of a copyright owner may be transferred to other individuals or organizations, just as other kinds of property may be sold or given away. The original owner need not transfer the entire copyright interest, however. A copyright can be divided and subdivided into small packages, each sold independently. This is referred to as the divisibility of copyright or, more graphically, as the *salami theory*. The original owner of a copyright begins with the whole salami and could sell it all, as is. Or it could be divvied up into little pieces, with the original owner perhaps retaining the main portion.

These small pieces of a copyright might include, for example, the right to reprint excerpts, the right to adapt into a screenplay, the right to publish first in the western United States, or the right to distribute the work for one year. When limited copyright interests are transferred in this piecemeal fashion, with the primary owner retaining the bulk of the rights, it is referred to as copyright **licensing.** The grantor of the license is called the *licensor,* and the party receiving the license is the *licensee.*

Copyright license agreements usually are negotiated contracts, and two principal types should be distinguished: An exclusive license is one in which the licensee is granted the sole authority to exercise the particular right in question. The license may be limited geographically or in duration. But as long as the license is in effect, no other person or organization—not even the principal copyright owner—may possess the same right. If the license is nonexclusive, on the other hand, the copyright owner may grant identical rights to additional parties.

Exclusive licenses typically carry a much higher price tag. For example, a radio station would expect to pay more for the exclusive right to broadcast a syndicated talk show within a certain geographic area than for the right to become one of perhaps three or four local stations carrying the program. Another distinction is that exclusive licenses must be in writing to be valid; nonexclusive licenses sometimes may rest entirely on oral agreements.[28]

In the entertainment industries copyright licensing plays a huge role, both as a way for the owners of copyrights to reap profits and as a way for other creators to obtain material for their projects. For example, suppose a motion picture company wants to produce a film about a warty, bug-eyed creature from outer space that charms youngsters on Earth. Pulling this production together may require the acquisition of several copyright licenses. Most notably, the production company will need to purchase motion picture rights from the author of the underlying screenplay (or novel, if the movie is to be based on a book). This license may cost anywhere from $50,000 to $10 million, depending on the bargaining power of the author. In addition, the producer might wish to integrate several pieces of recorded music into the film. This would require licenses from the owners of the musical compositions and also from the record companies that own the copyrights to the particular recorded versions.

When the film production company finishes its project, however, it will have created substantial copyright interests of its own. In addition to licensing distribution of the picture, the producer might license to a T-shirt company the right to market shirts with the space creature's face painted on the front. This kind of copyright license is called a grant of *merchandising rights.*

Copyright licensing can be an extremely complicated matter of contract and property law, and the agreements often are negotiated by lawyers who specialize in this field. That isn't always the case, however. It is common, for example, for the writer of a freelance magazine article to deal directly with an editor when determining what particular rights will be transferred to the magazine; the copyright stipulation might be stated in a simple sentence or two. And nonexclusive licenses for some kinds of uses (textbooks, for example) are routinely granted, though often a fee is required.

It is also true that communications professionals, in a rush to agree on an exciting idea, sometimes neglect important details about the duration, scope, and exclusivity of the copyright transfer. Such oversights can eventually lead to protracted legal conflict between the parties. Furthermore, inattention to the copyright transfer may be tantamount to squandered commercial opportunities. For example, a freelancer might write an essay and hastily sell it to a newspaper for $300, without specifically reserving any of the copyright. This apparent transfer of all rights would allow the newspaper to syndicate the essay to dozens of other publications and pocket $3000 in proceeds. The freelancer could have preserved the right to exploit the additional markets personally, following the initial publication, had an agreement with the newspaper editor contained language such as the following:

> In exchange for consideration of $300 paid to [freelancer's name], the *Daily News* is hereby granted a license of first North American serial rights to the essay titled "I Like Copyright." All other rights are retained by the author.

Electronic Rights

In recent years many copyright disputes have involved increasingly important *electronic rights,* the permission to make additional uses of copyrighted material in databases and online versions of periodicals. Authors and publishers alike are learning that electronic rights need to be distinctly addressed and separately negotiated.

This is at least one of the lessons from the contentious case of *Tasini v. New York Times Co.*[29] Six freelance authors were unhappy when they learned that articles they had written for the *Times* and a few other periodicals were in turn being provided to the powerful database NEXIS. The authors believed this was a separate publication of their writings, to which they had not consented and for which they had not been paid. The publishers, on the other hand, argued that providing electronic files to the database was simply an extension or "revision" of the periodicals which had already paid the authors for the right to run their articles.

The general practice of the publishers was to negotiate deadlines, length, and price with each freelancer. But they did not specifically mention the copyright terms. So, when the authors sued for copyright infringement, it was up to the courts to decide the scope of the freelancers' licenses. The federal district court in New York granted summary judgment in favor of the publishers, holding that the database represented merely a revised form of the periodicals, which the publishers had a right to undertake without securing additional permission from the freelance authors. But in 1999 the appeals court reversed, ruling that the database was not merely a revision of each periodical but rather a re-marketing of its various pieces—a separate publication of the freelance articles. The authors had retained all rights to their articles, beyond the first-publication rights for which they had been paid, the court held.

Music Licensing

Music licensing is a particularly complicated area of copyright law, and entire books have been written on the subject.[30] A few of the basic principles and practices are presented here because the use of music is vital to so many communications industries.

First of all, obtaining permission to use music may involve two different kinds of copyrights: One is in the song itself—the notes and lyrics, the musical composition; this copyright is typically owned by an individual music writer or by a music publishing company. The second copyright is in a desired recording of the song, referred to as a **sound recording;** this copyright is usually owned by a record company.

This principle is important to the chapter hypothetical, for example, where you sought to integrate popular recordings into the TV documentary. Because copyrights in the hit sound recordings are completely separate from copyrights in the underlying songs, you would need to clear two permissions for each recorded tune you wished to use. A license to use one of the recordings would be legally insufficient without an accompanying license to use the underlying song.

Music licenses come in many different forms. Three of the most important are synchronization licenses, master use licenses, and performance licenses.

Synchronization Licenses

Whenever film or video producers incorporate music, whether the music is prerecorded or recorded specifically for the production, they must obtain a license from the copyright owner of the composition. This is called a **synchronization license**—the permission to reproduce music in conjunction with video.

Synchronization licenses sometimes are obtained from the individual music writers or publishers who own the copyrights to the compositions. But often these licenses are obtained through agencies that represent the copyright owners, such as the Harry Fox Agency in New York. Synchronization licenses are typically nonexclusive, and granted for a flat fee determined in part by the value of the song and the prominence of the use. If a video producer intends to make his own, original rendition of the song, then the synchronization license may be the only music license he needs.

Master Use Licenses

If, in addition to using a musical composition, a video producer wishes to use a particular artist's existing recording of the composition, then a **master use license** must be obtained also. A master use license authorizes reproduction of a "master" recording for use in an audiovisual production such as a TV program or commercial. (The term *master* recording refers to the final copyrighted recording from which records, tapes, or compact discs are manufactured.)

Master use licenses usually are obtained directly from the record companies that own the copyrights in the sound recordings. Most record companies have special departments that negotiate and grant those licenses. The license fees are determined by a number of factors, such as the anticipated audience size, whether the recording will be featured or used in the background, and whether the use is for commercial or for nonprofit educational purposes.

Performance Licenses

Thus far we have looked at licenses that convey permission to reproduce music in the creation of another work. The right to reproduce music is separate from the right to *perform* it publicly, however. Music is publicly performed when it is actually presented to an audience in a commercial setting, for example by broadcasting a recording or by singing live on stage.

Recall that one of the basic, exclusive rights of a copyright owner is the right publicly to perform the copyrighted work. Sound recordings are an exception. Unlike most other classes of copyright, sound recordings *do not* include an exclusive right of public performance.[31] This means that anyone is free to play sound recordings in public, and to broadcast them, without having to obtain the permission of the copyright owner *of the sound recording*.

However, copyrights in the underlying musical compositions do enjoy all five of the exclusive rights, including the right to perform publicly. Therefore, any public performances of a copyrighted song *do* require permission from the copyright owner *of the composition*. The permission is obtained in the form of a **performance license.**

Consent is needed, for example, before a rock group may perform someone else's composition live at a concert. Furthermore, publicly playing a recording of a copyrighted song is also considered a "performance" of the underlying composition, so this too requires a license. Therefore, when a radio station plays recorded music on the air, copyright clearance is necessary. The same holds true for any other business that plays recordings of copyrighted songs for its customers—dance studios, nightclubs, shopping malls, restaurants, health clubs, and so on. Even when such establishments are merely playing a radio station for the benefit of customers—so-called storecasting—copyright permission may be required.[32] Again, the required copyright clearance is not needed for use of the sound recording per se, but for public performance of the underlying composition.

For example, in a 1986 case, rock star Bruce Springsteen and other owners of several popular musical compositions—including "Born in the USA," "Ghostbusters," and "Like a Virgin"—sued a small New Hampshire restaurant chain for performing the compositions without a license. The compositions were performed in some cases by musicians' live renditions and at other times by playing hit recordings of the compositions on a juke box. The federal district court noted that the

EXHIBIT 8.3   *Copyright Licenses for Music*

You need a . . .	In order to . . .
Synchronization license ☐	use a musical composition in a film or other new work
Master use license ☐	use a particular sound recording in a film or other work
Performance license ☐	publicly perform a composition, as by broadcasting a recording of the composition on radio

music was performed not for personal entertainment but as an integral part of the defendant's business. Therefore, they were public performances, and summary judgment was awarded in favor of the plaintiffs.[33] Exhibit 8.3 summarizes the licenses needed under specific circumstances.

Performance Rights Societies

As a practical matter, of course, the individual owners of musical compositions would find it virtually impossible to police all performances of their works and assure that licenses were obtained. Also, broadcast stations and other businesses would find it excessively burdensome to negotiate a license for each and every song they played. Therefore, performance licenses are handled in a different fashion—through performance rights societies.

The two main performance rights societies in the United States are Broadcast Music, Inc. (BMI), organized in 1939, and the American Society of Composers, Authors and Publishers (ASCAP), founded in 1914. Together they license performance rights to *millions* of musical compositions, on behalf of more than 150,000 songwriters and music publishers.

Essentially, the system works as follows. A music writer or publisher applies to one of the performance rights societies to become a member. In the membership agreement, the writer or publisher authorizes the society to grant nonexclusive performance rights in the member's compositions and to collect royalties on the member's behalf. This is accomplished through the sale of blanket licenses. Broadcast stations and other music-using businesses pay a yearly license fee to the performance rights organization, based on the gross receipts of the business. For commercial broadcast stations, the fee for each license is equal to about 2 percent of a station's revenues. Payment of this fee entitles the licensee to play or broadcast any songs in the society's repertory. The fees collected by the performance rights society are then disbursed to its members in the form of royalties. Royalty amounts are based on how frequently a particular member's music is performed, and this is determined by statistical sampling of actual broadcasts across the country.

Practically speaking, most broadcast stations have little choice but to purchase these blanket licenses from both ASCAP and BMI, thereby permitting the broadcast of virtually any popular tune. Even in the case of a TV station that airs only syndicated programming, the performance licenses are necessary. This is because TV shows contain plenty of music, and when the producers of those shows obtain music synchronization rights they usually do *not* also obtain performance rights on behalf of the stations that will actually "perform" the shows to the public. In the chapter hypothetical, then, you would need to negotiate synchronization rights for the musical works you wish to weave into your video production. You would not need to purchase performance rights on behalf of the stations that will air your program. In fact, you would view this as a waste, knowing that the stations already are likely to have blanket licenses.

Special Problem: Cable Retransmissions   A bitterly debated copyright question arose with the development of cable television: May cable operators intercept and retransmit broadcast signals without having to compensate the broadcasters, producers, and other program copyright owners? Or does the retransmission of a TV signal amount to a separate performance of a copyrighted work and thus a copyright infringement?

As cable systems in the 1970s began using microwave technology to import distant signals, thus fragmenting local broadcasters' audiences, the broadcasters became bitter over what seemed an unfair competitive advantage enjoyed by cable. While broadcasters spent roughly one-third of their budgets on programming costs, including copyright license fees, cablecasters obtained much of their programming free. Acting essentially as super antennas, cable systems simply plucked broadcast signals out of the air and retransmitted them to subscribers for a fee. Producers and broadcasters whose shows were being transmitted around the country without consent argued for greater control over the distribution of their product.

Nevertheless, the U.S. Supreme Court held in 1968 and again in 1974 that simultaneous cable retransmission did not constitute a separate performance within the meaning of the 1909 Copyright Act. The Court viewed cable systems more as antenna extensions for the TV viewer rather than performers of programming. Once a program is permitted to be broadcast, anyone with the technical ability to intercept and relay it is free to do so, the Court said. And this included commercial cable operators.[34]

Conventional TV broadcasters then pressed Congress for statutory changes. For distant broadcast signals—signals not originating in the cablecaster's service area—a complicated compromise was instituted in the 1976 act. Under the modern statute, public retransmission of a distant broadcast signal is considered a performance. But because Congress thought it too impractical to require that cable operators negotiate licenses for every retransmission of a broadcast, the act provides for a **compulsory licensing** system.[35] It allows cable companies to retransmit copyrighted broadcasts without consent, provided that the cablecaster pays a blanket license fee to the U.S. Copyright Office. The amount of the fee is set by statute and varies according to the size of the cable system. The compulsory license protects the cable operator as long as the retransmission is simultaneous with the original broadcast and the programming is not altered by the cable company.

After each year's royalty fees are collected, the Copyright Office is responsible for dividing them among the numerous copyright owners who file claim forms. The majority of the fund has been allocated to program syndicators and movie producers, with the rest going to sports leagues, commercial TV broadcasters, public TV, and music owners.

The compulsory license system covers only retransmissions of broadcasts; it does not cover cable-originated programming, such as that provided by MTV, HBO, or Showtime. Cable-oriented programming must be cleared for transmission through negotiations with the various copyright licensors who hold rights to the programming (motion picture studios, for example).

Also, the compulsory license is for distant signals only; the law did not require cablecasters to pay a license for picking up the signal of local television stations. A later law, the Cable Television Consumer Protection and Competition Act of 1992, dictated that cable systems *must carry* the signals of local TV stations that request carriage. And if a local station doesn't request carriage, the cablecaster nevertheless wishing to deliver the signal must negotiate for retransmission consent.

Under the Satellite Home Viewer Act of 1988 a similar compulsory license system was created for satellite retransmissions. A satellite carrier was authorized to retransmit a distant television broadcast signal to the public for private home viewing without the TV station's permission, as long as the satellite carrier paid royalties to the Copyright Office for later distribution.[36]

In 1999 Congress enacted the Satellite Home Viewer Improvement Act, which creates a copyright compulsory license authorizing satellite carriers to deliver *local* broadcast television stations to subscribers for the first time. It is up to each satellite carrier, however, to decide in which markets local signals will be offered.

International Protection

In today's global marketplace for news reports, motion pictures, music, books, computer programs, and other creative products, copyright protection is meaningfully effective only if it extends beyond the borders of the author's country. Without such protection, foreign copyright pirates can dump counterfeit copies into the marketplace without fear of legal reprisal. In fact, various estimates in recent years indicate that foreign rip-offs of U.S. creations are costing American companies tens of billions of dollars annually in lost revenues. Film and music companies are particularly concerned about a rise in Internet piracy around the globe.

However, there is no such thing as an international copyright that will automatically protect creations throughout the world. Instead, the legal mechanism

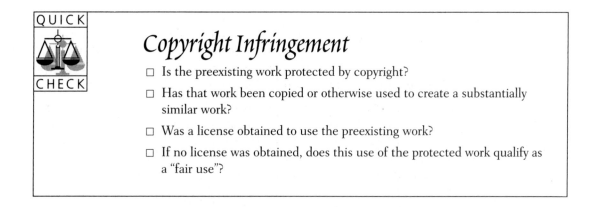

QUICK CHECK

Copyright Infringement

☐ Is the preexisting work protected by copyright?

☐ Has that work been copied or otherwise used to create a substantially similar work?

☐ Was a license obtained to use the preexisting work?

☐ If no license was obtained, does this use of the protected work qualify as a "fair use"?

necessary to allow copyright owners to enforce their rights in a foreign country is a treaty. In some cases the United States maintains bilateral copyright treaties with other nations. These are individual treaties between the United States and one other country, each granting reciprocal enforcement rights. More important, however, are the various multilateral treaties in which large groups of countries uniformly assent to basic copyright precepts and vow to enforce the copyrights on works created or published in any of the signatory countries.

The two principal multilateral treaties are the Berne Convention for the Protection of Literary and Artistic Property (called the Berne Convention) and the Universal Copyright Convention (UCC). The United States became a member of the UCC in 1955. More than seventy countries are members. The United States officially joined the Berne Convention, the oldest and most elaborate of all multilateral copyright treaties, in 1989. More than eighty countries have now ratified the Berne Convention, which began as a pact of ten European countries in 1886. American authors had urged participation in the Berne Convention for 100 years. But until recently some features of U.S. copyright law, such as the terms of protection, were incompatible with the Berne rules. To some extent, it remains to be seen whether recent state and federal moral rights legislation will be sufficient to meet the requirements of the Berne Convention.

Despite the advancement of international treaties, some countries still offer little or no copyright protection to foreign works. The Copyright Office supplies information on the current status of copyright relations with other nations.

The Fair Use Defense

There is one major exception to the principles of copyright protection and infringement discussed thus far. Known as the **fair use doctrine,** it gives people other than the copyright owner a limited privilege of using the copyrighted work without the owner's consent and without paying a royalty.

The fair use doctrine evolved from common law, beginning in the 1800s, as courts sought to balance the monopolistic rights of the copyright owner with the public interest in the dissemination of information. Beginning with the 1976 Copyright Act, the doctrine was formally incorporated into the statutes. Section 107 of the act codifies this important doctrine in the following language:

> Notwithstanding the [exclusive rights of copyright owners], the fair use of a copyrighted work . . . for purposes such as criticism, comment, news reporting, teaching (including multiple copies for classroom use), scholarship, or research, is not an infringement of copyright. In determining whether the use made of a work in any particular case is a fair use the factors to be considered shall include—
>
> 1. the purpose and character of the use, including whether such use is of a commercial nature or is for nonprofit educational purposes;
>
> 2. the nature of the copyrighted work;
>
> 3. the amount and substantiality of the portion used in relation to the copyrighted work as a whole; and
>
> 4. the effect of the use upon the potential market for or value of the copyrighted work.

Applying the Factors

Despite the statutory codification, fair use remains a relatively amorphous concept. It requires case-by-case determinations based on a weighing of the specific facts and the public interests at stake. Courts are left with considerable latitude to make equitable judgments, guided only by the four statutorily prescribed factors.

Purpose and Character of Use

With this factor, courts first identify the degree to which the unlicensed use serves some productive, publicly beneficial purpose, such as news reporting or teaching. Some such productive purpose typically must be present—as opposed to a use solely for entertainment purposes—in order for the use to be deemed fair. Additionally, courts look to whether the use is for a commercial, self-serving purpose or whether it is for a nonprofit or educational purpose. If the character of the use is predominantly commercial, this factor will weigh against fair use.

Nature of Copyrighted Work

Courts have drawn a variety of distinctions within the general confines of this second factor. Prior to the unconsented use, was the work published or unpublished? (Still-unpublished works are considered deserving of greater protection, thus weighing against fair use.) Is the copyrighted work primarily factual or fictional? (Factual works, such as new stories, are more susceptible to fair use.) Is the work out of print and no longer available for purchase? (If so, copying is more likely to be fair use.)

Portion of Work Used

This factor has both quantitative and qualitative elements. Courts will look to how much of the protected work was copied in relation to its whole. The smaller the amount used, the more likely it will be a fair use. But even if small percentages were taken, this factor may weigh against fair use if the copied portions were clearly the most important, most marketable elements of the copyrighted work.

Economic Effect

Finally, courts consider whether the unlicensed use will adversely affect the copyright owner. If the use has significantly usurped a portion of the market for the copyright, fair use will not be found. Courts have tended to consider the first and fourth factors as the most important, and the fourth as the single most important criterion for determining fair use.

Typical examples of fair use include quotation of excerpts in a book review for purposes of illustration; use in parody of some content from the work parodied; summary of a written speech or article, with brief quotations, in a news story; reproduction by a teacher or student of a small part of a work to illustrate a lesson; and incidental reproduction, in a TV news broadcast, of a copyrighted work located at the scene of the event being reported.

A District Court case that caught the attention of college campuses and copy shops is *Basic Books, Inc. v. Kinko's Graphics.* In this 1991 case several major book publishers sued the Kinko's photocopy chain alleging that Kinko's infringed the publishers' copyrights when it copied excerpts from books without permission, compiled them into course packets, and then sold them to college students. Kinko's claimed that its copying of excerpts was a fair use under Section 107 of the Copyright Act. The District Court concluded that the commercial copying was not a fair use and awarded the plaintiffs $510,000 in damages plus attorneys fees and court costs. The court analyzed the four fair use factors as follows:

1. Purpose and character of use: "Although Kinko's tries to impress this court with its purportedly altruistic motives," the judge wrote, "the facts show that Kinko's copying had the *intended purpose* of supplanting the copyright holder's commercially valuable right."[37] Therefore, this factor weighted heavily against fair use.

2. Nature of the copyrighted work: The books copied were factual in nature, and the court noted that such factual works as biographies, reviews, and commentary are believed to have a greater public value than fictional works. Therefore, copying of factual works is better tolerated under the copyright law. This factor weighed in favor of Kinko's.

3. Substantiality of portion used: The book passages copied in this case ranged from 5 percent to 25 percent of the works—often including entire chapters and in one instance a total of 110 pages. This amount was "grossly out of line

with accepted fair use principles," the court said in weighing this factor against fair use.[38]

4. Effect of use on market: Noting that Kinko's had 200 stores nationwide, the court concluded that the copying practice in question unfavorably affected the plaintiffs' sales of their books and their collection of permission fees. Therefore, this important factor weighed heavily against Kinko's.

The Sony Case

In 1984 and 1985 the U.S. Supreme Court decided two very difficult fair use cases. The first of these, *Sony Corp. of America v. Universal City Studios, Inc.,*[39] focused on whether home videotaping of TV programs is permitted under the fair use doctrine. The lawsuit was filed by Universal Studios and Walt Disney Productions, owners of a large number of copyrighted productions that are licensed for exhibition on network, local, and cable TV. In the late 1970s the studios were distressed by the burgeoning use of videotape recorders, which some people were using for unauthorized recording of the plaintiffs' productions. Surveys showed that the machines were used primarily for "time-shifting"—recording a program to view it once at a later time and then erasing it—though a substantial number of viewers also were accumulating libraries of tapes. Wide-scale taping could reduce the future demand for TV airings of the taped programs, the studios feared.

Yet the studios chose not to sue a sampling of individual tapers, recognizing that this would be a highly inefficient and ineffective way to curb the home taping practice. Rather, Universal and Disney sued Sony, the manufacturer of millions of Betamax recorders. Sony was a contributory infringer, the plaintiffs claimed, and they sought money damages and an injunction against future manufacture of the Betamax.

After a lengthy trial the District Court ruled in favor of Sony. The Court of Appeals reversed, holding that the studios were entitled to enjoin distribution of the recorders or to collect royalties on the sale of such equipment. It was a seemingly intractable issue that begged for a statutory solution. But Congress failed to act. The Supreme Court therefore had to resolve the issue.

In a 5–4 decision the Court ruled in favor of Sony, upholding the right to manufacture home recording devices without incurring copyright liability. In his majority opinion, Justice Stevens operated from this principle: that the mere sale of copying equipment is not contributory infringement if the product also has significant noninfringing uses. One common use of the Betamax satisfies this standard, Stevens wrote, because time-shifting in the home is a fair use. The Court briefly addressed the four fair use factors:

1. Time-shifting is generally done for a private, noncommercial purpose.

2. The copyrighted works were voluntarily placed on TV to be viewed free of charge by the general public.

3. Though entire works are copied, this doesn't have the usual effect of militating against fair use, because time-shifting merely enables viewers to see works they had indeed been invited to witness.

4. Plaintiffs at trial had been unable to show any actual harm as a result of time-shifting, the Court noted. Modern ratings methods would count the time-shifting audience, the Court said, and fears that time-shifting would reduce audiences for telecast reruns were based on mere speculation.

Four justices disagreed with the majority's rather shallow fair use assessment. The dissenters looked to the sample fair use situations in Section 107 and concluded that the fair use doctrine is intended only for productive uses—uses that provide some added public benefit, beyond that produced by the work itself, such as incorporation into a news report or teaching lesson. Time-shifting, though noncommercial, does not qualify as a productive use, the dissenters said. Furthermore, it should not be necessary for the copyright owners to prove actual harm. A potential of harm to the market for the copyright should be enough to militate against a finding of fair use. The studios had sufficiently identified potential harm in a number of ways, the dissenters concluded. For example, time-shifting could reduce the rerun audience, and consequently the license fees available to the studios for repeated showings. Also, advertisers might be willing to pay only for "live" audiences, if they believe Betamax viewers will delete the commercials.

In the end, it might be said that video machines with off-the-air taping capability are available in today's marketplace by the margin of one vote at the Supreme Court. The *Sony* case also demonstrated the inexact nature of the fair use doctrine, and it added little help for reducing the blurriness. A final word about *Sony:* Although the plaintiffs lost their case, the Court did not rule that all instances of home videotaping qualify as fair uses. The Court only needed to identify one such use, and it identified time-shifting. Neither *Sony* nor any other authoritative court decision stands for the proposition that unauthorized copying for personal entertainment purposes is always a fair use per se.

The Case of Ford's Memoirs

A year after *Sony* the Court made another attempt, in *Harper & Row Publishers v. Nation Enterprises,* to clarify the fair use doctrine. Former President Gerald Ford had contracted with Harper & Row to publish his memoirs. The agreement gave Harper & Row the exclusive right to license the first prepublication excerpts. As the manuscript neared completion, the publisher negotiated a deal with *Time* magazine in which *Time* would pay $25,000 in exchange for the right to excerpt 7500 words from Ford's account of his pardon of former President Richard Nixon. However, shortly before *Time's* exclusive was scheduled for release, a secret source provided *The Nation* magazine with a copy of the unpublished Ford manuscript. Working at a feverish pace in order to scoop *Time* magazine, editors at *The Nation* pulled quotes, paraphrases, and facts from the manuscript and published their own 2200-word article titled "The Ford Memoirs—Behind the Nixon Pardon." (About 15 percent of the article was in the form of direct excerpts from the manuscript; the rest was journalistic synopsis written by *The Nation*.) As a result of the *Nation* story, *Time* canceled its article and refused to pay Harper & Row for the first excerpt rights, which had now been usurped.

Harper & Row sued *The Nation* for copyright infringement and was awarded damages by the District Court. But the Court of Appeals reversed, holding that *The Nation*'s newsworthy publication was a fair use. Once again, the opportunity was presented for the Supreme Court to add some clarity to the fair use doctrine. In a 6–3 decision, the court sided with Harper & Row, ruling that *The Nation*'s unauthorized excerpts did not qualify as a fair use. And in contrast to its *Sony* opinion, the Court provided a lengthy and more thorough analysis of the fair use factors.

Writing for the majority, Justice Sandra Day O'Connor first recited the principle:

> We agree with the Court of Appeals that copyright is intended to increase and not to impede the harvest of knowledge. But we believe the Second Circuit gave insufficient deference to the scheme established by the Copyright Act for fostering the original works that provide the seed and substance of this harvest. The rights conferred by copyright are designed to assure contributors to the store of knowledge a fair return for their labors.[40]

Justice O'Connor then weighed the fair use factors as follows:

1. *Purpose of use.* The general purpose of *The Nation*'s use was news reporting, one of the sample fair use activities enumerated in Section 107 of the act. On the other hand, in its publication of verbatim excerpts *The Nation* in this case went beyond news reporting and actively sought to exploit the headline value of its own infringement, making a news event out of its unauthorized first publication. Therefore, the purpose of the use became largely commercial. The use had not merely the incidental effect but the intended purpose of supplanting the copyright holder's right of first publication and of drawing special attention to *The Nation*. In sum, then, the first factor was a close call but tended to weigh against fair use.

2. *Nature of copyrighted work.* The Ford manuscript was a factual, historical work, and the law generally recognizes a greater need to disseminate factual works than works of fiction or fantasy, Justice O'Connor acknowledged. However, another critical aspect of this work's nature was that it was unpublished, and the scope of fair use is narrower with respect to unpublished works. This is because it is of particular importance to an author to control the timing and quality of the first public appearance of his work. *The Nation* intruded upon a work that, by its nature, was still deserving of confidentiality

and a high degree of creative control by the copyright owners. Therefore, this factor also tended to lean against fair use.

3. *Substantiality of portion used.* In terms of raw amount, the passages actually copied by *The Nation*—about 300 words—were a very small portion of the total Ford manuscript. This fact tends to weigh in favor of fair use. On the other hand, Justice O'Connor said, this third factor also requires an evaluation of the qualitative nature of the taking. The passages concerning the Nixon pardon were recognized by the copyright holder as the focal point of the entire manuscript. From a qualitative perspective, the portion used was indeed substantial. In sum, this factor, too, was a close call that weighed slightly against fair use.

4. *Effect on market.* This last factor, the single most important one, was not a close call. "Rarely will a case of copyright infringement present such clear-cut evidence of actual damage" to the marketability of the copyright, wrote Justice O'Connor.[41] Specifically, she referred to the fact that Harper & Row lost its contract with *Time* and its ability to market first serial rights to the Nixon excerpts.

The three dissenters in the *Harper & Row* case, led by Justice Brennan, charged the majority with a failure to distinguish between the use of information and the appropriation of literary form, thus leading to an incorrect result. For example, on the critical fourth factor, Brennan acknowledged that *The Nation*'s publication led directly to *Time*'s cancellation of the Harper & Row contract. However, Brennan argued, the cancellation was not caused by the publication of a few copyrighted quotes but by the legitimate publication of significant information and ideas from the Ford manuscript. Wrote Justice Brennan: "In my judgment, the Court's fair use analysis has fallen to the temptation to find copyright violation based on a minimal use of literary form in order to provide compensation for the appropriation of information from a work of history."[42]

How might the video documentary in the chapter hypothetical fare if it tried to defend against infringement claims by asserting fair use? Not well, probably, given the commercial nature of the project and the fact that photos and songs are generally used in their entirety. Fair use would more likely be found for the sports columns, if the quoted portions were small in relation to the whole. What if the horse racing documentary had been produced for the Public Broadcasting System? How much more likely might a finding of fair use be?

News Video and Fair Use

One of the growing fair use battlegrounds concerns the use of externally produced videotape by television news programs. Hungry for dramatic video, and always running on deadline, TV stations may copy and broadcast newsworthy videotape produced by an external news service or by a home video buff without stopping to get copyright clearance. Should the fair use doctrine protect such use?

A sample case is *Los Angeles News Service v. KCAL-TV.*[43] The independent news service, LANS, provides news stories, photos, and video to its media subscribers. On April 29, 1992, rioting broke out in Los Angeles following a controversial court verdict. The LANS helicopter hovered above an intersection and with its live video camera captured dramatic scenes of a motorist named Reginald Denny being beaten in the street. One of the service's subscriber stations aired the live video, and LANS provided tape to a few other stations with which it had contracts. KCAL was not one of those stations. When it asked LANS for a license to broadcast the Denny tape that day, LANS declined. So KCAL obtained a copy of the tape from another station and broadcast it several times on its news programs. LANS sued for copyright infringement.

The federal district court said that KCAL was protected by the fair use doctrine, based on the fact that the tape was unique and highly newsworthy. But in 1997 the court of appeals reversed. It held that, even though KCAL was using the tape for a news purpose, it was also attempting to profit by exploiting the LANS coverage and—to make matters worse—presenting the tape as if it were its own. Furthermore, the court said, even though LANS could show little harm to its market based solely on the unauthorized use by KCAL, the proper question was whether LANS would be adversely affected if this kind of practice by KCAL were to occur more broadly. The court concluded that it surely would. Therefore, it was not fair use.

Freedom for Parody

Works of parody—those that mimic and poke fun at other author's works—long have been recognized by the courts as a form of social criticism as well as entertainment and thus deserving of some fair use protection against copyright infringement claims. In determining whether parodic works are fair uses, the analysis often focuses on the third factor, the substantiality of copying. The general rule is that this factor will weigh in favor of fair use so long as the parodist appropriates no greater amount of the original work than is reasonably necessary to recall or conjure up the object of the parody.

For example, in 1989 the rap group 2 Live Crew sought permission to record a parody of "Oh, Pretty Woman," the 1964 hit song by Roy Orbison. Acuff-Rose Music, which owned the copyright, refused to grant a license. 2 Live Crew nevertheless released its own, more shocking version. Acuff-Rose sued, claiming that the parody was in bad taste and would disparage the future value of its copyright. In *Campbell v. Acuff-Rose Music, Inc.*, a unanimous 1994 decision, the Supreme Court held that 2 Live Crew's parody could qualify as a fair use, and the case was sent back to the trial court for further factual determinations.[44] The Supreme Court's factor-by-factor analysis was as follows:

1. One purpose of 2 Live Crew's song clearly was commercial, which tends to weigh against fair use. However, the commercial nature of the use does not

automatically preclude a finding of fair use, nor does it necessarily even control the outcome of this first factor. Rather, it is a fact to be weighed along with other purposes of the use. In this case, 2 Live Crew's song reasonably could be perceived as commenting on, or criticizing, the original. Therefore, there was a parodic purpose as well as a commercial purpose to the work.

2. As to the nature of Orbison's original work, it was highly expressive and therefore fell within the core of copyright's protective purpose. This factor weighed against fair use, but that is typical in parody cases, the Court noted, because parodies almost invariably copy highly expressive, publicly known works.

3. The Court acknowledged this was a difficult but critical factor in parody cases: "Parody's humor, or in any event its comment, necessarily springs from recognizable allusion to its object through distorted imitation. . . . When parody takes aim at a particular original work, the parody must be able to 'conjure up' at least enough of that original to make the object of its critical wit recognizable." The Court noted that 2 Live Crew copied the characteristic opening bass riff of the original tune and that the first line of words copied the Orbison lyrics. But the Court remanded the case to the trial court to determine whether the amount taken was excessive, in light of 2 Live Crew's parodic purpose.

4. It is unlikely that a parody will negatively affect the market for the original copyright, either by acting as a direct substitute for it or by displacing the market for derivative works, the Court noted. This is because a parody and the original generally serve different market functions. Furthermore, the Court said, there is no protectable derivative market for criticism. "The market for potential derivative uses includes only those that creators of the original works would in general develop or license others to develop." Therefore, to the extent 2 Live Crew's song was criticism, it could not be deemed to invade the original copyright owner's market. On the other hand, 2 Live Crew's song comprised not only parody but also rap music, and potential harm to the derivative market for rap music would be proper to investigate. This fourth factor could weigh against fair use if it were shown that 2 Live Crew's parodic rap song supplanted the market for a non-parody, rap version of "Oh, Pretty Woman."

Thus the Supreme Court did not provide a satisfying, ultimate conclusion in the *Acuff-Rose* case. However, the Court's meticulous opinion, written by Justice Souter, does detail how the fair use factors are to be applied in parody cases. The case also serves as another reminder from the High Court that fair use controversies can be complicated and that they must be resolved through a case-by-case balancing of all relevant facts. The Court has consistently rejected any inclination by lower courts to draw bright-line rules in fair use cases.

Copyright and Advancing Technology

As the *Sony* case demonstrated, new technologies can swiftly rise to prominence, creating copyright dilemmas that leave Congress and the courts years behind in developing solutions. As of this writing, it is computerized manipulation of music, photos, and audiovisual works that is causing the biggest stir among artists and testing the bounds of copyright law.

In the music industry, digital sampling has become a commonplace technique for producing new rock recordings with sounds taken from other artists. Using a computerized recording device called a *sampler,* musical performances are duplicated in a manner that converts their sounds to digital bits of information. A recording engineer can then manipulate the recorded sounds in virtually limitless ways by giving them more echo, lowering the pitch, or combining them with other sounds, for example. A copyright infringement issue arises, however, when the manipulated sounds are appropriated from the copyrighted recordings of others, thus invading the exclusive right of the copyright owner to make derivative works.

In still photography a similar issue is presented by the use of photo-manipulating computer programs. With technology that became readily available in the late 1980s, photo images can be electronically copied into a computer and manipulated. For example, a picture of a sunset at the Grand Canyon could be altered by moving the sun lower on the horizon, brightening the color of the sky, and adding a few soaring prairie falcons, taken from other photos. Is the resulting computer picture an illegal adaptation of the other works, or is it an entirely new and distinct creation in its own right?

The answer may be a matter of degree. If substantial similarity exists between an original work and the electronically generated take-off and the amount of copying is more than minimal, the high-tech artist has probably committed copyright infringement (unless the fair use doctrine would apply). In other words, altering the protected graphic or musical works of others does not automatically insulate the high-tech manipulator from a copyright infringement claim. The infringement question is problematical, however, when the original artist's work isn't even recognizable to casual listeners or viewers of a drastically transformed, computer-generated composition.

Precedent-setting judicial decisions have yet to appear on the issue of high-tech copyright tinkering. In the meantime, the issue is liable to grow even more complicated as electronic manipulation expands into the audiovisual media. Already computers are used to "colorize" black-and-white movies and to speed up films (inconspicuously) to fit TV time slots. On the horizon is the digital capability to sample television programming and films and, perhaps, through a computer keyboard, to create a new audiovisual world that looks much like the world outside. Yet another problem area to surface in recent years is the application of copyright law in cyberspace—a topic that will be addressed in chapter 13.

Trademarks

Americans live in a marketplace brimming with trademarks. In ads, on packaging, on the sides of vehicles, in letterheads, as lapel buttons, on bumper stickers and matchbook covers—in every commercial medium, trademarks by the thousands compete for our attention. In essence, they are the beacons of capitalism. A **trademark** is any word, name, slogan, design, or symbol that is used in commerce to identify a particular product and distinguish it from others.

Akin to trademarks, and possessing the same basic legal protections, are service marks and trade names. A **service mark** is to services what a trademark is to products: It distinguishes the services of one company from another. A **trade name** is used to identify and distinguish the company itself. A single name, such as Sears, may serve as all three, identifying products, services, and the business itself. In this chapter the words *mark* or *trademark* are used to refer generally to all three forms of protected identification.

The main purpose of trademark protection is to increase the reliability of marketplace identification and thereby help consumers select goods and services. A distinctive trademark quickly identifies the origin of a product, and over time the mark may be equated with a particular level of quality. Thus trademarks may drastically reduce the time and costs that consumers would otherwise incur in searching for, verifying, and individually testing items in the marketplace. In short, trademark laws are intended to reduce consumer confusion. Secondarily, trademark protection also helps to assure fair economic returns for companies that achieve a consistent level of quality. In such cases the trademark itself becomes a valuable asset, a symbol of the earned goodwill of a business. Examples include:

- ☐ The words *Band-Aid* adhesive bandages, *Xerox* copiers, and *Frisbee* flying disks.

- ☐ The names *Levi's* jeans, *Hilton* hotels, and *Betty Crocker* baking mixes.

- ☐ The logos of McDonald's golden arches, the eye of CBS, and the shell insignia of Shell Oil.

- ☐ The slogans "Don't leave home without it" and "This Bud's for you."

It is important for mass communicators to know basic trademark principles, for several reasons. First, as a matter of accuracy, communicators should be able to recognize trademarks so they may be referred to properly—as capitalized, proper adjectives. Second, many communicators, particularly in advertising and public relations, are entrusted with the task of creating and ensuring the proper use of trademarks on behalf of employers and clients. And third, the mass media themselves often have trademarks to protect. The titles of newspapers, magazines, newsletters, TV programs, or a series of books can be trademarks, for example.

Like copyrights, trademarks are protected as a form of property. Owners of valid trademarks are granted exclusive rights to their use in commerce. Whereas copyrights are governed exclusively by federal statute, however, trademarks are governed both by federal and state law. The applicable federal law is the Trademark Act of 1946, also known as the Lanham Act.[45] The act, which underwent revisions in 1988, is primarily a national registration scheme, reserved for marks used in interstate or foreign commerce. Day-to-day administration is handled by the U.S. Patent and Trademark Office. Federal authority to govern trademarks rests on the commerce clause of the U.S. Constitution, contained in Article 1, Section 8.

At the state level, trademark rights are governed by a mixture of statutes and common law. As a general rule, statutes have been enacted to set up state registration systems and to specify the details of trademark ownership, transfer, and enforcement. Common law typically provides the basic principles of trademark creation and infringement. Considerable uniformity exists among state trademark laws. In 1949 the United States Trademark Association prepared the Model State Trademark Bill. As of 1995 that model had been adopted as the basis for trademark registration statutes in forty-six states.

Creation of Trademarks

As with copyrights, legal rights to trademarks arise automatically, apart from any particular governmental formalities. Unlike copyrights, however, the inception of trademark rights is not at the moment a word or symbol is first created or scribbled on paper. Rather, trademark rights stem from the actual use of a distinctive mark in commerce.

Use in Commerce

There is no bright standard for the amount of use required to establish trademark rights. However, the mark must be used in connection with the public distribution of goods or services; only then are legal rights to a trademark secured.

This principle flows from the general purpose of trademark protection. After all, it is not the creation of trademarks per se that the law is trying to encourage. The intent is to give a reasonable degree of competitive integrity to those marks actually in use. Not only is public use the key to trademark creation but rights also come to an end automatically when the mark is abandoned. Protection remains in effect as long as the mark is actively and continuously used by its owner.

In judging whether use of a mark has been sufficient to establish trademark rights, courts will consider whether the mark actually has been placed before a significant segment of the public and whether there has been a sincere effort to market the product or service on a commercial scale. The mark must be used in trade with actual customers before ownership rights begin. There is no legally sanctioned way to reserve a mark for future use.

Distinctiveness

In addition to use in commerce, distinctiveness is required for a valid trademark. This requirement, too, is central to the whole notion of a trademark—that the trademark user's goods be distinguished and that marketplace confusion be avoided. To accomplish this, the mark naturally must be different from existing trademarks and from terms or symbols commonly used in conjunction with similar products.

The most distinctive marks are those that would by themselves give no clue to the product. These may be coined terms that have no dictionary meaning, such as *Exxon* and *Kodak*. Or they can be common words applied in a unique, seemingly arbitrary way. Examples include *Ivory* soap and *Camel* cigarettes. Also considered sufficiently distinctive are suggestive terms that provide some clue to the product or service but not a vivid description. These include *Playboy* magazine and *Orange Crush* orange-flavored soft drink.

Entirely unacceptable, however, are attempts to appropriate *generic terms* as trademarks. These are common terms that are used in actually defining the kind of product or service in question. For example, the terms *cat food, root beer,* and *bicycle* cannot be taken from common usage and claimed as trademarks by individual producers of those products. The generic descriptions must remain available for other companies to use when describing their own products.

In most cases, terms that merely describe a characteristic of the product—such as *big, red,* or *fast*—also are insufficiently distinctive to claim as part of a trademark. In 1977, for example, the federal Court of Appeals ruled that the term *light* was either a generic term or a common descriptive word when applied to low-calorie beer. Therefore, neither the word not its phonetic equivalent, *lite,* may be appropriated as a trademark for beer. The court equated the use of the term to that of *white* bread; no one bakery could claim exclusive use of the word *white* in references to its product.[46]

However, some descriptive terms can attain trademark status if, over time, they acquire what is called a **secondary meaning.** Though the words initially are just descriptive, secondary meaning arises when consumers learn to associate the term with one particular producer or source. For example, a court in 1985 held that the service mark SEATS, for a computerized ticket reservation business, had through use acquired a secondary meaning in the context of reservation services and thus was a protected trademark.

When designs are intended as trademarks, they, too, must qualify as distinctive. Ordinary, common shapes, such as circles, squares, or hearts, cannot achieve trademark status unless a secondary meaning has been established.

Because a mark also must be distinctive in relation to other merchants' marks, trademark ownership can vest only in the first user of a particular mark. Other merchants who later use the same mark, or one confusingly similar, will not have met the distinctiveness test and may themselves be infringers. As a general rule, though, the distinctiveness test is limited to the user's particular geographical market. Often the first user has employed the identifying mark only within a limited territory of the United States. If so, other merchants who use the mark in entirely separate localities also are entitled to ownership rights in the mark. In essence, these subsequent users are really the first users within their distant geographical markets. However, the territorial rule has been limited to cases in which the subsequent merchants independently adopted the mark in good faith—that is, without trying to copy the mark or capitalize on its good reputation. Also, federal registration has the legal effect of precluding a good faith adoption by someone else anywhere in the United States because federal registration essentially serves as notice to all other businesses.

To avoid an embarrassing and costly conflict with an existing mark, the creators of a proposed new trademark should always conduct or commission a trademark availability search. In practice, these searches are performed by law firms, with assistance from companies that specialize in trademark searches. A computer database check is used to find similar words or designs among the trademarks officially registered with the federal or state governments. If the proposed mark appears to be available after this initial check, a more time-consuming search of specialized business directories and other publications may be conducted to determine whether some unregistered mark could pose a conflict.

In recent years a growing problem area in trademarks is that of Internet domain names—their distinctiveness, when protection attaches, the mechanics of registration. Domain names will be examined in detail in Chapter 13.

Trademark Registration

Legal rights to trademarks arise automatically through use, and those rights can continue to exist independently of registration. However, a number of valuable advantages flow from government registration, so it is advisable to register at both the state and federal levels.

Federal Registration

Under the federal Lanham Act, trademarks used in interstate or foreign commerce may be registered in the U.S. Patent and Trademark Office. The primary benefits of federal registration are as follows: First, it serves to create a legal presumption that the trademark is valid. This means that in a lawsuit for infringement, the burden of proof shifts to the defendant to show why the registered mark is undeserving of protection. Second, registration serves as nationwide notice of the registrant's claim of ownership. Therefore, a second user of the mark, in some other area of the country, cannot claim territorial ownership rights. Third, with federal registration comes the right to file infringement lawsuits in the federal courts. A fourth benefit is that registration simply serves as a deterrent against use by others.

Federally registered marks may be accompanied by the ® symbol as a warning to others. (Owners of unregistered marks may use the notice symbol ™, but the ® designation may be used only upon federal registration. See Exhibit 8.4.)

Federal registration lasts for ten years, provided that the mark continues to be used in interstate commerce. The registration is renewable every ten years, indefinitely, as long as the mark continues to meet the "use it or lose it" requirement.

EXHIBIT 8.4   *Trademark Marking*

These symbols or text may be used to identify a trademark:

TM	Used on goods to signify a claimed trademark
SM	Used in conjunction with services to signify a claimed service mark.
®	May be used only on marks that have been federally registered.
Reg. U.S. Pat. & Tm. Off.	May be used only on marks that have been federally registered. Sometimes printed some distance from the mark and referred to with an asterisk.

State Registration

Each state also offers a trademark registration scheme, usually through its secretary of state. The benefits of state registration are not as extensive as those of federal registration, however, so interstate merchants with federal registration often don't bother to obtain registration in individual states. Still, state registration is important for local businesses that do not qualify for federal protection.

State statutes typically specify that registration creates a legal presumption of valid ownership, and owners of state-registered trademarks may be entitled to enhanced damage awards for infringement. State registration generally is obtained much more quickly than federal registration—often within a few months of filing an application. As with federal registration, state registrations usually are renewable for successive ten-year periods, as long as the mark remains in use.

Infringement

The primary method of protecting a trademark against use by others is to file a lawsuit for infringement. The plaintiff may sue for money damages or an injunction against further use, or both. The basic legal test applied in infringement lawsuits is whether the allegedly infringing mark is similar enough to create a likelihood of confusion in the marketplace.

For example, *Playboy* magazine sued in federal court to enjoin another publisher from using the name *Playmen* as the title of its male-oriented magazine. The federal Court of Appeals held that *Playboy* was indeed entitled to the injunction because evidence suggested that product and source confusion would result from the similarities between the titles. Also, the court said the defendant's obvious purpose in adopting *Playmen* was to capitalize on the *Playboy* mark—another factor that may be considered when judging trademark infringement.[47]

Another magazine case involved Petersen Publishing, which has published *Teen* magazine since 1957, and Time, Inc., which has published *People* magazine since 1974. In 1997 each publisher was working independently on a new magazine, and each wanted to name its new magazine *Teen People*. When each learned of the other's plans, each was, of course, unhappy and ran down to the courthouse. *Teen* apparently abandoned its plan for naming the magazine, but when *Time* wanted to move ahead with its plan, Petersen sought an injunction. Based in part on the appearance of *Time*'s stipulated logo for the new publication, a jury concluded that its new publication would not create a likelihood of confusion. In 1999 the Court of Appeals affirmed the trial verdict.[48]

A different kind of confusion was at issue in a 1979 case in which the Dallas Cowboys Cheerleaders, a subsidiary of the Cowboys professional football team, sued to enjoin distribution of an adult motion picture, *Debbie Does Dallas*. The cheerleaders claimed that their distinctive uniform—white boots, white shorts, a blue bolero blouse, and a white vest decorated with blue stars and fringe—was a protected trademark. In one scene of the movie, which the Court of Appeals described as "a gross and revolting sex film,"[49] the lead actress appeared in a strikingly similar outfit. Advertising posters for the film also depicted the actress wearing the uniform.

The court first noted that although purely functional items do not qualify as trademarks, the cheerleaders' uniform in this case included many decorative aspects that had come to be associated with the Cowboys organization. Therefore, the uniform qualified as a trademark. As to the infringement, the court said infringement claims do not turn on whether consumers would be confused about who actually produced the item, in this case the film. Rather, it is confusion enough if the public could be led to believe that the mark's owner sponsored or otherwise approved of the trademark's use and that such association would tend to injure the plaintiff's business reputation. This standard was met, the court ruled, and upheld the injunction.

Generally speaking, infringement occurs only when similar or identical marks are used to identify similar or related kinds of products or services. That is to say, the infringer usually must be engaged in a competing type of business.

But sometimes trademark protection extends beyond the trademark holder's particular categories of products. Especially when the mark in question is highly distinctive and broadly known, such as *Exxon* and *Kodak,* attempts to capitalize on the mark may constitute infringement even when the upstart's products are very different from those produced under the original mark. The more distinctive and famous the mark, the more likely it is that consumers may think that even a different kind of product, if it bears that same name, must be from the same source.

Dilution

A lawsuit for infringement is not the only way in which trademark owners may protect the value of their marks. Roughly half the states have passed anti-dilution statutes. Under these statutes the trademark owner may seek an injunction to prevent **dilution** of a distinctive mark—even in the absence of public confusion or business competition between the parties.

Dilution may be defined as any activity that threatens to weaken the distinctive identity of a well-known mark or otherwise tarnish its reputation. To succeed on a dilution claim, the plaintiff needs to prove just two basic elements: (1) that the plaintiff's mark is indeed well known and distinctive, and (2) that the defendant's actions have raised a likelihood of dilution.

An example of dilution through tarnishment is the 1994 case of *Anheuser-Busch, Inc. v. Balducci Publications.* A humor magazine, *Snicker,* published on its back cover a mock advertisement for the fictitious product "Michelob Oily." The full-page ad depicted a replica of a can of Michelob beer pouring oil onto a fish, an oil-soaked rendition of the Anheuser-Busch eagle logo, and various "Michelob Oily" bottles and labels that closely resembled the brewery's actual products. The mock ad stated in bold type "ONE TASTE AND YOU'LL DRINK IT OILY." Actual Anheuser-Busch clip art was used to replicate the protected trademarks. The magazine publisher defended the mock ad as a parody intended to comment on a recent oil spill in the Gasconade River, a source of Anheuser-Busch's water supply.

Anheuser-Busch sued the magazine on several grounds, including trademark dilution under Missouri law. The trial court noted the magazine's substantial First Amendment right to engage in social commentary, and it dismissed the trademark dilution claim because, it said, there was no threat of tarnishing the plaintiff's trademarks through association with shoddy products. However, the federal Court of Appeals reversed. The appellate court held that the First Amendment did not necessarily protect against a dilution claim simply because the trademark is used in an editorial or artistic context. The First Amendment did not shield a parody that utilized protected trademarks to a degree greater than necessary to convey the point of the parody. Furthermore, a survey indicated that many people construed the ad parody as suggesting that Michelob beer actually contained some oil, thereby tarnishing the trademark's carefully developed image. Therefore, the ad parody was held to violate the anti-dilution statute, entitling Anheuser-Busch to an injunction prohibiting further distribution.[50]

For some trademark owners the most sinister problem is the improper use of the trademark in the everyday speech of the general public. A trademark is properly used as an adjective (Xerox copiers), but not as a noun (Where's the Xerox?) or verb (Please Xerox this). When such improper uses of the trademark become so commonplace as to overshadow the distinctive meaning of the mark, the mark may be deemed by courts to have become a generic term, no longer protectable as a trademark. This fate has befallen such former trademarks as *escalator* and *yo-yo,* for example. Some companies regularly buy advertising to remind communications professionals and consumers of the proper use of certain trademarks (Exhibit 8.5).

Recall that in the chapter hypothetical you designed a logo for your documentary, *Hooves.* Before adopting the design as your commercial symbol, it would have been wise to pay for a national trademark search. If the design is available,

you could obtain maximum protection by registering with the federal trademark office.

Unfair Competition

The property-based protections of copyright and, to a narrower extent, trademark are the most significant ways in which communicative creations are protected against unauthorized use. But in both areas several threshold requirements must be met before any protections apply. Sometimes materials are appropriated for business purposes in a manner that seems patently unfair, but no recourse is provided by either copyright or trademark law. In such cases the aggrieved party may find a business-related tort that would provide some legal relief.

There are a host of so-called business torts. Among them are trade libel, misappropriation of trade secrets, and interference with contractual relations. Invasion of the right of publicity, examined in Chapter 5, may be considered a business tort as well as a type of privacy tort. In terms of filling the gaps between copyright and trademark protection, though, the most important business tort is unfair competition.

Unfair competition is a broad legal term without any one specific definition. Historically, the concept developed as a tort primarily concerned with wrongful conduct by a commercial enterprise that results in business loss to another, ordinarily by the use of deceptive means to draw customers away from a competitor. Under modern state statutes the term is sometimes used even more broadly, as an umbrella term to cover such unlawful practice subcategories as false advertising. This book discusses false advertising in Chapter 10. Here, the concern is the common law notion of unfair competition as it may apply to protect communicative creations from unauthorized use by others.

One of the classic unfair competition cases is *International News Service v. Associated Press,* a 1918 Supreme Court decision. At the time the two news cooperatives were engaged in head-to-head competition in the business of providing timely news to hundreds of member newspapers across the country. In the course of this competition, INS resorted to copying AP news from bulletin boards (remember, this is 1918) and from early editions of AP member newspapers, quickly rewriting it, and then telegraphically transmitting it as its own product. Through this process the pirated INS news could appear in western papers issued at least as early as those served by AP.

The Associated Press sued, and it obtained a preliminary injunction against INS use of AP news until the competitive benefit of timeliness had passed. The U.S. Supreme Court upheld the injunction. It was not a matter of copyright infringement, the Court noted, because the factual substance of news is a matter of public domain. Therefore, AP could not prevent the purchaser of a newspaper—including INS—from spreading knowledge of its contents. However, the relationship between business competitors is subject to the additional limits of unfair competition law. Wrote the Court:

> [INS] admits that it is taking material that has been acquired by complainant as
> the result of organization and the expenditure of labor, skill, and money, and
> which is salable by complainant for money, and that defendant in appropriating
> it and selling it as its own is endeavoring to reap where it has not sown, and by
> disposing of it to newspapers that are competitors of complainant's members
> is appropriating to itself the harvest of those who have sown. Stripped of all

disguises, the process amounts to an unauthorized interference with the normal operation of complainant's legitimate business precisely at the point where the profit is to be reaped. . . .[51]

Contrast this with the 1997 case of *NBA v. Motorola, Inc.* Motorola manufactured the SportsTrax personal paging device, and Sports Team Analysis and Tracking Systems (STATS) supplied game information that is transmitted to the pager. The pager's inch-and-a-half square screen can display considerable information about basketball games in progress, including score changes, team foul status and the time remaining per quarter. The information is obtained from game broadcasts and is updated every two minutes, with a two-minute lag between the live action and when the information appears on the pager. The National Basketball Association sued, claiming unfair competition by misappropriation under New York law. But the federal court of appeals sided with Motorola and distinguished this case from INS:

> To be sure, some of the elements of a "hot-news" INS claim are met. The information transmitted to SportsTrax is . . . time-sensitive. Also, the NBA does provide . . . an information service like that available through Sports Trax. . . .
>
> However, there are critical [differences]. . . .
>
> With regard to the NBA's primary products—producing basketball games with live attendance and licensing copyrighted broadcasts of those games—there is no evidence that anyone regards SportsTrax . . . as a substitute."

Furthermore, as to the market for real-time game stats, SportsTrax is not free-riding off the NBA's own services, the court said. "Motorola and STATS expend their own resources to collect purely factual information. . . . They have their own network and assemble and transmit data themselves."[52] This was not a case of collecting facts from an NBA pager service and transmitting them to SportsTrax pagers, the court noted.

Among the most important ways that unfair competition law fills in the gaps left by copyright and trademark is by protecting titles. Mere titles of individual works, you will recall, are not protected by copyright law, and except for titles of periodicals, neither are they protected under trademark. Yet the palming off of a confusingly similar title may be enjoined under unfair competition law.

For example, in a 1979 case Orion Pictures sued a paperback book publisher to restrain it from using the title *A Little Romance* on a novel. The claim was made under the common law standard for unfair competition and also under Section 43(a) of the Lanham Act—a broad federal statute under which many unfair competition claims are made. The defendant had legitimately secured from the original French author the right to publish the novel in the United States, as Orion had purchased film rights to the story. But Orion came up with a new title for its film version, and the book publisher adopted the same title in an effort to capitalize on the substantial publicity that was being generated for the film. The title *A Little*

Romance had come to be associated in the public's mind with the particular Orion production, the court found. Therefore, the title could be protected from use by others if ordinary, prudent consumers would be misled or confused about the relationship between the works. Such confusion was likely in this case, the court ruled, and an injunction was granted.[53]

Summary Points

Copyrights are a form of property—property vitally important to individuals and businesses engaged in the production of entertainment and other forms of mass communication. Rights to copyright arise automatically, without legal formalities, and copyrights may be bought and sold much like other kinds of property.

Works are copyrightable if they qualify as original works of authorship fixed in any tangible medium of expression. Only the manner of expression is protected, not facts or ideas.

It is important to know whether copyrighted materials are works made for hire, for this distinction determines both the identity of the initial owner and the duration of protection.

In the professional world, interests in valuable copyrights are granted to others through licensing agreements. Music licensing is a particularly complicated field, with its own special rules.

The main legal avenue for enforcing copyrights is a civil lawsuit for infringement; often the key defense is the doctrine of fair use.

With the Copyright Act of 1976 the federal government has chosen to preempt the entire field of copyright law.

Trademarks, another form of intellectual property, are words, symbols, and other creations that are used to identify businesses, products, and services. Trademarks are protected under both state and federal law.

Trademark rights arise automatically through use of a distinctive mark in commerce, and protection is enhanced by government registration.

As a general rule, if no valid copyright or trademark exists in a particular creative work, it may be freely copied by others. However, if the unauthorized use is likely to deceive the public at the expense of another business enterprise, the tort of unfair competition may be alleged.

In the chapter hypothetical the racing documentary is clearly protected by copyright, to the extent it contains original material. The logo used to market the documentary also would be protected—under trademark law. Maximum protection for both the documentary and the logo could be achieved by registering these creations with the appropriate federal office. Some copyright problems also exist, however. Both the reproduction of magazine photographs and the copying of large portions of published columns are likely infringements. Furthermore, unauthorized integration of the sound recordings would infringe the copyrights of both the composition owners and the record companies.

Discussion Questions

1. Based on this chapter's discussion of music copyrights, do you think it would be a copyright violation to purchase a popular CD at a record store and then play it at a dorm party (without consent of the copyright owner and without an ASCAP or BMI license)? What if students are charged a fee to cover refreshments and entertainment at the party? Could you play the CD at a party if it were held at a cocktail lounge? Could you legally play the CD for an aerobics class you teach?

2. Following the *Kinko's* decision, some educators argued that Congress should enact a broader fair use exemption for education-oriented copying. Do you agree, or might a relaxation of copyright protections have counterproductive results? When music is played for the benefit of customers a copyright fee is usually owed to the owner of the composition. Should a similar fee be owed to authors or publishers when books are lent by a library?

3. If copyright law does not protect ideas, what is to stop a magazine, publishing company, or film studio from stealing the ideas in any materials you send to them? Should ethics, professionalism, and reputation be the only bars to stealing ideas, or should the law afford some special protection to ideas that are voluntarily submitted to others? What legal theories might be used to afford such protection? How about contract law?

4. Would it qualify as fair use to use an exact replica of cartoon character Bart Simpson in the masthead of a college newspaper? What if the Bart sketch were used in a political cartoon? Would it make a difference if Bart were being criticized in the political cartoon? Could an altered sketch of Bart—a parody—be used in the paper? In the masthead?

Key Terms

collaboration agreement
collective works
compilation
compulsory licensing
copyright
derivative works
dilution
fair use doctrine
generic term

intellectual property
joint work
licensing
master use license
moral rights
performance license
public domain
secondary meaning
service mark

sound recording   trademarks
source licensing   trade name
statutory damages   unfair competition
synchronization license   work made for hire

Web Resources

http://www.loc.gov/copyright/
U.S. Copyright Office, Library of Congress

http://www.copyright.com/
Copyright Clearance Center (for automated rights clearance)

http://www.uspto.gov/
U.S. Patent and Trademark Office

InfoTrac® College Edition

Copyright piracy is a major concern around the globe, especially as personal computer technology now makes it easier to copy and alter materials produced by the film and music industries. Find at least one article that provides details on an aspect of the pirating problem. Based on what you find, do you think there's a solution?

CHAPTER NINE

Chapter Outline

Corporate and Government Speech

Upon completing this chapter you should

- □ **understand** why corporate and government institutions are subject to speech restrictions that do not apply to other kinds of organizations or to individuals generally.
- □ **know** the principal Securities and Exchange Commission rules by which disclosure of corporate financial data is compelled and business news is scrutinized.
- □ **know** the limitations and rights that apply to corporate participation in candidate elections, ballot measures, and debates on public issues.
- □ **know** how government agencies and their employees are restricted in their ability to speak out on political matters.

Hypothetical

■ The Faulty Resort

Assume you are the director of corporate communications for Grand Hideaways, a resort/hotel chain listed on the New York Stock Exchange. A year ago the company boldly committed to building a huge coastal resort complex at a cost of $185 million. You have been in charge of all publicity, media relations, and financial news disclosures pertaining to the resort project.

This week has brought bad news, however. Construction of the resort was about one-third complete when a report by state geologists revealed for the first time that the resort site is directly adjacent to an active earthquake fault. The report has been made public, and the *Wall Street Journal* ran a short story indicating that design modifications might be required for your project. In a confidential board meeting a few days later, you learn that because of a stringent earthquake-safety ordinance major changes will need to be made to the structure. These changes will delay completion of the project by ten months and will cost $60 million—pushing the total cost of the project drastically over budget. You send a news release to the financial press, but in the release you deliberately downplay the extent of the company's financial problem. Because you don't want to scare off stockholders and potential investors, the release simply states that scheduled construction on the project "will be delayed by two or three months while workers install an estimated $5 million in special earthquake safety features." Would this less-than-honest news release be illegal?

Grand Hideaways faces a political challenge, too. Pending in the state legislature is a bill by Senator O'Riley that would require even more extensive safety precautions for buildings in fault zones. If the bill passes in its current form, Grand Hideaways would need to spend another $25 million in order to comply. Therefore, you plan to take the following actions: First, you plan to inform the state's voters directly of the potential economic costs of the bill, hoping that voters will ask their legislators to reject it. Second, as a gesture to help persuade the senator to amend the bill, you plan to contribute $50,000 of corporate assets to Senator O'Riley's reelection committee. Do either of these planned forms of political expression raise legal considerations?

Introduction

A substantial portion of today's communications experts work as public relations or public information professionals, and two of the biggest employers of those professionals are corporations and government. Corporations and government entities play unique and powerful roles in society, and their spokespersons consequently are subject to some special restrictions. These restrictions apply not because the content of their speech is unworthy; indeed, corporations and government employees can contribute much to public discourse on the most serious matters of national policy. Rather, restrictions are imposed because of the nature of the entities in question and the special responsibilities owed to their constituencies. It has long been thought that corporate and government speakers must be curtailed to some extent because their unique and powerful voices could threaten the integrity of the proverbial free marketplace of ideas.

Corporations are business entities created under authority of state law. They are considered artificial entities in the sense that they are accorded personalities, or legal status, entirely separate from the personalities of any individual stockholders or officers. Corporations can own property, incur debts, sue, and be sued in their own names, for example, quite apart from the activities of the individuals who own or manage the corporation. In this way corporations are different from partnerships or sole proprietorships, the other main forms of business ownership.

The states recognize many different kinds of corporations, such as professional corporations, non-profit corporations, and "close," often family-owned, corporations. This chapter details how the corporations that draw the greatest sentiment for speech caps are for-profit business corporations that amass capital—in some cases billions of dollars of capital—by selling shares through the public stock exchanges. These business corporations actually are owned by the investors, or stockholders, who in turn elect a board of directors to steer the corporation. By law, corporate directors are supposed to make decisions in a manner that serves the financial interests of the investors. The directors are deemed to occupy a position of special trust vis à vis the shareholders, sometimes referred to as a *fiduciary relationship*.

Government entities and employees, too, are often thought to occupy a corporate-like fiduciary position in relation to citizens and taxpayers. In fact, local governments are sometimes called *municipal corporations*. At first it might seem odd to suggest that government employees are in any way subject to extra speech restrictions, for the most visible icons of government—the elected politicians—often conjure up images of fast-talking, opinionated individuals on the campaign trail. But for purposes of this chapter it is important to realize that most government employees, including most government communications experts, are considered **civil service** employees. This term refers to nonelected government positions that are filled competitively on the basis of merit and not political considerations.

At the federal level, the Civil Service Act of 1883 established a system by which most federal employees are appointed on the basis of competitive examinations and then paid, retained, and promoted according to objective, apolitical standards. The states have enacted similar civil service statutes to cover employment at the state, county, and city levels. These civil service employees are expected to perform in a nonpartisan fashion.

Corporations and Investors

Business corporations raise capital in large part by offering to investors various kinds of stocks and bonds, known collectively as **corporate securities.** Once on the market, most types of securities may be freely traded, meaning bought and sold, by speculating investors. This trading is usually accomplished through a national stock exchange. Furthermore, owners of a certain class of stock called *common stock* are empowered to participate in corporate decision making by voting on candidates for the board of directors and also on some policy matters.

Business corporations and the stock markets, then, are complex and also fragile institutions. They are fragile in the sense that they depend on honest communications and absolute fairness with respect to all investors. Since the stock market Crash of 1929 and the Great Depression, corporate expression of significance to the investing public has been regulated heavily by the federal government; the agency in charge is the Securities and Exchange Commission.

The Securities and Exchange Commission

The Securities and Exchange Commission (SEC) is an independent federal regulatory agency headed by five commissioners appointed by the president. The SEC was created in the post-Depression era, via the Securities Exchange Act of 1934, to protect investors and ensure that corporate securities markets are fair and honest. The commission administers various securities laws enacted by Congress and has authority to pass its own regulations.

The SEC seeks to protect investors primarily by ensuring that corporations adequately disclose relevant information. For example, issuers of corporate stocks must file with the SEC registration statements containing financial and other pertinent data about the issuing corporation and the securities being offered. But the SEC's authority extends far beyond the policing of formal corporate reports. All corporate announcements of likely significance to investors may be scrutinized by the commission.

The commission uses a variety of enforcement tools to secure compliance with the federal laws pertaining to corporations and their securities. The SEC can go to federal District Court to obtain injunctions against fraudulent or misleading practices; it can conduct its own quasijudicial prosecutions of people charged with violating the securities laws; it can fine corporations that disobey the disclosure requirements or antifraud provisions; and it can suspend stockbrokers and investment advisers who violate the laws. Indeed, the entire realm of corporate financial and investor communications is heavily regulated, and the authority of the Securities and Exchange Commission is continually evident to those who are responsible for communicating corporate information.

Corporate Reports

Chapter 2 noted that government violates the First Amendment not only when it bans speech but also when it compels speech. This was true in *Miami Herald Co. v. Tornillo,* for example, in which Florida attempted to compel newspapers to run viewpoints opposing their editorials. The principle against mandatory speech generally holds true for nonmedia companies as well. For example, in the 1986 case of *Pacific Gas & Electric Co. v. Public Utilities Commission,* the Supreme Court held that a utility company could not be required to disseminate the views of a ratepayers' group. The utility, PG&E, had for many years distributed a newsletter to millions of customers in its monthly billing envelope. The newsletter contained editorials, feature stories, and tips on energy conservation. But when the California Public Utilities Commission ruled that PG&E must include in its billing envelope the opposing views of a ratepayers' group, the utility charged that its First Amendment rights had been violated. The Supreme Court agreed, noting that "for corporations as for individuals, the choice to speak includes within it the choice of what not to say."[1]

Despite this general rule, the government does indeed compel corporations to disclose considerable information for the benefit of investors. The disclosures are made through an array of formal documents and reports that are filed with the SEC, and the reports must follow government requirements as to form, content, and timing. These disclosure requirements have never been held to violate a corporation's First Amendment rights. Among the most important corporate filings are the following.

Securities Registration

A corporation may not offer any security for sale in interstate commerce unless it files first with the SEC a registration statement containing prescribed information. The registration statement is divided into two parts, the first of which is called a **prospectus.** The prospectus is a detailed financial document that also will be distributed to interested investors and brokers. The justification for this requirement is that a uniform prospectus format assists investors in evaluating securities offers. Corporations must also file with the SEC a registration form that contains additional corporate information not required in the prospectus.

Annual Report

Corporations with registered securities must file an **annual report** with the commission. The annual report provides a comprehensive overview of a corporation's business, and it must be filed at the end of a company's fiscal year. In most cases the annual report is filed on Form 10-K. This mandated report is separate from the slick, magazine-format annual reports that many companies produce for their shareholders.

Quarterly Report

Most companies must file a quarterly report on Form 10-Q for each of the first three fiscal quarters. The report includes unaudited financial statements and provides a continuing view of a corporation's financial position during the year.

Proxy Materials

Corporations must conduct shareholder meetings at least once a year at which the shareholders are entitled to vote on candidates for the board of directors and on matters of corporate policy. A **proxy statement** is a document intended to provide a company's shareholders with the information necessary to enable them to vote in an informed manner at the meeting. The statement typically also includes one or more proxy solicitations from people seeking authority to vote the shares of stockholders who will not attend the meeting. Copies of all proxy materials sent to shareholders must also be filed with the SEC. There the staff scrutinizes the materials to assure that they are in compliance with the numerous proxy regulations aimed at ensuring fair and complete disclosure.

Rule 10b-5

Less regimented than the government's disclosure and filing requirements are several laws that prohibit fraudulent or misleading corporate communications in any context relevant to investors. The most far-reaching of these laws is an SEC regulation known simply as **Rule 10b-5.** The rule reads as follows:

> It shall be unlawful for any person, directly or indirectly, by the use of any means or instrumentality of interstate commerce, or of the mails, or of any facility of any national securities exchange,
>
> (1) to employ any device, scheme, or artifice to defraud,
> (2) to make any untrue statement of a material fact or to omit to state a material fact necessary in order to make the statements made, in the light of the circumstances under which they were made, not misleading, or
> (3) to engage in any act, practice, or course of business which operates or would operate as a fraud or deceit upon any person, in connection with the purchase or sale of any security.[2]

At first glance, Rule 10b-5 is just a basic antifraud law that prohibits people from misleading others in connection with the purchase or sale of corporate stocks or bonds. The rule prohibits untrue statements of a material nature, meaning statements that would likely be considered by investors when deciding whether to purchase or sell securities. On the surface, then, 10b-5 is little different than state statutes that prohibit fraudulent statements by a person selling an automobile.

However, 10b-5 has enormously broad implications because of the manner in which corporate stocks are bought and sold in the United States. Rarely are stock transactions made face to face, like auto sales. Instead, stocks are bought and sold anonymously through national stock exchanges. The seller has no idea who the ultimate purchaser of the stock will be, nor does the purchaser have any idea of the identities of the sellers who have made their shares available on the exchange. Nevertheless, Rule 10-b applies, and this has led to two important ramifications.

First, 10b-5 works to prohibit **insider trading**—the purchase or sale of a corporation's securities by insiders in the corporation who are privy to material infor-

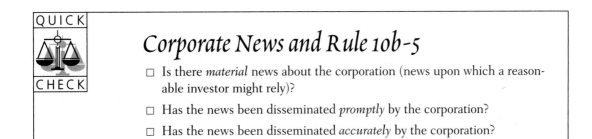

Corporate News and Rule 10b-5

☐ Is there *material* news about the corporation (news upon which a reasonable investor might rely)?

☐ Has the news been disseminated *promptly* by the corporation?

☐ Has the news been disseminated *accurately* by the corporation?

mation not available to outside investors. Even though the securities transactions are not made face to face and are essentially made with unidentified people, the insiders still are required to state all material facts to the other parties in the transaction. What this ultimately means is that an insider may not personally buy or sell the corporation's securities until the information relied upon by the insider has been made broadly available to the investing public. This is accomplished typically by the release of news reports to the financial press and general-circulation newspapers.

The second important and far-reaching ramification of 10b-5 is that corporations must promptly release financial news to the news media, and the releases must be accurate in all material respects. It's hard to find any other example in the law of a legal requirement that news releases be prompt and accurate. But whenever corporate financial news is not promptly or accurately disseminated, investors around the country are essentially buying or selling securities under false suppositions. By misleading these investors a corporation would violate Rule 10b-5.

The TGS Case

Both 10b-5 ramifications are illustrated in the classic case of *Securities and Exchange Commission v. Texas Gulf Sulphur Co.,* a 1968 decision in which a federal appeals court clarified the meaning of the rule. The case arose from exploratory drilling that Texas Gulf Sulphur (TGS) conducted in eastern Canada in 1963. The drilling revealed remarkably good deposits of copper and zinc. The handful of company insiders who knew of the confidential exploratory drilling results purchased TGS stock while the company moved ahead with a land acquisition program. When drilling resumed several months later, a few TGS officers, including the president and vice president, received daily progress reports but the reports were kept confidential. The reports revealed a substantial, commercially minable body of ore.

Meanwhile, rumors of a major ore strike began circulating throughout Canada, and eventually two New York newspapers ran unauthorized reports that implied a rich strike by TGS. With the aid of a public relations consultant, the company vice president drafted a press release designed to quell the rumors. The release, which appeared in several newspapers, read in part as follows:

> NEW YORK, April 12—The following statement was made today by Dr. Charles F. Fogarty, executive vice president of Texas Gulf Sulphur Company, in regard to the company's drilling operations near Timmins, Ontario, Canada. Dr. Fogarty said:
>
> "During the past few days, the exploration activities of Texas Gulf Sulphur in the area of Timmins, Ontario, have been widely reported in the press, coupled with rumors of a substantial copper discovery there. These reports exaggerate the scale of operations and mention plans and statistics of size and grade of ore that are without factual basis and have evidently originated by speculation of people not connected with TGS. . . .
>
> "The work done to date has not been sufficient to reach definite conclusions and any statement as to size and grade of ore would be premature and possibly misleading. When we have progressed to the point where reasonable and logical conclusions can be made, TGS will issue a definite statement to its stockholders and to the public in order to clarify the Timmins project."[3]

The effect of this release on the investing public was not certain, but the New York *Herald Tribune,* in a story headlined "Copper Rumor Deflated," quoted from the TGS release and backtracked from its earlier report of a major strike. Drilling continued for several more days before TGS made an official announcement of its find at a press conference. Based on the foregoing actions by TGS, the Securities and Exchange Commission prosecuted a complaint against the company for violation of Rule 10b-5.

The court stated that behind 10b-5 was the intent of Congress and the SEC that all members of the investing public should be subject to the same market risks. But the TGS insiders were not trading on equal footing with the outside investors, the court said. The insiders alone were in a position to evaluate the probability of what seemed from the outset to be a major ore strike; they alone could invest with the secure expectation that TGS stock prices soon would rise substantially. Such inequities based upon unequal access to information cannot be shrugged off as inevitable, the court said. Therefore, the court held that all transactions in TGS stock by the insiders apprised of the drilling results were in violation of 10b-5.

But the court did not stop there; it then addressed the legality of the April 12 news release. The SEC argued that issuance of the release also violated 10b-5 because the release painted a misleading and deceptive picture of the drilling progress. The court of appeals agreed, noting that government intended to prohibit any misleading statements made by or on behalf of corporations—irrespective of whether insiders are contemporaneously buying stock of the corporation and irrespective of whether the corporation had any ulterior purpose in making the statement. This is simply because a misleading statement of material information can seriously injure the investing public.

The court concluded that by downplaying the extent of the ore find the TGS release could have misled a reasonable investor. The court sent the case back to the District Court for a hearing on whether the release was indeed misleading. The district judge ultimately ruled that the news release was misleading and that it violated Rule 10b-5. These findings were upheld on a second appeal. TGS contended that the finding of a 10b-5 violation for mere negligence in the issuance of the press release infringed its First Amendment rights. But the court disagreed, holding that the corporate report on drilling operations was a kind of speech in the same category as corporate registration statements and prospectuses.[4]

Lawsuits by Investors

Since *Texas Gulf Sulphur,* dozens of other 10b-5 cases have reached the courts based on allegations that corporate news releases were misleading. Disgruntled investors, rather than the SEC, initiated most cases.[5] Though Rule 10b-5 does not expressly grant investors a right to file private lawsuits, the courts have long interpreted the rule to provide this right. Therefore, it is possible for vigilant and discontented investors to recover large damage awards through 10b-5 lawsuits. For a private investor to win a fraud case under 10b-5 the plaintiff must show:

1. That there was a false representation of material fact
2. That the defendant knew of the falsity or was reckless in making the representation
3. That the plaintiff reasonably relied on the information
4. That the plaintiff therefore suffered a financial loss

In the 1988 case of *Basic Inc. v. Levinson*[6] the Supreme Court faced the difficult issue of Rule 10b-5's application to secret merger negotiations. Combustion Engineering and Basic agreed to merge. The decision was reached after two years of merger discussions between the companies. During those two years Basic made three public statements denying that any merger negotiations were taking place. The statements were made in a media interview, a press release, and a shareholder report. Basic shareholders who sold their stock after the public denials filed a lawsuit claiming that Basic's statements were false and misleading in violation of Rule 10b-5. Basic argued that preliminary negotiations are not material facts and that it would be highly damaging to corporations and their shareholders if such negotiations could not be conducted in confidence.

The Supreme Court declared that an omitted fact is material if there is a substantial likelihood that a reasonable investor would consider its disclosure significant. The Court rejected a proposed rule that preliminary merger discussions do not become material until the negotiators have reached a basic agreement. Rather, materiality depends on the probability that the proposed transaction will be consummated and its likely significance to the value of the securities. Therefore, the Court remanded the case for a factual determination of whether a reasonable investor in this case would have placed significance on the misrepresented information.

However, the Court in *Basic v. Levinson* declined to answer the intriguing question of timing—the point at which a duty to disclose arises—as opposed to the question of material accuracy when an announcement is made. In other words, instead of issuing public statements that lied about the existence of merger talks, what if Basic had simply decided to remain silent on the topic? If the First Amendment is not interpreted to protect corporate lying of relevance to investors, should it at least provide corporations the right to determine when they will speak?

The Supreme Court in *Basic* indicated that management could consistently and safely say "No comment" in response to news reporters' questions about merger rumors—at least up to a point. But the Court declined to state the point at which disclosure of corporate activity becomes mandatory. Should a court give deference to management's judgment on whether merger talks have reached the point of being material? Or will courts not hesitate to second-guess corporations' judgments on the timing of newsworthy announcements? This remains quite uncertain.

Thus the *Basic* case is a good one for illustrating that corporate communicators under 10b-5 law find themselves in a uniquely perilous position. Political communicators can issue flat-out lies and, absent defamation, their speech is fully protected. But corporate communicators must pay special attention to difficult issues of materiality, timing, and accuracy—in an arena where vigilant investors and the SEC are on the lookout for missteps. In the future there are likely to be many more lawsuits concerning the timing of corporate news announcements, and those lawsuits are likely to contain serious First Amendment challenges to particular applications of Rule 10b-5.

It should at least be clear from the foregoing discussion that the news release issued in the chapter hypothetical could cause serious liability under Rule 10b-5. Recall that the release deliberately understated the estimate of the resort corporation's needed expenditure for earthquake safety features as well as the time frame for completion. This falsification would qualify as material because the disparity was of a magnitude that investors might consider relevant in determining the economic health of the company.

Corporations and Political Influence

Corporate political speech, unlike corporate investor-oriented speech, often has been declared by the courts as the kind of speech that lies at the very heart of First Amendment protection. Nevertheless, corporations also have been viewed with disdain and suspicion by many who fear that big companies are capable of dominating the nation's marketplace of political expression and destroying the integrity of the democratic system. Therefore, corporate political speech has been the target of many legislative restrictions, and the courts have upheld some of those restrictions.

Influencing Candidate Elections

The greatest concern about corporate political speech has centered on the ability of corporations to give large sums of money directly to selected political candidates or to use corporate funds to purchase advertising on behalf of candidates. This double-edged concern involves what the law calls **political contributions** and **independent expenditures.** A political contribution is a direct donation of money or some other asset to a candidate's campaign. It is the candidate, or the candidate's campaign committee, that will determine how the donation will be used to further the candidacy.

An independent expenditure, in contrast, is not given to or coordinated with the candidate. Rather, the donor independently spends money for a communication that advocates the election or defeat of a particular candidate. An example would be a TV commercial urging voters to "Elect Jefferson Smith to Senate," if the commercial were sponsored, written, and produced by a corporation without direction from the Smith campaign. News stories or commentaries run by *media* corporations, however, do not count as independent political expenditures subject to regulation.

Campaign Reform Statutes

Congress in 1971 enacted the comprehensive Federal Election Campaign Act (FECA),[7] an intricate package of legislation intended to curb corruption—and perceived corruption—in all phases of the federal election process. The act requires, for example, that campaign committees for federal candidates file detailed financial reports with the Federal Election Commission (FEC), listing contributions received and monies spent by the campaigns.

The act also places restrictions on political contributions to those campaigns and even on independent political expenditures. Individuals, for example, may contribute no more than $1000 to any one candidate in an election. And while they may make independent expenditures without limit, individuals must file a report with the FEC if expenditures exceed $250 during a year.

But for corporations the restrictions are much more severe. The act prohibits corporations from using their corporate funds to make contributions to candidates or to make independent expenditures for or against candidates. Federal regulations allow corporations to make limited, partisan communications to their own stockholders and executive personnel,[8] but they cannot use corporate funds to advise the general public how to vote on election day.

Though the Federal Election Campaign Act applies only to campaigns for federal elective office, the states have enacted their own campaign reform laws to cover statewide and local campaigns. Some state laws are modeled closely after the federal act and therefore prohibit partisan corporate contributions and expenditures.

Campaign Reforms vs. the First Amendment

For decades public sentiment has favored stricter campaign finance laws to curb the real or perceived influences of big money in elections. Constructing such laws can be difficult, however, considering that First Amendment rights of political speech are implicated at every turn. The first major court test was *Buckley v. Valeo,* a lawsuit challenging the constitutionality of many Federal Election Campaign Act provisions as they applied to individuals. In its 1976 ruling, the Supreme Court declared that contribution and expenditure limitations indeed implicate fundamental First Amendment interests. Wrote the Court:

> A restriction on the amount of money a person or group can spend on political communication during a campaign necessarily reduces the quantity of expression by restricting the number of issues discussed, the depth of their exploration, and the size of the audience reached. This is because virtually every means of communicating ideas in today's mass society requires the expenditure of money.[9]

The Court therefore employed strict scrutiny to determine whether the restrictions were narrowly drawn to prevent real problems of corruption or the appearance of corruption. In *Buckley* the Court upheld the $1000 contribution ceiling that applies to individuals because, it concluded, there is indeed an overriding justification in preventing the corruption that can spring from large contributions made directly to candidates. One the other hand, the Court held unconstitutional a similar provision in the original act that had limited the amount of independent expenditures that individuals could make on behalf of candidates. Political expenditures are even more closely connected with an individual's political expression than are contributions to candidates, the Court said, and the likelihood of candidate corruption is not as great with regard to independent expenditures.

However, the *Buckley* case concerned only the limitations on individuals, not the statutory prohibitions on corporate contributions and corporate independent expenditures. That issue was left to later cases, and in those cases the corporate bans on both contributions and expenditures generally have been upheld.

Like the Federal Election Campaign Act, the Michigan Campaign Finance Act prohibits corporations from using their funds to make contributions and expenditures in connection with candidates' campaigns. In 1990 the U.S. Supreme Court upheld the Michigan expenditure prohibition in *Austin v. Michigan Chamber of Commerce.* The central issue in the case was whether it is constitutional for government to prohibit a private, nonprofit corporation—the state Chamber of Commerce—from making an independent expenditure on behalf of a political candidate. The Court ruled that such restrictions are valid, at least where the nonprofit corporation is funded largely by for-profit business corporations.

The purposes of the state Chamber, as set out in its bylaws, were to promote economic conditions favorable to private enterprise, to train and educate its members, to foster ethical business practices, and to receive contributions and make expenditures for political purposes. The Chamber had more than 8000 dues-paying members, three-quarters of which were for-profit corporations. Though the Chamber had established a separate, segregated fund for making political contributions, the Chamber in 1985 sought to use its general treasury funds to place a newspaper advertisement supporting a candidate for the state legislature (Exhibit 9.1). Such an expenditure amounted to a felony under Michigan law.

The Supreme Court in *Michigan Chamber* acknowledged, as it had in *Buckley v. Valeo,* that a statute prohibiting or limiting independent expenditures for candidates does indeed burden freedom of expression—in this case corporate freedom of expression. But the Court nevertheless found that the prohibition was supported by a compelling state interest in avoiding corruption or the appearance of corruption. Wrote Justice Marshall for the majority:

> State law grants corporations special advantages—such as limited liability, perpetual life, and favorable treatment of the accumulation and distribution of assets—that enhance their ability to attract capital and to deploy their resources in ways that maximize the return on their shareholders' investments. These state-created advantages not only allow corporations to play a dominant role in the nation's economy, but also permit them to use "resources amassed in the economic marketplace" to obtain "an unfair advantage in the political marketplace." . . . We therefore have recognized that "the compelling governmental interest in preventing corruption supports the restriction of the influence of political war chests funneled through the corporate form."[10]

The Chamber argued that even if the law is constitutional as applied to business corporations, there is insufficient justification to support its application to nonprofit organizations. The Chamber argued that it was more like a voluntary political association than a for-profit corporation. But the Supreme Court disagreed, saying that because the Chamber accepted money from business corporations it could too easily serve as a conduit for political spending by corporations wishing to circumvent the prohibitions of the Michigan law.

Ideological Corporations

The Supreme Court has, however, carved out one constitutional exception to the prohibitions on corporate independent expenditures. It is an exception for some kinds of nonprofit, ideological corporations. *Federal Election Commission v. Massachusetts Citizens for Life, Inc.*[11] concerned a nonprofit, nonstock corporation that obtained contributions from regular donors and various fundraising activities for the purpose of promoting a right-to-life message. In 1978 Massachusetts Citizens for Life (MCFL) distributed a special election edition of its newsletter and admonished readers to vote for the pro-life candidates identified in the newsletter. A

EXHIBIT 9.1

Michigan Needs Richard Bandstra To Help Us Be Job Competitive Again

The Michigan State Chamber of Commerce, an organization of over 8,000 member companies, associations and local chambers of commerce, is committed to making Michigan more competitive for business investment and job creation. With that goal in mind, we'd like to share some facts with the electors in the 93rd House District before they vote in tomorrow's special election.

To be job competitive, Michigan needs to have fair regulatory policies on business regarding such important issues as workers' compensation and we need to encourage greater efficiency in state government by lowering the state personal income tax.

Currently, workers' compensation costs are 20% higher in Michigan than those in neighboring states. Why? Our eligibility standards are not the same as most other states. Too many people are allowed to qualify for too long a period of a time.

Many Grand Rapids businesses are competing with firms in other states having lower regulatory costs. Unless checked, this disadvantage may continue to cost Michigan jobs . . . jobs that are lost when businesses leave Michigan, expand out of state, or when out-state companies seeking to expand don't locate here in Michigan.

To ensure that Michigan is job competitive, we need legislators at the State Capitol who will show courage and stand up to special interests that advocate greater regulation and taxes.

The Michigan State Chamber of Commerce believes Richard Bandstra has the background and training to do the best job in Lansing for the people of the 93rd House District. We believe he will work to reduce workers' compensation costs and for an early rollback of the personal income tax rate.

The State Chamber is committed to job development in Michigan. We believe Richard Bandstra shares that commitment.

On Monday June 10th, Elect Richard Bandstra State Representative 93rd House District Special Election

MICHIGAN STATE CHAMBER OF COMMERCE

Not authorized by the Candidate Committee of Richard Bandstra
Paid for by the Michigan State Chamber of Commerce • Suite 400, 200 N. Washington Square • Lansing, Michigan 48933

complaint was filed with the Federal Election Commission alleging that the news-letter violated the Federal Elections Campaign Act.

The Supreme Court held that the newsletter did fall within the definition of an expenditure on behalf of candidates and therefore would be in violation of the statute. However, the Court went on to hold that the statute was unconstitutional as applied to nonprofit, ideological corporations such as MCFL. In his opinion for the Court, Justice Brennan noted that if MCFL were not organized in corporate form, its only obligations under the Campaign Act would be a few disclosure re-quirements that apply to unincorporated organizations that occasionally make political expenditures. But because MCFL happened to be incorporated, the or-ganization could not use its own funds to express opinions on candidates. Instead, it would have to establish a separate segregated fund to engage in indepen-dent spending. And because these funds are subject to substantial additional reg-ulation, the statute's practical effect might be to discourage protected political speech.

Such an infringement on First Amendment activity must be justified by a com-pelling government interest, the Court noted. In most other corporate expenditure cases that justification could be found in the need to restrict the influence of po-litical war chests built with corporate assets and to ensure that general-purpose corporate treasuries are not diverted for political purposes against the wishes of in-vestors. In short, the usual justification for the corporate expenditure prohibition is the compelling one of avoiding unfair deployment of corporate wealth for polit-ical purposes.

In this case, though, the usual justification did not apply. The Court said groups such as MCFL do not pose the same danger of corruption or misuse of cor-porate funds. This is because MCFL was formed specifically to disseminate po-litical ideas, not to amass capital and increase equity of investors. The Court therefore held that FECA's ban on independent political expenditures could not constitutionally apply to corporations that (1) are formed for the express pur-pose of promoting political ideas rather than engaging in business, (2) have no shareholders or others who have a claim to its assets, and (3) are not established or funded by for-profit business corporations.

Keep in mind, however, that this ruling in favor of nonprofit ideological corpo-rations applies only to their independent political expenditures. Campaign contri-butions by such corporations remain prohibited by FECA and state statutes.

Political Action Committees

The upshot of the *Michigan Chamber* and *MCFL* cases is that most corporations must abide by federal and state statutes prohibiting independent expenditures for or against candidates, and all presumably are bound by prohibitions against direct contributions to candidates. But the campaign laws do allow corporations a way to participate in elections: It is to establish what the FECA calls a **separate segre-gated fund,** more commonly referred to as a **political action committee** or

PAC. A corporation may establish, administer, and solicit contributions to a PAC, and the PAC is free to make partisan expenditures and contributions (within the contribution limits set by statute).[12]

The sponsoring corporation may appoint the PAC's officers, direct its political decision making, and pay for such operating costs as administrative salaries and office overhead—as long as no portion of the actual political fund comes from the corporate treasury. This is important to remember. The corporation's assets *cannot* be used to fund the actual campaign contributions or independent expenditures made by the PAC. Rather, donations are solicited specifically for that purpose, and the money contributed to the PAC is held in a separate bank account from the corporate assets. With the donated funds, PACs may make contributions to dozens or even hundreds of candidates, up to the limits specified by statute. (The limit under FECA is $5000 per candidate per election.) Furthermore, the Court in *Buckley v. Valeo* apparently cleared the way for PACs to make unlimited independent expenditures to communicate their views on candidates.

As of January 2000, there were 3835 federally registered PACs in the United States—down from a peak of 4268 PACs in 1988—and they disburse hundreds of millions of dollars a year to help their favored candidates get elected. About half of these PACs are sponsored by profit-making corporations. Others are sponsored by labor unions, trade organizations or other nonprofit organizations, and some are unconnected to any sponsoring organization.

PACs play a significant role—too significant, some say—in shaping American politics. Yet PACs are subject to considerable regulation. In addition to observing the contribution limit, PACs must comply with extensive recordkeeping and reporting requirements. For example, any PAC that makes expenditures or contributions to a federal candidate must register with the Federal Election Commission. The registration must include a PAC name that clearly provides the identity of the sponsoring organization. Following registration the PAC treasurer must maintain records of all monies received by the PAC and of all funds contributed to candidates or to other political organizations. The records must disclose the names and addresses of all people contributing more than $50 to the PAC. The treasurer also must file with the FEC, as often as monthly, a report of receipts and disbursements.[13]

One of the most controversial PAC restrictions under FECA—and one that directly curbs First Amendment freedoms—pertains to the manner in which PACs may solicit contributions. Generally, a corporation or its PAC may solicit only the company's stockholders and its executive or administrative personnel. Nonprofit corporations may solicit only members. A PAC may not solicit funds from the general public or even from rank-and-file employees of the sponsoring corporation. Naturally, this solicitation restriction reduces the amount of money a PAC can raise, which in turn reduces the amount that can be spent on candidates who share a PAC's concerns.

The Supreme Court dealt with the solicitation restriction in *Federal Election Commission v. National Right to Work Committee,* a 1982 ruling. The National Right to Work Committee (NRWC) was a nonprofit, nonstock corporation organized "to help make the public aware of the fact that American citizens are being required, against their will, to join and pay dues to labor organizations in order to earn a living."[14] To comply with the FECA prohibition on corporate contributions, NRWC in 1975 established a separate segregated fund to receive and make contributions on behalf of federal candidates. The NRWC sent letters to 267,000 individuals who had made prior donations to the organization, asking them to contribute to the new PAC. The NRWC maintained that these individuals qualified as members under the law. But the FEC ruled that a prior donation was not enough to qualify an individual as a member and that the solicitation was therefore illegal.

The Supreme Court sided with the FEC. The Court said the solicitation limitation is constitutional because it serves a compelling purpose: to ensure that the special advantages of the corporate form of ownership cannot be parlayed into huge political war chests that could be used to incur political debts from legislators who receive the contributions. With this purpose in mind, the Court interpreted the term *members* in the statute to refer only to people attached in some way to the corporate structure. Membership requires something more than merely making a contribution to a segregated fund. Rather, the Court said, Congress intended the term to apply to people who satisfy somewhat more formal requirements for association with the organization. A member must have "some relatively enduring and independently significant financial or organizational attachment to the organization," the Court said. Therefore, the NRWC solicitation was illegal.[15]

Further Reforms and "Soft Money"

In addition to administering PACs, corporations can participate in elections by contributing money to political party organizations. By contributing to the parties rather than to candidates directly, corporations take advantage of what some consider a loophole in the federal election laws. Often referred to as **soft money,** the contributions to parties may be made in unlimited amounts, without regulation, and the parties may then spend the money to help the candidates. In 2000, Congress was considering proposals to restrict contributions of soft money.

Around the country, lawmakers in many states also have been under pressure to clamp down on soft money contributions and to address other perceived loopholes or soft spots in state campaign finance laws. In January 2000 the U.S. Supreme Court issued a ruling that encouraged those who favor tighter restrictions. In *Nixon v. Shrink Missouri Government PAC,*[16] the Court upheld a Missouri statute that imposed limits on contributions to candidates ranging from $275 to $1,075, depending on the office being sought. A political action committee challenged the statute, claiming that the limits were too severe and were unsupported by sufficient evidence to withstand First Amendment scrutiny. But the Court, referring to its earlier decision in *Buckley v. Valeo,* said the states do not need "empirical evidence" of the corruption threshold when deciding where to draw the contribution limits. Rather, they may set the maximum allowed amounts based upon anecdotal evidence of money's corrosive influence and upon the perceptions of the electorate.

Influencing Public Issues

Corporate political expression has caused concern not only in terms of influencing the fortunes of candidates but also in terms of influencing sentiment on public issues. In many local and state jurisdictions a legislative issue may be formalized as a ballot measure and put to a public vote as a referendum or initiative. For example, a contentious debate over bear hunting might lead to a state proposal to ban bear hunting by amendment to the state constitution. This proposal then might appear as a ballot measure for the voters to decide. Or a local school district might propose a bond sale to finance new school construction, requiring voter approval within that district.

So the question arises: Should corporations be at liberty to use their assets to influence thinking on such issues, particularly after they are in the form of formal ballot measures? And even if government thought it wise to restrict corporate speech on issues, would a restriction of any degree be constitutional?

The Bellotti Case

The Supreme Court has spoken on this question, and its answer is viewed as definitive. In the 1978 case of *First National Bank of Boston v. Bellotti,* the Court distinguished corporate spending on candidates from spending on issues. With regard to the latter, the Court said, there did not exist the same opportunity for corruption; public officials would less likely be put in the position of owing favors. Therefore, with regard to public issues, a sufficiently compelling reason for restricting corporate expression was absent.

At issue in *Bellotti* was a Massachusetts law that prohibited corporations from making contributions or expenditures for the purpose of influencing the vote on any ballot measure other than one directly affecting the assets of the corporation. Several banks and business corporations wanted to spend money to publicize their opposition to a ballot proposal authorizing a graduated personal income tax. They sued to challenge the constitutionality of the state restriction on corporate political spending.

The Court began its analysis by noting that speech that would otherwise fall within the First Amendment's protection does not lose that protection simply because its source happens to be a corporation speaking out on issues that do not directly affect its assets. Rather, the question is whether the state has justifications so compelling as to override that protection. The Court acknowledged that the state's asserted interests in preventing corruption and preserving the integrity of the electoral process were indeed interests of the highest importance, theoretically. But in this case, the Court wrote, "there has been no showing that the relative voice of corporations has been overwhelming or even significant in influencing referenda in Massachusetts, or that there has been any threat to the confidence of the citizenry in government." Writing for the majority, Justice Powell continued:

> The risk of corruption perceived in cases involving candidate elections simply is not present in a popular vote on a public issue. To be sure, corporate advertising may influence the outcome of the vote; this would be its purpose. But the fact that advocacy may persuade the electorate is hardly a reason to suppress it.[17]

The *Bellotti* case is generally read as a blanket prohibition against restrictions on corporate freedom to express views on public issues. Some legal experts have noted, however, that the Court provided for the possibility of restrictions when it wrote: "If appellee's arguments were supported by record or legislative findings that corporate advocacy threatened imminently to undermine democratic processes, thereby denigrating rather than serving First Amendment interests, these arguments would merit our consideration." In essence, the Court did not rule that restrictions on issues speech were constitutionally impossible; it simply ruled that such restrictions would need solid and substantial evidence of their justification. To date, no ban on corporate discussion of issues has passed the strict constitutional hurdle required by the Court. (See Exhibit 9.2 for a diagram of corporate contribution and expenditure rights.)

When speaking out on public issues, however, corporations must be careful that they do not refer to particular candidates in a manner that crosses the line from a discussion of issues to an "independent expenditure" favoring or opposing candidates for office. Such would be the case if a for-profit corporation distributed a "voters' guide" on environmental issues and in the guide also identified certain "straight-thinking" political candidates who "deserve reelection."

Thinking back to the hypothetical problem at the beginning of this chapter, the *Bellotti* ruling apparently would assure that the resort corporation could legally wage a public information campaign against the earthquake safety bill pending in the legislature. Working to persuade the constituents of legislators in such a fashion is sometimes referred to as *grass roots lobbying* and it is a kind of speech on public issues. But the contribution of $50,000 to the senator's reelection campaign, which did not come from a separate segregated fund, most likely would violate a state statute against corporate political contributions.

Attribution Requirements

For many years state and federal laws have imposed various **attribution requirements** on mass political expression. Attribution laws typically state that any advertising, display, or handout materials that support or oppose particular candidates or ballot measures must also identify the sponsor of the message. The laws

EXHIBIT 9.2   *Corporate Participation in Elections*

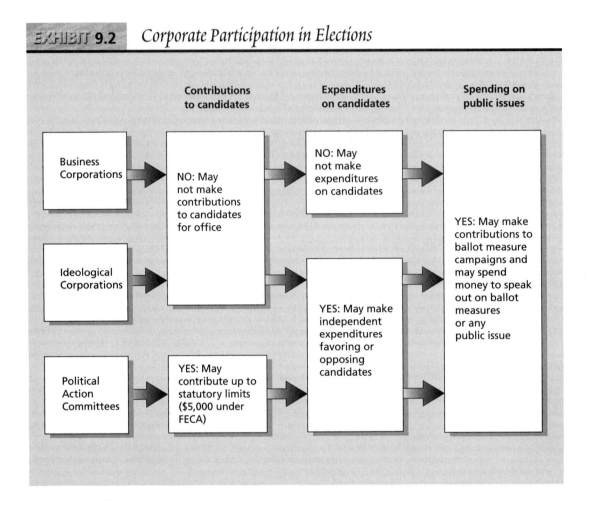

cover not only the advertising of registered campaigns themselves but also the independent expenditures of organizations stating opinions on candidates or ballot measures. It has long been thought that requiring attribution is one way to discourage political hit pieces laced with libel and lies.

These laws were thrown into doubt, however, by the 1995 Supreme Court ruling in *McIntyre v. Ohio Elections Commission.* Margaret McIntyre had distributed leaflets at a public meeting where the local schools superintendent planed to discuss an upcoming school tax referendum. The leaflets expressed McIntyre's opposition. Ohio law required that all such political messages intended to influence an election must contain the name and address of the person or organization issuing the message. But McIntyre's leaflets were signed only "concerned tax payers." McIntyre was fined $100 for violating the law.

The Supreme Court ruled that the Ohio statute violated the First Amendment, however. Wrote Justice Stevens for the Court: "Under our Constitution, anonymous pamphleteering is not a pernicious, fraudulent practice, but an honorable tradition of advocacy and of dissent. Anonymity is a shield from the tyranny of the majority."[18] The Court noted, for example, that the Federalist Papers urging ratification of the Constitution were written by James Madison, Alexander Hamilton, and John Jay, but were signed only "Publius." The Court said the Ohio law indiscriminately outlawed a whole category of speech without the overriding justification necessary for such a broad ban. It noted that, if libel is the concern, it can be discouraged via the state's more narrowly aimed libel laws.

The Court left open the possibility that some attribution laws would be constitutional. But in the five years following *McIntyre,* attribution requirements were struck down in several states. For example, Maine election law required that when a political action committee spent money to advocate a ballot measure the message had to list the name and address of the PAC that authorized the communication. The Yes For Life Political Action Committee wanted to run broadcast ads and distribute handbills urging voters to ban so-called partial-birth abortion in a November 1999 election. But it wanted to distribute its messages without the required disclosures, so it challenged the requirement. Following the *McIntyre* precedent, a federal district court held Maine's law unconstitutional.[19]

Governments and Political Influence

Government entities, like corporations, engender a special kind of public anxiety when they participate in the marketplace of speakers. Government bodies, after all, command substantial resources and authority, and they have the potential to dominate public discourse and intimidate the opposition. Most of this textbook has focused on the legal principles applicable when government attempts to serve as a censor of others' speech. But interesting problems are present when government itself seeks to be a voice in the marketplace.

Legally speaking, it has long been clear that government coercion of speech is constitutionally impermissible. In 1943, for example, the Supreme Court invalidated a West Virginia requirement that all public school children participate in a daily salute and pledge to the flag. Along with the decision the Court announced the sweeping principle that "If there is any fixed star in our constitutional constellation, it is that no official, high or petty, can prescribe what shall be orthodox in politics, nationalism, religion, or other matters of opinion."[20]

But if government may not coerce speech, to what extent may government at least speak to persuade the public on issues of the day? The only provision in the U.S. Constitution that expressly prohibits any kind of government speech is the First Amendment clause that bars Congress and the states from establishing religion. Beyond this, are there any implicit constitutional principles that should prevent a government entity from, say, telling voters how to cast their ballots in a referendum? The opposite side of this inquiry is equally intriguing. When a government body enacts a law specifically restricting the speech of its political subdivisions or its employees, does this law violate rights to free speech?

In most respects, the law on these questions is in an early stage of evolution. One exception is the free speech ramifications of the Hatch Act, a decades-old federal law that has been the subject of much litigation.

Government Employees and the Hatch Act

In 1939 Congress passed the Hatch Act to limit the political activities of federal civil service employees. The intent was to promote government neutrality and the public's trust, and to prevent political patronage from contaminating public service. Until recently the act contained sweeping language that read in part:

> An employee in an Executive agency or an individual employed by the government of the District of Columbia may not—
>
> (1) use his official authority or influence for the purpose of interfering with or affecting the result of an election; or
>
> (2) take an active part in political management or in political campaigns.[21]

The act does not concern official governmental action, but rather the individual political speech and activity of government employees. The act originally vested enforcement authority in the Civil Service Commission, authority that today lies in the successor agency, the Merit Systems Protection Board. Regulations passed by the Civil Service Commission in 1970 specified in greater detail the various activities deemed prohibited under the act, such as soliciting votes for a candidate, endorsing a candidate in a political ad, or addressing a political rally. But the foundation for those regulations, the sweeping statutory prohibition against taking part in campaigns, raised serious constitutional questions.

Constitutionality of the Act

The Hatch Act and its accompanying regulations survived a major constitutional challenge in *U.S. Civil Service Commission v. National Association of Letter Carriers,* a 1973 decision by the Supreme Court. In his majority opinion for the Court, Justice White identified four justifications for the Hatch Act restrictions: First, as an adjunct to the fundamental principle that government employees should administer the laws fairly and impartially, it is essential that federal employees not take an active role in partisan politics. Forbidding such activities as managing a partisan political campaign will reduce the hazards to fair and effective government, White said.

Second, it is important not only that government employees avoid making decisions on political grounds but that they also avoid the appearance of political bias. Otherwise, confidence in the system of representative government will erode to a disastrous extent, White noted.

A third justification is that the expanding government work force should not be employed to build a powerful, invincible, and perhaps corrupt political machine. Wrote Justice White:

> The experience of the 1936 and 1938 campaigns convinced Congress that these dangers were sufficiently real that substantial barriers should be raised against the party in power—or the party out of power, for that matter—using the thousands or hundreds of thousands of federal employees, paid for at public expense, to man its political structure and political campaigns.[22]

Finally, Justice White said the Hatch Act helped serve the goal that employment and advancement in government service should not depend on political performance. Government employees should be free from coercion to perform political chores for superiors, and an effective way to safeguard against such coercion is simply to prevent employees from engaging in political conduct.

The Court found these justifications sufficient to support the Hatch Act restrictions on otherwise protected political activity. Furthermore, the statute was not unconstitutionally vague. The accompanying regulations served to adequately guide employees, the Court said, and a procedure was in place by which employees uncertain about a proposed course of conduct could seek advice from the Civil Service Commission.

Still, numerous questions remained, and lower courts had to help draw the line between expression made in concert with a campaign, which was prohibited, and independent expressions of political opinion, which were permitted under the Hatch Act and protected by the First Amendment. For example, the Court of Appeals held that two Postal Service employees did not violate the Hatch Act by writing articles for union periodicals in which the employees advocated a particular candidate for president. The court wrote: "Absent a showing of concerted action with a partisan campaign or organization, petitioners' rights of freedom of political expression outweigh the asserted risk of inefficient or corrupt government administration.[23]

In another case, a federal employee wrote a letter to the editor of a Montana newspaper expressing his views on a state senatorial candidate's environmental record. The Merit Systems Protection Board ruled in 1983 that this publication was insufficient to constitute active participation in politics. Citing past appellate court decisions, the board noted that a critical distinction must be drawn between whether an employee has expressed independent, personal opinions on political issues, which is allowable, or whether an employee "with deliberation and as part of a concerted political action, has sought the election or defeat of political candidates."[24]

In the mid-1990s Congress revised the Hatch Act section quoted above, significantly narrowing the scope of prohibited political activity by federal employees. The revised section, absent the categorical ban on campaign activity, reads:

An employee may not engage in political activity—

(1) while the employee is on duty;

(2) in any room or building occupied in the discharge of official duties by an individual employed or holding office in the Government of the United States or any agency or instrumentality thereof;

(3) while wearing a uniform or official insignia identifying the office or position of the employee; or

(4) using any vehicle owned or leased by the Government of the United States or any agency or instrumentality thereof.[25]

State "Hatch Acts"

The states have enacted their own versions of the Hatch Act. The state laws typically apply to nonpartisan employees at both the state and local levels. As with the federal law, the state statutes do not attempt to rein in the political expression of government officials who are elected or appointed to partisan political posts.

In 1973 the Supreme Court of Florida held a portion of that state's Hatch Act unconstitutional because it provided that a knowing violation of the law was a misdemeanor. Imposition of criminal sanctions for political activity extends beyond the tradition of the federal Hatch Act, which simply allows for a penalty of discharge from public employment. The Florida court concluded that the criminal penalty was unconstitutional because it was not necessary for ensuring impartiality in public service. The court upheld the portion of Florida law that provided for dismissal from service.[26]

Employee Honoraria

The Hatch Act and state equivalents aim to limit the partisan political activities of rank-and-file government employees. But another increasing concern in recent years has been the acceptance by government employees of honoraria—compensation for making speeches or writing articles. Criticism has been most frequently leveled at members of Congress who supplemented their incomes by accepting substantial honoraria for speaking to special-interest groups. But there also has been criticism of honoraria paid to officials in the other branches of government. The underlying concern is that government officers not abuse their positions or create an appearance of improper influence by seeking or accepting appearance money.

In an effort to combat the rising criticism over honoraria, Congress passed the Ethics Reform Act of 1989, and in it prohibited the acceptance of honoraria by nearly all federal employees in all three branches of government. The act did not confine itself to high-level officials; it extended to hundreds of thousands of rank-and-file employees, prohibiting their acceptance of payment for appearances, speeches, or articles on any subject. A huge class of federal employees—

executive-branch employees earning from $11,900 to $86,500—challenged the constitutionality of the restriction. In the 1995 case of *United States v. National Treasury Employees Union,* the Supreme Court sided with the employees.

Unlike an isolated disciplinary action for disruptive expression, the Court noted, the honoraria ban was a broad, before-the-fact ban with great capacity to chill speech. Therefore, the government had a heavy burden to justify the law. It needed to show that the interests of both potential audiences and a vast group of employees in a broad range of expression are outweighed by that expression's necessarily harmful impact on the actual operation of government. This the government could not do.

Noting the honorarium typically paid to these employees was relatively minor and was for speech unrelated to their government jobs—such as occasional lectures or articles about their hobbies—the Court concluded that the government had not shown how such expression posed a threat to the proper performance of official duties. Therefore, as to this class of rank-and-file employees, the honoraria ban was held unconstitutional.[27] The Court specifically distinguished the honoraria ban from the restrictions of the Hatch Act, which were designed to combat demonstrated ill effects of government employees being used as partisan political spokespersons.

Official Government Persuasion

A different legal problem is presented when government agencies take official stands on issues and then use public monies to persuade the public. If the government speech is clearly partisan in nature, such as urging a particular vote on a ballot measure, courts have tended to find that the use of tax dollars for such expression is an abuse of government authority. Furthermore, state statutes may specifically prohibit a government agency from expending public time or money for partisan expression. On the other hand, governmental entities are heavily involved in educating the public on many issues—from the hazards of smoking to the benefits of conservation—and use of public funds for such purposes has not been thought to raise legal problems.

One of the most frequently cited cases in this area is *Stanson v. Mott,* a 1976 decision by the California Supreme Court. A taxpayer filed the lawsuit against the director of the California Department of Parks and Recreation, alleging that the department had illegally expended more than $5000 of public funds to promote passage of a statewide bond initiative. The bond proceeds were to be used to acquire park and recreational land. California's high court held that, at least in the absence of explicit legislative authorization, a public agency may not expend public funds to promote a partisan position in an election campaign. And in this case, the court said no such authorization existed. The department had express authority to disseminate information to the public relating to the bond election, but in doing so the department is obligated to provide a fair presentation of the facts and to avoid promotional speech, the court said.

The California court in *Stanson* cited a long-standing common law principle that an administrative department may spend public money only insofar as it is authorized by legislation. Furthermore, even where there is general authorization to disseminate information, the court said use of government funds to influence elections would raise serious constitutional questions: "A fundamental precept of this nation's democratic electoral process is that the government may not take sides in election contests or bestow an unfair advantage on one of the several competing factions,"[28] the court said.

A more complicated case was decided in 1978 by the Supreme Judicial Court of Massachusetts. In *Anderson v. City of Boston* taxpayers sought a declaratory judgment invalidating the city's proposed expenditures in support of a statewide referendum dealing with property tax assessments. The lawsuit was sparked when the city passed an ordinance authorizing it to spend funds "for the purposes of providing educational materials and disseminating information urging the adoption by the people of a proposed amendment to the Massachusetts Constitution relating to the classification of property for purposes of taxation."[29] Nearly $1 million were appropriated for this effort, and the mayor organized an Office of Public Information on Classification especially for the "educational" campaign.

The Massachusetts court began its analysis with the same issue addressed in *Stanson*: whether the city had express state authority to appropriate funds for the informational campaign. The court concluded that it did not. This conclusion was reached after reviewing the extensive state statutes pertaining to corporate political expenditures and reporting requirements and finding that municipal corporations were entirely absent from the legislation. This was interpreted as evidence of legislative intent that cities not engage in such activities.

But the Massachusetts court could not end its analysis with this ruling on legislative authorization. The city of Boston further argued that even if there were a legislative direction that it not use municipal funds to influence the outcome of a referendum, it had a First Amendment right to do so. The court found virtually no case law directly pertaining to this question of First Amendment rights for municipalities. Looking to the traditional applications of the First Amendment, however, the Massachusetts court concluded that the amendment has nothing to do with a state's determination to refrain from certain speech and to bar its various subdivisions from spending public funds for such speech. The U.S. Constitution does not forbid all government communications efforts that are other than purely informative and neutral, the court said, but neither does the Constitution guarantee that a government subdivision may engage in such speech.

Even assuming that government entities do possess First Amendment rights, however, the court in *City of Boston* noted that those rights could be overridden by a compelling interest. The court compared the plaintiffs' claim against the municipal corporation to a shareholders' lawsuit against a private corporation. "This action is thus an aspect of corporate democracy whose validity the Supreme Court seemingly acknowledged in *First National Bank v. Bellotti*," the Massachusetts court said.[30] The court also cited *First National Bank* for the proposition that it was possible for compelling justifications to exist that would allow for greater political speech restrictions on private corporations than on individuals. Likewise, the court said, there may exist special, compelling interests to support a speech restraint on the city. The court ended its lengthy analysis by concluding that a compelling interest did indeed exist—an interest in assuring fairness in elections and the appearance of fairness in the electoral process.

Summary Points

Both corporations and government entities occupy positions of special trust and power—with regard to shareholders, members, taxpayers, and the public at large—and therefore some significant reasons exist for controlling the speech of these institutions.

Corporate speech aimed at investors is heavily regulated by Congress and the Securities and Exchange Commission. Numerous kinds of disclosures such as annual reports and proxy statements are required, and they must be filed in the form prescribed by government.

In addition, all corporate announcements of interest to investors—including news releases and the statements made at press conferences—are subject to the antifraud provision known as Rule 10b-5.

The Federal Election Campaign Act (FECA), administered by the Federal Election Commission (FEC), is a complex package of legislation that controls virtually all phases of the federal election process. States also have campaign reform laws, often with provisions that mirror those in FECA.

Under FECA corporations are subject to numerous restrictions on political speech. To understand the applicability of these restrictions and the extent of constitutionally protected corporate speech, it is important to distinguish contributions from expenditures, business corporations from ideological corporations, and candidate elections from referenda.

Corporations may avoid restrictions on candidate contributions and expenditures by operating separate segregated funds, often called PACs. These PACs, however, are subject to many other regulations.

Political speech by government agencies and their employees also may be restricted. Active political participation by federal civil service employees, whether on or off duty, is prohibited by the Hatch Act. Official agency efforts to persuade the public on political matters also may be unlawful, under common law or constitutional principles.

In the chapter hypothetical, the less-than-honest news release for Grand Hideaways has the potential to mislead reasonable investors and would thus pose problems under the SEC Rule 10b-5. The grass roots persuasion campaign would qualify as protected corporate speech under *First National Bank v. Bellotti.* But the attempted corporate campaign contribution would likely be illegal under state law equivalents of FECA.

Discussion Questions

1. Suppose that, as director of communications for a large business corporation, you were asked to draft a news disclosure policy for your staff. To help assure that no violations of Rule 10b-5 occur, what content and timing guidelines would you include in your policy?
2. In ruling upon government restrictions on corporate political speech, the courts have given much attention to the First Amendment and have demanded a compelling justification for the restrictions. But judicial discussion of the First Amendment is sparse in cases pertaining to SEC restrictions on investor-oriented speech. Is there a valid legal distinction between political and financial speech? Is financial speech less important?
3. The Supreme Court in *First National Bank v. Bellotti* said it had no evidence that corruption would result from corporate spending to influence public issues. Can you think of any scenarios in which massive corporate spending on an issue *would* tend to compromise the objectivity of candidates or public officials? What if the spending were to drum up support for a particular U.S. senator's pending bill? If the senator also were up for reelection, would this spending be categorized as spending on an issue or might it amount to an illegal expenditure on behalf of a candidate?
4. Suppose, in the chapter hypothetical, that the state geology department became convinced that Senator O'Riley's earthquake safety bill was unnecessary and counterproductive. Could the public information officer for the department conduct a public persuasion campaign, using department funds, to sway public and legislative sentiment against the bill? Should there be any legal distinction between this and a situation in which the bill appears as a statewide ballot measure?

Key Terms

annual report	political expenditures
attribution requirements	prospectus
civil service	proxy statement
corporate securities	Rule 10b-5
insider trading	separate segregated fund
political action committee	soft money
political contributions	

Web Resources

http://www.sec.gov/
Federal Securities and Exchange Commission (SEC)

http://www.fec.gov
Federal Election Commission (FEC)

InfoTrac® College Edition

Campaign finance reform was among the hot topics in the year 2000 political races. Use PowerTrac to search for an article or commentary on corporate speech, the First Amendment, and the implications of Supreme Court precedent in this area. Do you think further restrictions on corporate contributions or expenditures are likely?

Chapter Outline

Commercial Speech

Upon completing this chapter you should

- ☐ **know** the extent of First Amendment protection afforded to commercial speech and how that protection has evolved.
- ☐ **understand** how deceptive advertising is regulated by the states and the federal government and, in particular, understand the role of the Federal Trade Commission in policing advertising.
- ☐ **know** which laws provide for criminal penalties against advertisers, which allow for private lawsuits by business competitors, and which allow for private lawsuits by consumers.
- ☐ **understand** how the courts determine when government can ban or otherwise regulate even truthful commercial advertising.
- ☐ **know** who—advertisers, ad agencies, and/or the media—can be held responsible for illegal advertising—and know the basic rules concerning media refusal of advertising.

Hypothetical

■ Guns and Subscribers

Suppose you are the publisher of a widely circulated magazine, *Guns Monthly,* for people whose hobbies include gun collecting, hunting, or target shooting, or who are otherwise interested in guns. You and your marketing advisers decide to institute an aggressive advertising campaign for the magazine. You purchase time on several TV stations for a thirty-second commercial to solicit new subscriptions. In the commercial a well-known professional baseball player, standing at what appears to be a shooting range, holds up a copy of the magazine and says: "During the off-season I relax by target shooting at gun clubs like this one. And I've also learned to count on *Guns Monthly* for top-quality articles, pictures, charts, and diagrams that help me enjoy and appreciate firearms." The baseball celebrity then urges viewers to call the number on the screen and order the magazine for the introductory price of $21.95 per year. The commercial also states that, along with the order, new subscribers will receive a free package of *Guns Monthly* foam ear plugs, "the ones specially designed to help protect a marksman's hearing."

A few things about the commercial are not exactly what they seem, however. The baseball player wasn't really at a gun club, but was taping the commercial on a realistic indoor set. In addition, the baseball player does not actually read *Guns Monthly.* In fact, he had never seen a copy prior to arriving to record the commercial. Also, the stated introductory price is actually a dollar higher than the magazine's usual introductory rate. The extra dollar is to partly recoup the cost of the ear plugs. Furthermore, although the *Guns Monthly* ear plugs do indeed help protect shooters' hearing, they are no different in this regard than any other brand of foam ear plugs.

Meanwhile, you are quite concerned with another matter. Congress has just passed legislation that bans all advertising for firearms. Such advertising accounts for more than half the ads carried in your magazine, so the ban could be devastating to you. Congress determined the ban was justified because tens of thousands of people are killed by firearms in this country each year, including 2000 of them accidentally. The advertising ban, Congress thought, would be one way to help reduce the demand and ultimately the prevalence of firearms in society.

Would the courts uphold the gun advertising ban as constitutional? Does your TV commercial violate any laws against deceptive advertising?

Introduction

Commercial speech—that which is intended to generate marketplace transactions—is a target of lawsuits and regulations from almost every conceivable direction. Indeed, in the midst of this chapter one might come to wonder whether the old common law phrase, *caveat emptor,* or "Let the buyer beware," is in any way a valid generalization about legal doctrine today. As far back as 1937, the Supreme Court declared that U.S. law had evolved to the point where it protected the trusting consumer as well as the suspicious. In the world of commerce, the Court said, "the rule of *caveat emptor* cannot be relied upon to reward fraud and deception."[1] Today in many respects it is the commercial advertiser who had best beware.

Yet even as the age of consumerism was bearing down upon commercial speech, this form of expression was gaining some measure of First Amendment status. Castigated as self-serving and socially worthless for most of this century, commercial speech can indeed benefit consumers and should not be subject to unbridled government restrictions, the Supreme Court has decided in recent years.

Many of the legal problems discussed elsewhere in this book are of significant concern to commercial messengers. These include time/place/manner restrictions (on billboards, for example), trade libel, commercial appropriation of name or likeness, copyright infringement, trademark infringement, and the common law tort of unfair competition. Such general legal concerns as breach of contract and fraud also arise occasionally in connection with the deceitful advertising or promotion of goods and services. It is not the purpose of this chapter, however, to revisit the legal principles covered earlier or to examine the broad field of commercial transactions law. Rather, this chapter looks at some of the specialized legal considerations faced by commercial speech—over and above the points of communications law made elsewhere in this book. The laws of concern in this chapter are statutes and administrative rules that restrict the content of commercial messages—messages that typically appear in the form of paid advertising.

Regulation of commercial speech is a matter of shared jurisdiction of the states and the federal government, which has broad authority to regulate on matters affecting interstate commerce. At the federal level, Congress has enacted laws that are enforced against advertisers by business competitors or by designated federal agencies, most notably the Federal Trade Commission (FTC). The FTC also is granted authority to enact its own regulations against deceptive advertising, consistent with the statutory mandate of Congress.

At the state level, legislatures pass laws that restrict commercial advertising content in the interest of protecting a state's consumers. Primary responsibility for enforcing the state statutes falls to state attorneys general and local prosecuting attorneys. But in some cases business competitors and even consumers are allowed to enforce the laws through private lawsuits.

Commercial Speech and the First Amendment

Historically, courts classified commercial speech as a form of expression unprotected by the First Amendment, thus open to the possibility of virtually unlimited regulation. Commercial speech was left unprotected because it was considered to be an entirely self-serving form of expression that contributed nothing to public discourse.

The Supreme Court endorsed this traditional view in the 1942 case of *Valentine v. Chrestensen*. In that case a man who had purchased a used navy submarine passed out leaflets urging people to come tour the vessel for a fee. Police stopped the man and informed him that a city ordinance prohibited distribution of commercial leaflets on the streets. (Educational or political leaflets were permitted.) A unanimous Supreme Court upheld the ordinance. The Court noted that streets are indeed proper places to communicate information and opinion freely and that local governments may not unduly burden or ban such expression. But the Court said it was "equally clear that the Constitution imposes no such restraint on government as respects purely commercial advertising."[2]

For three more decades the Court seemed to adhere to the *Valentine* approach with respect to commercial advertising. During that period the Court upheld a local ban on door-to-door magazine subscription solicitations (1951), a state ban on ads for eyeglass frames (1955), and a federal ban on broadcasting cigarette ads (1972).[3] In none of these cases did the Court indicate that the First Amendment was even an issue.

The Rise to Protection

In the mid-1970s, the Supreme Court's view of commercial speech shifted toward some degree of First Amendment protection. The first signal of this shift came in a 1975 case in which a Virginia newspaper editor had been convicted for running an ad that announced the availability of legal abortions in New York. At the time a Virginia state statute prohibited any abortion promotions. But the Supreme Court reversed the conviction and rejected the notion that commercial speech was totally without First Amendment protection.[4] Yet the abortion ad decision did not conclusively establish that purely commercial speech is constitutionally protected. The facts of the case did not lend themselves to that conclusion because the abortion ad did more than simply propose a commercial transaction; it contained factual material, clearly of public interest, about an important issue of the time. What would the Court say about a routine ad that simply announced a product and price and invited a purchase?

A year later, in the 1976 case of *Virginia State Board of Pharmacy v. Virginia Citizens Consumer Council, Inc.*, the Court squarely held that "pure commercial speech"—that which aims solely to propose a commercial transaction—is generally protected by the First Amendment. A Virginia statute had made it illegal for pharmacists to advertise prices for prescription drugs. The statute was challenged, not by pharmacists, but by an individual consumer and two nonprofit consumer groups. Their claim was that the First Amendment entitles the users of prescription drugs to receive information that pharmacists wish to communicate to them through advertising.

The Court first addressed the interesting point of First Amendment doctrine and acknowledged that the amendment does indeed confer a limited "right to receive information." Wrote Justice Harry Blackmun for the majority: "Freedom of speech presupposes a willing speaker. But where a speaker exists, as in the case here, the protection afforded is to the communication, to its source and to its recipients both."[5]

The Court next addressed the issue of whether purely commercial speech is excepted from First Amendment protection and concluded that it is not. Even assuming that the advertiser's interest is a purely economic one, Justice Blackmun wrote, that fact does not disqualify the speech for protection under the First Amendment. Economic motive does not mean the speech is without individual importance or social merit. And generally speaking, he said, society has a strong interest in the free flow of commercial information:

> As to the particular consumer's interest in the free flow of commercial information, that interest may be as keen, if not keener by far, than his interest in the day's most urgent political debate. . . . Advertising, however tasteless and excessive it sometimes may seem, is nonetheless dissemination of information as to who is producing and selling what product for what reason, and at what price.[6]

This did not end the discussion in *Virginia Pharmacy Board,* however, for the question remained: Was the advertising ban justified by reasons that outweighed the First Amendment protection? The state argued that the advertising ban was justified because of the need to maintain a high degree of professionalism on the part of licensed pharmacists. The state claimed that aggressive price competition would result from unlimited advertising and that this would divert pharmacists' attention from professional service and reduce their status to that of mere retailers. Justice Blackmun did not articulate a specific First Amendment standard for commercial speech, but he did conclude that the state's asserted justifications were simply insufficient to override protection. "Virginia is free to require whatever professional standards it wishes of its pharmacists; it may subsidize them or protect them from competition in other ways," Blackmun wrote. "But it may not do so by keeping the public in ignorance of the entirely lawful terms that competing pharmacists are offering."[7]

The following year the Supreme Court turned its attention to advertising in the professions. In *Bates v. State Bar of Arizona* two Arizona attorneys challenged a state disciplinary rule that prohibited lawyers from advertising their services in any mass medium. The state prohibition—which applied even to the mere advertisement of prices for legal services—was claimed by Arizona to be justified because advertising would allegedly (1) erode the profession's service orientation, (2) push fees higher because of increased overhead costs for lawyers, and (3) stir up more litigation in society.

But the Court, citing *Virginia Pharmacy Board,* held that blanket suppression of lawyers' advertising violated the First Amendment. To the extent attorneys' ads were false or misleading, they could be subject to restraint. Claims as to the quality of services might fall into this category, the Court said. But the Court ruled there is nothing inherently misleading about ads that announce the availability and terms of routine legal services. Nor was the Court persuaded that any of the state's proffered justifications were sufficient to suppress such ads. Justice Rehnquist dissented in *Bates,* arguing the traditional view that commercial advertisements are "not the sort of expression that the Amendment was adopted to protect."[8]

The *Central Hudson* Test

The *Virginia Pharmacy Board* decision set a strong precedent in favor of constitutional protection for commercial speech, and it is looked upon as a landmark case. The ruling did not clearly establish how much protection commercial advertising was afforded, however. It did not pronounce a test or standard of review for courts to use in later cases. That came in 1980, in the case of *Central Hudson Gas & Electric Co. v. Public Service Comm'n of New York.*[9]

Four-Part Test

In *Central Hudson* the Court was asked to determine the constitutionality of a New York state ban on promotional advertising by electric utilities. The ban had been instituted on grounds that advertising that promotes the use of electricity is contrary to the national policy of conserving energy.

In a majority opinion by Justice Lewis Powell, the Supreme Court observed a commonsense distinction between speech proposing a commercial transaction, which occurs in an area (commerce) traditionally subject to government regulation, and other kinds of speech. Therefore, the Court concluded that commercial speech is accorded lesser protection than other constitutionally guaranteed expression. The Court then set out the following four-step analysis to determine the constitutionality of regulation:

1. Is the commercial message either misleading or related to unlawful activity? If so, it is not constitutionally protected and may be banned. If not:

2. Does the government assert a substantial interest to be achieved by the restriction on speech?

3. Does the restriction directly advance this interest?

4. And is the restriction no more extensive than necessary to further the government's interest? If the answer to these last three questions is yes, the restriction on truthful commercial speech will be upheld.

Applying the test to the facts in *Central Hudson,* the Court concluded first that the commercial expression at issue was indeed protected speech because it was not argued to be inaccurate or related to unlawful activity. Further analysis was necessary. Second, the Court agreed that the state's interest in conserving energy was a substantial interest given the nation's dependence on energy sources beyond its control. Third, the Court also agreed that the advertising ban directly advanced the state's interest because there is a direct link between promotion and increased sales—in this case increased demand for electricity. On the fourth and final point, however, the Court ruled against the state. The advertising ban was a restriction more extensive than necessary to further the state's interest because the ban applied to all promotional advertising by the utility, regardless of its effect on energy use. Energy conservation, important as it is, could not justify suppressing information about electrical devices or services that would cause no increase in energy use, the Court said. Therefore, the ban was unconstitutional.

Part four of the *Central Hudson* test initially caused some confusion among lower courts. As stated in *Central Hudson,* the requirement is that a restriction on commercial speech be no more extensive than necessary. But does the term "necessary" mean *absolutely* necessary? No, the Court clarified in 1989; it means *reasonably* necessary. In order to be constitutional, an advertising restriction need not be the single least severe means of achieving the government's goal. Rather, the test requires a reasonable "fit" between the government's ends and the means chosen. The advertising restriction must be narrowly tailored to achieve the government's objective, but government is entitled to some reasonable choice among various well-tailored regulatory methods.[10]

Comparisons with Other Speech

The Supreme Court made it clear in *Central Hudson* and other cases that commercial speech is not protected to the same extent as speech that is primarily ideological or educational. One distinction is that protection for commercial speech is deemed lost if the expression is false or misleading. No similar exception exists for political speech. In some cases false political speech can be subject to a lawsuit for libel. But there is no general rule that misleading political speech is unprotected by the Constitution. Another distinction is that protection for purely commercial speech may be overcome by a *substantial* government interest. Most other forms of protected speech can be overridden only by a *compelling* justification.

Given the lesser degree of protection for commercial speech, it is sometimes critical to determine whether a communication is commercial or noncommercial. The Supreme Court has noted on several occasions that it does intend to draw a fine line, if necessary, and that the inclusion of some current political issue in a commercial message will not transform the overall nature of the expression. For example, in a footnote to the *Central Hudson* opinion the Court said that promotional advertising would not be accorded full First Amendment protection simply because the touted products or services may be tied to public concerns with the environment, energy, economic policy, health, or safety.

In *Bolger v. Youngs Drug Products Corp.* the Supreme Court was asked to judge the validity of a federal statute that prohibited the mailing of unsolicited contraceptive advertisements. The contraceptive manufacturer who challenged the statute routinely mailed informational pamphlets that discussed the desirability and availability of condoms in general, as well as mentioning the manufacturer's products in particular. Therefore, the Court's initial inquiry was whether the pamphlets were commercial or noncommercial. Despite the basic informational content and the discussion of public issues, the Court ruled that the mailings amounted to commercial speech. If a contrary rule were adopted, the Court said,

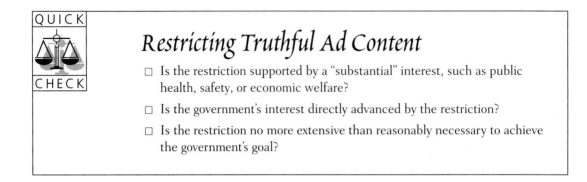

Restricting Truthful Ad Content

☐ Is the restriction supported by a "substantial" interest, such as public health, safety, or economic welfare?

☐ Is the government's interest directly advanced by the restriction?

☐ Is the restriction no more extensive than reasonably necessary to achieve the government's goal?

then other advertisers could "immunize false or misleading product information from government regulation simply by including reference to public issues."[11]

In *Bolger* the Court noted a few characteristics of the mailings that warranted their classification as commercial speech. They were the fact that (1) the company paid for the pamphlets, (2) that the pamphlets included references to a specific product, and (3) that the company had an economic motive for mailing the pamphlets. The Court declined to say whether all of these three characteristics were necessary elements of commercial speech, however. The bottom line is that commercial speech is protected to a lesser degree than most noncommercial speech, and the courts are likely to classify as commercial any speech from an organization whose primary objective in the communication is to prompt sales.

Ad Bans for Disfavored Products

Most commercial advertising regulation is aimed at false and misleading advertising, the kind that is unprotected by the First Amendment. This field of regulation is examined later in the chapter. But some restrictions also have been aimed at truthful advertising of lawful—though typically "disfavored"—products and services.

For example, in the *Bolger* case the federal statute at issue prohibited mailing of all unsolicited contraceptive ads, not just those that were false. In deciding that the manufacturer's mailings were commercial speech, First Amendment protection was diminished. But because the pamphlets were truthful, a moderate degree of protection remained. In order for the statute to be valid as applied to the plaintiff's truthful pamphlets, the government had to show that the restriction was carefully tailored to serve a substantial interest. The government asserted two interests. The first was to protect recipients from offense. The second was to allow parents to control their children's access to birth-control information. The Court ruled that these interests were insufficient, however, and held the statute unconstitutional as applied. The majority opinion noted that government can never shut off the flow of protected mailings for the mere reason of shielding people who might be offended. Furthermore, the ban on mailings would provide only a marginal degree of assistance to parents.

Another example of restrictions on truthful commercial speech—one that has been in effect for more than twenty years—is the federal ban on cigarette advertising in the broadcast media. The statute reads that "it shall be unlawful to advertise cigarettes on any medium of electronic communication subject to the jurisdiction of the Federal Communications Commission."[12] Note that here again, the approach of Congress was to restrict advertising of a controversial product rather than to ban or restrict the product itself. The Supreme Court upheld the statute in 1972 without issuing a written opinion. Recall, though, that this was prior to the *Virginia State Board* case in which the Court for the first time granted constitutional protection to purely commercial messages.

The Posadas *Case*

In the 1986 case of *Posadas de Puerto Rico Assocs. v. Tourism Co. of Puerto Rico* [13] a divided Supreme Court held that government's greater power to ban casino gambling completely includes the lesser power to ban advertising of casino gambling. Casino gambling is legal in the U.S. commonwealth of Puerto Rico. However, the Puerto Rican government, fearing a host of negative gambling-related effects upon its own populace, passed a statute that prohibited gambling advertisements directed at residents. Casino ads directed at nonresident tourists were permitted. The statute was challenged as unconstitutional on its face, and the Supreme Court split 5–4 on the issue.

Writing for the majority, Chief Justice Rehnquist applied the *Central Hudson* test as follows. First, he noted that the advertising at issue concerned a lawful activity and that the advertising was not being attacked as deceptive. Therefore, the remaining three steps of the *Central Hudson* analysis were applicable. *Substantial interest:* The government's interest was in the reduction of demand for casino gambling. It sought this reduction because, it said, gambling would lead to such harmful side effects as increased crime, prostitution, and corruption, and the infiltration of organized crime. These welfare and safety concerns were substantial, the Court majority held. *Directly advanced:* The Court held that the Puerto Rico Legislature's reasoning was sound when it concluded that advertising aimed at residents would increase the demand for gambling and that a ban on advertising would therefore lead directly to lower demand. *No broader than necessary:* Finally, the Court held that the ad ban was a narrow method by which to accomplish the government's goal:

> [T]he Puerto Rico Legislature surely could have prohibited casino gambling by the residents of Puerto Rico altogether. In our view, the greater power to completely ban casino gambling necessarily includes the lesser power to ban advertising of casino gambling. . . . It would be a strange constitutional doctrine which would concede to the legislature the authority to totally ban a product or activity, but deny to the legislature the authority to forbid the stimulation of demand for the product or activity through advertising. . . .[14]

The government was thus deemed to have met its burden under this restrictive application of the *Central Hudson* test, and the advertising ban was upheld.

The *Posadas* ruling came with a strong dissenting opinion by Justice Brennan, however. Brennan disagreed that Puerto Rico had a substantial justification for the ban. The actual legislative history indicates, he said, when the legislature legalized casino gambling it specifically concluded that it would *not* produce serious side effects in Puerto Rico. Further, Brennan doubted that the ad ban would directly advance the legislature's stated interests in reducing crime because the casinos remained open to residents and were actively promoted to tourists. And finally, Brennan said that the suppression of protected speech was a far broader action than attacking the perceived harms directly. For example, Puerto Rico should instead vigorously enforce its criminal statutes and establish limits on the level of permissible betting, Brennan said.

Thus the *Posadas* case left considerable uncertainty about just how the *Central Hudson* test would be applied in the future and whether it would be a significant hurdle for government. But in more recent cases the Supreme Court has consistently used the *Central Hudson* test to invalidate government restrictions. The trend appears to be toward more stringent protection of commercial speech.

The Liquor Cases

As one might guess, advertising for alcoholic beverages has been the subject of considerable state and federal regulation. Though the Twenty-First Amendment to the Constitution is interpreted to give the states great latitude to control alcohol, restrictions on liquor advertising may nevertheless raise serious First Amendment concerns. This is illustrated by Supreme Court cases in 1995 and 1996.

The first of these cases was *Rubin v. Coors Brewing Co.* Coors had applied to the Bureau of Alcohol, Tobacco, and Firearms for approval of proposed labels and ads that disclosed the alcohol content of its beer. The application was rejected on the ground that a federal statute specifically prohibited disclosure of the alcohol content of beer on labels or in ads. Coors sued for a declaratory judgment that the statute violated the First Amendment.

The government's main justification for the restriction was to prevent "strength wars" among brewers. Competition on the basis of alcohol strength would lead to greater alcoholism and its attendant social costs, the government said. The Court, in an opinion written by Justice Clarence Thomas, equated these interests to the health-and-welfare concerns at issue in *Posadas* and agreed they were substantial. However, the government encountered great difficulty with the next part of the *Central Hudson* test.

The Court reiterated that the government must show its regulation directly advances the asserted interests and that this cannot be established by mere speculation and conjecture. Rather, the government must demonstrate that its restriction will in fact alleviate real harms to a significant degree. This the government could not do in *Coors,* the Court held, because of the overall irrationality of the government's regulatory scheme. The Court noted, for example, that while the federal statute banned the disclosure of alcohol content on beer labels, it allowed and in some cases even required the disclosure of alcohol content for wine and spirits. "If combating strength wars were the goal, we would assume that Congress would regulate disclosure of alcohol content for the strongest beverages as well as for the weakest ones," Justice Thomas wrote.[15] Furthermore, the government was already allowing some brewers to signal high alcohol content through use of the term "malt liquor." In sum, the Court said, the challenged restriction could not actually be effective in preventing strength comparisons and alcoholism because of the government's own, countervailing laws and regulations.

In the Court's 1996 case, *44 Liquormart, Inc. v. Rhode Island,* the issue was whether the state could constitutionally prohibit the advertising of alcohol prices. In an effort to promote temperance in the consumption of alcohol, Rhode Island banned price advertising except at the place of sale. The theory behind the ban was that it would prevent public price wars, thereby minimizing discount shopping and the purchase and consumption of added amounts of alcohol. Seeking a declaratory judgment that the price-advertising ban was unconstitutional, 44 Liquormart sued. A unanimous Supreme Court held the ban invalid. Though the justices were split in their reasoning, all seemed to agree, at least, that Rhode Island's restriction was overly broad and therefore flunked the final prong of the *Central Hudson* test. Alcohol consumption could be tempered more directly and efficiently by setting minimum prices or increasing sales taxes, the Court noted. Four justices went further by repudiating the First Amendment analysis in *Posadas* and expressing nearly categorical hostility toward any regulation that seeks to manipulate consumers' behavior by keeping them in the dark about truthful, nonmisleading information.[16]

Casinos Revisited

In 1999 the Supreme Court handed down another decision on casino advertising, and this time a unanimous Court sided with the First Amendment. At issue in *Greater New Orleans Broadcasting Association, Inc. v. United States* was a federal statute that prohibits broadcasters from airing any commercials for gambling. The statute is broadly worded but also contains many exceptions. The Federal Communications Commission interpreted the statute to ban, among other things, any broadcast ads for privately owned casinos.

An association of Louisiana broadcasters challenged the restriction, for the stations wished to air promotional ads for casinos that are legal in Louisiana and neighboring Mississippi. The lower federal courts, applying the *Central Hudson* test in a manner consistent with the *Posadas* case, granted summary judgment in favor of the government. They concluded the government had a substantial interest in minimizing participation in gambling, in order to minimize gambling's social costs, and that the ad ban was a well-tailored way to serve that interest.

But the Supreme Court disagreed, holding the statute unconstitutional as applied to broadcasters in states where casinos are legal. Justice Stevens, writing for the Court, said the government cannot persuasively argue that the ban directly advances a substantial interest when the government's own prohibitions on gambling and gambling ads are so riddled with exceptions. For example, the statute in question prohibits all broadcast ads about privately operated casinos. But ads for tribal casino gambling, legalized by state compacts, are subject to no such ban. Furthermore, the Court said, the ad ban sacrifices an intolerable amount of truthful speech about lawful conduct when compared to the social ills government could reasonably hope the ban to eliminate. In a clear departure from *Posadas* reasoning, the Court held: "The power to prohibit or regulate particular conduct does not necessarily include the power to prohibit or regulate speech about that conduct."[17]

In a concurring opinion, Justice Thomas was even more forceful, reiterating a position he introduced in a concurrence to *44 Liquormart*:

> In cases such as this, in which the government's asserted interest is to keep legal users of a product or service ignorant in order to manipulate their choices in the marketplace, the Central Hudson test should not be applied because such an interest is *per se* illegitimate and can no more justify regulation of commercial speech than it can justify regulation of noncommercial speech."[18]

Though the majority of the Court remains content with the *Central Hudson* balancing approach, it is clear from *Greater New Orleans Broadcasting* that the Court will look very skeptically upon advertising bans for products or services that the government itself has determined should be available.

How about the ban on gun advertising posed in the chapter hypothetical? Would a federal ban likely be constitutional? Even more so than casino gambling or alcoholic beverages, gun ownership traditionally has been legal in the United States. Under the Second Amendment it might even be argued that private gun ownership is constitutionally protected (an issue not yet decided by the Supreme Court). Therefore, even though firearms are also a major public-safety concern, language in these recent cases suggests that a ban on advertising would be unconstitutional. Government's biggest hurdle would be showing that a ban on gun ads directly and significantly advanced government interests in public safety while the government allows guns themselves to be available with so few restrictions.

Required Disclosures

As an alternative to outright bans, advertisements for some legal products are required to contain specified language in the form of a warning, notice, or other disclosure. In fact, some legal authorities predict that disclosure requirements will become a highly fashionable legislative approach in years to come. This is because mandated disclosures are generally viewed as a less objectionable kind of restriction on free speech. As Chapter 2 detailed, forcing prescribed speech can indeed raise constitutional concerns. But courts have also stated, as a matter of basic First Amendment doctrine, that "disclaimers are preferred over blanket proscriptions of speech."[19]

Perhaps the best known of the disclosure requirements is the Federal Cigarette Labeling and Advertising Act.[20] Under that law all forms of cigarette advertising, including billboards, must contain one of four specified warning labels, such as: "SURGEON GENERAL'S WARNING: Smoking causes lung cancer, heart disease, emphysema, and may complicate pregnancy." The law also specifies that the warning statement must appear in conspicuous and legible type, in contrast with other printed material in the ad, and enclosed in a rectangle of a particular size.

Many other kinds of disclosure requirements have been enacted by the federal government and by the states. For example, the federal Food, Drug, and Cosmetic Act requires food and drug manufacturers to list ingredients on their product labels and on certain promotional materials used inside stores where the products are sold.[21] Also, some state laws require that advertisements include the price for certain kinds of products or services.

Deceptive Ads and the FTC

In *Virginia State Board of Pharmacy* the Supreme Court described the importance of commercial advertising in a free-enterprise system and to some extent elevated the legal status of that expression. The Court made no attempt, however, to raise the status of deceptive commercial advertising, considered a despicable practice in society since the era of traveling medicine shows and "snake oil" peddlers in the late 1800s and early 1900s. False or deceptive commercial advertising, which enjoys no First Amendment protection, has been declared unlawful in every U.S. jurisdiction.

Deceptive advertising is combated in many ways: by self-regulation groups within the advertising industry, by screening from the advertising media, by federal Lanham Act lawsuits filed by competitors, and by state attorneys general, for example. Historically, though, the predominant force against deceptive advertising has been the Federal Trade Commission.

Authority of the FTC

The FTC is an independent federal agency headed by five commissioners appointed by the president. No more than three of the commissioners may be from any one political party. Congress created the commission in 1914 and has given it increasingly broad statutory powers. The commission's basic authority is derived from Section 5 of the Federal Trade Commission Act, which charges the FTC with the responsibility to regulate "unfair or deceptive acts or practices in or affecting commerce."[22]

Under this broad directive the FTC combats a wide range of marketplace mischief, from fraudulent pricing and billing schemes to monopolistic practices. From the beginning, though, the FTC has also interpreted its mission to include the policing of advertising. The FTC Act does not define what constitutes an unlawful ad. Rather, the commission has been free to pave its own way through administrative rulemaking—with some guidance from the courts.

Regulatory Aggressiveness

As with other federal regulatory agencies, the FTC's aggressiveness has fluctuated somewhat over the years. During some periods the agency has been criticized by consumer advocates as an inactive and ineffective regulator. At other times the business community has complained that the agency was overbearing in its scrutiny of advertising.

In the 1960s two published reports, one sponsored by consumerist Ralph Nader and the other by the American Bar Association (ABA), were highly critical of the agency. The Nader report charged that the FTC was in disarray caused by poor management, that it lacked sufficient resources and enforcement authority, that it wasted its efforts on trivial matters, and that it should make scrutiny of modern advertising techniques a higher priority.[23] Soon after release of the Nader report, President Nixon asked the ABA to study the commission. The ABA report was nearly as harsh, concluding that drastic changes were essential if the FTC was to achieve its intended effectiveness in the field of consumer protection.[24]

Nixon appointed a new commission chairman and called upon Congress to help revitalize the FTC. Congress did just that by boosting the FTC's budget and by passing a series of statutes in the 1970s that significantly expanded the commission's powers. For example, the Federal Trade Commission Improvement Act,[25] which became law in 1975, strengthened the FTC's power to issue sweeping industrywide rules against certain advertising practices, and it gave the FTC power to sue in U.S. District Court for various forms of redress on behalf of consumers. By the late 1970s, during the zenith of the consumer movement, the FTC was operating as a potent force and was regarded by some as the most powerful of all regulatory agencies in the United States.

In the 1980s, however, in concert with the Reagan administration's emphasis on deregulation, the FTC seemed to back off from its aggressive, proactive role of the 1970s. Critics charged that the agency was abdicating its responsibility to scrutinize sophisticated, national advertising. But others defended the FTC, arguing that regulation had become too aggressive in the 1970s and that some retrenchment therefore was appropriate.

In 1989 the American Bar Association conducted a second study of the controversial FTC. This time members of the ABA's study panel could not agree on whether the FTC was prosecuting a sufficient number of claims against advertisers. But in its published report the panel did conclude: "[W]e are united in our belief that the FTC can and should do more to articulate its advertising law-enforcement agenda. . . . [T]oo rarely has the public received the message that the FTC believes it is important to move aggressively against false and deceptive advertising."[26]

After a decade of budget cuts, the FTC in the 1990s was not realistically in a position to devote the same amount of staff hours to advertising enforcement as it had in the late 1970s. On the other hand, the FTC during the Clinton administration did prosecute some high-profile claims against major advertisers, and it waged an expensive and exhaustive battle against telemarketing fraud across the country. Many of the FTC's enforcement actions in the 1990s concerned health and nutrition claims about food, and the FTC issued a special Enforcement Policy Statement on Food Advertising.[27] In the late 1990s the FTC also worked to promote closer media screening of weight-loss claims ("Operation Waistline") and exercise equipment claims ("Project Workout").

Procedures

At FTC headquarters and at ten regional offices around the country, staff members monitor broadcast commercials and examine the advertising in various other media. In addition, the FTC receives complaints about advertising from many sources, including consumers, consumer groups, members of Congress, local government agencies, and the competitors of alleged violators.

When the FTC receives a complaint or its own monitoring discloses a questionable advertisement, it must decide whether to launch a formal investigation. This decision is made on the basis of various criteria, including the apparent seriousness of the problem, the geographic scope of the advertising, and the current status of agency resources. The FTC tends to concentrate on national advertising and on claims relating to health or safety. When a business comes under investigation for potentially deceptive advertising, it may be asked to provide voluntarily a variety of information to the FTC. The agency also has the power to issue subpoenas to compel anyone to appear and testify or to produce documents.

Upon completion of an investigation, the FTC staff recommends a final course of action for the commissioners. One recommendation could be that the matter simply be closed. Another might be that the company in question be asked to agree on an informal settlement—usually by acceptance of a consent order that the company will discontinue the challenged advertising practice.

If the commission determines that a satisfactory voluntary settlement cannot be achieved, it typically will seek a binding **cease-and-desist order** to halt the illegal advertising. This process begins by issuing a formal, administrative complaint against the company in question. The case then goes to an administrative law judge, within the agency, who conducts a streamlined version of a trial and issues an initial decision. This decision may be appealed to the five-member commission. From the commission a company's next avenue of appeal is directly to the U.S. Court of Appeals.

As an alternative to the administrative proceeding, the commission may go to U.S. District Court and ask that a federal judge issue an injunction to halt the deceptive advertising. In such proceedings the FTC becomes a plaintiff, acting on behalf of consumers or business competitors.

Jurisdiction

Article I, Section 8 of the U.S. Constitution gives the federal government power to regulate commerce "among the several States." The commerce power has been interpreted very broadly by the courts; federal authority extends not only to interstate business activities but to any local activities that may affect interstate commerce. Congress in 1975 expressly passed this broad authority along to the FTC. In the FTC Improvement Act[28] the commission's jurisdiction was extended to "unfair or deceptive acts or practices in *or affecting* commerce." In practice, this means that the FTC can crack down on virtually any advertising campaign, no matter how local.

Furthermore, the FTC's jurisdiction over advertising extends beyond the traditional definition of that term as sponsored messages purchased in the mass media. The FTC may concern itself with any activity intended to draw public attention to a product, service, person, or organization for purposes of trade. Therefore, in addition to regulating magazine ads and television commercials, for example, the FTC may scrutinize product labels, packaging, direct mail, and promotional contests.

Deception: The Basic Elements

Since the early 1980s the Federal Trade Commission has defined **deceptive advertising**—or any deceptive business conduct—as "a material representation, omission, or practice that is likely to mislead a consumer acting reasonably under the circumstances."[29] The FTC must show that deception is probable, among reasonable members of the target audience, and that the deceptive content is "material"—that is, likely to be relied upon to the consumer's detriment (Exhibit 10.1).

Even with this articulated standard, determining whether a particular advertisement is deceptive can be thorny. Again, the application of legal standards to particular facts is by no means an exact science. In libel law, for example, determining whether a statement is one of fact or opinion can be quite problematic. The same is true for application of the fair use test in copyright law or the incitement standard in public safety cases. So it is here. Over the years, however, FTC adjudication of deceptive advertising cases has spawned some important principles for interpreting ads. For the most part these legal principles have been adopted by the states in their own efforts to combat deceptive ads. Some of the most important principles are described in the sections that follow.

EXHIBIT 10.1   *What makes an advertisement deceptive?*

According to FTC policy, an ad is deceptive if it contains a message—or an omission—that:

1. is likely to mislead consumers acting reasonably under the circumstances,

AND

2. is "material," meaning important to a consumer's decision to buy or use the product.

Representation or Omission

The first step in assessing an advertisement for potential deception is to determine what is actually being conveyed by the ad. Ad representations can be express or implied. Naturally, express product claims are the easiest to identify and measure against the truth. For example, an advertisement may not claim that a watch is waterproof unless the watch truly is waterproof, not merely water resistant. Similarly, advertisements could not legally claim that a shampoo cures split ends, that a battery lasts five years, or that a surfboard wax won't melt in the sun—unless the products indeed live up to those claims.

In a national advertising campaign for its Lady Kenmore brand dishwasher, Sears made this express claim: "With a Kenmore you'll never have to scrape or rinse again. Even dishes crusty with leftover food. Kenmore's fourteen powerful hot water jets scour every dish clean . . . with no scraping or pre-rinsing." Unfortunately, the "no scraping, no pre-rinsing" claim was not true. The claim apparently was made as part of a market "repositioning" strategy for the machine. But even the owner's manual, which customers received after they purchased the dishwasher, contradicted the claim by advising purchasers to soak and scour certain dishes. Therefore, in 1982 the federal Court of Appeals upheld an FTC order requiring Sears to cease and desist from making the claims.[30]

A large portion of the FTC's deceptive advertising cases involve implied representations. Although express claims in advertising are easy to identify, implied representations often are more subtle. Sometimes their very existence is debatable. In determining how consumers would likely interpret an ad, the FTC may rely solely on its own experience and intuition or it may consider such outside evidence as expert testimony or consumer surveys. Once the FTC concludes that the public would interpret an ad to include a particular implied message, however, that message is held up to the same scrutiny as an express claim. The actual intent of the advertiser is generally considered irrelevant, even if the advertiser's motives were entirely innocent.

For example, in the 1950s the FTC issued a cease-and-desist order against a businessman, David Erickson, who referred to himself as a "trichologist" and traveled around the country selling various hair and scalp preparations. Before visiting a city Erickson would place an advertisement in local papers. The typical ad contained a picture of Erickson attired in a white lab jacket of the sort customarily worn by and associated with members of the medical profession. The photo showed Erickson pointing to a clinical chart depicting the human scalp. In reality, Erikson had no medical training; his college education was limited to one semester in marketing. Based on the false implications concerning Erickson's credentials, as well as some express product claims about curing baldness, a federal court ordered enforcement of the FTC's order.[31]

Often the implied representation is that the advertiser's product is somehow unique. For example, in the hypothetical problem at the beginning of this chapter, the ad claimed that the *Guns Monthly* ear plugs were "*the* ones specially designed to protect a marksman's hearing." The foam ear plugs may indeed have been designed with that purpose in mind. However, the language of the ad might further imply that these particular ear plugs are somehow unique. If in fact they are no different than other foam ear plugs on the market, the ad could be deemed deceptive on that point.

Because implied representations are scrutinized to the same extent as express claims, an ad may be ruled deceptive even though it is literally true in every respect. For example, Bristol-Myers advertised for a time that doctors recommended the company's pain reliever, Bufferin, more than any other "leading brand" of over-the-counter analgesic. This is literally true. The FTC agreed that during the period of the advertising doctors recommended Bufferin more than Bayer, Excedrin, and Anacin, the other three leading brands at the time. But the commission also found that the implied message of the ads was that physicians recommend Bufferin more than any other over-the-counter, internal analgesic, not just the three other leading brands. Because doctors in fact recommended Tylenol, Ascriptin, and generic aspirin more often than Bufferin, the FTC found the implied message deceptive and the federal court upheld a cease-and-desist order.[32]

Another principle used in interpreting advertisements is that the overall impact is more determinative than isolated words or phrases. Or, as sometimes stated, text must yield to context. Furthermore, the overall impact of an ad is determined not only from the other words used in the ad but also from its visual messages. For example, a magazine ad might be dominated by a series of large, boldface headings arranged in a question-and-answer format. If the primary effect of the ad comes from these headings, which convey a deceptive message, some fine print wedged between the headings would be insufficient to rescue the ad.

Sometimes it is an omission of information that makes an advertisement deceptive. Of course, the FTC has never required that advertisers disclose everything they know about their products. However, unless they are otherwise informed, it is reasonable for consumers to make a few basic assumptions about advertised products. It is generally expected, for example, that advertised goods are new and in undamaged condition. If, in fact, the products being advertised are secondhand or flawed, failure to disclose this information in advertising will be deemed a deceptive omission.

Furthermore, if the nondisclosure is relevant to a point which the ad itself raised, the FTC has tended to insist that the full picture be conveyed. For example, the J.B. Williams Company used TV and print media to advertise its product, Geritol liquid and tablets, for the relief of iron-deficiency anemia. The ads emphasized that consumers who often feel tired and rundown may have "iron-poor blood" and that taking Geritol would make them feel stronger, fast. Looking at the overall impression created by the ads, the FTC found they were deceptive for their failure to disclose that for most people suffering from tiredness, the symptoms are not caused by iron deficiency and that Geritol would be of no benefit in such cases. The FTC therefore ordered that the advertiser affirmatively disclose this limiting fact whenever claiming generally that Geritol is an effective remedy for tiredness.[33]

Likely to Mislead Reasonable Consumer

In determining whether an advertisement is likely to mislead, the FTC will consider the characteristics of the specific audience at which the ad was targeted. For example, suppose the challenged ad is one for a dietary supplement and that it appeared in a medical journal circulated to physicians and a few other health professionals. The FTC would take into account the specialized background and sophistication of the readers in judging whether they would likely be misled. The ad in the medical journal might be deemed acceptable, even though the same ad, if placed in a supermarket tabloid, might be found deceptive. Conversely, advertisements aimed at young children will be judged in light of the immature nature of that target audience.

Aside from the consideration of the actual audience, however, the test of likely deception is an objective one. The commission considers whether a so-called reasonable member of the targeted group would likely have been misled under the circumstances. Again, this is an objective standard in the sense that it is not dependent upon how consumers actually reacted on a particular occasion. In theory, an ad could be ruled deceptive even if no consumer were actually misled by it; or, an ad might be deemed nondeceptive even though some consumers were misled. The FTC will not rule an ad illegal simply because some consumers interpreted the ad in an irrational fashion. But it is possible for an ad to have more than one reasonable interpretation.

One type of advertising claim that the FTC categorically will not rule deceptive is called **puffery,** or *puffing.* The term refers to the kind of commonplace, exaggerated sales talk that consumers should expect to encounter in the marketplace and that reasonable shoppers would know better than to rely upon. Put another way, puffery refers to the kind of product claims for which consumers would not expect to find factual documentation.

Sometimes it is difficult to distinguish between language that is mere puffery and that which an advertiser must be prepared to document. Generally, though, puffery comes in two forms. The first is general, subjective statements about a product's superiority. These are claims that by their very nature are not subject to verification—claims that a particular spaghetti sauce is the "best" available, that a new sports car is the "sexiest" model on the market, that a computer game is "terrific," or that a brand of bicycle is "in a class by itself," for example.

The second main branch of puffery includes claims that are simply too exaggerated to be taken literally. This would include, for example, the statement that a sewing machine "is almost human," or that a brand of golf ball "will reach the stratosphere." As noted earlier, sometimes literal truth will not prevent an ad from being ruled deceptive. Conversely, under the puffery principle, literal falsehood does not necessarily make an ad deceptive.

Materiality

Even if an advertising message is likely to mislead the public, the ad is not illegally deceptive unless the misleading claim is a material one. A **material representation** is one that is likely to influence a consumer's choice of a product or service. Express claims that in any way relate to an advertiser's product are generally presumed to be material. Implied claims are also presumptively material if they concern health or safety or if they relate to central characteristics of the product, such as its quality, cost, or performance. The courts generally have been willing to defer to the commission's expert judgment on whether a particular representation is material.

The materiality issue sometimes arises in cases involving product demonstrations, or mock-ups. A classic example is *Federal Trade Commission v. Colgate-Palmolive Co.,* a case from the early 1960s that went all the way to the U.S. Supreme Court. The case arose from a television ad campaign in which Colgate-Palmolive attempted to demonstrate that its shaving cream, Rapid Shave, could outshave all the rest. In a series of one-minute commercials, Rapid Shave was depicted as so effective that it could soften even the toughness of sandpaper. The announcer informed the audience: "To prove Rapid Shave's super-moisturizing power, we put it right from the can onto this tough, dry sandpaper." As the announcer continued speaking, Rapid Shave was applied to a substance that appeared to be sandpaper; immediately thereafter a razor was shown shaving the surface clean.

However, the substance resembling sandpaper was in fact a simulated prop, or mock-up, made of plexiglass to which sand had been applied. The Federal Trade Commission issued a complaint against Colgate and its advertising agency, charging that the commercials were deceptive. At the initial hearing an administrative law judge found that Rapid Shave could indeed shave sandpaper, though not quite as fast as in the commercials, and that the main reason real sandpaper had not been used in the ads was that television transmission made sandpaper look like nothing more than plain, colored paper on the TV screen. The administrative judge therefore dismissed the complaint on the ground that the mock-up misrepresentation was not a material one.

But the full commission saw things differently. The FTC ruled that the undisclosed use of plexiglass in the commercials was itself a material, deceptive practice—independent of underlying product claims. The Supreme Court agreed. It held that even if an advertiser has successfully conducted a test that proves a certain product claim, the advertiser may not convey to television viewers the false impression that they are seeing the test for themselves.

Wrote Chief Justice Earl Warren for the Court:

It has long been considered a deceptive practice to state falsely that a product ordinarily sells for an inflated price but that it is being offered at a special reduced price, even if the offered price represents the actual value of the product and the purchaser is receiving his money's worth. . . .

It has also been held a violation of §5 [of the FTC Act] for a seller to misrepresent to the public that he is in a certain line of business, even though the misstatement in no way affects the qualities of the product. . . .

It is generally accepted that it is a deceptive practice to state falsely that a product has received a testimonial from a respected source. In addition, the Commission has consistently acted to prevent sellers from falsely stating that their product claims have been "certified." We find these situations to be indistinguishable from the present case. We can assume that in each the underlying product claim is true and in each the seller actually conducted an experiment sufficient to prove to himself the truth of the claim. But in each the seller has told the public that it could rely on something other than his word concerning both the truth of the claim and the validity of his experiment. We find it an immaterial difference that in one case the viewer is told to rely on the word of a celebrity or authority he respects, in another on the word of a testing agency, and in the present case on his own perception of an undisclosed simulation.[34]

The Court in *Colgate* distinguished a hypothetical scenario in which a commercial extolled the goodness of ice cream while giving viewers a picture of a scoop of mashed potatoes appearing to be ice cream. Wrote Justice Warren:

In the ice cream case the mashed potato prop is not being used for additional proof of the product claim, while the purpose of the Rapid Shave commercial is to give the viewer objective proof of the claims made. If in the ice cream hypothetical the focus of the commercial becomes the undisclosed potato prop and the viewer is invited, explicitly or by implication, to see for himself the truth of the claims about the ice cream's rich texture and full color, and perhaps compare it to a rival product, then the commercial has become similar to the one now before us. Clearly, however, a commercial which depicts happy actors delightedly eating ice cream that is in fact mashed potatoes or drinking a product appearing to be coffee but which is in fact some other substance is not covered by the present [cease-and-desist] order.[35]

Prior Substantiation

In addition to the general standards for deception, the FTC has enforced an adjunct requirement called the **prior substantiation doctrine** since 1971. Under this doctrine advertisers must have reasonable evidence for all verifiable product claims before the claims are made. If an advertiser makes a claim without first possessing substantiation, it is considered a violation of Section 5 of the FTC Act—even if subsequent evidence shows that the product claim turned out to be true.

For example, in *Firestone Tire & Rubber Co. v. FTC,* the advertiser had claimed that its Wide Oval tires "stop 25 percent quicker." The FTC ruled that the advertisements were deceptive because they were made without adequate substantiation. In upholding the commission, the Court of Appeals wrote: "We are by no means sure that the Firestone Wide Oval tire does not 'stop 25% quicker.' But that is not our question."[36] Instead, the question was simply whether the claim was backed by the kind of evidence that consumers would expect upon hearing such claims.

The rationale behind the prior substantiation doctrine is that consumers cannot realistically make the kinds of tests or investigations necessary to determine whether product claims are actually true. Advertisers, on the other hand, often do possess the resources and expertise to conduct or commission thorough testing of their products. Therefore, it is considered fair and prudent public policy to place the burden of substantiation upon advertisers rather than consumers.

Shortly after the prior substantiation doctrine was instituted the FTC sent documentation demands to some entire industries, such as automobiles, tires, cold remedies, antiperspirants and deodorants, soaps, shampoos, and pet foods. Thus the FTC obtained data to help it detect unfounded claims, and the substantiation program probably helped to deter groundless statements in advertising. But usually the FTC issues substantiation demands in a more narrowly targeted, case-by-case fashion. A substantiation order is typically the commission's first step in dealing with an advertiser about which it has received complaints.

How much evidence is needed to satisfy the prior substantiation requirement? This depends upon the type of claim being made. A general standard applies whenever objectively verifiable advertising claims are made without reference to any specific level of proof. In all such cases, the advertising claim must be supported in advance by a reasonable basis for believing the claim is true. A reasonable basis does not necessarily mean irrefutable, scientific proof; the question is simply whether sufficient evidence had been gathered to satisfy a reasonably prudent businessperson.

However, when an advertisement itself represents that a product claim is supported by a particular level of proof, that particular level of proof must indeed be present. For example, if an ad refers to a "scientific report," a "major university

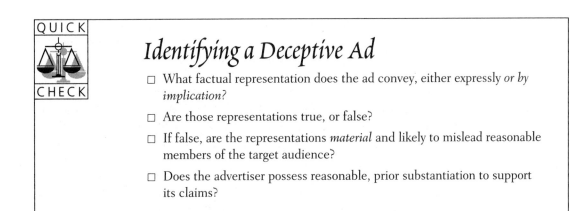

Identifying a Deceptive Ad

☐ What factual representation does the ad convey, either expressly *or by implication?*

☐ Are those representations true, or false?

☐ If false, are the representations *material* and likely to mislead reasonable members of the target audience?

☐ Does the advertiser possess reasonable, prior substantiation to support its claims?

study," a "survey of dentists," a "laboratory test," or a "medically proven" technique, the consumer is led to a heightened level of expectation that must be substantiated. These specific level-of-proof claims also may arise through visual implication. In a TV commercial, for instance, the use of white-coated technicians might suggest that the product claims are backed by scientific tests.

In the *Firestone Tire* case mentioned earlier, the FTC concluded that, by making a broad, 25-percent-quicker-stopping pledge, Firestone had implied that comprehensive scientific tests were the basis for the claim. Therefore, substantiation had to take that particular form. Upon investigation the FTC found that although tests had indeed been conducted, they were extremely limited in scope and were performed on a surface uncommon to American roadways. Given the sweeping nature of the advertising claim, the commission ruled that Firestone's substantiation was entirely inadequate to meet consumers' expectations.

FTC Rules and Guides

In addition to the general standards of deceptive advertising and the doctrine of prior substantiation, the FTC has promulgated scores of **trade regulation rules** and **industry guides** that brand particular kinds of advertising practices as deceptive. Both the rules and the guides, which are published in the *Code of Federal Regulations,* are intended to give greater specificity and clarity to the broad standard of deceptive advertising.

When the FTC enacts trade regulation rules it engages in formal, administrative lawmaking. The rules, passed in open proceedings following a public notice and comment period, become binding law in their own right. The functional effect of these rules is to narrow the inquiry conducted in a deceptive advertising pro`ceeding. Instead of adjudicating whether an advertiser violated the general and somewhat vague standards of deceptive trade practice, the inquiry is simply whether the defendant's ads violated the particular rule in question. If so, a cease-and-desist order will be issued. The trade regulation rules tend to be tailored to the problems of specific industries. For example, one rule declares that it is unlawfully deceptive for retail food chains to advertise products for sale in an area served by any of their stores that do not actually have the products in stock. Another rule lists a host of restrictions on how the retail gasoline industries may advertise games of chance for consumers.[37]

The industry guides issued by the FTC are designed to serve an educational, preventive function. Unlike the rules enacted by the FTC, the guides do not, technically speaking, have the status of law. The guides essentially are official, administrative interpretations of the law. The guides serve to put advertisers on notice that certain practices will be interpreted as violating the general deceptiveness standards and that the FTC will be inclined to file a complaint. As with the rules, many of the industry guides are designed for specific industries, such as pet food, tires, wrist watches, and even law book publishing. Several of the guides, however, are of general applicability to all industries. A few of the more important guides are summarized in the sections that follow.

Pricing

The FTC has published several guides pertaining to deceptive pricing. One of these guides addresses "former price comparisons"—the common advertising practice of offering a reduction from the advertiser's own, former price for a product. This is acceptable as long as the advertised former price is the actual price at which the product was offered to the public on a regular basis for a reasonably substantial period. The comparison is considered deceptive if the advertised former price is a fictitious, inflated one, established for the sole purpose of enabling the later offer of a huge, "bargain" reduction.

Another guide counsels on the use of the phrase "manufacturer's suggested retail price" or similar terms. Consumers have a right to assume that when a reduction from the suggested retail price is advertised, they will be getting a genuine bargain. Therefore, this form of advertising is considered deceptive if the suggested retail prices do not in fact correspond to prices at which a substantial number of sales were actually made. In other words, the manufacturer's list price cannot be a sham figure established merely to set up a deceptive, attention-grabbing comparison in local advertising campaigns.[38]

Use of the word *free* is also addressed in one of the FTC's published guides. When advertising claims such as "Buy 1—Get 1 Free" or "2-for-1 Sale" are made, consumers have a right to expect that they will actually pay nothing for the article represented to be free. Therefore, "a purchaser has a right to believe that the merchant will not directly and immediately recover, in whole or in part, the cost of the free merchandise or service by marking up the price of the article which must be purchased, by the substitution of inferior merchandise, or otherwise.[39]

Thinking back to the hypothetical problem at the beginning of this chapter, it is clear that the offer of a free package of ear plugs with the purchase of an introductory magazine subscription would run counter to this industry guide. That is because the introductory price was not the usual introductory price; it was an inflated price for the purpose of directly recouping the expense of the "free" merchandise.

Guarantees

Several guides speak to the advertising of warranties and guarantees. For example, if an ad mentions a written warranty or guarantee that is offered on an advertised product, the ad is also supposed to disclose that prior to sale prospective purchasers can see the warranty for complete details of its coverage. The guide recommends disclosure such as the following:

> The XYZ bicycle is warranted for 5 years. *Some restrictions may apply. See a copy of our warranty wherever XYZ products are sold.*

The guide also recommends that if the terms *lifetime* or *life* are used to describe the duration of a warranty or guarantee, the advertisement should disclose the life to which this representation refers. For example, is it the life of the product, the life of the purchaser, or the life of the purchaser's dog or cat?[40]

Endorsements

An elaborate set of guides pertains to the use of product endorsements or testimonials in advertising. An **endorsement** means any advertising message that consumers are likely to believe reflects the opinions or findings of a party other than the sponsoring advertiser.

As general considerations the FTC advises that endorsements must always reflect the honest beliefs or experience of the endorser and that they may not contain any representations that could not be substantiated if made directly by the advertiser. Furthermore, if an advertisement represents that the endorser uses the endorsed product, the endorser must indeed have been a legitimate user—both at the time the endorsement was given and throughout the period of the advertising campaign. This, you may recall, was another problem with the hypothetical problem for this chapter; the athlete endorser who claimed to read *Guns Monthly* was actually unfamiliar with the product.

Separate guides speak to the use of consumer endorsements and expert endorsements. For example, if a TV commercial presents endorsements by people who are represented as actual consumers, the ad should indeed use actual consumers—in both the audio and video portions of the commercial. Also, a consumer's endorsement should be used in an ad only if that consumer's experience is representative of what consumers generally will experience with the product.

As to experts, the FTC endorsement guides warn that whenever an ad represents, directly or by implication, that an endorser is an expert with respect to views conveyed, the endorser must indeed have the kind of expertise represented. Also, if the endorser makes claims about particular product features, the endorser must actually have exercised her expertise in evaluating the product. For example, an endorsement of a particular automobile by a person described as an engineer would imply that the endorser's training is in the design and performance of cars. If the endorser's field actually is chemical engineering, the endorsement would be deceptive.[41]

FTC Enforcement Devices

For the most part, compliance with the laws against deceptive advertising is obtained through voluntary and cooperative action. This cooperation is achieved by way of FTC staff advice to businesses, advisory opinions issued by the commission, and the publication of industry guides. But in some cases the FTC resorts to formal litigation to obtain binding orders against offenders. The most common enforcement tools used by the FTC include:

☐ **Cease-and-desist orders.** An FTC cease-and-desist order is similar to an injunction, except that it is issued by the commission, not by a court, following a formal hearing. Each order details the specific advertising practices to be prohibited. If a cease-and-desist order is violated, the FTC can levy fines against the advertiser. Sometimes after the FTC begins cease-and-desist litigation, but before the commission makes a formal ruling, the advertiser agrees to settle. In this case the advertiser agrees to an FTC **consent order,** which has the same binding effect as a cease-and-desist order. Most FTC cases end in a consent order.

☐ **Corrective advertising.** In some cases, the FTC may order an advertiser to make certain disclosures in future ads for the purpose of clearing up the false impressions caused by prior, deceptive advertising. This can be highly embarrassing for the advertiser, but it is deemed appropriate if the deceptive advertising campaign would otherwise leave long-lasting mis-impressions in consumers' minds. For example, in the late 1970s the FTC ordered Warner-Lambert Company to conspicuously state in its future advertising for Listerine mouthwash: "Contrary to prior advertising, Listerine will not help prevent colds or sore throats or lessen their severity."[42] The order applied to the next $10 million of Listerine advertising—roughly one year's worth.

☐ **Court injunctions.** The FTC also has authority to seek the imposition of certain remedies by a federal District Court. One of these remedies is an injunction. The injunction is a valuable remedy for the FTC because it can be obtained fairly quickly. Via injunction, an allegedly deceptive advertising practice can be halted temporarily, pending the outcome of the commission's own adjudicative procedure.

☐ **Civil and criminal penalties.** The FTC may seek court imposition of civil penalties against any person or business entity that knowingly violates a trade regulation rule. Each violation can bring a maximum penalty of $10,000. Furthermore, each day that a defendant remains in noncompliance may be treated as a separate violation. When the falsely advertised products are food, drugs, or cosmetics and there is an intent to mislead, the advertiser may be

EXHIBIT 10.2   *Sample Case: FTC v. SlimAmerica, Inc.*
77 F.Supp.2d 1263 (1999)

The Facts

In 1995 SlimAmerica began promoting a weight-loss program called the Super-Formula Program, consisting of three separate diet pills. Ads for the product appeared in hundreds of newspapers and magazines, making such claims as the following:

"Yes, utterly amazing as it seems, someone has finally combined three of the world's most powerful weight-loss weapons ever into one explosive Super-Formula Program that is absolutely guaranteed to blast up to 49 pounds off you in only 29 days!"

"Blasts Away Up to 50% of Your Body Fat in Record Time . . . Obliterates Up to 5 Inches From Your Waistline . . . And Zaps 3 Inches From Your Thighs Before You Know It."

Some of the ads also contained an endorsement from a physician who was identified as a past president of The American College of Nutrition. Next to the endorsement appeared a photo of a man in a white coat.

The Federal Trade Commission sued for an injunction against SlimAmerica's advertising and for consumer restitution.

The Holding

At least four of SlimAmerica's express and implied claims were held deceptive and in violation of federal law:

Weight loss claims: The ads represented that Super-Formula users would lose specified weight amounts in a brief time without dieting or exercise. This representation was false.

Evidence shows that to lose one pound of weight, the average person needs a deficit of about 3500 calories between caloric intake and output. "Although drugs may make it easier to achieve this deficit, they cannot alter this basic equation."

Size reduction claims: The ads represented that Super-Formula would cause substantial, specified reductions of waist and thigh sizes without dieting or exercise. Again, false. "There is no plausible scientific or medical evidence supporting claims that diet products can make size reductions exclusively from specific areas of the body."

Lack of substantiation: The ads implied that the weight loss and size-reduction claims had been scientifically validated in clinical studies. But they were not. To the extent SlimAmerica provided any studies, they were filled with serious methodological and technical flaws. The only blind study of the Super-Formula ingredients, completed pursuant to a court order, showed that subjects who took a placebo fared nearly as well.

The endorsement: Ads represented that the product was endorsed by a former president of a recognized physicians' organization specializing in nutrition. But in fact, the physician, who had retired nearly twenty years earlier, had never even been a member of the organization. Further, the accompanying photo was that of a younger man who was not the physician.

Therefore, the FTC's request for an injunction is granted, and SlimAmerica is ordered to pay more than $8 million for consumer restitution.

convicted of a misdemeanor. First offenses are punishable by up to $5000 or six months' imprisonment.

Though these remedies give the FTC Act some sharp teeth, note that the remedial power rests exclusively with the commission. Courts have held consistently that no private lawsuit can be maintained for violation of the FTC Act. In other words, consumers or business competitors who believe they have been damaged by deceptive advertising cannot personally sue the offending advertiser under the act; they must rely on the FTC to act.

Lanham Act Lawsuits

The Lanham Act was described in Chapter 8 as the federal government's trademark protection law. In addition to trademark protection, however, Section 43(a) of the act provides businesspeople with a legal tool against false advertising by others in the marketplace. Section 43(a), as revised in 1988, reads in part as follows:

> Any person who . . . in commercial advertising or promotion, misrepresents the nature, characteristics, qualities, or geographic origin of his or her or another person's goods, services, or commercial activities, shall be liable in a civil action by any person who believes that he or she is or is likely to be damaged by such act.[43]

Thus Section 43(a) specifically authorizes private party, civil lawsuits in federal court based upon false advertising of goods or services sold in interstate commerce. As federal courts have described it on several occasions, Section 43(a) of the Lanham Act creates a "distinct federal statutory tort designed to afford broad protection against various forms of unfair competition and false advertising."[44] A typical use of this statute is a lawsuit by a business against one of its competitors, alleging false comparative advertising.

The statute uses the language "any person . . . likely to be damaged" in describing who may file a lawsuit. However, courts generally have held that this language does not include consumers. Consumers do not have authority to file lawsuits under Section 43(a), the judicial reasoning goes, because the Lanham Act was enacted exclusively to protect commercial interests from unscrupulous commercial conduct.

The Lanham Act, then, is a federal vehicle, used with increasing frequency in the last decade or so by people or businesses to sue others for competitive harm inflicted by false advertising. The plaintiff need not be in direct business competition with the alleged violator, though plaintiffs often are. The ability to file a Lanham Act lawsuit is predicated simply on whether the plaintiff suffered some harm to its competitive position in the marketplace.

For example, you may recall from Chapter 5 the 1988 case in which filmmaker Woody Allen sued a clothing store for unauthorized exploitation of his identity by use of a convincing look-alike in a magazine ad. A federal court awarded summary judgment to Allen based on Section 43(a) of the Lanham Act, even though Allen was not in competition with the clothing store. It was enough, the court said, that the defendant misrepresented its relationship with Allen and that the misrepresentation could damage Allen's stature in the marketplace.[45]

Elements of a Claim

A false advertising claim under Section 43(a) of the Lanham Act rests on the following elements:

1. A false representation of fact made by an advertiser about a product or service

2. A representation that deceives, or has a tendency to deceive, a substantial segment of the intended audience

3. A representation that is material, in that it is likely to influence purchasing decisions

4. The false representation results or is likely to result in injury to the plaintiff

These elements are similar to those that the FTC must prove when it prosecutes a deceptive advertising case. The most significant difference is that the particular plaintiff in a Lanham Act case must prove that it is, in fact, likely to be injured commercially by the defendant's false and misleading ad claims.

It is the burden of the plaintiff to prove that a challenged advertising claim is actually false. To accomplish this, of course, a particular claim must be identified and then tested. In Lanham Act cases the falsity element cannot be proved by a mere showing that the advertiser lacked substantiation.

As with FTC prosecutions, a Lanham Act case can attack either explicit product claims or an advertiser's implied product claims, as they would be understood by the target audience. The existence of implied claims is typically established in court through consumer survey evidence that shows how the targeted consumers interpret the advertisement. Once the existence of implied promises is established, they, too, must meet the truthfulness requirement of Section 43(a).

Sample Cases

Business enterprises tend to be quite vigilant of their competitors' advertising, as a couple of Lanham Act cases illustrate.

Tambrands, manufacturer of a twenty-minute home pregnancy test kit called First Response, sued a competitor for false and misleading advertising in 1987. The competitor, manufacturer of the E.P.T. Plus pregnancy test kit, claimed in national advertising that users would learn for sure whether they are pregnant "in as fast as ten minutes." However, the federal District Court found that although positive results generally were available in ten minutes, negative results could not be confirmed until thirty minutes had elapsed. This was significantly misleading because more than half the women who purchase the kits want to confirm that they are not pregnant. For these purchasers, the kit was, in truth, a thirty-minute test. The court therefore issued an injunction prohibiting the competitor from advertising that its kit was a ten-minute test or that its kit was the "fastest" on the market.[46]

Another Lanham Act case involved the two leading national competitors in the ready-to-serve orange juice market. Tropicana Products had aired a 30-second television commercial described by the federal Court of Appeals as follows:

> The commercial shows the renowned American Olympic athlete Bruce Jenner squeezing an orange while saying "It's pure, pasteurized juice as it comes from the orange," and then shows Jenner pouring the fresh-squeezed juice into a Tropicana carton while the audio states "It's the only leading brand not made with concentrate and water."[47]

Coca-Cola Company, maker of Minute Maid orange juice, sued Tropicana for false advertising under the Lanham Act. Coke claimed the ad was false because it represented that Tropicana's product contained unprocessed, fresh-squeezed juice when in fact the juice is heated to 200 degrees Fahrenheit (pasteurized) and then sometimes frozen prior to packaging. The Court of Appeals found that the ad indeed made a false representation, that the representation could cause consumers to change their product choice and therefore injure Coke, and that Coke was likely to prevail in the lawsuit. The court therefore directed the trial judge to issue a preliminary injunction in favor of Coke.

Plaintiff's Remedies

A variety of legal remedies are available to victorious plaintiffs in Lanham Act lawsuits. These remedies include injunctions, corrective advertising orders, product recalls, and monetary damages.

By far the remedy most likely to be obtained is an injunction prohibiting the defendant from continuing its false advertising. Actually, injunctive relief is often dished out in two stages. The first stage is a preliminary injunction. To secure a preliminary injunction the plaintiff must convince a judge that the defendant's advertising is causing irreparable harm to the plaintiff and that the plaintiff, ultimately, is likely to prevail at trial. In order to demonstrate irreparable harm, plaintiffs typically argue that the offending advertising confuses consumers and diverts customers from the plaintiff. The value of a preliminary injunction is that it can be obtained quickly. A preliminary injunction is used to stop an offending ad campaign in its tracks, sometimes months before a full-scale proceeding is held to determine whether the advertising is, in fact, unlawful. If at trial it is formally concluded that the defendant's advertising is false and misleading, the court will issue a permanent injunction.

Of the other remedies available in Lanham Act cases, the only one that is commonly sought is monetary damages. However, damages are rarely awarded. This is because a tougher standard of proof applies to damage claims than to requests for injunctive relief. To obtain damages, a plaintiff must show that purchasers were actually deceived by the defendant's false advertising and that this deception caused direct injury to the plaintiff. This standard is difficult to prove. If it is proved, however, a defendant can be ordered to compensate the plaintiff for lost sales. In cases involving national advertisers this compensation could amount to millions of dollars.

State Advertising Laws

All fifty states have enacted their own statutes prohibiting false advertising and other deceptive business practices. Remember that commercial speech regulation is an area of law in which the federal government shares jurisdiction with the states. The theory is that this shared jurisdiction will result in an effective regulatory partnership: The federal government will naturally serve as the premier regulator of national advertising, the presumption goes, and the states will complement these efforts by scrutinizing local and regional advertising. In the 1980s, however, as the Federal Trade Commission was perceived as retreating from a decade of zealous (some would say overzealous) regulation, the states began to play an increasingly prominent role in regulating local and national ads alike.

The state statutes are sometimes called *baby FTC acts* for they typically are modeled to some extent on the federal FTC Act.[48] Furthermore, the state courts, when ruling on questions of deception under state law, are often guided by federal interpretations of the FTC Act. States are not actually bound by interpretations of the federal law, however. A state might declare a certain advertising practice unlawful even though it has not been declared so by federal authorities. Also, there is considerable variation among the states with respect to their statutory definitions of advertising, the government offices designed to enforce the law, and the kinds of legal remedies available.

As a general rule state enforcement efforts are considered a valid exercise of joint jurisdiction unless the state efforts are actually counterproductive to the federal government's statutes and regulations. In some cases, comprehensive federal regulation of particular industries has been held to preempt state regulation.

Government Prosecution

Governmental responsibility to enforce state antideception statutes may be vested in a state attorney general, local criminal prosecutors, a separate state agency, or some combination. Authorities may be empowered to obtain injunctions, sue for civil penalties, or prosecute false advertising as a misdemeanor.

Traditionally, state advertising statutes were rarely enforced by authorities because attorneys general and local prosecutors have many other law enforcement responsibilities that, quite frankly, are seen as higher priorities. However, state regulatory efforts have gained greater stature in recent years as the states have joined forces to combat large-scale advertising problems.

Some of the coordinated state effort has come from the National Association of Attorneys General (NAAG). This organization has no legal authority to pass laws. But NAAG has on several occasions passed resolutions or guidelines pertaining to misleading advertising. Some resolutions, for example, have asked the federal government to investigate a particular advertising practice. On other occasions NAAG has passed guidelines that serve to warn advertisers that certain practices are likely to be prosecuted by the various state attorneys general under the states' laws against false and misleading advertising.

Another vehicle for state cooperation has been multistate enforcement campaigns. Several states occasionally will agree to collectively pursue a particular advertiser, or group of advertisers, under the states' false advertising statutes. Typically it is the various state attorneys general that prosecute the claims, but these multistate enforcement efforts are quite separate from the advisory efforts of NAAG. Which states take part in a multistate enforcement campaign depends on the nature of the problem and the geographic region in which the questionable advertising is most prevalent. At the multistate level, recent enforcement efforts have been aimed at food advertising and at ads that make environmental claims, for example.

Private Lawsuits

Unlike the federal FTC Act, most of the state antideception statutes authorize private lawsuits against advertisers; enforcement does not depend exclusively on the vigilance and resources of government officials. Furthermore, unlike the Lanham Act most state laws provide that lawsuits may be filed by consumers, not just by people who suffer competitive harm.

In most states a plaintiff who sues for false advertising may sue for an injunction or for compensatory damages. If the advertiser willfully attempted to mislead, plaintiffs may be awarded an additional sum in the form of punitive damages. Some state statutes also authorize consumers to file **class actions** against illegal advertisers. A class action is a kind of lawsuit in which one or more named plaintiffs sue as representatives of a large number of people, all of whom share a similar complaint against the defendant. For example, a class could include thousands of consumers who presumably were induced to buy a particular product by false and misleading advertising claims.

Federal Preemption

If a state advertising law aims to restrict truthful ads then it can be challenged under the First Amendment. But another way advertisers have combatted state controls—whether they pertain to truthful or deceptive advertising—is by raising the issue of federal preemption. Some federal statutes contain language that specifically reserves an area of regulation exclusively for the federal government.

For example, both NAAG and a multistate enforcement effort had their sails trimmed by the Supreme Court, on preemption grounds, in *Morales v. Trans World Airlines, Inc.* The case arose from airline advertising guidelines adopted by NAAG that stipulated any fuel tax or other airfare surcharge must be included in advertised fare prices. The attorneys general of Texas and a few other states sent letters to TWA, Continental, and British Air, notifying them that some of their ads were contrary to the NAAG guidelines and were considered in violation of those states' false advertising laws. The airlines sued to enjoin prosecution, arguing that any state regulation on advertising of airlines' rates was preempted by federal law.

The Supreme Court agreed. In the 1992 ruling the Court held that enforcement of the NAAG airfare advertising guidelines through state consumer-protection laws was preempted by the Airline Deregulation Act of 1978. A section in that act specifically prohibits states from enforcing any law relating to airline rates, routes, or services, and that was held to include laws on the advertising of rates. The purpose behind the preemption provision was to give airlines, which typically operate across many states, a single regulator in matters pertaining to rates.[49]

Some state and local attempts to regulate cigarette advertising have also been held to be preempted. This is because the Federal Cigarette Labeling and Advertising Act contains a preemption clause that reads: "No requirement or prohibition based on smoking and health shall be imposed under State law with respect to the advertising or promotion of any cigarettes."[50] In one case, the U.S. Court of Appeals invalidated a New York City ordinance that had banned tobacco advertising on taxis unless anti-smoking, public-health messages were also displayed. The court noted that the ordinance was enacted for the laudable purpose of warning the public about the dangers of smoking. Nevertheless, the law ran afoul of the express federal statute that sought to establish national uniformity in cigarette advertising rules.[51]

In contrast, however, the California Supreme Court held that a civil lawsuit by several California cities and counties against R.J. Reynolds Tobacco Co. and its old Joe Camel ad campaign was not preempted. The lawsuit alleged that the ad campaign targeted minors and induced them to make illegal cigarette purchases. (In California it is illegal for minors to purchase cigarettes.) The claim was filed under a general state statute prohibiting unfair business practices. The state's high court construed the federal preemption clause narrowly and held that the claim against R.J. Reynolds was not preempted because it was not actually a legal action "based on smoking and health," the words used in the federal preemption section. Rather, the court said, the legal claim was predicated on a more general obligation not to engage in unfair competition by advertising illegal conduct or encouraging others to violate the law.[52] In 1997 R.J. Reynolds agreed to pay $10 million in a settlement and also agreed to suspend its Joe Camel campaign.

Meanwhile, in the mid-1990s state after state began filing lawsuits against the major cigarette makers to recover Medicaid money spent treating people with smoking-related illnesses. In 1998 the cigarette industry and the states agreed to a settlement—the biggest legal settlement in U.S. history. The cigarette makers would pay $206 billion to the states over twenty-five years. But in addition, the deal called for several restrictions on advertising. For example, the industry agreed to a phased-in ban on billboard ads, transit ads, clothing with brand logos, and cartoon characters in advertising. Because these restrictions were part of a negotiated settlement, not state regulation, they do not run afoul of federal preemption.

Liability for Illegal Ads

Under general legal principles of civil and criminal liability, a defendant usually cannot be held legally responsible unless at fault. In other words, some degree of error on the defendant's part, be it negligence, recklessness, or an intent to defraud, generally must be found. In deceptive advertising cases—whether based on the Lanham Act, state statutes, or FTC authority—this principle generally has worked to remove the advertising media from the chain of liability. This is because in most cases newspapers, magazines, broadcast stations, and other media are not in a position to check each submitted advertisement for accuracy, nor are the media generally privy to the kind of information that reasonably would cause a submitted ad to be looked upon with suspicion.

In addition to these general principles, some state and federal statutes specifically limit the potential liability of the advertising media. For example, a California statute specifies that false advertising liability does not apply to any medium that "broadcasts or publishes an advertisement in good faith, without knowledge of its false, deceptive, or misleading character."[53] However, the media could be liable when the media knew of an ad's material falsehoods when the ad was run or when they perhaps contributed to writing or designing the deceptive message.

As a further safeguard, the advertising media and advertising agencies sometimes include in their contracts with advertisers an indemnity clause. These clauses state that in the event the medium or ad agency is found liable on the basis of information provided by the advertiser, the advertiser shall agree to indemnify the medium or agency for its losses.

Rejection of Advertising

As private businesses, the mass media generally are free to accept or reject advertising—provided that they don't violate antidiscrimination or antimonopoly laws or breach their advertising contracts. This traditional rule has been recognized by the U.S. Supreme Court, which has held that the First Amendment does not give advertisers a right of access to the media—not even to the government-regulated broadcast media.[54]

Exceptions may occur, however. In 1988 the U.S. Court of Appeals upheld a preliminary injunction requiring a soap opera magazine to publish advertisements for a soap opera newsletter. The magazine *Soap Opera Digest* had carried ads for *Soap Opera Now!*, a newsletter, from 1983 to 1987. Then the magazine refused to continue publishing the newsletter's ads. The newsletter sued, alleging that the refusal to run its ads constituted an antitrust violation—in this case exclusionary conduct by a competitor without a normal business justification. The trial judge found that the defendant magazine commanded 84 percent of the market for soap opera publications and that the antitrust claim therefore raised a legitimate issue for litigation under the Sherman Act, which prohibits monopolistic practices. Because the magazine could be deemed an essential advertising vehicle for the newsletter, the judge ordered that the ads be published, pending the outcome of the trial. The Court of Appeals affirmed in an unpublished opinion.[55] (Sometimes courts withhold their opinions from publication in the official reports when they do not want the opinion to be cited in court as precedent.)

Also, Congress and the Federal Communications Commission do require that under certain circumstances broadcast stations run political ads submitted by individual candidates. These rules will be examined in Chapter 11. There are no similar rules for access by commercial advertisers, however.

The issue of access to the media and the media's right to reject advertising often arise in the context of student publications. One such case was discussed in Chapter 2; it involved a decision by public high school principals in Las Vegas to prohibit ads for birth control services in campus newspapers. The prohibition was upheld by the U.S. Court of Appeals. When ads are refused by student publications at public schools, the distinction between a public forum publication and a laboratory publication may be important. If, as in the Las Vegas case, the publication is operated as a learning lab and is not a public forum, administrators have great discretion to set reasonable policies and reject particular content, including ads. If the publication is a public forum administrators lose this control. However, the student editors of the forum papers presumably can freely decide to reject ads.

Summary Points

Commercial speech is accorded a lesser degree of First Amendment protection than most other kinds of speech. Truthful commercial speech can be regulated if the government has a substantial interest in doing so. And commercial speech is entirely without First Amendment protection if it is false or misleading or if it advertises an illegal product.

In the *Central Hudson* case the Supreme Court articulated a four-part test for resolving constitutional challenges to advertising regulation. The 1986 *Posadas de Puerto Rico* case demonstrated that the Court's test leaves much room for differing interpretation.

As an alternative to banning truthful ads for disfavored products, regulators have been more inclined to require that the ads contain warning messages. Disclosure statements also have been mandated for other kinds of commercial advertising. Thus far, the required disclosures have not been held to violate advertisers' First Amendment rights.

False or deceptive commercial speech is subject to attack from many directions, including the Federal Trade Commission, state attorneys general, local prosecutors, competitors, and consumers. Historically, it was the FTC that advertisers most had to fear, and commission rulings over the years have provided much guidance for advertisers and the states on how commercial messages should be interpreted.

The federal Lanham Act has been used frequently in recent years by businesses that wish to halt what they see as misleading advertising by their competitors. The Lanham Act was designed to protect the integrity of the commercial marketplace.

State statutes against false and misleading advertising often authorize lawsuits directly by consumers who believe they have been misled by an advertiser. State law enforcement authorities also have banded together in some cases, using their various state statutes collectively to combat the practices of major national or regional advertisers.

One of the problems presented in the chapter hypothetical was a proposed ban on gun advertising. Such a ban would have difficulty passing the *Central Hudson* test. Surely a substantial interest—public safety—is at stake. But it would be tough to prove that the ad ban directly advances that interest and that the restriction is no more extensive than necessary. The chapter hypothetical also presented problems relating to a *Guns Monthly* promotional ad. The fact that the baseball player in the commercial was on a set, not at a gun club, would most likely be considered an immaterial part of the ad. But other claims in the ad would violate FTC industry guides requiring that spokespeople actually be familiar with the product and that "free" merchandise actually be free. Also, the implication that the earplugs are somehow unique might qualify as deceptive.

Discussion Questions

1. In light of the decision in *Bates v. State Bar of Arizona* and the development of the *Central Hudson* test, do you think advertising bans on any of the professions could be constitutionally valid? Could physicians be prevented from truthfully advertising their services and fees in TV commercials or on billboards? Might any substantial justifications exist for such a ban?

2. Based on the principles discussed in this chapter, is there any limit on the government's ability to require warning messages in product advertising? For example, suppose Congress enacted a law stating that all magazine ads for guns must contain a boldface message citing various gun fatality and injury statistics and warning consumers about particular dangers relating to gun storage and transportation. Further suppose that the law requires the warning message to be enclosed in a box equal to one-third of the total space purchased for the ad. Should this be considered a substantial restriction on

advertising, thereby invoking the *Central Hudson* test? At what point does a warning notice requirement work as a de facto ban on advertising?

3. Do you think the definition for misleading advertising should encompass ads that are *likely* to mislead reasonable consumers, as the current FTC standard reads, or should plaintiffs and prosecutors have to prove that an ad *actually did mislead* reasonable consumers? Some members of the advertising industry have argued in favor of the latter standard. Or, do you think the standard should move the other direction, prohibiting advertising that could result in *possible* deception? This was the standard used in the 1970s.

4. A common advertising technique is to link a particular product with some other gratifications. For many years Marlboro cigarettes have been linked to the serenity and ruggedness of wide open pastures, for example, and in an early 1990s TV campaign Old Milwaukee beer was linked to parties with the "Swedish Bikini Team." Legally speaking, why don't such ads qualify as deceptive messages?

Key Terms

cease-and-desist order
class action
consent order
corrective advertising
deceptive advertising
endorsement

industry guides
material representation
prior substantiation doctrine
puffery
trade regulation rules

Web Resources

http://www.ftc.gov/bcp/guides/guides.htm
Federal Trade Commission, Advertising Policy Statements and Guidance

http://www.aaf.org/relations.htm
American Advertising Federation, Government Relations

InfoTrac® College Edition

Health, nutrition, and fitness claims in advertising have come under increasing scrutiny in recent years. Find an article about falsity, deception, or unfairness in this broad class of advertising. Read the article carefully to determine of the problems discussed are truly legal problems.

Chapter Outline

Broadcast and Cable Regulation

Upon completing this chapter you should

☐ **understand** the rationales for government regulation of ownership and content in the electronic media.

☐ **know** the process and criteria by which broadcast stations are licensed and relicensed and by which cable TV companies are awarded local franchises.

☐ **understand** some of the most important content controls enforced by the Federal Communications Commission.

☐ **appreciate** the First Amendment issues arising from regulation of broadcast stations and cable TV.

Hypothetical

■ Air Time for a Crackpot?

Suppose you are the station manager for a television station in a small city. The owner lives nearby but rarely visits the station. She gives you wide latitude to make the day-to-day decisions at the station, with the simple directive that you "don't do anything that could cost us our license."

It's an election year and that has brought you some extra headaches at the station. In the interest of public service you scheduled a live debate at your studio between the two major-party candidates for a seat in the state legislature. You purposely declined to invite the third candidate, who is running as an independent and lags well behind in the polls. Frankly, you believe the independent candidate is a crackpot who would detract from the quality of the debate, which is scheduled ten days before the general election.

Then the third candidate phones you and demands to be included. He says federal law requires you to include all candidates in the debate. And if you exclude him, he says, he will have a right to free response time on your station. Is he right about this? While you're mulling this over, the candidate also advises you that he wants to buy three sixty-second commercial spots on your station, to air two days before the election during drive time. You would prefer to simply decline. Or you would like to quote him rates equivalent to the very highest you charge any advertiser. Is it your business and First Amendment prerogative to make these decisions, or does the law intervene here?

Meanwhile, a local viewer has sent a nasty letter to the station owner, complaining that the station is not meeting its obligations to children. The viewer said she has examined the station's public file and that you are not providing enough programming to meet the educational needs of young viewers. In the file you specifically noted that you are running the cartoon show "The Flintstones," to teach youngsters lessons about family relationships, and that you are rerunning the old sit-com "Gilligan's Island," to help kids learn about survival skills. Isn't this good enough? Don't you have a First Amendment right to make these judgments?

Introduction

The legal restrictions discussed so far in this book apply both to print and electronic media. Libel law, invasion of privacy, copyright, trespass—these are everyday concerns for professionals in print and electronic media alike, and the principles are the same regardless of medium. However, the electronic mass media are burdened by numerous regulatory restrictions over and above the laws that apply to communicators generally.

Consumers today may choose from a continually expanding array of electronic media services. This chapter will focus on two of the traditional giants: broadcasting and cable television. Chapter 13 will look at the legal issues presented by the most rapidly growing medium, the Internet.

The fact is that broadcasters, and to a lesser extent cable operators, are subject to licensing schemes, mandatory technical standards, ownership limitations, and even political content regulations—many of which would be considered intolerable if applied to America's print media. This chapter examines the ways in which government controls access to the broadcast and cable media and directly supervises the performance of those industries. In the broadcast field, the federal government exercises exclusive regulatory jurisdiction. The key players are Congress and the Federal Communications Commission. Jurisdiction over cable TV is shared by the federal government and the local municipalities that provide access to utility poles and underground conduits.

Keep in mind as you read this chapter that the law of broadcast and cable television changes more rapidly than any other area of law discussed in this book. Sometimes the changes are relatively minor adjustments of FCC regulations. But the changes can also be bold. For example, several times in this chapter we will refer to the Telecommunications Act of 1996. The Act made sweeping changes to broadcast and cable law, particularly with regard to ownership and licensing. Largely a package of deregulatory legislation, the 1996 Act encourages greater competition among electronic media industries. Yet, within weeks after enactment of the Act, there were formal efforts in Congress to repeal portions of it. This is the fluid nature of electronic media law.

The Rudiments of Broadcast Regulation

The term **broadcasting** is used narrowly in this chapter to mean the transmission of radio or television signals for intended reception by the general public. Broadcasting is distinguished from transmissions that are intended for a select number of identified receivers, such as communications for police cars, ambulances, aircraft, military stations, and satellites. These are called *point-to-point communications.* Broadcasting must also be distinguished from methods of delivery that do not use the airwaves, such as the delivery of television programming by terrestrial cable.

Use of the Spectrum

Broadcasting is achieved by harnessing electromagnetic energy of particular wavelengths. Electromagnetic energy takes many forms, among them X rays, ultraviolet rays, visible light, and the electric current that powers household appliances. The range of electromagnetic waves that can be used for broadcasting is called the **radio spectrum.** The radio spectrum is an amazing resource, a form of radiant energy by which communications can be sent thousands of miles at the speed of light. From a legal perspective, though, one of the most significant aspects of the radio spectrum is its limited availability.

A Limited Resource

America's first radio station went on the air in 1920 and soon was followed by hundreds of others. By the mid-1920s radio chaos existed in some parts of the country. Station signals interfered with one another, threatening the viability of an exciting and influential medium. The Supreme Court described the situation as it existed in 1926:

> New stations used any frequencies they desired, regardless of the interference thereby caused to others. Existing stations changed to other frequencies and increased their power and hours of operation at will. The result was confusion and chaos. With everybody on the air, nobody could be heard.[1]

This predicament arose so quickly because the radio spectrum is a finite resource. The spectrum can accommodate only a limited number of different broadcast frequencies. And if two or more stations attempt to broadcast at the same frequency within a given geographical area, the result is *interference* that makes the broadcast signals worthless. (When done deliberately, such as between hostile nations during wartime, interference with radio signals is called *jamming*.) The bottom line was that the benefits of broadcast would be obliterated if stations and individuals were permitted to transmit at any wavelength, with any power, and at any time they chose.

In an attempt to salvage the new medium, the secretary of commerce in the mid-1920s fashioned an allocation scheme. This scheme included the assignment of a specified frequency to each station. The secretary also attempted to limit the power and hours for operation so that multiple stations could share particular frequencies. Still, the federal government was overwhelmed with frequency requests, and when a federal court ruled that the secretary of commerce had no authority to impose restrictions on broadcasters, the coordination effort was abandoned. In 1926, with nearly 1,000 unregulated stations on the air across America, President Calvin Coolidge appealed to Congress to enact a comprehensive radio law.

Government Options

Congress was faced with essentially three options for dealing with domestic use of the choked and chaotic airwaves in the mid-1920s:

The first possibility was to commandeer the airwaves and create an entirely public system in which all broadcast stations were owned and operated by the government. This would ensure orderly use of the electromagnetic spectrum over which radio waves are carried because government, as the manager, would coordinate its stations to operate only at a frequency and level of power that would avoid interference with one another. Further, the government would operate only the number of stations it deemed necessary to meet society's needs.

A second option was simply to let the private marketplace evolve on its own, with individual spectrum disputes resolved in the courts. This laissez-faire approach had philosophical appeal, but it would put tremendous pressure on the court system to fashion case-by-case solutions. The courts would be left with the specialized task of administering a complicated patchwork of stations.

The third option was essentially halfway between the other two: Private ownership of broadcast stations would be allowed but only in accord with a government allocation process. Under this option listeners could benefit from the creativity and competitiveness of commercial broadcasters and from the exhaustive oversight of government.

Government opted for the third course of action. With the Radio Act of 1927, Congress created a Federal Radio Commission to divvy up the radio spectrum and assign frequencies to radio stations. The Radio Act determined the legal framework for the future. It firmly established the notion that the radio spectrum would be treated as a public resource in which no individual could claim a property right. The spectrum was to be treated much like a national waterway, where the individual users are private concerns, but the waterway itself is controlled by government.

The Communications Act of 1934

The Radio Act was replaced by the Communications Act of 1934—the basic legislation that governs broadcasting today. Under the Communications Act, the Radio Commission was renamed the Federal Communications Commission (FCC), and its jurisdiction was expanded to cover other forms of electronic communication, including telephone.

The Communications Act, as amended over the years, is a voluminous package of statutes found in Title 47 of the *United States Code*. As it relates to broadcasting, the act states its purpose as follows:

> It is the purpose of this Act, among other things, to maintain the control of the United States over all the channels of interstate and foreign radio transmission; and to provide for the use of such channels, but not the ownership thereof, by persons for limited periods of time, under licenses granted by Federal authority, and no such license shall be construed to create any right, beyond the terms, conditions, and periods of the license. . . .[2]

The Communications Act specifically states that the FCC is not granted the power of censorship and that the agency shall not "interfere with the right of free speech by means of radio communication."[3] But this censorship prohibition has been interpreted narrowly by the courts. Another piece of guiding language in the act—a phrase often cited in court opinions—is that the FCC shall carry out its prescribed powers "as public convenience, interest, or necessity requires."[4] This public interest directive has been interpreted to confer considerable powers of judgment upon the commission.

The right of Congress to enact broadcast regulations, and in turn to delegate authority to the FCC, is derived from the interstate commerce clause of the U.S. Constitution.[5] Initially some broadcasters questioned whether federal jurisdiction could extend to broadcast signals that did not cross state lines. But the federal government argued that its jurisdiction extended to all radio signals because even purely local transmitting can interfere with the signals that do cross state lines. The Supreme Court sided with the federal government on this point in 1933.[6] Furthermore, the federal government has laid claim to exclusive jurisdiction over broadcast regulation; the ability of states to regulate even broadcasters operating entirely within their borders has been preempted by Congress and the FCC.

The FCC

The Federal Communications Commission is a large, independent agency headed by five commissioners. The commissioners, appointed for five-year terms by the president, ultimately are responsible for policy-making—within the statutory confines set by Congress and the constitutional limitations as defined by the courts. No more than three commissioners may be from any one political party. The commission has the power to pass its own regulations and to adjudicate disputes within its realm of authority. Decisions of the commission may be appealed directly to the U.S. Court of Appeals—and ultimately to the U.S. Supreme Court.

The FCC is an agency with highly technical and specialized responsibilities. In addition to regulating radio and television broadcasting, the commission today is charged with regulating interstate and international communications by wire, satellite, and cable. The FCC employs a large staff, organized into different bureaus according to the agency's functional areas of expertise. Broadcasting is handled by the agency's Mass Media Bureau. About one-fifth of the FCC's staff employees work in field jobs around the country, where they monitor usage of the radio spectrum, inspect broadcast stations, conduct operator examinations, track down unauthorized transmitters, and gather technical data for the commission's use.

The FCC's primary task of allocating usage of the radio spectrum actually involves three separate processes. They are spectrum allocation, band allotment, and channel assignment.

Spectrum allocation is the task of reserving certain portions of the radio spectrum for particular uses. For example, certain frequency ranges within the radio spectrum are reserved exclusively for use by AM radio, FM radio, VHF television, UHF television, police and fire communications, satellite communications, and so on. Broadcasting is just one of many uses the radio spectrum must accommodate. In fact, the vast majority of the usable radio spectrum is allocated to government, military, and space communications.

Band allotment is the task of deciding how many channels will be available within each usage area. For example, the FM radio band, which is located between 88 and 108 megahertz within the radio spectrum, is allotted one hundred assignable channels. The challenge for the FCC has been to allot as many channels as possible while at the same time ensuring that the band width of each channel is sufficient to provide a buffer against signal interference.

Channel assignment is the process of deciding which applicants will be awarded which channels. This is formally accomplished through station licensing. Applicants deserving of a license are authorized to broadcast at a particular channel, meaning a particular frequency. This frequency is essentially the station's address on the radio spectrum. All three processes—allocation, allotment, and assignment—present difficult challenges to the FCC and all have been controversial in recent years as the commission has attempted to make room on the spectrum for new services and technologies.

In addition to allocating the spectrum, the FCC dictates many other aspects of the broadcast industry. It sets technical standards for the operation of stations, for example, and it even has enacted rules pertaining to stations' employment practices. But most interesting of all, from a legal point of view, is that the FCC enforces numerous restrictions on the content of broadcasts. Much of this broadcast regulation, particularly the restrictions on content, raises serious constitutional questions. Do broadcasters enjoy First Amendment protection? If so, how can the extensive regulation by Congress and the FCC be justified?

Limited First Amendment Status

In the latter half of this century Americans have come to rely on the broadcast media as sources of serious news and public affairs programming as well as for entertainment. Today, in fact, many people depend on broadcast media as their *primary* source of news. Yet broadcasting has never been accorded the full range of First Amendment privileges enjoyed by the print media.

In the early days of broadcasting, the judicial view was essentially that broadcast communication was merely a cheap form of entertainment—an inferior form of speech that deserved little protection. (The courts took a similar view of motion pictures in the early 1900s.) A 1932 case serves well to illustrate the early disparity between print and broadcasting: In Los Angeles the Reverend Bob Shuler had been granted a broadcast license in the name of his Trinity Methodist Church. Shuler was a rigid moralist who took it upon himself to wage war against the vice and corruption that existed in the city during the Prohibition era. Shuler went on the air two evenings a week, and by the late 1920s "Bob Shuler's Civil Talk" was one of the most popular radio shows in Los Angeles. Shuler used his program to make ruthless attacks on government officials and other individuals and groups. He charged that the mayor was letting a gangster run the city, that the police chief was protecting organized crime, and that the district attorney took bribes. Shuler also made disparaging statements about Jews and the Catholic church.

Then it came time for Shuler to renew his radio license. During a lengthy review hearing he faced high-powered opposition. Ultimately, the Federal Radio Commission decided not to renew the license, and it ordered Shuler off the air immediately. The basis for the decision was that Shuler's broadcasts were sensationalized and factually reckless attacks and therefore were not in the public interest. The federal Court of Appeals upheld the commission, holding that the agency was within its rights to pull the license in an effort to prevent abusive, defamatory broadcasts in the future.[7]

What makes the Shuler case particularly revealing is that it was decided less than a year after the Supreme Court's landmark ruling in *Near v. Minnesota*.[8] In *Near,* which was discussed in Chapter 2, authorities sought an injunction to prevent J.M. Near from continuing to disseminate scurrilous charges against local public officials. Like Shuler, Near had made a habit of attacking those who violated Prohibition; he railed against public officials who failed to shut down gambling and other vices; he even distributed anti-Semitic statements. In many respects the facts of the *Near* case are strikingly similar to those in Shuler's—except for one critical fact: Near made his comments in a newspaper. The Supreme Court struck down the injunction against Near as an unconstitutional prior restraint. Yet the Court of Appeals did not apply this fresh precedent to Shuler's case.

The Scarcity Rationale

As the content of broadcasting became more sophisticated, it also became necessary for the courts to explain in greater detail exactly why the broadcast media should be legally distinctive. Several regulatory justifications have been articulated over the years. For example, it is sometimes stated that broadcasters are public trustees of the airwaves. Courts have also said that broadcasting is distinctive because it enters homes in an intrusive fashion and that it possesses a unique power to influence the audience, especially children.

However, the primary justification for broadcast regulation is known as the **scarcity rationale.** In essence the rationale is that because the usable radio spectrum is limited and cannot accommodate everyone who might wish to be a broadcaster, it is incumbent upon government to manage access to the spectrum. And because government must limit access to a select number of broadcasters, it might as well grant access to those broadcasters who would use the spectrum best.

Given the spectrum chaos that transpired in the mid-1920s, the scarcity rationale seems like a logical basis for some kinds of regulations. However, application of the scarcity rationale to justify content regulations has been particularly controversial for decades, and it remains so today. The U.S. Supreme Court squarely faced the issue of broadcast content restrictions in *Red Lion Broadcasting Co. v. FCC;* in that 1969 case the Court made its most elaborate defense of the scarcity rationale. In *Red Lion* the Court upheld two content restrictions, the Political Editorial Rule and the Personal Attack Rule, both of which require broadcasters to provide air time for certain individuals to respond to criticism. (The details of these rules are discussed later in this chapter.) *Red Lion* is a landmark decision because it firmly established spectrum scarcity as the main justification for government intervention in broadcasting. (See the *Red Lion* case excerpt that follows.) It is interesting to compare *Red Lion* with the Court's 1974 decision in

Miami Herald Co. v. Tornillo, discussed in Chapter 2, in which the Court unanimously struck down a statute that attempted to give political candidates a right of reply in newspapers.

Red Lion Broadcasting Co. v. FCC

395 U.S. 367 (1969)

From the opinion of the Court by Justice White:

The broadcasters challenge the fairness doctrine and its specific manifestations in the personal attack and political editorial rules on conventional First Amendment grounds, alleging that the rules abridge their freedom of speech and press. Their contention is that the First Amendment protects their desire to use their allotted frequencies continuously to broadcast whatever they choose, and to exclude whomever they choose from ever using that frequency. . . .

Although broadcasting is clearly a medium affected by a First Amendment interest, differences in the characteristics of new media justify differences in the First Amendment standards applied to them. For example, the ability of new technology to produce sounds more raucous than those of the human voice justifies restrictions on the sound level, and on the hours and places of use, of sound trucks so long as the restrictions are reasonable and applied without discrimination.

Just as the Government may limit the use of sound-amplifying equipment potentially so noisy that it drowns out civilized private speech, so may the Government limit the use of broadcast equipment. The right of free speech of a broadcaster, the user of a sound truck, or any other individual does not embrace a right to snuff out the free speech of others. . . . The lack of know-how and equipment may keep many from the air, but only a tiny fraction of those with resources and intelligence can hope to communicate by radio at the same time if intelligible communication is to be had, even if the entire radio spectrum is utilized in the present state of commercially acceptable technology.

It is this fact, and the chaos which ensured from permitting anyone to use any frequency at whatever power level he wished, which made necessary the enactment of the Radio Act of 1927 and the Communications Act of 1934. . . . It was this reality which at the very least necessitated first the division of the radio spectrum into portions reserved respectively for public broadcasting and for other important radio uses such as amateur operation, aircraft, police, defense, and navigation; and then the subdivision of each portion, and assignment of specific frequencies to individual users or groups of users. Beyond this, however, because the frequencies reserved for public broadcasting were limited in number, it was essential for the Government to tell some applicants that they could not broadcast at all because there was room for only a few.

Where there are substantially more individuals who want to broadcast than there are frequencies to allocate, it is idle to posit an unabridgeable First Amendment right to broadcast comparable to the right of every individual to speak, write, or publish. . . .

. . . A license permits broadcasting, but the licensee has no constitutional right to be the one who holds the license or to monopolize a radio frequency to the exclusion of his fellow citizens. There is nothing in the First Amendment which prevents the Government from requiring a licensee to share his frequency with others and to conduct himself as a proxy or fiduciary with obligations to present those views and voices which are representative of his community and which would otherwise, by necessity, be barred from the airwaves.

This is not to say that the First Amendment is irrelevant to public broadcasting. On the contrary, it has a major role to play as the Congress itself recognized in §326, which forbids FCC interference with "the right of free speech by means of radio communication." . . . But the people as a whole retain their interest in free speech by radio and their collective right to have the medium function consistently with the ends and purposes of the First Amendment. It is the right of the viewers and listeners, not the right of the broadcasters, which is paramount. It is the purpose of the First Amendment to preserve an uninhibited marketplace of ideas in which truth will ultimately prevail, rather than to countenance monopolization of that market, whether it be by the Government itself or a private license. . . .

Rather than confer frequency monopolies on a relatively small number of licensees, in a Nation of 200,000,000, the Government could surely have decreed that each frequency should be shared among all or some of those who wish to use it, each being assigned a portion of the broadcast day or the broadcast week. The ruling and regulations at issue here do not go quite so far. They assert that under specified circumstances, a licensee must offer to make available a reasonable amount of broadcast time to those who have a view different from that which has already been expressed on his station. . . . As we have said, the First Amendment confers no right on licensees to prevent others from broadcasting on "their" frequencies and no right to an unconditional monopoly of a scarce resource which the Government has denied others a right to use. . . .

In view of the scarcity of broadcast frequencies, the Government's role in allocating those frequencies, and the legitimate claims of those unable without government assistance to gain access to those frequencies for expression of their views, we hold the regulations and ruling at issue here are both authorized by statute and constitutional.

Is the Rationale Still Valid?

With the *Red Lion* decision, the Supreme Court puts its imprimatur on the notion that broadcasting is different from print—constitutionally different—and that government has the power to compel responsible use of the limited spectrum resource. Few would have questioned that the spectrum was indeed a scarce re-source in the 1920s or that government needed to step in with some regulations to alleviate a chaotic situation in the early years of broadcasting. However, in later decades the broadcast industry grew increasingly critical of government's regula-tory forays into matters other than purely technical, spectrum-usage issues. Fur-thermore, in the years since the *Red Lion* decision legal authorities have argued increasingly that the scarcity rationale—the key underpinning for broadcast regu-lation—is no longer a valid concept.

A reexamination of the scarcity rationale is needed, some argue, because cir-cumstances have changed dramatically since the 1920s and even since 1969, the year *Red Lion* was decided. Though the spectrum remains a finite resource, tech-nically speaking, the argument is that today's marketplace is overflowing with so many channels of communication—broadcast and otherwise—that in practical terms the consumer is faced with a virtual barrage of programming choices.

For example, in the late 1960s there were roughly 6,000 radio stations and 700 television stations operating in the United States. But by 1990 those numbers had increased to about 11,000 radio stations and 1,500 TV stations. The increases are attributable in part to enhanced broadcast technology that uses spectrum space more efficiently and to more sophisticated allotment of the spectrum. In addition, U.S. consumers today are served by roughly 8,000 cable TV systems, some of which provide 50 channels or more. In reality Americans are served by many more radio and TV outlets than daily newspapers. Yet newspapers are not subject to gov-ernment regulation and broadcasters are—on the ground of spectrum scarcity.

In 1986 the U.S. Court of Appeals bluntly attacked the logic behind the scar-city rationale and questioned whether the concept would long remain one of con-stitutional significance. Wrote the court:

> . . . [T]he line drawn between the print media and the broadcast media, resting as it does on the physical scarcity of the latter, is a distinction without a differ-ence. Employing the scarcity concept as an analytic tool, particularly with respect of new and unforeseen technologies, inevitably leads to strained reasoning and artificial results.
>
> It is certainly true that broadcast frequencies are scarce but it is unclear why that fact justifies content regulation of broadcasting in a way that would be intol-erable if applied to the editorial process of the print media. All economic goods are scarce, not least the newsprint, ink, delivery trucks, computers, and other re-sources that go into the production and dissemination of print journalism. Not everyone who wishes to publish a newspaper, or even a pamphlet, may do so. Since scarcity is a universal fact, it can hardly explain regulation in one context and not another. . . .

There may be ways to reconcile *Red Lion* and *Tornillo* but the "scarcity" of broadcast frequencies does not appear capable of doing so. Perhaps the Supreme

Court will one day revisit this area of the law and either eliminate the distinction between print and broadcast media . . . or announce a constitutional distinction that is more usable than the present one.[9]

The FCC itself has expressed some doubts about the continued legal validity of the scarcity concept, and the agency has acted since the mid 1980s to deregulate some aspects of broadcasting. Though the broadcast industry now is nearly a century old, its underlying First Amendment status may be on the verge of further evolution. This is pure speculation, of course. But in a 1984 opinion the Supreme Court did acknowledge mounting criticism of the scarcity rationale and hinted that it might reconsider its constitutional approach to broadcasting if it were to receive "some signal from Congress or the FCC that technological developments have advanced so far that some revision of the system of broadcast regulation may be required."[10] Should the Supreme Court use a future case to overturn its *Red Lion* justification for regulation, the relationship between broadcasters and the government could be drastically altered and much of the current broadcast law could be rendered obsolete.

As of the year 2000, however, the broadcast media still did not enjoy the same First Amendment freedoms as print media, and the scarcity rationale was still fully operative in the eyes of the law. And for those seeking a license, frequencies did indeed appear scarce. Despite the rapid growth of alternative electronic media, the demand for radio and television broadcast frequencies remained far greater than the supply. In 1999 the FCC received more than 30,000 inquiries from persons wishing to start radio stations, though in many cities it had been years since an open frequency was available.

Station Licensing

Significant legal consequences can flow from the conclusion that the broadcast spectrum is a scarce public resource. One consequence is that broadcasting can be subjected to a government licensing scheme and to various operational rules that would not be acceptable in other media. This book focuses on the law that directly affects communication *content,* rather than the law that pertains to such operational aspects as business licensing and hiring practices. In this section, however, we will take a streamlined look at the FCC's broadcast licensing practices and related ownership and equal employment opportunity (EEO) rules. In each case, these rules have been structured and restructured with an eye on influencing broadcast content, and in each case these rules have been controversial.

The Communications Act of 1934 specifically requires would-be broadcasters to apply for a license, and the act authorizes the FCC to grant licenses if the applicant will serve "the public interest." Beyond the vague public interest standard, however, the Communications Act leaves it largely to the commission to determine how the day-to-day licensing decisions shall be made. What minimum qualifications will be required of any applicant? If there are several applicants for one available frequency, how will the FCC decide among them? When the term of a license expires, will the existing licensee be accorded a preference for renewal? Or should the preference go to a new applicant?

These kinds of sticky policy questions led the FCC down a path of elaborate and controversial licensing criteria and time-consuming, expensive procedures that backlogged the agency. Thus in recent years the FCC has looked increasingly to awarding some kinds of licenses on the basis of an auction or a lottery. Such methods are quicker, and they lessen the potential for political favoritism or "political correctness" to creep into the licensing process. On the other hand, many believe that to parcel out licenses based on auctions or lotteries is to abdicate the responsibility to license in the public interest. These critics argue that, while it may be more difficult and cumbersome, the government is obligated to award broadcast licenses on some assessment of merit.

All local broadcast stations must have an FCC license. A license is not required to operate a network, however, because a network is not directly engaged in broadcasting. As a practical matter, all of the major TV networks do hold broadcast licenses, but this is because each network also owns several stations in lucrative markets, not because the networks provide programming to affiliates.

The Initial License

To obtain an initial license for a broadcast station, an applicant must follow several procedural steps and must meet certain basic qualifications. If a frequency is available and there is no opposition to the application and no competition for the frequency, granting the license is a fairly routine matter. In all cases, though, the applicant must meet certain basic qualifications established by the FCC.

Basic Qualifications

The basic qualifications required of all broadcast licensees fall into the following categories:

Technical. Applicants must show that their stations will comply with FCC standards pertaining to such technical matters as transmission facilities, interference avoidance, and signal quality.

Financial. Applicants must have adequate capital to support their proposals. The traditional guide has been that an applicant should have sufficient funds to operate the proposed station for a few months with little or no advertising revenue.

Character. Applicants must be of good character—as measured by a lack of serious legal violations in one's past. The FCC is likely to deny a license to anyone who has previously lied to the commission, engaged in fraudulent programming, or committed felonies such as federal drug offenses.

Citizenship/ownership. Applicants must be U.S. citizens and their applications must be consistent with station ownership limitations. (Ownership limitations are discussed later in this chapter.)

Equal employment opportunity (EEO). Applicants must submit formal plans for assuring that women and members of minority groups will have a fair chance of being employed at the station. The plan must indicate how the licensee will actively recruit minorities. (The EEO rules are discussed later in the chapter.)

The FCC is generally not concerned with the specific programming intentions of license applicants. However, the commission can refuse a license even when the criteria are met, if the commission is doubtful that granting the license would serve the public interest. Therefore, in addition to meeting the basic requirements, prudent applicants will show the FCC how the proposed programming is based on some assessment of local community needs.

In the 1970s the FCC required that all applicants conduct formal research of the communities in which they proposed to broadcast. The research included random-sample telephone surveys and personal interviews with members of certain local institutions. This elaborate community study was called **ascertainment,** and it was an onerous requirement. However, in the 1980s, as part of an FCC move toward partial deregulation, the commission dropped the formal ascertainment requirement. Today community research by a broadcast applicant is strictly voluntary, but some kind of ascertainment effort is often made because it helps convince the FCC that the license proposal is indeed in the public interest.

A broadcast station's particular call letters, which can become an integral part of a station's local marketing effort, may be requested by the licensee. (See Exhibit 11.1.)

The Contested Application

In some cases members of a community may contact the FCC to formally oppose an application. This formal opposition may complicate the license process by forcing the FCC to conduct a full hearing, which would not be required otherwise. In order to force a hearing the complaining party must have legal standing to formally oppose the application. This means that the people opposing an application must have a direct and substantial stake in the outcome.

Often it has been existing station owners in the local community who have opposed the licensing of a new station. An existing licensee has standing to complain, for example, that the proposed new station would cause significant interference with the existing station's signal. And if this allegation can be proved at a hearing, the application would be doomed unless it could be amended to solve the problem.

More controversial has been the complaint by an existing licensee that the new station would siphon off advertising revenue, thereby working an economic hard-

EXHIBIT 11.1 *Station Identification and Call Signs*

Since the early days of wireless telegraphy, radio stations have had their own identification. Under international agreement, since 1927 the alphabet has been divided among nations for basic call sign use. The United States, for example, is assigned three letters—N, K, and W—to serve as initial call letters for the exclusive use of its radio stations. It also shares the initial letter A with some other countries. The letter A is assigned to the Army and Air Force; N to the Navy and Coast Guard; and K and W to domestic stations, both government and non-government.

. . . Generally speaking, those beginning with K are assigned to stations west of the Mississippi River and in U.S. territories and possessions, while those beginning with W are assigned to broadcast stations east of the Mississippi. . . .

Since the beginning of broadcasting, stations have had the privilege of requesting specific call signs. In requesting their preferences for certain letters of the alphabet, broadcasters have presented combinations of names, places, or slogans. For example, the letters NBC are used for stations owned by the National Broadcasting Company, CBS for those of the Columbia Broadcasting System, and ABC for the American Broadcasting Companies. Examples of individual station call letters are: WGN, Chicago ("World's Greatest Newspaper"); WACO, Texas (Waco, Texas); WTOP, Washington, D.C. ("Top of the Dial"); WMTC, Vancleve, KY ("Win Men to Christ"); WGCD, Chester, S.C. ("Wonderful Guernsey Center of Dixie"); and KABL, Oakland, CA, selected its letters to represent San Francisco's famous cable cars. If a new broadcast station makes no specific request, it is assigned a call sign by the FCC. . . .

With the advent of FM and TV in 1941, new calls signs for all such stations were not assigned. Rather, since many FM and TV stations were operated by the same AM licensee in the same license area, the general practice was for the associated FM or TV station to simply add "-FM" or "-TV" to the call sign of the co-owned AM station. . . .

—FCC Information Bulletin

ship on the existing station and decreasing its ability to provide quality programming. Should this kind of economic argument ever be considered sufficient grounds to deny a new broadcast license? For many years the FCC entertained these complaints, so long as the protesting licensee alleged that granting the new license would have a deleterious effect on the overall delivery of public service programming—not just on the complaining station's profits. However, in 1988 the commission announced that it would no longer consider economic consequences as a ground for denying a license.[11]

Listeners or citizen groups also may have standing to inject formal complaints into the licensing process. Standing for local citizen groups was ordered, in fact, by the Court of Appeals in 1966.[12] However, a license will not be rejected simply because a group of local listeners might object to an applicant's proposed musical format. Citizens' complaints are more common in conjunction with license renewals, when it may be argued that a licensee has not lived up to promises for public affairs programming.

Competing Applications

The most complicated licensing scenario arises when two or more qualified applicants are vying for the same frequency. These are called *mutually exclusive applications,* because only one of the applicants can be granted the license, to the necessary exclusion of the others. In this circumstance the FCC historically conducted a **comparative proceeding** in which it weighed the merits of the two or more competing applicants. When the applicants were fairly evenly qualified, the comparative process could become quite elaborate. It involved the filing of initial documentation, a period for collection of evidence by the applicants, a period for filing written testimony with the agency, a hearing before an administrative law judge, and then another period for applicants to file their final pleadings—all before the administrative law judge rendered a decision. The judge's decision often was appealed to the commission itself. For the applicant this route was an expensive and time-consuming proposition. The full comparative process sometimes took three years.

Until 1993 the FCC arrived at its decision in comparative proceedings by considering several factors beyond the basic qualifications for a station license. The commission looked principally at the following six factors:

1. diversification of control of mass media: In the interest of promoting independence and diversity in broadcasting, the FCC would prefer the applicant with fewer existing ownership interests in mass media.

2. full-time participation in station: This was commonly referred to as *integration of ownership with management.* In the interest of better accountability and predictability, hands-on owners were preferred over absentee owners. Further preference was given to hands-on applicants who were women or minorities.

3. proposed program service: minor differences in programming proposals were considered irrelevant. However, the FCC took note of exceptional proposals for public affairs programming.

4. past broadcast record: Unusually good or bad prior behavior in broadcasting was considered in the comparison of applicants.

5. efficient use of the frequency: Applications were seen as having extra merit if they proposed to use equipment that made fuller geographic use of the frequency than would competing applicants.

6. character of the applicants: In the comparative proceeding the FCC would consider character deficiencies that were not quite serious enough to cause disqualification at the basic qualifications stage.[13]

For each factor the FCC determined whether one of the competing applicants deserved what was called a *preference,* or *enhancement,* and if so, by how much. For example, in a comparative proceeding between applicants A and B, Applicant A might be given a "slight" preference for full-time participation in management and a "moderate" preference for proposed public affairs programming. Applicant B might get a moderate preference for efficient frequency use but a "substantial" preference for diversification of control. In this case, Applicant B would be granted the license.

However, in 1993 the above-described comparative process was suspended by the FCC, in response to a court decision, while the agency began to study other options. In *Bechtel v. FCC,* a broadcast license applicant attacked the second comparative factor, integration of ownership with management, as unconstitutionally arbitrary. The federal court of appeals agreed. The FCC attempted to defend the integration policy by arguing that on-site owners, because of their direct financial interest, are more likely than absentee owners to make sure the station complies with all FCC rules and responds to community needs. But the court found no evidence to support the FCC's claims, and it wrote: "The fact that corporate America generally does not insist upon the integration of ownership and management casts doubt on the Commission's rosy speculations about the benefits of integration."[14]

Thus with one of its comparative preferences invalidated by the Court of Appeals, the FCC decided to suspend the entire process and conduct a fresh, thorough review of the other preferences as well. Years passed, and hundreds of radio and TV license applications were on hold.

The Auction Solution

In 1999 the FCC gave the final go-ahead to a process that altogether discards the thorny thicket of comparative proceedings. With nudging from Congress, the FCC's new process awards commercial licenses among competing applicants on the basis of an auction. The license goes to the highest bidder, and the bid money to the U.S. Treasury. An auction process for mutually exclusive applications was authorized in the Telecommunications Act of 1996 and then mandated in the Balanced Budget Act of 1997.[15]

More specifically, the process now in place is called an "electronic simultaneous multiple-round auction," which the FCC hopes will prove to be both efficient and fair. Instead of selling licenses one at a time, a number of related licenses are grouped together and auctioned simultaneously. The pre-qualified bidders can bid on any of the licenses offered, and the auction closes when bidding has ceased on all licenses in the group. Bidding is multiple-round, meaning that the bids are not sealed, and a bidder has the opportunity to top the high bid from the previous round. The FCC has set up an automated auction system that allows it to process hundreds or even thousands of bids, which are made via personal computer. Progress of an auction can be tracked by bidders and other interested persons through the FCC's Web site.

Through its rulemaking process, the FCC announces the spectrum to be auctioned at least four months in advance. Applications to participate in the auction must be submitted to the FCC at least 30 days in advance, along with a refundable deposit. The size of the deposit determines which licenses the applicant may bid upon. Each license is assigned a minimum level of acceptable bid.

Remember that the auction process is used only for broadcast frequencies for which there were mutually exclusive applications. If an available frequency is identified and draws only one application, it will be awarded upon demonstration of the basic qualifications.

Minority Ownership

In a 1978 policy statement the FCC announced that minority ownership and participation in management could be considered in comparative hearings as a plus to be weighed with the other comparative factors when awarding licenses. In order for the minority ownership preference to apply, the applicant had to be a member of a racial minority group who would actively participate in the day-to-day management of the station. The justification behind this policy was a finding by the FCC that the views of racial minorities were inadequately represented in the broadcast media, that greater representation of minority viewpoints would enrich the entire audience, and that promoting hands-on minority ownership would help accomplish the desired diversity in programming.[16]

In 1990 the minority ownership preference narrowly withstood a constitutional challenge before the U.S. Supreme Court. In *Metro Broadcasting, Inc. v. FCC* the Court held, 5–4, that granting a preference to license applicants who are racial minorities does not violate the Fifth Amendment's guarantee of due process and equal treatment by government. In the majority opinion, Justice Brennan stated that the minority ownership policy is valid because it is substantially related to achievement of an important governmental objective—programming diversity. Drawing from language in prior decisions, Brennan wrote:

> The Government's role in distributing the limited number of broadcast licenses is not merely that of a "traffic officer"; rather it is axiomatic that broadcasting may be regulated in light of the rights of the viewing and listening audience and that the widest possible dissemination of information from diverse and antagonistic sources is essential to the welfare of the public. Safeguarding the public's right to receive a diversity of views and information over the airwaves is therefore an integral component of the FCC's mission.[17]

The minority ownership preference is substantially related to this diversity-in-programming objective, Brennan wrote, because "evidence suggests that an owner's minority status influences the selection of topics for news coverage and the presentation of editorial viewpoint, especially on matters of particular concern to minorities.[18]

Justice O'Connor wrote a stern dissenting opinion in *Metro Broadcasting*, in which she accused the majority of applying the wrong standard. Her opinion began as follows:

> At the heart of the Constitution's guarantee of equal protection lies the simple command that the Government must treat citizens as *individuals,* not as simply components of a racial, religious, sexual or national class. Social scientists may debate how peoples' thoughts and behavior reflect their background, but the Constitution provides that the Government may not allocate benefits and burdens among the individuals based on the assumption that race or ethnicity determines how they act or think. To uphold the challenged programs, the Court [majority] departs from these fundamental principles and from our traditional requirement that racial classifications are permissible only if necessary and narrowly tailored to achieve a compelling interest.[19]

Thus, while Brennan and the slim majority found an "important" or "substantial" government interest sufficient, O'Connor believed a much stricter, "compelling" justification was necessary to uphold a race-based preference. O'Connor added that the interest in increasing the diversity of broadcast viewpoints "is simply too amorphous, too insubstantial, and too unrelated to any legitimate basis for employing racial classifications."[20]

Early in 1992 the U.S. Court of Appeals held that a similar FCC preference in favor of women applicants was an unconstitutional violation of male applicants' rights under the equal-treatment component of the Fifth Amendment. The majority opinion was written by Judge Clarence Thomas, shortly before his confirmation to the Supreme Court. Thomas noted that the majority in *Metro Broadcasting* found substantial empirical evidence supporting a link between minority ownership of stations and the stations' programming practices. But this case was different, he said: "Whatever the merit of these assumptions as applied to cohesive ethnic cultures, it simply is not reasonable to expect that granting preferences to women will increase programming diversity."[21]

Then in 1995 the U.S. Supreme Court decided *Adarand Constructors, Inc. v. Pena.*[22] The *Adarand* case did not involve broadcast licenses; rather, it concerned a Colorado preferential policy for minority contracting firms. But the case is significant because the Court overruled the standard used to decide *Metro Broadcasting,* thus calling into question once again the constitutionality of the FCC's minority ownership preference.

Of the five justices in the *Metro Broadcasting* majority, only Justice Stevens remained in 1995. And in *Adarand,* Justice O'Connor wrote for the majority. In *Adarand* the Court held that race-based programs, state or federal, are constitutional only if they further a *compelling* governmental objective and only if they are the least intrusive means of accomplishing that objective. Following *Adarand,* FCC chairman Reed Hundt said the agency intended to keep its minority preference policy and would justify it under the Court's strict standard.

Soon the FCC's entire comparative process was eliminated. But when the new auction system was adopted, it included this special accommodation: In order to help ensure that small businesses and businesses owned by minority groups and women have a good opportunity to succeed in the auctions, the FCC will award "new entrant" bidding credits to applicants with no, or few, media properties. Applicants with no controlling interests in other broadcast, cable or daily newspaper properties will receive a 35 percent bidding credit. If such an applicant makes a winning bid of $1 million, for example, the applicant will actually pay a reduced amount of $650,000 to the U.S. Treasury. Applicants with no more than three existing media properties will receive a bidding credit of 25 percent. It remains to be seen whether this new system will meet the FCC's diversity goals and whether it will survive constitutional scrutiny in court.

License Renewals

Broadcast licenses are awarded for a specified term of years, not for perpetuity. Under the Telecommications Act of 1996, Congress extended license terms to a maximum of 8 years for both television and radio. When the license term expires the licensee must apply for renewal. As with the application for an initial license, the renewal process can be complicated by community opposition. Again, the FCC is authorized to grant renewals only "if the Commission finds that the public interest, convenience, and necessity would be served thereby."[23]

Though the grant of an initial license does not create a vested property right in the frequency, station owners may nevertheless invest millions of dollars in capital in their operations. Therefore, a decision to deny renewal is potentially a decision of great financial ramifications. The threat of nonrenewal is real, but in practice nonrenewals are statistically rare.

The Renewal Process

The basic procedure for broadcast license renewal was drastically streamlined in the early 1980s as part of the FCC's push toward partial deregulation. Most notably the FCC eliminated much of the paperwork previously imposed on broadcasters at renewal time—lengthy forms that had been used to document a station's performance. It moved to a five-question renewal application form that become known as "postcard renewal." And more recently, the FCC's goal is to eliminate paper altogether with an online system.

The renewal application must be filed at the FCC four months before expiration of the license. In addition, the stations must make a series of announcements over the air, beginning six months before the expiration of their licenses. The announcements advise viewers or listeners that the station's license will soon expire and that comments regarding the renewal may be filed with the FCC by a particular date. Members of the public may register informal objections to the renewal or they may file a formal petition to deny the application.

An item of particular importance during renewal time is a station's **public inspection file.** This is a file containing not only a copy of the renewal application but also copies of program lists, public issues lists, letters from the public, political access records, and ownership and employment reports. The public file must be available for inspection at the station's offices during regular business hours throughout the term of the license. (See Exhibit 11.3 on page 434.)

Grounds for Nonrenewal

The FCC does not conduct a full investigation into the performance of every licensee who has applied for renewal. Instead, the agency usually depends on public comment to draw its attention to a licensee who might not deserve renewal.

The FCC may deny renewal for a variety of reasons unrelated to the licensee's programming content. Among the more likely reasons for nonrenewal are failure to follow the renewal application procedures; lying to the FCC (on application forms or in required reports, for example); fraudulent behavior in the billing of advertisers or in the operation of consumer contests or promotions; unauthorized transfer of the license; or some other development that would run afoul of the basic requirements discussed earlier. Often it is a combination of such problems that leads to nonrenewal. The Telecommunications Act of 1996 specifies that renewal applications shall be granted if the station has served the public interest, if there have been no serious violations of the Communications Act or FCC rules, and if no other violations of FCC rules suggest a pattern of abuse.[24]

Programming content by itself rarely is grounds for nonrenewal. (And if it were, serious First Amendment questions might be raised.) However, objectionable programming may well cost a station its license when coupled with grossly negligent management or with efforts to hide information from the FCC. For example, in one case the FCC informed a radio station at renewal time that listeners had complained of vulgar, indecent programs on the station and that the FCC had obtained tapes of the programs. The FCC invited the licensee to respond to the allegations. The owner responded at that time, and again at a hearing, that he had not been aware of the vulgar programs and that upon first learning of the problem from the FCC he had fired the employee responsible. However, evidence showed that numerous complaints had indeed been made directly to the owner prior to the FCC investigation. The FCC denied the renewal, not on the ground that the programming was illegal, but solely on the ground that the owner had lied to the FCC: "The licensee's misrepresentations and false statements, *in and of themselves,* constitute grounds for denial," wrote the commission. The denial was upheld by the Court of Appeals.[25]

In 1978 the commission denied renewal to a campus radio station at the University of Pennsylvania. For many months listeners had complained that programming on the student-run station was laced with obscenity. Complaints also were made about technical violations and about the conduct of students at the station. Yet the university, which held the license, took few steps to cure the problems at its station until after the FCC began a formal investigation at renewal time. The commission denied renewal solely on the ground that the university licensee had abdicated managerial control over its own station.[26]

Even when a licensee has indeed performed irresponsibly or violated FCC rules, the commission is likely to employ a form of punishment less severe than nonrenewal. One popular form of punishment is to renew for a short term, such as two years. The FCC is also authorized in the Communications Act to assess fines—called *forfeitures*—against stations that violate specific FCC rules. Forfeitures can be imposed at renewal time or at any other time during the operation of the station.

Renewal Expectancy

Historically, as a broadcast license approached its expiration date, a new applicant could try to wrestle the frequency away from the current licensee. A new applicant who met the basic qualifications could force a comparative hearing similar to the one described previously for initial licenses; the same factors would be weighed to determine which applicant would best serve the public interest. But in a comparative renewal proceeding there was one additional consideration: Should the current licensee be accorded any degree of preference over the challengers?

Public interest reasons do exist for giving some comparative advantage—called a **renewal expectancy**—to the current licensee. For one, renewals provide greater certainty of performance, as opposed to regularly awarding licenses to challengers who might or might not live up to their paper proposals. The current licensee has an established track record, and even if this record is not outstanding, it may be wiser to renew the license than to turn the frequency over to a novice applicant. Second, renewals foster stability in industry ownership—stability that may be highly important to employees and investors. Finally, and perhaps most important, a likelihood of renewal encourages licensees to invest heavily in their stations, just as the owners of other kinds of businesses invest in their enterprises to improve performance over the long term.

In light of these considerations, the FCC for decades offered the possibility of a renewal expectancy to incumbent broadcasters embroiled in a comparative renewal proceeding. The renewal expectancy was one of the several factors weighed in the comparative process. It was not automatic, but rather was awarded to broadcasters who had compiled commendable records of serving the public interest. The better the broadcaster's record in terms of serving the public interest, the greater the weight of the renewal expectancy.

In the Telecommunications Act of 1996, however, Congress eliminated comparative renewal proceedings. Instead, the FCC is directed to first decide whether an existing station's license deserves to be renewed. If the answer is no, only then may the FCC open the frequency to new applications. This is known as a "two-step" approach to renewals. It means considerable certainty for broadcasters, as long as they do not neglect their public interest obligations. They must still demonstrate compliance with FCC rules that are directly grounded in public service philosophy, such as the children's programming requirement for TV (discussed later in this chapter) and the requirement of an EEO hiring process.

Transfer of Licenses

Just like other businesses, commercial broadcast stations can accumulate substantial monetary value in their physical assets and consumer goodwill. When a station owner decides to leave the broadcast business or move to another location, the owner naturally will seek to sell the station during a license term and obtain full value for the business. It would make little sense to let the license expire and then attempt to sell the broadcast facility. Owners instead wish to sell a station that is an ongoing, licensed enterprise.

But it would make little sense for the government to operate an elaborate licensing scheme based on public interest standards and then allow the licenses to be transferred at will. Therefore, the Communications Act requires that all license transfers must first be approved by the FCC, based on a finding that the transfer would serve "the public interest, convenience, and necessity."[27]

It is the responsibility of the station purchaser to file a transfer application with the FCC prior to closing the deal with the licensee. The FCC then gives public notice of the application on its Internet home page and allows a thirty-day comment period. In most cases the transfer (technically called an *assignment* of the license) is approved shortly thereafter, unless serious questions are raised through informal public complaints or in formal petitions to deny the application. A similar application and public-comment process is followed when a station owned in corporate form undergoes a major stock transfer (technically called a *transfer of control*).

A burning legal issue some decades ago was whether listeners and viewers could force the FCC to consider their objections to proposed changes in entertainment programming formats before approving license transfers. The FCC's position was that the choice of entertainment formats should be left entirely to the judgment of the licensee and that market forces could be relied upon to promote enough diversity in programming to serve the public interest. But the public was angered in some locales where new owners arrived and eliminated an existing format, such as classical music, from the service area. In 1981 the Supreme Court sided with the FCC in *FCC v. WNCN Listeners Guild*. The Court concluded that the FCC was acting reasonably and within its legal mandate from Congress when it determined that "the market, although imperfect, would serve the public interest as well or better by responding quickly to changing preferences and by inviting experimentation with new types of programming." Furthermore, the Court concluded that the FCC's policy did not conflict with the First Amendment rights of listeners. Referring to its earlier decision in *Red Lion*, the Court wrote: "Although observing that the interests of the people as a whole were promoted by debate of public issues on the radio, we did not imply that the First Amendment grants individual listeners the right to have the Commission review the abandonment of their favorite entertainment programs."[28]

Ownership Limitations

The FCC has long advocated that the public interest is served in part by providing the public with a large number of different broadcast voices, as opposed to allowing media ownership to concentrate in the hands of a few. The assumption behind this is that a large number of station owners equates to greater diversity in programming. This assumption is challenged by industry experts who say that it is market preferences that ultimately determine the nature of programming, not the individual proclivities of media owners. Nevertheless, the FCC traditionally has adhered to the philosophy that new owners should be encouraged to enter the broadcast field and that no one owner should be allowed to amass unlimited numbers of broadcast licenses. So Congress and the FCC have maintained numerous categorical limits on the concentration of ownership.

The deregulation-minded FCC of the 1980s and early 1990s sought to relax or eliminate many of the ownership restrictions, believing they were no longer necessary to assure a multitude of broadcast voices. Congressional leaders and minority groups at the time generally favored keeping the restrictions in place, however. By the mid-1990s, Congress appeared more inclined to remove or relax some of the limits, and this was accomplished with the Telecommunications Act of 1996. The most important ownership limits, historically, and their current status, include the following:

One to a Market

The one-to-a-market rule, also called the *duopoly rule,* limited a licensee to one VHF television station or one AM-FM radio combination within a single service area. A licensee could not possess two AM radio stations in a market, for example, or an AM station and a VHF television station. The rule did not apply to UHF television stations, which traditionally were weak competitors and could benefit from affiliation with another station in the market. When the one-to-a-market rule was adopted in 1970 it applied prospectively only; licensees who owned duopolies were allowed to keep them. Also, the FCC was inclined to grant waivers of the rule in large markets already served by thirty or more broadcast voices.

In 1992 the FCC cast aside the duopoly rule as it had applied to radio. The FCC's new rule permitted ownership of three to six radio stations per market, depending on the market size. The Telecom Act of 1996 further extended the limit to five to eight radio stations per market, depending on market size.

In 1999 the FCC also revised the duopoly rule for television. The new rule permits common ownership of two TV stations in the same market area if at least eight full-power independent stations will remain after the merger. The rule also allows common ownership of two stations in a market if a station is failing financially and a same-market licensee is the only available buyer.

Newspaper Cross-Ownership

Also categorically prohibited is the granting of any radio or television license to an applicant who owns a daily newspaper servicing the same market. The rationale behind this rule is that ownership of a newspaper and, say, a TV station, in the same community vests too much journalistic power in a single owner—just as would the ownership of two or three TV stations. Here again, the rule was applied prospectively only; newspaper–broadcast combinations in existence prior to 1975 were allowed to continue without a required divestiture. This cross-ownership rule was not modified by the Telecom Act of 1996, but as of this writing the rule was under review by the FCC.

National Ownership

The duopoly and cross-ownership rules limit ownership within a given market area. But the FCC has for several decades also limited the total number of stations that can be owned nationwide. In 1953 the commission adopted an ownership limit of seven AM radio stations, seven FM stations, and seven TV stations. The 7–7–7 rule was immediately challenged in court as an arbitrary, categorical judgment that in regard to a particular applicant might have no genuine bearing on the public interest. The Supreme Court upheld the commission, however.[29]

In 1984 the FCC expanded the national multiple ownership limits to 12–12–12, and the commission stated its intention to eventually eliminate the national caps altogether. In 1992 the commission raised the national radio ownership limits to 30 AM stations and 30 FM. Relaxation of the limits was warranted, the commission believed, because with thousands of different TV and radio licensees in the country, it had become less necessary for the government to use its regulatory power to assure diversity in broadcast voices. Furthermore, the FCC hoped the relaxed limits would help attract new investors to an economically ailing radio industry. However, the commission's action was sharply criticized by minority broadcasters and some members of Congress, who saw the action as too drastic and an undeserved concession to media conglomerates.

Despite the controversy, however, the Telecom Act of 1996 repealed all national ownership limits for radio, allowing one person or company to own an unlimited number. The Act also repealed the 12-station national cap for television, though a TV owner's reach may not exceed 35 percent of the national audience.

Application of the FCC's various ownership limitations is complicated by the fact that licensees often are not individuals but corporate enterprises with several or perhaps thousands of shareholders. How many shares must an investor own before that investor is considered a broadcast owner for purposes of these rules? The FCC's rules indicate that it is concerned only with "cognizable" ownership interests. This generally means an ownership level of at least 5 percent of the broadcast company.

EXHIBIT 11.2 *The Telecommunications Act of 1996*

The Telecommunications Act of 1996 was the most sweeping revision of communications law since the Communications Act of 1934. Listed here are some of the most significant provisions for broadcasters and cable operators.

Ownership Limits

- Repealed all limits on the number of radio or television stations one person or entity may own nationwide.

- Increased the national audience reach limitation for TV station owners to 35 percent (formerly, 25 percent).

- Raised the cap on the number of radio stations a party may own in one market (formerly 3 to 6, now 5 to 8, depending on size of the market).

Licensing

- Authorized television and radio license terms of 8 years (up from 5 and 7 years respectively).

- Eliminated comparative renewal proceedings for broadcast licensees.

Competition

- Repealed most price caps on cable operators, effective March 1999—or sooner if a cable operator faces "effective competition."

- Repealed regulations that had prevented telephone companies from offering video programming services and thus opened the door to direct telco-cable competition.

TV Violence

- Required TV industry to develop a ratings system for programming that contains sexual, violent, or other objectionable material.

- Required that new TV sets, beginning in 1997, include "V-chip" technology to allow blocking of objectionable programming.

The ownership rules summarized above are likely to undergo further change in the near future. The Telecom Act of 1996 required the FCC to review broadcast ownership rules every two years to determine whether the rules remain necessary to protect the public interest (see Exhibit 11.2).

EEO Rules

As noted earlier, the FCC maintains **equal employment opportunity (EEO) rules** requiring broadcasters to devise and follow formal procedures for assuring that women and members of minority groups will have a fair chance of being employed at the station. The rules go beyond the many non-discrimination laws to which employers are subject at the federal, state, and local levels (i.e., the Age Discrimination and Employment Act, the Equal Pay Act, and the Civil Rights Act of 1964).The EEO rules require broadcasters actively to recruit minorities for employment.

The commission's EEO rules hit a snag, however, in a 1998 court decision. A Lutheran church operated two Missouri radio stations that aired music and religious programming. Both stations were housed on church property and helped carry out the church's religious mission. After receiving the stations' license renewal applications, the FCC requested more information about their affirmative action efforts. Also, the NAACP filed a petition to deny the renewals, contending that the church's EEO program was deficient. The church answered that its low percentage of minority employees was because of its hiring criteria, "knowledge of Lutheran doctrine" and "classical music training." Further, little outside recruiting was done because employees were drawn from the church's own seminary. Therefore, the station's minority employee percentage did not come close to matching the percentage of minorities in the service area.

The FCC held that many positions at the station, such as secretaries and engineers, were not connected to espousing religion and that the stations violated EEO regulations by failing to recruit minorities for those positions. The church challenged the FCC's ruling on constitutional grounds, arguing that the affirmative action requirement violated the equal protection component of the Fifth Amendment.

In *Lutheran Church-Missouri Synod v. FCC*, the D.C. Circuit Court of Appeals began its analysis by noting that the EEO rules, as written at the time, required more than an outreach program. The rules actually instructed broadcasters to make race-conscious hiring decisions so that minorities employed at a station would not be "underrepresented" in comparison to the local population. Because the rules were attempting to influence ultimate decisions, the court applied a strict scrutiny test under the *Adarand* precedent. In its stinging opinion, the court criticized much about the FCC's logic and application of the regulations. But, most important, the court was not convinced of a compelling justification for the race-based rules:

> The Commission has unequivocally stated that its EEO regulations rest solely on its desire to foster "diverse" programming content. . . . The Commission never defines exactly what it means by "diverse programming." The government's formulation of the interest seems too abstract to be meaningful. . . . We do not mean to suggest that race has no correlation with a person's tastes or opinions. We doubt, however, that the Constitution permits the government to take account of racially based differences, much less encourage them. One might well think such an approach antithetical to our democracy. Indeed, its danger is poignantly illustrated by this case. It will be recalled that one of the NAACP's primary concerns was its belief that the Church had stereotyped blacks as uninterested in classical music.[30]

The FCC's ruling against the church therefore was reversed and remanded.

The *Lutheran Church* case did not cause the FCC to back away from EEO rules, however. In January 2000 the commission adopted revised EEO rules intended to correct the defects identified by the appeals court. The revised rules focus on outreach efforts. Broadcasters have the flexibility to design their own outreach programs, such as sending vacancy announcements to recruitment organizations, participating in minority job fairs, and establishing internship programs. Broadcasters still must file employment profile data with the FCC, but the commission will not use the data to assess EEO compliance, to make licensing decisions, or to otherwise second-guess broadcasters' ultimate hiring decisions. The revised rules also permit religious broadcasters to establish religious belief or affiliation as a job qualification for all station employees.[31]

Broadcast Content Controls

In the field of broadcast regulation it is controls over content that spark the greatest controversy. Legally, content controls raise the most serious First Amendment questions. From an operational perspective content controls are often burdensome and confusing for the staff people who make the daily programming decisions at broadcast stations. This section looks at a few of the most important areas of content regulation.

Political Broadcasting

By far the most complicated of the current content restrictions are those pertaining to political broadcasting by candidates for public office. Political speech is in no way prohibited. But broadcasters are required to give certain candidates access to their broadcast facilities, to treat all political candidates equally, and to give candidates preferential advertising rates at certain times of the year.

The basic requirements have been in place for many years and are statutory in origin. But FCC rules and policies play a major rule in determining exactly how the statutory provisions are interpreted and enforced, and these rules are, of course, subject to change.

Equal Opportunities Rule

Section 315(a) of the Communications Act provides that whenever a legally qualified candidate for public office uses broadcast time, the station must afford equal opportunity to all other candidates in the race. This is known as the **equal opportunities rule,** sometimes also called the *equal time rule.*

The key antecedent to a broadcaster's obligations under the rule is a "use" of broadcast time by a declared candidate during a political campaign. Use of time by a candidate triggers the broadcaster's obligations to provide equal opportunities. Therefore, it is important for broadcasters to recognize when a candidate has "used" broadcast time in the eyes of the FCC.

The FCC currently defines "use" as any positive appearance of a candidate, by voice or picture, that is identifiable to the broadcast audience. The typical campaign commercial, then, would qualify as broadcast use by a candidate. An appearance on a TV variety show or a charity telethon also would be considered a use in most cases. So would a product commercial or public-service announcement featuring the candidate. There is no requirement that the appearance contain a political message; nonpolitical appearances are still uses if they occur after the candidacy has been declared.

An interesting problem arose when former screen actor Ronald Reagan began campaigning for the presidency in the 1970s. Broadcast stations around the country could hardly resist airing some of Reagan's old films, such as the classic *Bedtime for Bonzo*. But would broadcasting those films amount to a "use" of airtime by a candidate and thus raise equal opportunity obligations by the station? In 1976 the FCC ruled that showing the movies would indeed amount to a use, noting that even nonpolitical appearances can be highly beneficial for a candidate, to the detriment of other candidates who may be struggling to become better known.[32] In 1992 the FCC revised its definition of use to require that the appearances be controlled, approved, or sponsored by the candidate. But this gave considerable political discretion to broadcasters, and the FCC returned to its original definition in 1994.

Exemption for News

By statute, candidate appearances in certain kinds of programs are not considered a candidate use of broadcast time. These programs include the following:

1. Bona fide newscasts

2. Bona fide news interview programs

3. Bona fide news documentaries

4. On-the-spot coverage of bona fide news events, including political conventions and debates[33]

The term *bona fide* in this list refers to news coverage that is genuine and impartial, based on sincere journalistic judgment and not used to advance the candidacy of a particular individual. Without the news exemptions, broadcasters might shy away from covering legitimate political news for fear that it would create a flood of equal opportunity obligations. Such a reluctance to cover important news would be contrary to the public interest, of course, and contrary to the intent of the equal opportunities rule.

Determining whether a news exemption applies is not always easy, and broadcasters sometimes request declaratory rulings from the FCC before going ahead with programming plans. In determining whether a program qualifies as a bona fide news interview, for example, the FCC considers three factors: (1) whether the program is regularly scheduled, (2) whether the broadcaster, not the candidate, controls the program, and (3) whether the broadcaster's decisions on format and participants are based on reasonable, good-faith journalistic judgment. Using these criteria, the commission generally holds that TV talk shows are bona fide news interview shows.

In 1984 an interesting use question arose when William Branch, a TV news reporter in Sacramento, sought election to a nearby town council. Branch appeared in newscasts about three minutes per day on average. The station calculated that it would be required to provide thirty-three hours of free response time to Branch's opponents if he continued to work on air during the campaign. The station therefore told Branch he would need to take an unpaid leave of absence during his campaign. Branch sought a ruling that his continued appearance as a newscaster would not be considered a use of broadcast time. But in *Branch v. FCC*[34] the Court of Appeals ruled otherwise. Branch had argued that his appearances did not trigger the equal opportunities rules because they were part of bona fide newscasts. But the court distinguished between coverage of a candidate and coverage by a candidate. Congress exempted coverage of legitimate news events, the court said, to protect a station's ability to exercise broad discretion in choosing which newsworthy events to present to the public. Sometimes an appearance of a candidate is itself a newsworthy item and thus deserves to be exempt. However, when a candidate simply covers a news event involving other people, the appearance is unrelated to the news content and therefore is not exempt.

Special Problem: Debates

Political debates and news conferences have been particularly troublesome under the equal opportunities rule. In the early 1960s the FCC interpreted the spot news exemption to apply only if the appearance of a candidate was incidental to the coverage of a separate news event. Candidates themselves could not be the event. This interpretation meant that televised political debates and press conferences were considered broadcast uses that required stations to provide equal time to opposing candidates who did not appear in the original coverage.

But in 1975 the commission overruled its earlier interpretation. Upon a closer examination of congressional intent it decided that a debate was exempt if sponsored by an organization other than the candidates themselves or the broadcaster and if the broadcaster made a good-faith, journalistic judgment that the debate was newsworthy. Similarly, the commission decided that press conferences by candidates were exempt if broadcasters reasonably judged them as newsworthy enough for spot coverage. Minor-party candidates appealed the FCC's rulings, but the Court of Appeals upheld the commission's altered interpretation of the Communications Act.[35]

In 1983 the commission went one step further, ruling that even a debate sponsored by the broadcaster can quality as bona fide spot news so long as the broadcaster has designed the format and invited candidates on a good-faith judgment of news value. The key is simply whether the broadcaster has arranged and covered the debate based on a good-faith judgment of newsworthiness. If so, the broadcast does not qualify as use by a candidate, and candidates excluded from the debate acquire no equal opportunity rights.[36]

Based on this ruling, how would you answer the question posed in this chapter's opening hypothetical? Recall that you had arranged a debate at your station between the two leading candidates for office. Though a third, minor candidate demanded equal time, you would not have to meet that demand because you made a good-faith judgment that a debate between the two leading candidates alone was a bona fide news event.

The Meaning of Equal Opportunity

Nonexempt use of broadcast time by a political candidate automatically activates the equal opportunities rule. Section 315(a) of the Communications Act, as applied by the FCC, works as follows: After the initial use of broadcast time by a legally qualified candidate (Candidate A), any other legally qualified candidate in the same race (Candidates B and C) may demand equal opportunity to appear on the station. The demand must be made within seven days of the initial use by Candidate A. Broadcast stations are not required to directly notify campaign opponents each time a candidate makes use of the station's airtime. However, stations must keep a detailed, public file of candidate uses.

Equal opportunity means precisely that. It means that Candidate B must be afforded an opportunity to reach essentially the same size audience as Candidate A, for the same length of time, at the same cost. If Candidate A purchased a sixty-second commercial at 2 A.M., the opponent must be given an opportunity to purchase sixty seconds in the wee morning hours at the same rate. If Candidate A's appearance was free during prime time as part of an entertainment show, Candidate B has a right to the same number of minutes during prime time at no charge. The time slot need not be exactly the same, as long as the requesting candidates reaches a comparable audience. The broadcaster has discretion to determine precisely how its equal opportunity obligations will be met; a candidate does not have the right to demand access to a particular program, hour, or day.

There is no requirement that Candidates B and C use their equal opportunity time to address the same matters raised in Candidate A's initial appearance. In fact, the responding candidates may use the time in any way they choose, and Section 315 warns that the broadcaster "shall have no power of censorship over the material broadcast under the provisions of this section." This means that the broadcaster must stand aside and refrain from editing even those political uses that may contain vulgar or defamatory remarks. In light of this no censorship mandate, it would seem logical that a broadcaster should not be subject to liability if the political use is indeed defamatory—and the Supreme Court has so ruled.[37] The candidates themselves are responsible for what they say on the air, however.

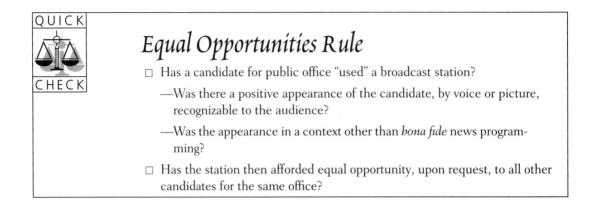

QUICK CHECK

Equal Opportunities Rule

☐ Has a candidate for public office "used" a broadcast station?

—Was there a positive appearance of the candidate, by voice or picture, recognizable to the audience?

—Was the appearance in a context other than *bona fide* news programming?

☐ Has the station then afforded equal opportunity, upon request, to all other candidates for the same office?

The Candidate Access Rule

To avoid the potentially onerous obligations of the equal opportunities rule, broadcasters may be tempted to refuse any access by candidates in the first place. Nothing in Section 315 would prevent this. However, a companion section of the Communications Act, Section 312(a)(7), specifies that a broadcast license may be revoked for "willful or repeated failure to allow reasonable access to or to permit purchase of reasonable amounts of time for the use of a broadcasting station by a legally qualified candidate for Federal elective office on behalf of his candidacy." What this means is that—in regard to *federal* candidates—a broadcaster may not categorically exclude access or otherwise deny reasonable requests to purchase political time.

The Supreme Court interpreted the reasonable access requirement in *CBS, Inc. v. FCC,* a 1981 decision. The Jimmy Carter campaign for president had sought to purchase thirty minutes of prime time from each of the major TV networks in December 1979, just after Carter announced he would seek reelection. The networks refused on grounds that it was too early in the political season and that the requested access would disrupt their programming. But the FCC ruled that the networks, which also were broadcast licensees, had violated the reasonable access requirement. The Supreme Court agreed. Wrote Chief Justice Burger:

> Broadcasters are free to deny the sale of air time prior to the commencement of a campaign, but once a campaign has begun, they must give reasonable good faith attention to access requests from "legally qualified" candidates for federal elective office. Such requests must be considered on an individual basis, and broadcasters are required to tailor their responses to accommodate, as much as reasonably possible, a candidate's stated purposes in seeking air time. In responding to access requests, however, broadcasters may also give weight to such factors as the amount of time previously sold to the candidate, the disruptive impact on regular programming, and the likelihood of requests for time by rival candidates under

the equal opportunities provision of §315(a). These considerations may not be invoked as pretexts for denying access; to justify a negative response, broadcasters must cite a realistic danger of substantial program disruption—perhaps caused by insufficient notice to allow adjustments in the schedule—or of an excessive number of equal time requests. . . . If broadcasters take the appropriate factors into account and act reasonably and in good faith, their decisions will be entitled to deference. . . . But if broadcasters adopt "across-the-board policies" and do not attempt to respond to the individualized situation of a particular candidate, the Commission is not compelled to sustain their denial of access.[38]

The Court concluded that the networks had not adequately considered the president's request on an individual basis.

In 1991 a legally qualified candidate for the New Hampshire Republican presidential primary, Michael Steven Levinson, requested three-hour blocks of free, prime-time programming from two noncommercial TV stations. The stations denied the request, and each offered five prime-time minutes instead. Levinson filed a complaint with the FCC, but the agency ruled that the stations' actions were reasonable. The stations had cited two main reasons for their denial of the access request: First, the three-hour request would have a highly disruptive effect on each station's programming. And second, with at least nineteen candidates in the race for the Republican nomination, the potential equal time requests under Section 315 would be unduly burdensome.[39]

The access requirement of Section 312(a)(7) applies only to federal candidates. State and local candidates have no similar right of access. If a station does sell time to a candidate for state or local office, however, the equal opportunities rule is applicable.

Advertising Rates

One way to keep candidate use to a minimum, it might seem, would be to charge higher-than-usual advertising rates to candidates. However, the law requires just the opposite. Section 315(b) of the Communications Act reads:

> The charges made for the use of any broadcast station by any person who is a legally qualified candidate for any public office in connection with his campaign for nomination for election, or election, to such office shall not exceed—
>
> 1. During the 45 days preceding the date of a primary or primary runoff election and during the 60 days preceding the date of a general or special election in which such person is a candidate, the lowest unit charge of the station for the same class and amount of time for the same period; and
>
> 2. At any other time, the charges made for comparable use of such station by other users thereof.

This means that during most of the year stations must charge candidates no more than they would charge commercial advertisers for the same kind and frequency of advertising. During the 45- and 60-day periods preceding elections, however, candidates are entitled to an even better deal: They can be charged no more than the lowest unit rate enjoyed by a commercial advertiser during the same time slot.

For example, suppose that a TV station's usual ad rate for a thirty-second spot during prime time is $200. Discounts are given to advertisers who buy with great frequency, however, and one commercial advertiser who bought the most spots is actually being charged $125 per unit for those spots. Within the 45- or 60-day period prior to an election, a candidate wishing to buy a prime-time, thirty-second spot could be charged no more than $125—the lowest unit rate—even if the candidate purchases just a single spot. During other times of the year, the candidate could be charged no more than the $200 that commercial advertisers normally would be charged for a single spot.

In practice, implementing the lowest unit rate requirement can be quite complicated. In 1990 the FCC sent inspectors out to thirty TV stations to conduct an audit of compliance with the political broadcasting rules. The agency found that at most of the stations candidates were paying more for commercials than were other advertisers. One reason for this, the FCC found, was that candidates were generally being sold nonpreemptible, fixed time commercials. This is a different and more expensive class of advertisement than the preemptible commercials generally purchased by most other advertisers. Because the lowest unit rate requirement applies only to advertisements within the same class, the audited TV stations were not necessarily in violation. Nevertheless, the FCC was concerned that candidates were not being fully apprised of their options. In 1992 the agency issued new disclosure requirements. Every station now must give a written disclosure statement to any candidate inquiring about advertising. The statement should include a description of all available classes of time, the lowest unit charge for each class, and the privileges associated with each class.

The special ad rate provisions apply only to candidate uses of broadcast time. The lowest unit rate and comparable rate requirements of Section 315 do not apply to other kinds of advertising that may have a political message, such as an interest group's ad in support of a particular ballot initiative or referendum.

Remnants of the Fairness Doctrine

The foregoing discussion of sections 315 and 312 depicts a fairly complicated set of provisions, each mandated by Congress and implemented by the FCC. Historically, though, these provisions were not the most controversial or omnipresent content controls that broadcasters faced. That distinction went to the **fairness doctrine.**

The fairness doctrine originated with the old Federal Radio Commission, and the doctrine was refined in the 1940s by the FCC, operating under its general mandate to supervise broadcasting in the public interest. The theory behind the doctrine was that there was simply not enough room in the radio spectrum for every religious, political, or social school of thought to have its own separate station on the air. Therefore, it was the duty of each broadcast licensee to make sure that a full range of viewpoints was presented. Specifically, the fairness doctrine required that all broadcasters (1) devote a reasonable amount of their programming to controversial issues of public importance, and (2) provide contrasting viewpoints on those issues.

The commission did not establish a rigid formula; equal time was not required, as it is for candidates under Section 315. Rather each licensee was simply expected to act in good faith to cover issues and to air contrasting views. Nevertheless, the fairness doctrine caused considerable problems for broadcasters and for the FCC. Audience complaints to the commission were numerous, and litigation was common, particularly under the second prong of the doctrine. Some broadcast observers claimed that the doctrine was stifling robust debate of the issues rather than encouraging it.

In 1987 the FCC formally abandoned the fairness doctrine. In its *Syracuse Peace Council* decision,[40] the commission eliminated the doctrine on several grounds. Most notably, the commission said the doctrine inhibited rather than enhanced the coverage of controversial issues and that, given the many media voices in today's marketplace, the doctrine was probably an unconstitutional interference with the editorial discretion of broadcasters.

Over the years the main trunk of the fairness doctrine acquired three specialized offshoots. When the commission axed the doctrine it did not eliminate the offshoots, however, and so they presumably remain in full effect. The offshoots are referred to as *the personal attack rule, the political editorial rule,* and *the Zapple rule.*

Personal Attacks

The **personal attack rule** is activated whenever a person or small group is subject to a character attack during broadcast presentations on public issues. Within one week the station must notify the individuals who were attacked, send them tapes, transcripts, or summaries of what was said, and offer a reasonable opportunity to respond on the air.

Under the personal attack rule the response time must be offered free, even if the original attack was made by an individual who had purchased broadcast time from the station. The response time need not be equal, just reasonable. If the personal attack occurred during a network show, the individual affiliate nevertheless must assure that the obligations of the rule are met.

The burden on broadcasters from the personal attack rule is lessened significantly by some exemptions. The rule does not apply to personal attacks on foreign groups or foreign public figures or to attacks that occur during bona fide newscasts. Nor does the rule apply to attacks made by political candidates or their representatives against other candidates.

Political Editorials

If a station broadcasts an editorial in which declared candidates for public office are endorsed or opposed, the **political editorial rule** requires that the candidates who were not endorsed be accorded reasonable opportunity to respond. Here again, the response time must be offered free. It is the station's obligation to notify the opposed candidates within twenty-four hours after the editorial aired—or prior to airing, if the editorial is broadcast within three days before the election. Note that political editorials are in no way prohibited; stations simply must provide notification of response time to opposed candidates.

A station can insist that response time be used by spokespersons for opposed candidates rather than the candidates themselves. This avoids a collision between the political editorial rule and the rigid requirements of Section 315.

The Zapple Rule

Even when a candidate does not appear on the air in voice or picture, a type of equal opportunities situation arises when a broadcaster sells or gives time to the supporters of a candidate. The supporters of the opponent are entitled to equal time on the air under what has come to be known as the **Zapple rule.** This rule is not a Section 315 requirement of the Communications Act. Rather, it is an outgrowth of the fairness doctrine. Like the equal opportunities rule, though, the Zapple rule applies only during campaign periods, there is no requirement that the response time be free, and bona fide news programming is exempt.

Children's Television

Consumers and the government long have been concerned about the quality of children's programming on TV and about the potentially overbearing effects of commercials aimed at youngsters. Congress addressed both concerns in the Children's Television Act of 1990.[41] The act required the FCC to adopt specific rules limiting the number of commercial minutes during children's programming. Furthermore, the commission was ordered to consider at renewal time whether the licensee has met the commercial limits and also the extent to which the licensee has served the "educational and informational needs of children." The FCC issued rules and policies that went into effect in 1991.

Commercial Limits

The commercial limits apply to programs originally produced and broadcast primarily for an audience of children 12 years old and younger. During such programming, commercials must be limited to 10.5 minutes per hour on weekends and 12 minutes an hour on weekdays. Commercials are defined by the FCC as air time sold for purposes of selling a product or service. TV stations are required to maintain records in their public inspection files, demonstrating compliance with these limits.

Of particular concern in recent years has been the growth of so-called program-length commercials. The commission defines a **program-length commercial** as "a program associated with a product, in which commercials for that product are aired."[42] A children's program becomes a program-length commercial if a product associated with the program appears in commercial spots not separated from the start or close of the program by at least sixty seconds of unrelated material. Any children's program found to be a program-length commercial will count in its entirety toward the commercial limits.

Programming Requirements

Throughout its license term, every commercial TV station is required to serve the educational and informational needs of children aged 16 or younger, both through its overall programming and through programming that is *specifically designed* to meet those needs (referred to as "core" children's programming). Given the traditional leadership of public television in the area of children's programming, the commission decided not to apply this programming content requirement to noncommercial stations. Licensees are not required to target programs to all ages of children in the 16-and-under range. However, at renewal time a broadcaster is expected to have aired programming specifically designed to serve the needs of children of at least some age within that range.

Educational and informational programming is defined as that which furthers the positive development of children in any respect, including children's cognitive/intellectual or emotional/social needs. Initially the commission established no guidelines, however, for the kind of programs that would qualify and for the minimum amount of such programming that must be aired.

In 1996 the FCC adopted new rules and guidelines to strengthen enforcement and eliminate the squishiness of the original rules. They revised rules are as follows:[43]

"Core" children's programming is defined as that which has as a *significant purpose* serving the educational needs of children; it must be aired between 7 A.M. and 10 P.M.; it must be regularly scheduled at least weekly; and it must be at least a half-hour program. In comments accompanying the new rules, the FCC stated that "core" children's programming does not include general audience and entertainment programming (such as reruns of old sitcoms, presumably).

At license renewal time, FCC staff will automatically deem a broadcaster in full compliance with the programming requirements if the station aired on average at least three hours per week of such core programming. As an alternative, stations can also earn quick staff approval by demonstrating that they aired a combination of core programming and packages of other educational programming, such as

EXHIBIT 11.3   *The Public Inspection File*

The FCC requires all TV and radio stations to maintain a local public inspection file at their main studios, available for viewing during regular business hours. The file also may be electronic, available to view on a studio computer terminal or on a Web site. Stations must keep the following in the file:[44]

- A copy of the current FCC broadcast license
- Applications filed with the FCC (such as a renewal application)
- Signal contour maps
- The current ownership report, listing owners' names
- Any FCC materials relating to an investigation
- A political file, documenting time requested by and provided to candidates
- Annual employment reports, documenting efforts to recruit minorities
- Copies or recent, written comments from the public
- An issues/programs list of programming that discussed specific local issues
- Children's Television Act reports on programming and commercial limits

public service announcements, specials and short-form programs that are equivalent to at least three hours per week of core programming. If a station does not meet either of these guidelines, the FCC staff will refer the matter to the full Commission to determine if the educational needs of children have been sufficiently met in some other fashion.

TV stations must file a "children's television programming report" with the FCC quarterly (see Exhibit 11.3). In addition, stations must identify their educational children's programming, both on air and in programming guides.[45]

Other Content Controls

Congress and the FCC also control the content of broadcasting in many other ways. A few are described here.

Sponsor Identification

The Communications Act requires that all paid broadcast messages include the identity of the sponsor.[46] With most commercial ads for products or services the sponsorship is clearly built into the message. But with paid political or public service messages the sponsor might not be inherently obvious. Therefore, the FCC has adopted special rules to assure that noncommercial messages include an adequate sponsor identification notice. For example, FCC rules on televised ads for political candidates require all such ads to include a visual sponsor ID. The identification must be in letters equal to at least 4 percent of vertical screen height and the ID must be on the air for at least four seconds.

Indecency

For many years the FCC has maintained rules against the broadcast of "indecent" material during hours when children are likely to be in the audience. Active enforcement of the indecency prohibition seems to come in cycles, with the last major enforcement push running from about the mid-1980s to the mid-1990s. The indecency rules are discussed in detail in Chapter 12.

Hoaxes

In the early 1990s the FCC received complaints about several on-air radio station hoaxes. In one case that took place during the Persian Gulf War, a station in St. Louis, Missouri, interrupted what appeared to be regular music programming and announced: "Attention: civil defense warning. The United States is under nuclear attack." This was accompanied by a variety of sound effects, including muffled screams and explosions and a loud tone similar to the distress signal associated with the Emergency Broadcasting System. The broadcast was intended as satire, but some listeners didn't understand it that way. The FCC in 1991 assessed a $25,000 fine against the station for violating a Communications Act prohibition on transmitting false distress signals.

In another case a Los Angeles station aired an apparent murder confession that generated a police investigation and substantial publicity. Nearly a year passed before the station's management and the public learned that the confession was a hoax. The FCC subjected the Los Angeles station to a costly and embarrassing inquiry pursuant to the general investigative powers contained in Section 403 of the Communications Act. Ultimately, no formal punishment was handed down because management was not involved in the hoax. But in egregious cases the commission presumably could initiate a license revocation hearing.

The cluster of radio hoaxes convinced the FCC that it needed a specific rule on hoaxes—a rule that would give the commission greater flexibility to levy forfeitures and other forms of punishment for harmful on-air hoaxes. In 1992 the FCC adopted a new rule that prohibits the broadcast of false information concerning a crime or catastrophe if it is foreseeable that the broadcast could cause substantial public harm and if the broadcast does in fact directly cause substantial harm.[47] Legal experts for the broadcast industry criticized the rule as an awkward and unwise attempt at content regulation. If the proposed regulation were adopted, one expert wondered, could radio stations legally rebroadcast Orson Welles' classic "War of the Worlds" production?

Cable Television

Cable television systems began operating in the United States in the 1940s, not many years after broadcast television became commercially viable. The early cable systems were established primarily to deliver clear TV pictures to communities where mountains or other barriers prevented good reception of over-the-air signals. For the typical system, a large antenna was constructed adjacent to the community, usually on a hilltop. This allowed the collection of a high-quality signal from TV stations in the vicinity, and the signal was delivered via cables directly to homes in the community. It was originally called *community antenna television,* or CATV, and cable operators were no more than passive relayers of area TV signals.

But over the years cable operators began offering additional programming services by importing signals from distant stations and in some cases by originating their own local programming. The 1960s and 1970s brought dramatic technical advances to the cable industry: satellite and microwave receiving stations, improved coaxial cable hardware, and signal conversion boxes for the home. In the 1980s many systems were delivering 25 or even 50 channels to their subscribers, and the future promised two-way, interactive programming services. By the 1990s nearly two-thirds of American homes were served by cable.

Cable had become a major mass medium in its own right and a worrisome competitor for the broadcast TV industry. Cable TV upset the established regulatory scheme and presented tremendously difficult legal challenges to Congress, the FCC, and local governments.

First Amendment Status

One of the most hotly debated questions in cable TV law has been whether cable can be regulated at all. Industry representatives and some legal scholars have argued that cable companies deserve the same full-strength First Amendment shield accorded newspapers and other print media. A cable system does not broadcast over the public airwaves, after all, so there is no problem of clogging a naturally occurring, physically scarce resource. There is no physical limit to the number of cable channels that can be delivered to a home. Nor is there a necessary physical limit to the number of cable operators that can serve a community. Just as another newspaper or two could always decide to circulate in a town, another cable operator could, in theory, string its lines. Without a physically scarce resource at issue, the critical regulatory rationale described in *Red Lion* would appear inapplicable.

A prevailing constitutional approach among the lower courts was evident by the late 1980s: Cable regulations not based on content were given the intermediate-scrutiny test articulated by the Supreme Court in *United States v. O'Brien.*[48] A regulation would be upheld if it advanced an important governmental interest unrelated to the suppression of speech and if the regulation did not burden substantially more speech than necessary. When assessing the validity of content-based regulations, on the other hand, courts were tending to use strict scrutiny, requiring a *compelling* justification.

The judicial trend, then, was to treat cable operators much like the print media, with substantial First Amendment protection.

It wasn't until 1994, however, that the Supreme Court verified this indeed was the proper standard for the cable medium. At issue in *Turner Broadcasting System v. FCC* was the validity of a statute requiring cable operators to carry the signals of local broadcast stations. The Court first needed to determine whether cable, for purposes of First Amendment analysis, could be accorded the relaxed constitutional protection that applies to broadcasting. The Court concluded that it could not. Wrote Justice Kennedy for the Court:

> [T]he rationale for applying a less rigorous standard of First Amendment scrutiny to broadcast regulation, whatever its validity in the cases elaborating it, does not apply in the context of cable regulation. The justification for our distinct approach to broadcast regulation rests upon the unique physical limitations of the broadcast medium. . . . [C]able television does not suffer from the inherent limitations that characterize the broadcast medium. Indeed, given the rapid advances in fiber optics and digital compression technology, soon there may be no practical limitation on the number of speakers who may use the cable medium.[49]

Therefore, the Court held, cable TV regulations should be scrutinized under the same, strict First Amendment standards applicable generally to nonbroadcast media.

Of course, this does not mean that all government regulation of cable is invalid. Unique aspects of the cable medium may still justify restrictions that generally would not be valid if applied to other media. Particularly if the regulations are not content-based, they may be upheld by the courts.

The Cable Acts
In the 1970s cable became a heavily regulated industry. Every level of authority was involved—the federal government, the states, and especially cities and counties. Local municipalities by and large awarded the franchises, and in exchange they demanded rate limits, programming promises, and community access channels. Cities and counties also set standards for such things as equipment and franchise application and renewal procedures. The FCC also had an interest in national regulation of cable, largely because of the medium's possible effects on broadcast media. Different levels of government were essentially vying for control over cable, and the blossoming cable industry was caught in an increasingly harsh and uncertain legal environment.

The courts began to enter the picture, and some regulations were invalidated. But it had become obvious by the early 1980s that national coordination was necessary.

Congress enacted the Cable Communications Policy Act of 1984 in an effort to clarify the regulatory picture.[50] The Cable Act for the first time established a national policy for cable regulation, and it allocated regulatory responsibility to the different levels of government. In the end the act actually helped to deregulate some aspects of cable. Major features of the 1984 act included the following:

☐ Local governments were recognized in the act as proper authorities to issue cable franchises. The act permits a municipality to award one or more franchises within its jurisdiction.

□ Franchising governments have authority to request that cable operators reserve channels for public access, educational, and governmental uses.

□ Franchising authorities generally are prohibited from establishing requirements for specific kinds of programming.

□ Technical standards relating to the facilities and equipment of a cable system are set primarily by the FCC.

□ Cable companies are generally prohibited from owning TV stations that share any portion of the same service area.

The 1984 Cable Act represented a major compromise between cable operators and various levels of government. Nevertheless, the future of the Cable Act was not peaceful. On the one hand, cable operators challenged the constitutionality of provisions in the act. And on the other hand, broadcasters, some consumer groups and members of Congress pushed for additional regulation.

In 1992, Congress did enact more regulation, over a presidential veto, with the Cable Television Consumer Protection and Competition Act. The 1992 act was prompted to a large extent by consumer complaints about the rising costs of cable service and a lack of cable competition. The act authorized cable rate regulation by the FCC and by municipalities; it prohibited cities from awarding exclusive cable franchises; and it directed the FCC to develop and enforce additional technical standards for cable. The act also contained various provisions intended to protect broadcasters from the growing competition from cable.

However, the Telecommunications Act of 1996 in turn repealed many provisions of the 1992 act, including the highly contentious cable rate regulations. The prevailing view in Congress at the time was that ultimately consumers would be better served by allowing market forces to determine how the cable industry would grow, compete and invest in new technology. Under the 1996 act cable price caps were to be phased out, except for the caps on "basic tier" cable programming services. Price caps were repealed immediately for small cable operators, those with annual revenues under $25 million. Further, price caps could end immediately for any other cable operator that faced "effective competition" in its market from other video programming services.[51]

To say that regulation of cable has been unsettled would be a profound understatement. It is a difficult chore, however. Many over-the-air TV broadcasters are wary of cable as a competitor and miffed by the fact that cable operators can deliver programming without incurring the production costs. Cable operators promise continually expanding consumer choice and wondrous technology, if only government will stand aside and allow the industry to expand. And government is trying to mold and remold the rules so that both industries can prosper—along with satellite, telephone companies, and other potential providers of video programming.

Following are summaries of some of the areas that have drawn considerable legal attention to date.

Franchising

Cable companies must install their lines on utility poles or underground, typically beneath or adjacent to streets. Because cities and counties control the rights-of-way to these facilities, local governments logically have assumed the task of franchising cable operators. In most cases a city in need of a cable system will consider competitive bids from several companies. Each bid will outline a specific proposal as to construction time, number of channels, subscriber rates, quality of equipment, and other factors. The city typically chooses one of the companies to construct and operate the system under an exclusive franchise for a set number of years. When the franchise expires the cable company may apply to the city for renewal.

Within this franchise process are many opportunities for constitutional conflict, however, as municipalities seek to saddle cable operators with various franchise prerequisites. The best case for illustrating the legal labyrinth of cable franchising is *City of Los Angeles v. Preferred Communications, Inc.*[52] The case arose when a cable operator, Preferred Communications, sought to lease space on city utility poles so it could provide cable TV service. The city responded that the company could not lease space unless it first obtained a cable TV franchise from the city, and it refused to grant a franchise because Preferred had not participated in the competitive process used by the city to award a single franchise for the area. Preferred went to federal court, claiming that it was a First Amendment violation to refuse access when the utility poles contained excess physical capacity. Preferred also claimed that the franchise process was unconstitutional because it discriminated against franchise applicants based on content considerations.

The federal District Court in Los Angeles in 1990 issued rulings on numerous motions for summary judgment made by both parties. The district judge employed the intermediate scrutiny *O'Brien* test to determine the constitutionality of city regulations that imposed an incidental burden on speech. But for restrictions that directly curtailed expression the court used the strictest level of scrutiny, requiring the city to show that its restrictions were precisely tailored to serve a compelling government interest.

Based on these tests the trial judge ruled that the following were direct restrictions on speech and were unconstitutional: eight mandatory public access channels; the consideration of overall owner character in awarding franchises; a state-of-the-art technology requirement; and a requirement that the cablecaster create a community advisory board, subject to city approval.

The court also invalidated two indirect restrictions on speech: One was the limitation of one cable operator per franchise area; the other was a requirement of a $10,000 filing fee.

The District Court upheld the city's requirement that local individuals or groups participate in the ownership and operation of the system. It also upheld the requirement of a 5 percent franchise fee, the requirement that franchisees be financially and technically qualified, the requirement that the city have access to poles and towers erected by the cable company, and the requirement that the city have a right to inspect company business records.

Cable Content

Restrictions on the content of cable transmissions raise the greatest potential First Amendment problems. The cable acts impose little in the form of content-based restrictions. But Congress and the FCC are free to impose content rules through separate legislation.

Many of the broadcast content regulations discussed earlier in this chapter are, in fact, also applied to cable. Thus far they have been the source of very few lawsuits by cablecasters, however, because cable operators primarily deal with secondary transmissions; broadcasters are initially responsible for most of the programming transmitted on cable. To the extent that cable operators do originate their own programming, however, they are subject to rules nearly identical to many of the broadcast restrictions, including the lowest unit rate provision, the personal attack rule, the political editorial rule, and the equal opportunities rule for political candidates.[53] The commercial time limits of the Children's Television Act explicitly apply to cable as well.

One kind of restriction that has generated successful court challenges by cablecasters is prohibitions against indecency. In the 1985 case of *Cruz v. Ferre,*[54] for example, a federal Court of Appeals held that the kind of indecency prohibition that applies to broadcast cannot constitutionally be applied to cable. The court distinguished cable as a less invasive medium without the same compelling justifications for content controls. This issue is discussed further in Chapter 12.

Access Channels

Franchising authorities are permitted under the 1984 Cable Act to require that cable operators set aside channels for public access, educational, and government use—sometimes called **PEG channels.** Cablecasters have challenged the constitutional authority of cities to require PEG channels, with some success. But if the mandated number of PEG channels is not too extensive, the requirement is likely to be valid.

This raises another interesting question: Who is legally responsible for the content on these mandated PEG channels? The 1984 Cable Act stated that cable operators could not exercise any editorial control over outside parties' use of PEG channels, except to censor obscenity. At the same time, the cable operator was granted sweeping immunity from any libel, obscenity, incitement, invasion of privacy, or false advertising problems that may occur during use of a PEG channel.

So, only the PEG channel users themselves would be liable for any torts or crimes arising from their expression.

In the 1992 Cable Television Consumer Protection and Competition Act, the Congress went a step further by permitting—though not requiring—cable operators to screen out "indecent" or offensive sexually oriented material on their public access channels. "Indecent" material covers a much broader range of programming than obscenity, as we'll see in Chapter 12, and most of it is protected expression under the First Amendment. This screening authority under the 1992 act thus raised another interesting question: Does censorship by a private cable company, when done under specific authority of a statute, amount to "government action" that raises First Amendment concerns? In 1995 a federal court of appeals said no—that the screening by a private cable operator could not be attributed to government and therefore the First Amendment is not violated.[55] On review, the U.S. Supreme Court was a bit more equivocal in its ruling, but nevertheless affirmed that this particular provision did not violate the First Amendment: "[T]he permissive nature of the provision, coupled with its viewpoint-neutral application, is a constitutionally permissible way to protect children from the type of sexual material that concerned Congress."[56]

Apart from this limited provision, however, the general rule is that once a public-access channel is set up at the demand of a franchising government, the government is prohibited from controlling the expression on that channel (by the First Amendment), and the cable operator also is generally prohibited from exercising control over content (by statute). For example, when the City Council of Kansas City, Missouri, learned that the Ku Klux Klan intended to make regular use of the local access channel, the council decided to close the channel. Instead, it was to be converted to a local programming channel controlled by the cable operator. But the Klan went to court, and a federal district judge ruled that the First Amendment prevented the city from closing the access channel if its purpose was to keep the Klan off the channel. The court characterized the channel as a public forum that could not be manipulated by government in a manner that discriminated among viewpoints.[57] The city eventually agreed to reinstate the public access channel and pay the Klan's legal fees.

Syndicated Programming

Over the years various content-related rules have been imposed on cable operators in an effort to protect broadcasters. Of the rules currently in effect one of the most notable is the **syndicated exclusivity rule,** or *syndex,* for short. In the contract negotiated between a supplier of syndicated programs and a broadcast station, the syndicator typically will agree that the station will be the exclusive carrier of the show in the station's local broadcast area. Under the syndex rule the station possessing such exclusive contract rights may forbid any cable company from importing the syndicated program into the community from another, distant source. The FCC repealed its syndex rule in 1980, but reinstated it in 1988.[58]

Must-Carry

Certainly among the boldest efforts to protect the broadcast industry are the must-carry rules. In the Cable Television Consumer Protection and Competition Act of 1992, Congress required cable operators to carry the signals of local, full-power television stations, both commercial and noncommercial, up to specified limits. The number of channels that must be set aside for local broadcast stations depends upon the size of the cable system.[59]

This **"must-carry" law** was intended to protect the market for broadcasters who might otherwise find themselves effectively edged out by cablecasters who chose instead to import distant signals and other cable programming. Without the audience attained through local cable systems, a broadcaster could find it difficult to earn sufficient advertising revenue, or viewer contributions, to continue operation.

As mentioned earlier, the must-carry law was challenged in the 1994 Supreme Court case of *Turner Broadcasting System v. FCC*. Numerous cable operators and cable programmers alleged that the must-carry provisions violated their First Amendment rights. For cable operators, the must-carry provisions reduced the number of channels over which they may exercise unfettered control. For cable programmers, the must-carry law rendered it more difficult to attain carriage on the more limited limited number of channels remaining.

While the Supreme Court's 1994 *Turner* ruling did clarify the First Amendment standard applicable to cable, it did not ultimately resolve the dispute over the must-carry rules. The Court determined that the rules were not content based; the rules did not impose a burden on cable operators or programmers by reason of the views or programs carried. Therefore, the Court said, the must-carry provisions should be analyzed under the intermediate scrutiny test of *O'Brien*. The content-neutral law would be upheld if the government could demonstrate that the law significantly advanced important government interests. But the Court at this point became fractured, with some justices finding the must-carry provisions unconstitutional on their face, one justice finding them constitutional without need for further inquiry, and other justices desiring additional factual findings. The case was sent back to the district court for additional fact finding.

In 1997 the case was back at the Supreme Court, and again the justices were sharply divided. But by a 5–4 majority the Court upheld the must-carry requirement. Writing for the majority, Justice Kennedy noted a trend toward concentrated ownership of multiple cable systems and toward ownership or affiliation agreements with cable programmers. There was sufficient evidence collected by Congress, the Court majority found, that these increasingly powerful cable systems would tend to drop local broadcast signals in favor of their affiliated national programmers. Evidence also made it reasonable to conclude that this would cause economic hardship for many stations. By assuring cable carriage and concomitant higher audiences for local TV, more stations will secure the revenues they need to succeed. Therefore, the majority held, the must-carry requirement serves the important governmental interests of preserving free, over-the-air local television for the public, promoting a multiplicity of programming voices, and promoting fair competition in the market for TV programming.

Furthermore, Justice Kennedy concluded the law was no broader than necessary. As a result of must-carry, broadcast stations gained carriage on 5,880 cable channels nationwide. This was not an overly broad burden on the half-million cable channels that existed at the time, Kennedy concluded.

Justice O'Connor filed a strong dissenting opinion, however, in which she accused the majority of making too many assumptions and granting too much deference to Congress, given the seriousness of the First Amendment issue at stake. O'Connor said there was insufficient evidence to conclude the broad must-carry approach was actually necessary to prevent a significant reduction in the multiplicity of broadcast programming sources or to prevent anticompetitive conduct by cable systems. Instead, she said, must-carry should be applied more narrowly, only in markets where a need to protect the economic viability of TV stations is actually demonstrated.[60]

Retransmission Consent

An added complexity to the law of must-carry is the companion regulation known as **retransmission consent,** which became effective in 1993. In the FCC regulation, which was specifically authorized by Congress, commercial television stations must elect every three years between retransmission consent and must-carry status. Local cable operators must be notified of the decision. For those stations that elect retransmission consent — typically popular stations with greater bargaining power — a local cable system is *not allowed* to retransmit the signal without first negotiating a retransmission agreement with the station. This may mean that a cable system will have to pay a popular station for the right to carry its signal in the cable lineup.[61]

Entry by Telephone Companies

One of the most intriguing disputes in the communications industry in recent years has been whether the nation's regional telephone companies should be permitted to enter the business of providing cable television services. The cable TV industry vigorously opposed such a move, worried that the giant telephone companies, sometimes called "telcos," could come to dominate programming and threaten the profitability of local cable operators. Some regulators were concerned, too, about the monopolistic effect of allowing telephone companies to expand their scope of communication services by becoming cable providers.

Telephone and cable TV companies are regulated under two different models. The telephone companies are classified as "common carriers" that provide the means for two-way, personal communication rather than information or entertainment content for the public. The telephone companies are subject to public utility regulation by the states. Cable operators, on the other hand, are regulated mainly at the federal and local levels as programmers, not passive channel providers.

Technologically speaking, though, the telephone companies are quite well equipped to enter the cable TV business in grand fashion. Whereas most cable firms use coaxial wire to transmit their programming, the telephone companies have laid vast networks of optical fiber. The fiber is more costly, but it also offers potentially huge advantages. Most notably, fiber optic cables have far greater channel capacity and can deliver a higher quality picture over longer distances. In theory these fiber networks could be adapted to deliver literally hundreds of channels of programming, including sophisticated two-way programming.

The telephone companies understandably had been interested in entering the field of cable TV. Until 1996, however, their full-scale entry had been blocked by two legal hurdles. First, under the 1982 Justice Department/AT&T consent decree the nation's regional Bell operating companies were prohibited from offering information services. Antitrust concerns were the basis for the consent decree, which split a portion of AT&T into smaller, regional companies and essentially limits those companies to providing common carrier, telecommunication services. The second hurdle was a provision in the 1984 Cable Act that prohibited any telephone company from providing television programming to subscribers. Both the limits of the consent decree and the Cable Act could be waived in limited circumstances, but the telephone companies were pushing for more sweeping changes in the law—changes that would allow them to compete head-to-head with existing cable operators.

With the Telecommunications Act of 1996 the telcos got their wish. The Act repealed telco-cable cross-ownership restrictions and authorized telcos to offer video services, either by distributing programming as a cable TV system or by establishing an "open video system" for disseminating programming on a common carrier basis.

Summary Points

The electronic media are subject to far greater regulation than the print media. For broadcast media the main justification for regulation is spectrum scarcity, as articulated in the case of *Red Lion Broadcasting v. FCC*. The constitutional justification for cable TV regulation is less well established, but municipalities long have exerted regulatory power by virtue of their control over rights-of-way for the cables themselves.

The chief regulatory agency for most electronic media is the Federal Communications Commission. Since the late 1970s the FCC has been in a deregulatory mood in some respects, but many complicated restrictions remain in effect. Also, some key restrictions are in the form of statutes enacted by Congress.

The federal government has preempted almost all aspects of broadcast regulation through the Communications Act of 1934. Cable TV is regulated by both the federal government and the states, primarily through cities and counties. This system of shared jurisdiction over cable is outlined in the Cable Act of 1984.

The ultimate power over broadcasting is the government's licensing power, controlled by the FCC. For cable TV, it is primarily municipalities that decide who will be awarded a franchise.

Among the currently enforced content restrictions, the most complicated and potentially burdensome provisions are those relating to political broadcasting. Chief among these provisions is the equal opportunities rule. It applies to programming by both broadcasters and cable operators, and it is triggered when a candidate uses airtime in the medium.

The electronic media industries are subject to various ownership restrictions intended to ensure that consumers are served by multiple media voices and diversity in programming. These rules often change, however, and some were modified or eliminated under the Telecommunications Act of 1996.

In the chapter hypothetical, you would be free to exclude the independent candidate from your radio debate without triggering the equal opportunities rule, so long as the debate was a good-faith effort to convey news—not a veiled effort to promote a particular candidate. Because the candidate is running for a state office, not a federal post, you also could decline the request for commercial time without violating the access provision of the Communications Act. You could not, however, grant commercial time and then charge your very highest rate.

Discussion Questions

1. The *Red Lion* decision seems to rest entirely on the notion of spectrum scarcity. Specifically, what technological advances have been employed over the last two decades to call into question the continued validity of the scarcity rationale? Do you think these advantages are *legally* sufficient to warrant a reconsideration of the *Red Lion* principle?

2. Suppose the Supreme Court took the drastic step of overturning *Red Lion* and declaring invalid the current licensing scheme for broadcast. What kind

of legal rules could be applied instead to ensure orderly use of frequencies and sufficient certainty to prompt capital investment in stations?

3. The legal restraints on broadcast station ownership—such as the one-to-a-market rule and the national reach limits—have proved highly controversial. Do you think the FCC makes a valid assumption that greater diversity of broadcast owners will equate to greater diversity in programming? Is any other rationale sufficient to warrant caps on ownership by a single individual or corporation?

4. Do you think the lowest-unit-rate limitation for candidate commercials is working in the public interest, or is it merely a statutory perk in favor of candidates? If the rate limitation does work to ensure more political speech on the airwaves, is the benefit to the public sufficient to warrant the compliance burdens placed upon broadcasters?

5. When the telephone companies become cable programmers, will this threaten the continued viability of the TV broadcast industry, and if so, should this be a concern of Congress? If TV networks could contract for large, regional telephone companies to carry network programming, would the networks be interested in maintaining local affiliates?

Key Terms

ascertainment
band allotment
broadcasting
channel assignment
comparative proceeding
Equal Employment Opportunity
    requirement
equal opportunities (equal time) rule
fairness doctrine
must-carry law
PEG channels
personal attack rule

political editorial rule
program-length commercial
public inspection file
radio spectrum
renewal expectancy
retransmission consent
scarcity rationale
spectrum allocation
syndicated exclusivity rule
wireless cable
Zapple rule

Web Resources

http://www.fcc.gov/mmb
Federal Communications Commission, Mass Media Bureau

http://www.nab.org/legal
National Association of Broadcasters, Legal & Regulatory Affairs

http://www.ncta.com/home.html
National Cable Television Association

InfoTrac® College Edition

In recent years there has been increasing talk of electronic media "convergence"—the melding of cable, film, broadcast, telephone, and Internet industries to provide greater electronic innovations and efficiencies to the consumer. Are government regulators ready for this? Will the law likely clear the way for these mergers, or slow them down? Find an *InfoTrac* article or piece of commentary that discusses these questions.

Chapter Outline

Obscenity and Indecency

Upon completing this chapter you should

- ☐ **understand** the Supreme Court's basic approach to review of obscenity and pornography controls.
- ☐ **know** how the Court defines obscenity and the difficulties in applying the definition.
- ☐ **know** the means by which local, state, and federal governments today attempt to control sexually explicit materials, including those that are not strictly obscene.
- ☐ **know** how print and broadcast media are treated differently in the regulation of indecent language and depictions.

Hypothetical

■ Steamy Ads

Imagine that you're employed as the advertising director for a pharmaceutical company that manufactures condoms, among other things. One day the company's top executives decide to take a new, aggressive advertising stance. You are asked to write and produce two ads for the condoms, one to appear in magazines around the country, and the other to appear during evening hours on cable TV channels and on a few over-the-air TV stations. You decide to break new ground with a particularly erotic, attention-grabbing campaign.

The magazine ad features a full-page photograph of a nude man and nude woman sitting in the center of a large bed, facing one another, looking into each other's eyes with expressions of excitement, with hands caressing each other's shoulders. The woman's breasts are clearly visible. So is the tip of the man's penis, covered with a fluorescent pink condom. The heading reads: "Passion brand condoms. Hot colors for the hottest sexual experience."

The thirty-second TV commercial depicts virtually the same bedroom scene, but with live action, music, and other sound effects. The models are shown in the same nude position, kissing and caressing each other's upper torsos. Again a portion of the pink condom is visible. After several seconds of this action the announcer breaks in to give the pitch for Passion brand.

Would the media violate obscenity or indecency laws by running your ads? Would you violate the law even by sending the ads to the media through the mail?

Introduction

This chapter deals primarily with sexual content in public communication, though violence and plain old profanity to some extent also figure into the laws against obscenity and indecency. For most of the mainstream mass media, sexual content raises occasional ethical and professional issues, but rarely legal ones. Yet this area of law seems destined to remain forever in the spotlight of heated public debate; it brings basic free speech philosophy to the fore; and it does snare individual media, writers, and artists from time to time.

Sexual expression is something that America has had a very difficult time coming to terms with, though this country isn't alone in that regard. To some degree, public tension and a sense of taboo about sexual expression can be found in most cultures, both now and throughout recorded history. Sexually explicit materials can evoke intense and wide-ranging responses, from all-consuming curiosity to embarrassment, excitement, lust, or moral indignation.

In America today sexual expression in general elicits seemingly intractable, polarized opinions. What conclusions can be drawn, for example, when people respond with outrage to graphic sexual depictions? Some take this as proof that the American audience is backwardly puritan or immature in its views about sex. To others the outrage is seen as an appropriate response to immaturity and immorality by the communicators.

Sexual expression is a topic that also is accompanied by much irony in the United States. Evidence suggests that Americans aren't very sophisticated in their knowledge of sex. In 1990, for example, 55 percent of a nationwide sample reportedly flunked a much-publicized Kinsey Institute multiple choice test on facts about sexual habits and problems.[1] Yet this is a society in which sexual innuendo, sex-oriented talk shows, and graphic sexual entertainment seem pervasive. An even more sobering irony, perhaps, is that the culture has wrestled so extensively with the allowable boundaries of sexual depictions, while highly graphic portrayals of violence have been accepted in cinema and on TV screens with comparatively little protest and virtually no legal constraint.

It is in this heated and confusing climate that legal controls on sexual expression exist. The courts have worked hard to strike some middle ground. But just when it seems a legal truce has been achieved, another emotional conflict makes its way into headlines, either locally or nationally. In the 1990s this legal struggle spread to music lyrics, art museum exhibits, and websites.

Before moving on, it's important to note a few terms that will be used in this chapter. **Pornography** is a broad term used to describe all material that is sexually explicit and intended primarily for the purpose of sexual arousal. **Obscenity** is a word that has taken on a narrower, legal meaning. It is a class of sexual material so offensive that it is deemed by the Supreme Court to have virtually no First Amendment protection; almost all jurisdictions have declared it illegal. An inherent difficulty in this area of law is the task of articulating specific standards for obscenity. **Indecency** is a term with special legal meaning in the electronic media. It refers to a class of speech that is restricted on the broadcast airwaves even though it is not necessarily obscene and would be legally allowable in other avenues of expression.

History of Pornography

Though graphic depictions of sex on videotape and in glossy magazines are, of course, a development of the modern media and society, sexual expression is not a modern aberration. The following account of the history of sexual expression is from the 1986 final report of the U.S. Attorney General's Commission on Pornography:

> The use of comparatively explicit sexual references for the purpose of entertainment or arousal is hardly a recent phenomenon. Greek and Roman drama and poetry was frequently highly specific, and the works of Aristophanes, Catallus, Horace, and Ovid, to name just a few, contain references to sexual activity that, by the standards of the time, are highly explicit. Scenes of intercourse have been found on the walls of the brothel at Pompeii. . . .

Similar observations can be made about later historical periods and about other cultures. . . .

We can be fairly certain that sexually explicit descriptions and depictions have been around in one form or another almost since the beginning of recorded history, and we can also be fairly certain that its regulation by law in a form resembling contemporary regulation of sexually explicit materials is a comparatively recent phenomenon. It is difficult, however, to draw useful conclusions from this aspect of the history. . . .

[I]t is a mistake to draw too many conclusions about social tolerance and social control from the presence or absence of laws or law enforcement practices. There is little indication that sexual *conduct* was part of classical drama, and the very fact that many sexual references were veiled (however thinly) rather than explicit indicate that some sense of taboo or social stigma has always been in most societies attached to public discussion of sexuality. Yet although some degree of inhibition obviously attached to public descriptions and depictions of sexual acts, it is equally clear that the extent of these inhibitions has oscillated throughout history. In somewhat cyclical fashion, social tolerance of various practices has been at times limited and at times extensive. To conclude that inhibition, in some form or another, of public discussion and representations of sexual practices is a totally modern phenomenon is to overstate the case and to misinterpret the evidence from earlier times. But to assume that public discussions and descriptions of sexuality were, prior to 1850, always as inhibited as they were in English speaking countries from 1850 to 1950 is equally mistaken. . . .

Throughout the seventeenth and eighteenth centuries, common law courts in England were only occasionally asked to take action against the kind of material that would then have been considered pornographic. Even when asked, the courts were often reluctant to respond. In 1708, for example, James Read was indicted in London for publishing an extremely explicit book entitled The Fifteen Plagues of a Maidenhead. The Queen's Bench court, however, dismissed the indictment. . . . [Lord Justice Powell explained that the book "indeed tends to the corruption of good manners, but that is not sufficient for us to punish."] . . .

The history of the English experience with sexually explicit materials is largely paralleled by the experiences in other European countries, and the English colonies, including those in North America. As the world entered the nineteenth century, it remained the case that in most of the world there was greater tolerance for sexually explicit writing, printing, and drawing than there would be fifty years later. . . .[2]

Early American Obscenity Law   By the mid-1800s, American law had clearly moved toward declaring sexually explicit materials illegal. Earlier prosecutions are on record against sex-oriented materials, both in England and in the American colonies. But these prosecutions were relatively rare. Courts throughout the 1700s, perhaps sensing a can of worms and lacking a clear mandate from the public, were reluctant to take action against sexually explicit materials. For example, in England in 1748 John Cleland published an explicit novel called *Memoirs of a Woman of Pleasure,* also known as *Fanny Hill,* without public outcry, government censorship, or legal prosecution.

When the law did occasionally intervene in the 1700s, it was not truly directed at sexual depictions. Rather, prosecutions were aimed at attacks on religion. Courts were not inclined to intervene in defense of some broad and cloudy notion of decency. But they would take action if the material containing sexual depictions amounted to religious blasphemy, a well-established crime of that era.

In the 1800s, though, the climate began to change. In Great Britain and the United States prevailing societal views about sexual morality were becoming increasingly strict. At the same time, economical printing technology was making explicit descriptions of sexual activity increasingly available to the general public. Increasingly available, too, was pictorial material, especially with the development of photography. Social and legal confrontations were imminent. In England private groups such as the Society for the Suppression of Vice demanded prosecutions for obscene libel, as it was then called, and people were frequently convicted throughout the 1800s for pure sexual explicitness.

Developments in America were similar. In 1821 Vermont passed the country's first statute prohibiting the publication or distribution of obscene materials. By the mid-1800s, production and distribution of obscenity was a crime throughout most of the United States. And in this country, as in Great Britain, much of the clamor for enforcement came from private watchdog organizations. Most prominent were the Watch and Ward Society in Boston and the New York Society for the Suppression of Vice.

New York grocer Anthony Comstock became the nation's best-known and vigorous crusader against explicit sexual materials. He was largely responsible for the 1873 enactment of a strict, federal postal law against mailing obscenity. Sometimes referred to as the Comstock Act, the law is still on the books in modified form.[3] Soon after the law's enactment Comstock was appointed a special agent of the Post Office Department to help enforce the act. Shortly before his death in 1915 Comstock boasted that he had convicted more than 3,000 people on obscenity charges and had destroyed 160 tons of obscene materials, including hundreds of thousands of pictures and books.[4] In this climate of vigorous prosecution sexually explicit materials were still produced, but they were indeed forced underground. Materials were no longer advertised or circulated openly.

Obscenity and the Constitution

By the early 1900s obscenity prosecution had become too zealous. The fervor against sexual materials had overstepped reasonable bounds. Increasingly, prosecutions were aimed at mainstream books and films that contained substantial educational or artistic merit—not materials that were pornographic.

For example, in the late 1920s Mary Ware Dennett decided her two sons should have some basic sex education, but she wasn't satisfied with any of the publications available on that topic. She wrote a pamphlet and titled it "The Sex Side of Life." She gave copies to her sons and later had the pamphlet published. Dennett then was prosecuted for mailing an obscene publication, found guilty by a jury, and fined $300, even though the sole purpose of the booklet was educational.[5]

Even works of obvious literary merit by well-known writers were caught in the effort to rid society of smut. In 1927 Boston authorities notified booksellers that the further sale of two recently published books, *Elmer Gantry* by Sinclair Lewis and *An American Tragedy* by Theodore Dreiser, would be deemed grounds for obscenity prosecution. And in New York, the novel *Lady Chatterley's Lover* by D. H. Lawrence was held obscene by a trial court in 1944.[6]

In the late 1950s the U.S. Supreme Court finally entered the fray. The Court began to closely scrutinize materials that had been pronounced obscene, and it employed the First Amendment as a safeguard against rash and sweeping judgments by government officials. It was in the 1957 case of *Roth v. United States*[7] that the Court laid the general foundation for today's approach to obscenity law. It is an approach based on two main principles: First, the Court said in *Roth* that there is indeed a category of sexual expression—called *obscenity*—that is without First Amendment protection. As a result, this kind of speech may be banned by the states and by the federal government. No compelling interest or any other particular level of justification need be shown in order to punish this unprotected category of expression.

But the second key principle established by *Roth* is that it is for the Court to establish the definition of obscenity—a definition born of constitutional principle—and to ensure that the definition is properly applied. The Court in *Roth* went on to fashion a narrow definition for obscenity, limiting it to hard core sexual material that is utterly without redeeming social value. Sexual expression that did not fit the strict definition was protected by the First Amendment and could not be banned. The constitutional definition, which has been modified by the Court since, led to a substantial curtailment of obscenity prosecutions throughout the country.

The Rationale for Controls

Though the Supreme Court's approach prevented government sanctions against most sexual expression, some legal experts questioned whether the Court had sufficient justification to take *any* category of sexual material and place it entirely outside the purview of the First Amendment. This was an exception to the usual balancing approach in which some specific harm from expression must be identified before the First Amendment yields. But the Court has reiterated on many occasions that obscenity is categorically excluded from constitutional protection, even when the material is distributed only to a willing adult audience. One of the

Court's most thorough defenses of the categorical obscenity exclusion came in *Paris Adult Theatre I v. Slaton*, a 5 – 4 decision against the First Amendment claims of two adult movie theaters in Atlanta. Wrote Chief Justice Burger for the Majority in the 1973 case:

> [I]t is argued there are no scientific data which conclusively demonstrate that exposure to obscene material adversely affects men and women or their society. It is urged on behalf of the petitioners that, absent such a demonstration, any kind of state regulation is "impermissible." We reject this argument. . . . From the beginning of civilized societies, legislatures and judges have acted on various unprovable assumptions. . . . The sum experience, including that of the past two decades, affords an ample basis for legislatures to conclude that a sensitive, key relationship of human existence, central to family life, community welfare, and the development of human personality, can be debased and distorted by crass commercial exploitation of sex. Nothing in the Constitution prohibits a State from reaching such a conclusion and acting on it legislatively simply because there is no conclusive evidence or empirical data.[8]

Not all Supreme Court justices have agreed with the categorical obscenity approach, however. In *Roth,* three justices dissented: two who thought that all sexually oriented expression should be protected, and one who thought the definition approach was impracticable. Justice William Brennan, who crafted the majority opinion in *Roth,* had changed his mind by 1973. Brennan had come to view the *Roth* approach as unworkable and as a threat to personal liberty because, he became convinced, a definition could not be articulated with sufficient clarity to ensure fair and consistent application. Brennan explained his change of mind in a dissent to the *Paris Adult Theatre* case.

Brennan wrote: "Our experience with *Roth* requires us not only to abandon the effort to pick out obscene materials on a case-by-case basis, but also to reconsider a fundamental postulate of *Roth:* that there exists a definable class of sexually oriented expression that may be totally suppressed by the Federal and State governments."[9]

The Presidential Commissions

Two presidential commissions have contributed to the debate over whether obscenity is harmful to society and whether it warrants prohibition. The first of these, called the President's Commission on Obscenity and Pornography, was created in 1967 and issued its report in 1970. The commission spent $2 million, sponsored some of its own research, and ultimately concluded there was no reliable evidence suggesting that exposure to explicit sexual materials was a cause of delinquent or criminal behavior. The commission therefore recommended that all legislation prohibiting the sale or distribution of sexual materials to consenting adults be repealed—a recommendation that was never followed. The commission did support continued prohibitions on public display and unsolicited mailing, however.

The second commission, called the Attorney General's Commission on Pornography, was formed at the request of President Reagan in 1985 and issued its report a year later. Sometimes referred to as the Meese Commission after Attorney General Edwin Meese, this second commission had only a quarter the funding of the earlier commission. Its conclusions and recommendations were significantly different, too, and some critics charged that the Meese Commission was determined from the beginning to find pornography harmful. The commission conducted several public hearings, examined explicit films and magazines, visited adults-only bookstores, and consulted current research by social scientists. The commission concluded that exposure to sexually explicit materials that are violent or sexually degrading leads to more aggressive attitudes toward women and probably to a higher incidence of sexual violence. The commission therefore recommended that local, state, and federal prosecutors more zealously seek convictions for violators of obscenity laws, including laws against distribution to consenting adults.

Defining Obscenity

The debate over the wisdom of attempting to ban obscenity will surely continue. Constitutionally speaking, though, the Supreme Court has made it clear that such materials may be banned—if the materials truly meet the Court's standard for obscenity. Constitutional rights may hinge entirely on the wording of the Court's obscenity definition and whether the definition was properly applied to the material in question. Appellate courts have been stuck with the time-consuming burden of reviewing sexually explicit material and determining whether juries had properly determined they were obscene.

The standard that the Court first began to articulate in *Roth* went through a period of some tinkering. Then in 1973 the Court finally settled on the definition it has used ever since. The current standard was stated in *Miller v. California*,[10] a case decided the same day as *Paris Adult Theatre*. Under what has come to be known as the *Miller* test, material may constitutionally be deemed obscene only if:

1. The average person, applying contemporary community standards, would find that the work taken as a whole appeals to the prurient interest

2. The work depicts or describes in a patently offensive way sexual conduct specifically defined by the applicable state law

3. The work, taken as a whole, lacks serious literary, artistic, political, or scientific value

All portions of this test must be proved in court before material can be labeled obscene, stripped of its constitutional protection, and punished.

Prurient Interest First a prosecutor must convince a judge or jury that the material in question was designed to appeal to a **prurient interest.** This means that the material was intended to excite lewd, lascivious, shameful, or morbid thoughts about sex. Material that provokes only normal, healthy sexual desires does not fall into this category.[11]

Distinguishing normal sexual desires from lewd, deviant ones has, of course, proved a somewhat confusing task. In making the determination jurors are not simply to impose their own views but are to judge how the average person in that community would respond to the materials. By average person it is meant adults who are neither the most prudish nor the most tolerant. The average person concept does not include children—unless they were the intended audience for the material.

In *Miller* the Court concluded that the obscenity definition should accommodate varying community standards because

> our nation is simply too big and too diverse for this Court to reasonably expect that such standards could be articulated for all 50 States in a single formulation. . . . It is neither realistic nor constitutionally sound to read the First Amendment as requiring that the people of Maine or Mississippi accept public depiction of conduct found tolerant in Las Vegas, or New York City.[12]

As reasonable as this might sound, however, some constitutional experts have excoriated this approach. It is, critics say, the only place in constitutional law where the protections of the Constitution may be allowably narrower in some parts of the country than in others. Geographically, anti-obscenity statutes may designate the applicable community to be the city, county, or state where the materials were distributed.

It is important to note that although the community standards portion of the *Miller* test does allow for some degree of variation across the country, the discretion of juries is limited. Whether determining questions of prurient interest or patent offensiveness, juries do not necessarily have the final word. Trial judges and appellate courts are free to review juries' obscenity determinations and to overturn them if they are not limited to the narrow class of material that the Supreme Court actually had in mind. This was made abundantly clear by the Court in *Jenkins v. Georgia,* a case that will be discussed shortly.

Finally, the prurient interest determination is to be made by considering the work as a whole. This means that a small, sexually oriented portion of a work may not be looked at in isolation when deciding the prurient interest question. Nor, on the other hand, would one page of political commentary protect a hundred-page picture book filled with shamefully graphic sex scenes. The overall tenor and intent of the work is the determining factor.

Patent Offensiveness

The second part of the *Miller* test serves to further clarify the first by requiring that any material deemed obscene must show or describe sexual conduct, and it must do so in a patently offensive manner. Furthermore, in order to be valid, obscenity statutes must specify the kinds of sexual content they intend to regulate. By way of example the Supreme Court in *Miller* said that statutes could prohibit the following:

☐ Patently offensive representations or depictions of ultimate sexual acts, normal or perverted, actual or simulated

☐ Patently offensive representations or descriptions of masturbation, excretory functions, and lewd exhibition of the genitals

In sum, the Supreme Court has applied the **patent offensiveness** part of the *Miller* test to limit obscenity to hard core materials. Community standards may be considered when determining patent offensiveness. But in no case may a local judge or jury, under the guise of community standards, extend the obscenity definition to works other than the hard core variety.

In *Jenkins v. Georgia,* decided a year after *Miller,* the Supreme Court reversed an obscenity conviction for showing the popular film *Carnal Knowledge,* starring Jack Nicholson, Art Garfunkel, Ann-Margaret and Candice Bergen. The movie was about two lifelong male friends and their troubled sex lives. Though the film contained occasional scenes of nudity and simulated sexual intercourse, the actors' bodies were not the main focus of those scenes. At no time was there any exhibition of the actors' genitals, lewd or otherwise. The unanimous Court held that the movie plainly did not meet the *Miller* standard for obscenity, despite what the jury thought. Wrote Justice William Rehnquist for the majority:

> Even though questions of "appeal to the prurient interest" or of patent offensiveness are "essentially questions of fact," it would be a serious misreading of *Miller* to conclude that juries have unbridled discretion in determining what is "patently offensive." . . . Appellant's showing the film "Carnal Knowledge" is simply not the "public portrayal of hard core sexual conduct for its own sake, and for ensuing commercial gain" which we said was punishable in *Miller.*[13]

Thus for two decades the nation's lower courts have been on notice that the *Miller* standard encompasses only hard core representations of sexual conduct. Though citizens may complain to authorities, and jurors may be offended, mere depictions of nudity or the use of some sexual terms, for instance, cannot be deemed patently offensive under *Miller.*

Nearly all judicial declarations of obscenity under the *Miller* test have involved materials that were pictorial in nature. In rare instances, however, descriptions of sexual conduct by words alone—orally or in writing—can amount to obscenity. Soon after *Miller* was decided the Supreme Court upheld an obscenity conviction based on the book titled *Suite 69.* The book had no pictures either on the cover or on the inside. But according to the Court the prose consisted "entirely of repetitive descriptions of physical, sexual conduct, 'clinically' explicit and offensive to the point of being nauseous."[14]

Lack of Serious Value

Material that appeals to a prurient interest through patently offensive representations of sexual conduct is still not obscene unless taken as a whole it lacks serious literary, artistic, political, or scientific value. This final part of the *Miller* test is to ensure that obscenity laws do not operate to deprive society of works that may honestly contribute to the marketplace of ideas.

This third part of the test, unlike the first two, is not determined with reference to local community standards. Art or literature experts, for example, may be called in from distant parts of the country to explain to a jury the value of the material in question. The Supreme Court made this point clear in a 1987 case, *Pope v. Illinois*, in which the Court remanded the obscenity convictions of two clerks at adult bookstores. At the defendants' trials the juries had been instructed that, under the third part of the *Miller* test, they must determine whether ordinary adults in the state of Illinois would believe that the magazines in question contained value. The Supreme Court ruled that the instruction was in error because, unlike the first two parts of the obscenity standard, literary, artistic, political, or scientific value is not to be determined in terms of contemporary community standards. "The proper inquiry," wrote Justice White for the majority, "is not whether an ordinary member of any given community would find serious literary, artistic, political, or scientific value in allegedly obscene material, but whether a reasonable person would find such value in the material."[15] This final part of the *Miller* test is a national, reasonable person standard.

Nevertheless, this serious value element has generated much difference of opinion and judicial inconsistency. *Penthouse* magazine will serve to illustrate. *Penthouse* is a slick men's magazine with a worldwide circulation of about 5 million, and it is widely available in the United States. It is sometimes called *soft core* pornography and considered in the same general category as *Playboy*—a magazine that the Meese Commission categorized as "plainly non-obscene."[16] However, a few courts have been convinced that *Penthouse* is distinctly more explicit, that its depictions are offensive enough to qualify as hard core under the second part of the *Miller* test. This determination has led to interesting judicial discussions about whether *Penthouse* also qualifies as obscene under the third part of the *Miller* test.

In 1980 the Supreme Court of Louisiana said no, that *Penthouse* was saved by the third part of the test. The case, *State v. Walden Book Co.,* involved a criminal proceeding against five booksellers in which the state sought to have the June 1980 issue of *Penthouse* declared obscene. The retailers chose to remove the publication from their shelves rather than contest the proceeding. But the magazine publisher intervened to counter the obscenity charge. The court agreed with the trial judge that the magazine appealed to the prurient interest and contained patently offensive depictions of sexual conduct. But the magazine wasn't obscene, the court held, because it contained serious political, scientific, and literary value.

The Louisiana court said that under the third part of the *Miller* test it was necessary to treat the whole magazine as a unit and to weigh those portions of the magazine that possess serious value against those that do not. Of the magazine's 228 pages, the court determined that 65 were full-page ads, 67 contained articles with serious value, and 96 contained material lacking serious value. Among the items with constitutionally sufficient value were an article about the U.S. banking industry and the Organization of Petroleum Exporting Countries, a critique of the volunteer army, an analysis of new cameras on the market, and a consumer report on a new car. "These articles are not a sham," the court said, but are "of a kind frequently and traditionally found in periodicals of general interest."[17] In a concurrent opinion, one justice wrote: "This [justice] regards restrictions by government of what type of literature our citizens may or may not read as the most obscene element in the case."[18]

That same year, however, the federal Court of Appeals concluded that *Penthouse* magazine could be deemed obscene. The case, *Penthouse v. McAuliffe,*[19] arose after a Georgia sheriff's obscenity enforcement program had convinced magazine retailers to pull both *Playboy* and *Penthouse* magazines from the shelves. The publishers sought a declaratory judgment, stating that their magazines were not obscene. The appellate court declared *Playboy* nonobscene under all three parts of the *Miller* test. But the court found *Penthouse* distinctly different. Rather summarily, the court concluded that the magazine appealed to the prurient interest. As to the second part of the *Miller* test, the court said photographs suggesting that a female model was engaged in masturbation were indeed patently offensive. Patently offensive descriptions of sexual conduct also were contained in the magazine's letters from readers sections, the court said. The court's opinion then focused on the final part of the *Miller* test.

The *McAuliffe* court stressed that the "taken as a whole" language from the *Miller* test is not quantitative, but instead requires an overall judgment about the publication's editorial mission. Even though *Penthouse* contained articles of literary merit, the court said, these articles were overshadowed by the magazine's many patently offensive descriptions of sexual conduct. It was a close call, the court acknowledged, but when taken as a whole, the magazine was not one of serious value.

The *McAuliffe* decision is a questionable one, in which the court found itself critiquing the comparative literary merit of articles in *Playboy* and *Penthouse.* And it should be noted that, as of 1996, no criminal determination of obscenity has ever been upheld against *Penthouse.* (In *McAuliffe,* the court merely refused to grant the magazine's request for an official declaration that it was not obscene.) However, these *Penthouse* cases do illustrate the difficulty courts face in applying the third part of the *Miller* standard, and the cases would seem to indicate that *Penthouse,* at least in some communities in 1980, represented the borderline between clearly protected speech and obscenity. This is not to say that anything more graphic than *Penthouse* magazine is necessarily obscene, however. Far from it. Judges and juries on many occasions have concluded that particular materials far more graphic than *Penthouse*—including videotapes that boastfully label themselves as "XXX-rated"—were not obscene.

Now consider the chapter hypothetical in light of the *Miller* test. The magazine and cable TV ads for Passion condoms did depict sexual activity to some extent and that is one key ingredient of obscenity. However, it is unlikely that the ads as described could be deemed to cater to a prurient, shameful interest. Furthermore, even with the tip of a condom-covered penis showing, this fact alone would not bring the ads into line with the kinds of materials that have been declared as hard core and patently offensive. Unclear from the hypothetical, however, was whether the male's sex organ as depicted was in an obvious state of arousal. If it were, do you think that would be enough to qualify the ads as obscene?

Exception: Child Pornography

Though the *Miller* test is now well established as the dividing line between sexual expression that may be banned and that which is protected, one exception exists. The Supreme Court held in the 1982 case of *New York v. Ferber*[20] that government may prohibit the dissemination of child pornography—material showing children engaged in sexual conduct—regardless of whether the material is obscene according to *Miller.*

The Court acknowledged that laws against child pornography, like obscenity statutes, run the risk of suppressing protected speech by becoming too heavy handed. Nevertheless, the Court said states are entitled to greater leeway when combatting pornographic depictions of children. This is because the use of juveniles as pornography subjects is intrinsically related to the sexual abuse of children, the Court said, and government's interest in safeguarding the physical and mental well-being of children is compelling. Whether the work appeals to the prurient interest bears no connection to the real issue—direct harm to children. Likewise, the other two parts of the *Miller* formulation are also irrelevant in these cases, the Court ruled.

As a result, statutes banning child pornography need not limit their reach to obscene materials under the *Miller* standard. A federal statute, for example, makes it a crime for any person to induce a minor to "engage in any sexually explicit conduct for the purpose of producing any visual depiction of such conduct." A first offense is punishable by a fine of as much as $100,000 or ten years in prison, or both.[21] The federal statute is limited to instances in which visual materials are intended for distribution by mail or other means of interstate or foreign commerce, but states have similar criminal prohibitions that apply to local distribution of child pornography. The constitutionality of these federal and state statutes has been upheld by federal courts on several occasions.

With the Child Pornography Act of 1996 Congress expanded federal law to combat the use of computer-generated images that merely "appear to be" of children engaged in sexual conduct. This was a new twist. Prior child porno laws had always sought to prevent harm to real children used in the creation of explicit images. But the theory was that child pornography, real as well as "virtual," may provoke activity by child molesters. This portion of the statute was challenged, and in 1999 the Ninth Circuit Court of Appeals declared the virtual pornography sections unconstitutionally overbroad. The court noted that the Supreme Court had allowed blanket prohibitions on child pornography because of the harm caused in its creation, not because of alleged consequences of viewing the material.[22]

Attacking Obscenity

The *Miller* test is at the core of American obscenity law. Yet, as important—and perplexing—as that constitutionally based test may be, it is only the beginning to understanding the complicated matter of actually prosecuting and otherwise curbing obscenity in the United States. *Miller* determines which expression may be prohibited. It does not demand such intervention, however. It is up to the various government jurisdictions to enact and enforce their own obscenity laws. These laws may not prohibit speech in more sweeping terms than *Miller* allows. In addition, individuals may be prosecuted only in accord with certain procedural and privacy safeguards. These are constitutional safeguards in addition to those directly provided by the narrow obscenity definition.

State Statutes   The vigor of obscenity law enforcement varies significantly in states, counties, and cities. For the most part this deviation is due to differences in resources and enforcement priorities, not to differences in the wording of obscenity laws. Virtually all states have statutes that define obscenity pursuant to *Miller* and make it a crime to produce, distribute, sell, or exhibit such materials. (See Exhibits 12.1 and 12.2).

State statutes authorize a range of punishments for obscenity violations, with the strongest penalties reserved for repeat offenders and for those engaged in ambitious commercial obscenity operations. For example, distributing an obscene videotape to acquaintances in a college dorm typically would qualify as a misdemeanor, punishable by a fine of perhaps $1,000 and/or up to six months in jail. On the other hand, commercial importation of large quantities of obscene tapes and publications would qualify in many states as a felony, punishable by hefty fines and/or several years in state prison.

EXHIBIT 12.1   *From the Texas Penal Code*

§ 43.21. Definitions

"Obscene" means material or a performance that:

(A) the average person, applying contemporary community standards, would find that taken as a whole appeals to the prurient interest in sex;

(B depicts or describes:

  (i) patently offensive representations or descriptions of ultimate sexual acts, normal or perverted, actual or simulated, including sexual intercourse, and sexual bestiality; or

  (ii) patently offensive representations or descriptions of masturbation, excretory functions, sadism, masochism, lewd exhibition of the genitals, the male or female genitals in a state of sexual stimulation or arousal, covered male genitals in a discernably turgid state, or a device designed and marketed as useful primarily for stimulation of the human genital organs; and

(C) taken as a whole, lacks serious literary, artistic, political, and scientific value.

. . . .

§ 43.23. Obscenity

(a A person commits an offense if, knowing its content and character, he wholesale promotes or possesses with intent to wholesale promote any obscene material or obscene device.

(b) An offense under Subsection (a) of this section is a felony of the third degree.

(c) A person commits an offense if, knowing its content and character, he:

(1) promotes or possesses with intent to promote any obscene material or obscene device; or

(2) produces, presents, or directs an obscene performance or participates in a portion thereof that is obscene or that contributes to its obscenity.

(d) An offense under Subsection (c) of this section is a Class A misdemeanor.

Federal Statutes

This country operates under a dual system of criminal law and that holds true in the field of obscenity: both the states and the federal government have statutory prohibitions against obscenity. The *United States Code* contains almost thirty sections pertaining to obscenity. Among them are the following:

☐ It is a federal crime to knowingly use the mail to send obscene material, to import it into the United States, or to transport it between states by any method.[23]

☐ It is a crime to transmit obscene material by broadcast or by cable television.[24]

☐ Customs officers are authorized to seize any apparently obscene materials being imported into the United States and hold them until a District Court judgment is obtained.[25]

EXHIBIT 12.2   *Oregon's Different Approach*

The fact that the U.S. Constitution is interpreted not to provide protection for *Miller*-type obscenity doesn't preclude broader protection for sexual expression under state constitutions. In 1987 the Supreme Court of Oregon turned that state in a unique direction when it ruled that, under the Oregon Constitution, obscenity is protected expression.

In the case of State v. *Henry*,* the owner of an adult bookstore argued that Oregon's obscenity statute was inconsistent with the state constitutional provision that "no law shall be passed . . . restricting the right to [express oneself] freely on any subject whatever." Oregon's high court, the final authority on the state constitution, agreed on historical grounds and invalidated the statute. The court noted that the Oregon Constitution's free speech guarantee is worded even more forcefully than the First Amendment, and the court said exceptions are strictly limited to classes of speech—such as perjury—that were prohibited by law at the time the constitution was adopted. Sexual expression, the court concluded, was not among the historical prohibitions. On the contrary, it is the kind of expression that framers of the federal and state constitutions probably intended to protect.

"The problem with the United States Supreme Court's approach to obscene expression," wrote the Oregon court, "is that it permits government to decide what constitutes socially acceptable expression, which is precisely what [James] Madison decried." The court noted that the very purpose of free speech guarantees is to protect expression that *fails* to conform to community standards. "We hold," the court concluded, "that characterizing expression as 'obscenity' under any definition, be it *Roth, Miller* or otherwise, does not deprive it of protection under the Constitution."**

*State v. Henry, 732 P.2d 9 (Or. 1987).
**Henry, 17.

☐ It is unlawful to make obscene communications by means of the telephone for a commercial purpose.[26]

Title 18 of the federal Code also contains several sections that specify potent civil remedies and criminal penalties—including devastating property forfeitures—against racketeer influenced and corrupt organizations. This cluster of statutes aimed at organized crime, known cumulatively as the *RICO Act,* has been used in recent years against organizations with a track record of peddling obscenity.

For example, in a 1990 case against a husband and wife and their chain of bookstores and video rental stores in northern Virginia, a jury found obscene six magazines and four videotapes distributed by the company. But the conviction was not limited to a basic violation of the federal statute against interstate obscenity distribution. The defendants also were convicted of participating in a pattern of racketeering activity under the RICO Act, based on these and fifteen prior obscenity convictions. This allowed much harsher punishment, including complete forfeiture of all shares of stock in the corporation, as well as forfeiture of corporate assets, real estate, and motor vehicles—any property that supported the defendants in the conduct of their business or was derived from the business proceeds. U.S. marshals immediately padlocked the doors of the shops, and the forfeiture included books and magazines that were not obscene and would otherwise be constitutionally protected.

Nevertheless, the Court of Appeals held that the sweeping forfeitures did not violate the First Amendment. Obscenity is listed as one of the predicate offenses constituting racketeering activity. The court therefore reasoned:

> The defendants may not launder their money derived from racketeering activities by investing it in bookstores, videos, magazines and other publications. The First Amendment may be used as a shield, but it is not a shield for criminal activity.
>
> To follow the defendants' argument would allow criminals to protect their loot by investing it in newspapers, magazines, radio and television stations. Carried to its logical end, this reasoning would allow the Colombian drug lords to protect their enormous profits by purchasing the New York Times or the Columbia Broadcasting System.[27]

Some states have enacted their own RICO statutes and, following the federal model, have listed obscenity violations among the predicate offenses—along with drug offenses, extortion, and other offenses often associated with organized crime. The U.S. Supreme Court in 1989 upheld the application of Indiana's RICO statute to obscenity violations, holding that the harsher RICO punishments were not an unconstitutional deterrent to protected speech. However, the Court also held that seizure of a place of business and all its contents is unconstitutional unless there has first been an adversarial hearing to determine that there was indeed an obscenity violation. A seizure cannot be accomplished under a RICO statute merely on probable cause that obscenity violations had occurred.[28]

In its final report, the Meese Commission concluded that both state and federal statutes against obscenity generally were adequate but that enforcement was lax. Except in instances of child pornography, the commission said prosecuting obscenity cases was apparently regarded as a low priority by law enforcement personnel in the mid-1980s. And when convictions were obtained, sentencing typically was light. The commission reported that courts tend to impose only small fines and unsupervised probation, even though the statutes permit harsher sentencing, because "to a significant extent, those involved in the sentencing process tend not to perceive obscenity violations as serious crimes."[29]

The Knowledge Requirement

In order to be constitutional, obscenity statutes must contain a requirement of guilty knowledge on the part of the violator. This mirrors a principle that applies throughout criminal law. It means that for a conviction the defendant must have been aware of the actions that led to the violation. In the law this requisite degree of criminal knowledge is called **scienter.**

The obscenity defendant need not have known that the material in question actually violated the statute. But it is necessary that the defendant at least had knowledge of the general nature of the material. For example, suppose a video store owner were prosecuted because one videotape stocked in the store was believed to be obscene by local authorities. To obtain a conviction the prosecutor would have to convince the jury—beyond a reasonable doubt—that the defendant was aware of the sexually explicit and offensive nature of the tape. It would be a complete defense for the store owner if he had ordered the tape by its nondescript title and had never personally viewed it or otherwise become aware of its hard-core contents.

Scienter may be proved by circumstantial evidence, however. In a 1988 case, the Court of Appeals of Texas upheld the conviction of an adult bookstore clerk who had sold a magazine to an undercover police officer. The magazine cover depicted a woman performing oral sodomy on a man, while another man was having sexual intercourse with her. The magazine was sealed with a sticker stating that "this literary material has been sealed prior to the exhibition for sale of this literary material. . . . The clerk who has sold this material has exhibited no knowledge of the contents of this literary material. . . ." The court said the sexually explicit cover, along with the fact that the clerk was surrounded in the shop by rows of magazines with similar covers, was sufficient evidence to conclude that the defendant was indeed aware of the nature of the material.[30]

In a more difficult case, a Texas appellate court upheld the conviction of an adult book and video store manager whose routine was simply to arrive at the store to collect the day's receipts and then leave. The court said the jury could indeed have found scienter beyond a reasonable doubt because (1) the manager, even in those brief visits, could not have missed seeing near the cash register the shelves of videotapes with highly explicit pictures on the boxes, and (2) the manager had written a memo instructing store clerks on how to deal with vice officers, thereby suggesting that he was aware the operation was illegal.[31]

Private Possession

Despite the unqualified declarations in many Supreme Court cases that obscenity is not protected by the First Amendment, those cases have invariably dealt with some aspect of obscenity distribution. The matter of private possession has been squarely considered by the Court only on one occasion—the 1969 case of *Stanley v. Georgia*.[32] And in that case the Court held that the mere private possession of obscenity cannot constitutionally be made a crime.

The case arose when police entered the defendant's home with a search warrant to look for evidence of an illegal gambling business. In his bedroom they found three reels of film, which the police viewed and deemed to be obscene. The defendant was convicted under Georgia law for possession of obscene matter, but the Supreme Court reversed. With private possession alone as the issue, the Court found a different set of interests than in other obscenity cases. The defendant had asserted a constitutional right to read or observe what he pleased in the privacy of his own home and to be free from the threat of state inquiry into the contents of his library. The state's asserted interest was essentially to protect the defendant's mind—to control the moral content of his thoughts—and the Court ruled this mission inconsistent with the First Amendment.

Stanley v. Georgia represents an intriguing departure from the Supreme Court's usual vein of pronouncements on obscenity. It means that technically speaking, obscenity does indeed have some constitutional protection. As a practical matter, however, the case has proved to be of limited importance. Later Supreme Court cases have made it clear that the *Stanley* exception is strictly limited to possession in the home. Mailing, importation, or interstate transportation of obscenity, even though for the sole purpose of private use, may be prohibited.[33] Furthermore, even home possession is not protected when the material in question is child pornography. The Supreme Court ruled in 1990 that government could punish the mere private possession of photographs showing children in sexually explicit poses.[34]

Prior Restraint

In *Near v. Minnesota,* the landmark 1931 case that established the general doctrine against prior restraint (discussed in Chapter 2), the Supreme Court listed a few exceptional kinds of cases in which prior restraint would be allowable. One was enforcement against obscenity. In practice obscenity prosecutions typically are initiated only after the material in question has been distributed or exhibited in the marketplace, thus giving rise to complaints. However, prior restraints against obscenity do have a long tradition, particularly with respect to motion pictures and use of the mails, and censorship is acceptable as long as certain procedural safeguards are followed.

Motion Picture Censorship

In 1915 the Supreme Court took the position that a state could require distributors of films to submit them to a government agency for approval prior to exhibition. This procedure was constitutional, the Court said, because motion pictures were merely entertainment for profit and were not protected by the First Amendment.[35] In the aftermath of this decision, such censorship became widespread in the United States, typically through local film review boards.

In a 1952 case the Court reversed its constitutional stance on films, stating that "motion pictures are a significant medium for the communication of ideas."[36] The Court declared films to be protected by the First Amendment, and it held unconstitutional a New York law that had authorized the banning of "sacrilegious" movies. However, the Court specifically left open the possibility that obscene films could be censored if done in accordance with a properly drafted law.

Then in 1965, in *Freedman v. Maryland,*[37] the Court described the procedural safeguards necessary in order for censorship of obscene films to pass constitutional muster. First, the burden of proving whether the film is obscene must rest with the censor, not the exhibitor. Second, the system must provide for a prompt judicial review of any preliminary restraint to make sure it is based on probable obscenity. Finally, a restraint of indefinite duration may be based only on a final judicial determination that the film is actually obscene.

In *Freedman* the Court struck down the Maryland censorship scheme for its failure to incorporate these safeguards. Under the Maryland law a motion picture exhibitor had to first obtain a license for each film by submitting it to the state Board of Censors. If the license was denied the burden was placed on the exhibitor to initiate a court proceeding to challenge the board's ruling. Obtaining the judicial review could take months, and meanwhile exhibition of the film—a film that might ultimately be ruled nonobscene—was prohibited. Thus the Maryland procedure lacked all the required safeguards and was constitutionally unacceptable.

Applying the *Freedman* standards again in 1980 the Supreme Court affirmed that a Texas public nuisance statute was unconstitutional. In *Vance v. Universal Amusement Co.*,[38] a county attorney had decided to have an adults-only movie theater declared a public nuisance and to obtain an injunction to prevent the future showing of allegedly obscene films. A state statute specifically listed exhibition of obscene material as one activity that could be enjoined as a nuisance. Texas argued that such a restraint is no more inhibitive than the criminal statutes against obscenity and that it is therefore constitutional. But the Supreme Court disagreed. Under the Texas procedure, the Court noted, a prior restraint of indefinite duration could be issued against films that had not been finally adjudicated to be obscene. And a film exhibitor who decided to disobey the injunction presumably could be subject to contempt proceedings, even if the films ultimately were found to be nonobscene. A 5–4 majority of the Court therefore found the Texas approach too similar to the problem in *Freedman*.

Curbing Non-Obscene Material

One of the basic principles of this chapter has been that unless it is found by a court to fit the legal definition of obscenity, sexual expression enjoys First Amendment protection and cannot be banned. However, as discussed in Chapter 2, even protected expression sometimes may be controlled as to the time, place, or manner of its exhibition. Such attempts are particularly common with respect to sexual expression.

Postal Controls   As noted earlier in this chapter, the U.S. Post Office Department in the late 1800s and early 1900s engaged in a vigorous—even fanatic—campaign to confiscate pornographic materials from the mails. But that era has passed, and after the *Roth* decision of 1957 the ability of postal authorities to unilaterally withhold sex-oriented mailings essentially has been restricted to materials that will be prosecuted as obscene. Furthermore, today's Postal Service generally may not open and inspect first-class mail.

Congress, however, has passed two powerful laws designed to protect postal customers from receiving unsolicited sexual materials, while at the same time relieving the Postal Service of the role of censor. The laws, which took effect in about 1970, apply to materials beyond those that would qualify as obscene. These federal statutes work as follows.

39 U.S.C. §3008

Under this statute, whoever mails any advertisement "which the *addressee in his sole discretion* [italics added] believes to be erotically arousing or sexually provocative" is subject to a Postal Service order to refrain from any further mailings to that customer. The order to refrain from further mailings is sent at the postal customer's request, without a government assessment of the material in question. It is an effective way for individuals to assure their removal from a particular company's mailing list.

39 U.S.C. §3010

This law allows individuals to register their names with the Postal Service, stating that they do not wish to receive any sexually oriented advertisements through the mails. The Postal Service compiles a reference list of these names and makes it available to mailers. Any mailer who sends such advertisements to a person whose name has been listed for thirty days violates the law. *Sexually oriented advertisement* is defined as any ad that depicts or explicitly describes in a predominantly sexual context human genitalia, any act of natural or unnatural sexual intercourse, any act of sadism or masochism, or any other erotic subject directly related to the foregoing.

Unlike Section 3008, Section 3010 is a potentially effective screen against initial mailings from any company. It is not necessary that the mail patron first receive an objectionable advertisement. On the other hand, Section 3010 is more restricted in the sense that it applies only to mailings that meet the statutory definition of sexually oriented advertisement.

Sections 3008 and 3010 can work to prevent companies from mailing not only obscenity but also constitutionally protected material to particular individuals, and the statutes cause these companies the additional headache of having to constantly update mailing lists under force of law. Nevertheless, because it is postal customers, not government officials, who make the decision to block mailings, the laws have been held constitutional. Mailers have no First Amendment right to communicate through private mailboxes to unwilling recipients, the courts have held.[39]

Local Zoning   In many instances community disgust over sexual expression is prompted not so much by the existence of any particular content as it is by the nature of establishments in which such materials are commonly sold. Businesses specializing in adult

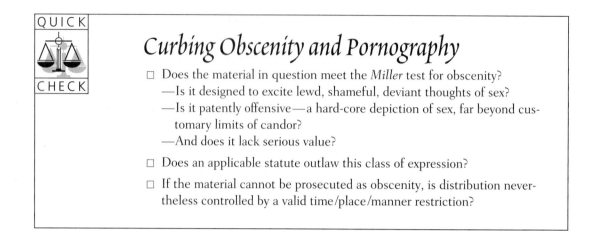

QUICK CHECK

Curbing Obscenity and Pornography

☐ Does the material in question meet the *Miller* test for obscenity?
   —Is it designed to excite lewd, shameful, deviant thoughts of sex?
   —Is it patently offensive—a hard-core depiction of sex, far beyond customary limits of candor?
   —And does it lack serious value?

☐ Does an applicable statute outlaw this class of expression?

☐ If the material cannot be prosecuted as obscenity, is distribution nevertheless controlled by a valid time/place/manner restriction?

entertainment—bookstores, video shops, peep shows, and the like—often are associated with garish lights and offensively explicit signs and displays, with undesirable clientele, and perhaps with nearby prostitution and other crimes. Case-by-case prosecution for obscenity is not necessarily the answer for neighborhoods concerned about maintaining an attractive environment. For this purpose many communities have relied on zoning.

Local zoning ordinances have been used to control establishments for sex-oriented expression in a variety of respects. One of these is location. Some communities have enacted zoning laws that attempt to disperse pornography outlets by prohibiting their location within a specified distance of one another. The theory behind dispersal zoning is that, by scattering adult businesses around town, no one neighborhood will suffer from a concentration of them. Other communities have taken the opposite approach, allowing adult businesses to locate only in designated business districts.

Zoning laws also are used to regulate the way in which adult businesses operate and how they look to passersby. For example, an ordinance might specify that sexually explicit pictures may not be displayed on the exterior of adult businesses. Some communities also require that certain kinds of adult businesses obtain conditional-use permits before they begin operation. This is a potentially heavy-handed zoning technique in which an adult business, in order to qualify for location within a certain zone, must first agree to abide by established operating criteria. These criteria might include the size of the establishment and hours of operation.

In all cases zoning ordinances describe the adult businesses they regulate in terms broader than the *Miller* definition of obscenity. This, after all, is central to the idea of regulation through zoning—to exert some control over establishments that specialize in explicit sexual expression without having to prosecute particular materials as obscene. Of course, to the extent zoning ordinances affect expression beyond the legally obscene, they also raise serious First Amendment concerns.

In 1976 and again in 1986 the U.S. Supreme Court upheld zoning regulations pertaining to the location of adult establishments.[40] In the first case no majority of the justices could agree to one particular rationale. But in the more recent case, *City of Renton v. Playtime Theatres, Inc.,* the majority agreed to uphold the law under a time/place/manner analysis. To be valid as a time/place/manner regulation, you may recall, a restriction must be content neutral, must serve a substantial government interest, and must allow alternate avenues of communication.

The owners of two theaters in Renton, Washington, wanted to exhibit explicit adult films. They were stymied, however, by a zoning ordinance that prohibited adult movie theaters from locating within 1,000 feet of any residential zone, single- or multiple-family dwelling, church, park, or school. The theater owners sued, seeking a declaratory judgment that the ordinance was too restrictive and violated their First Amendment rights.

Writing for the majority, Justice Rehnquist acknowledged that the Renton ordinance did not fit neatly into the content-neutral category because the law treated theaters specializing in adult movies differently from other theaters. Nevertheless, the ordinance still qualified as content neutral, he said, because it was aimed not at the content of films shown in adult theaters but at the secondary effects of such theaters on the surrounding community. The ordinance by its terms was designed to prevent crime, protect the city's retail trade, maintain property values, and generally protect the quality of neighborhood life, not to suppress the expression of unpopular views, Rehnquist wrote.

These aims also qualified as a substantial government interest. And even though the city of Renton apparently had not experience any problems related to adult theaters, it was justified in relying on the experiences of other cities when it determined that the restrictions were needed. Finally, as to reasonable, alternative avenues of communication, the Court said the ordinance left more than 5 percent of the city's land area open for use as adult theater sites. This was sufficient, the Court concluded.

Justice Brennan wrote a lengthy dissent in *Renton,* arguing that the ordinance was not properly categorized as content neutral. And even if it were, Brennan wrote, he still would have ruled it unconstitutional. In Brennan's view, the law was overly restrictive as to theater sites and was too speculative concerning the problems adult theaters would induce.

As a result of *Renton* communities have considerable latitude to use their zoning power to control the channels of adult expression. Ordinances are unconstitutional, however, if their real effect would be to zone protected sexual expression entirely out of existence. Also, zoning laws generally cannot be applied retroactively. That is, zoning is a prospective planning device; if enacted to immediately eradicate existing businesses, it may violate owners' Fifth Amendment property rights.

Funding Conditions

In 1989 highly controversial photographs appeared in art exhibits funded by the National Endowment for the Arts (NEA), a federal agency that awards grants to artists, studios, and art museums. A grant had been used to fund an exhibit of photographs by the late Robert Mapplethorpe, and several of the photos contained explicit sexual poses with homosexual themes. In response to the resulting public outcry, Congress passed an amendment to the NEA's 1990 reauthorization bill, directing the NEA to ensure that "artistic excellence and artistic merit are the criteria by which [grant] applications are judged, taking into consideration general standards of decency and respect for the diverse beliefs and values of the American public."[41]

Four performance artists who were later denied funding then filed a lawsuit, alleging their applications were rejected on political grounds in violation of their First Amendment rights; they challenged the decency provision. But the U.S. Supreme Court upheld the statute in 1998. Justice O'Connor, writing for the 8–1 majority in *National Endowment v. Finley,* emphasized that the statute only requires the NEA *consider* decency notions in the grant-awarding process; it doesn't categorically prohibit awards to projects that many would deem indecent. Furthermore, though the terms may be vague, O'Connor noted, this is not a criminal statute involving punishment. It merely requires the NEA to consider certain factors in its decisions to award public dollars, and this doesn't interfere with First Amendment rights. Congress has wide latitude to set spending priorities and to allocate funding according to criteria, the Court said.[42]

Women's Rights

Various jurisdictions have attempted to curb sexually explicit materials beyond those that are obscene by declaring such materials a violation of women's civil rights and in some cases providing for civil lawsuits against the distributors. These efforts have not been successful, however. The leading case is *American Booksellers Association v. Hudnut,* a Court of Appeals decision from 1985. The case involved an Indianapolis ordinance that declared pornography a form of illegal discrimination against women. Pornography was defined broadly under the ordinance as "the graphic sexually explicit subordination of women, whether in pictures or in words," that also includes depictions of women in any of several enumerated degrading roles.[43] The ordinance prohibited trafficking in such pornography and it gave anyone injured by someone who had seen or read pornography a right to sue the maker or seller. The ordinance did not limit its scope to patently offensive materials or to materials lacking in serious value or to expression that panders to a prurient interest. Thus the ordinance concerned a potentially much wider range of material than that which would qualify as obscene. Several retail book and video stores and bookstore and publishing associations challenged the ordinance.

The Court of Appeals declared that "we accept the premises of this legislation. Depictions of subordination tend to perpetuate subordination. The subordinate status of women in turn leads to affront and lower pay at work, insult and injury at home, battery and rape in the streets."[44] But this was not enough to save the ordinance. The court noted that almost any kind of speech, from popular TV programs to religious teaching, may have some negative effect on individuals or society. That is no justification to ban the speech, however. In declaring the ordinance a blatant infringement on protected speech, the court said: "Under the First Amendment the government must leave to the people the evaluation of ideas," and there exists "an absolute right to propagate opinions that the government finds wrong or even hateful."[45]

Indecency

The broadcast media are considered scarce resources that are also particularly accessible and persuasive, and thus they are subject to additional content regulation, as discussed in Chapter 11. This also holds true in the area of sexual expression. Although obscenity prohibitions are rarely a serious concern for mainstream mass media in America, the additional restrictions that apply to mainstream broadcast media can indeed be a frequent concern.

The Public Airwaves

Since 1927 federal law has prohibited the broadcast of obscene *or indecent* material. Today the ban is codified within the general criminal statutes. The provision reads as follows: "Whoever utters any obscene, indecent, or profane language by means of radio communication shall be fined not more than $10,000 or imprisoned not more than two years, or both."[46] Enforcement is not left entirely to prosecutions by the U.S. Justice Department, however. The Federal Communications Commission is specifically empowered by the Communications Act to penalize broadcasters who violate the statute.[47]

Though the statute is worded broadly, a long time passed before broadcasters and the FCC seriously tangled over obscene or indecent content. And even more years went by before the court challenge arose to determine the statute's constitutionality and the valid scope of FCC power in this area. From 1964 to 1974 the FCC investigated several radio programs in response to complaints from listeners and began groping for standards on where to draw the line. In a couple of instances the commission levied fines against the broadcasters. One case involved the use of allegedly indecent words during an interview with a rock musician; the other case concerned blatant sexual innuendo during call-in-talk shows of the topless radio genre. But the broadcasters paid their fines without a court test of the critical First Amendment issue: May broadcasters be punished for content that is considered indecent but is not legally obscene?

In 1975 the FCC formulated a definition for the term **indecency,** seeking to give broadcasters clearer notice and to distinguish the term from the *Miller* definition of obscenity. The FCC defined indecency as material that

> describes or depicts, in terms patently offensive as measured by contemporary community standards for the broadcast medium, sexual or excretory activities or organs, at times of day when there is a reasonable risk that children may be in the audience.[48]

The definition is significantly broader than that for obscenity: There is no requirement of appeal to prurient interest and no built-in protection for material that contains political or artistic value.

Seven Dirty Words

Finally in 1978 the Supreme Court issued a landmark ruling on the constitutionality of banning indecency. The case, *Federal Communications Commission v. Pacifica Foundation,* arose as follows: About two o'clock on a Tuesday afternoon a New York radio station broadcast a recording of a twelve-minute monologue titled "Filthy Words," by satiric comedian George Carlin. The monologue focused on seven words which, by Carlin's own description, "you couldn't say on the public airwaves." In the monologue taped before a live audience, Carlin listed the words and proceeded to repeat them, over and over again, demonstrating many phrases in which each is used. The words were *shit, piss, fuck, cunt, cocksucker, motherfucker* and *tits.*

The monologue aired on the FM station during part of a larger discussion about society's attitude toward language. The station warned in advance that the recording included language that might offend listeners. Nevertheless, a man who apparently missed the warning heard a portion of the monologue while driving with his young son. He later wrote a complaint to the FCC, stating that, although he could understand the "record's being sold for private use, I certainly cannot understand the broadcast of same over the air that, supposedly, you control."[49] About a year later the FCC issued a declaratory order stating that the station owner, Pacifica Foundation, could have been subject to sanctions. No formal sanctions were actually imposed, but the order was placed in the station's license file for the FCC to consider in the event of any further complaints. Pacifica appealed to the courts.

The Supreme Court, in a 5–4 decision, upheld the FCC order. Even though the recording was not obscene and would be protected in other contexts, the Court said the FCC action in this particular case was justified for two reasons: First, broadcasting has a uniquely pervasive presence in Americans' lives. Patently offensive, indecent material presented over the airwaves confronts a person in the privacy of the home, where the individual's right to be let alone outweighs the First Amendment rights of the intruder. And the Court said turning off the radio is no solution. Wrote Justice John Paul Stevens: "To say that one may avoid further offense by turning off the radio when he hears indecent language is like saying that the remedy for an assault is to run away after the first blow."[50]

The second and perhaps more important justification was that the broadcast program was uniquely accessible to children. "Pacifica's broadcast could have enlarged a child's vocabulary in an instant,"[51] Stevens said, before parents would have a reasonable opportunity to exercise control. Broadcasting cannot easily be monitored minute to minute, unlike media such as magazines, the Court said, which parents must deliberately bring into the home.

The Court majority in *Pacifica* emphasized that its ruling was a narrow one, resting on a nuisance rationale—a sort of time/place/manner restriction—in which context is all important. The time of the day, the composition of the audience, and the content of the program in which the language appears are important variables that, in another case, could produce a different result, the Court noted.

Recent Enforcement

Thus the FCC had obtained a court victory in *Pacifica,* but a narrow one. For almost a decade following *Pacifica* the FCC took a very limited approach to enforcing the indecency prohibition. The commission restricted its investigations to material broadcast before 10 P.M., when significant numbers of children were most likely to be in the audience, and to programs that involved the repeated use of offensive words for their shock value. For several years not a single broadcast was held in violation of the law.

Then in 1987 the FCC adopted a new, get-tough standard. It ruled in three separate cases that radio broadcasts had violated the indecency prohibition, and formal warnings were issued to the stations. One broadcast consisted of excerpts from a play in which two homosexuals dying of AIDS discuss their sexual fantasies in telephone conversations. The second case, against a University of California campus radio station in Santa Barbara, concerned a song that contained several graphic references to sexual organs and activities. The third case involved "The Howard Stern Show," which featured raunchy, sex-oriented humor in a call-in radio format.[52]

Two of the radio broadcasts had aired after 10 P.M., the time period previously termed as a **safe harbor,** when broadcasters could air adult-oriented programming without the threat of indecency sanctions. But the FCC had decided, rather off-handedly, to reduce the safe harbor to the period between midnight and 6 A.M.

In 1988 the FCC turned to television as well, ruling that a prime-time broadcast of the movie *Private Lessons* was indecent. The move, aired on KZKC-TV in Kansas City, Missouri, was about a housekeeper's seduction of a 15-year-old boy, and it included scenes of frontal nudity and a sex-oriented theme. The FCC ruled that the explicit nudity and fondling and the overall emphasis on sexual activity

Curbing Broadcast Indecency

☐ Does the material describe or depict sexual or excretory activities?

☐ Is the material patently offensive—as measured by modern community standards *for broadcast?*

☐ Did the material air during a time when children are likely to be in the audience, as opposed to the FCC's "safe harbor" yours?

were presented "in a pandering and titillating fashion," and the commission voted to fine the station $2,000.[53]

Meanwhile, Congress, too, had decided the time was right to clamp down on TV sex and raunchy radio humor. In 1988 it passed a statute ordering the FCC to enforce the anti-indecency law twenty-four hours a day. Thus Congress and the FCC had moved well beyond the narrow enforcement circumstances that the Supreme Court had approved in *Pacifica*. Clearly, it was time for the courts to make another constitutional assessment in the midst of the politically charged maneuvering over indecency.

In 1991 the federal Court of Appeals issued a predictable opinion on the twenty-four hour ban in *Action for Children's Television v. Federal Communications Commission.*[54] The court said broadcasts that are indecent but not obscene are protected by the First Amendment, and it interpreted *Pacifica* to mean that some kind of safe harbor for adult programming was constitutionally required. Therefore, the court struck down the twenty-four hour ban. As to the expanse of the safe harbor, the court did not dictate particular hours. Rather, it directed the FCC to conduct a thorough research and hearing process and then to set reasonable safe harbor hours on the basis of solid audience data concerning children. Stated in terms of the constitutional standard, the restriction on protected indecent speech will be valid only if narrowly tailored to serve the compelling public interest in safeguarding children.

Based on additional data collected by the FCC, Congress included a section in the Public Telecommunications Act of 1992 stating that indecent material may be broadcast only between the hours of midnight to 6 A.M. An exception permitted public broadcast stations that go off the air at midnight to broadcast indecent material after 10 P.M. In 1993 the FCC adopted regulations to implement the new statutory restriction on indecency. But the new statute and regulations were again challenged on the ground that they unconstitutionally infringed upon the First Amendment rights of adults.

In 1995, in another case named *Action for Children's Television v. FCC*, a full panel of the Court of Appeals ruled that the FCC had demonstrated sufficiently compelling justification for protecting children aged 17 and under against indecency up to midnight. Wrote the court:

> The data on broadcasting that the FCC has collected reveal that large numbers of children view television or listen to the radio from the early morning until late in the evening, that those numbers decline rapidly as midnight approaches, and that a substantial portion of the adult audience is tuned into television or radio broadcasts after midnight. We find this information sufficient to support the safe harbor parameters that Congress has drawn.[55]

Thus the court held there was sufficient evidence to justify anti-indecency enforcement up to midnight, and it held the limited midnight-to-6 A.M. safe harbor for indecency did not unduly burden the First Amendment rights of adult viewers and listeners.

Nevertheless, the court held the midnight safe-harbor time unconstitutional because of the disparity built into the statute: For some stations the safe harbor period began at 10 P.M. The safe-harbor distinction drawn by Congress between the two categories of broadcasters bore no apparent relationship to the compelling interest in protecting children, the court said. Therefore, the court ruled that all stations must be permitted to broadcast indecency beginning at 10 P.M. as long as some stations are permitted to do so. As of January 2000, the safe harbor for indecency remained 10 P.M. to 6 A.M.

In another 1995 case, yet again named *Action for Children's Television v. FCC*,[56] the Court of Appeals upheld the FCC's multi-step procedure for imposing indecency forfeitures against broadcasters. Following this case, the FCC promptly moved forward on about one hundred pending indecency cases. In one case, the FCC announced a $1.7 million settlement agreement with Infinity Broadcasting Corp. The FCC had initiated proceedings against the company for airing allegedly indecent material during "The Howard Stern Show." Infinity's first settlement installment of $1 million was the largest amount ever paid to the U.S. Treasury by a broadcast licensee. (See Exhibit 12.3 for one of the forfeiture letters sent during the FCC crackdown period of the late 1980s to mid-1990s. It provides an example of what the FCC considers indecent and the manner in which stations are notified.)

Another question about broadcast indecency prohibitions has been whether they would apply to the content of news programming. The FCC has never suggested that a blanket indecency exemption exists for news programs. Yet it is questionable whether the *Pacifica* balancing approach would permit punishment of legitimate news content, and the FCC has in recent years dismissed audience complaints against a handful of news programs.

For example, in 1989 National Public Radio's news program, "All Things Considered," aired a segment on organized crime. The broadcast included portions of a tape-recorded phone conversation between an alleged mobster and an associate. During the conversation the words *fuck* and *fucking* were used ten times.

EXHIBIT 12.3   **Federal Communications Commission**   **FCC 92-223**

Before the
Federal Communications Commission
Washington, D.C. 20554

LETTER

Released: May 26, 1992

CERTIFIED MAIL, RETURN RECEIPT REQUESTED

KGB Incorporated   C5-732/MD
Licensee, Radio Station KGB-FM
7150 Engineer Road
San Diego, CA 92111

Dear Licensee:

This letter constitutes a Notice of Apparent Liability for a forfeiture pursuant to Section 503(b) of the Communications Act of 1934, as amended.

On April 24, 1991, after receiving complaints alleging that Station KGB-FM, San Diego, California, may have broadcast indecent language in violation of 18 U.S.C. Section 1464, we asked for your comments concerning certain material broadcast during the "Friday Morning Blow-Out Show" of February 23, March 16, and April 13, 1990, at approximately 8 a.m. Transcripts of the relevant material, taken from transcripts and tapes submitted with the complaints, were attached to our inquiry and are again appended here.

You have replied that the February 23, 1990, broadcast of the song "Candy Wrapper" was an error and that the song was broadcast despite KGB's policy that this particular recording, the cause of previous Commission indecency enforcement actions, should never be aired. You state that the employee responsible was admonished and that the record has been destroyed.

You admit that the written lyrics of the song "Sit on My Face," which aired March 16 and April 13, 1990, are offensive and should not have been broadcast. You contend, however, that the lyrics as aired are difficult to decipher "due to the English accent and the ambient noise that surrounds the performance." You state that, after receiving complaints about it, this record, too, was destroyed .

Section 1464 of Title 18 of the United States Code prohibits utterances of "any obscene, indecent or profane language by means of radio communication." Pursuant to Sections 312(a)(6) and 503(b)(1)(D) of the Communications Act, the Commission has statutory authority to take appropriate administrative action when licensees broadcast material in violation of 18 U.S.C. Section 1464. The Commission has defined indecency as language or material that, in context, depicts or describes, in terms patently offensive as measured by contemporary community standards for the broadcast medium, sexual or excretory activities or organs. The United States Court of Appeals for the District of Columbia Circuit has upheld the Commission's authority to restrict the broadcast of indecent material at times when there is a reasonable risk that children may be in the audience. *Action for Children's Television v. FCC*, 852 F.2d 1332 (D.C. Cir. 1988).

We believe that the subject broadcasts fit squarely within the definition of indecency. They contained patently offensive language concerning sexual activities and organs and occurred at a time of day when children were likely to have been in the listening audience. We have reviewed the recordings of the broadcasts in question and are not persuaded by your apparent contention that the offensive lyrics of the song "Sit on My Face," as actually aired, were not sufficiently understandable to constitute a violation. Moreover, while your asserted policy against the broadcast of indecent material, and particularly the song "Candy Wrapper," is laudable, the implementation of this policy was clearly deficient. This is especially disturbing given the station's acknowledged awareness that "Candy Wrapper" had been found by the Commission to be indecent.

Thus. it appears that on February 23, March 16, and April 13, 1990, Station KGB-FM violated 18 U.S.C. Section 1464 by airing indecent programming. Accordingly, pursuant to Section 503(b) of the Communications Act, KGB Incorporated is hereby advised of its apparent liability for a forfeiture of twenty-five thousand dollars ($25,000).

The amount specified was reached after consideration of the factors set forth in Section 503(b)(2) of the Act and the guidelines described in our *Policy Statement, Standards for Assessing Forfeitures,* 6 FCC Rcd 4695 (1991), *recon. pending.* Under these standards, $12,500 is the base forfeiture for the transmission of indecent or obscene material. The violation in this case is exacerbated, however, because the broadcast of indecent material was repeated and, with respect to the broadcast of the song "Candy Wrapper," was egregious, given the prior Commission determination that that particular material was indecent. *See WIOD, Inc.,* 6 FCC Rcd 3704 (MMB Oct. 26, 1989). Weighing these various considerations, we find that a forfeiture in the amount of $25,000 is appropriate.

In regard to this forfeiture proceeding, you are afforded a period of thirty (30) days from the date of this letter "to show, in writing, why a forfeiture penalty should not be imposed or should be reduced, or to pay the forfeiture. Any showing as to why the forfeiture should not be imposed or should be reduced shall include a detailed factual statement and such documentation and affidavits as may be pertinent." 47 C.F.R. § 1.80(f)(3). Other relevant provisions of Section 1.80 of the Commission's Rules are summarized in the attachment to this letter.

This letter was adopted by the Commission on May 15, 1992.

BY DIRECTION OF THE COMMISSION

Donna R. Searcy
Secretary

1

FCC 92-223 **Federal Communications Commission** EXHIBIT **12.3**

continued

ATTACHMENTS

Station KGB-FM, San Diego, CA
"Friday Morning Blow-Out"

MV: Male Voice

February 23, 1990, at 8:37 a.m.

MV: We're going to have a little adjunct to the Friday Morning Blow-Out here. We've had so many requests for this today that we're going to play it right now. This is the Candy Wrapper Song on 101, KGB-FM .

(Song:)

It was another Pay Day and I was tired of being a Mr. Goodbar, when I saw Miss Hershey standing behind the Powerhouse on the corner of Clark and 5th Avenue. I whipped out my Whopper and whispered, Hey Sweettart, how'd you like to Crunch on my Big Hunk for a Million Dollar Bar? Well, she immediately went down on my Tootsie Roll and you know, it was like pure Almond Joy. I couldn't help but grab her delicious Mounds 'cause it was easy to see that this little Twix had the Red Hots. It was all I could do to hold back a Snicker and a Krackle as my Butterfinger went up her tight little Kit Kat, and she started to scream Oh, Henry! Oh, Henry! Soon she was fondling my Peter Paul and Zagnuts and I knew it wouldn't be long before I blew my Milk Duds clear to Mars and gave her a taste of the old Milky Way. She asked if I was into M & M's and I said, Hey, Chicklet, no kinky stuff. I said, Look you little Reese Piece, don't be a Zero, be a Life Saver, why don't you just take my Whatchamacallit and slip it up your Bit-O-Honey. Oh, what a piece of Juicy Fruit she was too. She screamed Oh, Crackerjack. You're better than the Three Musketeers! as I rammed my Ding Dong up her Rocky Road and into her Peanut Butter Cup. Well, I was I was giving it to her Good 'n Plenty, and all of a sudden, my Starburst. Yeah, as luck would have it, she started to grow a bit Chunky and complained of a Wrigley in her stomach. Sure enough, nine months later, out popped a Baby Ruth.

March 16, 1990, between 8 and 8:20 a.m.;
and April 13, 1990, approximately 8 a.m.

Male Chorus:
Sit on my face and tell me that you love me. I'll sit on your face and tell you I love you, too. I love to hear you moralize when I'm between your thighs. You blow me away. Sit on my face and let my lips embrace you. I'll sit on your face and then I'll love you (?) truly. Life can be fine, if we both sixty-nine. If we sit on faces (?) the ultimate places to play.(?) We'll be blown away.

A listener complained to the FCC that the tape, which had been presented as court evidence against the alleged mobster, was indecent for broadcast. The FCC voted 4–1 that in light of the legitimate news context, the broadcast was not patently offensive and thus not indecent.[57] Context, then, is a factor the FCC will consider before concluding that programming is indecent.

In the past few years FCC indecedy sanctions have again become less frequent, perhaps because most broadcast stations got the message that Congress and the FCC were serious about enforcement. Still, the FCC continues to fine a handful of broadcasters each year. For example, in January 2000 the FCC imposed a forfeiture order of $35,000 on WQAM-AM in Miami for a series of alleged violations that occurred over five days as radio personalities joked and sang lyrics that were laced with raw sexual terms and innuendo.[58]

Cable TV

Nudity, coarse language, and explicit sexual scenes have been available through cable TV services to a greater extent than through broadcast TV. Predictably, many attempts have been made to curtail this kind of programming. Thus far, however, the courts have not extended the *Pacifica* doctrine to the cable medium and have struck down regulatory attempts that go beyond obscenity.

For example, in *Cruz v. Ferre* the Court of Appeals held unconstitutional a Miami ordinance that sought to prohibit the distribution of indecent material through cable. In this 1985 case the court noted that *Pacifica* rested on the double justification of broadcasting's pervasive presence and, more important, its accessibility to children. But in the cable medium those justifications are absent:

> Cablevision does not "intrude" into the home. The Cablevision subscriber must affirmatively elect to have cable service come into his home. Additionally, the subscriber must make the additional affirmative decision whether to purchase any "extra" programming services, such as HBO. . . . The Supreme Court's reference to "a nuisance rationale" is not applicable to the Cablevision system, where there is no possibility that a noncable subscriber will be confronted with materials carried only on cable.[59]

And, as to the shielding of children:

> Again parents must decide whether to allow Cablevision into the home. Parents decide whether to select supplementary programming services such as HBO. These services publish programming guides which identify programs containing "vulgarity," "nudity," and "violence." Additionally, parents may obtain a "lockbox" or "parental key" device enabling parents to prevent children from gaining access to "objectionable" channels of programming.[60]

Thinking back to the chapter hypothetical, the condom ad, which is not likely obscene, is much more likely to be deemed indecent for broadcast. This is because almost any showing of actual sex organs might be judged patently offensive as measured by contemporary community standards for the broadcast medium. However, in cable TV it is still the obscenity standard, not indecency, that is the boundary for allowable expression. Furthermore, even in broadcast there must be safe-harbor time when adult material such as this can be aired legally as long as it is not obscene.

It is worth remembering, though, that the hypothetical question on indecency—to the extent it concerns broadcast TV—is more a springboard for conjecture than an exercise with pat answers. This owes largely to the fact that the law of indecency is young, and the few judicial decisions to date have focused on radio. TV broadcasters today are confronted with much uncertainty in this area, and they have been reluctant to test the boundaries of video indecency.

In the spring of 2000 the U.S. Supreme Court was expected to announce a ruling in the case of *United States v. Playboy Entertainment Group*. At issue in the case is whether the federal government may require sexually explicit premium cable channels to provide fully effective signal blocking during hours outside the safe harbor, as stipulated by the Telecommunications Act of 1996. The case might provide a definitive answer on whether indecency restrictions may constitutionally be applied to cable.

Telephone   A relatively recent phenomenon has been the growth of so-called dial-a-porn services that offer taped erotic messages or live sexual conversation over the telephone. People using the service have been billed by way of their credit card accounts or, more significantly, through their regular telephone bills. Parents began complaining to legislators, phone companies, and the FCC about the easy access of these services to children and the fact that some minors had unknowingly run up huge phone bills listening to dial-a-porn.

In 1988 Congress amended the Communications Act to prohibit dial-a-porn. A total ban was imposed, making it illegal for adults as well as children to have access to sexually explicit messages over the phone. This legislation raised interesting constitutional questions: Could the government legally regulate sexual expression within commercial telephone messages aimed at consenting people? If so, could it ban messages that are indecent or only those that are obscene? The matter reached the Supreme Court in *Sable Communications of California, Inc. v. FCC.*[61] The Court upheld the statute, but only to the extent that it banned obscene messages. The Court reiterated that obscenity is not protected by the First Amendment and that its distribution could be prohibited even to willing adults. The Court equated the statute to the ban on distribution of obscene materials through the mails, which the Court similarly upheld in 1971.

In *Sable* all nine justices agreed, however, that the telephone restriction was unconstitutionally overboard to the extent that it prohibited sexual messages that were merely indecent. Sexual expression that is indecent but not obscene is protected by the First Amendment and may be banned totally only if the ban is narrowly tailored to promote a compelling interest, the Court noted. Though a compelling interest did exist—protecting children from the potentially harmful effects of such messages—an outright ban on sexual messages to adults and children alike was by no means a narrowly tailored law. It was more like burning the house to roast the pig, the Court said. The government could not limit the adult population to only what is fit for children, the Court ruled, when other solutions exist for keeping dial-a-porn messages out of the reach of children.

Following the *Sable* ruling, Congress altered the statute and the FCC issued new regulations in order to eliminate children's access to indecent phone messages by less restrictive means. The statute now specifies that if the telephone company performs the billing, dial-a-porn calls will not be connected unless the telephone subscriber has requested access to such messages in writing. This is referred to as *reverse blocking*. FCC regulations specify other conditions for delivery of indecent dial-a-porn messages. Most notably, transmission of the message would be prohibited unless payment by credit card was made in advance or unless the dial-a-porn provider required a special access code, issued only to adults. These less-sweeping restrictions were upheld by the Court of Appeals in 1991 as a "narrowly tailored effort to serve the compelling interest of preventing minors from being exposed to indecent telephone messages."[62]

Summary Points

Whether explicit sexual expression causes any significant harm to society has been, and remains, a hotly debated issue. Even without solid evidence of harm, however, the U.S. Supreme Court has allowed obscenity to be banned and has approved lesser controls on other kinds of sexual expression.

The Supreme Court has devised a three-part definition of obscenity, called the *Miller test,* which serves as the dividing line between sexual expression protected by the First Amendment and that which is not. Under the Miller test, material can be judged obscene only if it is aimed at prurient interest in sex, contains patently offensive depictions or descriptions of sexual conduct, and lacks serious literary, artistic, political, or scientific value.

Obscenity may be subject to prior restraint, but only if based on a prompt judicial determination of obscenity; determining what is obscene cannot be left to the discretion of administrators.

The local distribution of sexually explicit material, whether obscene or not, may be controlled as to time, place, and manner. This is most often accomplished through zoning ordinances.

In the broadcast media, Congress has prohibited indecency as well as obscenity. Whether punishment for indecency is constitutional, however, depends on the circumstances. Sanctions against indecency will be upheld if significant numbers of children were likely in the broadest audience.

In the chapter hypothetical the magazine ad for condoms would be highly unlikely to violate obscenity laws, even though the man's genitals were partially visible in the ad. Simple nudity is insufficient to qualify as obscenity under the *Miller* standard, unless coupled with some kind of sexual activity. The TV commercial poses a greater legal danger, however, under the FCC's indecency standard, unless the ad would run only during safe harbor hours.

Discussion Questions

1. If it were up to you to devise a new, more workable legal standard for obscenity, how would you do so? Should the purpose of the communicator be considered? Should evidence of harmful effects be required, or should a presumption of moral harm be sufficient? Should the standard take into account whether the audience is willing or unwilling?

2. In his concurring opinion in the 1987 case of *Pope v. Illinois,* Supreme Court Justice Antonin Scalia said the justices' variety of opinions evidenced a "need for reexamination of *Miller.*" If the Court were to undertake such a reexamination, what would be the most likely outcome? Some minor adjustments in the obscenity definition? Or do you think the current Court would be willing to consider a whole new approach to obscenity and the First Amendment?

3. This chapter has examined two main approaches to controlling sexually explicit depictions: One is to describe a class of expression—obscenity—that is without First Amendment protection and thus open to criminal punishment. Another approach is to rely on zoning laws and other quasi time/place/manner restrictions to keep all adult materials confined to places where they are unlikely to offend unwilling audiences or cause identified negative effects. Which of these approaches do you think is most effective? Which is most compatible with First Amendment ideals? Which best addresses legitimate moral concerns of society?

4. Thus far courts have drawn a distinction between over-the-air broadcasting and cable TV and have concluded that the FCC's indecency prohibition cannot be applied to the latter. Cable is a less intrusive medium, the courts have said. Is this a valid distinction? Is electing to have a TV set in the home an affirmative action to the same extent as electing to subscribe to cable? And if a parent elects not to have cable TV in the home, is this a practical way of protecting children if indecent cable programming is nonetheless readily available in the community?

Key Terms

indecency

Miller test

obscenity

patent offensiveness

pornography

prurient interest

safe harbor

scienter

Web Resources

http://www.fiawol.demon.co.uk/FAC/
Feminists Against Censorship

http://www.4decency.org/main.htm
Dallas Association for Decency

http://www.usdoj.gov/criminal/ceos/index.html
U.S. Department of Justice, Child Exploitation and Obscenity Section

InfoTrac® College Edition

In recent years many critics of the film and television industries have argued for legal restrictions on graphic and gratuitous violence in those media. Find an *InfoTrac* article that examines this idea. Do you think the legal approaches to obscenity or indecency could serve as models for crafting violence restrictions, consistent with the First Amendment?

CHAPTER THIRTEEN

Chapter Outline

The Internet

Hypothetical

■ An e-Mail Exposed

You are the operator of an Internet bulletin-board service called SweatNet, for people who are interested in exercise, fitness, and nutrition. Subscribers to your service post information, advice, and personal observations for the benefit of other SweatNet users. A SweatNet promotional brochure makes the following claims:

> Our trained staff is on duty 24 hours a day to assure that only sincere, helpful postings about exercise and nutrition remain on the system. In addition, we monitor postings to make sure they are properly categorized under our dozens of user-friendly headings. SweatNet is quite simply the best newsgroup available for fitness buffs.

At SweatNet headquarters employees called "board leaders," referred to less formally as "cyber bouncers," are employed to review newly posted items. Their primary duty is to assure that postings fit the general purposes of SweatNet, that is, to provide helpful information and perspectives on staying fit. Board leaders also make sure that new postings are properly categorized. Beyond these tasks, however, the board leaders are directed to "stay as hands-off as possible," and they are not authorized to edit the postings. SweatNet user postings become available to other subscribers immediately, even before screening by board leaders. Postings may be reviewed within minutes after they arrive or as late as a day later, depending on volume.

A SweatNet subscriber in another state was using a friend's computer to send some e-mail messages. However, the subscriber couldn't resist peeking at an e-mail message directed to his friend from his friend's physician. The message was about a new diet book the friend was thinking of following. The physician advised against it and was highly critical of the book and its foreign author, saying that the author and his diet are a fraud. The subscriber copied the doctor's e-mail message, without asking anyone's permission, and posted it to the SweatNet bulletin board. It remained on the service for several hours until, following a complaint from the book author, it was removed. As it turns out, the physician's accusations about the author are false, and the author intends to sue your service and the subscriber for defamation.

Would SweatNet be liable for the defamatory message posted by its subscriber? What states or countries would have jurisdiction? Did SweatNet or its subscriber violate any other laws?

Introduction

For some years communications technology experts have predicted that the separate media of cable television, telephone, and computer will converge to deliver personalized, interactive, multimedia services—services that will stagger the imagination in their vastness, their aural and visual pizzazz, and their responsiveness to consumer fancy. Making all this possible is the **Internet,** a global network that links together tens of thousands of smaller computer networks and millions of host computers. It is a network of networks. No one country, government agency, or company is in charge of the Internet. It has no master organizational plan or hierarchy of command. It is a fairly haphazard, cyberspace community linking universities, special-interest groups, government agencies, private companies of every kind, and an estimated 150 million individual users worldwide as of 2000.

Congress in 1996 enacted a major telecommunications bill intended to promote rapid deployment of Internet technologies by private industry.[1] By removing many regulatory barriers, the bill for the first time allowed cable and telephone companies to compete in one another's businesses, to form cross-industry alliances, and to begin "bundling" communication services for the public. Still, it remains too early to say whether a new, interactive medium will fully develop for the average consumer, how soon it will become readily available, and whether it will be widely embraced by consumers.

We do know that the Internet has developed, over the past decade or so, into a serious communications medium. Commercial online services, including so-called e-commerce, have grown into a multi-billion-dollar industry. Furthermore, a huge volume of information is exchanged through such interactive services as electronic mail, conferencing, electronic bulletin boards and USENET newsgroups, databases, and electronic publications. The Internet can be described as a many-to-many mass medium in which the users themselves generate much of the content for other users.

The unique nature of the Internet medium, coupled with the unorthodox manner in which many net services operate, has created enough perplexing legal problems to warrant an entire chapter in *Communications Law*. This chapter will examine some new legal topics but also will revisit some areas of law discussed earlier. Thus, it serves as a good review chapter for the entire book.

In many ways the law is struggling to keep pace with this rapidly expanding medium. Keep in mind that cyberspace law—or *cyberlaw*—is in the early stages of its evolution. Authoritative case law from the higher appellate courts remains scant, and in many instances analogies must be drawn to older cases from other media.

Jurisdiction Issues

One of the most exciting features of the Internet is its international, border-defying scope. With the simple click of a mouse, users can dart from websites in the United States to sites in Asia or South America. Similarly, e-mail messages can be sent at the speed of light to the next city, a neighboring state, or a distant continent. Furthermore, even when an Internet destination is strictly domestic (say, from Baltimore to Denver), the Internet connection may run through computers in Canada or Mexico. This borderless nature of the Internet poses some special challenges for the legal concept of jurisdiction.

As we have seen earlier in this book, mass communicators often expose themselves to the possibility of legal proceedings in numerous, distant jurisdictions. For example, a Pennsylvania company that launches a national advertising campaign risks being pulled into court in Texas or California if it violates those states' false-advertising laws. However, with traditional mass communicators this multiple-jurisdiction legal exposure is a calculated decision. An advertiser or newspaper can limit its distribution efforts to a few select states if it wishes, and legal jurisdiction over the communicator might likewise be limited to those states.

The Internet is much different. Once an information service connects to the Internet it generally becomes available to any Internet user, anywhere on the globe. Though new technology will allow service providers to distribute selectively, most Internet providers now have little control over who will access their services, and where. Does this mean the service provider is subject to lawsuits in every state and nation around the world? And how about the individual Internet *users* who upload messages? Are they subject to the jurisdiction of every sovereign on the globe?

Interstate Jurisdiction

As we saw in Chapter 1, a court cannot decide a case unless it has jurisdiction over the parties, whether they be individuals or corporations. This is called **personal jurisdiction.** Furthermore, a federal or state court cannot simply claim jurisdiction over any parties it wishes. Rather, jurisdiction is limited by the **due process clause** of the 14th Amendment to the U.S. Constitution. The due process clause, as interpreted by the Supreme Court, mandates fundamental fairness in all legal proceedings.

Within the United States, jurisdiction issues typically arise when a court in one state attempts to exert its power over a defendant resident in another state. The states have so-called long-arm statutes that declare personal jurisdiction in the broadest possible terms. But this jurisdiction remains limited by the U.S. Constitution. The due-process rule is that a court may not exercise personal jurisdiction unless there are sufficient "minimum contacts" between the defendant and the state in which the court is located—the **forum state.** These contacts must be such that the defendant "should reasonably anticipate being haled into court" in that state.[2] The rule applies not only to state courts but also to the federal district courts located in each state.

This due-process, minimum-contacts test for jurisdiction is easily satisfied when an individual defendant actually resides in the forum state, when a business is incorporated in the forum state, or when a defendant maintains significant property in the state. But jurisdiction also can be based on less formal contacts, and the contacts need not be physical. As the Supreme Court has explained:

> Although a territorial presence frequently will enhance a potential defendant's affiliation with a State and reinforce the reasonable foreseeability of suit there, it is an inescapable fact of modern commercial life that a substantial amount of business is transacted solely by mail and wire communications across state lines, thus obviating the need for physical presence within a State in which business

is conducted. So long as a commercial actor's efforts are "purposefully directed" toward residents of another State, we have consistently rejected the notion that an absence of physical contacts can defeat personal jurisdiction there.[3]

On the other hand, courts have also held that the mere act of making a phone call or sending a fax message or other electronic communication to the forum state is not sufficient grounds, by itself, for personal jurisdiction.[4]

In cyberspace, then, aggressive information services—those that deliberately spread advertising and marketing campaigns nationwide and maintain subscribers in every state—should assume they will be subject to jurisdiction throughout the country. These services have "purposefully directed" significant commercial activity into each state. But a contrary rule should apply to small, locally oriented information services that are only passively available in other states and to individual users whose electronic postings may, by mere happenstance, be viewed by net browsers in another state.

And indeed, this is the trend. Though courts in some early cases asserted jurisdiction solely because a passive World Wide Web site was accessible in the forum state, most courts now are requiring some kind of more purposive, deliberate communication aimed at residents of the forum state. A couple of cases will illustrate.

Cybersell, Inc., a Florida corporation, was formed by a business school student and his professor father to provide Web consulting services. On its own website the business featured a "Cybersell" logo over a depiction of the planet earth and a caption that read "Professional Services for the World Wide Web." The site also invited potential customers to send an e-mail requesting further information. Meanwhile, another company also called Cybersell had begun doing business in Arizona and had obtained a federal service mark registration for "Cybersell." Cybersell AZ eventually filed an infringement complaint against Cybersell FL in federal district court in Arizona. In 1997 the federal court of appeals held that Cybersell FL could not be hauled into court in Arizona because the company had not purposefully availed itself of the privilege of conducting business activities in Arizona. The court noted that Cybersell FL's website was predominantly "a passive home page" and did not specifically and actively seek to sign up Arizona residents as customers. Nor was it possible actually to sign on as a customer through the website.[5]

More aggressive, interactive websites are at greater risk of multiple-state jurisdiction, however. This is especially true if there is evidence of significant site traffic with residents of the state in question. One case involved a California company named CyberGold that launched a website to promote a planned mailbox service. Browsers of the site were encouraged to add their names to a list that essentially subscribed them to the service. A Missouri company sued CyberGold for alleged trademark infringement, and the lawsuit was filed in a federal court in Missouri. The court concluded that CyberGold could indeed be required to defend the suit in that distant state, though CyberGold's only contact with Missouri residents was its website. This was not simply a passive site, the court said, noting that the site had more than 100 hits by Missouri residents and was designed to initiate a business relationship.[6]

International Jurisdiction

The prospect of having to defend one or more lawsuits in distant states could have a chilling effect upon cyberspace communicators. Yet, the added burden and expense is relatively minor compared to the prospect of defending charges in other countries, where the law may be substantially less favorable to communicators. The potential problems of international jurisdiction were illustrated vividly in December 1995: Prosecutors in Germany warned CompuServe, an Ohio-based on-line information service, that about 200 of its newsgroups contained material that might violate German obscenity laws. CompuServe responded by closing the adult-oriented newsgroups to all of its 4 million customers worldwide. That set off protests from subscribers and free speech advocates in the United States, who resented the notion of one country's effectively censoring cyberspace for the rest of the world.

Within a few months, CompuServe resolved the problem technologically by providing special new software that allowed parents to screen out objectionable services. Nevertheless, the former head of CompuServe's German operations was prosecuted and convicted in Germany of violating local obscenity laws by failing to block access to the explicit photos back in 1995. In 1999 a German appeals court reversed the conviction on the ground that the blocking technology was not available in 1995. Nevertheless, the incident depicts the special kind of legal headaches that cyberspace communicators may face internationally.

Not only may other nations' laws differ drastically on such content matters as defamation, privacy, and pornography, but each nation also is free to set its own jurisdictional rules. Other nations may claim jurisdiction over a United States information service, for example, without the minimum contacts required under the due process clause of the U.S. Constitution.

No matter what another nation's jurisdictional rules are, a more practical issue in many instances is whether an American defendant need worry about lawsuits filed in other countries. Unless the defendant owns assets in the foreign country, the court may have little or no leverage to enforce a judgment against the defendant. In that case, foreign officials must seek cooperation from the U.S. justice system; they must request that a U.S. court enforce the foreign judgment. However, U.S. courts may refuse to enforce foreign judgments if they were based on legal standards inconsistent with the U.S. Constitution.

Liability Issues   Another threshold issue in cyberlaw is the degree to which Internet service providers should be liable for the material they transmit. The problem is particularly acute with operators of electronic **bulletin board** or **newsgroup** services.

These services allow system users to post messages of their own to a central location and to read the postings of other users. Typically the service provider exercises minimal control over the newsgroup postings, which immediately become available to other users. This is part of the great appeal of these services—that they offer an opportunity for unfiltered, real-time discourse and information-sharing among people with common interests.

However, many Internet service providers (**ISPs**) do exert some control over their newsgroups and bulletin boards in order to keep them commercially viable. This control may consist of simply cleaning up the postings occasionally to assure they are properly categorized. Or, it may involve more aggressive editing, either by human editors or by special computer programs that screen out highly offensive language or graphics.

Common Law Models of Liability

Under common law, the standard of liability for communication torts generally depends upon the degree of editorial control that the defendant assumed and exercised, or could have been expected to exercise. Therefore, certain models of liability have evolved. These common law models are as follows.

Publishers   These are the creators, editors, and packagers of disseminated information; they have assumed extensive control over the product, therefore they are held to the greatest degree of accountability for content. Examples are newspapers and television stations. They are in the chain of tort liability even for material that they do not originate, such as letters to the editor. (Some exceptions exist for material the publisher could not reasonably be expected to verify. These exceptions include the wire-service privilege in defamation cases, discussed in Chapter 4, and statutes protecting the media when they unknowingly disseminate misleading advertisements, discussed in Chapter 10.)

Distributors   The distributors of a publication are those who were not involved in its creation but who actively disseminate it—such as libraries, bookstores, and newsstands. Distributors traditionally have not been held liable for the content unless they actually knew of its harmful character. For example, under the Restatement (Second) of Torts' rule of liability for defamation, "one who only delivers or transmits defamatory matter published by a third person is subject to liability if, but only if, he knows or has reason to know of its defamatory character."[7]

Common Carriers and Conduits   Virtually no legal responsibility is assigned to common carriers or conduits for information, such as telephone companies or private mail carriers, even if they are aware of the offensive nature of the communication. Conduits essentially set up an avenue by which others, the true disseminators, may communicate directly. Conduits assume no role in selecting or screening particular content and may even be prevented by law from doing so.

Computer newsgroup services do not neatly fit into one of these traditional common law models of communications liability. They may possess some attributes of publishers, some attributes of distributors, and some attributes of common carriers or conduits. Further complicating the matter is the great variation in screening and editing policies among electronic bulletin-board operators. Nevertheless, courts have referred to these models when determining liability for electronic system operators on a case-by-case basis.

Liability Under the First Amendment

The common law distinctions in liability among publishers, distributors, and common carriers have essentially been adopted and further developed as a matter of First Amendment doctrine. For example, in several obscenity cases the U.S. Supreme Court has addressed the permissible extent of liability for book and magazine distributors.

In the 1959 case of *Smith v. California,*[8] a bookstore proprietor had been convicted of violating a local ordinance that prohibited possession of obscene material in a store, regardless of whether the proprietor was actually familiar with the material. The Court reversed and struck down the ordinance because without requiring proof of knowledge, or **scienter,** it would inhibit the valid exercise of freedom of expression and restrict the public's access to constitutionally protected material, not just obscenity. Again in a 1966 case, the Court wrote: "The Constitution requires proof of scienter to avoid the hazard of self-censorship of constitutionally protected material and to compensate for the ambiguities inherent in the definition of obscenity."[9] And in 1974, constitutionally sufficient scienter for a distributor was described by the Supreme Court as a showing that the defendant knew "the contents of the materials he distributed and that he knew the character and nature of the materials."[10]

Given this common law and constitutional history, we would expect many Internet cases to wrestle with the publisher-distributor-conduit analysis to determine the liability status of ISPs. A few such cases are discussed in the sections that follow, but recent federal statutes have to some extent preempted this traditional analysis and have clarified potential legal liability for ISPs.

Defamation in Cyberspace

The Internet, with its informality, its myriad interactive services and its often-anonymous users, would seem to be the perfect environment for defamation. And in fact, there has been no shortage of Internet defamation cases, or *cyber-libel.* By 2000, dozens of cyberspace defamation decisions had been published by courts around the country. But many more cases, including some rulings from high-ranking courts, are surely on the way.

Internet defamation cases generally fall into two categories: (1) lawsuits against the originators or primary publishers of libelous content, such as e-mail authors and the creators of website content, and (2) lawsuits against the Internet service providers or system operators. Cases of the first kind have been fairly straightforward, following the general rules of defamation liability as presented in Chapter 4. But cases of the second type have generated some Internet-specific law.

ISP Liability

Two often-cited libel cases from the early 1990s addressed the issue of ISP liability for material posted by electronic bulletin board users. However, the cases reached different conclusions and led to a special provision in the Telecommunications Act of 1996.

The CompuServe and Prodigy cases

In *Cubby v. CompuServe Inc.*, CompuServe was sued for allegedly libelous statements made by a third party and disseminated in the service's Journalism Forum. The statements became available to users immediately upon being uploaded into the system, and CompuServe did not monitor the posting. CompuServe sought summary judgment on the grounds that it was an electronic distributor, not a publisher; that it did not know of the libelous character of the statements; and that as a matter of law it could not be held liable. The federal district court in New York agreed and granted summary judgment in favor of CompuServe. Wrote the court:

> Technology is rapidly transforming the information industry. A computerized database is the functional equivalent of a more traditional newsvendor, and the inconsistent application of a lower standard of liability to an electronic news distributor such as CompuServe than that which is applied to a public library, bookstore, or newsstand would impose an undue burden on the free flow of information. Given the relevant First Amendment considerations, the appropriate standard of liability to be applied to CompuServe is whether it knew or had reason to know of the allegedly defamatory . . . statements.[11]

In *Stratton Oakmont, Inc. v. Prodigy Services Co.*,[12] an investment banking firm sued Prodigy for defamatory statements posted by an unknown user on the Prodigy bulletin board "Money Talk." But in this case a New York state court declined to categorize Prodigy as a distributor. Rather, it concluded that Prodigy was a publisher because the company advertised to the public that it controlled the content of its bulletin boards and because it did in fact exercise some control, both through a software program that screened out certain offensive words and through "board leaders" who were contracted to enforce Prodigy's content guidelines against material in bad taste. Even though Prodigy's control over content was far from complete and was often exercised long after the material became available to users, the state court concluded that Prodigy had assumed the role of publisher and could therefore be held liable.

The upshot of *Prodigy* was that it penalized the ISP for exercising some editorial control and attempting to clean up the content of its bulletin boards. Apparently the ISP would have been better off, legally speaking, to exercise altogether no control and allow bad-taste submissions to clutter its site. This result jolted the online community and sparked an outcry that convinced Congress to insert a "Good Samaritan" provision into the Telecommunications Act of 1996.

Protection Under the Telecom Act

Many bulletin-board services across the country operate in a fashion similar to Prodigy's, or to SweatNet in our chapter hypothetical. Through these services the quantity and speed of information flow often is such that it could not possibly be screened and edited as it arrives. On the other hand, the fact that the information comes from many unknown and untrained sources makes it a virtual necessity that some minimal monitoring take place to protect the decency and commercial attractiveness of the service.

To encourage such editing, Congress passed, in section 230 of the Telecommunications Act of 1996, a provision that reads: "No provider or user of an interactive computer service shall be treated as the publisher or speaker of any information provided by another information content provider." The intent of this provision is to encourage Good Samaritan blocking and screening of "offensive material."[13] The statute appears to nullify the court's approach in Prodigy.

The leading case under the new statute is *Zeran v. America Online, Inc.* Following the fatal Oklahoma City bombing in 1995, someone posted to AOL's electronic bulletin boards several bogus messages claiming to be ads for "Naughty Oklahoma" T-shirts. The messages contained offensive slogans disparaging the bombing victims, and attached was the name "Ken Z" and a Seattle phone number that belonged to Zeran. He received many abusive phone calls from people offended by the messages. Zeran then notified AOL that the ads were a hoax and demanded their deletion. AOL did delete the messages and terminated the sender's account, but it was unable to determine the true identity of the hoaxer, who soon set up new accounts and re-posted versions of the offensive messages. Zeran sued AOL, claiming that it was negligent in failing to remove the defamatory messages immediately.

The federal district court granted summary judgment for AOL, holding that it was immunized by section 230. In 1998 the 4th Circuit Court of Appeals boldly affirmed. Wrote the court:

> By its plain language, § 230 creates a federal immunity to any cause of action that would make service providers liable for information originating with a third-party user of the serevice. Specifically, § 230 precludes courts from entertaining claims that would place a computer service provider in a publisher's role. Thus, lawsuits seeking to hold a service provider liable for its exercise of a publisher's

traditional editorial functions—such as deciding whether to publish, withdraw, postpone or alter content—are barred. . . . None of this means, of course, that the original party who posts defamatory messages would escape accountability.[14]

It remains to be seen whether other federal courts will interpret section 230 just as broadly. Even under the statute, it would appear that ISPs could occasionally be held liable for defamation under the traditional standards for *distributors*. That is, an ISP could be held legally accountable for disseminated material that it did actually review and should have recognized as libelous.

Recall the chapter hypothetical about the SweatNet bulletin-board service. Based on the principles discussed in the foregoing sections, and considering the passage of section 230 and the *Zeran* case, could SweatNet be liable for the defamation distributed through its service?

User Liability   Most of the published cases on cyberspace defamation to date are cases against the actual originators of libelous content—the users who upload messages to electronic bulletin-boards and newsgroups. These cases have been fairly predictable. The creators of a libelous communication are always in the chain of potential liability, regardless of medium. An interesting issue that has arisen, however, is whether bulletin-board services are covered by state retraction statutes.

Illustrating this issue is the 1995 case of *It's in the Cards, Inc. v. Fuschetto*, a case between a sports memorabilia dealer in Wisconsin and another dealer in New York. The two men had communicated frequently by phone and e-mail and in the course of these communications had arranged to visit each other in New York. One of the dealers became ill, however, and suggested the meeting be postponed. This led to a series of e-mail communications in which the men argued over the cost of tickets that had already been purchased for an airline, a Knicks game, and *The David Letterman Show*. Consequently, the New York dealer posted allegedly defamatory notes on SportsNet, a computer bulletin-board service, and the Wisconsin dealer sued.

The defendant argued that the lawsuit was improper because the plaintiff failed to comply with the Wisconsin retraction statute. That statute specifies that no libel claim may be filed against a "newspaper, magazine, or periodical" unless the persons responsible for the publication have first been notified of the error, in writing, and given a chance to correct. The trial court granted the defendant's motion for summary judgment on the grounds that the bulletin-board notes amounted to a "periodical" under the statute, thus requiring a prior demand for retraction. But the Wisconsin Court of Appeals reversed and remanded the case for trial. Posting a message to the SportsNet bulletin board was a random, computerized communication, not a publication that appears at regular intervals and therefore not a periodical under the usual meaning of that term, the court ruled. In addition, the court noted that the retraction statute was enacted years before cyberspace was even envisioned and that it was not within the court's domain to rewrite the statute. Rather, it was the job of the legislature alone to extend the statute to cyberspace if it so desired.[15]

Privacy Online

Computer communications provide unique and alarming opportunities for invasion of personal privacy. This has been recognized by Americans and by their legal system for many years. We saw in Chapter 6, for example, that the Supreme Court in 1989 declined a Freedom of Information Act request to view the contents of a file in the government's criminal-history database. The Court said access to the computerized "clearinghouse of information" could constitute an unwarranted invasion of personal privacy—even though the individual file entries all came from public documents.[16] As sophisticated databases, e-mail, networked communications, and online business transactions become increasingly prevalent, special privacy issues are arising.

Electronic Mail

One of the festering questions about cyberspace is the extent to which personal e-mail messages are protected under privacy law. Is it a violation of law for an investigative journalist to access others' e-mail messages? May an employer monitor employees' e-mail? How about the nosy friend in the hypothetical that began this chapter? Was it a legal violation to read the e-mail note from the doctor?

The relevant law comes primarily from three sources. First, the common law privacy tort known as **intrusion** may apply if the e-mail user had a reasonable expectation of privacy and if that expectation was invaded in a highly offensive manner. The intrusion tort was discussed in Chapter 5. Application of the tort to e-mail invasions is uncertain from one case to another, however, because e-mail users will not always have the requisite expectation of privacy. For example, in some workplaces employees are on notice that e-mail messages are periodically monitored or that copies of all messages are automatically stored by the system administrator.

Many seemingly analogous cases have dealt with privacy of telephone communications and have concluded that interception of calls can amount to a tort.[17] However, e-mail is in some ways less secure, and less private, than traditional communications by phone or letter. For example, e-mail messages travel through a system server, and some systems automatically create backup copies of all messages as a precaution against system failures. These backup copies may remain available for inspection even after the sender and receiver have erased their copies. Particularly in the workplace, employees will not always have a reasonable expectation of privacy for e-mail messages, and courts have so held.[18]

A second source of relevant law is state criminal statutes that specifically prohibit various forms of electronic surveillance or interception of private communications. The language in these statutes varies greatly, but some apply a strict all-party-consent rule.[19] These statutes would prevent secret, employer monitoring of e-mail messages unless all parties to those messages consented. Some employers and e-mail service providers utilize user agreements that disclose monitoring procedures, thereby avoiding problems with such statutes.

Another source of relevant law is the Electronic Communications Privacy Act (ECPA) of 1986, which added numerous sections to the federal code. This is potentially an important source of law to combat e-mail snooping nationwide. One provision of the act was introduced in Chapter 5, the so-called wiretap statute that prohibits the actual or attempted interception, disclosure, or use of an electronic communication by any person or entity—including government and electronic communication services—without the prior consent of at least *one* of the parties to the communication.[20] Other key provisions in the act prohibit accessing communications that are stored in a computer system without specified authorization.[21]

A limitation of the ECPA is illustrated by the case of *Jessup-Morgan v. America Online, Inc.* Terry Jessup began a relationship with her soon-to-be husband, Phillip Morgan, while he was still married to Barbara Smith. While a divorce was pending between Morgan and Smith, Jessup played a Zeran-like hoax on Smith. Jessup impersonated Smith by posting a message with the name "Barbeeedol" to an America Online message board, soliciting "just about any kind of sex I can have with someone other than myself." The message included the phone number where Smith was living with her parents and children, and disturbing phone calls followed. Smith's lawyer served AOL with a subpoena seeking the identity of the message sender, and AOL complied. Jessup sued AOL, claiming that its release of her name violated the ECPA and related privacy laws. But a federal court dismissed the case, holding the ECPA was not applicable. The statute prohibits disclosing the contents of an electronic communication to any person, entity or government. But the term "contents" refers to the substance of the message, the court said, not to the identity of the AOL account customer.[22]

The language of the ECPA seems tailor-made to problems of snooping in the e-mail medium. But there remains some uncertainty about exactly how the act will apply to e-mail monitoring or even to the kind of informal snooping described in the chapter hypothetical. As of 2000 there were few reported cases involving application of the ECPA to private monitoring of e-mail.[23] As with state statutes and common law privacy torts, employers and e-mail service providers can protect themselves against liability under the ECPA by publishing their e-mail monitoring, copying, or disclosure policies and then abiding by them.

Data Collection and the Web

The past few years have seen increasing concern over the collection of data about individuals, without their knowledge, as they navigate and interact with the World Wide Web. As people travel through the Web, they leave electronic markers, and sometimes other information, at each visited page. The trail of these markers is sometimes called the *clickstream,* and it may reveal such information as the visitor's e-mail address, the type of computer used, and the URL pathway by which the visitor arrived at a particular Web page. Sophisticated software makes it possible to track website visits and to accumulate such data as the length of time spent on each page and the number of return visits generated by a page. Many websites ask visitors voluntarily to provide additional information, and of course, any actual online ("e-commerce") transactions also create a record.

Many Web visitors do not understand the degree to which the information they voluntarily provide or involuntarily leave behind can be accumulated and sold for commercial purposes—a practice called **online profiling.** When they do realize it, there often is a sense that privacy is being invaded. Even where individuals have voluntarily provided information at a particular website, they may be angered to find that it is being made available to other commercial interests in quite different contexts. A special concern has been the collection from children of product preference information and other data.

Recognizing the anxiety of consumers over Web privacy, many software companies and other organizations have been devising systems to protect anonymity, ensure transmission security, prevent children from utilizing sites, and even rate websites for the degree of privacy they guarantee. Efforts toward industry self-regulation also have been significant.

Internet-specific government regulation also has begun. Such government agencies as the Federal Communications Commission and the Federal Trade Commission have been examining Web privacy issues for some years. In 1997 the FTC issued a report urging the online industry to adopt website policies that fully inform users of a site's privacy practices for various kinds of information, provide users with choices on how information is used, and allow consumers access to the information that has been collected about them.[24]

In 1999 Congress enacted the **Children's Online Privacy Protection Act (COPPA),** which became effective in April 2000.[25] The act specifies the circumstances under which online businesses can collect or use data from children under 13. Under COPPA, operators of commercial websites aimed at children must provide online notices of their information practices, indicating in clear language the kinds of information collected, how it is used, and whether it is disclosed to third parties. Also, before collecting any personal information from a child, the site operator must obtain verifiable parental consent. If a website does not first obtain parental consent, it cannot set information-gathering "cookies" on a child's computer, for example, or ask questions about toy and game preferences.

Information Security

Such private information as bank account records, credit card information, business records, and personal data is being transferred to or from databases, via the Internet, with increasing regularity. More and more businesses are utilizing cyberspace to conduct their transactions with customers and clients. But if a business or entire industry—the banking industry, for example—is to use cyberspace in this fashion, there must be a way to ensure the security of information transmitted electronically.

Therefore, in the 1990s sophisticated **encryption systems** became readily available. These are software systems that encode any electronic communications using secret codes or "keys" that effectively lock the data out of reach of professional hackers or amateur snoops. Clearly, some form of encryption is increasingly necessary to protect the security and privacy of communications and the integrity of university, commercial, and government databases.

However, substantial controversy has arisen in recent years concerning the federal government's efforts to set the standards for encryption technology. As private encryption software has become increasingly sophisticated in recent years, the government has become concerned that it may lose the ability to monitor electronic communications for legitimate law enforcement purposes such as tracking computer fraud, international drug rings, terrorists and organized crime.

Through the National Security Agency and the National Institute of Standards and Technology, the federal government has worked for decades to develop highly secure systems for encrypting messages, and in recent years it has sought to enforce a national standard. In 1993 the Clinton Administration proposed a national encryption standard referred to as the **Clipper Chip** system. The system was based on a classified algorithm and a special microprocessor. Most important, though, the system included "spare key" technology, officially called **key escrow.** With these spare keys and a proper warrant, the government would always be equipped to decode electronic information. The government also announced export restrictions on competing encryption technology as a way to ensure adoption of the single standard.

However, the Clipper proposal and export restrictions proved highly controversial, and as of this writing it had not actually been adopted as a national standard by industry. Computer software companies have argued for the right to produce their own, possibly superior, encryption technology and the right to market that technology worldwide. Furthermore, civil liberties groups have opposed the notion of a national encryption standard that would always guarantee the government easy access to electronic information networks.

In 1999 the 9th Circuit Court of Appeals held that the government's export restrictions on computer encryption codes violated the First Amendment. The case arose after a University of Illinois professor developed a new encryption method and sought to distribute instructions on its use. The government informed the professor that his method was subject to licensing restrictions. The professor sued, challenging the constitutionality of the regulations. In holding the government's restrictions unconstitutional, a three-judge panel of the 9th Circuit noted that the professor and other scientists "have been effectively chilled from engaging in valuable scientific expression." However, late in 1999 the full 9th Circuit voted to grant a rehearing in the case and the earlier court opinion was withdrawn.[26]

Creative Property in Cyberspace

For creators and owners of copyrighted material and trademarks, the Internet has been a mixed blessing. On the one hand, advancing digital technology and the exponential growth of the Internet have given these intellectual-property holders a fast and inexpensive way to disseminate material to a worldwide audience of online users. But, on the other hand, Internet dissemination provides a tantalizing avenue for unauthorized copying and manipulation of the protected work. The threat is especially severe to copyrights.

Other technologies have proved convenient tools for copyright infringement, of course. Chief among these have been photocopy machines and video recorders, as we saw in Chapter 8. However, modern digital technology presents a copyright infringement threat of vastly greater scope. Consider the following applications.

Music   The technology has recently become available for transmitting digitized sound recordings. As the quality of sound reproduction continues to improve, some say it is opening the floodgates to music piracy via computer and distribution via the Internet.

Pictures   Relatively inexpensive scanners are being used in homes and offices to digitize copyrighted photographs from books and magazines. These electronic versions can easily be transferred to and from Internet sites.

Software   Computer software is protected by copyright, and small-time copying infringements have long been common. But the economic harm to software companies can be especially severe when, for example, game software is distributed without authorization via the Internet.

Text   Textual material is especially easy to copy, transmit, alter, and market via the Internet, and tracing the chain of wrongdoing can quickly become a virtual impossibility.

Clearly, copyright law must provide adequate protection to authors if the Internet is to reach its full potential as a medium for society's most serious and creative work. As one legal scholar explained the problem: "If all kinds of works of authorship, particularly those of intense creativity and imagination, are to embark willingly on the cyber-road, then authors require some assurance that the journey will not turn into a hijacking."[27]

Some observers have suggested that the Copyright Act itself must be rewritten to address the new realities of cyberspace. However, the basic precepts of copyright law remain sound. What is needed is additional case law to clarify how existent copyright principles apply in cyberspace. We will look at a few recurring problem areas.

Copyright's Exclusive Rights

Recall from Chapter 8 that copyright owners possess five exclusive rights. These include the rights to distribute, reproduce, adapt, perform, and publicly display the protected works.[28] Copyright infringement may occur when one or more of these activities is undertaken without consent.

In the context of online media, however, there remain fundamental, unsettled questions about when these exclusive rights are triggered. For example, does the mere transmission of protected material over the Internet constitute a public "distribution" of the work, and therefore a possible infringement? Does Internet availability constitute public "display"? When protected material is uploaded to or downloaded from a bulletin-board service or database, does this act by itself constitute a "reproduction" of the work? If a Web site creator includes a hypertext link to another site without consent, does this amount to an unauthorized "display" of the other site?

The Frena Case

The 1993 case of *Playboy Enterprises v. Frena* directly addressed such questions. The defendant, George Frena, operated an electronic bulletin-board service called Techs Warehouse BBS. For a fee, subscribers could log onto the service and browse through files of photographs, some of which contained adult subject matter. Subscribers also could download high-quality copies of the photos to their own home computers.

The problem, however, was that 170 of the photos found available on Frena's service were taken, without consent, from copyrighted magazines of Playboy Enterprises. Furthermore, the files had been downloaded by at least one customer. Playboy sued for copyright infringement, and, because Frena admitted the photos were displayed on his service, Playboy moved for summary judgment.

In his defense, Frena argued that *he* never uploaded Playboy's photos onto his bulletin-board service; rather a subscriber had uploaded the photos, at which time they became immediately available to other subscribers. Assuming this is true, did defendant Frena actually violate any of the exclusive rights guaranteed to copyright owners when he simply allowed the photos to remain in the system? The federal district court said yes.

First, the court held that Frena usurped Playboy's exclusive right of public distribution: "There is no dispute that Defendant Frena supplied a product containing unauthorized copies of a copyrighted work," the court wrote. "It does not matter that Defendant Frena claims he did not make the copies."[29] Furthermore, the court held that Frena infringed upon Playboy's public display rights. The court noted that under the Copyright Act the concept of "display" is a broad one that covers the showing of an image on any viewing apparatus, electronic or otherwise, and connected with any sort of information storage and retrieval system. Also, the display was "public" because it was available for viewing by a substantial number of persons, in this case subscribers.

New Liability Shield: the DMCA

The Frena case remains instructive on how the Internet may infringe upon a copyright holder's exclusive rights. However, the question of when an Internet service provider can be held liable for that infringement is now governed by federal statute.

You may recall from earlier in this chapter that the Telecommunications Act of 1996 includes at least a partial immunity from liability for ISPs, declaring that they shall not be treated as the "publishers" of any information posted by others. That act further states, however, that it shall not alter existing law pertaining to copyright.[30]

A later act specifically dealt with the matter of copyright infringement liability for Internet service providers. In 1998 Congress enacted the **Digital Millennium Copyright Act (DMCA),** a complicated package of legislation that implemented various international treaty provisions and made some high-tech-era adjustments to U.S. copyright law. One of these is a DMCA section that generally insulates ISPs from copyright infringement liability for material posted by others. Referred to in its own right as the Online Copyright Infringement Liability Limitation Act,[31] the statute states that an ISP, including libraries and educational institutions, shall not be liable for copyright infringement when transmitting or temporarily storing material placed by others on the ISP's site, provided the transmission or storage is an automatic, technical process and the ISP did not specifically select the work for copy or display. In other words, as long as the ISP is "passive." ISPs are, however, expected to remove posted material once they are notified that it is infringing copyright.

Fair Use

Another recurring problem is the scope of fair use in cyberspace. Recall from Chapter 8 that in some limited circumstances useful forms of unauthorized copying may be tolerated as fair use and thus not copyright infringement. In determining whether unauthorized uses are fair use, the courts consider four factors: the purpose of the use, the nature of the copyrighted work, the amount and substance of the work used, and the effect upon the market.

In some cases, these fair use principles can be applied in cyberspace without much difficulty. For example, in *Playboy Enterprises v. Frena* the defendant also argued that even if he had intruded upon Playboy's exclusive rights, this intrusion was so minimal as to warrant classification as a fair use. The court quickly rejected this argument, however. In its examination of the four factors, the court found that Frena's use of the photos was clearly commercial, that the photos belonged in the highly protected category of entertainment, that the photos were a key part of several of Playboy's magazines, and that this kind of electronic distribution could deny Playboy significant revenue.

In the world of digital technology and the Internet, however, the parameters of fair use often are not so clear. For example, unauthorized copying of a systematic, institutional nature is frowned upon by the courts, whereas individual, isolated acts of copying are much more likely to qualify as fair uses.[32] But on the Internet it is quite uncertain what the courts will consider "systematic" copying or distribution. Suppose you attach an electronic copy of a newsletter to an e-mail message you send to a friend. Your friend then forwards the scanned newsletter, at one touch of a key, to a preset e-mail list of fifty colleagues in his media corporation. Would this amount to an unacceptable, systematic form of copying? Legally speaking, should it be considered the same as making fifty separate photocopies of the newsletter and mailing them?

Trademarks and Domain Names

Although most creative-property issues online involve copyrights, another significant cyberlaw problem has been the relationship between trademark rights and "domain names." Domain names are the Internet site addresses used by individuals and organizations. For example, an employee working at SweatNet in our chapter hypothetical might use the e-mail address *jdoe@sweatnet.com*. The *sweatnet.com* portion is the domain name, and this protocol or format applies both to e-mail and Web addresses, also called universal resource locators or URLs.

For most of the 1990s an organization called Network Solutions, Inc. (NSI) was exclusively responsible for registering commercial domain names in the United States. Operating under a special agreement with the federal government, NSI assigned domain names on a first-come, first-served basis. It charged a $100 fee to assign the requested name for a two-year period, and then a renewal fee thereafter. NSI would not assign a domain name that was currently registered by someone else.

As of this writing the domain name registration and management system is in a state of transition as the government moves ahead with plans to utilize other registrars in addition to NSI for the increasingly burdensome task of handling tens of thousands of domain name registration requests annually. New commercial registrars are being accredited by The Internet Corporation for Assigned Names and Numbers (ICANN). Internet business may soon have a choice among dozens of competing organizations through which to register URLs, and some details of the registration process are likely to change. However, a source of legal frustration that apparently will continue is this: The domain name registration process does not include a trademark search prior to assigning a requested domain name. Trademark owners therefore have increasingly found that other businesses have been assigned domain names confusingly similar to the existing trademarks.

In some cases this confusion has been intentional, as individuals called "cybersquatters" or "cyberpirates" have rushed to register domain names containing others' trademarks. They may have no intention of utilizing the domain name themselves, but rather hope to extract a payment from the trademark owners at a later date, when the trademark owners seek to use the domain name for a website. In other instances, cyberpirates may actually use the names to attract more traffic to their own sites, sometimes by intentionally misleading the public.

In most instances, similarities between registered Internet domain names and others' preexisting trademarks arise more innocently. In any event, legal action often has been the result. For example, Planned Parenthood Federation of America owns a registered service mark in its name and operates a website for sexual health, contraception, family planning, and abortion information at the domain name "ppfa.org." In 1996 Richard Bucci, an active opponent of abortion, registered with NSI the domain name "plannedparenthood.com" and set up a website at that address, where he provided links to anti-abortion literature. Claiming a likelihood of confusion with its service mark, Planned Parenthood sought a preliminary injunction under the federal Lanham Act to prevent Bucci's use of the domain name. Following a lengthy analysis, a federal district court concluded that consumer confusion was indeed likely and enjoined Bucci from using "Planned Parenthood" to identify any internet site—despite his valid registration.[33]

In an effort to give trademark owners more options for protecting their marks in cyberspace, Congress late in 1999 enacted the Anticybersquatting Consumer Protection Act (ACPA). It creates a new form of civil action that may be filed against persons who, in "bad faith," register domain names identical to or confusingly similar to an existing, distinctive trademark. An intent to capitalize financially on the goodwill of the trademark owner or to harm the goodwill of the trademark owner will be considered "bad faith." Under the ACPA a trademark owner may be awarded statutory damages of up to $100,000, as well as cancellation or reassignment of the disputed domain name.[34]

Adult Material on the Net

Nothing in the developing field of cyberspace law has generated more emotion than efforts to curb sexually explicit materials on the Net. The prevalence of sex-oriented chat groups online and, more recently, a flood of photographically explicit sites on the World Wide Web, have outraged many who view it as an invasion into homes across America of pornography that is within easy reach of children. For others it is the effort to censor that infuriates; they see it as the oppressive hand of government in an otherwise pristine frontier of wide-open speech.

The Framework for Regulation Through most of the 1990s there was much speculation about the proper framework, or model, for regulating content on the Internet. Often that speculation occurred in the context of sexually explicit content, where the perceived clash between morality and the First Amendment is most pronounced. Furthermore, sexual expression is the only type of content to date that Congress has attempted to regulate directly on the Internet.

Should the Internet be accorded the same First Amendment freedom as a newspaper or magazine, making it subject to regulation only of speech that is itself excepted from First Amendment protection? Or, should the Internet be regarded more like broadcast media, subject to regulation of content that would otherwise be fully protected speech?

Recall from Chapter 11 that the main justification for regulation of broadcast, including content, is the scarcity rationale articulated by the Supreme Court in *Red Lion Broadcasting Co. v. FCC*. Because available broadcast frequencies are a scarce national resource, the Court said, their content may be regulated in the public interest.[35] But such a rationale would hardly seem justifiable for the Internet, which utilizes an expanding "superhighway" infrastructure of enormous capacity and without limits set by nature. Furthermore, the Court's 1994 ruling in *Turner Broadcasting System v. FCC* strongly suggested that full First Amendment protection would apply to the Internet. In *Turner* the Court said that *cable* TV, unlike broadcast TV, possessed the same First Amendment shield as newspapers and other nonbroadcast media.[36]

The Court finally had a chance to directly address the First Amendment status of the Internet in a 1997 decision. But before we turn to that case, remember that this First Amendment framework discussion is irrelevant if the expression in question amounts to obscenity under the *Miller* test. Obscenity is an unprotected form of speech, as discussed in Chapter 12, and it may be banned in the Internet just as in any other medium.

This is illustrated by the 1996 case of *United States v. Thomas*. A husband and wife in California began operating the Amateur Action Computer Bulletin Board System from their home. The system included e-mail, chat lines, public messages, and photo files that subscribers could download to their own computers. Nonsubscribers who connected to the system could view introductory screens that contained sexually explicit descriptions of the files and a message that read, "Welcome to AABBS, the Nastiest Place On Earth." Subscribers, after paying a fee, could access all files and view highly graphic photos of sexual conduct. A U.S. postal inspector received a complaint about AABBS from an individual in Tennessee, which led to a thorough federal investigation. The Thomases were eventually convicted of violating federal obscenity laws by using a means of interstate commerce—a combined computer/telephone system—for the purpose of disseminating obscene materials across state lines. On appeal, the Thomases argued that the federal anti-obscenity statute did not apply to the transmission of "intangible" objects such as the electronic photo files. The federal Court of Appeals disagreed, however, and upheld the convictions.[37]

**The Commu-
nications
Decency Act**

In 1996 Congress enacted the Communications Decency Act (CDA), a portion of the Telecommunications Act of 1996. The CDA read, in part, as follows:

> Whoever in interstate or foreign communications knowingly uses any interactive computer service to display, in a manner available to a person under 18 years of age, any comment, request, suggestion, proposal, image, or other communication that, in context, depicts or describes, in terms patently offensive as measured by contemporary community standards, sexual or excretory activities or organs, regardless of whether the user of such service placed the call or initiated the communication, shall be fined (up to $250,000) or imprisoned not more than two years, or both.[38]

Thus the CDA attempted to ban from the Internet any sexual expression that was patently offensive or indecent, though not necessarily obscene, unless that offensive expression could be effectively shielded from minors. Recall from Chapter 12 that the Supreme Court in *FCC v. Pacifica Foundation* upheld a similar federal ban on "indecent" material in the broadcast media—during hours when children are likely to be in the audience.[39] Would the Court similarly uphold the CDA?

On the same day the CDA was signed into law, the American Civil Liberties Union and nineteen other groups joined to file a First Amendment lawsuit against the Act. The plaintiffs charged that the CDA ban was far too broad and would threaten the ability of the Internet to serve as a medium of free expression, education, and commerce for adults. Furthermore, the groups alleged, there exist less drastic alternatives that would more effectively protect children, including user-based blocking technology that allows parents to screen out whatever words or images they deem inappropriate.

The case found its way to the Supreme Court, and in *Reno v. ACLU*[40] the Court in 1997 invalidated those portions of the CDA that attempted to restrict speech other than that which is strictly obscene. In the majority opinion by Justice Stevens, the court distinguished this case from *Pacifica*. In *Pacifica*, the issue was an FCC order that applied to a medium that had historically received limited First Amendment protection and which was invasive. In broadcast, content warnings could not adequately protect the unsuspecting listener or viewer. By contrast, the Internet had no such history of content regulation. Furthermore, it is not as invasive as radio or TV, the Court noted. Users seldom encounter websites "by accident," but must take a series of affirmative steps to access specific material. The Court equated this case to its earlier decision in *Sable Communications v. FCC*, in which the Court invalidated a portion of a federal statute that sought to ban indecent "dial-a-porn" messages on the telephone.

The Child Online Protection Act   After the Supreme Court invalidated portions of the Communications Decency Act in *Reno v. ACLU,* Congress decided to try again. In 1998 it passed the Child Online Protection Act (COPA). The Act provided in part that:

> Whoever knowingly and with knowledge of the character of the material, in interstate or foreign commerce by means of the World Wide Web, makes any communication for commercial purposes that is available to any minor and that includes any material that is harmful to minors shall be fined not more than $ 50,000, imprisoned not more than 6 months, or both.[41]

COPA defined "harmful to minors" in a manner similar to the *Miller* test for obscenity, but with a broader swipe, prohibiting material patently offensive "with respect to minors." Purveyors of explicit Web material could avoid liability by requiring use of a credit card or other screening device to access a site.

The law was to become effective late in 1998, but the ACLU and a group of other plaintiffs challenged the act, and the federal district court issued a preliminary injunction against the statute's enforcement. In *ACLU v. Reno (Reno II),*[42] the district court acknowledged that protecting minors from harmfully explicit material was a compelling government interest, but it also concluded that COPA was written too broadly and would have a chilling effect on constitutionally protected adult speech. The court said that less burdensome methods, such as the use of filtering software, existed to protect minors.

Summary Points

Internet technology is progressing at a pace faster than the law's ability to evolve, and on some recurring issues, such as state and international jurisdiction and online copyright manipulation, authoritative case law is still scarce.

When defamation is placed on the Internet by users, a key issue is whether Internet service providers (ISPs) may be held accountable. It appears a new federal statute will shield ISPs from liability in most cases.

Cyberspace technology raises various privacy and security concerns. One area in drastic need of more case law is that of e-mail privacy. A combination of privacy torts and state and federal statutes may be used to resolve e-mail privacy disputes.

Copyrights on the Internet face a particularly precarious position. Copyrighted material is subject to easy copying, manipulation, and distribution. However, basic principles of copyright protection do apply to the Net. The Digital Millennium Copyright Act gives ISPs a safe harbor against many infringement claims.

Many legal disputes are arising over the relationship between registered trademarks and registered Internet domain names. Some of these disputes involve the unscrupulous seizing of domain names by cyberpirates.

Direct regulation of Internet content was attempted by the Communications Decency Act of 1996, but portions of the Act were promptly held unconstitutional by the Supreme Court.

Key Terms

bulletin-board service

Clipper Chip

Children's Online Privacy
   Protection Act

Digital Millennium Copyright Act

due process clause

forum state

Internet

intrusion

ISPs

key escrow

newsgroup

online profiling

personal jurisdiction

scienter

Web Resources

http://www.cdt.org/
Center for Democracy & Technology

http://www.eff.org/
Electronic Frontier Foundation

http://www.epic.org/privacy/
Electronic Privacy Information Center

http://www.ciec.org/
Citizens Internet Empowerment Coalition

http://www.gseis.ucla.edu/iclp/hp.html
The UCLA Online Institute for Cyberspace Law and Policy

InfoTrac® College Edition

Recent government task forces have explored ways to improve the registration process for domain names and to handle disputes over domain names and trademarks. Find an *InfoTrac* article that discusses controversies or developments in the handling of domain names.

Appendix

SELECTED PROVISIONS OF THE U.S. CONSTITUTION

Article I, Section 8 — Powers of Congress

The Congress shall have power . . . to promote the progress of science and useful arts, by securing for limited times to authors and inventors the exclusive right to their respective writings and discoveries. . . .

Article III, Section 1 — Judicial Powers

The judicial power of the United States, shall be vested in one supreme court, and in such inferior courts as the Congress may from time to time ordain and establish. . . .

Amendment I

Congress shall make to law respecting an establishment of religion, or prohibiting the free exercise thereof; or abridging the freedom of speech, or of the press; or the right of the people peaceably to assemble, and to petition the Government for a redress of grievances.

Amendment IV

The right of the people to be secure in their persons, houses, papers, and effects, against unreasonable searches and seizures, shall not be violated. . . .

Amendment VI

In all criminal prosecutions, the accused shall enjoy the right to a speedy and public trial, by an impartial jury of the State and district wherein the crime shall have been committed . . . and . . . to have compulsory process for obtaining witnesses in his favor. . . .

Amendment X

The powers not delegated to the United States by the Constitution, nor prohibited by it to the States, are reserved to the States respectively, or to the people.

Amendment XIV

. . . . No State shall make or enforce any law which shall abridge the privileges or immunities of citizens of the United States; nor shall any State deprive any person of life, liberty, or property, without due process of law; or deny to any person within its jurisdiction the equal protection of the laws.

Glossary of Legal Terms

Absolutist theory. The view that First Amendment freedoms should be absolute, that the amendment should be interpreted literally to protect expression against any government regulations.

Acquittal. A verdict after a criminal trial that the defendant has not been proven guilty beyond a reasonable doubt.

Action. A lawsuit.

Actual damages. Compensatory damages based on evidence of actual harm to the plaintiff, as opposed to *presumed* damages.

Actual malice. The constitutional standard of fault that a public-figure plaintiff must prove to win a libel case against the media. Publishing with knowledge of falsity or with reckless disregard for the truth.

Administrative regulations. Laws enacted by administrative agencies, such as the FCC.

Affidavit. A written statement given voluntarily and under oath. For example, in a libel case, affidavits of witnesses might be used to support a motion for summary judgment.

Affirmed. In the practice of appellate courts, a ruling to uphold the decision of a lower court.

Answer. The defendant's formal response to a plaintiff's allegations as stated in a civil complaint.

Appellant. The party who appeals a court judgment to a higher court. Sometimes called the *petitioner*.

Appellate court. A court with jurisdiction to hear appeals and review the rulings of trial courts.

Appellee. The party against whom an appeal is taken. Sometimes called the *respondent*.

Appropriation. The commercial use of a person's name or likeness without consent. One of the commonly recognized forms of invasion of privacy; sometimes called *misappropriation*.

Arraignment. A criminal proceeding in which an accused is brought before the court to hear the charge against him or her and to enter a plea of "guilty" or "not guilty."

Ascertainment. A process of determining the needs and issues of a community, conducted by applicants for FCC broadcast licenses.

Bench trial. A trial in which all factual and legal determinations are made by a judge, without the presence of a jury.

Bill of Rights. The first ten amendments to the U.S. Constitution, ratified by the states in 1791.

Breach of contract. A legally inexcusable failure to perform as obligated under a contract.

Brief. A persuasive document prepared by the lawyer arguing a case in court. It sets forth the factual and legal arguments being made on the client's behalf.

Case law. Law derived from the previous, published decisions of appellate courts.

Cause of action. Particular facts entitling a person to a claim for legal redress. For example, a sloppy news story could provide a *cause of action* for libel and a *cause of action* for invasion of privacy.

Cease-and-desist order. An order from an administrative agency prohibiting a person or business from continuing specified conduct.

Certiorari. A discretionary order commonly used by the U.S. Supreme Court to indicate that the Court has agreed to review a case. This action by the Court is referred to as granting *cert*.

Change of venue. Moving a lawsuit to another place for trial, often to avoid the effects of extensive media publicity.

Civil law. The law pertaining to non-criminal matters in which one person or business sues another to obtain some legal relief.

Clear and present danger. A standard adopted by the U.S. Supreme Court to determine when government may forbid speech encouraging violence or civil unrest.

Codes. Systematic compilations of laws, such as the statutes or administrative regulations of a state.

Collaboration agreement. A contract between the joint authors of a copyrightable work.

Common law. Legal rules and principles that originate solely from judicial decisions, as distinguished from the laws enacted by legislatures.

Comparative license hearing. An FCC administrative proceeding to determine who shall receive a broadcast license among two or more competing applicants.

Compelling state interest. A rigorous standard that government must meet to justify restrictions on First Amendment freedoms. Justification of the highest order. Government may restrict some kinds of speech on a lesser showing of *substantial* state interest.

Compilation. A copyrightable work formed by the creative assembly of preexisting works or information.

Complaint. A legal document that begins a lawsuit by stating the plaintiff's grievance and the remedy being sought. The initial *pleading* filed in a civil case.

Compulsory licensing. A system allowing copyrighted works to be used without negotiation or consent in exchange for mandatory payment of a set license fee.

Concurring opinion. An appellate court opinion in which one or more judges agree with the majority ruling but state different or additional reasons.

Constitutional law. Law concerning the basic organization and powers of government and the individual liberties enumerated in constitutions.

Contempt of court. Willful disobedience of a judicial order, punishable by a fine or time in jail.

Content-neutral restriction. Government action that restrains expression in a particular place or medium but is *not* based on the content of the message.

Continuance. A court order postponing a trial or other proceedings to a later time or day.

Contract. A legally enforceable agreement made either orally or in writing.

Copyright. An intangible property right granted by federal statute to the authors of literary, musical, and pictorial works.

Court reports. Volumes containing the judicial opinions of a particular court or jurisdiction.

Criminal law. The state and federal statutes that define criminal offenses and punishment. Criminal cases are brought to trial, or *prosecuted,* by government lawyers.

Damages. Money awarded in court to a person unlawfully harmed by another. Damages are *compensatory,* if awarded as the measure of injury suffered, or *punitive,* if awarded in addition as punishment for outrageous conduct.

Deceptive advertising. Advertising deemed illegal under state or federal statutes because of its capacity to mislead reasonable consumers.

Defamation. Communication that unjustly harms the reputation of another person. Includes the torts of *libel* and *slander.*

Defendant. In a civil case, the person or business being sued. In a criminal case, the person being prosecuted.

Demurrer. A motion to dismiss a civil case, alleging that the plaintiff's complaint fails to state grounds for a valid legal claim.

Derivative work. A copyrightable production formed by creatively altering or adapting a preexisting work.

Dictum. A superfluous comment in a judicial opinion; a statement that is not necessary to the court's decision and therefore does not carry the force of precedent.

Discovery. The ascertainment of relevant facts, prior to trial, by the parties to a lawsuit. Formal discovery tools used by lawyers include oral depositions, requests to produce documents, and mental examinations.

Dissenting opinion. An appellate court opinion by one or more judges explaining their disagreement with the decision of the majority.

Diversity action. A lawsuit that comes within the jurisdiction of the federal courts because the parties are citizens of different states.

Doctrine of judicial review. Principle that the courts have authority to review and declare unconstitutional the actions of other branches of government.

Due care. The degree of care that an ordinarily prudent person would have exercised under the same circumstances.

EEO rules. Rules enacted by the FCC requiring that broadcast licensees follow specific steps to assure *equal employment opportunity* at their broadcast stations.

Equal time rule. Federal statute requiring that whenever one candidate for public office "uses" broadcast time, the station must allow equal opportunity to all other candidates in the race. Also called the *equal opportunities rule.*

Executive privilege. A privilege that exempts presidential documents from disclosure requirements.

Executive session. A governmental meeting, or portion of a meeting, that is closed to the public.

Expressive conduct. A hybrid form of expression in which conduct, such as burning a flat, is performed in a manner intended to convey a particular message. Also called *symbolic speech.*

Fair comment privilege. A common law defense to libel; a privilege to make statements of honest opinion on matters of public interest.

Fair report privilege.	A defense against libel claims, applied to fair and accurate reports of public proceedings. Also known as the *public record privilege.*
Fair use doctrine.	A privilege to use copyrighted material for limited, productive purposes without the owner's consent.
Fairness doctrine.	An FCC rule requiring, among other things, that broadcasters provide contrasting viewpoints on public issues. The main provisions of the doctrine were abandoned by the FCC in 1987.
False light.	A tortious representation of an individual in a false and highly offensive manner before the public. Recognized in many states as a form of invasion of privacy.
FCC.	Federal Communications Commission. A federal agency, headed by five appointed commissioners, that enacts and administers laws pertaining to broadcasting and other electronic communications.
Federal circuits.	Judicial divisions for the U.S. Courts of Appeal. In the federal court system the nation is divided geographically into 12 appellate circuits.
Freedom of Information Act (FOIA).	An act of Congress requiring that most documents of federal agencies be open to public inspection.
FTC.	Federal Trade Commission. A federal agency, headed by five appointed commissioners, that regulates advertising and other business practices.
Gag order.	A restrictive court order directing attorneys, witnesses or other trial participants not to discuss the case with the media. Sometimes a gag order is aimed at the media, directing them not to report on legal proceedings until their conclusion.
Grand jury.	A body of citizens whose duty is to determine whether probable cause exists to formally charge someone with a crime.
Holding.	The central legal principle to be drawn from a court decision.
Hung jury.	A jury that cannot reach a verdict.
Impartial jury.	A jury that begins trial in an open-minded, unprejudiced frame of mind. A provision of the Sixth Amendment.
Implied consent.	Consent reasonably assumed from signs, actions, silence, or tradition.
Incitement standard.	A stricter version of the clear-and-present danger test, adopted by the U.S. Supreme Court to determine when speech is sufficiently dangerous that it may be punished.
Indecency.	A category of sexually explicit material, broader than obscenity, that is prohibited in the broadcast media during times when children are likely to be in the audience.
Indictment.	The formal accusation issued by a grand jury against a person charged with a crime.
Industry guides.	Detailed descriptions of what the FTC considers to be illegal advertising practices, published by the FTC to put advertisers on notice.
Injunction.	A court order that a defendant act, or refrain from acting, in a particular manner.
Intellectual property.	Products of the mind, including copyrights, trademarks and patents, that have legal status apart from any physical property in which they may be embodied.
Intrusion.	A tort consisting of a highly offensive invasion of a person's physical seclusion or private affairs. One of the legally recognized forms of invasion of privacy.
Joint work.	A work in which two or more co-creators share the copyright.

Jurisdiction. Authority of government and its courts to make and enforce laws and to decide cases. Limited by territorial and subject-matter boundaries.

Jury admonitions. A judge's orders or warnings to the jury concerning its duty to consider only the admissible evidence.

Justiciable controversy. A real and substantial controversy which is appropriate for judicial examination, as opposed to a controversy that is hypothetical, academic or moot.

Law of equity. Historically, a separate system of law developed in England for the purpose of granting remedies other than money damages. An injunction, for example, is referred to as an *equitable* remedy.

Liable. Legally responsible; obliged to pay compensation.

Libel. A false communication that wrongfully injures the reputation of another. In many jurisdictions *libel* refers only to defamation that occurs in writing; oral defamation is called *slander*.

Litigant. A party to a lawsuit; a plaintiff or defendant.

Litigation. A case or lawsuit.

Majority opinion. A written, appellate court opinion in which a majority of the court's judges join.

Malicious prosecution. A tort committed by the unjustifiable initiation of criminal or civil proceedings.

Material representation. A statement upon which an average consumer or investor might reasonably rely when making a purchasing decision.

Miller test. The current test for determining when sexually explicit material is obscene and unprotected by the First Amendment. Adopted by the U.S. Supreme Court in *Miller v. California,* 1973.

Model release. A written consent form, signed by people who appear in photographs to be used commercially.

Motion. A formal request that a judge make some kind of ruling in favor of the applicant. Examples: motion for a continuance, motion for summary judgment, motion to suppress evidence.

Negligence. Failure to exercise due care; lack of care that a reasonable person would have exercised under the circumstances. A fault standard used in tort law.

Neutral reportage. A libel defense recognized in some jurisdictions; allows a reporter to publish allegations made by one newsworthy person about another, even if the reporter suspects the allegations are untrue.

Newsworthiness defense. A defense to lawsuits for public disclosure of private facts.

Obscenity. Hard-core, sexually explicit material that lacks First Amendment protection. Defined by the U.S. Supreme Court in *Miller v. California,* 1973.

Opinion. A written explanation that accompanies the judgment of an appellate court. The *majority* or *plurality* opinion expresses the court's decision and may be accompanied by *concurring* and *dissenting* opinions. A *per curiam* opinion is an unsigned opinion representing the whole court.

Ordinances. Laws adopted by cities, counties, and other units of local government.

Outrage.	An independent tort comprised of intentional, outrageous conduct that causes severe emotional distress. May be called *intentional infliction of emotional distress,* or another name, depending on jurisdiction.
Overbreadth doctrine.	Judicial principle that a law must be declared unconstitutional if it could, in some instances, be applied to punish protected speech.
PEG channels.	Cable television channels reserved for public access, educational and government use.
Per curiam.	"By the court," A per curiam appellate opinion is an unsigned opinion that represents the court as a whole, as distinguished from an opinion signed by a particular judge.
Performance right.	The right to publicly perform a copyrighted work. Copyright owners of musical compositions typically authorize a clearinghouse such as ASCAP or BMI to license performance rights in their works.
Personal attack rule.	An FCC rule requiring broadcast licensees to offer reply time to persons who suffer character attacks during broadcast discussions on public issues.
Plaintiff.	The person who initiates a civil lawsuit.
Pleadings.	Court documents which contain the parties' formal allegations of their respective claims or defenses. Examples include the plaintiff's *complaint* and the defendant's *answer.*
Political action committees (PACs).	Formally known as *separate segregated funds,* they make political expenditures and contributions, as allowed by law, using funds derived from voluntary donations.
Political editorial rule.	An FCC rule requiring that when a broadcast licensee airs an editorial opposing a candidate for public office, the candidate must be offered airtime to respond.
Pornography.	A broad term that may refer to any sexually explicit material, including obscenity.
Precedent.	A previously decided case that guides judges in future cases presenting the same issue of law.
Preliminary hearing.	In criminal cases, a hearing to determine whether the government has enough evidence against the accused to warrant a full-blown trial.
Prior restraint.	A government restraint on expression that is imposed prior to publication or other dissemination to the public, as distinguished from sanctions imposed following publication.
Prior substantiation doctrine.	The FTC requirement that advertisers possess reasonable substantiation for all verifiable product claims before the claims are made.
Program-length commercial.	A television program associated with a particular product, in which commercials for that product are aired. Under FCC policy, the entire program counts as commercial time.
Public domain.	In copyright law, a term applied to works that no longer have copyright protection and therefore may be used by the public without consent.
Public forum.	A government-provided place or medium that is specifically designed or traditionally used for free speech by the public.
Public inspection file.	A file that every broadcast station is required to keep, for viewing by the public upon request. It contains such items as ownership reports, program lists, and a copy of the station's license renewal application.
Puffery.	Exaggerated, figurative advertising claims that consumers would not assume to be grounded in factual documentation.

Punitive damages. A monetary sum awarded to a plaintiff, over and above the amount needed to compensate the plaintiff for his property loss or injury. Punitive damages, also called *exemplary damages,* are awarded in order to punish a defendant for malicious conduct.

Remand. To send a case from the appellate court back down to the trial court where it was originally heard.

Renewal expectancy. A preference given to the current broadcast licensee in a comparative renewal proceedings, based on meritorious broadcast performance.

Respondent. The party against whom an appeal is made. Also called the *appellee.*

Restraining order. An interim court order forbidding the defendant from engaging in allegedly harmful behavior. Typically it is effective until a full proceeding can be conducted on the plaintiff's application for a permanent *injunction.*

Retraction statutes. Laws in about thirty states that encourage potential libel plaintiffs to request, and the media to run, timely retractions of defamatory reports.

Rhetorical hyperbole. Emotional, exaggerated name-calling that an audience would not take as fact and therefore is not defamatory.

Right of publicity. The legal right of individuals to control and profit from the commercial use of their own identities. See *appropriation.*

Rule 10b-5. A regulation of the Securities and Exchange Commission that requires corporations to disseminate their financial news promptly and accurately.

Safe harbor. The hours of the day during which broadcasters legally may air material that is *indecent* and inappropriate for children.

Scarcity rationale. The primary legal justification for broadcast regulation, based on the face that the radio spectrum is limited and cannot accommodate all who might wish to be broadcasters.

Seditious libel. Communication intended to encourage or incite overthrow of the government. Historically a serious crime.

Sequestration. Keeping all of the jurors together during the course of a trial, typically by housing them in a hotel, in an effort to prevent the jury from being influenced by out-of-court information.

Shield laws. Laws that give journalists special protection against having to provide subpoenaed information to authorities. About half the states have adopted shield laws, usually by statute.

Slander. Defamation communicated orally rather than in writing. See *libel.*

Smith Act. A federal statute the punishes the advocacy of overthrowing government by force or violence.

Source licensing. The acquisition of music performance rights by the producers of syndicated TV programs that use the music, as opposed to each TV station individually purchasing the music performance licenses to cover programs they air.

Special damages. In libel cases, a type of compensatory damages based solely on evidence of direct, monetary harm.

Standing. A direct, tangible, legally protectible stake in a legal controversy. It is a basic principle of law that a party must have standing in order to sue.

State action. Government activity that restricts a Constitutional freedom, as opposed to restrictions imposed by private individuals or groups.

Statute of limitations. The time within which a lawsuit must be filed. Statutes of limitations vary among the states and among different kinds of lawsuits.

Statutory law. Law enacted by legislative bodies, including Congress and the state legislatures, as opposed to common law.

Stay. A court order that stops or temporarily suspends a judicial proceeding or the enforcement of a law or judgment.

Strict scrutiny. In constitutional law, the strictest level of judicial review for statutes and other actions of government. Under strict scrutiny, government action that impedes freedom of speech can be valid only if the action is found to serve a compelling public interest.

Subpoena. A command, backed by legal authority, to appear at a designated time and place to give testimony that is deemed relevant to a legal proceeding. A *subpoena duces tecum* commands a person to turn over stipulated notes, photographs, video tape or other documentary evidence.

Summary judgment. A common procedure for ending a lawsuit prior to trial. A party to a lawsuit is entitled to summary judgment in his favor if there is no disputable issue of fact and established legal rules clearly dictate that he would prevail at trial.

Sunshine Act. The federal open-meetings law. It requires public access to the meetings of about fifty federal agencies, including the Federal Trade Commission and the Federal Communications Commission.

Symbolic speech. A form of expression in which conduct, such as burning a flag, is performed in a manner that conveys a particular message. Also called *expressive conduct.*

Synchronization right. The right, granted by license, to incorporate copyrighted music into a video production.

Syndicated exclusivity rule. An FCC rule by which TV stations possessing exclusive contracts with syndicators may prohibit any cable company from importing the same syndicated program into the community from a distant source.

Time, place, manner restriction. A government limitation on speech that is not based on the content of expression. Such a restrictions is more likely to be constitutionally valid than an outright ban or a content-based limitation.

Torts. A wrongful acts, other than breaches of contract, for which the law gives the injured party some legal remedy against the wrongdoer in civil court. Examples include invasion of privacy, trespass, libel, infliction of mental distress, and negligence.

Trade libel. Intentional disparagement of the quality of a product, resulting in monetary loss. Also called *product disparagement.*

Trademark. A distinctive mark used in commerce to identify and authenticate the goods of a particular manufacturer. *Trade names* and *service marks* perform similar functions for business names and their services.

Trademark dilution. Any use of a term that would tend to weaken the distinctiveness of a protected trademark.

Trespass. An intentional, unconsented entry upon property rightfully controlled by others.

Trial court. A court in which civil cases or criminal proceedings begin. A court authorized to hear evidence and determine the facts when they are in dispute.

U.S. Courts of Appeals. The intermediate appellate courts in the federal judicial system. Divided into eleven geographic circuits across the country. Cases typically are heard by panels of three judges.

U.S. District Court. In the federal judicial system, a trial court with general jurisdiction. Each state has at least one U.S. District Court.

U.S. Supreme Court.	The nation's highest-ranking court; the court of last resort. An appellate court consisting of the chief justice of the United States and eight associate justices.
Unfair competition.	The use of deceptive means to unfairly gain competitive advantage in commerce, considered a tort in many jurisdictions.
Venue.	The county or district in which a criminal or civil case may properly be filed and adjudicated.
Voir dire.	The questioning of prospective jurors to determine if they should sit on the jury in a particular case.
Work made for hire.	In copyright law, a work of authorship created for an employer and owned by the employer from the moment of creation.
Zapple rule.	An FCC regulation that supplements the equal time rule. It requires that whenever supporters of a political candidate are afforded broadcast time, supporters of opposing candidates must be given equal opportunity.

Notes

Chapter 1

1. See College Savings Bank v. Florida Prepaid Postsecondary Education Expense Board, 119 S.Ct. 2219 (1999). **2.** One of the most important constitutional cases of all time is Marbury v. Madison, 2 L.Ed. 60 (1803), in which the U.S. Supreme Court held that laws repugnant to the Constitution are void and that it is the province of the Court to make that determination.

Chapter 2

1. John Milton, *Areopagitica,* in *The Works of John Milton,* ed. William Haller (New York: Columbia University Press, 1931), 346. **2.** Leonard W. Levy, *Emergence of a Free Press* (New York: Oxford University Press, 1985), 9. **3.** See Levy's *Emergence,* Chapter 7, for a detailed account of the laws adopted immediately after the American Revolution. **4.** See Sir William Blackstone, *Commentaries on the Laws of England,* 1765–1769, Book 4, Chapter 11, ed. William Carey Jones (San Francisco: Bancroft-Whitney, 1916), 152. **5.** Jefferson to Edward Carrington, January 16, 1787, *A Jefferson Profile as Revealed in His Letters,* ed. Saul K. Padover (New York: J. Day Co., 1956), 44–45. **6.** Alexander Meiklejohn, *Free Speech and Its Relation to Self-Government* (New York: Kennikat Press, 1948), 88–89. **7.** Frederick Siebert, *Freedom of the Press in England,* 1476–1776 (Urbana, Ill.: University of Illinois Press, 1952), 7. **8.** Barron v. Mayor and City Council of Baltimore, 7 Pet. 243 (1833). **9.** Gitlow v. New York, 268 U.S. 652 (1925). **10.** Gitlow, 666. **11.** Barnes v. Glen Theatre, Inc., 111 S. Ct. 2456, 2460 (1991). **12.** City of Dallas v. Stanglin, 109 S. Ct. 1591, 1595 (1989). **13.** Texas v. Johnson, 109 S. Ct. 2533, 2539–2540 (1989). **14.** United States v. Eichman, 110 S. Ct. 2404 (1990). **15.** Near v. Minnesota, 283 U.S. 697, 718–719 (1931). **16.** Bantam Books, Inc. v. Sullivan, 372 U.S. 58, 70 (1963). **17.** City of Lakewood v. Plain Dealer Publishing Co., 486 U.S. 750, 757 (1988). **18.** Skywalker Records, Inc. v. Navarro, 739 F. Supp. 578, 583 (S.D. Fla. 1990). **19.** Skywalker Records, 598–599. See also Playboy Enterprises v. Meese, 639 F. Supp. 581 (D.D.C. 1986), where court held the government's threat to publish a list of pornography retailers was an unconstitutional attempt to suppress sales of *Playboy* Magazine. **20.** Bantam Books, 67. **21.** Doe v. University of Michigan, 721 F. Supp. 852, 853 (E.D. Mich. 1989). **22.** R.A.V. v. City of St. Paul, 505 U.S. 377 (1992). **23.** Simon & Schuster v. Crime Victims Board, 502 U.S. 105, 115 (1991). **24.** Arkansas Writers' Project, Inc. v. Ragland, 481 U.S. 221, 227–229 (1987). **25.** The Commission on Freedom of the Press, *A Free and Responsible Press* (Chicago: University of Chicago Press, 1947). **26.** John Merrill, *The Imperative of Freedom* (New York: Hastings House, 1974). **27.** Jerome Barron, *Access to the Press—A New First Amendment Right,* 80 HARV. L. REV. 1641 (1967). **28.** Miami Herald Publishing Co. v. Tornillo, 418 U.S. 241, 256, 258 (1974). **29.** Red Lion Broadcasting Co. v. FCC, 395 U.S. 367 (1969). **30.** Keller v. State Bar of California, 496 U.S. 1 (1990). **31.** Southworth v. Grebe, 151 F.3d 717 (7th Cir. 1998). **32.** Board of Regents of the University of Wisconsin v. Southworth, 120 S.Ct. 1346 (2000). **33.** Heffron v. International Society for Krishna Consciousness, 452 U.S. 640 (1981). **34.** See, for example, Gannett Satellite Information Network, Inc. v. Township of Pennsauken, 709 F. Supp. 530 (D.N.J. 1989). **35.** See, for example, Sebago Inc. v. Alameda, 259 Cal. Rptr. 918 (Ct. App. 1989). **36.** Meiklejohn, *Free Speech,* 17. **37.** Dissent of Justice Douglas in Dennis v. United States, 341 U.S. 494, 590 (1951). **38.** Dissent of Justice Douglas in Scales v. United States, 367 U.S. 203, 270 (1961). **39.** Miller v. California, 413 U.S. 15, 23 (1973). **40.** Zechariah Chafee, *Free Speech in the United States* (Cambridge, Mass.: Harvard University Press, 1941), 31. **41.** Hustler Magazine, Inc. v. Falwell, 108 S. Ct. 876, 879 (1988). **42.** Central Hudson Gas & Electric Corp. v. Public Service Commission, to 100 S. Ct. 2343 (1980). **43.** Heffron v. International Society for

Krishna Consciousness, 452 U.S. 640 (1981).   **44.** United States v. O'Brien, 391 U.S. 367 (1968).
45. Texas v. Johnson, 2544.   **46.** See Southeastern Promotions vs. Conrad, 420 U.S. 546 (1975),
where it was unlawful prior restraint to deny auditorium access for the theatrical production *Hair*.
47. See, for example, Greer v. Spock, 424 U.S. 828 (1976).   **48.** Arkansas Educational TV Commission v. Forbes, 523 U.S. 666 (1998).   **49.** See, for example, Gambino v. Fairfax County School
Board, 564 F.2d 157 (4th Cir. 1977).   **50.** The substantial disruption standard comes primarily
from an often-cited Supreme Court decision upholding the right of students to wear black armbands
to school: Tinker v. Des Moines Independent Sch. Dist., 393 U.S. 503 (1969).   **51.** Hazelwood
School District v. Kuhlmeier, 484 U.S. 260 (1988).   **52.** See "First National Survey Since *Hazelwood* Says Censorship Now a 'Fact of Life,'" *Student Press Law Center Report,* 11 (Fall 1990): 3.
53. Kincaid v. Gibson, 1999 U.S. App. LEXIS 21385 (6th Cir. 1999).   **54.** Planned Parenthood of
S. Nevada, Inc. v. Clark County School Dist., 887 F.2d 935 (9th Cir. 1989).   **55.** Rust v. Sullivan,
111 S. Ct. 1759 (1991).   **56.** FCC v. League of Women Voters of California, 468 U.S. 364 (1984).
57. The leading case is Snepp v. United States, 444 U.S. 507 (1980).

Chapter 3

1. Schenck v. United States, 249 U.S. 47, 52 (1919).   **2.** Whitney v. California, 274 U.S. 357, 376
(1927).   **3.** Yates v. United States, 354 U.S. 298 (1957).   **4.** The Smith Act can be found at 18
U.S.C. §2385 (1988).   **5.** Brandenburg v. Ohio, 395 U.S. 444 (1969).   **6.** Hess v. Indiana, 414
U.S. 105 (1973).   **7.** New York Times Company v. United States, 403 U.S. 713, 720 (1971).   **8.**
New York Times, 725.   **9.** New York Times, 742.   **10.** New York Times, 730.   **11.** New York
Times, 756.   **12.** United States v. Progressive, Inc., 467 F. Supp. 990, 996 (W.D. Wis. 1979).
13. Progressive, 993.   **14.** Flynt v. Weinberger, 762 F.2d 134 (D.C. Cir. 1985).   **15.** Olivia N. v.
National Broadcasting Co., 178 Cal. Rptr. 888, 891 (Ct. App. 1981).   **16.** Olivia N., 892.   **17.**
DeFilippo v. National Broadcasting Co., 446 A.2d 1036 (R.I. 1982).   **18.** Herceg v. Hustler Magazine, Inc., 814 F.2d 1017, 1023 (5th Cir. 1987).   **19.** Zamora v. Columbia Broadcasting System,
480 F.Supp. 199, 206 (1979).   **20.** Facts taken from unbylined news story, "Boy, 10, Accused of
Hiding Homemade Bomb at School," *The Daily News of Los Angeles,* December 8, 1990, p. N1.
21. Weirum v. RKO General, Inc., 539 P.2d 36, 41 (Cal. 1975).   **22.** Walt Disney Productions,
Inc. v. Shannon, 276 S.E.2d 580, 585 (Ga. 1981).   **23.** McCollum v. CBS, Inc., 249 Cal. Rptr.
187, 190 (Ct. App. 1988).   **24.** Waller v. Osbourne, 763 F. Supp. 1144 (M.D. Ga. 1991). (See also
Vance v. Judas Priest, in which it was alleged that a suicide and an attempted suicide were the result
of subliminal messages hidden in the record album *Stained Glass.* A Nevada trial court ultimately
ruled in favor of the musical group in 1990. But earlier in the proceedings it was held that if there
were subliminal messages, they would not be protected by the First Amendment. 16
Media.L.Rep. 2241).   **25.** Smith v. Linn, 563 A.2d 123 (Pa. Super. Ct. 1989).   **26.** Winter v. G.
P. Putnam's Sons, 938 F.2d 1033, 1037 (9th Cir. 1991).   **27.** Rice v. Paladin Enterprises, 128 F.3d
233, 267 (4th Cir. 1997), cert denied, 523 U.S. 1074 (1998).   **28.** Planned Parenthood of the Co-
lumbia/Willamette v. American Coalition of Life Activists, 41 F. Supp. 2d 1130 (D. Ore. 1999).
29. See Roman v. City of New York, 442 N.Y.S.2d 945 (Sup. Ct. of N.Y. 1981), holding that a duty
of care is not owed to someone with whom a clinic had never personally dealt.   **30.** Eimann v. Soldier of Fortune Magazine, Inc. 880 F.2d 830, 834, 838 (5th Cir. 1989).   **31.** Braun v. Soldier of
Fortune Magazine, Inc., 968 f.2d 1110 (11th Cir. 1992).   **32.** See Yuhas v. Mudge, 322 A.2d 824
(N.J. Super. Ct. 1974) and *Walters v. Seventeen Magazine,* 241 Cal. Rptr. 101 (Ct. App. 1987).   **33.**
Way v. Boy Scouts of America, 856 S.W.2d 230 (1993).   **34.** James Brooke, Lawsuit Tests Lethal
Power of Words, *The New York Times,* Feb. 14, 1996, at A12.   **35.** James Brooke, Lawsuit Tests
Lethal Power of Words, N.Y. Times, Feb. 14, 1996, at A12.

Chapter 4

1.   From the concurring opinion of Justice Stewart in Rosenblatt v. Baer, 383 U.S. 75, 92 (1966).
2. William L. Prosser, *Handbook of the Law of Torts* (St. Paul, Minn.: West Publishing Co., 1971),
737.   **3.** See Garrison v. Louisiana, 379 U.S. 64 (1964), in which the Court found Louisiana's criminal defamation statute unconstitutional.   **4.** In 1990 a weekly newspaper editor was charged with
criminal libel in South Carolina, but the charges were dropped before a preliminary hearing. See *The
News Media & The Law* (summer 1990) 14: 10.   **5.** This is similar to the working definition sug-

gested by lawyer Bruce W. Sanford, one of the nation's top authorities on libel, in his treatise *Libel and Privacy: The Prevention and Defense of Litigation* (New York: Harcourt Brace Jovanovich, 1987), 76.   **6.** RESTATEMENT (SECOND) OF TORTS §559 (1977).   **7.** For an example of a case based on product disparagement, see Bose Corp. v. Consumers Union of United States, Inc., 466 U.S. 485 (1984).   **8.** Melody Petersen, *Farmers' Right to Sue Grows,* N.Y. Times, June 1, 1999, at A1.   **9.** Raymer v. Doubleday & Co., 615 F.2d 241, 244 (5th Cir. 1980).   **10.** Corporate Training Unlimited, Inc. v. National Broadcasting Co., 868 F. Supp. 501 (E.D.N.Y. 1994).   **11.** For example, Sierra Breeze v. Superior Court, 149 Cal. Rptr. 914 (Ct. App. 1978).   **12.** For example, Schermerhorn v. Rosenberg, 426 N.Y.S.2d 274 (App. Div. 1980).   **13.** Kaelin v. Globe Communications Corp., 162 F.3d 1036 (9th Cir. 1998).   **14.** Moriatry v. Lippe, 249 A.2d 326, 333 (Conn. 1972).   **15.** Evarts v. Downey, 16 Media L. Rep. 2449 (N.Y. Sup. Ct. 1989).   **16.** Newton v. National Broadcasting Company, 930 F.2d 662, 666 (9th Cir. 1990).   **17.** Newton v. National Broadcasting Company, 677 F. Supp. 1066, 1067 (D. Nev. 1987).   **18.** Towne v. Eisner, 245 U.S. 418, 425 (1918).   **19.** Drotzmanns, Inc. v. McGraw-Hill, Inc., 500 F.2d 830 (8th Cir. 1974).   **20.** Cardiff v. Brooklyn Eagle, 75 N.Y.S.2d 222 (Sup. Ct. 1947).   **21.** Philadelphia Newspapers, Inc. v. Hepps, 475 U.S. 767, 776 (1986).   **22.** Hepps, 786.   **23.** Milkovich v. Lorain Journal Co., 110 S. Ct. 2695, 2698 (1990).   **24.** Milkovich, 2705–2707.   **25.** These factors were articulated in Ollman v. Evans, 750 F.2d 970 (D.C. Cir. 1984), a pre-Milkovich opinion that proved highly influential for courts around the country.   **26.** Moyer v. Amador Valley Joint Union High School Dist., 275 Cal. Rptr. 494 (Ct. App. 1990).   **27.** Stevens v. Tillman, 661 F. Supp. 702 (N.D. Ill. 1986).   **28.** Gaylord Broadcasting Co. v. Francis, 1999 Tex. App. LEXIS 8786.   **29.** Immuno AG v. Moor-Jankowski, 566 N.Y.S.2d 906, 917 (1991).   **30.** Harris v. Minvielle, 19 So. 925, 928 (La. 1896).   **31.** Michigan United Conservation Club v. CBS News, 665 F.2d 110, 112 (6th Cir. 1981).   **32.** RESTATEMENT (SECOND) OF TORTS, comment to §564A (1977).   **33.** Neiman-Marcus Co. v. Lait, 107 F. Supp. 96 (D.N.Y. 1952).   **34.** New York Times Co. v. Sullivan, 376 U.S. 254 (1964).   **35.** New York Times Co. v. Sullivan, 376 U.S. 254, 279 (1964).   **36.** Herbert v. Lando, 441 U.S. 153 (1979).   **37.** Masson v. New Yorker Magazine, Inc., 111 S. Ct. 2419 (1991).   **38.** Harte-Hanks Communications, Inc. v. Connaughton, 109 S. Ct. 2678, 2698 (1989).   **39.** World Boxing Council v. Cosell, 715 F. Supp. 1259 (S.D.N.Y. 1989).   **40.** Newson v. Henry, 443 So. 2d 817 (Miss. 1983).   **41.** Meisler v. Gannett Co., 12 F.3d 1026 (11th Cir. 1994).   **42.** Rosenbloom v. Metromedia, Inc. 403 U.S. 29, 43 (1971).   **43.** Gertz v. Robert Welch, Inc. 418 U.S. 323, 347 (1974).   **44.** Kassel v. Gannett Co. Inc., 16 Media L. Rep. 1814, 1821 (1st Cir. 1989).   **45.** Gertz, 366.   **46.** Rosenblatt v. Baer, 383 U.S. 75, 85 (1966).   **47.** For example, compare Johnston v. Corinthian Television Corp., 583 P.2d 1101 (Okla. 1978), and Richmond Newspapers, Inc. v. Lipscomb, 362 S.E.2d 32 (Va. 1987).   **48.** See Garrison v. Louisiana, 379 U.S. 64 (1964).   **49.** Associated Press v. Walker and Curtis Publishing Co. v. Butts, reported together at 388 U.S. 130 (1967).   **50.** Rosanova v. Playboy Enterprises, 411 F. Supp. 440, 443 (S.D. Ga. 1976).   **51.** See Wolston v. Reader's Digest Ass'n, 443 U.S. 157 (1979). (Man who was cited for contempt because of his failure to testify before a grand jury investigating Soviet spy activities had not thrust himself into the controversy over espionage. Held not a public figure.)   **52.** Bose Corp. v. Consumers Union, 508 F. Supp. 1249 (D. Mass. 1981).   **53.** Rosanova v. Playboy Enterprises, 580 F.2d 859 (5th Cir. 1978).   **54.** Street v. National Broadcasting Co., 645 F.2d 1227, 1235 (6th Cir. 1981).   **55.** See Vitale v. National Lampoon, Inc., 449 F. Supp. 442 (E.D. Pa. 1978) and Pring v. Penthouse Int'l., Ltd., 695 F.2d 438 (10th Cir. 1982).   **56.** See Logan v. District of Columbia, 447 F. Supp. 1328 (1978) and Wynberg v. National Enquirer, Inc., 564 F. Supp. 924 (1982).   **57.** See Andrew Radolf, "Landmark Libel Case?" *Editor & Publisher,* May 20, 1989, 9–10.   **58.** Gertz, 349.   **59.** Examples, as of this writing, included Massachusetts [Stone v. Essex County Newspapers, Inc., 330 N.E.2d 161 (1975)] and Oregon [Wheeler v. Green, 593 P.2d 777 (1979)].   **60.** Dun & Bradstreet, Inc. v. Greenmoss Builders, Inc., 472 U.S. 749, 758 (1985).   **61.** Newell v. Field Enters, Inc., 415 N.E.2d 434, 446–447 (Ill. App. Ct. 1980).   **62.** Stokes v. CBS Inc., 25 F.Supp.2d 992 (Minn. 1998).   **63.** Friedman v. Israel Labour Party, 957 F. Supp. 701 (E.D. Penn., 1997).   **64.** RESTATEMENT (SECOND) OF TORTS §611 comment i (1977).   **65.** Edwards v. National Audubon Society, Inc., 556 F.2d 113, 120 (2d Cir. 1977).   **66.** In re United Press International, 16 Media L. Rep. 2401, 2407 (D.D.C. 1989).   **67.** Gay v. Williams, 486 F. Supp. 12 (D. Alaska 1979). See also Brown v. Courier-Herald Publishing Co., 700 F. Supp. 534 (S.D. Ga. 1988).   **68.** CAL. CIV. CODE §48a (West 1982).   **69.** Anderson v. Liberty Lobby, Inc., 477 U.S. 242 (1986).   **70.** Layayette Morehouse, Inc. v. Chronicle Publishing Co., 37 Cal.app.4th 855 (1995). **71.** Burnett v. National Enquirer, 193 Cal. Rptr. 206 (Ct. App. 1983). **72.** The Libel Reform Project of the Annenberg Washington Program, *Proposal for the Reform of Libel Law* (Washington, D.C.: Northwestern University, 1988), 7.

Chapter 5

1. Warren and Brandeis, "The Right of Privacy," 4 Harv L. Rev. 193, 196 (1890). **2.** Restatement (Second) of Torts, §652C comment d (1977). **3.** Zacchini v. Scripps-Howard Broadcasting Co., 97 S. Ct. 2849 (1977). **4.** Ali v. Playgirl, Inc., 447 F. Supp. 723, 727 (S.D.N.Y. 1978). **5.** Murray v. New York Magazine, 267 N.E.2d 256 (N.Y. 1971). **6.** Spellman v. Simon & Schuster, 3 Media L. Rep. 2406 (N.Y. Civ. Ct. 1978). **7.** Anderson v. Fisher Broadcasting Co., 712 P.2d 803 (Or. 1986). **8.** Cher v. Forum International, Ltd., 692 F.2d 634 (9th Cir. 1982). **9.** Carson v. Here's Johnny Portable Toilets, Inc., 698 F.2d 831 (6th Cir. 1983). **10.** Midler v. Ford Motor Co., 849 F.2d 460 (9th Cir. 1988). **11.** Allen v. Men's World Outlet, Inc., 679 F. Supp. 360 (S.D.N.Y. 1988). **12.** White v. Samsung Electronics, 971 F.2d 1397 (9th Cir. 1992). **13.** Hoffman v. Capital Cities/ABC, 33 F.Supp.2d 867 (C.D.Cal., 1999). **14.** For a case that addresses details of the surviving right, see The Martin Luther King Center v. American Heritage Products, 296 S.E. 2d 697 (Ga. 1982). **15.** Cal. Civ. Code §3344.1 (2000). **16.** Comedy III Productions v. Gary Saderup, Inc., 80 Cal.Rptr.2d 464 (1998). **17.** See Factors etc., Inc. v. Pro Arts, Inc., 579 F.2d 215 (2nd Cir. 1978) in which the court ruled against a poster of Elvis Presley that contained the words "in Memory" and the date of the singer's death as a mere use of his likeness and not protected expression about a newsworthy event. **18.** Neff v. Time, Inc., 406 F. Supp. 858 (W.D. Pa. 1976). **19.** Daily Times Democrat v. Graham, 162 So. 2d 474 (Ala. 1964). **20.** Cox Broadcasting Corp. v. Cohn, 420 U.S. 469, 494 (1975). **21.** Cox Broadcasting, 496. **22.** Florida Star v. BJF, 109 S. Ct. 2603, 2613 (1989). **23.** Times Mirror Co. v. Superior Court (Doe), 244 Cal. Rptr. 556 (Ct. App. 1988). **24.** Virgil v. Sports Illustrated, 424 F. Supp. 1286, 1289 (S.D. Cal. 1976). **25.** McNamara v. Freedom Newspapers, Inc., 802 S.W.2d 901 (Tex. Ct. Appl. 1991). **26.** Diaz v. Oakland Tribune, 188 Cal.Rptr. 762 (1983). **27.** See Doe v. Roe, 400 N.Y.S.2d 668 (Sup. Ct. 1977), where a New York court enjoined distribution of a book about plaintiff's psychiatric treatment. **28.** Melvin v. Reid, 297 P. 91 (Cal. 1931). **29.** Leverton v. Curtis Publishing Co., 192 F.2d 974, 977–978 (3d Cir. 1951). **30.** Cantrell v. Forest City Publishing Co., 419 U.S. 245, 248 (1974). **31.** Times, Inc. v. Hill, 385 U.S. 374 (1967). **32.** For example, Mississippi thus far has not recognized false light claims [see Mitchell v. Random House, Inc., 865 F.2d 664 (5th Cir. 1989)], nor has the Ohio Supreme Court [see Angelotta v. ABC, 820 F.2d 806 (6th Cir. 1987)]. **33.** Huskey v. National Broadcasting Co., 632 F. Supp. 1282, 1288 (N.D. Ill. 1986). **34.** Miller v. National Broadcasting Co., 232 Cal. Rptr. 668 (Ct. App. 1986). **35.** Mark v. King Broadcasting, 618 P.2d 512, 519 (Wash. Ct. App. 1980). **36.** Shulman v. Group W Productions, Inc., 955 P.2d 469 (Cal Sup. Ct. 1998). **37.** California v. Greenwood, 486 U.S. 35 (1988). **38.** Shulman at 493–94. **39.** Dietemann v. Time, Inc., 449 F.2d 245, 249 (9th Cir., 1971). **40.** Dietemann, 249. **41.** Desnick v. American Broadcasting Companies, Inc., 44 F.3d 1345, 1353 (7th Cir. 1995). **42.** Sanders v. ABC, 978 P.2d 67 (Cal. Sup. Ct. 1999). **43.** Pearson v. Dodd, 410 F.2d 701, 705 (D.C. Cir. 1969). **44.** Galella v. Onassis, 353 F. Supp. 196 (S.D.N.Y. 1972), 487 F.2d 986 (2d Cir. 1973), 533 F. Supp. 1076 (S.D.N.Y. 1982). **45.** Galella v. Onassis, 353 F. Supp. 196, 227–228 (S.D.N.Y. 1972). **46.** For example, see Wilkins v. NBC, 84 Cal.Rptr.2d 329 (Ct. App. 1999), concerning a "Dateline NBC" investigation of the pay-per-phone-call industry; and Deteresa v. ABC, 121 F.3d 460 (9th Cir. 1997), concerning secret audio taping of O.J. Simpson's flight attendant. **47.** Food Lion, Inc. v. Capital Cities/ABC, Inc., 1999 U.S. App. LEXIS 26373 (4th Cir.). **48.** Hustler Magazine v. Falwell, 108 S. Ct. 876 (1988). **49.** Hustler, 879. **50.** Armstrong v. H & C Communications, Inc., 575 So.2d 280, 282 (1991). **51.** KOVR-TV, Inc. v. Superior Court, 37 Cal.Rptr.2d 431, 435 (1995). **52.** Smith v. Daily Mail Publishing Co., 99 S. Ct. 2667 (1979). **53.** 18 U.S.C. §2511 (2000). **54.** In re King World Productions, Inc., 898 F.2d 56 (6th Cir. 1990). **55.** Fla. Stat. §934.01–934.03 (1991). **56.** Cal. Penal Code §630–632 (2000). **57.** 47 C.F.R. §73.1206 (1999). **58.** See the protection From Personal Intrusion Act of 1997, H.R. 2448, 105th Cong., and the Personal Privacy Protection Act, S. 2103, 105th Cong. (1998) and the Personal Privacy Protection Act, H.R. 97, 106th Cong. (1999). **59.** Cal. Civ.Code § 1708.8 (1999).

Chapter 6

1. Houchins v. KQED, Inc., 438 U.S. 1, 2594 (1978).   **2.** See Le Mistral, Inc. v. Columbia Broadcasting System, 402 N.Y.S.2d 815 (App. Div. 1978), in which a television state was held liable for trespass.   **3.** See Desnick v. American Broadcasting Companies, Inc., 44 F.3d 1345, 1351–52 (7th Cir. 1995).   **4.** Special Force Ministries v. WCCO Television, 584 N.W.2d 789, 792 (Minn. Ct. of Appeals, 1998).   **5.** Miller v. National Broadcasting Co., 232 Cal. Rptr. 668 (Ct. App. 1986).
6. Florida Publishing Co. v. Fletcher, 340 So. 2d 914 (Fla. 1976).   **7.** Wilson v. Layne, 526 U.S. 603 (1999).   **8.** Hanlon v. Berger, 526 U.S. 808 (1999).   **9.** Berger v. Hanlon, 129 F.3d 505 (9th Cir. 1997).   **10.** Cal. Penal Code §602 (2000).   **11.** Stahl v. State, 665 P.2d 839 (Okla. Crim. 1983).   **12.** See Cal. Penal Code §409.5 (2000), which outlines the authority of peace officers to close disaster areas and specifies an exception for news people.   **13.** Leiserson v. City of San Diego, 229 Cal. Rptr. 22 (Ct. App. 1986).   **14.** See State v. Lashinsky, 404 A.2d 1121 (1979), in which New Jersey's Supreme Court upheld the conviction of a press-pass-carrying photographer for arguing with a state trooper at the scene of a fatal automobile accident.   **15.** Daily Herald v. Munro, 838 F.2d 380 (9th Cir. 1988). See also National Broadcasting Co. v. Cleland, 697 F.Supp. 1204 (N.D. Ga. 1988).   **16.** Houchins v. KQED, Inc., 438 U.S. 1 (1978).   **17.** NY CLS Correc. § 660 (1999).   **18.** KQED, Inc. v. Vasquez, C-90-1383, 1991 U.S. Dist. LEXIS 19791 (N.D. Cal. 1991). See also Garrett v. Estelle, 556 F.2d 1274 (5th Cir. 1977), involving camera access to a Texas execution.   **19.** California First Amendment Coalition v. Calderon, 150 F.3d 976 (9th Cir. 1998).
20. The Government in the Sunshine Act is at 5 U.S.C. §552b (2000).   **21.** The Freedom of Information Act is at 5 U.S.C. §552 (2000).   **22.** See 13 U.S.C. §9 (2000).   **23.** See 26 U.S.C. §6103 (1988).   **24.** See 35 U.S.C. §122 (2000).   **25.** Justice Department v. Julian, 108 S. Ct. 606 (1988).   **26.** United States v. Nixon, 418 U.S. 683 (1974).   **27.** The New York Times v. NASA, 920 F.2d 1002 (D.C. Cir. 1990).   **28.** Linda Greenhouse, "Agencies Get New Power to Withhold Investigative Reports," *New York Times,* October 29, 1986, p. A18.   **29.** U.S. Department of Justice v. Reporter's Committee for Freedom of the Press, 109 S.Ct. 1468, 1477 (1989).   **30.** Reporter's Committee at 1482.   **31.** Accuracy in Media, Inc. v. National Park Service, 194 F.3d 120, 123 (D.C. Cir., 1999).   **32.** The FOI Service Center, a project of the Reporters Committee for Freedom of the Press, is at 800 18th Street N.W., Washington, D.C. 20006.   **33.** The Electronic Freedom of Information Act Amendments, Pub. L. No. 104–231, 110 Stat. 3048, 1–12 (1996) (codified in various sections of 5 U.S.C. 552).   **34.** See M. L. Stein, "Access to Drivers' Records Limited," *Editor & Publisher,* September 23, 1989, 28.   **35.** Borreca v. Fasi, 369 F.Supp. 906, 909 (D. Haw. 1974).   **36.** Snyder v. Ringgold, 40 F.Supp.2d 714 (Dist. of Maryland, 1999).
37. Los Angeles Free Press, Inc. v. City of Los Angeles, 88 Cal. Rptr. 605, 609–610 (Ct. App. 1970).   **38.** Colo. Rev. Stat. §24-72-204 (1999).

Chapter 7

1. For example, in 1991 the State Bar of California sponsored a survey to determine the "legal literacy" level of adults in that state. The president of the state bar gave Californians a "C-" on their knowledge of the legal system and concluded, "The test scores reveal that our citizens are dangerously misinformed about basic laws which permeate their day-to-day lives." *California Lawyer,* June 1991, p. 68.   **2.** Nebraska Press Ass'n v. Stuart, 427 U.S. 539, 547, 561 (1976).   **3.** Irvin v. Dowd, 366 U.S. 717, 727 (1961).   **4.** Rideau v. State of Louisiana, 373 U.S. 723, 726 (1963).
5. Sheppard v. Maxwell, 384 U.S. 333, 348 (1966).   **6.** Sheppard, 355–362.   **7.** *Report of the President's Commission on the Assassination of John F. Kennedy* (Washington, D.C.: U.S. Government Printing Office, (1964), 231–240.   **8.** Rita J. Simon, *Does the Court's Decision in Nebraska Press Association Fit the Research Evidence on the Impact on Jurors of News Coverage?,* 29 Stan L. Rev. 515 (Feb. 1977).   **9.** John Kaplan, *Of Babies and Bathwater,* 29 Stan L. Rev. 621 (Feb. 1977).   **10.** American Bar Association, *Standards Relating to Fair Trial and Free Press* (1968).   **11.** Nebraska Press, 559.   **12.** Nebraska Press, 570.   **13.** C.B.S. v. U.S. District Court, 729 F.2d 1174, 1180 (9th Cir. 1984).   **14.** Procter & Gamble v. Bankers Trust Co., 78 F.3d 219, 225 (6th Cir. 1996).
15. Ex parte: State Record Co., 504 S.E.2d 592 (S.C. Sup. Ct. 1998).   **16.** See "CNN Noriega Tapes Gag Order Stands," *The News Media & the Law,* Winter 1991, pp. 6–7.   **17.** Criminal Action v. McVeigh, 964 F.Supp. 313 (D. Colo. 1997).   **18.** ABA Model Rules of Professional Conduct, Rule 3.6(a) (1983).   **19.** Gentile v. State Bar of Nevada, 111 S. Ct. 2720 (1991).

20. Seattle Times Co. v. Rhinehart, 467 U.S. 20 (1984).   **21.** Richmond Newspapers, Inc. v. Virginia, 448 U.S. 555, 561 (1980).   **22.** Richmond Newspapers, 573.   **23.** Richmond Newspapers, 576, 580.   **24.** Richmond Newspapers, 581.   **25.** Richmond Newspapers, 582.   **26.** Globe Newspaper Co. v. Superior Court, 457 U.S. 596 (1982).   **27.** Press-Enterprise Co. v. Superior Court (Press-Enterprise I), 464 U.S. 501 (1984).   **28.** Press-Enterprise Co. v. Superior Court (Press-Enterprise II), 478 U.S. 1, 4 (1986).   **29.** For example, see Westmoreland v. Columbia Broadcasting System, Inc., 752 F.2d 16 (2nd Cir. 1984).   **30.** For example, see Wilson v. American Motors Corp., 759 F.2d 1568 (11th Cir. 1985).   **31.** Estes v. Texas, 381 U.S. 532 (1965).   **32.** Chandler v. Florida, 449 U.S. 560, 574 (1981).   **33.** In re J.S., 438 A.2d 1125 (Vt. Sup. Ct., 1981).   **34.** Smith v. Daily Mail Publishing Co., 99 S. Ct. 2667 (1979).   **35.** Jeffries v. State of Mississippi, 724 So.2d 897 (Miss. Sup. Ct., 1998).   **36.** Press-Enterprise II, 13.   **37.** For example, see In re Application of CBS, Inc. (Salerno), 828 F.2d 958 (2d Cir. 1987).   **38.** Branzburg v. Hayes, 408 U.S. 665, 682 (1972).   **39.** Shoen v. Shoen, 48 F.3d 412 (9th Cir. 1995).   **40.** United States v. Smith, 135 F.3d 963, 970–71 (5th Cir. 1998).   **41.** Delaney v. Superior Court, 789 P.2d 934 (Cal. 1990).   **42.** For a case in which the court ordered a media defendant to disclose its news source, see Miller v. Transamerican Press, Inc., 621 F.2d 721 (5th Cir. 1980). For a case in which a disclosure order was overturned, see Mitchell v. Superior Court, 690 P.2d 625 (Cal. 1984).   **43.** Cohen v. Cowles Media Co., 111 St. Ct. 2513, 2518 (1991).   **44.** Cohen v. Cowles Media Co., 479 N.W.2d 387 (Minn. 1992).   **45.** Zurcher v. Stanford Daily, 436 U.S. 547 (1978).   **46.** 42 U.S.C. § 2000aa (2000).   **47.** In re Farber, 394 A.2d 330 (N.J. 1978). (Farber was released when the defendant was found not guilty of homicide.)   **48.** See United States v. Dickinson, 465 F.2d 496 (5th Cir. 1972).   **49.** See in re Providence Journal, 820 F.2d 1342 (1st Cir. 1986), and In re Misener, 213 Cal. Rptr. 569 (1985).   **50.** U.S. v. Cable News Network, Inc., 865 F.Supp 1549 (1994).   **51.** See Bridges v. State of California, 314 U.S. 252 (1941).

Chapter 8

1. The Copyright Act of 1976 is contained in Title 17 of the *United States Code*.   **2.** 17 U.S.C. § 102(a) (2000).   **3.** 17 U.S.C. § 102(a) (2000).   **4.** See Nichols v. Universal Pictures Corp., 45 F.2d 119 (2nd Cir. 1930), holding that the degree of complexity and development is what separates unprotected literary ideas from protected characters and sequences.   **5.** 17 U.S.C. § 103 (2000).   **6.** J. R. O'Dwyer Co. v. Media Marketing Int., 755 F. Supp. 599 (1991).   **7.** Feist Publications, Inc. v. Rural Telephone Service Co., 111 S. Ct. 1282, 1294 (1991).   **8.** See Williams v. Weisser, 78 Cal. Rptr. 542 (Ct. App. 1969), involving unauthorized distribution of a professor's class notes.   **9.** See Chamberlain v. Feldman, 89 N.E. 2d 863 (N.Y. 1949), regarding the ownership rights in a Mark Twain manuscript.   **10.** 17 U.S.C. § 201(b) (2000).   **11.** Community for Creative Non-Violence v. Reid, 109 S. Ct. 2166 (1989).   **12.** 17 U.S.C. § 101 (2000).   **13.** Definitions of forty copyright terms are found in Section 101 of the act.   **14.** 17 U.S.C. § 105 (2000).   **15.** For example, see Georgia v. Harrison Co., 548 F.Supp. 110 (N.D. Ga. 1982), holding that state statutes are not subject to copyright protection.   **16.** The duration provisions are found in Sections 302 to 304 of the Copyright Act.   **17.** Estate of Martin Luther King v. CBS, Inc., 194 F3d 1211 (11th Cir. 1999).   **18.** In the 1980s ten states enacted moral rights legislation, led by California's Art Preservation Act, CAL. CIV. CODE § 987. The other states were Connecticut, Louisiana, Massachusetts, Maine, New Jersey, New Mexico, New York, Pennsylvania, and Rhode Island.   **19.** See 17 U.S.C. § 106A (2000).   **20.** Application forms are supplied free by the Copyright Office, Publications Section LM-455, Library of Congress, Washington, D.C. 20559.   **21.** 17 U.S.C. § 401(a) (2000).   **22.** 17 U.S.C. § 106 (2000).   **23.** Rogers v. Koons, 751 F. Supp. 474 (S.D.N.Y. 1990).   **24.** Bright Tunes Music Corp. v. Harrisongs Music, Ltd., 420 F. Supp. 177, 180 (S.D.N.Y. 1976).   **25.** 17 U.S.C. § 504(c) (2000).   **26.** RSO Records, Inc. v. Peri, 596 F. Supp. 849 (S.D.N.Y. 1984).   **27.** 17 U.S.C. § 2319 (2000).   **28.** 17 U.S.C. § 204(a) (2000).   **29.** Tasini v. New York Times Co., 192 F.3d 356 (2nd Cir. 1999).   **30.** For a particularly thorough treatment, see Al Kohn and Bob Kohn, *The Art of Music Licensing* (Englewood Cliffs, NJ: Prentice-Hall, 1992).   **31.** 17 U.S.C. § 114(a). In 1978 the Register of Copyrights recommended to Congress that performance rights be added for sound recordings. Bills to that effect have been introduced, but have not passed.   **32.** One of the leading "storecasting" cases is Sailor Music v. Gap Stores, Inc., 668 F.2d 84 (2nd Cir. 1981). See also International Korwin Corp. v. Kowalczyk, 855 F.2d 375 (7th Cir. 1988).   **33.** Sailor Music v. Mai Kai of Concord, Inc., 640 F. Supp. 629 (D.N.H. 1986).   **34.** See Fortnightly

Corp. v. United Artists, 392 U.S. 390 (1968) and Teleprompter Corp. v. CBS, 415 U.S. 394 (1974). **35.** 17 U.S.C. § 111 (2000). **36.** 17 U.S.C. § 119 (2000). **37.** Basic Books, Inc. v. Kinko's Graphics, 758 F. Supp. 1522, 1531 (S.D.N.Y. 1991). **38.** Kinko's, 1534. **39.** Sony Corp. of America v. Universal City Studios, Inc., 464 U.S. 417 (1984). **40.** Harper & Row Publishers v. Nation Enterprises, 471 U.S. 539, 545–546 (1985). **41.** Harper & Row, 567. **42.** Harper & Row, 590. **43.** Los Angeles News Service v. KCAL-TV,108 F.3d 1119 (9th Cir. 1997). **44.** Campbell v. Acuff-Rose Music, Inc., 114 S. Ct. 1164 (1994). For a contrasting case, see Walt Disney Productions v. Air Pirates, 581 F.2d 751 (9th Cir. 1978), in which the copying of Disney cartoon characters was too extensive to qualify as fair use. **45.** Lanham Act. 15 U.S.C. § 1051 et. seq. **46.** Miller Brewing Co. v. G. Heileman Brewing Co., 561 F.2d 75 (7th Cir. 1977). **47.** Playboy Enterprises, Inc. v. Chuckleberry Publishing, Inc., 687 F.2d 563 (2nd Cir. 1982). **48.** Time, Inc. v. Petersen Publishing Co., 173 F.3d 113 (2nd Cir. 1999). **49.** Dallas Cowboys Cheerleaders, Inc. v. Pussycat Cinema, Ltd., 604 F.2d 200, 202 (2nd Cir. 1979). **50.** Anheuser-Busch, Inc. v. Balducci Publications, 28 F.3d 769 (8th Cir. 1994). **51.** International News Service v. Associated Press, 248 U.S. 215, 239 (1918). **52.** NBA v. Motorola, Inc., 105 F.3d 841 (2nd Cir. 1997). **53.** Orion Pictures Co., Inc. v. Dell Publishing Co., Inc., 471 F.Supp. 392 (S.D.N.Y. 1979).

Chapter 9

1. Pacific Gas & Electric Co. v. Public Utilities Commission, 475 U.S. 1, 16 (1986). **2.** 17 C.F.R. §240.10b-5 (2000). **3.** Securities and Exchange Commission v. Texas Gulf Sulphur Co., 401 F.2d 833, 845 (2nd Cir. 1968). **4.** Securities and Exchange Commission v. Texas Gulf Sulphur Co., 446 F.2d 1301 (2nd Cir. 1971). **5.** For examples of shareholder lawsuits based on corporate news releases see Lewis v. Chrysler Corp., 949 F.2d 644 (3rd Cir. 1991) and Brickman v. Tyco Toys, Inc., 731 F. Supp 101 (S.D.N.Y. 1990). **6.** Basic Inc. v. Levinson, 108 S. Ct. 978 (1988). **7.** 2 U.S.C. §441b(a) (1999). **8.** See 11 C.F.R. §114.3 (2000). **9.** See 11 C.F.R. §114.5 (2000). **10.** Buckley v. Valeo, 424 U.S. 1, 19 (1976). **11.** Federal Election Commission v. Massachusetts Citizens for Life, Inc., 479 U.S. 238 (1986). **12.** The federal regulations pertaining to the detailed operation of PACs are found in Title 11 of the CODE OF FEDERAL REGULATIONS. **13.** Federal Election Commission v. National Right to Work Committee, 459 U.S. 197, 199 (1982). **14.** National Right to Work, 204. **15.** Nixon v. Shrink Missouri Government PAC, 2000 U.S. LEXIS 826. **16.** First National Bank of Boston v. Bellotti, 435 U.S. 765, 790 (1978). **17.** McIntyre v. Ohio Elections Commission, 512 U.S. 334, 357 (1995). **18.** Yes for Life PAC v. Webster, 1999 U.S. Dist. LEXIS 17829 (Maine). See also Buckley v. American Constitutional Law Foundation, Inc., 525 U.S. 182 (1999), holding unconstitutional a requirement that petition circulators wear ID badges. **19.** West Virginia State Board of Education v. Barnette, 319 U.S. 624, 642 (1943). **20.** 5 U.S.C. §7324(a)(2) (1988). **21.** U.S. Civil Service Commission v. National Ass'n of Letter Carriers, 413 U.S. 548, 565 (1973). **22.** Biller v. U.S. Merit Systems Protection Board, 863 F.2d 1079, 1091 (2d Cir. 1988). **23.** Special Counsel v. Biggs, 16 M.S.P.B. 355 (1983). **24.** 5 U.S.C. §7324(a) (1999). **25.** Swinney v. Untreiner, 272 So. 2d 805 (Fla. 1973). **26.** United States v. National Treasury Employees Union, 130 L.Ed.2d 964 (1995). **27.** Stanson v. Mott, 551 P.2d 1, 9 (Cal. 1978). **28.** Anderson v. City of Boston, 380 N.E.2d 628, 631 (Mass. 1978). **29.** Anderson, 640 n.19.

Chapter 10

1. FTC v. Standard Education Society, 302 U.S. 112, 116 (1937). **2.** Valentine v. Chrestensen, 316 U.S. 52, 54 (1942). **3.** Breard v. Alexandria, 341 U.S. 622 (1951), Williamson v. Lee Optical of Oklahoma, 348 U.S. 483 (1955), and Capital Broadcasting Co. v. Mitchell, 405 U.S. 1000 (1972). **4.** Bigelow v. Virginia, 421 U.S. 809 (1975). **5.** Virginia State Board of Pharmacy v. Virginia Citizens Consumer Council, Inc., 425 U.S. 748, 756 (1976). **6.** Virginia Pharmacy Board, 763 and 765. **7.** Virginia Pharmacy Board, 770. **8.** Bates v. State Bar of Arizona, 433 U.S. 350, 404 (1977). **9.** Central Hudson Gas & Electric Corp. v. Public Service Comm'n of New York, 447 U.S. 557 (1980). **10.** Board of Trustees v. Fox, 492 U.S. 469, 480 (1989). **11.** Bolger v. Youngs Drug Products Corp., 103 S. Ct. 2875, 2881 (1983). **12.** See 15 U.S.C. §1335 (1999), adopted in 1969. **13.** Posadas de Puerto Rico Assocs. v. Tourism Co. of Puerto Rico, 478 U.S. 328 (1986). **14.** Posadas, 346. **15.** Rubin v. Coors Brewing Co., 131 L.Ed.2d 532, 543 (1995). **16.** 44

Liquormart, Inc. v. Rhode Island, 64 U.S.L.W. 4313 (1996). **17.** Greater New Orleans Broadcasting Association, Inc. v. United States, 527 U.S. 173 (1999). **18.** Greater New Orleans Broadcasting, p. 182. **19.** Consumers Union v. General Signal Corp., 724 F.2d 1044, 1053 (2nd Cir. 1983). **20.** 15 U.S.C. §1333 (a) and (b) (1999). **21.** See 21 U.S.C. §343(q) (1999). **22.** 15 U.S.C. §45(a)(1) (1999). **23.** Edward Cox, Robert Fellmeth, and John Schulz, *The Nader Report on the Federal Trade Commission* (New York: Barron Press, 1969). **24.** American Bar Association, *Report of the ABA Commission to Study the Federal Trade Commission* (1969), p. 3. **25.** Federal Trade Commission Improvement Act, Pub. L. 93-637, tit. 2, 88 Stat. 2193 (1975). **26.** Report of the ABA Section of Antitrust Law Special Committee to Study the Role of the Federal Trade Commission, 58 Antitrust L.J., 43 (1989). **27.** 59 Fed. Reg. 28388 (1994). **28.** 15 U.S.C. §45(a) (1999). **29.** See Amrep Corp. v. FTC, 768 F.2d 1171 (10th Cir. 1985). **30.** Sears, Roebuck and Co. v. FTC, 676 F.2d 385 (9th Cir. 1982). **31.** Erickson v. FTC, 272 F.2d 318 (7th Cir. 1959). **32.** Bristol-Meyers Co. v. FTC, 738 F.2d 554 (2nd Cir. 1984). **33.** J. B. Williams Company v. FTC, 381 F.2d 884 (6th Cir. 1967). **34.** Federal Trade Commission v. Colgate-Palmolive Co., 380 U.S. 374, 387–390 (1965). **35.** Colgate, 393. **36.** Firestone Tire & Rubber Co. v. FTC, 481 F.2d 246, 251 (6th Cir. 1973). **37.** See 16 C.F.R. §424 and §419 (2000). **38.** Guides Against Deceptive Pricing, 16 C.F.R. §§233.1 to 233.5 (2000). **39.** Guide Concerning Use of the Word "Free" and Similar Representations, 16 C.F.R. §251.1 (2000). **40.** Guides for the Advertising of Warranties and Guarantees, 16 C.F.R. §§239.1 to 239.5 (2000). **41.** Guides Concerning Use of Endorsements and Testimonials, 16 C.F.R. §§255 to 255.5 (2000). **42.** See Warner-Lambert Co. v. FTC, 562 F.2d 749 (D.C. Cir. 1977), in which the court upheld the corrective order, with some language modification. **43.** Lanham Act §43(a), 15 U.S.C. §1125(a) (1999). **44.** For example, see Estate of Presley v. Russen, 513 F. Supp. 1339, 1376 (D.N.J. 1981). **45.** Allen v. Men's World Outlet, Inc., 679 F. Supp. 360 (S.D.N.Y. 1988). **46.** Tambrands, Inc. v. Warner-Lambert Co., 673 F. Supp. 1190 (S.D.N.Y. 1987). **47.** Coca-Cola v. Tropicana Products, Inc., 690 F.2d 312, 314 (2d Cir. 1982). **48.** For examples of state statutes pertaining to deceptive advertising, see Sections 349 and 350 of the New York General Business Law and Section 17500 et seq. of the California Business & Professions Code as well as Section 1750 et seq. of the California Civil Code. **49.** Morales v. Trans World Airlines, Inc., 504 U.S. 347 (1992). **50.** 15 U.S.C. 1334(b) (1999). **51.** Vango media, Inc. v. City of New York, 34 F.3d 68 (2nd Cir. 1994). **52.** Mangini v. R. J. Reynolds Tobacco Co. 31 Cal.Rptr.2d 358 (1994). **53.** Cal. Bus. & Prof. Code §17502 (West 1987). See also 15 U.S.C. §54 (1988), a section of the Federal Trade Commission Act that specifically exempts the mass media from *criminal* liability for false advertising. **54.** CBS v. Democratic National Committee, 423 U.S. 94 (1973). **55.** Soap Opera Now, Inc. v. Network Publishing Corp., 867 F.2d 1424 (2nd Cir. 1988).

Chapter 11

1. NBC v. United States, 319 U.S. 190, 212 (1943). **2.** 47 U.S.C. §301 (1999). **3.** 47 U.S.C. §326 (1999). **4.** See 47 U.S.C. §303. The *public interest* phrase also appears in §307(a) (1999). **5.** U.S. Const., art. I, §8. **6.** U.S. v. Nelson Brothers, 289 U.S. 266 (1933). **7.** Trinity Methodist Church v. FRC, 62 F.2d 850 (D.C. Cir. 1932). **8.** Near v. Minnesota, 283 U.S. 697 (1931). **9.** Telecommunications Research and Action Center v. FCC, 801 F.2d 501, 508 (D.C. Cir. 1986). **10.** FCC v. League of Women Voters of California, 468 U.S. 364, 376 n.11 (1984). **11.** Policies Regarding Detrimental Effects of Proposed New Broadcast Stations on Existing Stations, 3 F.C.C.R. 638 (1988). **12.** Office of Communications of United Church of Christ v. FCC, 359 F.2d 994 (D.C. Cir. 1966). **13.** For a good summary of the now-defunct comparative evaluation process, see West Michigan Broadcasting Co. v. FCC, 735 F.2d 601, 604–607 (D.C. Cir. 1984). **14.** Bechtel v. FCC, 10 F.3d 875, 880 (D.C. Cir. 1993). **15.** 47 U.S.C. §309(j) (1999). **16.** Statement of Policy on Minority Ownership of Broadcasting Facilities, 68 F.C.C.2d 979 (1978). **17.** Metro Broadcasting, Inc. v. FCC, 110 S. Ct. 2997, 3010 (1990). **18.** Metro Broadcasting, 3017. **19.** Metro Broadcasting, 3028–3029. **20.** Metro Broadcasting, 3034. **21.** Lamprecht v. FCC, 958 F.2d 382 (D.C. Cir. 1992). **22.** Adarand Constructors, Inc. v. Pena, 115 S.Ct. 2097 (1995). **23.** 47 U.S.C. §307(c) (1999). **24.** Telecommunications Act of 1996, section 204 (codified at 47 U.S.C. §309). **25.** Robinson v. FCC, 334 F.2d 534 (D.C. Cir. 1964). **26.** In re Application of the Trustees of the University of Pennsylvania, 69 F.C.C.2d 1394 (1978). **27.** 47 U.S.C. §310(d) (1999). **28.** FCC v. WNCN Listeners Guild, 450 U.S. 582, 601, 604 (1981).

29. United States v. Storer Broadcasting Co., 351 U.S. 192 (1956).   **30.** Lutheran Church–Missouri Synod v. FCC., 141 F.3d 344, 354–55 (D.C. Cir. 1998).   **31.** See FCC Report and Order, FCC 00–20.   **32.** Adrian Weiss, 58 F.C.C.2d 342 (1976).   **33.** 47 U.S.C. §315(a)(1999).   **34.** Branch v. FCC, 824 F.2d 37 (D.C. Cir. 1987).   **35.** Chisholm v. FCC, 538 F.2d 349 (D.C. Cir. 1976).   **36.** Petitions of Henry Geller et al., 95 F.C.C.2d 1236 (1983).   **37.** Farmers Educational & Cooperative Union v. WDAY, Inc., 360 U.S. 525 (1959).   **38.** CBS, Inc. v. FCC, 453 U.S. 367, 386–387 (1981).   **39.** Letter to Michael Levinson, 7 F.C.C.R. 1457 (1992).   **40.** Syracuse Peace Council, 2 F.C.C.R. 5043 (1987). The commission's authority to repeal the fairness doctrine was upheld in Syracuse Peace Council v. FCC, 867 F.2d 654 (1989).   **41.** Children's Television Act of 1990, 47 U.S.C. §§303a, 303b, 394 (2000).   **42.** 56 Fed. Reg. 19611 (1991).   **43.** See 47 C.F.F. §73.671 for the rules on children's programming.   **44.** For the rules concerning local public inspection files, see 47 C.F.R. 73.3526 (2000)   **45.** The children's TV programming rules are found at 47 C.F.R. §73.671 (2000).   **46.** 47 U.S.C. §317 (1999).   **47.** 57 Fed. Reg. 28638 (1992) (codified at 47 C.F.R. §73.1217).   **48.** United States v. O'Brien, 391 U.S. 367 (1968).   **49.** Turner Broadcasting System v. FCC, 129 L.Ed.2d 497, 514 (1994).   **50.** The 1984 Cable Act is codified at 47 U.S.C. §§521–559.   **51.** Telecommunications Act of 1996, section 301(b) and (c) (codified at 47 U.S.C. §543).   **52.** This controversy has been handled by the District Court through a number of separate orders. For example, see Preferred Communications, Inc. v. City of Los Angeles, No. CV 83-5846, 1991 U.S. Dist. LEXIS 19577 (C.D. Cal. 1991).   **53.** See 47 C.F.R. §76.205 (2000) regarding equal opportunities for origination cablecasts by political candidates.   **54.** Cruz v. Ferre, 755 F.2d 1415 (11th Cir. 1985).   **55.** Alliance for Community Media v. FCC, 56 F.3d 105 (D.C. Cir. 1995).   **56.** Denver Area Educational Telecommunications Consortium v. FCC, 518 U.S. 727, 747 (1996) (together with Alliance for Community Media v. FCC).   **57.** Missouri Knights of the Ku Klux Klan v. Kansas City, 723 F. Supp. 1343 (W.D. Mo. 1989).   **58.** The syndicated exclusivity rule is at 47 C.F.R. §76.151 (2000).   **59.** For the must-carry statutes and regulations, see 47 U.S.C. §§534, 535 (1999); 47 C.F.R. §76.56 (2000).   **60.** The Supreme Court's two decisions in Turner Broadcasting System v. FCC are at 512 U.S. 622 (1994) and 520 U.S. 180 (1997).   **61.** The retransmission consent statute and regulation are at 47 U.S.C. §325(b)(1) (1999) and 47 C.F.R. §76.64 (2000).

Chapter 12

1. Jean Seligmann, "A New Survey on Sex," *Newsweek*, September 17, 1990, 72.   **2.** Attorney General's Commission on Pornography, *Final Report* (Washington, D.C.: U.S. Department of Justice, 1986), 233–240.   **3.** 18 U.S.C. § 1461 (1999).   **4.** See Frederick Schauer, *The Law of Obscenity* (Washington, D.C.: Bureau of National Affairs, 1976), 8–29.   **5.** See United States v. Dennett, 39 F.2d 564 (2d Cir. 1930) (conviction overturned on appeal).   **6.** See generally, Paul S. Boyer, *Purity in Print: The Vice-Society Movement and Book Censorship in America* (New York: Scribners, 1968).   **7.** Roth v. United States, 354 U.S. 476 (1957).   **8.** Paris Adult Theatre I v. Slaton, 413 U.S. 49, 60 (1973).   **9.** Paris Adult Theatre, 103.   **10.** Miller v. California, 413 U.S. 15 (1973).   **11.** The Court discussed the meaning of prurient interest in Brockett v. Spokane Arcades, Inc., 105 S. Ct. 2794 (1985).   **12.** Miller, 32.   **13.** Jenkins v. Georgia, 418 U.S. 153, 160–161 (1974).   **14.** Kaplan v. California, 413 U.S. 115, 116–117 (1973).   **15.** Pope v. Illinois, 481 U.S. 497, 500 (1987).   **16.** Attorney General's *Final Report*, 271.   **17.** State v. Walden Book Co., 386 So. 2d 342, 346 (La. 1980).   **18.** Walden Book Co., 349.   **19.** Penthouse v. McAuliffe, 610 F.2d 1353 (5th Cir. 1980).   **20.** New York v. Ferber, 458 U.S. 747 (1982).   **21.** 18 U.S.C. § 2251 (1999).   **22.** Free Speech Coalition v. Reno, 198 F.3d 1083 (9th Cir., 1999).   **23.** 18 U.S.C. §§ 1461, 1462 (1999).   **24.** 18 U.S.C. §§ 1464, 1468 (1999).   **25.** 19 U.S.C. § 1305 (1999).   **26.** 47 U.S.C. § 223 (1999).   **27.** U.S. v. Pryba, 900 F.2d 748, 755 (4th Cir. 1990).   **28.** Fort Wayne Books, Inc. v. Indiana, 109 S. Ct. 916 (1989).   **29.** Attorney General's *Final Report*, 368.   **30.** Glass v. State, 761 S.W.2d 806 (Tex. 1988).   **31.** Beier v. State, 681 S.W.2d 124 (Tex. 1984).   **32.** Stanley v. Georgia, 89 S. Ct. 1243, 1248 (1969).   **33.** For example, see United States v. 12 200-Ft. Reels, 413 U.S. 123 (1973).   **34.** Osborne v. Ohio, 110 S. Ct. 1691 (1990).   **35.** Mutual Film Corp. v. Ohio Industrial Commission, 236 U.S. 230 (1915).   **36.** Burstyn v. Wilson, 343 U.S. 495, 501 (1952).   **37.** Freedman v. Maryland, 380 U.S. 51 (1965).   **38.** Vance v. Universal Amusement Co., 445 U.S. 308 (1980).   **39.** See Rowan v. Post Office, 397 U.S. 728 (1970) and Pent-R-Books v. U.S. Postal Service, 328 F. Supp. 297 (E.D.N.Y. 1971).   **40.** Young v. American Mini Theatres, Inc.,

427 U.S. 50 (1976), and City of Renton v. Playtime Theatres, Inc., 475 U.S. 41 (1986). **41.** 20 U.S.C. §954(d)(1). **42.** National Endowment v. Finley, 524 U.S. 569 (1998). **43.** American Booksellers Association v. Hudnut, 771 F.2d 323, 324 (7th Cir. 1985). **44.** American Booksellers, 329. **45.** American Booksellers, 327–328. **46.** 18 U.S.C. § 1464 (1999). **47.** See 47 U.S.C. §§ 307, 308, 213 (a)(6) (1999). **48.** In re Citizen's Complaint Against Pacifica Foundation Station WBAI(FM), 56 F.C.C.2d 94, 98 (1975). **49.** Federal Communications Commission v. Pacifica Foundation, 438 U.S. 726, 730 (1978). **50.** Pacifica, 748. **51.** Pacifica, 749. **52.** See 2 F.C.C.R. 2692, 2703, and 2705 (1987). **53.** Media Central (KZKC-TV), No. 88-213 (FCC June 23, 1988). **54.** Action for Children's Television v. Federal Communications Commission, 932 F.2d 1504 (D.C. Cir. 1991). **55.** Action for Children's Television v. FCC, 58 F.3d 654, 665 (D.C.Cir. 1995). **56.** Action for Children's Television v. FCC, 59F.3d 1249 (D.C.Cir. 1995). **57.** See "FCC Refuses to Find News Broadcasts Indecent," *The News Media & The Law,* Spring 1991, 29. **58.** In the Matter of WQAM License Limited Partnership, FCC File No. 918 ED 030 (Jan. 2000). **59.** Cruz v. Ferre, 755 F.2d 1415, 1420 (11th Cir. 1985). **60.** Cruz, 1420. **61.** Sable Communications of California, Inc. v. FCC, 492 U.S. 115 (1989). **62.** Information Providers' Coalition for Defense of the First Amendment v. FCC, 928 F.2d 866, 872 (9th Cir. 1991).

Chapter 13

1. See the Telecommunications Act of 1996. **2.** World-Wide Volkswagen Corp. v. Woodson, 444 U.S. 286, 297 (1980). **3.** Burger King Corp. v. Rudzewicz, 471 U.S. 462, 476 (1985). **4.** See, for example, Superfos Investments Ltd. v. FirstMiss Fertilizer, Inc., 774 F. Supp. 393, 397–98 (E.D. Va. 1991). **5.** Cybersell,Inc. v. Cybersell, Inc., 130 F.3d 414 (9th Cir. 1997). **6.** Maritz, Inc. v. CyberGold, Inc., 947 F.Supp. 1328 (E.D. Mo. 1996). **7.** Restatement (Second) of Torts § 581(1). **8.** Smith v. California, 361 U.S. 147 (1959). **9.** Mishkin, v. New York, 383 U.S. 502, 511 (1966). **10.** Hamling et al. v. United States, 418 U.S. 87, 123 (1974). **11.** Cubby v. CompuServe Incorporated, 776 F. Supp. 135, 141 (S.D.N.Y. 1991). **12.** Stratton Oakmont, Inc. v. Prodigy Services Co., 23 Media L. Rep. 1794 (N.Y. Sup. Ct. 1995). **13.** 47 U.S.C. § 230 (1999). **14.** Zeran v. American Online, Inc., 129 F.3d 327, 329–31 (4th Cir. 1998), cert. denied, 118 S. Ct. 2341. **15.** It's in the Cards, Inc. v. Fuschetto, 535 N.W. 2d 11 (Wisc. App. 1995). **16.** U.S. Department of Justice v. Reporter's Committee for Freedom of the Press, 109 S. Ct. 1468 (1989). **17.** For example, see Nader v. General Motors Corp., 255 N.E.2d 765 (N.Y. 1970). **18.** For example, see Smyth v. Pillsbury Company, 914 F.Supp. 97, 101 (E.D. Penn. 1996). **19.** For example, see Cal. Penal Code § 630–632 (West 1988 & Supp. 1992). **20.** 18 U.S.C. § 2511 (1999). **21.** 18 U.S.C. §§2701 et seq. **22.** Jessup-Morgan v. America Online, Inc., 20 F.Supp.2d 1105 (E.D. Mich. 1998). **23.** For a case involving the ECPA and *government's* ability to search electronic communications, see Steve Jackson Games, Inc. v. United States Secret Service, 816 F.Supp. 432 (W.D. Tex. 1993). **24.** Federal Trade Commission, Public Workship on Consumer Privacy on the Global Information Infrastructure (Jan. 20, 1997). **25.** The Children's Online Privacy Protection Act is codified at 15 U.S.C. §§6501–6506. **26.** Bernstein v. U.S. Dept. of Justice, 192 F.3d 1308 (9th Cir. 1999). **27.** Jane C. Ginsburg, *Putting Cars on the Information Superhighway: Authors, Exploiters, and Copyright in Cyberspace,* 95 Colum. L. Rev. 1466, 1467 (Oct. 1995). **28.** The Copyright Act of 1976, 17 U.S.C. § 106. **29.** Playboy Enterprises v. Frena, 839 F. Supp. 1552, 1556 (M.D. Fla. 1993). **30.** The Telecommunications Act of 1996, Title V § 509 (codified at 47 U.S.C. 230(d)(2)). **31.** Online Copyright Infringement Liability Limitation Act, 17 U.S.C. §512 (1999). **32.** American Geophysical Union v. Texaco, Inc., 37 F.3d 881 (2d Cir. 1994). **33.** Planned Parenthood v. Bucci, 1997 U.S. Dist. LEXIS 3338 (S.D.N.Y. 1997). **34.** P.L. No. 106–113, Div. B, §1000(a)(9), 113 Stat. 1536, codified primarily at 15 U.S.C. §1125 (1999). **35.** Red Lion Broadcasting Co. v. FCC, 395 U.S. 367 (1969). **36.** Turner Broadcasting System v. FCC, 129 L.Ed.2d 497 (1994). **37.** United States v. Thomas, 74 F.3d 701 (6th Cir. 1996), cert. denied, 117 S. Ct. 74 (1996). **38.** Communications Decency Act of 1996, Section 502 (to be codified at 47 U.S.C. § 223(d)). **39.** Federal Communications Commission v. Pacifica Foundation, 438 U.S. 726 (1978). **40.** Reno v. ACLU, 521 U.S. 844 (1997). **41.** Child Online Protection Act, 47 U.S.C. §231 (1998). **42.** ACLU v. Reno (Reno II), 31 F.Supp.2d 473 (E.D. Penn. 1999).

Subject Index

Case Index